E-commerce Essentials

FIRST EDITION

Kenneth C. Laudon
New York University

Carol Guercio Traver
Azimuth Interactive, Inc.

PEARSON

Boston   Columbus   Indianapolis   New York   San Francisco   Upper Saddle River
Amsterdam   Cape Town   Dubai   London   Madrid   Milan   Munich   Paris   Montreal   Toronto
Delhi   Mexico City   São Paulo   Sydney   Hong Kong   Seoul   Singapore   Taipei   Tokyo

Editor In Chief: Stephanie Wall
Executive Editor: Bob Horan
Director of Editorial Services: Ashley Santora
Director of Marketing: Maggie Moylan
Senior Marketing Manager: Anne Fahlgren
Senior Managing Editor: Judy Leale
Senior Project Manager: Karalyn Holland
Procurement Specialist: Michelle Klein
Creative Director: Blair Brown
Senior Art Director: Janet Slowik

Cover Designer: DePinho Design
Cover Image: Shutterstock VLADGRIN
Media Editor: Denise Vaughn
Media Project Manager: Lisa Rinaldi
Full Service Project Management: Azimuth Interactive, Inc.
Composition: Azimuth Interactive, Inc.
Printer/Binder: Edwards Brothers, Inc.
Cover Printer: Lehigh-Phoenix Color/Hagarstown
Text Font: ITC Veljovic Std. Book, 9.5pt

Credits and acknowledgements borrowed from other sources and reproduced, with permission, in this textbook appear on page C-1.

Library of Congress Cataloging-in-Publication Information Is Available

10 9 8 7 6 5 4 3 2 1

PEARSON

ISBN 10: 0-13-354498-2
ISBN 13: 978-0-13-354498-5

PREFACE

We wrote *E-commerce Essentials* for undergraduate students who are looking for a shorter, yet in-depth introduction to the field of e-commerce. We focus on concepts that will help you understand and take advantage of the evolving world of opportunity offered by e-commerce, which is dramatically altering the way business is conducted and driving major shifts in the global economy.

Just as important, we have tried to create a book that is thought-provoking and current. We use the most recent data available, and focus on companies that you are likely to encounter on a daily basis in your everyday life, such as Facebook, Google, Twitter, Amazon, YouTube, Pinterest, eBay, and many more that you will recognize, as well as some exciting startups that may be new to you. We also have up-to-date coverage of the key topics in e-commerce today, from privacy and piracy, to government surveillance, cyberwar, social, local and mobile marketing, Internet sales taxes, intellectual property, and more. You will find here the most up-to-date and comprehensive overview of e-commerce today.

The e-commerce concepts you learn in this book will make you valuable to potential employers. The e-commerce job market is expanding rapidly. Many employers expect new employees to understand the basics of e-commerce, social and mobile marketing, and how to develop an e-commerce presence. Every industry today is touched in at least some way by e-commerce. The information and knowledge you find in this book will be valuable throughout your career.

WHAT'S DIFFERENT ABOUT E-COMMERCE ESSENTIALS?

You may be familiar with our book, *E-commerce. Business. Technology. Society*, now in its 10th edition. *E-commerce Essentials* has been designed for courses where a shorter book is desired.

E-commerce Essentials retains all the features that have made *E-commerce. Business. Technology. Society* the market-leading text on e-commerce, including:

- The most up-to-date data with the latest developments and information from leading industry sources
- Lively and clear writing that increases student interest, attention, and curiosity
- A clear conceptual foundation and pedagogy
- Video case studies and Learning Tracks (additional content) online

The major differences between the two books are:

- *E-commerce Essentials* is about half the length (around 450 pages versus around 800) and one chapter shorter. Two chapters on e-commerce marketing and e-commerce advertising in *E-commerce Business. Technology. Society.* have been combined into a single chapter (E-commerce Marketing and Advertising Concepts).
- All the important concepts have been retained but some figures and tables and advanced discussions have been eliminated or shortened.
- Opening and closing case studies and Insight On cases have been shortened without losing their pedagogical message or lively writing style.

WHAT'S NEW IN E-COMMERCE 2013

E-commerce today is greatly different from e-commerce only five years ago. The iPhone was introduced in 2007. The iPad tablet was first introduced in 2010 and has already gone through four generations! The smartphone and tablet devices have changed e-commerce into a social, local, and mobile experience.

Headlines

- Social, Mobile, Local: Content about social networks, the mobile platform, and local e-commerce appears throughout the book.
  - » Social networks such as Facebook, Twitter, and LinkedIn continue their rapid growth, laying the groundwork for a "social e-commerce platform" and continued expansion of social marketing opportunities.
  - » The mobile Internet platform composed of smartphones and tablet computers takes off and becomes a major factor in search, marketing, payment, retailing and services, and online content. Mobile device use poses new security and privacy issues as well.
  - » Location-based services lead to explosive growth in local advertising and marketing.
- Online privacy continues to deteriorate, driven by a culture of self-revelation and powerful technologies for collecting personal information online without the knowledge or consent of users.
- Internet security risks increase; cyberwarfare becomes a new way of conducting warfare among nation-states and a national security issue.

Business

- E-commerce revenues surge after the recession.
- Internet advertising growth resumes, at a faster rate than traditional advertising.
- Social marketing/advertising grows faster than search or display advertising.
- E-books take off and expand the market for text, supported by the iPad, Kindle, Nook, and iPhone.
- Streaming of popular TV shows and movies (Netflix, Amazon, and Hulu.com) becomes a reality, as Internet distributors and Hollywood and TV producers strike deals for Web distribution that also protects intellectual property.
- "Free" and "freemium" business models compete to support digital content.
- New mobile payment platforms emerge to challenge PayPal.
- B2B e-commerce exceeds pre-recession levels as firms become more comfortable with digital supply chains.

Technology

- Smartphones, tablets, and e-book readers, along with associated software applications, and coupled with 3G/4G cellular network expansion, fuel rapid growth of the mobile platform.

- Investment in cloud computing increases, providing the computing infrastructure for a massive increase in online digital information and e-commerce.
- Cloud-based streaming services for music and video replace sales of downloads and physical product.
- Nearly a million software apps fuel growth in app sales, marketing, and advertising; transforming software production and distribution.
- Touch interface operating systems emerge: Windows 8 introduced with a touch screen interface, mimicking Apple's iOS and Google Android smartphones.
- The cost of developing sophisticated Web sites continues to drop due to declining software and hardware prices and open source software tools.
- Internet and cellular network capacity is challenged by the rapid expansion in digital traffic generated by mobile devices; bandwidth caps begin to appear in 2012.
- Internet telecommunications carriers support differential pricing to maintain a stable Internet; opposed by Net neutrality groups pushing non-discriminatory pricing.

Society
- The mobile, "always on" culture in business and family life continues to grow.
- Congress considers legislation to regulate the use of personal information for behavioral tracking and targeting consumers online.
- States heat up the pursuit of taxes on Internet sales by Amazon and others.
- Intellectual property issues remain a source of conflict with significant movement toward resolution in some areas, such as Google's deals with Hollywood and the publishing industry, and Apple's and Amazon's deals with e-book and magazine publishers.
- P2P piracy traffic declines as paid streaming music and video gains ground, although digital piracy of online content remains a significant threat to Hollywood and the music industry.
- Governments around the world increase surveillance of Internet users and Web sites in response to national security threats; Google continues to tussle with China and other countries over censorship and security issues.

Since it began in 1995, electronic commerce has grown in the United States from a standing start to a $362 billion retail, travel, and media business and a $4.1 trillion business-to-business juggernaut, bringing about enormous change in business firms, markets, and consumer behavior. Economies and business firms around the globe are being similarly affected. During this relatively short time, e-commerce has itself been transformed from its origin as a mechanism for online retail sales into something much broader. Today, e-commerce has become the platform for media and new, unique services and capabilities that aren't found in the physical world. There is no physical world counterpart to Facebook, Twittter, Google search, or a host of other recent online innovations from Groupon and iTunes to Tumblr. Welcome to the new e-commerce!

Although e-commerce today has been impacted by the worldwide economic recession, in the next five years, e-commerce in all of its forms is still projected to continue growing at high single-digit rates, becoming the fastest growing form of commerce. Just as automobiles, airplanes, and electronics defined the twentieth century, so will e-commerce of all kinds define business and society in the twenty-first century. The rapid movement toward an e-commerce economy and society is being led by both established business firms such as Walmart, Ford, IBM, JCPenney, and General Electric, and newer entrepreneurial firms such as Google, Amazon, Apple, Facebook, Yahoo, Twitter, YouTube, and Pinterest. Students of business and information technology need a thorough grounding in electronic commerce in order to be effective and successful managers in the next decade. This book is written for tomorrow's managers.

BUSINESS. TECHNOLOGY. SOCIETY.

We believe that in order for business and technology students to really understand e-commerce, they must understand the relationships among e-commerce business concerns, Internet technology, and the social and legal context of e-commerce. These three themes permeate all aspects of e-commerce, and therefore, in each chapter, we present material that explores the business, technological, and social aspects of that chapter's main topic.

Given the continued growth and diffusion of e-commerce, all students—regardless of their major discipline—must also understand the basic economic and business forces driving e-commerce. E-commerce has created new electronic markets where prices are more transparent, markets are global, and trading is highly efficient, though not perfect. E-commerce has a direct impact on a firm's relationship with suppliers, customers, competitors, and partners, as well as how firms market products, advertise, and use brands. Whether you are interested in marketing and sales, design, production, finance, information systems, or logistics, you will need to know how e-commerce technologies can be used to reduce supply chain costs, increase production efficiency, and tighten the relationship with customers. This text is written to help you understand the fundamental business issues in e-commerce.

The Web and e-commerce have caused a major revolution in marketing and advertising in the United States. We have a full chapter devoted to discussing how marketing and advertising dollars are moving away from traditional media, and towards online media and their huge audiences, creating significant growth in search engine marketing, targeted display advertising, online rich media/video ads, and social marketing techniques. This chapter includes an in-depth look at social, local, and mobile marketing using the most current examples.

E-commerce is driven by Internet technology. Internet technology, and information technology in general, is perhaps the star of the show. Without the Internet, e-commerce would be virtually nonexistent. Accordingly, we provide three chapters specifically on the Internet and e-commerce technology, and in every chapter we provide continuing coverage by illustrating how the topic of the chapter is being shaped by new information technologies. For instance, Internet technology drives developments in security and payment systems, marketing strategies and advertising, financial applications, media distribution, business-to-business trade, and retail e-commerce. We discuss the rapid growth of the mobile digital platform, the emergence of cloud computing, new open source software tools and applications that enable Web 2.0, and new types of Internet-based information systems that support electronic business-to-business markets.

E-commerce is not only about business and technology, however. The third part of the equation for understanding e-commerce is society. E-commerce and Internet technologies have important social consequences that business leaders can ignore only at their peril. E-commerce has challenged our concepts of privacy, intellectual property, and even our ideas about national sovereignty and governance. Google, Facebook, Apple, Amazon, and assorted advertising networks maintain profiles on millions of shoppers and consumers worldwide. The proliferation of illegally copied music and videos on the Internet, and the growth of social networking sites often based on displaying copyrighted materials without permission, are challenging the intellectual property rights of record labels, Hollywood studios, and artists. And many countries—including the United States—are demanding to control the content of Web sites displayed within their borders for political and social reasons. Tax authorities in the United States and Europe are demanding that e-commerce sites pay sales taxes just like ordinary brick and mortar stores on mainstreet. As a result of these challenges to existing institutions, e-commerce and the Internet are the subject of increasing investigation, litigation, and legislation. Business leaders need to understand these societal developments, and they cannot afford to assume any longer that the Internet is borderless, beyond social control and regulation, or a place where market efficiency is the only consideration. In addition to an entire chapter devoted to the social and legal implications of e-commerce, each chapter contains material highlighting the social implications of e-commerce.

FEATURES AND COVERAGE

Strong Conceptual Foundation The book emphasizes the three major driving forces behind e-commerce: business development and strategy, technological innovations, and social controversies and impacts. Each of these driving forces is represented in every chapter, and together they provide a strong and coherent conceptual framework for understanding e-commerce. We analyze e-commerce, digital markets, and e-business firms just as we would ordinary businesses and markets using concepts from economics, marketing, finance, sociology, philosophy, and information systems. We strive to maintain a critical perspective on e-commerce and avoid industry hyperbole.

Some of the important concepts from economics and marketing that we use to explore e-commerce are transaction cost, network externalities, information asymmetry, social networks, perfect digital markets, segmentation, price dispersion, targeting, and positioning. Important concepts from the study of information systems and technologies play an important role in the book, including Internet standards and protocols, client/server computing, multi-tier server systems, cloud computing, mobile digital platform and wireless technologies, and public key encryption, among many others. From the literature on ethics and society, we use important concepts such as intellectual property, privacy, information rights and rights management, governance, public health, and welfare.

From the literature on business, we use concepts such as business process design, return on investment, strategic advantage, industry competitive environment, oligopoly, and monopoly. We also provide a basic understanding of finance and accounting issues, and extend this through an "E-commerce in Action" case that critically examines the financial statements of Amazon. One of the witticisms that emerged from the early years of e-commerce and that still seems apt is the notion that e-commerce changes everything except the rules of business. Businesses still need to make a profit in order to survive in the long term.

Currency Important new developments happen almost every day in e-commerce and the Internet. We try to capture as many of these important new developments as possible in each annual edition. You will not find a more current book for a course offered during the 2013 academic year. Many other texts are already six months to a year out of date before they even reach the printer. This text, in contrast, reflects extensive research through October 2012, just weeks before the book hits the press.

Real-World Business Firm Focus and Cases From Akamai Technologies to Google, Microsoft, Apple, and Amazon, to Facebook, Twitter, and Tumblr, to Netflix, Pandora, and Elemica, this book contains hundreds of real-company examples and over 60 more extensive cases that place coverage in the context of actual dot.com businesses. You'll find these examples in each chapter, as well as in special features such as chapter-opening, chapter-closing, and "Insight on" cases. The book takes a realistic look at the world of e-commerce, describing what's working and what isn't, rather than presenting a rose-colored or purely "academic" viewpoint.

In-depth Coverage of Marketing and Advertising The text includes a chapter devoted solely to e-commerce marketing and advertising. Marketing concepts, including social, mobile, and local marketing, market segmentation, targeting and re-targeting ads, personalization, clickstream analysis, bundling of digital goods, long-tail marketing, and dynamic pricing, are used throughout the text.

In-depth Coverage of B2B E-commerce We devote an entire chapter to an examination of B2B e-commerce. In writing this chapter, we developed a unique and easily understood classification schema to help students understand this complex arena of e-commerce. This chapter covers four types of Net marketplaces (e-distributors, e-procurement companies, exchanges, and industry consortia) as well as the development of private industrial networks and collaborative commerce.

Current and Future Technology Coverage Internet and related information technologies continue to change rapidly. The most important changes for e-commerce include dramatic price reductions in e-commerce infrastructure (making it much less expensive to develop sophisticated Web sites), the explosive growth in the mobile platform based on smartphones, tablet computers, cloud storage, and expansion in the development of social technologies, which are the foundation of online social networks.

What was once a shortage of telecommunications capacity has now turned into a surplus, PC prices and sales have continued to fall, smartphone and tablet sales have soared, Internet high-speed broadband connections are now typical and are continuing to show double-digit growth, and wireless technologies such as Wi-Fi and cellular broadband are transforming how, when, and where people access the Internet. While we thoroughly discuss the current Internet environment, we devote considerable attention to describing Web 2.0 and emerging technologies and applications such as the advanced network infrastructure, fiber optics, wireless Web and 4G technologies, Wi-Fi, IP multicasting, and future guaranteed service levels.

Up-to-Date Coverage of the Literature This text is grounded in the e-commerce research literature. We have drawn especially on the disciplines of economics, marketing, and information systems and technologies, as well as law journals and broader social science research journals including sociology and psychology. In addition, we use the latest reports of leading industry sources such as eMarketer, comScore, Hitwise, Nielsen, and Gartner; newspapers such as the *New York Times* and *Wall Street Journal*; and industry publications such as *Computerworld* and *InformationWeek*, among others. Figures and tables sourced to "authors' estimates" reflect analysis of data from the U.S. Department of Commerce, estimates from various research firms, historical trends, revenues of major online retailers, consumer online buying trends, and economic conditions.

Special Attention to the Social and Legal Aspects of E-commerce We have paid special attention throughout the book to the social and legal context of e-commerce. Chapter 8 is devoted to a thorough exploration of four ethical dimensions of e-commerce: information privacy, intellectual property, governance, and protecting public welfare on the Internet. We have included an analysis of the latest Federal Trade Commission and other regulatory and nonprofit research reports, and their likely impact on the e-commerce environment.

Writing That's Fun to Read We've aimed for this book to be fun to read and easy to understand. This is not a book written by committee—you won't find a dozen different people listed as authors, co-authors, and contributors on the title page. We have a consistent voice and perspective that carries through the entire text and we believe the book is the better for it.

OVERVIEW OF THE BOOK

The book is organized into four parts.

Part 1, "Introduction to E-commerce," provides an introduction to the major themes of the book. Chapter 1 defines e-commerce, and defines the different types of e-commerce. Chapter 2 introduces and defines the concepts of business model and revenue model, describes the major e-commerce business and revenue models for both B2C and B2B firms, and introduces the basic business concepts required throughout the text for understanding e-commerce firms including industry structure, value chains, and firm strategy.

Part 2, "Technology Infrastructure for E-commerce," focuses on the technology infrastructure that forms the foundation for all e-commerce. Chapter 3 thoroughly describes how today's Internet works. A major focus of this chapter is mobile technology, Web 2.0 applications, and the near-term future Internet that is now under development and will shape the future of e-commerce. Chapter 4 builds on the Internet chapter by focusing on the steps managers need to follow in order to build a commercial Web presence. This e-commerce infrastructure chapter covers the systems analysis and design process that should be followed in building an e-commerce Web presence; the major decisions regarding outsourcing site development and/or hosting; and how to choose software, hardware, and other tools that can improve Web site performance. It also has a section on developing a mobile Web site and mobile applications. Chapter 5 focuses on Internet security and payments, building on the e-commerce infrastructure discussion of the previous chapter by describing the ways security can be provided over the Internet. This chapter defines digital information security, describes the major threats to security, and then discusses both the technology and policy solutions available to business managers seeking to secure their firm's sites. This chapter concludes with a section on Internet payment systems including mobile payment systems.

Part 3, "Business Concepts and Social Issues," focuses directly on the business concepts and social-legal issues that surround the development of e-commerce. Chapter 6 focuses on e-commerce consumer behavior, the Internet audience, online marketing technologies and branding, and social, local, and mobile marketing. Chapter 7 provides a thorough introduction to the social and legal environment of e-commerce. Here, you will find a description of the ethical and legal dimensions of e-commerce, including a thorough discussion of the latest developments in personal information privacy, intellectual property, Internet governance, jurisdiction, and public health and welfare issues such as pornography, gambling, and health information.

Part 4, "E-commerce in Action," focuses on real-world e-commerce experiences in retail and services, online media, auctions, portals, and social networks, and business-to-business e-commerce. These chapters take a sector approach rather than a conceptual approach as used in the earlier chapters. E-commerce is different in each of these sectors. Chapter 8 takes a close look at the experience of firms in the retail marketplace for both goods and services. Chapter 9 explores the world of online content and digital media, and examines the enormous changes in online publishing and entertainment industries that have occurred over the last two years, including streaming movies, e-books, and online newspapers. Chapter 10 explores the online world of social networks, auctions, and portals. Chapter 11 explores the world of B2B e-commerce, describing both electronic Net marketplaces and the less-heralded, but very large arena of private industrial networks and the movement toward collaborative commerce.

PEDAGOGY AND CHAPTER OUTLINE

The book's pedagogy emphasizes student cognitive awareness and the ability to analyze, synthesize, and evaluate e-commerce businesses. While there is a strong data and conceptual foundation to the book, we seek to engage student interest with lively writing about e-commerce businesses and the transformation of business models at traditional firms.

Each chapter contains a number of elements designed to make learning easy as well as interesting.

Learning Objectives A list of learning objectives that highlights the key concepts in the chapter guides student study.

Chapter-Opening Cases Each chapter opens with a story about a leading e-commerce company that relates the key objectives of the chapter to a real-life e-commerce business venture.

Pinterest:
A Picture Is Worth A Thousand Words

Like all of the most successful e-commerce companies, Pinterest taps into a simple truth. In Pinterest's case, the simple truth is that people love to collect things, and show off their collections to others. And like other Internet firms that have goals of global scope, such as Google, Facebook, and Amazon, Pinterest also has a global mission: to connect everyone in the world through the things they find interesting. How? Founded in 2009 by Ben Silbermann, Evan Sharp, and Paul Sciarra and launched in March 2010, Pinterest allows you to create virtual scrapbooks of images, video, and other content that you "pin" to a virtual bulletin board or pin board on the Web site. For instance, on a recent August day, the home page of the site was populated with a truly eclectic collection of images: luscious chocolate chip cookies, crochet high-heeled shoes, an intricate and colorful Japanese painting of a tiger, an R2D2 trash can, and a close-up of various nail designs, among others. Categories range from Animals to Videos, with Food & Drink, DIY & Crafts, and Women's Fashion among the most popular. Find something that you particularly like? In addition to "liking" and perhaps commenting on it, you can re-pin it to your own board, or follow a link back to the original source. Find someone whose taste you admire or who shares your passions? You can follow one or more of that pinner's boards to keep track of everything she or he pins.

According to comScore, Pinterest is one of the fastest growing Web sites it has ever tracked, growing an astounding 4,377% from May 2011 to May 2012. Reportedly the fastest Web site in history to reach 10 million visitors a month, Pinterest currently has around 20 million monthly visitors, an estimated 70% to 80% of them women. According to some tracking services, it is now the third largest social network in the United States, behind Facebook and Twitter. It is also one of the "stickiest" sites on the Web—according to comScore, users spend an average of 80 minutes per session on Pinterest, and almost 60% of users with accounts visit once or more a week. Jeff Jordan, a partner at Andreessen Horowitz, a venture capital firm and investor in Pinterest, says he has seen

© Blaize Pascall / Alamy

| 3

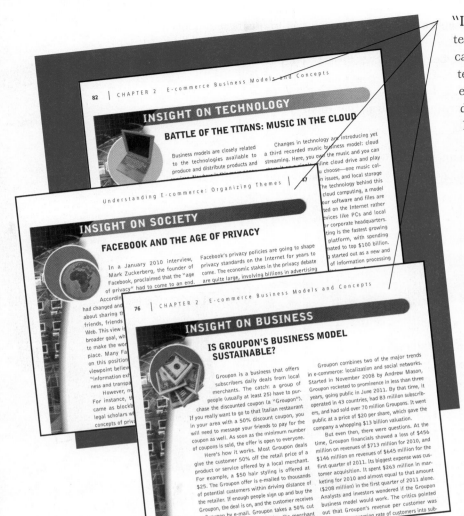

"Insight on" Cases Each chapter contains three real-world cases illustrating the themes of technology, business, and society. These cases take an in-depth look at relevant topics to help describe and analyze the full breadth of the field of e-commerce. The cases probe such issues as the ability of governments to regulate Internet content, how to design Web sites for accessibility, the challenges faced by luxury marketers in online marketing, and smartphone security.

Margin Glossary Throughout the text, key terms and their definitions appear in the text margin where they are first introduced.

Real-Company Examples Drawn from actual e-commerce ventures, well over 100 pertinent examples are used throughout the text to illustrate concepts.

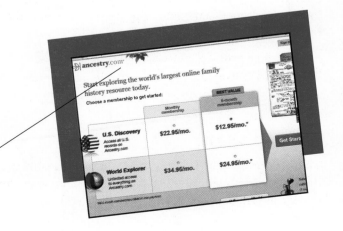

Chapter-Closing Case Studies Each chapter concludes with a robust case study based on a real-world organization. These cases help students synthesize chapter concepts and apply this knowledge to concrete problems and scenarios such as evaluating Pandora's freemium business model, ExchangeHunter-Jumper's efforts to build a brand, and the fairness of the Google Books settlement.

Chapter-Ending Pedagogy Each chapter contains extensive end-of-chapter materials designed to reinforce the learning objectives of the chapter.

Key Concepts Keyed to the learning objectives, Key Concepts present the key points of the chapter to aid student study.

Review Questions Thought-provoking questions prompt students to demonstrate their comprehension and apply chapter concepts to management problem solving.

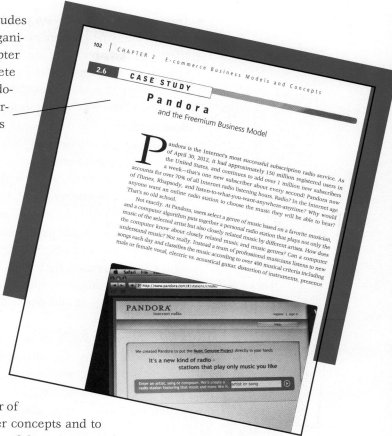

Projects At the end of each chapter are a number of projects that encourage students to apply chapter concepts and to use higher level evaluation skills. Many make use of the Internet and require students to present their findings in an oral or electronic presentation or written report. For instance, students are asked to evaluate publicly available information about a company's financials at the SEC Web site, assess payment system options for companies across international boundaries, or search for the top 10 cookies on their own computer and the sites they are from.

Web Resources Web resources that can extend students' knowledge of each chapter with projects, exercises, and additional content are available at www.azimuth-interactive.com/essentials1e. The Web site contains the following content provided by the authors:

- Additional projects, exercises, and tutorials
- Information on how to build a business plan and revenue models
- Essays on careers in e-commerce

SUPPORT PACKAGE

The following supplementary materials are available to qualified instructors through the Online Instructor Resource Center. Contact your Prentice Hall sales representative for information about how to access them.

- **Instructor's Manual with solutions** This comprehensive manual pulls together a wide variety of teaching tools so that instructors can use the text easily and effectively. Each chapter contains an overview of key topics, a recap of the key learning objectives, additional topics for class discussion and debate, lecture tips, discussion of the chapter-ending case, and answers to the Case Study Questions, Review Questions, and Student Projects.

- **Test Bank** For quick test preparation, the author-created Test Bank contains multiple-choice, true/false, and short-essay questions that focus both on content and the development of critical/creative thinking about the issues evoked by the chapter. The Test Bank is available in Microsoft Word and TestGen format. The TestGen is also available in WebCT and BlackBoard-ready format. TestGen allows instructors to view, edit, and add questions.

- **PowerPoint lecture presentation slides** These slides illustrate key points, tables, and figures from the text in lecture-note format. The slides can be easily converted to transparencies or viewed electronically in the classroom. The slides also include additional questions for the opening cases and the "Insight on" vignettes throughout the book. These questions are very useful for in-class discussions, or quizzes.

- **Video Cases** The authors have created a collection of video case studies that integrate short videos, supporting case study material, and case study questions. Video cases can be used in class to promote discussion or as written assignments. See the following page for a list of video cases available for this edition.

- **Learning Tracks** These additional essays, created by the authors, provide instructors and students with more in-depth content on selected topics in e-commerce. See the following page for a list of Learning Tracks available for this edition.

VIDEO CASES

Chapter 1	1.1 The Future of E-commerce
Chapter 2	2.1 Deals Galore at Groupon
Chapter 3	3.1 Google Data Center Efficiency Best Practices
	3.2 NBA: Competing on Global Delivery
Chapter 4	4.1 ESPN Goes to eXtreme Scale
	4.2 Data Warehousing at REI: Understanding the Customer
Chapter 5	5.1 Cyberespionage: The Chinese Threat
	5.2 Stuxnet and Cyberwarfare
	5.3 IBM Zone Trusted Information Channel (ZTIC)
	5.4 Open ID and Web Security
Chapter 6	6.1 The Power of Like
	6.2 Nielsen Online Campaign Ratings
Chapter 7	7.1 Facebook Privacy
	7.2 What Net Neutrality Means for You
	7.3 Lawrence Lessig on Net Neutrality
Chapter 8	8.1 Etsy: A Marketplace and a Community
Chapter 9	9.1 YouTube's 7th Birthday
Chapter 10	10.1 Mint Returns for Goodwill's eBay Auctions of Thrift-Store Finds
Chapter 11	11.1 Ford AutoXchange B2B Marketplace

LEARNING TRACKS

Chapter 1	1.1 Global E-commerce Europe
	1.2 Global E-commerce Latin America
	1.3 Global E-commerce China
Chapter 6	6.1 Basic Marketing Concepts
	6.2 Social Media Marketing - Facebook
	6.3 Social Media Marketing - Twitter
	6.4 Social Media Marketing - Blogging

ACKNOWLEDGMENTS

Pearson Education sought the advice of many excellent reviewers, all of whom strongly influenced the organization and substance of this book. The following individuals provided extremely useful evaluations of our e-commerce texts:

Deniz Aksen, Koç University (Istanbul)

Carrie Andersen, Madison Area Technical College

Dr. Shirley A. Becker, Northern Arizona University

Prasad Bingi, Indiana-Purdue University, Fort Wayne

Christine Barnes, Lakeland Community College

Cliff Butler, North Seattle Community College

Joanna Broder, University of Arizona

James Buchan, College of the Ozarks

Ashley Bush, Florida State University

Mark Choman, Luzerne City Community College

Andrew Ciganek, Jacksonville State University

Daniel Connolly, University of Denver

Tom Critzer, Miami University

Dursan Delen, Oklahoma State University

Abhijit Deshmukh, University of Massachusetts

Brian L. Dos Santos, University of Louisville

Robert Drevs, University of Notre Dame

Akram El-Tannir, Hariri Canadian University, Lebanon

Kimberly Furumo, University of Hawaii at Hilo

John H. Gerdes, University of California, Riverside

Philip Gordon, University of California at Berkeley

Allan Greenberg, Brooklyn College

Bin Gu, University of Texas at Austin

Peter Haried, University of Wisconsin-La Crosse

Sherri Harms, University of Nebraska at Kearney

Sharon Heckel, St. Charles Community College

David Hite, Virginia Intermont College

Gus Jabbour, George Mason University

Ellen Kraft, Georgian Court University

Gilliean Lee, Lander University

Zoonky Lee, University of Nebraska, Lincoln

Andre Lemaylleux, Boston University, Brussels

Haim Levkowitz, University of Massachusetts, Lowell

Yair Levy, Nova Southeastern University

Richard Lucic, Duke University

John Mendonca, Purdue University

Dr. Abdulrahman Mirza, DePaul University

Kent Palmer, MacMurray College

Karen Palumbo, University of St. Francis

Wayne Pauli, Dakota State University

Jamie Pinchot, Thiel College

Kai Pommerenke, University of California at Santa Cruz

Barry Quinn, University of Ulster, Northern Ireland

Michelle Ramim, Nova Southeastern University

Jay Rhee, San Jose State University

Jorge Romero, Towson University

John Sagi, Anne Arundel Community College

Patricia Sendall, Merrimack College

Dr. Carlos Serrao, ISCTE/DCTI, Portugal

Neerja Sethi, Nanyang Business School, Singapore

Amber Settle, DePaul CTI

Vivek Shah, Texas State University-San Marcos

Seung Jae Shin, Mississippi State University

Sumit Sircar, University of Texas at Arlington

Hongjun Song, University of Memphis

Pamela Specht, University of Nebraska at Omaha

Esther Swilley, Kansas State University

Tony Townsend, Iowa State University

Bill Troy, University of New Hampshire

Susan VandeVen, Southern Polytechnic State University

Hiep Van Dong, Madison Area Technical College

Mary Vitrano, Palm Beach Community College

Andrea Wachter, Point Park University

Catherine Wallace, Massey University, New Zealand

Biao Wang, Boston University

Haibo Wang, Texas A&M International University

Harry Washington, Lincoln University

Rolf Wigand, University of Arkansas at Little Rock

Erin Wilkinson, Johnson & Wales University

Alice Wilson, Cedar Crest College

Dezhi Wu, Southern Utah University

Gene Yelle, SUNY Institute of Technology

David Zolzer, Northwestern State University

We would like to thank eMarketer, Inc. and David Iankelevich for their permission to include data and figures from their research reports in our text. eMarketer is one of the leading independent sources for statistics, trend data, and original analysis covering many topics related to the Internet, e-business, and emerging technologies. eMarketer aggregates e-business data from multiple sources worldwide.

In addition, we would like to thank all those at Pearson Prentice Hall who have worked so hard to make sure this book is the very best it can be. We want to thank Bob Horan, Executive Editor of the Pearson Prentice Hall MIS and business law list, and Karalyn Holland, Senior Production Project Manager, for their support; Judy Leale for overseeing production of this project; and DePinho Design for the outstanding cover design. Very special thanks to Robin Pickering, Megan Miller, and Will Anderson at Azimuth Interactive, Inc., for all their hard work on the production of, and supplements for, this book.

A special thanks also to Susan Hartman, Executive Editor for the first and second editions and to Frank Ruggirello, Publisher at Addison-Wesley when we began this project, and now Vice President and Editorial Director at Benjamin-Cummings.

Finally, last but not least, we would like to thank our family and friends, without whose support this book would not have been possible.

Kenneth C. Laudon
Carol Guercio Traver

Brief Contents

PART 1 Introduction to E-commerce

1	THE REVOLUTION IS JUST BEGINNING	2
2	E-COMMERCE BUSINESS MODELS AND CONCEPTS	34

PART 2 Technology Infrastructure for E-commerce

3	E-COMMERCE INFRASTRUCTURE: THE INTERNET, WEB, AND MOBILE PLATFORM	68
4	BUILDING AN E-COMMERCE PRESENCE: WEB SITES, MOBILE SITES, AND APPS	120
5	E-COMMERCE SECURITY AND PAYMENT SYSTEMS	162

PART 3 Business Concepts and Social Issues

6	E-COMMERCE MARKETING AND ADVERTISING CONCEPTS	206
7	ETHICAL, SOCIAL, AND POLITICAL ISSUES IN E-COMMERCE	258

PART 4 E-commerce in Action

| 8 | ONLINE RETAIL AND SERVICES | 310 |

| 9 | ONLINE CONTENT AND MEDIA | 346 |

| 10 | SOCIAL NETWORKS, AUCTIONS, AND PORTALS | 382 |

| 11 | B2B E-COMMERCE: SUPPLY CHAIN MANAGEMENT AND COLLABORATIVE COMMERCE | 412 |

Contents

PART 1 Introduction to E-commerce

1 THE REVOLUTION IS JUST BEGINNING   2

Learning Objectives   2

Pinterest: A Picture Is Worth A Thousand Words   3

1.1 E-commerce: The Revolution Is Just Beginning   5

The First 30 Seconds   7

What Is E-commerce?   7

Why Study E-commerce?   8

Eight Unique Features of E-commerce Technology   8

   Ubiquity   8

   Global Reach   9

   Universal Standards   10

   Richness   10

   Interactivity   10

   Information Density   11

   Personalization/Customization   11

   Social Technology: User Content Generation and Social Networking   11

Web 2.0: Play My Version   11

Types of E-commerce   13

   Business-to-Consumer (B2C) E-commerce   13

   Business-to-Business (B2B) E-commerce   14

   Consumer-to-Consumer (C2C) E-commerce   14

   Social E-commerce   14

   Mobile E-commerce (M-commerce)   15

   Local E-commerce   15

Growth of the Internet and the Web   15

1.2 E-commerce: A Brief History   17

E-commerce 1995–2000: Invention   18

E-commerce 2001–2006: Consolidation   20

E-commerce 2007—Present: Reinvention   20

Insight on Business: Is the Party Already Over?   22

1.3   *Understanding E-commerce: Organizing Themes*   23

Technology: Infrastructure   23

Business: Basic Concepts   24

Society: Taming the Juggernaut   24

Insight on Society: Facebook and the Age of Privacy   25

Academic Disciplines Concerned with E-commerce   27

Technical Approaches   27

Behavioral Approaches   27

1.4   *Case Study: The Pirate Bay: The World's Most Resilient Copyright Infringer?*   28

1.5   *Review*   30

Key Concepts   30

Questions   32

Projects   32

| 2 | E-COMMERCE BUSINESS MODELS AND CONCEPTS | 34 |

Learning Objectives   34

Tweet Tweet: What's Your Business Model?   35

2.1   *E-commerce Business Models*   37

Introduction   37

Eight Key Elements of a Business Model   37

Value Proposition   37

Revenue Model   38

Market Opportunity   40

Competitive Environment   40

Competitive Advantage   41

Market Strategy   41

Organizational Development   42

Management Team   42

2.2   *Major Business-to-Consumer (B2C) Business Models*   42

Insight on Business: Is Groupon's Business Model Sustainable?   44

E-tailer   45

Community Provider   45

Content Provider   45

Portal   46

Transaction Broker   46

    Insight on Technology: Battle of the Titans: Music in the Cloud   47

Market Creator   48

Service Provider   48

2.3   *Major Business-to-Business (B2B) Business Models*   49

E-distributor   49

E-procurement   50

Exchanges   50

Industry Consortia   50

Private Industrial Networks   51

2.4   *E-commerce Enablers*   51

2.5   *How the Internet and the Web Change Business: Strategy, Structure, and Process*   51

Industry Structure   53

Industry Value Chains   54

Firm Value Chains   55

Firm Value Webs   56

Business Strategy   57

2.6   *Case Study: Pandora and the Freemium Business Model*   60

2.7   *Review*   63

Key Concepts   63

Questions   65

Projects   65

PART 2 Technology Infrastructure for E-commerce

3   **E-COMMERCE INFRASTRUCTURE: THE INTERNET, WEB, AND MOBILE PLATFORM**   **68**

Learning Objectives   68

Google Glass: Augment My Reality   69

3.1   *The Internet: Technology Background*   71

The Evolution of the Internet: 1961—the Present   72

The Internet: Key Technology Concepts   73

    Packet Switching   73

    Transmission Control Protocol/Internet Protocol (TCP/IP)   74

    IP Addresses   76

    Domain Names, DNS, and URLs   76

Client/Server Computing   77
The New Client: the Mobile Platform   79
The Internet "Cloud Computing" Model: Software and Hardware as a
        Service   80
Other Internet Protocols and Utility Programs   81
        Internet Protocols: HTTP, E-mail Protocols, FTP, Telnet, and SSL/TLS   82
        Utility Programs: Ping and Tracert   83

3.2   *The Internet Today*   83
The Internet Backbone   85
Internet Exchange Points   86
Campus Area Networks   87
Internet Service Providers   88
Intranets and Extranets   90
Who Governs the Internet?   90

3.3   *The Future Internet Infrastructure*   91
Limitations of the Current Internet   91
The Internet2® Project   92
The First Mile and the Last Mile   93
        Fiber Optics and the Bandwidth Explosion in the First Mile   93
        The Last Mile: Mobile Internet Access   94
The Future Internet   96
        The Internet of Things   96

3.4   *The Web*   97
Hypertext   98
Markup Languages   99
        HyperText Markup Language (HTML)   99
        Insight on Technology: Is HTML5 Ready for Prime Time?   100
        eXtensible Markup Language (XML)   101
Web Servers and Clients   102
Web Browsers   104

3.5   *The Internet and the Web: Features and Services*   104
E-mail   104
Instant Messaging   104
Search Engines   105
Online Forums and Chat   105
Streaming Media   106
Cookies   107
Web 2.0 Features and Services   107
        Online Social Networks   107
        Blogs   107
        Really Simple Syndication (RSS)   108

Podcasting   108

Wikis   108

Music and Video Services   108

Internet Telephony   109

Intelligent Personal Assistants   109

3.6   *Mobile Apps: The Next Big Thing Is Here*   109

Platforms for Mobile Application Development   110

App Marketplaces   110

Insight on Business: Apps For Everything: The App Ecosystem   111

3.7   *Case Study: Akamai Technologies: Attempting to Keep Supply Ahead of Demand*   112

3.8   *Review*   115

Key Concepts   115

Questions   118

Projects   119

| **4** | **BUILDING AN E-COMMERCE PRESENCE: WEB SITES, MOBILE SITES, AND APPS** | **120** |

Learning Objectives   120

Tommy Hilfiger Replatforms   121

4.1   *Imagine Your E-commerce Presence*   123

What's the Idea? (The Visioning Process)   123

Where's the Money: Business and Revenue Model   123

Who and Where Is the Target Audience   124

What Is the Ballpark? Characterize the Marketplace   124

Where's the Content Coming From?   125

Know Yourself: Conduct a SWOT analysis   126

Develop an E-commerce Presence Map   127

Develop a Timeline: Milestones   128

How Much Will This Cost?   128

4.2   *Building an E-commerce Presence: A Systematic Approach*   129

Pieces of the Site-building Puzzle   130

Planning: the Systems Development Life Cycle   130

Systems Analysis/Planning: Identify Business Objectives, System Functionality, and Information Requirements   131

System Design: Hardware and Software Platforms   132

Building the System: In-house Versus Outsourcing   133

Build Your Own versus Outsourcing   133

Host Your Own versus Outsourcing   136

Testing the System   136
     Insight on Business: Curly Hair and Appillionaires   137
Implementation and Maintenance   138

4.3   *Choosing Software and Hardware*   138
Simple Versus Multi-tiered Web Site Architecture   138
Web Server Software   139
     Site Management Tools   139
     Dynamic Page Generation Tools   140
Application Servers   141
E-commerce Merchant Server Software Functionality   142
     Online Catalog   143
     Shopping Cart   143
     Credit Card Processing   143
Merchant Server Software Packages (E-commerce Suites)   143
Web Services and Open Source Options   144
The Hardware Platform   145
Right-Sizing Your Hardware Platform: The Demand Side   145
Right-Sizing Your Hardware Platform: the Supply Side   145

4.4   *Other E-Commerce Site Tools*   **146**
Web Site Design: Basic Business Considerations   146
Tools for Web Site Optimization   147
Tools for Interactivity and Active Content   148
     Common Gateway Interface (CGI)   148
     Active Server Pages (ASP)   149
     Java, Java Server Pages (JSP), and JavaScript   149
     Web 2.0 Design Elements   150

4.5   *Developing a Mobile Web Site and Building Mobile Applications*   150
Planning and Building a Mobile Web Presence   151
Mobile Web Presence: Design Considerations   152
Mobile Web Presence: Performance and Cost Considerations   153
     Insight on Technology: Building a Mobile Presence   155

4.6   *Case Study: Orbitz Charts Its Mobile Trajectory*   156

4.7   *Review*   158
Key Concepts   158
Questions   160
Projects   161

5 E-COMMERCE SECURITY AND PAYMENT SYSTEMS 162

Learning Objectives 162

Cyberwar: MAD 2.0 163

5.1 *The E-commerce Security Environment* 165
The Scope of the Problem 165
What Is Good E-commerce Security? 167
Dimensions of E-commerce Security 167

5.2 *Security Threats in the E-commerce Environment* 169
Malicious Code 170
Potentially Unwanted Programs (PUPs) 172
Phishing and Identity Theft 172
Hacking, Cybervandalism, Hacktivism, and Data Breaches 174
Credit Card Fraud/Theft 174
Spoofing (Pharming) and Spam (Junk) Web Sites 175
Denial of Service (DOS) and Distributed Denial of Service (DDOS) AttackS 175
Sniffing 176
Insider Attacks 176
Poorly Designed Server and Client Software 177
Social Network Security Issues 177
Mobile Platform Security Issues 178
Cloud Security Issues 178
Insight on Technology: Think Your Smartphone Is Secure? 179

5.3 *Technology Solutions* 180
Protecting Internet Communications 180
Encryption 180
Symmetric Key Encryption 182
Public Key Encryption 182
Public Key Encryption Using Digital Signatures and Hash Digests 183
Digital Certificates and Public Key Infrastructure (PKI) 186
Limitations to Encryption Solutions 186
Securing Channels of Communication 187
Secure Sockets Layer (SSL) and Transport Layer Security (TLS) 187
Insight on Society: Web Dogs and Anonymity: Identity 2.0 188
Virtual Private Networks (VPNs) 190
Protecting Networks 190
Firewalls 190
Protecting Servers and Clients 191
Operating System Security Enhancements 191

Anti-Virus Software   191

5.4   *E-commerce Payment Systems*   191
Online Credit Card Transactions   192
Limitations of Online Credit Card Payment Systems   194
Alternative Online Payment Systems   194
Mobile Payment Systems: Your Smartphone Wallet   195
Digital Cash and Virtual Currencies   195

5.5   *Electronic Billing Presentment and Payment*   196
Market Size and Growth   196

5.6   *Case Study: Online Payment Marketplace: Goat Rodeo*   198

5.7   *Review*   201
Key Concepts   201
Questions   203
Projects   204

PART 3 Business Concepts and Social Issues

6   E-COMMERCE MARKETING AND ADVERTISING CONCEPTS   206

Learning Objectives   206

Facebook: Does Social Marketing Work?   207

6.1   *Consumers Online: the Internet Audience and Consumer Behavior*   209
Internet Traffic Patterns: the Online Consumer Profile   209
Intensity and Scope of Usage   210
Demographics and Access   210
Type of Internet Connection: Broadband and Mobile Impacts   212
Media Choices and Multitasking: The Internet versus Other Media Channels   212
Profiles of Online Consumers   212
The Online Purchasing Decision   213
Shoppers: Browsers and Buyers   216
What Consumers Shop for and Buy Online   217
Intentional Acts: How Shoppers Find Vendors Online   217
Why More People Don't Shop Online   218

6.2   *Digital Commerce Marketing and Advertising Strategies and Tools*   218

The Web Site as a Marketing Platform: Establishing the Customer
Relationship   219

Online Marketing and Advertising Tools   220

Search Engine Marketing and Advertising   221

Display Ad Marketing   225

E-mail Marketing   228

Affiliate Marketing   229

Lead Generation Marketing   230

Sponsorship Marketing   230

Social Marketing and Advertising: Sharing and Engaging   230

Blog Marketing and Advertising   232

Game Advertising   233

Viral Marketing   233

Mobile and Local Marketing and Advertising   234

Mobile Marketing and Advertising   234

App Marketing   235

*Insight on Business: Mobile Marketing: Land Rover Seeks Engagement on the Small
Screen*   236

Local Marketing: The Social-Mobile-Local Nexus   237

Multi-Channel Marketing: Integrating Online and Offline Marketing   237

Long Tail Marketing   241

Insight on Technology: The Long Tail: Big Hits and Big Misses   242

6.3   *Understanding the Costs and Benefits of Online Marketing
Communications*   243

Online Marketing Metrics: Lexicon   243

How Well Does Online Advertising Work?   246

The Costs of Online Advertising   249

6.4   *Case Study: Instant Ads: Real-Time Marketing on Exchanges*   252

6.5   *Review*   254

Key Concepts   254

Questions   256

Projects   257

7   ETHICAL, SOCIAL, AND POLITICAL ISSUES IN E-COMMERCE   258

Learning Objectives   258

Internet Free Speech: Who Decides?   259

7.1   *Understanding Ethical, Social, and Political Issues in E-commerce*   261

A Model for Organizing the Issues   261

Basic Ethical Concepts: Responsibility, Accountability, and Liability   264
Ethical Principles   264

7.2   *Privacy and Information Rights*   265
Information Collected at E-commerce Sites   267
Social Networks and Privacy   267
Mobile and Location-Based Privacy Issues   269
Profiling and Behavioral Targeting   269
The Internet and Government Invasions of Privacy: E-commerce
        Surveillance   271
Legal Protections   272
    Informed Consent   272
        The Federal Trade Commission's Fair Information Practices Principles   274
        The European Data Protection Directive   276
Private Industry Self-Regulation   277
Technological Solutions   278

7.3   *Intellectual Property Rights*   278
Types of Intellectual Property Protection   279
Copyright: the Problem of Perfect Copies and Encryption   279
    Fair Use Doctrine   280
    The Digital Millennium Copyright Act of 1998   281
Patents: Business Methods and Processes   283
    E-commerce Patents   283
Trademarks: Online Infringement and Dilution   284
    Trademarks and the Internet   286
    Cybersquatting and Brandjacking   286
    Cyberpiracy   287
    Metatagging   287
    Keywording   288
    Linking   288
    Framing   289

7.4   *Governance*   289
Who Governs the Internet and E-commerce?   289
    Can the Internet Be Controlled?   291
    Public Government and Law   292
Taxation   292
Net Neutrality   293
    Insight on Business: Internet Sales Tax Battle   294

7.5   *Public Safety and Welfare*   295
Protecting Children   296
Cigarettes, Gambling, and Drugs: Is the Web Really Borderless?   297

Insight on Society: The Internet Drug Bazaar   298

7.6   *Case Study: The Google Books Settlement: Is It Fair?*   300

7.7   *Review*   304

    Key Concepts   304

    Questions   307

    Projects   307

PART 4 E-commerce in Action

8   ONLINE RETAIL AND SERVICES   310

    Learning Objectives   310

Blue Nile Sparkles for Your Cleopatra   311

8.1   *Online Retail*   314

    Online Retailing   315

        E-commerce Retail: The Vision   315

        The Online Retail Sector Today   316

        Multi-Channel Integration   318

8.2   *Online Retail Business Models*   319

    Virtual Merchants   320

    Multi-Channel Merchants: Bricks-and-Clicks   320

    Catalog Merchants   321

    Manufacturer-Direct   322

    Common Themes in Online Retailing   323

        Insight on Technology: Using the Web to Shop 'Till You Drop   325

8.3   *Online Services*   324

8.4   *Online Financial Services*   326

    Online Financial Consumer Behavior   327

    Online Banking and Brokerage   327

        Multi-Channel vs. Pure Online Financial Services Firms   329

        Financial Portals and Account Aggregators   329

    Online Mortgage and Lending Services   330

    Online Insurance Services   330

    Online Real Estate Services   331

8.5   *Online Travel Services*   332

Why Are Online Travel Services So Popular?   332

The Online Travel Market   333

Online Travel Industry Dynamics   333

Insight on Society: Phony Reviews   335

8.6   *Online Career Services*   336

It's Just Information: the Ideal Web Business?   336

8.7   *Case Study: OpenTable: Your Reservation Is Waiting*   338

8.8   *Review*   340

Key Concepts   340

Questions   344

Projects   344

| 9 | ONLINE CONTENT AND MEDIA | 346 |

Learning Objectives   346

YouTube and the Emerging Internet Broadcasting System (IBS)   347

9.1   *Online Content*   349

Content Audience and Market: Where Are the Eyeballs and the Money?   350

Media Utilization   350

Internet and Traditional Media: Cannibalization versus Complementarity   351

Media Revenues   351

Three Revenue Models for Digital Content Delivery: Subscription, A La Carte, and Advertising-Supported (Free and Freemium)   351

Online Content Consumption   352

Free or Fee: Attitudes About Paying for Content and the Tolerance for Advertising   355

Digital Rights Management (DRM) and Walled Gardens   355

9.2   *The Online Publishing Industry*   356

Online Newspapers   356

Audience Size and Growth   357

Newspaper Business Models   358

E-Books and Online Book Publishing   359

Insight on Society: Can Apps and Video Save Newspapers?   360

Amazon and Apple: The New Digital Media Ecosystems   361

What Are the Challenges of the Digital E-Book Platform?   362

Interactive Books: Converging Technologies   363

Magazines Rebound on the Tablet Platform   363

9.3   The Online Entertainment Industry   364

Online Entertainment Audience Size and Growth   366

Television and Premium Video   367

Movies   368

Music   371

Insight on Technology: Hollywood and the Internet: Let's Cut a Deal   372

Games   373

9.4   Case Study: Zynga Bets on Online Games   376

9.5   Review   378

Key Concepts   378

Questions   380

Projects   380

10	**SOCIAL NETWORKS, AUCTIONS, AND PORTALS**	**382**

Learning Objectives   382

Social Network Fever Spreads to the Professions   383

10.1   Social Networks and Online Communities   385

What Is an Online Social Network?   386

The Growth of Social Networks and Online Communities   386

Turning Social Networks into Businesses   388

Types of Social Networks and Their Business Models   388

Social Network Features and Technologies   389

The Future of Social Networks   389

Insight on Technology: FaceBook Has Friends   391

10.2   Online Auctions   392

Defining and Measuring the Growth of Auctions and Dynamic Pricing   392

Risks and Costs of Auctions for Consumers and Businesses   393

Market-Maker Benefits: Auctions as an E-commerce Business Model   393

Why Are Auctions So Popular? Benefits and Costs of Auctions   394

Benefits of Auctions   394

Types and Examples of Auctions   395

When to Use Auctions (and for What) in Business   397

Auction Prices: Are They the Lowest?   398

When Auction Markets Fail: Fraud and Abuse in Auctions   399

10.3   E-commerce Portals   400

The Growth and Evolution of Portals   400

Types of Portals: General-purpose and Vertical Market   401

Insight on Business: The Transformation of AOL   402

Portal Business Models   403

10.4 *Case Study: eBay Evolves*   405

10.5 *Review*   407
Key Concepts   407
Questions   410
Projects   410

---

11   B2B E-COMMERCE: SUPPLY CHAIN MANAGEMENT AND COLLABORATIVE COMMERCE   412

Learning Objectives   412

Volkswagen Builds Its B2B Platform   413

11.1 *B2B E-commerce and Supply Chain Management*   415
Defining and Measuring the Growth of B2b Commerce   416
The Evolution of B2B Commerce   416
The Growth of B2B E-commerce 2000–2016   417
Potential Benefits and Challenges of B2B E-commerce   418
The Procurement Process and the Supply Chain   419
Types of Procurement   419
Insight on Society : Where's My iPad? Supply Chain Risk and Vulnerability   420
Trends in Supply Chain Management and Collaborative Commerce   422
Just-in-Time and Lean Production   423
Supply Chain Simplification   423
Supply Chain Black Swans: Adaptive Supply Chains   423
Accountable Supply Chains: Labor Standards   424
Sustainable Supply Chains: Lean, Mean and Green   426
Electronic Data Interchange (EDI)   426
Supply Chain Management Systems: Mobile B2B in Your Palm   427
Collaborative Commerce   429
Social Networks and B2B: The Extended Social Enterprise   430
Main Types of Internet-based B2B Commerce   430

11.2 *Net Marketplaces*   431
Types of Net Marketplaces   431
E-distributors   432
E-procurement   433
Exchanges   435
Industry Consortia   436

11.3 *Private Industrial Networks*   438
What Are Private Industrial Networks?   438
Private Industrial Networks and Collaborative Commerce   439

Insight on Business: Walmart Develops a Private Industrial Network 440

11.4 *Case Study: Elemica: Cooperation, Collaboration, and Community* 442

11.5 *Review* 444
    Key Concepts 444
    Questions 447
    Projects 448

Index   *I-1*

References and Credits   *RC-1*

PART 1

■ **CHAPTER 1**
The Revolution Is Just Beginning

■ **CHAPTER 2**
E-commerce Business Models and Concepts

Introduction to E-commerce

CHAPTER 1

The Revolution Is Just Beginning

LEARNING OBJECTIVES

After reading this chapter, you will be able to:

- Define e-commerce.
- Identify and describe the unique features of e-commerce technology and discuss their business significance.
- Recognize and describe Web 2.0 applications.
- Describe the major types of e-commerce.
- Discuss the origins and growth of e-commerce.
- Understand the evolution of e-commerce from its early years to today.
- Identify the factors that will define the future of e-commerce.
- Describe the major themes underlying the study of e-commerce.

Pinterest:

A Picture Is Worth a Thousand Words

Like all of the most successful e-commerce companies, Pinterest taps into a simple truth. In Pinterest's case, the simple truth is that people love to collect things, and show off their collections to others. And like other Internet firms that have goals of global scope, such as Google, Facebook, and Amazon, Pinterest also has a global mission: to connect everyone in the world through the things they find interesting. How? Founded in 2009 by Ben Silbermann, Evan Sharp, and Paul Sciarra and launched in March 2010, Pinterest allows you to create virtual scrapbooks of images, video, and other content that you "pin" to a virtual

© Blaize Pascall / Alamy

bulletin board or pin board on the Web site. Find someone whose taste you admire or who shares your passions? You can follow one or more of that pinner's boards to keep track of everything she or he pins.

According to comScore, Pinterest is one of the fastest growing Web sites it has ever tracked, growing an astounding 4,377% from May 2011 to May 2012. Reportedly the fastest Web site in history to reach 10 million visitors a month, by mid-2012, Pinterest had around 20 million monthly visitors, an estimated 70% to 80% of them women. According to some tracking services, it is now the third largest social network in the United States, behind Facebook and Twitter. It is also one of the "stickiest" sites on the Web—according to comScore, users spend an average of 80 minutes per session on Pinterest, and almost 60% of users with accounts visit once or more a week.

For consumers, Pinterest can function both as a source of inspiration and aspiration. It has proven to be very popular for creating shopping wish lists and a great way to get ideas. Retailers, in particular, have taken notice and for good reason: several recent reports have shown that Pinterest helps drive shoppers to make purchases. For example, a study of 25,000 online stores using the Shopify e-commerce platform found there was as much traffic originating from Pinterest as from Twitter, and that Pinterest users spend an average of $80 each time they make an online purchase, twice the amount of Facebook users. Bizrate Insights found that almost a third of online shoppers surveyed

SOURCES: "Going Mobile with Pinterest," Pinterestinvite.org, accessed August 13, 2012; "Pinterest Gives Copyright Credit to Etsy, Kickstarter, SoundCloud," by Sarah Kessler, Mashable.com, July 19, 2012; "A Mobile Shopping App Takes an Interest in Pinterest," by Katie Deatsch, InternetRetailer.com, July 11, 2012; "Pinterest Tops Tumblr in National Popularity?," by Stephanie Mlot, *PC Magazine*, June 28, 2012; "Pinterest Whets Consumer Desire with Images that Turn Window Shoppers into Online Buyers," by Matt Butter, *Forbes*, June 6, 2012; "Gemvara Raises $25 Million," by Stefany Moore, InternetRetailer.com, June 5, 2012; "Pinterest Raises $100 Million with $1.5 Billion Valuation," by Pui-Wing Tam, *Wall Street Journal*, May 17, 2012; "Japanese E-commerce Company Rakuten Invests in Pinterest," by Zak Stambor, InternetRetailer.com, May 17, 2012; "Now on Pinterest: Scams," by Riva Richmond, *New York Times*, May 16, 2012; "Pinterest Plagued by More Scams, Fake Android Apps," by Fahmida Y. Rashid, PCMag.com, April 30, 2012; "Nearly 1/3 Online Shoppers Have Made Purchases from What They've Seen on Pinterest," by Zak Stambor, InternetRetailer.com, April 25, 2012; "E-commerce Giants Amazon and eBay Add Pinterest Buttons," by Kate Kaye, ClickZ.com, April 11, 2012; "Interest in Pinterest Skyrockets," by Zak Stambor, InternetRetailer.com, March 23, 2012; "Is Pinterest the Next Napster," by Therese Poletti, *Wall Street Journal*, March 14, 2012; "A Site That Aims to Unleash the Scrapbook Maker in All of Us," by Jenna Wortham, *New York Times*, March 11, 2012; "Pinterest Releases Optional Code to Prevent Unwanted Image Sharing," by Andrew Webster, Theverge.com, February 20, 2012; "A Scrapbook on the Web Catches Fire," by David Pogue, *New York Times*, February 15, 2012.

have made a purchase based on what they'd seen on Pinterest and other image-sharing sites; an even higher percentage (37%) have seen items they want to buy but have not yet purchased. As a result, savvy retailers are starting to work Pinterest into their marketing mix. A recent Responsys study found that almost 25% of large retailers are highlighting Pinterest in their marketing e-mail, and it will likely soon overtake YouTube as the third most promoted social media site in retailers' e-mails behind Facebook and Twitter. eBay and Amazon are also getting into the act, and have added Pinterest buttons that allow users to share product images and page links directly from eBay and Amazon.

On the mobile front, Pinterest introduced its own iPhone app in March 2011 and has frequently updated it since then, and an iPad app is also available for purchase. However, rather than develop additional stand-alone apps for Android, BlackBerry, or Windows smartphones, Pinterest chose a different route: to create a mobile version of the Web site using HTML5. Unlike an app, Pinterest Mobile runs inside the smartphone's browser rather than as a stand-alone program, and is able to serve multiple platforms.

Despite all the recent good news for Pinterest, there are some significant issues lurking just behind the scenes that may cloud its future; chief among them is copyright infringement. The basis of Pinterest's business model involves users potentially violating others' copyrights by posting images without permission and/or attribution. Pinterest has provided an opt-out code to enable other sites to bar its content from being shared on Pinterest, but some question why they should have to take action when Pinterest is creating the problem. Further, the code does not necessarily resolve the issue since it does not prevent someone from downloading an image and then uploading it to Pinterest. Another thing Pinterest has done to try to ameliorate the problem is to automatically add citations (attribution) to content coming from certain specified sources, such as Flickr, YouTube, Vimeo, Etsy, Kickstarter, and SlideShare, among others. It also complies with the Digital Millenium Copyright Act, which requires sites to remove images that violate copyright, but this too requires the copyright holder to be proactive and take action to demand the images be removed. Some have suggested that Pinterest follow YouTube's lead and implement a filter system, coupled with a revenue sharing platform. Although no major copyright cases have been filed against it so far, how Pinterest resolves this issue may have a major impact on its ultimate success. Pinterest is also not immune to the spam and scams that plague many e-commerce initiatives. Pinterest has acknowledged the problem and has promised to improve its technology.

Another issue facing Pinterest is competition. Will Pinterest be like MySpace, destined to be eclipsed by a later entrant? Although some similar firms preceded Pinterest into the "visual collection" space, such as Polyvore and StyleCaster, Pinterest can be considered a first mover and as such has some significant advantages. However, other competitors are quickly springing up, such as Juxtapost (which allows private boards), Manteresting (aimed at the male demographic), and most recently, The Fancy. The Fancy has a revenue model based on linking its users to transactions, taking a 10% cut of purchases in the process, has backing from co-founders of both Twitter and Facebook, and could become a formidable rival to Pinterest.

I n 1994, e-commerce as we now know it did not exist. In 2012, less than 20 years later, around 150 million American consumers spent about $362 billion, and businesses more than $4.1 trillion, purchasing goods and services online or via a mobile device. A similar story has occurred throughout the world. And in this short period of time, e-commerce has been reinvented not just once, but twice.

The early years of e-commerce, during the late 1990s, were a period of business vision, inspiration, and experimentation. It soon became apparent, however, that establishing a successful business model based on those visions would not be easy. There followed a period of retrenchment and reevaluation, which led to the stock market crash of 2000–2001, with the value of e-commerce, telecommunications, and other technology stocks plummeting. After the bubble burst, many people were quick to write off e-commerce. But they were wrong. The surviving firms refined and honed their business models, ultimately leading to models that actually produced profits. Between 2002–2008, retail e-commerce grew at more than 25% per year. Today, we are in the middle of yet another transition: a new and vibrant social, mobile, and local model of e-commerce growing alongside the more traditional e-commerce retail sales model exemplified by Amazon.

1.1 E-COMMERCE: THE REVOLUTION IS JUST BEGINNING

Table 1.1 describes the major trends in e-commerce in 2013. Social networks are becoming a new e-commerce platform that will rival traditional e-commerce platforms by providing search, advertising, and payment services to vendors and customers. The mobile platform based on smartphones like the iPhone, tablet computers like the iPad, and netbooks has also finally arrived with a bang, making true mobile e-commerce a reality.

More and more people and businesses are using the Internet to conduct commerce; smaller, local firms are learning how to take advantage of the Internet as Web services and Web site tools become very inexpensive. New e-commerce brands emerge while traditional retail brands such as Sears, JCPenney, and Walmart further extend their multi-channel, bricks-and-clicks strategies and retain their dominant retail positions by strengthening their Internet operations. At the societal level, other trends are apparent. The Internet has created a platform for millions of people to create and share content, establish new social bonds, and strengthen existing ones through social networks, blogging, and video-posting sites. These same social networks have created significant privacy issues. The major digital copyright owners have increased their pursuit of online file-swapping services with mixed success, while reaching broad agreements with the big technology players like Apple, Amazon, and Google to protect intellectual property rights. States have successfully moved toward taxation of Internet sales, while Internet gaming sites have been severely curtailed through criminal prosecutions in the United States. Sovereign nations have expanded their surveillance of, and control over, Internet communications and content as a part of their anti-terrorist activities and their

TABLE 1.1	MAJOR TRENDS IN E-COMMERCE 2012–2013

BUSINESS

- A new "social e-commerce" platform continues to emerge based on social networks and supported by advertising.
- A new app-based online economy grows alongside traditional Internet e-commerce.
- Retail e-commerce in the United States continues double-digit growth (over 15%), building on its 2010 and 2011 resurgence, after slow growth in 2008 and 2009 due to the recession.
- Facebook continues to grow, with more than 1 billion active users worldwide.
- Twitter continues to grow, with more than 140 million active users worldwide.
- Mobile retail e-commerce explodes to more than $11 billion in the United States.
- Localization of e-commerce expands with group marketing and localized tracking of mobile consumers.
- Search engine marketing continues to challenge traditional marketing and advertising media as more consumers switch their eyes to the Web.
- B2B supply chain transactions and collaborative commerce in the United States continue to strengthen and grow beyond the $4.1 trillion mark.

TECHNOLOGY

- A mobile computing and communications platform based on iPhones, BlackBerrys, and other smartphones, netbook computers, and the iPad (the "new client") becomes a reality and begins to rival the PC platform.
- More than 1 million apps in Apple's and Google's app stores create a new platform for online transactions, marketing, and advertising.
- Computing and networking component prices continue to fall dramatically.
- As firms track the trillions of online interactions that occur each day on the Web, a flood of data, typically referred to as "Big Data," is being produced.
- Cloud computing completes the transformation of the mobile platform by storing consumer content and software on Internet servers and making it available to any consumer-connected device from the desktop to a smartphone.

SOCIETY

- Consumer- and user-generated content, and syndication in the form of social networks, tweets, blogs, and wikis, continue to grow and provide an entirely new self-publishing forum.
- The amount of data the average American consumes each day (currently around 34 gigabytes) continues to increase.
- Social networks encourage self-revelation, while threatening privacy.
- E-books finally gain wide acceptance and today account for about half of all book sales.
- Conflicts over copyright management and control continue.
- Participation by adults in social networks on the Internet increases; Facebook becomes ever more popular in all demographic categories.
- Taxation of Internet sales becomes more widespread and accepted by large online merchants.
- Surveillance of Internet communications by both repressive regimes and Western democracies grows.
- Concerns over commercial and governmental privacy invasion increase as firms provide government agencies with access to private personal information.
- Internet security continues to decline as major sites are hacked and lose control over customer information.

traditional interest in snooping on citizens. Privacy seems to have lost some of its meaning in an age when millions create public online personal profiles.

THE FIRST 30 SECONDS

It is important to realize that the rapid growth and change that has occurred in the first 17 years of e-commerce represents just the beginning—what could be called the first 30 seconds of the e-commerce revolution. The same technologies that drove the first decade and a half of e-commerce (described in Chapter 3) continue to evolve at exponential rates. This underlying ferment in the technological groundwork of the Internet and Web presents entrepreneurs with new opportunities to both create new businesses and new business models in traditional industries, and also to destroy old businesses. Business change becomes disruptive, rapid, and even destructive, while offering entrepreneurs new opportunities and resources for investment.

Improvements in underlying information technologies and continuing entrepreneurial innovation in business and marketing promise as much change in the next decade as was seen in the last decade. The twenty-first century will be the age of a digitally enabled social and commercial life, the outlines of which we can barely perceive at this time. Analysts estimate that by 2016, consumers will be spending about $542 billion and businesses about $5.7 trillion in online transactions. In 2020, industry analysts are calling for e-commerce to be about 17% of all retail sales (Deatsch, 2010). It appears likely that e-commerce will eventually impact nearly all commerce, and that most commerce will be e-commerce by the year 2050.

As a business or technology student, this book will help you perceive and understand the opportunities and risks that lie ahead. By the time you finish, you will be able to identify the technological, business, and social forces that have shaped the growth of e-commerce and extend that understanding into the years ahead.

WHAT IS E-COMMERCE?

Our focus in this book is **e-commerce**—the use of the Internet, the World Wide Web (Web) and mobile apps to transact business. Although the terms Internet and Web are often used interchangeably, they are actually two very different things. The Internet is a worldwide network of computer networks, and the Web is one of the Internet's most popular services, providing access to billions of Web pages. An app (short-hand for application) is a software application. The term is typically used when referring to mobile applications, although it is also sometimes used to refer to desktop computer applications as well. (We describe the Internet, Web, and apps more fully later in this chapter and in Chapter 3 and Chapter 4.) More formally, we focus on digitally enabled commercial transactions between and among organizations and individuals. Each of these components of our working definition of e-commerce is important. *Digitally enabled transactions* include all transactions mediated by digital technology. For the most part, this means transactions that occur over the Internet, the Web and/or via mobile apps. *Commercial transactions* involve the exchange of value (e.g., money) across organizational or individual boundaries in return for products and services. Exchange of value is important for understanding the limits of e-commerce. Without an exchange of value, no commerce occurs.

e-commerce
the use of the Internet, the Web, and apps to transact business. More formally, digitally enabled commercial transactions between and among organizations and individuals

The professional literature sometimes refers to e-commerce as "digital commerce" in part to reflect the fact that in 2012, apps account for a small but growing amount of e-commerce revenues. For our purposes, we consider "e-commerce" and "digital commerce" to be synonymous.

WHY STUDY E-COMMERCE?

E-commerce technology is different and more powerful than any of the other technologies we have seen in the past century. E-commerce technologies—and the digital markets that result—are bringing about fundamental, unprecedented shifts in commerce. While other technologies transformed economic life in the twentieth century, the evolving Internet and other information technologies are shaping the twenty-first century.

Prior to the development of e-commerce, the marketing and sale of goods was a mass-marketing and sales force–driven process. Information about prices, costs, and fees could be hidden from the consumer, creating profitable "information asymmetries" for the selling firm. **Information asymmetry** refers to any disparity in relevant market information among parties in a transaction. One of the shifts that e-commerce is bringing about is a reduction in information asymmetry among market participants (consumers and merchants). Preventing consumers from learning about costs, price discrimination strategies, and profits from sales becomes more difficult with e-commerce, and the entire marketplace potentially becomes highly price competitive. At the same time, online merchants gain considerable market power over consumers by using consumer personal information in ways inconceivable 10 years ago.

EIGHT UNIQUE FEATURES OF E-COMMERCE TECHNOLOGY

Table 1.2 lists eight unique features of e-commerce technology that both challenge traditional business thinking and explain why we have so much interest in e-commerce. These unique dimensions of e-commerce technologies suggest many new possibilities for marketing and selling—a powerful set of interactive, personalized, and rich messages are available for delivery to segmented, targeted audiences. E-commerce technologies make it possible for merchants to know much more about consumers and to be able to use this information more effectively than was ever true in the past.

Each of the dimensions of e-commerce technology and their business significance listed in Table 1.2 deserves a brief exploration, as well as a comparison to both traditional commerce and other forms of technology-enabled commerce.

Ubiquity

In traditional commerce, a **marketplace** is a physical place you visit in order to transact. For example, television and radio typically motivate the consumer to go some place to make a purchase. E-commerce, in contrast, is characterized by its **ubiquity**: it is available just about everywhere, at all times. It liberates the market from being restricted to a physical space and makes it possible to shop from your desktop, at home, at work, or even from your car, using mobile e-commerce. The result

information asymmetry
any disparity in relevant market information among parties in a transaction

marketplace
physical space you visit in order to transact

ubiquity
available just about everywhere, at all times

TABLE 1.2	EIGHT UNIQUE FEATURES OF E-COMMERCE TECHNOLOGY
E-COMMERCE TECHNOLOGY DIMENSION	**BUSINESS SIGNIFICANCE**
Ubiquity—Internet/Web technology is available everywhere: at work, at home, and elsewhere via mobile devices, anytime.	The marketplace is extended beyond traditional boundaries and is removed from a temporal and geographic location. "Marketspace" is created; shopping can take place anywhere. Customer convenience is enhanced, and shopping costs are reduced.
Global reach—The technology reaches across national boundaries, around the earth.	Commerce is enabled across cultural and national boundaries seamlessly and without modification. "Marketspace" includes potentially billions of consumers and millions of businesses worldwide.
Universal standards—There is one set of technology standards, namely Internet standards.	There is a common, inexpensive, global technology foundation for businesses to use.
Richness—Video, audio, and text messages are possible.	Video, audio, and text marketing messages are integrated into a single marketing message and consuming experience.
Interactivity—The technology works through interaction with the user.	Consumers are engaged in a dialog that dynamically adjusts the experience to the individual, and makes the consumer a co-participant in the process of delivering goods to the market.
Information density—The technology reduces information costs and raises quality.	Information processing, storage, and communication costs drop dramatically, while currency, accuracy, and timeliness improve greatly. Information becomes plentiful, cheap, and accurate.
Personalization/Customization—The technology allows personalized messages to be delivered to individuals as well as groups.	Personalization of marketing messages and customization of products and services are based on individual characteristics.
Social technology—User content generation and social networks.	New Internet social and business models enable user content creation and distribution, and support social networks.

is called a **marketspace**—a marketplace extended beyond traditional boundaries and removed from a temporal and geographic location. From a consumer point of view, ubiquity reduces *transaction costs*—the costs of participating in a market. To transact, it is no longer necessary that you spend time and money traveling to a market.

Global Reach

E-commerce technology permits commercial transactions to cross cultural, regional, and national boundaries far more conveniently and cost-effectively than is true in

marketspace

marketplace extended beyond traditional boundaries and removed from a temporal and geographic location traditional commerce. As a result, the potential market size for e-commerce merchants is roughly equal to the size of the world's online population (more than 2.2 billion) (Internet Worldstats, 2012). The total number of users or customers an e-commerce business can obtain is a measure of its **reach**. In contrast, most traditional commerce is local or regional—it involves local merchants or national merchants with local outlets and does not easily cross national boundaries to a global audience.

reach
the total number of users or customers an e-commerce business can obtain

Universal Standards

universal standards
standards that are shared by all nations around the world

One strikingly unusual feature of e-commerce technologies is that the technical standards of the Internet, and therefore the technical standards for conducting e-commerce, are **universal standards**—they are shared by all nations around the world. In contrast, most traditional commerce technologies differ from one nation to the next. For instance, television and radio standards differ around the world, as does cell phone technology. The universal technical standards of the Internet and e-commerce greatly lower *market entry costs*—the cost merchants must pay just to bring their goods to market. At the same time, for consumers, universal standards reduce *search costs*—the effort required to find suitable products. And by creating a single, one-world marketspace, where prices and product descriptions can be inexpensively displayed for all to see, *price discovery* becomes simpler, faster, and more accurate. Users of the Internet, both businesses and individuals, also experience *network externalities*—benefits that arise because everyone uses the same technology.

Richness

richness
the complexity and content of a message

Information **richness** refers to the complexity and content of a message. Traditional markets, national sales forces, and small retail stores have great richness: they are able to provide personal, face-to-face service using aural and visual cues when making a sale. The richness of traditional markets makes them a powerful selling or commercial environment. Prior to the development of the Web, there was a trade-off between richness and reach: the larger the audience reached, the less rich the message. The Internet has the potential for offering considerably more information richness than traditional media such as printing presses, radio, and television because it is interactive and can adjust the message to individual users.

Interactivity

interactivity
technology that allows for two-way communication between merchant and consumer

Unlike any of the commercial technologies of the twentieth century, with the possible exception of the telephone, e-commerce technologies allow for **interactivity**, meaning they enable two-way communication between merchant and consumer and among consumers. Traditional television, for instance, cannot ask viewers questions or enter into conversations with them, or request that customer information be entered into a form. In contrast, all of these activities are possible on an e-commerce Web site and are now commonplace with smartphones, social networks, and Twitter.

Information Density

The Internet and the Web vastly increase **information density**—the total amount and quality of information available to all market participants, consumers, and merchants alike. E-commerce technologies reduce information collection, storage, processing, and communication costs. At the same time, these technologies greatly increase the currency, accuracy, and timeliness of information—making information more useful and important than ever. As a result, information becomes more plentiful, less expensive, and of higher quality.

information density
the total amount and quality of information available to all market participants

Personalization/Customization

E-commerce technologies permit **personalization**: merchants can target their marketing messages to specific individuals by adjusting the message to a person's name, interests, and past purchases. Today this is achieved in a few milliseconds and followed by an advertisement based on the consumer's profile. The technology also permits **customization**—changing the delivered product or service based on a user's preferences or prior behavior. Given the interactive nature of e-commerce technology, much information about the consumer can be gathered in the marketplace at the moment of purchase. With the increase in information density, a great deal of information about the consumer's past purchases and behavior can be stored and used by online merchants. The result is a level of personalization and customization unthinkable with existing commerce technologies.

personalization
the targeting of marketing messages to specific individuals by adjusting the message to a person's name, interests, and past purchases

customization
changing the delivered product or service based on a user's preferences or prior behavior

Social Technology: User Content Generation and Social Networking

The Internet and e-commerce technologies have evolved to be much more social by allowing users to create and share content in the form of Web and Facebook pages, text, videos, music, and photos with a worldwide community. All previous mass media in modern history, including the printing press, use a broadcast model (one-to-many) where content is created in a central location by experts, such as professional writers, and audiences are concentrated in huge aggregates to consume a standardized product. The Internet and e-commerce technologies have the potential to invert this standard media model by giving users the power to create and distribute content on a large scale, and permit users to program their own content consumption. The Internet provides a unique, many-to-many model of mass communication.

WEB 2.0: PLAY MY VERSION

Many of the unique features of e-commerce and the Internet come together in a set of applications and social media technologies referred to as Web 2.0. The Internet started out as a simple network to support e-mail and file transfers among remote computers. The Web started out as a way to use the Internet to display simple pages and allow the user to navigate among the pages by linking them together electronically. You can think of this as Web 1.0. By 2007 something else was happening. The Internet and the Web had evolved to the point where users could create, edit, and distribute content to others; share with one another their preferences, bookmarks, and online personas; participate in virtual lives; and build online communities. This

Web 2.0

a set of applications and technologies that allows users to create, edit, and distribute content; share preferences, bookmarks, and online personas; participate in virtual lives; and build online communities

"new" Web was called by many **Web 2.0,** and while it draws heavily on the "old" Web 1.0, it is nevertheless a clear evolution from the past.

Let's take a quick look at some examples of Web 2.0 applications and sites:

- Twitter is a social network/micro-blogging service that encourages users to enter 140-character messages ("tweets") in answer to the question "What are you doing?" Twitter has more than 140 million active users worldwide, sending around 340 million tweets per day and more than 10 billion tweets a month.

- YouTube is the world's largest online consumer-generated video-posting site. YouTube is now morphing into a premium video content distributor and video producer, offering feature-length movies, television series, and its own original content.

- Instagram is a mobile photo-sharing application available for Androids and iPhones that allows users to easily apply a variety of different photo filters and borders, and then post the photos to social networks such as Facebook, Twitter, Foursquare, Tumblr and Flickr.

- Wikipedia allows contributors around the world to share their knowledge and in the process has become the most successful online encyclopedia, far surpassing "professional" encyclopedias such as Encarta and Britannica. Wikipedia is one of the largest collaboratively edited reference projects in the world.

- Tumblr is a combination of blog platform and social network. It allows users to easily post text, photos, links, music, videos and more. As of June 2012, Tumblr hosted almost 60 million blogs, containing almost 25 billion posts. On a typical day, users make over 65 million posts (Tumblr.com, 2012). Tumblr has more than doubled in size since September 2011.

What do all these Web 2.0 applications and sites have in common? First, they rely on user- and consumer-generated content. These are all "applications" created by people, especially people in the 18–34 year-old demographic, and in the 7–17 age group as well. "Regular" people (not just experts or professionals) are creating, sharing, modifying, and broadcasting content to huge audiences. Second, easy search capability is a key to their success. Third, they are inherently highly interactive, creating new opportunities for people to socially connect to others. They are "social" sites because they support interactions among users. Fourth, they rely on broadband connectivity to the Web. Fifth, many of them are currently only marginally profitable, and their business models are unproven despite considerable investment. Nevertheless, the potential monetary rewards for social sites with huge audiences is quite large. Sixth, they attract extremely large audiences when compared to traditional Web 1.0 applications, exceeding in many cases the audience size of national broadcast and cable television programs. These audience relationships are intensive and long-lasting interactions with millions of people. In short, they attract eyeballs in very large numbers. Hence, they present marketers with extraordinary opportunities for targeted marketing and advertising. They also present consumers with the opportunity to rate and review products, and entrepreneurs with ideas for future business ventures. Last, these sites act as application development platforms where users can contribute and use software applications for free. Briefly, it's a whole new world from what has gone before.

TYPES OF E-COMMERCE

There are several different types of e-commerce and many different ways to characterize them. For the most part, we distinguish different types of e-commerce by the nature of the market relationship—who is selling to whom. Social, mobile, and local e-commerce can be looked at as subsets of these types of e-commerce.

Business-to-Consumer (B2C) E-commerce

The most commonly discussed type of e-commerce is **business-to-consumer (B2C) e-commerce**, in which online businesses attempt to reach individual consumers. B2C commerce includes purchases of retail goods, travel services, and online content. Even though B2C is comparatively small (about $342 billion in 2012 in the United States), it has grown exponentially since 1995, and is the type of e-commerce that most consumers are likely to encounter (see **Figure 1.1**).

business-to-consumer (B2C) e-commerce

online businesses selling to individual consumers

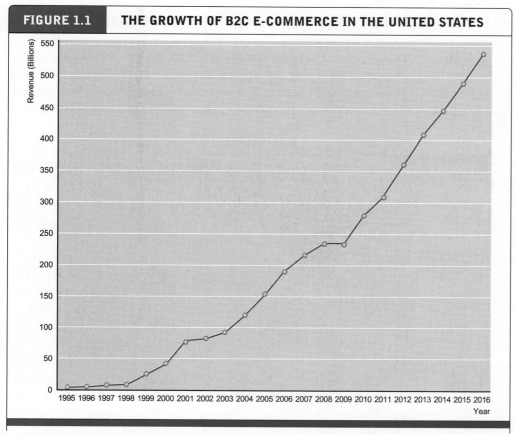

| FIGURE 1.1 | THE GROWTH OF B2C E-COMMERCE IN THE UNITED STATES |

In the early years, B2C e-commerce was doubling or tripling each year. Although B2C e-commerce growth in the United States slowed in 2008–2009 due to the economic recession, it resumed growing at about 13% in 2010 and continued to grow at double-digit rates in 2011 and 2012.

SOURCES: Based on data from eMarketer, Inc., 2012a; authors' estimates.

Business-to-Business (B2B) E-commerce

business-to-business (B2B) e-commerce
online businesses selling to other businesses

Business-to-business (B2B) e-commerce, in which businesses focus on selling to other businesses, is the largest form of e-commerce, with about $4.1 trillion in transactions in the United States in 2012 (see **Figure 1.2**). There was an estimated $11.5 trillion in business-to-business exchanges of all kinds, online and offline, suggesting that B2B e-commerce has significant growth potential. The ultimate size of B2B e-commerce is potentially huge.

Consumer-to-Consumer (C2C) E-commerce

consumer-to-consumer (C2C) e-commerce
consumers selling to other consumers

Consumer-to-consumer (C2C) e-commerce provides a way for consumers to sell to each other, with the help of an online market maker such as eBay or Etsy, or the classifieds site Craigslist. In C2C e-commerce, the consumer prepares the product for market, places the product for auction or sale, and relies on the market maker to provide catalog, search engine, and transaction-clearing capabilities so that products can be easily displayed, discovered, and paid for.

Social E-commerce

social e-commerce
e-commerce enabled by social networks and online social relationships

Social e-commerce is e-commerce that is enabled by social networks and online social relationships. It is sometimes also referred to as Facebook commerce, but in actuality is a much larger phenomenon that extends beyond just Facebook. The growth of social e-commerce is being driven by a number of factors, including the increasing popularity of social sign-on (signing onto Web sites using your Facebook or other social network ID), network notification (the sharing of approval or disapproval of products,

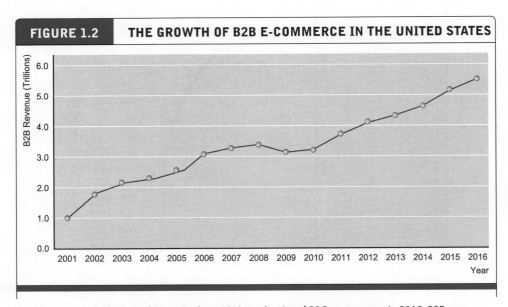

FIGURE 1.2   THE GROWTH OF B2B E-COMMERCE IN THE UNITED STATES

B2B e-commerce in the United States is about 10 times the size of B2C e-commerce. In 2016, B2B e-commerce is projected to be about $5.6 trillion. (Note: Does not include EDI transactions.)
SOURCES: Based on data from U.S. Census Bureau, 2012; authors' estimates.

services, and content via Facebook's Like button or Twitter tweets), online collaborative shopping tools, and social search (recommendations from online trusted friends).

Mobile E-commerce (M-commerce)

Mobile e-commerce, or m-commerce, refers to the use of mobile devices to enable transactions on the Web. Described more fully in Chapter 3, m-commerce involves the use of cellular and wireless networks to connect laptops, smartphones such as the iPhone, Android, and BlackBerry, and tablet computers such as the iPad to the Web. Once connected, mobile consumers can conduct transactions, including stock trades, in-store price comparisons, banking, travel reservations, and more.

mobile e-commerce (m-commerce)
use of mobile devices to enable transactions on the Web

Local E-commerce

Local e-commerce, as its name suggests, is a form of e-commerce that is focused on engaging the consumer based on his or her current geographic location. Local merchants use a variety of online marketing techniques to drive consumers to their stores. Local e-commerce is the third prong of the social, mobile, local e-commerce wave. **Table 1.3** summarizes the various forms of e-commerce.

local e-commerce
e-commerce that is focused on engaging the consumer based on his or her current geographic location

GROWTH OF THE INTERNET AND THE WEB

The technology juggernauts behind e-commerce are the Internet and the Web. Without both of these technologies, e-commerce as we know it would be impossible. We

TABLE 1.3	MAJOR TYPES OF E-COMMERCE
TYPE OF E-COMMERCE	EXAMPLE
B2C—business-to-consumer	Amazon is a general merchandiser that sells consumer products to retail consumers.
B2B—business-to-business	Go2Paper.com is an independent third-party marketplace that serves the paper industry.
C2C—consumer-to-consumer	On a large number of Web auction sites such as eBay, and listing sites such as Craigslist, consumers can auction or sell goods directly to other consumers.
Social e-commerce	Facebook is both the leading social network and social e-commerce site.
M-commerce—mobile e-commerce	Mobile devices such as tablet computers and smartphones can be used to conduct commercial transactions.
Local e-commerce	Groupon offers subscribers daily deals from local businesses in the form of "Groupons," discount coupons that take effect once enough subscribers have agreed to purchase.

Internet

worldwide network of computer networks built on common standards

describe the Internet and the Web in some detail in Chapter 3. The **Internet** is a worldwide network of computer networks built on common standards. Created in the late 1960s to connect a small number of mainframe computers and their users, the Internet has since grown into the world's largest network. It is impossible to say with certainty exactly how many computers and other wireless access devices such as smartphones are connected to the Internet worldwide at any one time, but the number is clearly more than 1 billion. The Internet links businesses, educational institutions, government agencies, and individuals together, and provides users with services such as e-mail, document transfer, shopping, research, instant messaging, music, videos, and news.

One way to measure the growth of the Internet is by looking at the number of Internet hosts with domain names. (An *Internet host* is defined by the Internet Systems Consortium as any IP address that returns a domain name in the in-addr.arpa domain, which is a special part of the DNS namespace that resolves IP addresses into domain names.) In January 2012, there were over 888 million Internet hosts in over 245 countries, up from just 70 million in 2000 (Internet Systems Consortium, 2012).

The Internet has shown extraordinary growth patterns when compared to other electronic technologies of the past. It took radio 38 years to achieve a 30% share of U.S. households. It took television 17 years to achieve a 30% share. It took only 10 years for the Internet/Web to achieve a 53% share of U.S. households once a graphical user interface was invented for the Web in 1993.

World Wide Web (the Web)

the most popular service that runs on the Internet; provides easy access to Web pages

The **World Wide Web (the Web)** is the most popular service that runs on the Internet infrastructure. The Web is the "killer app" that made the Internet commercially interesting and extraordinarily popular. The Web was developed in the early 1990s and hence is of much more recent vintage than the Internet. We describe the Web in some detail in Chapter 3. The Web provides access to billions of Web pages indexed by Google and other search engines. These pages are created in a language called *HTML (HyperText Markup Language)*. HTML pages can contain text, graphics, animations, and other objects. You can find an exceptionally wide range of information on Web pages, ranging from the entire collection of public records from the Securities and Exchange Commission, to the card catalog of your local library, to millions of music tracks and videos. The Internet prior to the Web was primarily used for text communications, file transfers, and remote computing. The Web introduced far more powerful and commercially interesting, colorful multimedia capabilities of direct relevance to commerce. In essence, the Web added color, voice, and video to the Internet, creating a communications infrastructure and information storage system that rivals television, radio, magazines, and even libraries.

There is no precise measurement of the number of Web pages in existence, in part because today's search engines index only a portion of the known universe of Web pages, and also because the size of the Web universe is unknown. Google reported that its system had, as of July 2008, identified 1 trillion unique URLs, although many of those pages did not necessarily contain unique content. Today, it is likely that Google indexes at least 120 billion Web pages, if not more. In addition to this "surface" or "visible" Web, there is also the so-called "deep Web" that is reportedly 1,000 to

5,000 times greater than the surface Web. The deep Web contains databases and other content that is not routinely indexed by search engines such as Google. Although the total size of the Web is not known, what is indisputable is that Web content has grown exponentially since 1993.

The most significant technology that can reduce barriers to Internet access is the wireless mobile platform. In 2012, around 122 million people (over 50% of Internet users in the United States) used a mobile device to access the Internet, and this number is expected to grow to 199 million (75% of all Internet users in the United States) by 2016 (eMarketer, Inc., 2012b). **Figure 1.3** illustrates the rapid growth projected for mobile Internet access during the period 2009–2016.

1.2 E-COMMERCE: A BRIEF HISTORY

Although e-commerce is not very old, it already has a tumultuous history. The history of e-commerce can be usefully divided into three periods: 1995–2000, the period of invention; 2001–2006, the period of consolidation; and 2007–present, a period of

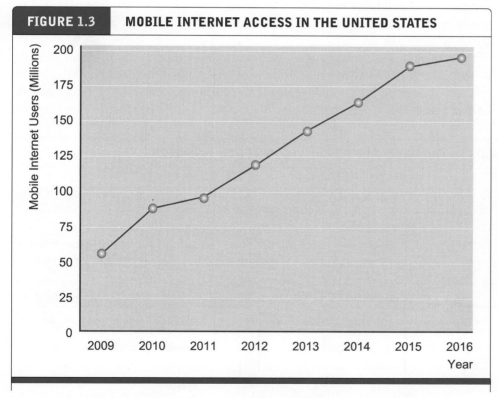

FIGURE 1.3 — MOBILE INTERNET ACCESS IN THE UNITED STATES

Growth in the number of mobile Internet users will provide a significant stimulus to mobile e-commerce.
SOURCE: Based on data from eMarketer, Inc., 2012b.

reinvention with social, mobile, and local expansion. The following examines each of these periods briefly, while **Figure 1.4** places them in context along a timeline.

E-COMMERCE 1995–2000: INVENTION

The early years of e-commerce were a period of explosive growth and extraordinary innovation, beginning in 1995 with the first widespread use of the Web to advertise products. During this Invention period, e-commerce meant selling retail goods, usually quite simple goods, on the Internet. There simply was not enough bandwidth for more complex products. Marketing was limited to unsophisticated static display ads and not very powerful search engines. The Web policy of most large firms, if they had one at all, was to have a basic static Web site depicting their brands. The rapid growth in e-commerce was fueled by over $125 billion in venture capital. This period of e-commerce came to a close in 2000 when stock market valuations plunged, with thousands of companies disappearing (the "dot-com crash").

A number of key e-commerce concepts were developed in this period. For computer scientists and information technologists, the early success of e-commerce was a powerful vindication of a set of information technologies that had developed over a period of 40 years—extending from the development of the early Internet, to the PC, to local area networks. The vision was of a universal communications and computing environment that everyone on Earth could access with cheap, inexpensive computers—a worldwide universe of knowledge stored on HTML pages created by hundreds of millions of individuals and thousands of libraries, governments, and scientific institutes.

For economists, the early years of e-commerce raised the prospect of a nearly perfect competitive market: where price, cost, and quality information are equally distributed, a nearly infinite set of suppliers compete against one another, and customers have access to all relevant market information worldwide. The Internet would spawn

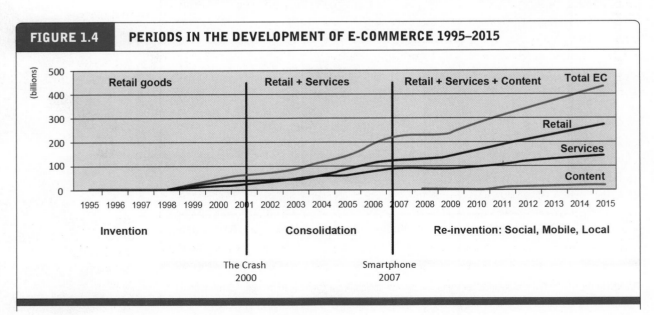

FIGURE 1.4 **PERIODS IN THE DEVELOPMENT OF E-COMMERCE 1995–2015**

digital markets where information would be nearly perfect—something that is rarely true in other real-world markets. Merchants in turn would have equal direct access to hundreds of millions of customers. In this near-perfect information marketspace, transaction costs would plummet because search costs—the cost of searching for prices, product descriptions, payment settlement, and order fulfillment—would all fall drastically.

Prices and even costs would be increasingly transparent to the consumer, who could now know exactly and instantly the worldwide best price, quality, and availability of most products. Information asymmetry would be greatly reduced. Given the instant nature of Internet communications, the availability of powerful sales information systems, and the low cost involved in changing prices on a Web site (low menu costs), products could be dynamically priced to reflect actual demand, ending the idea of one national price, or one suggested manufacturer's list price. In turn, market middlemen—the distributors and wholesalers who are intermediaries between producers and consumers, each demanding a payment and raising costs while adding little value—would disappear (**disintermediation**). Manufacturers and content originators would develop direct market relationships with their customers. This vision was called **friction-free commerce.**

For real-world entrepreneurs and business firms and their investors, instead of friction-free commerce, e-commerce represented an extraordinary opportunity to earn far above normal returns on investment. The e-commerce marketspace represented access to millions of consumers worldwide who used the Internet and a set of marketing communications technologies (e-mail and Web pages) that was universal, inexpensive, and powerful. These new technologies would permit marketers to practice what they always had done—segmenting the market into groups with different needs and price sensitivity, targeting the segments with branding and promotional messages, and positioning the product and pricing for each group—but with even more precision. In this new marketspace, extraordinary profits would go to **first movers**—those firms who were first to market in a particular area and who moved quickly to gather market share. In a "winner take all" market, first movers could establish a large customer base quickly, build brand name recognition early, create an entirely new distribution channel, and then inhibit competitors (new entrants) by building in switching costs for their customers through proprietary interface designs and features available only at one site. The idea for entrepreneurs was to create near monopolies online based on size, convenience, selection, and brand. Online businesses using the new technology could create informative, community-like features unavailable to traditional merchants. These "communities of consumption" also would add value and be difficult for traditional merchants to imitate. The thinking was that once customers became accustomed to using a company's unique Web interface and feature set, they could not easily be switched to competitors. In the best case, the entrepreneurial firm would invent proprietary technologies and techniques that almost everyone adopted, creating a network effect. A **network effect** occurs where all participants receive value from the fact that everyone else uses the same tool or product (for example, a common operating system, telephone system, or software application such as a proprietary

disintermediation
displacement of market middlemen who traditionally are intermediaries between producers and consumers by a new direct relationship between producers and consumers

friction-free commerce
a vision of commerce in which information is equally distributed, transaction costs are low, prices can be dynamically adjusted to reflect actual demand, intermediaries decline, and unfair competitive advantages are eliminated

first mover
a firm that is first to market in a particular area and that moves quickly to gather market share

network effect
occurs where users receive value from the fact that everyone else uses the same tool or product

instant messaging standard or an operating system such as Windows), all of which increase in value as more people adopt them.

Thus, the early years of e-commerce were driven largely by visions of profiting from new technology, with the emphasis on quickly achieving very high market visibility. The source of financing was venture capital funds. The ideology of the period emphasized the ungoverned "Wild West" character of the Web and the feeling that governments and courts could not possibly limit or regulate the Internet; there was a general belief that traditional corporations were too slow and bureaucratic, too stuck in the old ways of doing business, to "get it"—to be competitive in e-commerce. Young entrepreneurs were therefore the driving force behind e-commerce, backed by huge amounts of money invested by venture capitalists. The business emphasis was on digital disruption of entire industries, deconstructing (destroying) traditional distribution channels, and disintermediating existing channels, using new pure online companies who aimed to achieve impregnable first-mover advantages.

E-COMMERCE 2001–2006: CONSOLIDATION

In the second period of e-commerce, from 2000 to 2006, a sobering period of reassessment of e-commerce occurred, with many critics doubting its long-term prospects. Emphasis shifted to a more "business-driven" approach rather than being technology driven; large traditional firms learned how to use the Web to strengthen their market positions; brand extension and strengthening became more important than creating new brands; financing shrunk as capital markets shunned start-up firms; and traditional bank financing based on profitability returned.

During this period of consolidation, e-commerce changed to include not just retail products but also more complex services such as travel and financial services. This period was enabled by widespread adoption of broadband networks in American homes and businesses, coupled with the growing power and lower prices of personal computers that were the primary means of accessing the Internet, usually from work or home. Marketing on the Internet increasingly meant using search engine advertising targeted to user queries, rich media and video ads, and behavioral targeting of marketing messages based on ad networks and auction markets. The Web policy of both large and small firms expanded to include a broader "Web presence" that included not just Web sites, but also e-mail, display, and search engine campaigns; multiple Web sites for each product; and the building of some limited community feedback facilities. E-commerce in this period was growing again by more than 10% a year.

E-COMMERCE 2007—PRESENT: REINVENTION

Beginning in 2007 with the introduction of the iPhone, to the present day, e-commerce has been transformed yet again by the rapid growth of online social networks, widespread adoption of consumer mobile devices such as smartphones and tablet computers, and the expansion of e-commerce to include local goods and services. The defining characteristics of this period are often characterized as the "social, mobile, local" online world. In this period, entertainment content begins to develop as a major source of e-commerce revenues and mobile devices become entertainment centers, as well as on-the-go shopping devices for retail goods and services. Marketing is transformed by the increasing use of social networks, word-of-mouth, viral marketing, and much more powerful data repositories and analytic tools for truly personal marketing. Firms' online policies expand in the attempt to build a digital presence that surrounds the online consumer with coordinated marketing messages based on their social network memberships, use of search engines and Web browsers, and even their personal e-mail messages, social networks, the mobile platform, and local commerce. This period is as much a sociological phenomenon as it is a technological or business phenomenon. Few of the new mobile, social, and local firms in this period have been able to monetize their huge audiences into profitable operations yet, but many eventually will. The *Insight on Business* case, *Is the Party Already Over?*, examines the rise of yet another Internet investment bubble, this time centered around social media, and the fall-out resulting from the problems surrounding Facebook's initial public offering.

Table 1.5 summarizes e-commerce in each of these three periods.

TABLE 1.5	EVOLUTION OF E-COMMERCE	
1995–2000 INVENTION	2001–2006 CONSOLIDATION	2007–PRESENT RE-INVENTION
Technology driven	Business driven	Mobile technology enables social, local, and mobile commerce
Revenue growth emphasis	Earnings and profits emphasis	Audience and social network connections emphasis
Venture capital financing	Traditional financing	Smaller VC investments; early small-firm buyouts by large online players
Ungoverned	Stronger regulation and governance	Extensive government surveillance
Entrepreneurial	Large traditional firms	Entrepreneurial social and local firms
Disintermediation	Strengthening intermediaries	Proliferation of small online intermediaries renting business processes of larger firms
Perfect markets	Imperfect markets, brands, and network effects	Continuation of online market imperfections; commodity competition in select markets
Pure online strategies	Mixed "bricks-and-clicks" strategies	Return of pure online strategies in new markets; extension of bricks-and-clicks in traditional retail markets
First-mover advantages	Strategic-follower strength; complementary assets	First-mover advantages return in new markets as traditional Web players catch up
Low-complexity retail products	High-complexity retail products and services	Retail, services, and content

INSIGHT ON BUSINESS

IS THE PARTY ALREADY OVER?

In 2011 and early 2012, with the successful initial public offerings (IPOs) of LinkedIn, Zynga, Groupon, and Pandora Media, rampant interest in the forthcoming Facebook IPO, and increased venture capital investment in other social media companies such as Twitter, many felt the times were reminiscent of the dot-com bubble of 1998–2000. And, in an eerie similarity, just as the dot-com bubble burst to a crash in mid-2000, so too has the new "social media" bubble shown signs of serious leakage.

The problems first began to surface with the eagerly anticipated Facebook IPO in May 2012. Facebook went public with a valuation of over $100 billion, the biggest IPO valuation ever, and a share price of $38, making it unlikely that its shares would experience the traditional first day "pop" in price that was the hallmark of Internet IPOs back in the heyday of the dot-com bubble. Investors both large and small were inevitably disappointed as the shares declined rather than rose from their initial price. As spring turned into summer there was more bad news. With the release of Facebook's first public quarterly earnings report in July, which showed slowing growth in the total number of users and a net loss of $157 million, as well as continued uncertainty over how Facebook would be able to monetize its user base, the shares continued to lose value. By August, its share price had declined by more than 40% to the $20 range, cutting Facebook's valuation almost by half, to around $65 billion. At the same time, other Internet-related public companies, such as Zynga and Groupon, which had also gone public with much fanfare, were experiencing similar troubles. Zynga's share price experienced a precipitous drop, by more than 75% from its high, as investors became concerned that a company built on virtual goods

like online games might not have staying power. Questions about Groupon's business model and accounting methods, as well as slower growth and revenue that was below expectations, reduced its gleam for investors as well as its share price.

So, is the bloom totally off the social media rose? Is the party really already over? The answer is not by a long shot. The "old guard"—Amazon, Google, and Apple—are all doing just fine. Some of the "new guard," such as LinkedIn, are holding relatively steady. And the news for start-ups remains rosy. Starting an Internet-related company has, in some ways, never been easier or more potentially profitable. The technology required to begin a business has become very inexpensive and much more accessible, and, if necessary, many aspects of the process can be outsourced. It's the idea that is paramount. If it takes off and goes viral, the company can be worth millions before you even realize it. Pinterest, examined in the opening case, is a case in point. Other recent success stories include Yammer, a social network for businesses that was started in 2008 and acquired by Microsoft in June 2012 for $1.2 billion, and Instagram, started in 2009 and acquired by Facebook for $1 billion in April 2012. As a result, many believe that this is still a phenomenal time to be an entrepreneur. Venture capital firms remain undaunted and have raised billions for new funds that are ready to invest. These venture capital firms believe that today's world is much different from the earlier dot-com era, and that the barriers to creating a global start-up have never been lower. As a result, despite the turmoil in the stock markets, many young companies are still raising seed capital based on high valuations. Silicon Valley remains at the epicenter, but other areas, such as New York City, with its proximity to media, advertising and fashion industries, are also seeing increased activity.

Sectors that remain particularly hot include, not surprisingly, anything related to the mobile platform, and security. In the first quarter of 2012, the number of venture capital investments in the mobile sector reached an all-time high, with many of the deals related to mobile photo or video technology, which some have dubbed the Instagram Effect. Mobile payments are another strong area, with Square, which enables cell phones to accept credit card payments, attracting the majority of attention. Launched in October 2010, Square already is valued at more than $1 billion and has an alliance with Starbucks that is likely to make it even more valuable.

On the security front, start-ups attracting significant investments include Bit9, a leader in advanced threat protection that has tripled its client base in two years; Lookout, which blocks malware and spyware on mobile devices; Zenprise, which brings business-level security to consumer phones; Appthority, which tracks suspicious behavior by mobile apps; and Solera Networks, which tracks intrusions in real time. Interest in security start-ups has also been heightened by some big-ticket acquisitions, including Apple's purchase of AuthenTec for $356 million and EMC Corporation's acquisition of NetWitness for a reported $400 million.

So while the party may have slowed for the moment on Wall Street, in the rest of the Internet world, it is by no means over!

■■■ **SOURCES:** "In Silicon Valley, Finding the Next Big Thing in the Ordinary," by Steven M. Davidoff, *New York Times*, August 14, 2012; "Groupon Posts Mixed Results, and Stock Falls," by Quentin Hardy, *New York Times*, August 13, 2012; "A Steep Climb Back for Facebook's Stock," by Somini Sengupta, *New York Times*, August 12, 2012; "Security Start-Ups Catch Fancy of Investors," by Nicole Perlroth and Evelyn M. Rusli, *New York Times*, August 5, 2012; "In Sliding Internet Stocks, Some Hear Echo of 2000," by David Streitfeld and Evelyn M. Rusli, *New York Times*, July 27, 2012; "Facebook Delivers an Earnings Letdown," by Somini Sengupta, *New York Times*, July 26, 2012; "The News Isn't Good for Zynga, Maker of Farmville," by David Streitfeld and Jenna Wortham, *New York Times*, July 25, 2012; "Venture Capital Investments Pick Up, with Strong Emphasis on Mobile," by Eliza Kern, Gigaom.com, July 16, 2012; "A Reality Series Finds Silicon Valley Cringing," by David Streitfeld, *New York Times*, July 9, 2012; "For Tech Start-Ups, New York Has Increasing Allure," by Joshua Brustein, *New York Times*, May 27, 2012.

1.3 UNDERSTANDING E-COMMERCE: ORGANIZING THEMES

Understanding e-commerce in its totality is a difficult task for students and instructors because there are so many facets to the phenomenon. No single academic discipline is prepared to encompass all of e-commerce. After teaching the e-commerce course for several years and writing this book, we have come to realize just how difficult it is to "understand" e-commerce. We have found it useful to think about e-commerce as involving three broad interrelated themes: technology, business, and society.

TECHNOLOGY: INFRASTRUCTURE

The development and mastery of digital computing and communications technology is at the heart of the newly emerging global digital economy we call e-commerce. To understand the likely future of e-commerce, you need a basic understanding of the information technologies upon which it is built. E-commerce is above all else a technologically driven phenomenon that relies on a host of information technologies as well as fundamental concepts from computer science developed over a 50-year period. At the core of e-commerce are the Internet and the World Wide Web, which we describe in detail in Chapter 3. Underlying these technologies are a host of complementary technologies: cloud computing, personal computers, smartphones, tablet computers, local area networks, relational and non-relational databases, client/server computing, data mining, and fiber optics, to name just a few.

To truly understand e-commerce, you will need to know something about packet-switched communications, protocols such as TCP/IP, client/server and cloud computing, mobile digital platforms, Web servers, HTML5, CSS, and software programming tools such as Flash and JavaScript on the client side, and Java, PHP, Ruby on Rails, and ColdFusion on the server side. All of these topics are described fully in Part 2 of the book (Chapters 3–5).

BUSINESS: BASIC CONCEPTS

While technology provides the infrastructure, it is the business applications—the potential for extraordinary returns on investment—that create the interest and excitement in e-commerce. New technologies present businesses and entrepreneurs with new ways of organizing production and transacting business. New technologies change the strategies and plans of existing firms: old strategies are made obsolete and new ones need to be invented. New technologies are the birthing grounds where thousands of new companies spring up with new products and services. New technologies are the graveyard of many traditional businesses, such as record stores and bookstores. To truly understand e-commerce, you will need to be familiar with some key business concepts, such as the nature of digital markets, digital goods, business models, firm and industry value chains, value webs, industry structure, digital disruption, and consumer behavior in digital markets, as well as basic concepts of financial analysis. We'll examine these concepts further in Chapter 2, Chapter 6, and also Chapters 8 through 11.

SOCIETY: TAMING THE JUGGERNAUT

With more than 193 million adult Americans now using the Internet, many for e-commerce purposes, and more than 2.2 billion users worldwide, the impact of the Internet and e-commerce on society is significant and global. Increasingly, e-commerce is subject to the laws of nations and global entities. You will need to understand the pressures that global e-commerce places on contemporary society in order to conduct a successful e-commerce business or understand the e-commerce phenomenon. The primary societal issues we discuss in this book are individual privacy, intellectual property, and public welfare policy.

Since the Internet and the Web are exceptionally adept at tracking the identity and behavior of individuals online, e-commerce raises difficulties for preserving privacy—the ability of individuals to place limits on the type and amount of information collected about them, and to control the uses of their personal information. Read the *Insight on Society* case, *Facebook and the Age of Privacy,* to get a view of some of the ways e-commerce sites use personal information.

Because the cost of distributing digital copies of copyrighted intellectual property—tangible works of the mind such as music, books, and videos—is nearly zero on the Internet, e-commerce poses special challenges to the various methods societies have used in the past to protect intellectual property rights, such as copyright and patents. The global nature of e-commerce also poses public policy issues of equity,

INSIGHT ON SOCIETY

FACEBOOK AND THE AGE OF PRIVACY

In a January 2010 interview, Mark Zuckerberg, the founder of Facebook, proclaimed that the "age of privacy" had to come to an end. According to Zuckerberg, social norms had changed and people were no longer worried about sharing their personal information with friends, friends of friends, or even the entire Web. This view is in accordance with Facebook's broader goal, which is, according to Zuckerberg, to make the world a more open and connected place. Supporters of Zuckerberg's viewpoint believe the 21st century is an age of "information exhibitionism," a new era of openness and transparency.

However, not everyone is a true believer. Privacy—limitations on what personal information government and private institutions can collect and use—is a founding principle of democracies. A decade's worth of privacy surveys in the United States show that well over 80% of the American public fear the Internet is a threat to their privacy.

With more than 1 billion users worldwide, and about 190 million in North America, Facebook's privacy policies are going to shape privacy standards on the Internet for years to come. The economic stakes in the privacy debate are quite large, involving billions in advertising and transaction dollars. Social network sites such as Facebook use a model based on building a database of hundreds of millions of users who post personal information, preferences, and behaviors, and who are encouraged, or deceived, into relinquishing control over their information, which is then sold to advertisers and outside third parties. The less privacy Facebook's users want or have, the more Facebook profits.

Facebook's current privacy policies are quite a flip-flop from its original privacy policy in 2004, which promised users near complete control over who could see their personal profile. The default option then was that only immediate friends who you invited were given access. Other users in your network could not get much information about you at all. People outside that network could find nothing about you. This was the privacy environment that millions of Facebook users originally signed up for. However, every year since 2004, Facebook has attempted to extend its control over user information and content, usually without notice. For instance, in 2007, Facebook introduced the Beacon program, which was designed to broadcast users' activities on participating Web sites to their friends. After a public outcry, Facebook terminated the Beacon program in 2009, and paid $9.5 million to settle a host of class action lawsuits.

In 2009, undeterred by the Beacon fiasco, Facebook unilaterally decided that it would publish users' basic personal information on the public Internet, and announced that whatever content users had contributed belonged to Facebook, and that its ownership of that information never terminated. However, as with the Beacon program, Facebook's efforts to take permanent control of user information resulted in users joining online resistance groups and it was ultimately forced to withdraw this policy as well.

In 2009, Facebook also introduced the Like button, and in 2010 extended it to third-party Web sites to alert Facebook users to their friends' browsing and purchases. In 2011, it began publicizing users' "likes" of various advertisers in Sponsored Stories (i.e., advertisements) that included the users' names and

(continued)

profile pictures without their explicit consent, without paying them, and without giving them a way to opt out. This resulted in yet another class action lawsuit, which Facebook settled for $20 million in June 2012. As part of the settlement, Facebook agreed to make it clear to users that information like their names and profile pictures might be used in Sponsored Stories.

In 2011, Facebook enrolled all Facebook subscribers into its facial recognition program without notice. When a user uploads photos, the software recognizes the faces, tags them, and creates a record of that person/photo. Later, users can retrieve all photos containing an image of a specific friend. Any friend can be tagged, and the software suggests the names of friends to tag when you upload the photos. This too raised the privacy alarm, forcing Facebook to make it easier for users to opt out.

In May 2012, Facebook went public, creating more pressure on it to increase revenues and profits to justify its stock market value. Shortly thereafter, Facebook announced that it was launching a mobile advertising product that pushes ads to the mobile news feeds of users based on the apps they use through the Facebook Connect feature, without explicit permission from the user to do so. Facebook may also decide to track what people do on their apps. It also announced Facebook Exchange, a program that allows advertisers to serve ads to Facebook users based on their browsing activity while not on Facebook. Privacy advocates have raised the alarm yet again and more lawsuits have been

filed by users who claim that Facebook has invaded their privacy by tracking their Internet use even after they have logged off from Facebook. Although Facebook is not yet combining this data with its own database of user personal information, there are concerns that it may do so in the future. And that database is truly huge. For instance, an Austrian law student was able to use the European Union's stronger privacy protections to force Facebook to release a copy of the data that Facebook had compiled on him over a three-year period. He received 1,222 pages covering 57 categories of personal data, such as date and time of log-ins, geographic location, deleted Wall posts and messages, e-mail addresses, and more. In response to increased European Union scrutiny of its data collection practices, Facebook recently agreed to provide users with more information about the data it stores, and will begin rolling out the new policy in Europe and Canada, and then later in the United States.

It appears that Zuckerberg's proclamation that the age of privacy is over was premature. Instead, Facebook's posture on privacy may turn out to be an enduring headache and perhaps ultimately its Achilles heel. As Facebook itself noted in its S-1 filing with the Securities and Exchange Commission, if it adopts "policies or procedures related to areas such as sharing or user data that are perceived negatively by our users or the general public," its revenue, financial results, and business may be significantly harmed. And this, more than anything else, may be the savior for privacy at Facebook.

■■ **SOURCES:** "Facebook to Face Senate Hearing on Facial Recognition," by Katy Bachman, AdWeek.con, July 16, 2012; "Facebook to Target Ads Based on App Usage," by Shayndi Raice, *Wall Street Journal*, July 6, 2012; "Facebook's Facial-Recognition Acquisition Raises Privacy Concerns," by Samantha Murphy, Mashable.com, June 25, 2012; "Facebook Exchange Ads Raise Privacy Concerns," by Mikal E. Belicove, CNBC.com, June 21, 2012; "Facebook About to Launch Facebook Exchange, Real-Time Ad Bidding," by Jessica Guynn, *Los Angeles Times*, June 13, 2012; "Facebook Suit Over Subscriber Tracking Seeks $15 Billion," by Kit Chellel and Jeremy Hodges, Bloomberg.com, May 19, 2012; Facebook Inc. Form S-1/A filed with the Securities and Exchange Commission, May 16, 2012; "Facebook and Your Privacy," by Consumer Reports Staff, ConsumerReports.org, May 3, 2012; "Facebook Offers More Disclosure to Users," by Kevin J. O'Brien, *New York Times*, April 12, 2012; "German State to Sue Facebook over Facial Recognition Feature," by Emil Protalinski, ZDnet.com, November 10, 2011; "Facebook Aims to Simplify Privacy Settings," by Somini Sengupta, *New York Times*, August 23, 2011; "Facebook Again in Spotlight on Privacy," by Geoffrey Fowler, *Wall Street Journal*, June 8, 2011; "Facebook Redesigns Privacy Controls," by Ben Worthen, *Wall Street Journal*, May 27, 2010; "How Facebook Pulled a Privacy Bait and Switch," by Dan Tynan, *PC World*, May 2010; *The Constitution of the Roman Republic*, Andrew Lintott, Oxford University Press, 1999.

equal access, content regulation, and taxation. What rights do nation-states and their citizens have with respect to the Internet, the Web, and e-commerce? We address issues such as these in Chapter 8, and also throughout the text.

ACADEMIC DISCIPLINES CONCERNED WITH E-COMMERCE

The phenomenon of e-commerce is so broad that a multidisciplinary perspective is required. There are two primary approaches to e-commerce: technical and behavioral.

Technical Approaches

Computer scientists are interested in e-commerce as an exemplary application of Internet technology. They are concerned with the development of computer hardware, software, and telecommunications systems, as well as standards, encryption, and database design and operation. Management scientists are primarily interested in building mathematical models of business processes and optimizing these processes. They are interested in e-commerce as an opportunity to study how business firms can exploit the Internet to achieve more efficient business operations.

Behavioral Approaches

In the behavioral area, information systems researchers are primarily interested in e-commerce because of its implications for firm and industry value chains, industry structure, and corporate strategy. The information systems discipline spans the technical and behavioral approaches. For instance, technical groups within the information systems specialty also focus on data mining, search engine design, and artificial intelligence. Economists have focused on consumer behavior at Web sites, pricing of digital goods, and on the unique features of digital electronic markets. The marketing profession is interested in marketing, brand development and extension, consumer behavior on Web sites, and the ability of Internet technologies to segment and target consumer groups, and differentiate products. Economists share an interest with marketing scholars who have focused on e-commerce consumer response to marketing and advertising campaigns, and the ability of firms to brand, segment markets, target audiences, and position products to achieve above-normal returns on investment.

Management scholars have focused on entrepreneurial behavior and the challenges faced by young firms who are required to develop organizational structures in short time spans. Finance and accounting scholars have focused on e-commerce firm valuation and accounting practices. Sociologists—and to a lesser extent, psychologists—have focused on general population studies of Internet usage, the role of social inequality in skewing Internet benefits, and the use of the Web as a social network and group communications tool. Legal scholars are interested in issues such as preserving intellectual property, privacy, and content regulation.

No one perspective dominates research about e-commerce. The challenge is to learn enough about a variety of academic disciplines so that you can grasp the significance of e-commerce in its entirety.

1.4 **CASE STUDY**

The Pirate Bay:
The World's Most Resilient Copyright Infringer?

The Pirate Bay (TPB) is one of the world's most popular pirated music and content sites, offering free access to millions of copyrighted songs and thousands of copyrighted Hollywood movies. In July 2012, The Pirate Bay reported that it had almost 6 million registered users, despite the fact that it has been subjected to repeated legal efforts to shut the site down. In fact, the authorities pursuing TPB must feel as if they are engaged in a never-ending game of Whack-a-mole, as each time they "whack" TPB, it somehow manages to reappear. But the battle is far from over. The Internet is becoming a tough place for music and video pirates in part because of enforcement actions, but more importantly because of new mobile and wireless technologies that enable high-quality content to be streamed for just a small fee.

TPB is part of a European social and political movement that opposes copyrighted content and demands that music, videos, TV shows, and other digital content be free and unrestricted. It does not operate a database of copyrighted content. Neither does it operate a network of computers owned by "members" who store the content, nor create, own, or distribute software (like BitTorrent and most other so-called P2P

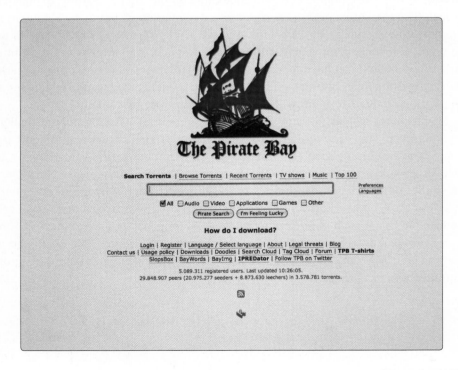

© Tommy (Louth) / Alamy

networks) that permit such networks to exist in the first place. Instead, TPB simply provides a search engine that responds to user queries for music tracks, or specific movie titles, and generates a list of search results that include P2P networks around the world where the titles can be found. By clicking on a selected link, users gain access to the copyrighted content, but only after downloading software and other files from that P2P network.

TPB claims it is merely a search engine providing pointers to existing P2P networks that it does not itself control. From a broader standpoint, TPB's founders also claim that copyright laws in general unjustly interfere with the free flow of information on the Internet, and that in any event, they were not violating Swedish copyright law, which they felt should be the only law that applied. And they further claimed they did not encourage, incite, or enable illegal downloading. Nevertheless, the defendants have never denied that theirs was a commercial enterprise, fueled primarily by advertising.

However, the First Swedish Court in Stockholm declared TPB's four founders guilty of violating Swedish copyright law, and sentenced each to one year in prison and payment of $3.5 million in restitution to the plaintiffs, all Swedish divisions of the major record label firms (Warner Music, Sony, and EMI Group among them). The court found that the defendants had incited copyright infringement by the file sharers by providing a Web site with search functions, easy uploading and storage, and a tracker linked to the Web site. The court also said that the four defendants had been aware of the fact that copyrighted material was shared with the help of their site and that the defendants were engaged in a commercial enterprise, the basis of which was encouraging visitors to violate the copyrights of owners. In fact, the primary purpose of TPB was to violate copyrights in order to make money for the owners (commercial intent).

TPB has appealed the court judgment, has paid no fine, and its owners have, as yet, never spent a night in jail. Since then, though, TPB has been hounded by lawsuits, police raids, and confiscation of servers in countries around the world. A number of countries have refused to allow Internet service providers to host TPB, or link to TPB, no matter where in the world its servers are located although TPB has in some cases been able to circumvent this by frequently changing its IP address. TPB has caused England, France, Malaysia, Finland, and most recently the United States, to consider strong intellectual property protection laws such as the IP Protect act that will prevent domestic search engines and ISPs from linking to infringing sites.

The TPB case is just the latest in a saga of court cases involving the record industry, which wants to preserve its dominance of copyrighted music, and Internet users who want free music. Legal victories over copyright infringers and stronger government enforcement of copyright laws have not proven to be the magic bullets that miraculously solve all the problems facing the music industry, which has had to drastically change its business model and decisively move towards digital distribution platforms. In 2011, sales of music in a purely digital format accounted for more revenue than sales of music in a physical format. With new media delivery platforms gaining traction, the copyright owners—record companies, artists, and Hollywood studios—have struck licensing deals with the technology platform owners and distributors. Consumers benefit from near instant access to high-quality music tracks and videos without the hassle of P2P software downloads. Content owners get a growing revenue

SOURCES: alexa.com/siteinfo/thepiratebay.se, July 10, 2012; "Pirate Bay Founder Submits Emotional Plea for Pardon," by Ernesto, Torrentfreak.com, July 7, 2012; "The Pirate Bay Evades ISP Blockade with IPv6, Can Do It 18 Quintillion More Times," by Sebastian Anthony, Extremetech.com, June 8, 2012; "World's Biggest Ad Agency Keelhauls 2,000 Pirate Sites," by Natalie Apostolu, *The Register*, June 14, 2011; "Internet Piracy and How to Stop It," *New York Times*, June 8, 2011; "The "Pirate Bay: Five Years After the Raid," by Ernesto, Torrentfreak.com, May 31, 2011; "Why Google Would Defend Pirate Bay?," by Parmy Olson, *Forbes*, May 19, 2011; "The Protect IP Act: COICA Redux," by Abigail Phillips, Electronic Frontier Foundation, May 12, 2011; "Preventing Real Online Threats to Economic Creativity and Theft of Intellectual Property (Protect IP Act) of 2011," United States Senate, 112th Congress, 1st Session, 2011; "Pirate Bay Keeps Sinking: Another Law Suit Coming," by Stan Schroeder, mashable.com, June 22, 2010; "Idea Man of LimeWire at a Crossroads," by Joseph Plambeck, *New York Times*, May 23, 2010; "Pirate Bay Sunk by Hollywood Injunction For Now," by Charles Arthur, *The Guardian*, May 17, 2010; "British Put Teeth in Anti-Piracy Proposal," by Eric Pfanner, *New York Times,* March 14, 2010.

stream and protection for their copyrighted content. TPB and other pirate sites may not be able to compete with new and better ways to listen to music and view videos.

> ## Case Study Questions
>
> 1. Do you think TPB can continue to survive in a global Internet world? Why or why not?
> 2. Why is legislation like The Protect IP Act opposed by Google and civil liberties groups?
> 3. Why does cloud computing threaten pirate sites?

1.5   REVIEW

KEY CONCEPTS

- Define e-commerce.
- E-commerce involves digitally enabled commercial transactions between and among organizations and individuals. Digitally enabled transactions include all those mediated by digital technology, meaning, for the most part, transactions that occur over the Internet, the Web and/or via mobile apps. Commercial transactions involve the exchange of value (e.g., money) across organizational or individual boundaries in return for products or services.

- Identify and describe the unique features of e-commerce technology and discuss their business significance.

There are eight features of e-commerce technology that are unique to this medium:
- *Ubiquity*—available just about everywhere, at all times.
- *Global reach*—permits commercial transactions to cross cultural and national boundaries.
- *Universal standards*—shared by all nations around the world.
- *Richness*—refers to the complexity and content of a message.
- *Interactivity*—allows for two-way communication between merchant and consumer.
- *Information density*—is the total amount and quality of information available to all market participants.
- *Personalization* and *customization*—merchants can target their marketing messages to specific individuals by adjusting the message.
- *Social technology*—provides a many-to-many model of mass communications.

- Describe and identify Web 2.0 applications.

- A set of applications has emerged on the Internet, loosely referred to as Web 2.0. These applications attract huge audiences and represent significant new opportunities for e-commerce revenues. Web 2.0 applications such as social networks, photo- and video-sharing sites, and blog platforms support very high levels of interactivity compared to other traditional media.

■ Describe the major types of e-commerce.

There are five major types of e-commerce:
- B2C involves businesses selling to consumers and is the type of e-commerce that most consumers are likely to encounter.
- B2B e-commerce involves businesses selling to other businesses and is the largest form of e-commerce.
- C2C is a means for consumers to sell to each other. In C2C e-commerce, the consumer prepares the product for market, places the product for auction or sale, and relies on the market maker to provide catalog, search engine, and transaction clearing capabilities so that products can be easily displayed, discovered, and paid for.
- Social e-commerce is e-commerce that is enabled by social networks and online social relationships.
- M-commerce involves the use of wireless digital devices to enable transactions on the Web.
- Local e-commerce is a form of e-commerce that is focused on engaging the consumer based on his or her current geographic location.

■ Understand the evolution of e-commerce from its early years to today.

E-commerce has gone through three stages: innovation, consolidation, and reinvention. The early years of e-commerce were a period of explosive growth, beginning in 1995 with the first widespread use of the Web to advertise products and ending in 2000 with the collapse in stock market valuations for dot-com ventures.
- The early years of e-commerce were a technological success, with the digital infrastructure created during the period solid enough to sustain significant growth in e-commerce during the next decade, and a mixed business success, with significant revenue growth and customer usage, but low profit margins.
- E-commerce during its early years did not fulfill economists' visions of perfect friction-free commerce, or fulfill the visions of entrepreneurs and venture capitalists for first-mover advantages, low customer acquisition and retention costs, and low costs of doing business.
- E-commerce entered a period of consolidation beginning in 2001 and extending into 2006.
- E-commerce entered a period of reinvention in 2007 with the emergence of the mobile digital platform, social networks and Web 2.0 applications that attracted huge audiences in a very short time span.

■ Describe the major themes underlying the study of e-commerce.

E-commerce involves three broad interrelated themes:
- *Technology*—To understand e-commerce, you need a basic understanding of the information technologies upon which it is built, including the Internet and the Web, and a host of complementary technologies.
- *Business*—While technology provides the infrastructure, it is the business applications—the potential for extraordinary returns on investment—that create the interest and excitement in e-commerce.

- *Society*—Understanding the pressures that global e-commerce places on contemporary society is critical to being successful in the e-commerce marketplace. The primary societal issues are intellectual property, individual privacy, and public policy.

QUESTIONS

1. What is e-commerce?
2. What is information asymmetry?
3. What are some of the unique features of e-commerce technology?
4. What is a marketspace?
5. What are three benefits of universal standards?
6. Compare online and traditional transactions in terms of richness.
7. What is Web 2.0? Give examples of Web 2.0 sites and explain why you included them in your list.
8. Give examples of B2C, B2B, C2C, and social, mobile, and local e-commerce besides those listed in the chapter materials.
9. How are the Internet and the Web similar to or different from other technologies that have changed commerce in the past?
10. Describe the three different stages in the evolution of e-commerce.
11. Define disintermediation and explain the benefits to Internet users of such a phenomenon. How does disintermediation impact friction-free commerce?
12. What are some of the major advantages and disadvantages of being a first mover?
13. Discuss the ways in which the early years of e-commerce can be considered both a success and a failure.
14. What are five of the major differences between the early years of e-commerce and today's e-commerce?

PROJECTS

1. Define "social e-commerce" and describe why it is a new form of advertising, search, and commerce.

2. Search the Web for an example of each of the major types of e-commerce described in Section 1.1. Create an electronic slide presentation or written report describing each Web site (take a screenshot of each, if possible), and explain why it fits into the category of e-commerce to which you have assigned it.

3. Choose an e-commerce Web site and assess it in terms of the eight unique features of e-commerce technology described in Table 1.2. Which of the features does the site implement well, and which features poorly, in your opinion? Prepare a short memo to the president of the company you have chosen detailing your findings and any suggestions for improvement you may have.

4. Given the development and history of e-commerce in the years from 1995–2012, what do you predict we will see during the next five years of e-commerce? Describe some of the technological, business, and societal shifts that may occur as the Internet continues to grow and expand. Prepare a brief electronic slide presentation or written report to explain your vision of what e-commerce will look like in 2016.

5. Follow up on events at Pinterest and other social network sites since September 2012 (when the opening case was prepared). Prepare a short report on your findings.

CHAPTER 2

E-commerce Business Models and Concepts

After reading this chapter, you will be able to:

- Identify the key components of e-commerce business models.
- Describe the major B2C business models.
- Describe the major B2B business models.
- Understand key business concepts and strategies applicable to e-commerce.

Tweet Tweet:

What's Your Business Model?

Twitter, the social network site based on 140-character text messages, is the latest in a series of unpredicted developments on the Internet. Twitter provides a platform for users to express themselves, by creating content and sharing it with followers who sign up to receive someone's tweets. Although Twitter was the breakout social network of 2012, like most social network sites, Twitter faces the problem of how to make a profit. In 2011, Twitter produced $140 million in revenue but zero profits despite over $1 billion in funding since its inception. Management is still trying

© Kennedy Photography / Alamy

to understand how best to exploit the buzz and user base it has unexpectedly created.

Twitter began in 2006 as a Web-based version of popular text messaging services provided by cell phone carriers. The basic idea was to marry short text messaging on cell phones with the Web and its ability to create social groups. You start by establishing a Twitter account online. By typing a short message called a "tweet" online or to a code on your cell phone (40404), you can tell your followers what you are doing, or whatever else you might want to say. You are limited to 140 characters, but there is no installation required and no charge.

Coming up with solid numbers for Twitter is not easy. By 2012, Twitter had an estimated 500 million registered users worldwide generating 340 million daily tweets, although it is not clear how many continue to actively use the service after signing up. According to Twitter, it had 140 million "active" users worldwide as of March 2012. But according to eMarketer, there are actually far fewer active U.S. adult users (those who use Twitter at least once a month): eMarketer estimates their number to be around 30 million. Industry observers believe Twitter is the second largest social network worldwide, behind Facebook. Experts believe that the vast majority of tweets are generated by a small percentage of users. Twitter also has an estimated 60% churn rate: only 40% of users remain more than one month.

So how can Twitter make money from its users and their tweets? What's its business model and how might it evolve over time? To start, consider the company's assets and customer value proposition. The main asset is user attention and audience size (eyeballs

SOURCES: "Twitter Stats," Business.twitter.com/basics/what-is-twitter, August 22, 2012; "Twitter Embraces Changing Identity" by Nick Bilton, *New York Times*, July 30, 2012; "Analyst: Twitter Passed 500M Users in June 2012, 140M of Them in US; Jakarta 'Biggest Tweeting' City," by Ingrid Lunden, Techcrunch.com, July 30, 2012; "Apple Officials Said to Consider Stake in Twitter," by Evelyn M. Rusli and Nick Bilton, *New York Times*, July 27, 2012; "Twitter's Mobile Ads Begin to Click," by Shira Ovide, *Wall Street Journal*, June 28, 2012; "Microsoft's Bing Extends Twitter Search Deal," by David Roe, Cmswire.com, September 2011; "40 Fast Facts on Twitter," by Jennifer Lawinski, August 8, 2011; "Twitter Raises Big Bucks to Buy Back Shares," Denverpost.com, July 23, 2011; "How Twitter Makes Money," by Harry Gold, ClickZ.com, April 26, 2011, "Twitter to Launch Geo-targeted Promoted Tweets and Data for Marketers," by Sarah Shearnman, Brandrepublic.com, April 7, 2011; "Twitter Users: A Vocal Minority," by Paul Verna, eMarketer, March 2011; "Twitter as Tech Bubble Barometer," by Spencer E. Ante, Amir Efrati, and Anupreeta Das, *Wall Street Journal*, February 10, 2011; "Promoted Promotions," Blog.twitter.com, October 4, 2010; "The Blogosphere: Colliding with Social and Mainstream Media" by Paul Verna, eMarketer, September 21, 2010; "Will Twitter's Ad Strategy Work," by Erica Naone, Technology Review, April 15, 2010; "Twitter Rolls Out Ads," by Jessica Vascellaro and Emily Steel, *Wall Street Journal*, April 14, 2010.

per day). The value proposition is "get it now" or real-time news. An equally important asset is the database of tweets that contains the comments, observations, and opinions of the audience, and the search engine that mines those tweets for patterns.

How can these assets be monetized? Advertising, what else! In April 2010, Twitter announced its first foray into the big-time ad marketplace with Promoted Tweets. Promoted Tweets are Twitter's version of Google's text ads. In April 2011, Twitter announced that it would offer geo-targeted Promoted Tweets. Many companies are now using the service, ranging from Best Buy, to Ford, to Starbucks, to Virgin America. According to Twitter, Promoted Tweets are producing greater engagement with viewers than traditional Web advertisements.

A second Twitter monetization effort announced in June 2010 is called Promoted Trends. "Trends" is a section of the Twitter home page that lets users know what's hot, what a lot of people are talking about. A company can place a Promoted Trends banner at the top of the Trends section and when users click on the banner, they are taken to the follower page for that movie or product. Promoted Trends are reportedly Twitter's most consistent source of revenue, costing advertisers between $100,000 to $120,000 a day.

In October 2010, Twitter launched Promoted Accounts, which are suggestions to follow various advertiser accounts based on the list of accounts that the user already follows. Like Promoted Tweets, Promoted Accounts can be geo-targeted. Twitter added Enhanced Profile Pages for brands in February 2012. For a reported $15,000 to $25,000, companies get their own banner to display images, and the ability to pin a tweet to the top of the company's Twitter stream. In March 2012, Twitter began testing Promoted Tweets and Promoted Accounts on iOS and Android devices, and by June 2012 was reporting that it was generating the majority of its revenues from ads on mobile devices rather than on its Web site.

Another monetizing service is temporal real-time search. In 2010, Twitter entered into agreements with Google, Microsoft, and Yahoo to permit these search engines to index tweets and make them available to the entire Internet. This service gives free real-time content to the search engines as opposed to archival content. It is unclear who's doing whom a service here, and the financial arrangements are not public. Microsoft extended the deal for two years in September 2011, but Google let its deal with Twitter expire.

Freemium is another possibility. Twitter could ask users to pay a subscription fee for premium services such as videos and music downloads. However, it may be too late for this idea because users have come to expect the service to be free. But Twitter's most likely steady revenue source might be its database of hundreds of millions of real-time tweets. Major firms such as Starbucks, Amazon, Intuit, and Dell have used Twitter to understand how their customers are reacting to products, services, and Web sites, and then make corrections or changes in those services and products.

The possibilities are endless, and just about any of the above scenarios offer some solution to the company's problem, which is a lack of profits. Regardless, in July 2012, Apple was said to be interested in making a strategic investment in Twitter at a valuation in the absolutely astounding $10 billion range.

The story of Twitter illustrates the difficulties of turning a good business idea with a huge audience into a successful business model that produces revenues and even profits.

Thousands of firms have discovered they can spend other people's invested capital much faster than they can get customers to pay for their products or services. In most instances of failure, the business model of the firm is faulty from the beginning. In contrast, successful e-commerce firms have business models that are able to leverage the unique qualities of the Web, provide customers real value, develop highly effective and efficient operations, avoid legal and social entanglements that can harm the firm, and produce profitable business results. In addition, successful business models must scale. The business must be able to achieve efficiencies as it grows in volume. But what is a business model, and how can you tell if a firm's business model is going to produce a profit?

In this chapter, we focus on business models and basic business concepts that you must be familiar with in order to understand e-commerce.

2.1   E-COMMERCE BUSINESS MODELS

INTRODUCTION

A **business model** is a set of planned activities (sometimes referred to as *business processes*) designed to result in a profit in a marketplace. The business model is at the center of the business plan. A **business plan** is a document that describes a firm's business model. A business plan always takes into account the competitive environment. An **e-commerce business model** aims to use and leverage the unique qualities of the Internet and the World Wide Web.

EIGHT KEY ELEMENTS OF A BUSINESS MODEL

If you hope to develop a successful business model in any arena, not just e-commerce, you must make sure that the model effectively addresses the eight elements listed in **Table 2.1**. These elements are: value proposition, revenue model, market opportunity, competitive environment, competitive advantage, market strategy, organizational development, and management team. Many writers focus on a firm's value proposition and revenue model. While these may be the most important and most easily identifiable aspects of a company's business model, the other elements are equally important when evaluating business models and plans, or when attempting to understand why a particular company has succeeded or failed. In the following sections, we describe each of the key business model elements more fully.

Value Proposition

A company's value proposition is at the very heart of its business model. A **value proposition** defines how a company's product or service fulfills the needs of customers. To develop and/or analyze a firm's value proposition, you need to understand why

---

business model
a set of planned activities designed to result in a profit in a marketplace

business plan
a document that describes a firm's business model

e-commerce business model
a business model that aims to use and leverage the unique qualities of the Internet and the World Wide Web

value proposition
defines how a company's product or service fulfills the needs of customers

TABLE 2.1	KEY ELEMENTS OF A BUSINESS MODEL
COMPONENTS	KEY QUESTIONS
Value proposition	Why should the customer buy from you?
Revenue model	How will you earn money?
Market opportunity	What marketspace do you intend to serve, and what is its size?
Competitive environment	Who else occupies your intended marketspace?
Competitive advantage	What special advantages does your firm bring to the marketspace?
Market strategy	How do you plan to promote your products or services to attract your target audience?
Organizational development	What types of organizational structures within the firm are necessary to carry out the business plan?
Management team	What kinds of experiences and background are important for the company's leaders to have?

customers will choose to do business with the firm instead of another company and what the firm provides that other firms do not and cannot. From the consumer point of view, successful e-commerce value propositions include: personalization and customization of product offerings, reduction of product search costs, reduction of price discovery costs, and facilitation of transactions by managing product delivery.

Revenue Model

revenue model
describes how the firm will earn revenue, produce profits, and produce a superior return on invested capital

A firm's **revenue model** describes how the firm will earn revenue, generate profits, and produce a superior return on invested capital. We use the terms *revenue model* and *financial model* interchangeably. The function of business organizations is both to generate profits and to produce returns on invested capital that exceed alternative investments. Profits alone are not sufficient to make a company "successful." In order to be considered successful, a firm must produce returns greater than alternative investments. Firms that fail this test go out of existence.

Although there are many different e-commerce revenue models that have been developed, most companies rely on one, or some combination, of the following major revenue models: the advertising model, the subscription model, the transaction fee model, the sales model, and the affiliate model.

advertising revenue model
a company provides a forum for advertisements and receives fees from advertisers

In the **advertising revenue model**, a Web site that offers its users content, services, and/or products also provides an audience to advertisements and receives fees from advertisers. Those Web sites that are able to attract the greatest viewership or that have a highly specialized, differentiated viewership and are able to retain user attention ("stickiness") are able to charge higher advertising rates. Yahoo, for instance, derives a significant amount of revenue from display and video advertising.

In the **subscription revenue model**, a Web site that offers its users content or services charges a subscription fee for access to some or all of its offerings. For instance, the online version of *Consumer Reports* provides access to premium content, such as detailed ratings, reviews, and recommendations, only to subscribers, who have a choice of paying a $6.95 monthly subscription fee or a $30.00 annual fee. Companies successfully offering content or services online on a subscription basis include Match.com and eHarmony (dating services), Ancestry.com (see **Figure 2.1**) and Genealogy.com (genealogy research), Microsoft's Xboxlive.com (video games), Rhapsody.com (music), and Hulu.com.

In the **transaction fee revenue model**, a company receives a fee for enabling or executing a transaction. For example, eBay provides an online auction marketplace and receives a small transaction fee from a seller if the seller is successful in selling the item. E*Trade, an online stockbroker, receives transaction fees each time it executes a stock transaction on behalf of a customer.

In the **sales revenue model**, companies derive revenue by selling goods, information, or services to customers. Companies such as Amazon (which sells books, music, and other products), LLBean.com, and Gap.com, all have sales revenue models.

subscription revenue model
a company offers its users content or services and charges a subscription fee for access to some or all of its offerings

transaction fee revenue model
a company receives a fee for enabling or executing a transaction

sales revenue model
a company derives revenue by selling goods, information, or services

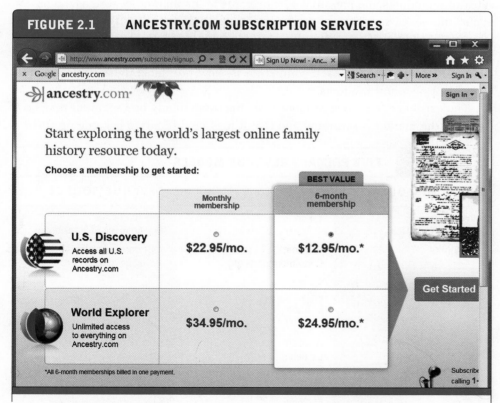

FIGURE 2.1   ANCESTRY.COM SUBSCRIPTION SERVICES

Ancestry.com offers a variety of different membership options for different subscription fees.
SOURCE: Ancestry.com, 2012.

affiliate revenue model

a company steers business to an affiliate and receives a referral fee or percentage of the revenue from any resulting sales

In the **affiliate revenue model**, sites that steer business to an "affiliate" receive a referral fee or percentage of the revenue from any resulting sales. For example, MyPoints makes money by connecting companies with potential customers by offering special deals to its members. When they take advantage of an offer and make a purchase, members earn "points" they can redeem for freebies, and MyPoints receives a fee. Community feedback sites such as Epinions receive much of their revenue from steering potential customers to Web sites where they make a purchase.

Table 2.2 summarizes these major revenue models.

Market Opportunity

market opportunity

refers to the company's intended marketspace and the overall potential financial opportunities available to the firm in that marketspace

The term **market opportunity** refers to the company's intended **marketspace** (i.e., an area of actual or potential commercial value) and the overall potential financial opportunities available to the firm in that marketspace. The market opportunity is usually divided into smaller market niches. The realistic market opportunity is defined by the revenue potential in each of the market niches where you hope to compete.

marketspace

the area of actual or potential commercial value in which a company intends to operate

Competitive Environment

competitive environment

refers to the other companies operating in the same marketspace selling similar products

A firm's **competitive environment** refers to the other companies selling similar products and operating in the same marketspace. It also refers to the presence of substitute products and potential new entrants to the market, as well as the power of customers and suppliers over your business. We discuss the firm's environment later in the chapter. The competitive environment for a company is influenced by several factors: how many competitors are active, how large their operations are, what the market share of each competitor is, how profitable these firms are, and how they price their products.

The existence of a large number of competitors in any one segment may be a sign that the market is saturated and that it may be difficult to become profitable.

TABLE 2.2	FIVE PRIMARY REVENUE MODELS	
REVENUE MODEL	EXAMPLES	REVENUE SOURCE
Advertising	Yahoo	Fees from advertisers in exchange for advertisements
Subscription	WSJ.com Consumerreports.org	Fees from subscribers in exchange for access to content or services
Transaction Fee	eBay E*Trade	Fees (commissions) for enabling or executing a transaction
Sales	Amazon L.L.Bean Gap iTunes	Sales of goods, information, or services
Affiliate	MyPoints	Fees for business referrals

On the other hand, a lack of competitors could either signal an untapped market niche ripe for the picking, or a market that has already been tried without success because there is no money to be made. Analysis of the competitive environment can help you decide which it is.

Competitive Advantage

Firms achieve a **competitive advantage** when they can produce a superior product and/or bring the product to market at a lower price than most, or all, of their competitors. Firms also compete on scope. Some firms can develop global markets, while other firms can only develop a national or regional market. Firms that can provide superior products at the lowest cost on a global basis are truly advantaged.

Firms achieve competitive advantages because they have somehow been able to obtain differential access to the factors of production that are denied to their competitors—at least in the short term. Perhaps the firm has been able to obtain very favorable terms from suppliers, shippers, or sources of labor. Or perhaps the firm has more experienced, knowledgeable, and loyal employees than any competitors. Maybe the firm has a patent on a product that others cannot imitate, or access to investment capital through a network of former business colleagues or a brand name and popular image that other firms cannot duplicate.

One rather unique competitive advantage derives from being a first mover. A **first-mover advantage** is a competitive market advantage for a firm that results from being the first into a marketplace with a serviceable product or service. If first movers develop a loyal following or a unique interface that is difficult to imitate, they can sustain their first-mover advantage for long periods. Amazon provides a good example. However, in the history of technology-driven business innovation, most first movers often lack the **complementary resources** needed to sustain their advantages, and often follower firms reap the largest rewards. Indeed, many of the success stories we discuss in this book are those of companies that were slow followers—businesses that gained knowledge from failure of pioneering firms and entered into the market late.

Companies are said to **leverage** their competitive assets when they use their competitive advantages to achieve more advantage in surrounding markets. For instance, Amazon's move into the online grocery business leverages the company's huge customer database and years of e-commerce experience.

Market Strategy

No matter how tremendous a firm's qualities, its marketing strategy and execution are often just as important. The best business concept, or idea, will fail if it is not properly marketed to potential customers.

competitive advantage
achieved by a firm when it can produce a superior product and/or bring the product to market at a lower price than most, or all, of its competitors

first-mover advantage
a competitive market advantage for a firm that results from being the first into a marketplace with a serviceable product or service

complementary resources
resources and assets not directly involved in the production of the product but required for success, such as marketing, management, financial assets, and reputation

leverage
when a company uses its competitive advantages to achieve more advantage in surrounding markets

market strategy
the plan you put together
that details exactly how
you intend to enter a new
market and attract new
customers

Everything you do to promote your company's products and services to potential customers is known as marketing. **Market strategy** is the plan you put together that details exactly how you intend to enter a new market and attract new customers.

For instance, Twitter, YouTube, and Pinterest have a social network marketing strategy that encourages users to post their content on the sites for free, build personal profile pages, contact their friends, and build a community. In these cases, the customer is the marketing staff!

Organizational Development

Although many entrepreneurial ventures are started by one visionary individual, it is rare that one person alone can grow an idea into a multi-million dollar company. In most cases, fast-growth companies—especially e-commerce businesses—need employees and a set of business procedures. In short, all firms—new ones in particular—need an organization to efficiently implement their business plans and strategies. Many e-commerce firms and many traditional firms that attempt an e-commerce strategy have failed because they lacked the organizational structures and supportive cultural values required to support new forms of commerce.

**organizational
development**
plan describes how the
company will organize the
work that needs to be
accomplished

Companies that hope to grow and thrive need to have a plan for **organizational development** that describes how the company will organize the work that needs to be accomplished.

Management Team

management team
employees of the company
responsible for making the
business model work

Arguably, the single most important element of a business model is the **management team** responsible for making the model work. A strong management team gives a model instant credibility to outside investors, immediate market-specific knowledge, and experience in implementing business plans. A strong management team may not be able to salvage a weak business model, but the team should be able to change the model and redefine the business as it becomes necessary.

Eventually, most companies get to the point of having several senior executives or managers. How skilled managers are, however, can be a source of competitive advantage or disadvantage. The challenge is to find people who have both the experience and the ability to apply that experience to new situations.

Read *Insight on Business: Is Groupon's Business Model Sustainable?* for a look at some of the issues involved in developing a successful business model.

2.2 MAJOR BUSINESS-TO-CONSUMER (B2C) BUSINESS MODELS

Business-to-consumer (B2C) e-commerce, in which online businesses seek to reach individual consumers, is the most well-known and familiar type of e-commerce. **Table 2.3** illustrates the major business models utilized in the B2C arena.

TABLE 2.3	B2C BUSINESS MODELS			
BUSINESS MODEL	VARIATIONS	EXAMPLES	DESCRIPTION	REVENUE MODEL
E-tailer	Virtual Merchant	Amazon iTunes Bluefly	Online version of retail store, where customers can shop at any hour of the day or night without leaving their home or office	Sales of goods
	Bricks-and-Clicks	Walmart.com Sears.com	Online distribution channel for a company that also has physical stores	Same
	Catalog Merchant	LLBean.com LillianVernon.com	Online version of direct mail catalog	Same
	Manufacturer-Direct	Dell.com Mattel.com SonyStyle.com	Manufacturer uses online channel to sell direct to customer	Same
Community Provider		Facebook LinkedIn Twitter Pinterest	Sites where individuals with particular interests, hobbies, common experiences, or social networks can come together and "meet" online	Advertising, subscription, affiliate referral fees
Content Provider		WSJ.com CBSSports.com CNN.com ESPN.com Rhapsody.com	Information and entertainment providers such as newspapers, sports sites, and other online sources that offer customers up-to-date news and special interest how-to guidance and tips and/or information sales	Advertising, subscription fees, affiliate referral fees
Portal	Horizontal/General	Yahoo AOL MSN Facebook	Offers an integrated package of content, content-search, and social network services: news, e-mail, chat, music downloads, video streaming, calendars, etc. Seeks to be a user's home base	Advertising, subscription fees, transaction fees
	Vertical/Specialized (Vortal)	Sailnet	Offers services and products to specialized marketplace	Same
	Search	Google Bing Ask.com	Focuses primarily on offering search services	Advertising, affiliate referral
Transaction Broker		E*Trade Expedia Monster Travelocity Hotels.com Orbitz	Processors of online sales transactions, such as stockbrokers and travel agents, that increase customers' productivity by helping them get things done faster and more cheaply	Transaction fees
Market Creator		eBay Etsy Amazon Priceline	Web-based businesses that use Internet technology to create markets that bring buyers and sellers together	Transaction fees
Service Provider		VisaNow.com Carbonite RocketLawyer	Companies that make money by selling users a service, rather than a product	Sales of services

INSIGHT ON BUSINESS

IS GROUPON'S BUSINESS MODEL SUSTAINABLE?

Groupon is a business that offers subscribers daily deals from local merchants. The catch: a group of people have to purchase the discounted coupon (a "Groupon"). As soon as the minimum number of coupons is sold, the offer is open to everyone. Most Groupon deals offer the customer 50% off the retail price of a product or service offered by a local merchant. The Groupon offer is e-mailed to thousands of potential customers within driving distance of the retailer. If enough people sign up and buy the Groupon, the deal is on, and the customer receives a Groupon by e-mail. Groupon takes a 50% cut of the revenue, leaving the merchant with 50%.

Who wins here? The customer gets products and services at steeply discounted prices. Groupon gets a hefty percentage of the coupon's face value. The merchant receives many customers. While merchants may lose money on these single offers, they are hoping to generate repeat purchases, loyal customers, and a larger customer base.

Groupon combines two of the major trends in e-commerce: localization and social networks. Groupon rocketed to prominence in less than three years, going public in June 2011. But even then, there were questions. At the time, Groupon financials showed a loss of $456 million on revenues of $713 million for 2010, and $146 million on revenues of $645 million for the first quarter of 2011. Groupon was spending so much on marketing that it was having a difficult time turning a profit despite healthy revenues. Analysts and investors wondered if the Groupon business model would work.

The company responded by arguing that this was typical of the early years of Amazon, Netflix, and even Google. While a company focuses on growing its customer base, revenues per customer and profits will decline. Senior management said that large customer acquisition costs would continue for a few years, as would losses, until it reached sufficient size.

But questions continue to abound. Much of the skepticism regarding Groupon's prospects for future growth stems from small businesses expressing dissatisfaction with their results. Many companies have found that the deals only attracted customers who were willing to spend the bare minimum for services. Today, the jury is still out. In the last six months of 2011, nearly 800 daily deal sites went out of business. At the same time, some heavy hitters have joined the fray: Google Offers and Amazon Local. During that time, Groupon's stock price has steadily dropped from its initial price. On the plus side, its revenue for the first six months of 2012 compared to the same time period in 2011 almost doubled to over $1 billion, and it showed its first profit ever, even if it was only a comparatively meager $27 million. Groupon has begun to overhaul its sales and payment systems and is introducing new technology to makes its sales force more efficient. It has also acquired a number of companies that it believes will help it in the small and medium-sized business market.

Nevertheless, many are still skeptical about whether the company can continue to push towards further profits. In 2012, two of its biggest venture backers sold their Groupon stock. However, other prominent Groupon backers have increased their holdings. Groupon's earliest and largest backer, New Enterprise Associates, has held onto its full stake of shares since the company went public. Which of these companies is making the right choice?

■ **SOURCES:** "Groupon's New Operations Czar Grasps Shaky Helm," by Alistair Barr, Reuters, August 22, 2012; "Groupon Investors Give Up," by Shayndi Raice and Shira Ovide, *Wall Street Journal*, August 20, 2012; "Ready to Ditch the Deal," by Stephanie Clifford and Claire Cain Miller, *New York Times*, August 17, 2012; "Groupon Posts Mixed Results, and Stock Falls," by Quentin Hardy, *New York Times*, August 13, 2012; "Google Offers a Two-Pronged Attack on Groupon's Business Model," by Chunka Mui, Forbes, June 29, 2011; "How Does Groupon Work? Is Its Business Model Sustainable?" by Don Dodge, Dondodge.wordpad.com, June 11, 2011; "Is Groupon's Business Model Sustainable?" by Michael de la Merced, *New York Times*, June 8, 2011.

E-TAILER

Online retail stores, often called **e-tailers**, come in all sizes, from giant Amazon to tiny local stores that have Web sites. E-tailers are similar to the typical bricks- and-mortar storefront, except that customers only have to connect to the Internet to check their inventory and place an order. Some e-tailers, which are referred to as "bricks-and-clicks," are subsidiaries or divisions of existing physical stores and carry the same products. REI, JCPenney, Barnes & Noble, Walmart, and Staples are examples of companies with complementary online stores. Others, however, operate only in the virtual world, without any ties to physical locations. Amazon, Blue Nile, and Drugstore.com are examples of this type of e-tailer. Several other variations of e-tailers—such as online versions of direct mail catalogs, online malls, and manufacturer-direct online sales—also exist.

Given that the overall retail market in the United States in 2012 was around $3.7 trillion, the market opportunity for e-tailers is very large (Bureau of Economic Analysis, 2012). Every Internet user is a potential customer. Customers who feel time-starved are even better prospects, since they want shopping solutions that will eliminate the need to drive to the mall or store. The e-tail revenue model is product-based, with customers paying for the purchase of a particular item.

> **e-tailer**
> online retail store

COMMUNITY PROVIDER

Although community providers are not a new entity, the Internet has made such sites for like-minded individuals to meet and converse much easier, without the limitations of geography and time to hinder participation. **Community providers** are sites that create an online environment where people with similar interests can transact (buy and sell goods); share interests, photos, videos; communicate with like-minded people; receive interest-related information; and even play out fantasies by adopting online personalities called avatars. The social network sites Facebook, LinkedIn, Twitter, and Pinterest, and hundreds of other smaller, niche sites all offer users community-building tools and services.

The basic value proposition of community providers is to create a fast, convenient, one-stop site where users can focus on their most important concerns and interests, share the experience with friends, and learn more about their own interests. Community providers typically rely on a hybrid revenue model that includes subscription fees, sales revenues, transaction fees, affiliate fees, and advertising fees from other firms that are attracted by a tightly focused audience. Both the very large social network sites such as Facebook, Twitter, and LinkedIn, as well as niche sites with smaller dedicated audiences, are ideal marketing and advertising territories.

> **community provider**
> sites that create a digital online environment where people with similar interests can transact (buy and sell goods); share interests, photos, and videos; communicate with like-minded people; and receive interest-related information

CONTENT PROVIDER

Although there are many different ways the Internet can be useful, "information content," which can be defined broadly to include all forms of intellectual property, is one of the largest types of Internet usage. **Intellectual property** refers to all forms of human expression that can be put into a tangible medium such as text, CDs, or on

> **intellectual property**
> refers to all forms of human expression that can be put into a tangible medium such as text, CDs, or on the Web

the Web. **Content providers** distribute information content, such as digital video, music, photos, text, and artwork, over the Web. It is estimated that U.S. consumers spent more than $19 billion for online content such as movies, music, videos, television shows, e-books, and newspapers during 2012.

content provider
distributes information content, such as digital news, music, photos, video, and artwork, over the Web

Content providers make money by charging a subscription fee, or by giving away their content and charging advertisers for access to the audience. For instance, in the case of Rhapsody.com, a monthly subscription fee provides users with access to thousands of music tracks. Other content providers, such as WSJ.com (the *Wall Street Journal* online newspaper), *Harvard Business Review*, and many others, charge customers for content downloads in addition to or in place of a subscription fee. The *Insight on Technology* case, *Battle of the Titans: Music in the Cloud*, discusses how changes in Internet technology are driving the development of new business models in the online content market.

Online content is discussed in further depth in Chapter 9.

PORTAL

portal
offers users powerful Web search tools as well as an integrated package of content and services all in one place

Portals such as Yahoo, MSN, and AOL offer users powerful Web search tools as well as an integrated package of content and services, such as news, e-mail, instant messaging, calendars, shopping, music downloads, video streaming, and more, all in one place. Initially, portals sought to be viewed as "gateways" to the Internet. Today, however, the portal business model is to be a destination site. They are marketed as places where consumers will want to start their Web searching and hopefully stay a long time to read news, find entertainment, and meet other people (think of destination resorts). Portals do not sell anything directly—or so it seems—and in that sense they can present themselves as unbiased. Portals generate revenue primarily by charging advertisers for ad placement, collecting referral fees for steering customers to other sites, and charging for premium services.

Although there are numerous portal/search engine sites, the top five sites (Google, Yahoo, MSN/Bing, AOL, and Ask.com) gather more than 95% of the search engine traffic because of their superior brand recognition. Many of the top sites were among the first to appear on the Web and therefore had first-mover advantages. Being first confers advantage because customers come to trust a reliable provider and experience switching costs if they change to late arrivals in the market. By garnering a large chunk of the marketplace, first movers—just like a single telephone network—can offer customers access to commonly shared ideas, standards, and experiences.

TRANSACTION BROKER

transaction broker
site that processes transactions for consumers that are normally handled in person, by phone, or by mail

Sites that process transactions for consumers normally handled in person, by phone, or by mail are **transaction brokers**. The largest industries using this model are financial services, travel services, and job placement services. The online transaction broker's primary value propositions are savings of money and time. In addition, most transaction brokers provide timely information and opinions. Sites such as Monster.com offer job searchers a national marketplace for their talents and employers a national resource for that talent. Both employers and job seekers are attracted by the convenience and currency of information. Online stock brokers charge commissions

INSIGHT ON TECHNOLOGY

BATTLE OF THE TITANS: MUSIC IN THE CLOUD

The Internet has enabled two new music business models: the online store download-and-own model used by Amazon or Apple's iTunes where you purchase songs and store them on your computer or devices, and the subscription service model used by Rhapsody, Pandora, and many others where for a monthly fee you can listen to an online library of songs streamed to your devices. In this business model you don't own the music, and if you miss a payment, it's gone.

Changes in technology are introducing yet a third recorded music business model: cloud streaming. Here, you own the music and you can store it on a single online cloud drive and play it from any device you choose—one music collection, no coordination issues, and local storage for offline playback. The technology behind this new business model is cloud computing, a model of computing where your software and files are stored on servers located on the Internet rather than on your local devices like PCs and local servers in your office or corporate headquarters.

In 2012, Apple, Amazon, and Google introduced their cloud-based music models. The resulting competition is a battle royale amongst Internet titans to preserve existing advantages for each firm, and to dominate the future of music distribution.

Amazon was the first to announce its cloud music service, in March 2011. Using a "music locker" business model, Amazon's Cloud Player allows you to upload music files, store the music on Cloud Player, and play the music on any number of supported digital devices.

Amazon's announcement was followed by Google's announcement in May 2011 of its own music locker service, called Google Music Beta, and now known as Google Play. Both Amazon and Google planned on beating Apple's cloud offering to market. In June 2011, Apple finally joined the party, announcing its own cloud service player and storage system, iCloud.

It's still too early to tell which of these giants will prevail in the music distribution business, but all will continue to be the dominant players. While there are mostly similarities among the various cloud services (they all will play on any device you choose), some differences may have business significance. For instance, Google and Amazon require users to upload their music, which can take many hours or even days, and some of your music tracks might be very low quality. Apple's service matches your local collection and places high-quality versions of the music online automatically.

Music is just the first online content to go onto cloud servers. It will soon be followed by movies, television shows, books, and magazines, and revenues in these online markets are growing at double digits. None of the titans plan to miss out on this opportunity for cloud-based business models and mobile digital devices. There's also money for the content producers. The streaming music cloud services promise to provide a rich and stable stream of revenue for the content producers and artists. Instead of fighting each other, for once it appears the content owners and the Internet content distributors have reached a consensus on a mutually profitable business model for content.

SOURCES: "Web Services to Drive Future Growth for Amazon," by Trefis Team, Forbes.com, August 21, 2012; "Top Cloud Services for Storing and Streaming Music," by Paul Lilly, PCWorld, July 29, 2012; "Apple's Stash of Credit Card Numbers is Its Secret Weapon," by Nick Bilton, *New York Times*, June 11, 2012; "The Cloud That Ate Your Music," by Jon Pareles, *New York Times*, June 22, 2011; "Amazon's and Google's Cloud Services Compared," by Paul Boutin, *New York Times*, June 6, 2011; "Apple, Google, Facebook Turn N.C. Into Data Center," *Computerworld*, June 3, 2011; "For a Song, Online Giants Offer Music in a Cloud," by Walter Mossberg, *Wall Street Journal*, May 19, 2011; "Apple's Cloud Music Service Might Crush the Competition," by Mikko Torikka, VentureBeat.com, May 19, 2011; "Amazon Beats Apple and Google to Cloud Music," by Dean Takahashi, VentureBeat.com, March 28, 2011.

that are considerably less than traditional brokers, with many offering substantial deals, such as cash and a certain number of free trades, to lure new customers.

Transaction brokers make money each time a transaction occurs. Each stock trade, for example, nets the company a fee, based on either a flat rate or a sliding scale related to the size of the transaction. Attracting new customers and encouraging them to trade frequently are the keys to generating more revenue for these companies. Job sites generate listing fees from employers up front, rather than charging a fee when a position is filled.

MARKET CREATOR

market creator
builds a digital environment where buyers and sellers can meet, display products, search for products, and establish a price for products

Market creators build a digital environment in which buyers and sellers can meet, display products, search for products, and establish prices. Prior to the Internet and the Web, market creators relied on physical places to establish a market. There were few private digital network marketplaces prior to the Web. The Web changed this by making it possible to separate markets from physical space. A prime example is Priceline, which allows consumers to set the price they are willing to pay for various travel accommodations and other products (sometimes referred to as a reverse auction) and eBay, the online auction site utilized by both businesses and consumers. Market creators make money by either charging a percentage of every transaction made, or charging merchants for access to the market.

For example, eBay's auction business model is to create a digital electronic environment for buyers and sellers to meet, agree on a price, and transact. This is different from transaction brokers who actually carry out the transaction for their customers, acting as agents in larger markets. At eBay, the buyers and sellers are their own agents. Each sale on eBay nets the company a commission based on the percentage of the item's sales price, in addition to a listing fee. eBay is one of the few Web sites that has been profitable from the beginning. Why? One answer is that eBay has no inventory or production costs. It is simply a middleman.

The market opportunity for market creators is potentially vast, but only if the firm has the financial resources and marketing plan to attract sufficient sellers and buyers to the marketplace. As of June 30, 2012, eBay had more than 113 million active registered users, and this makes for an efficient market (eBay, 2012). There are many sellers and buyers for each type of product, sometimes for the same product, for example, laptop computer models.

SERVICE PROVIDER

service provider
offers services online

While e-tailers sell products online, **service providers** offer services online. There's been an explosion in online services that is often unrecognized. Web 2.0 applications such as photo sharing, video sharing, and user-generated content (in blogs and social network sites) are all services provided to customers. Google has led the way in developing online applications such as Google Maps, Google Docs, and Gmail. More personal services such as online medical bill management, financial and pension planning, and travel recommender sites are showing strong growth.

Service providers use a variety of revenue models. Some charge a fee, or monthly subscriptions, while others generate revenue from other sources, such as through advertising and by collecting personal information that is useful in direct marketing. Some services are free but are not complete. For instance, Google Apps' basic edition is free, but a business edition with advanced tools costs $5/user/month or $50/user/year. Much like retailers who trade products for cash, service providers trade knowledge, expertise, and capabilities for revenue.

Obviously, some services cannot be provided online. For example, dentistry, medical services, plumbing, and car repair cannot be completed via the Internet. However, online arrangements can be made for these services. Online service providers may offer computer services, such as information storage (as does Carbonite), or provide legal services (RocketLawyer).

The basic value proposition of service providers is that they offer consumers valuable, convenient, time-saving, and low-cost alternatives to traditional service providers or—in the case of search engines and most Web 2.0 applications—they provide services that are truly unique to the Web. The market opportunity for service providers is as large as the variety of services that can be provided and potentially is much larger than the market opportunity for physical goods. Consumers' increasing demand for convenience products and services bodes well for current and future online service providers.

2.3 | MAJOR BUSINESS-TO-BUSINESS (B2B) BUSINESS MODELS

In Chapter 1, we noted that business-to-business (B2B) e-commerce, in which businesses sell to other businesses, is more than 10 times the size of B2C e-commerce, even though most of the public attention has focused on B2C. For instance, it is estimated that revenues for all types of B2B e-commerce in the United States totalled around $4.12 trillion in 2012, compared to about $362 billion for all types of B2C e-commerce. Clearly, most of the dollar revenues in e-commerce involve B2B e-commerce. Much of this activity is unseen and unknown to the average consumer. The major business models utilized in the B2B arena are e-distributor, e-procurement, exchanges, industry consortia, and private industrial networks.

E-DISTRIBUTOR

Companies that supply products and services directly to individual businesses are **e-distributors**. W.W. Grainger, for example, is the largest distributor of maintenance, repair, and operations (MRO) supplies. MRO supplies are thought of as indirect inputs to the production process—as opposed to direct inputs. In the past, Grainger relied on catalog sales and physical distribution centers in metropolitan areas. Its catalog of equipment went online in 1995 at Grainger.com, giving businesses access to more than 1 million items. Company purchasing agents can search by type of product, such as motors, HVAC, or fluids, or by specific brand name.

E-distributors are owned by one company seeking to serve many customers. However, as with exchanges (described on the next page), critical mass is a factor. With

e-distributor
a company that supplies products and services directly to individual businesses

e-distributors, the more products and services a company makes available on its site, the more attractive that site is to potential customers. One-stop shopping is always preferable to having to visit numerous sites to locate a particular part or product.

E-PROCUREMENT

e-procurement firm
creates and sells access to digital electronic markets

Just as e-distributors provide products to other companies, **e-procurement firms** create and sell access to digital electronic markets. Firms such as Ariba, for instance, have created software that helps large firms organize their procurement process by creating mini-digital markets for a single firm. Ariba creates custom-integrated online catalogs (where supplier firms can list their offerings) for purchasing firms. On the sell side, Ariba helps vendors sell to large purchasers by providing software to handle catalog creation, shipping, insurance, and finance. Both the buy and sell side software is referred to generically as "value chain management" software.

EXCHANGES

exchange
an independent digital electronic marketplace where suppliers and commercial purchasers can conduct transactions

Exchanges garnered most of the attention and early funding in the B2B arena because of their potential market size even though today they are a small part of the overall B2B picture. An **exchange** is an independent digital electronic marketplace where hundreds of suppliers meet a smaller number of very large commercial purchasers. Exchanges are owned by independent, usually entrepreneurial start-up firms whose business is making a market, and they generate revenue by charging a commission or fee based on the size of the transactions conducted among trading parties. They usually serve a single vertical industry such as steel, polymers, or aluminum, and focus on the exchange of direct inputs to production and short-term contracts or spot purchasing. For buyers, B2B exchanges make it possible to gather information, check out suppliers, collect prices, and keep up to date on the latest happenings all in one place. Sellers, on the other hand, benefit from expanded access to buyers. The greater the number of sellers and buyers, the lower the sales cost and the higher the chances of making a sale. The ease, speed, and volume of transactions are referred to as *market liquidity*.

In theory, exchanges make it significantly less expensive and time-consuming to identify potential suppliers, customers, and partners, and to do business with each other. In reality, as will be discussed in Chapter 11, B2B exchanges have had a difficult time convincing thousands of suppliers to move into singular digital markets where they face powerful price competition, and an equally difficult time convincing businesses to change their purchasing behavior away from trusted long-term trading partners.

INDUSTRY CONSORTIA

industry consortia
industry-owned vertical marketplaces that serve specific industries

Industry consortia are industry-owned *vertical marketplaces* that serve specific industries. In contrast, *horizontal marketplaces* sell specific products and services to a wide range of companies. Vertical marketplaces supply a smaller number of companies with products and services of specific interest to their industry, while horizontal marketplaces supply companies in different industries with a particular type of product and services. For example, Exostar is an online trading exchange for the aerospace and defense industry, founded by BAE Systems, Boeing, Lockheed Martin, Raytheon, and Rolls-Royce in 2000. Exostar connects with more than 300 procurement systems and has registered more than 70,000 trading partners in 95 countries around the world.

PRIVATE INDUSTRIAL NETWORKS

Private industrial networks constitute about 75% of all B2B expenditures by large firms. A **private industrial network** (sometimes referred to as a private trading exchange or PTX) is a digital network (often but not always Internet-based) designed to coordinate the flow of communications among firms engaged in business together. The network is owned by a single large purchasing firm. Participation is by invitation only to trusted long-term suppliers of direct inputs. These networks typically evolve out of a firm's own enterprise resource planning (ERP) system, and are an effort to include key suppliers in the firm's own business decision making. For instance, Walmart operates one of the largest private industrial networks in the world for its suppliers, who on a daily basis use Walmart's network to monitor the sales of their goods, the status of shipments, and the actual inventory level of their goods.

We discuss the nuances of B2B commerce in more detail in Chapter 12.

private industrial network
digital network designed to coordinate the flow of communications among firms engaged in business together

2.4   E-COMMERCE ENABLERS

No discussion of e-commerce business models would be complete without mention of a group of companies whose business model is focused on providing the infrastructure necessary for e-commerce companies to exist, grow, and prosper. These are the e-commerce enablers: the Internet infrastructure companies. They provide the hardware, operating system software, networks and communications technology, applications software, Web designs, consulting services, and other tools that make e-commerce over the Web possible. While these firms may not be conducting e-commerce per se (although in many instances, e-commerce in its traditional sense is in fact one of their sales channels), as a group they have perhaps profited the most from the development of e-commerce. We will discuss many of these players in the following chapters.

2.5   HOW THE INTERNET AND THE WEB CHANGE BUSINESS: STRATEGY, STRUCTURE, AND PROCESS

Now that you have a clear grasp of the variety of business models used by e-commerce firms, you also need to understand how the Internet and the Web have changed the business environment in the last decade, including industry structures, business strategies, and industry and firm operations (business processes and value chains).

In general, the Internet is an open standards system available to all players, and this fact inherently makes it easy for new competitors to enter the marketplace and offer substitute products or channels of delivery. The Internet tends to intensify competition. Because information becomes available to everyone, the Internet inherently shifts power to buyers who can quickly discover the lowest-cost provider on the Web. On the other hand, the Internet presents many new opportunities for creating value, for branding products and charging premium prices, and for enlarging an already powerful offline physical business such as Walmart or Sears. These features of the Web work to the advantage of merchants.

Recall Table 1.2 in Chapter 1 that describes the truly unique features of e-commerce technology. **Table 2.4** suggests some of the implications of each unique feature

TABLE 2.4	EIGHT UNIQUE FEATURES OF E-COMMERCE TECHNOLOGY
FEATURE	SELECTED IMPACTS ON BUSINESS ENVIRONMENT
Ubiquity	Alters industry structure by creating new marketing channels and expanding size of overall market. Creates new efficiencies in industry operations and lowers costs of firms' sales operations. Enables new differentiation strategies.
Global reach	Changes industry structure by lowering barriers to entry, but greatly expands market at same time. Lowers cost of industry and firm operations through production and sales efficiencies. Enables competition on a global scale.
Universal standards	Changes industry structure by lowering barriers to entry and intensifying competition within an industry. Lowers costs of industry and firm operations by lowering computing and communications costs. Enables broad scope strategies.
Richness	Alters industry structure by reducing strength of powerful distribution channels. Changes industry and firm operations costs by reducing reliance on sales forces. Enhances post-sales support strategies.
Interactivity	Alters industry structure by reducing threat of substitutes through enhanced customization. Reduces industry and firm costs by reducing reliance on sales forces. Enables Web-based differentiation strategies.
Personalization/ Customization	Alters industry structure by reducing threats of substitutes, raising barriers to entry. Reduces value chain costs in industry and firms by lessening reliance on sales forces. Enables personalized marketing strategies.
Information density	Changes industry structure by weakening powerful sales channels, shifting bargaining power to consumers. Reduces industry and firm operations costs by lowering costs of obtaining, processing, and distributing information about suppliers and consumers.
Social technologies	Changes industry structure by shifting programming and editorial decisions to consumers. Creates substitute entertainment products. Energizes a large group of new suppliers.

for the overall business environment—industry structure, business strategies, and operations.

INDUSTRY STRUCTURE

E-commerce changes industry structure, in some industries more than others. **Industry structure** refers to the nature of the players in an industry and their relative bargaining power. An industry's structure is characterized by five forces: *rivalry among existing competitors,* the *threat of substitute products, barriers to entry into the industry,* the *bargaining power of suppliers,* and the *bargaining power of buyers.* When you describe an industry's structure, you are describing the general business environment in an industry and the overall profitability of doing business in that environment. E-commerce has the potential to change the relative strength of these competitive forces (see **Figure 2.2**).

E-commerce can affect the structure and dynamics of industries in very different ways. Consider the recorded music industry, an industry that has experienced significant change because of the Internet and e-commerce. Historically, the major record companies owned the exclusive rights to the recorded music of various artists,

industry structure
refers to the nature of the players in an industry and their relative bargaining power

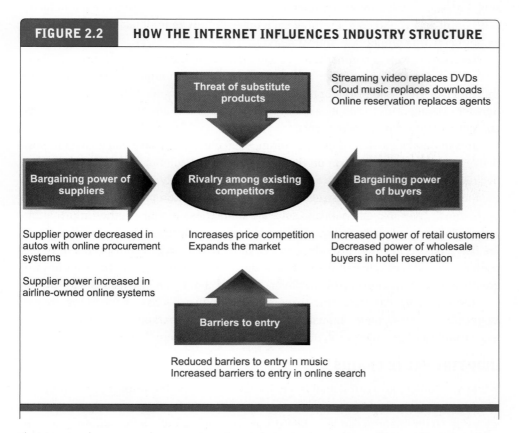

| FIGURE 2.2 | HOW THE INTERNET INFLUENCES INDUSTRY STRUCTURE |

Threat of substitute products

Streaming video replaces DVDs
Cloud music replaces downloads
Online reservation replaces agents

Bargaining power of suppliers

Rivalry among existing competitors

Bargaining power of buyers

Supplier power decreased in autos with online procurement systems

Supplier power increased in airline-owned online systems

Increases price competition
Expands the market

Increased power of retail customers
Decreased power of wholesale buyers in hotel reservation

Barriers to entry

Reduced barriers to entry in music
Increased barriers to entry in online search

The Internet and e-commerce have many impacts on industry structure and competitive conditions. From the perspective of a single firm, these changes can have negative or positive implications depending on the situation. In some cases, an entire industry can be disrupted, while at the same time, a new industry is born. Individual firms can either prosper or be devastated.

and the distribution channels were national and local music stores selling CDs. With the entrance into the online marketplace of firms selling pirated music, substitute providers such as Napster and Kazaa nearly demolished the music label business. With Apple and Amazon selling digital tracks, music stores were suddenly out of business. In the travel industry, entirely new middlemen such as Travelocity have entered the market to compete with traditional travel agents. After Travelocity, Expedia, Cheap-Tickets, and other travel services demonstrated the power of e-commerce marketing for airline tickets, the actual owners of the airline seats—the major airlines—banded together to form their own Internet outlet for tickets, Orbitz, for direct sales to consumers (although ultimately selling the company to a private investor group). Clearly, e-commerce and the Internet create *new industry dynamics* that can best be described as the give and take of the marketplace, the changing fortunes of competitors.

Yet in other industries, the Internet and e-commerce have strengthened existing players. In the chemical and automobile industries, e-commerce is being used effectively by manufacturers to strengthen their traditional distributors. In these industries, e-commerce technology has not fundamentally altered the competitive forces—bargaining power of suppliers, barriers to entry, bargaining power of buyers, threat of substitutes, or rivalry among competitors—within the industry. Hence, each industry is different and you need to examine each one carefully to understand the impacts of e-commerce on competition and strategy.

Inter-firm rivalry (competition) is one area of the business environment where e-commerce technologies have had an impact on most industries. In general, the Internet has increased price competition in nearly all markets. It has been relatively easy for existing firms to adopt e-commerce technology and attempt to use it to achieve competitive advantage vis-à-vis rivals.

It is impossible to determine if e-commerce technologies have had an overall positive or negative impact on firm profitability in general. Each industry is unique, so it is necessary to perform a separate analysis for each one. Clearly, e-commerce has shaken the foundations of some industries, in particular, information product industries (such as the music, newspaper, book, and software industries) as well as other information-intense industries such as financial services. In these industries, the power of consumers has grown relative to providers, prices have fallen, and overall profitability has been challenged. In other industries, especially manufacturing, the Internet has not greatly changed relationships with buyers, but has changed relationships with suppliers. Increasingly, manufacturing firms in entire industries have banded together to aggregate purchases, create industry digital exchanges or marketplaces, and outsource industrial processes in order to obtain better prices from suppliers.

INDUSTRY VALUE CHAINS

value chain

the set of activities performed in an industry or in a firm that transforms raw inputs into final products and services

While an industry structural analysis helps us understand the impact of e-commerce technology on the overall business environment in an industry, a more detailed industry value chain analysis can help identify more precisely just how e-commerce may change business operations at the industry level. One of the basic tools for understanding the impact of information technology on industry and firm operations is the value chain. The concept is quite simple. A **value chain** is the set of activities performed in an industry or in a firm that transforms raw inputs into final products and services. Each of these activities adds economic value to the final product; hence, the term *value chain* as an interconnected set of value-adding activities. **Figure 2.3** illustrates the six generic players in an industry value chain: suppliers, manufacturers, transporters, distributors, retailers, and customers.

By reducing the cost of information, the Internet offers each of the key players in an industry value chain new opportunities to maximize their positions by lowering costs and/or raising prices. For instance, manufacturers can reduce the costs they pay for goods by developing Web-based B2B exchanges with their suppliers. Manufacturers can develop direct relationships with their customers through their own Web sites, bypassing the costs of distributors and retailers. Distributors can develop highly efficient inventory management systems to reduce their costs, and retailers can develop highly efficient customer relationship management systems to strengthen their service to customers. Customers in turn can use the Web to search for the best quality, fastest delivery, and lowest prices, thereby lowering their transaction costs and reducing prices they pay for final goods. Finally, the operational efficiency of the entire industry can increase, lowering prices and adding value to consumers, and helping the industry to compete with alternative industries.

FIRM VALUE CHAINS

The concept of value chain can be used to analyze a single firm's operational efficiency as well. The question here is: How does e-commerce technology potentially affect the value chains of firms within an industry? A **firm value chain** is the set of activities a firm engages in to create final products from raw inputs. Each step in the process of

firm value chain
the set of activities a firm engages in to create final products from raw inputs

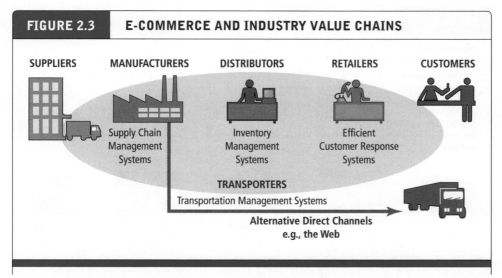

| **FIGURE 2.3** | **E-COMMERCE AND INDUSTRY VALUE CHAINS** |

SUPPLIERS   MANUFACTURERS   DISTRIBUTORS   RETAILERS   CUSTOMERS

Supply Chain Management Systems

Inventory Management Systems

Efficient Customer Response Systems

TRANSPORTERS
Transportation Management Systems

**Alternative Direct Channels
e.g., the Web**

Every industry can be characterized by a set of value-adding activities performed by a variety of actors. E-commerce potentially affects the capabilities of each player as well as the overall operational efficiency of the industry.

production adds value to the final product. In addition, firms develop support activities that coordinate the production process and contribute to overall operational efficiency. **Figure 2.4** illustrates the key steps and support activities in a firm's value chain.

The Internet offers firms many opportunities to increase their operational efficiency and differentiate their products. For instance, firms can use the Internet's communications efficiency to outsource some primary and secondary activities to specialized, more efficient providers without such outsourcing being visible to the consumer. In addition, firms can use the Internet to more precisely coordinate the steps in the value chains and reduce their costs. Finally, firms can use the Internet to provide users with more differentiated and high-value products. For instance, Amazon uses the Internet to provide consumers with a much larger inventory of books to choose from, at a lower cost, than traditional book stores. It also provides many services—such as instantly available professional and consumer reviews, and information on buying patterns of other consumers—that traditional bookstores cannot.

FIRM VALUE WEBS

value web

networked business ecosystem that coordinates the value chains of several firms

While firms produce value through their value chains, they also rely on the value chains of their partners—their suppliers, distributors, and delivery firms. The Internet creates new opportunities for firms to cooperate and create a value web. A **value web** is a networked business ecosystem that uses Internet technology to coordinate the value chains of business partners within an industry, or at the first level, to coordinate the value chains of a group of firms. **Figure 2.5** illustrates a value web.

A value web coordinates a firm's suppliers with its own production needs using an Internet-based supply chain management system. We discuss these B2B systems in Chapter 11. Firms also use the Internet to develop close relationships with their logistics partners. For instance, Amazon relies on UPS tracking systems to provide its

FIGURE 2.4 | E-COMMERCE AND FIRM VALUE CHAINS

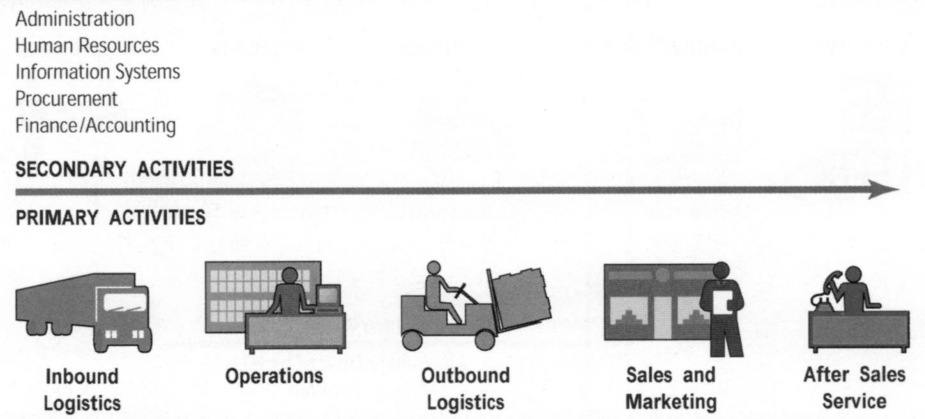

Administration
Human Resources
Information Systems
Procurement
Finance/Accounting

SECONDARY ACTIVITIES

PRIMARY ACTIVITIES

Inbound Logistics · Operations · Outbound Logistics · Sales and Marketing · After Sales Service

Every firm can be characterized by a set of value-adding primary and secondary activities performed by a variety of actors in the firm. A simple firm value chain performs five primary value-adding steps: inbound logistics, operations, outbound logistics, sales and marketing, and after sales service.

FIGURE 2.5	INTERNET-ENABLED VALUE WEB

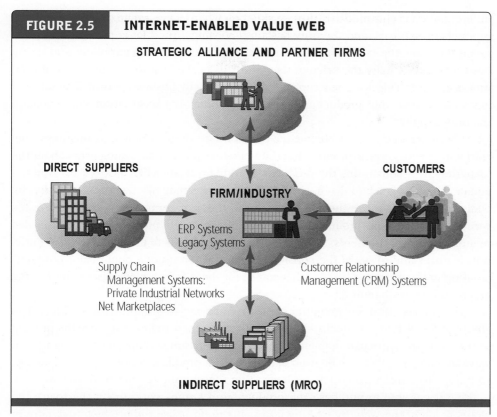

Internet technology enables firms to create an enhanced value web in cooperation with their strategic alliance and partner firms, customers, and direct and indirect suppliers.

customers with online package tracking, and it relies on the U.S. Postal Service systems to insert packages directly into the mail stream. Amazon has partnership relations with hundreds of firms to generate customers and to manage relationships with customers. (Online customer relationship management systems are discussed in Chapter 6.)

BUSINESS STRATEGY

A **business strategy** is a set of plans for achieving superior long-term returns on the capital invested in a business firm. A business strategy is therefore a plan for making profits in a competitive environment over the long term. **Profit** is simply the difference between the price a firm is able to charge for its products and the cost of producing and distributing goods. Profit represents economic value. Economic value is created anytime customers are willing to pay more for a product than it costs to produce. There are four generic strategies for achieving a profitable business: differentiation, cost, scope, and focus. We describe each of these below. The specific strategies that a firm follows will depend on the product, the industry, and the marketplace where competition is encountered.

A strategy of **differentiation** refers to all the ways producers can make their products unique and distinguish them from those of competitors. The opposite of

business strategy
a set of plans for achieving superior long-term returns on the capital invested in a business firm

profit
the difference between the price a firm is able to charge for its products and the cost of producing and distributing goods

differentiation
refers to all the ways producers can make their products unique and different to distinguish them from those of competitors

commoditization

a situation where there are no differences among products or services, and the only basis of choosing products is price

differentiation is **commoditization**—a situation where there are no differences among products or services, and the only basis of choosing a product is price. When price alone becomes the basis of competition and there are many suppliers and many customers, eventually the price of the good falls to the cost to produce it. And then profits are zero! This is an unacceptable situation for any business person. The solution is to differentiate your product and to create a monopoly-like situation where you are the only supplier.

There are many ways businesses differentiate their products. A business may start with a core generic product, but then create expectations among users about the "experience" of consuming the product—"Nothing refreshes like a Coke!" or "Nothing equals the experience of driving a BMW." Businesses may also augment products by adding features to make them different from those of competitors. And businesses can differentiate their products further by enhancing the products' abilities to solve related consumer problems. The purpose of marketing is to create these differentiation features and to make the consumer aware of the unique qualities of products, creating in the process a "brand" that stands for these features. We discuss marketing and branding in Chapter 6.

The Internet and the Web offer some unique ways to differentiate products. The ability of the Web to personalize the shopping experience and to customize the product or service to the particular demands of each consumer are perhaps the most significant ways in which the Web can be used to differentiate products. E-commerce businesses can also differentiate products by leveraging the ubiquitous nature of the Web (by making it possible to purchase the product from home, work, or on the road); the global reach of the Web (by making it possible to purchase the product anywhere in the world); richness and interactivity (by creating Web-based experiences for people who use the product, such as unique interactive content, videos, stories about users, and reviews by users); and information density (by storing and processing information for consumers of the product, such as warranty information on all products purchased through a site or income tax information online).

Adopting a *strategy of cost competition* means a business has discovered some unique set of business processes or resources that other firms cannot duplicate. Business processes are the atomic units of the value chain. For instance, the set of value-creating activities called Inbound Logistics in Figure 2.4 is in reality composed of many different collections of activities performed by people on the loading docks and in the warehouses. These different collections of activities are called *business processes*—the set of steps or procedures required to perform the various elements of the value chain.

The Internet offers some new ways to compete on cost, at least in the short term. Firms can leverage the Internet's ubiquity by lowering the costs of order entry (the customer fills out all the forms, so there is no order entry department); leverage global reach and universal standards by having a single order entry system worldwide; and leverage richness, interactivity, and personalization by creating customer profiles online and treating each individual consumer differently—without the use of an expensive sales force that performed these functions in the past. Finally, firms can leverage the information intensity of the Web by providing consumers with detailed information on products, without maintaining either expensive catalogs or a sales force.

While the Internet offers powerful capabilities for intensifying cost competition, which makes cost competition appear to be a viable strategy, the danger is that competitors have access to the same technology. Assuming they have the skills and organizational will to use the technology, competitors can buy many of the same cost-reducing techniques in the marketplace. Even a skilled labor force can be purchased, ultimately. However, self-knowledge, proprietary tacit knowledge (knowledge that is not published or codified), and a loyal, skilled workforce are in the short term difficult to purchase. Therefore, cost competition remains a viable strategy.

Two other generic business strategies are scope and focus. A *scope strategy* is a strategy to compete in all markets around the globe, rather than merely in local, regional, or national markets. The Internet's global reach, universal standards, and ubiquity can certainly be leveraged to assist businesses in becoming global competitors. Yahoo, for instance, along with all of the other top 20 e-commerce sites, has readily attained a global presence using the Internet. A *focus strategy* is a strategy to compete within a narrow market segment or product segment. This is a specialization strategy with the goal of becoming the premier provider in a narrow market. For instance, L.L.Bean uses the Web to continue its historic focus on outdoor sports apparel; and W.W. Grainger—the Web's most frequently visited B2B site—focuses on a narrow market segment called MRO: maintenance, repair, and operations of commercial buildings. The Internet offers some obvious capabilities that enable a focus strategy. Firms can leverage the Web's rich interactive features to create highly focused messages to different market segments; the information intensity of the Web makes it possible to focus e-mail and other marketing campaigns on small market segments; personalization—and related customization—means the same product can be customized and personalized to fulfill the very focused needs of specific market segments and consumers.

Industry structure, industry and firm value chains, value webs, and business strategy are central business concepts used throughout this book to analyze the viability of and prospects for e-commerce sites. In particular, the case studies found at the end of each chapter are followed with questions that may ask you to identify the competitive forces in the case, or analyze how the case illustrates changes in industry structure, industry and firm value chains, and business strategy.

Pandora
and the Freemium Business Model

Pandora is the Internet's most successful subscription radio service. As of April 30, 2012, it had approximately 150 million registered users in the United States, and continues to add more than 1 million new subscribers a week—that's one new subscriber about every second! Pandora now accounts for more than 70% of all Internet radio listening hours.

At Pandora, users select a genre of music based on a favorite musician, and a computer algorithm puts together a personal radio station that plays not only the music of the selected artist but also closely related music by different artists. A team of professional musicians listens to new songs each day and classifies the music according to more than 400 musical criteria including male or female vocal, electric vs. acoustical guitar, distortion of instruments, presence of background vocals, strings, and various other instruments.

Pandora's founders, Will Glaser and Tim Westergren, launched Pandora in 2005. Their biggest challenge was how to make a business out of a totally new kind of online radio station when competing online stations were making music available for free, many

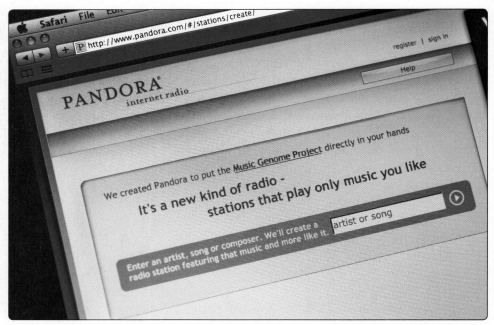

© NetPhotos / Alamy

without advertising, and online subscription services were streaming music for a monthly fee and finding some advertising support as well. Online music illegally downloaded from P2P networks for free was also a significant factor, as was iTunes, which by 2005 was a roaring success, charging 99 cents a song with no ad support. The idea of a "personal" radio station playing your kind of music was very new.

Pandora has run through a litany of business models, including giving away free hours of access and then asking subscribers to pay, an advertising-supported model with tiered service, and deals with major online content providers to add 'Buy' buttons to songs being played. None of these proved to be a smash success. In late 2009, the company launched Pandora One, a premium service that offered no advertising, higher quality streaming music, a desktop app, and fewer usage limits. The service cost $36 a year. By July 2010, Pandora had 600,000 subscribers to its premium service, about 1% of its then 60 million users. Pandora reported $55 million in annual revenue in 2009 and $137 million in 2010, with about $120 million coming from advertising and $18 million from subscriptions. Pandora's "new" business model has proven so successful that it filed for an initial public offering in early 2011, and went public in June 2011. For 2012, revenues again doubled, to $274 million. with about 87% ($239 million) coming from advertising and the remainder from subscriptions and other sources. However, it has not yet shown a profit, and does face competition from services such as Spotify, which also is using the freemium strategy.

As Chris Anderson, author of *Free: The Future of a Radical Price*, has pointed out, since the marginal cost of digital products is typically close to zero, providing free product does not cost much, and potentially enables you to reach many more people and if the market is very large, even getting just 1% of that market to purchase could be very lucrative. There are many other examples of successful freemium model companies. For many traditional print media like newspapers and magazines, the freemium model may be their path to survival. But it won't work for every online business.

Pandora is an example of the "freemium" business revenue model. The model is based on giving away some services for free to 99% of the customers, and relying on the other 1% of the customers to pay for premium versions of the same service. While it clearly has worked for Pandora, there is ongoing debate among e-commerce CEOs and venture capitalists about the effectiveness of the freemium model. While freemium can be an efficient way to gather a large group of potential customers, companies have found that it's a challenge to convert eyeballs into those willing to pay. Absent subscriber revenue, firms need to rely on advertising revenues.

MailChimp's story is both a success and a cautionary tale. The company lets anyone send e-mail newsletters to customers, manage subscriber lists, and track the performance of an e-mail marketing campaign. Despite the powerful tools it gives marketers, and its open applications programming interface, after 10 years in business, the company had only 85,000 paid subscribers.

In 2009, CEO Ben Chestnut decided that it was time to implement new strategies to attract additional customers. MailChimp began giving away its basic tools and charging subscription fees for special features. In just over a year, MailChimp went from 85,000 to 450,000 users. E-mail volume went from 200 million a month to around

SOURCES: "When Freemium Fails," by Sarah E. Needleman and Angus Loten, *Wall Street Journal*, August 22, 2012; "Evernote Opens Up about Tripling Its Revenue," by Patrick Hoge, Bizjournals.com, July 27, 2012; "MailChimp Announces Integration with Customer Analytics Platform," press release, July 26, 2012; "Pandora Faces Rivals for Ears and Ads," by Ben Sisario, *New York Times*, June 20, 2012; "Evernote by the Numbers: 34M Users, 1.4M Paying, and the Relative Merits of Different Platforms," by Ingrid Lunden, Techcrunch.com, June 19, 2012; Pandora Media Inc. Annual Report on Form 10-K, March 2012; "An Interview with Phil Libin (Evernote)," Doeswhat.com, February 25, 2012; "Glam Media Completes Ning Acquisition," press release, December 5, 2011; "Gling? Glam Buys Ning for $200 Million, Mostly in Stock," by Kara Swisher, Allthingsd.com, September 20, 2011; "Pandora IPO Prices at $16; Valuation $2.6 Billion," by Eric Savitz, Blogs.forbes.com, June 14, 2011; "Social-Networking Site Ning: Charging Users Works for Us," by Jennifer Valentino-DeVries, *Wall Street Journal*, April 13, 2011; "Explainer: What Is the Freemium Business Model," by Pascal-Emmanuel Gobry, *San Francisco Chronicle*, April 8, 2011; "Shattering Myths About 'Freemium' Services: Mobility is Key," by Martin Scott, WirelessWeek, April 7, 2011; "Evernote Statistics—89% User Acquisition via Word of Mouth," Plugged.in, April 5, 2011; Pandora Media Inc, Amendment No. 2 to Form S-1, filed with Securities and Exchange Commission, April 4, 2011; "Going Freemium: One Year Later," by Ben Chestnut, Blog.mailchimp.com, September 27, 2010; "Update on Omnivore, New 3 Strikes Rule," by Ben Chestnut, Blog.mailchimp.com, August 27, 2010; "How To Avoid The Traps and Make a 'Freemium' Business Model Pay," Anna Johnson, Kikabink.com, June 14th, 2010; "6 Ways for Online Business Directories to Convert More Freemium to Premium," BusinessWeek.com, April 14, 2010; "Case Studies in Free-mium: Pandora, Dropbox, Evernote, Automattic and MailChimp," by Liz Gannes, Gigacom.com, Mar. 26, 2010; *Free: The Future of a Radical Price*, by Chris Anderson, Hyperion, 2009.

700 million. Most importantly, the number of paying customers increased more than 150%, while profit increased more than 650%! Although the company also saw a significant increase in abuse of its system, they developed an algorithm that helped them to find and eliminate spammers using their service. For MailChimp, freemium has been worth the price. It currently supports more than 2 million subscribers worldwide, sending 3.2 billion e-mails per month.

However, Ning, a company that enables users to create their own social networks, tried freemium and came to a different conclusion. Marc Andreessen, co-author of Mosaic, the first Web browser, and founder of Netscape, launched Ning in 2004. With his assistance, the company has raised $119 million in funding. Despite being the market's leading social network infrastructure platform, Ning was having a common problem—converting eyeballs into paying customers. While 13% of customers were paying for some premium services, the revenue was not enough. The more free users Ning acquired, the more it cost the company.

In May 2010, Ning announced the impending end of the freemium model. The company shed staff, going from 167 to 98, and began using 100% of its resources to capture premium users. Since shifting to a three-tier paid subscription model, Ning has experienced explosive growth, increasing the number of paying customers from 17,000 to more than 100,000 and growing revenue by more than 500%. By September 2011, Ning had more than 100 million registered user social profiles and its social networks reached more than 60 million monthly unique users. In December 2011, Ning was acquired by Glam Media, a leading social media company, for $200 million.

So when does it make sense to include freemium in a business plan? It makes sense when the product is easy to use and has a very large potential audience, preferably in the millions. It's helpful if a large user network increases the perceived value of the product (i.e., a dating service). An extremely important part of the equation is that the variable costs of providing the product or service to additional customers for free must be low.

For example, Evernote, a personal note-taking service, added freemium to its business model and has since grown its user base to 34 million. The company has over 1.4 million paying users. Typically, 2% to 5% of freemium users convert from free product to the paid version. Evernote currently has a conversion rate of around 4–5%, within the range of what is expected. But Evernote has also discovered that the longer a subscriber remains an active user, the more likely he or she is to convert to a premium subscription. For instance, 12% of those who continue to use Evernote for at least two years become premium subscribers. Evernote currently is taking in about $30 million in revenues and recently raised funding of $100 million that valued the company at $1 billion, clear proof that the freemium model can add tremendous value.

Companies also face challenges in terms of what products and/or services to offer for free versus what to charge for (this may change over time), the cost of supporting free customers, and how to price premium services. Further, it is difficult to predict attrition rates, which are highly variable at companies using freemium. So, while freemium can be a great way to get early users and to provide a company with a built-in pool for upgrades, it's tough to determine how many users will be willing to pay and willing to stay.

A freemium strategy makes sense for companies such as Pandora, where there is a very low marginal cost, approaching zero, to support free users. It also makes sense for a company where the value to its potential customers depends on a large network, like Facebook. Freemium also works when a business can be supported by the percentage of customers who are willing to pay, like Pandora or Evernote, especially when there are other revenues like affiliate and advertising fees that can make up for shortfalls in subscriber revenues. Freemium has also become the standard model for most apps, with over 75% of the top 100 apps in Apple's app store using a freemium strategy.

Case Study Questions

1. Compare Pandora's original business model with its current business model. What's the difference between "free" and "freemium" revenue models?

2. What is the customer value proposition that Pandora offers?

3. Why did MailChimp ultimately succeed with a freemium model but Ning did not?

4. What's the most important consideration when considering a freemium revenue model?

2.7 REVIEW

KEY CONCEPTS

■ Identify the key components of e-commerce business models.

A successful business model effectively addresses eight key elements:
- *Value proposition*—how a company's product or service fulfills the needs of customers.
- *Revenue model*—how the company plans to make money from its operations.
- *Market opportunity*—the revenue potential within a company's intended marketspace.
- *Competitive environment*—the direct and indirect competitors doing business in the same marketspace.
- *Competitive advantage*—the factors that differentiate the business from its competition, enabling it to provide a superior product at a lower cost.
- *Market strategy*—the plan a company develops that outlines how it will enter a market and attract customers.
- *Organizational development*—the process of defining all the functions within a business and the skills necessary to perform each job, as well as the process of recruiting and hiring strong employees.
- *Management team*—the group of individuals retained to guide the company's growth and expansion.

■ **Describe the major B2C business models.**

There are a number of different business models being used in the B2C e-commerce arena. The major models include the following:
- *Portal*—offers powerful search tools plus an integrated package of content and services; typically utilizes a combined subscription/advertising revenue/transaction fee model; may be general or specialized (vortal).
- *E-tailer*—online version of traditional retailer; includes virtual merchants (online retail store only), bricks-and-clicks e-tailers (online distribution channel for a company that also has physical stores), catalog merchants (online version of direct mail catalog), and manufacturers selling directly over the Web.
- *Content provider*—information and entertainment companies that provide digital content over the Web; typically utilizes an advertising, subscription, or affiliate referral fee revenue model.
- *Transaction broker*—processes online sales transactions; typically utilizes a transaction fee revenue model.
- *Market creator*—uses Internet technology to create markets that bring buyers and sellers together; typically utilizes a transaction fee revenue model.
- *Service provider*—offers services online.
- *Community provider*—provides an online community of like-minded individuals for networking and information sharing; revenue is generated by advertising, referral fees, and subscriptions.

■ **Describe the major B2B business models.**

The major business models used to date in the B2B arena include:
- *E-distributor*—supplies products directly to individual businesses.
- *E-procurement*—single firms create digital markets for thousands of sellers and buyers.
- *Exchange*—independently owned digital marketplace for direct inputs, usually for a vertical industry group.
- *Industry consortium*—industry-owned vertical digital market.
- *Private industrial network*—industry-owned private industrial network that coordinates supply chains with a limited set of partners.

■ **Understand key business concepts and strategies applicable to e-commerce.**

The Internet and the Web have had a major impact on the business environment in the last decade, and have affected:
- *Industry structure*—the nature of players in an industry and their relative bargaining power by changing the basis of competition among rivals, the barriers to entry, the threat of new substitute products, the strength of suppliers, and the bargaining power of buyers.
- *Industry value chains*—the set of activities performed in an industry by suppliers, manufacturers, transporters, distributors, and retailers that transforms raw inputs into final products and services by reducing the cost of information and other transaction costs.
- *Firm value chains*—the set of activities performed within an individual firm to create final products from raw inputs by increasing operational efficiency.

- *Business strategy*—a set of plans for achieving superior long-term returns on the capital invested in a firm by offering unique ways to differentiate products, obtain cost advantages, compete globally, or compete in a narrow market or product segment.

QUESTIONS

1. What is a business model? How does it differ from a business plan?
2. What are the eight key components of an effective business model?
3. What are Amazon's primary customer value propositions?
4. Describe the five primary revenue models used by e-commerce firms.
5. Why is targeting a market niche generally smarter for a community provider than targeting a large market segment?
6. What are some of the specific ways that a company can obtain a competitive advantage?
7. Besides advertising and product sampling, what are some other market strategies a company might pursue?
8. What elements of Groupon's business model may be faulty?
9. Besides the examples given in the chapter, what are some other examples of vertical and horizontal portals in existence today?
10. What are the major differences between virtual storefronts, such as Drugstore.com, and bricks-and-clicks operations, such as Walmart.com? What are the advantages and disadvantages of each?
11. Besides news and articles, what other forms of information or content do content providers offer?
12. What is a reverse auction? What company is an example of this type of business?
13. What are the key success factors for exchanges? How are they different from portals?
14. How have the unique features of e-commerce technology changed industry structure in the travel business?
15. Who are the major players in an industry value chain and how are they impacted by e-commerce technology?
16. What are four generic business strategies for achieving a profitable business?
17. What is the difference between a market opportunity and a marketspace?

PROJECTS

1. Select an e-commerce company. Visit its Web site and describe its business model based on the information you find there. Identify its customer value proposition, its revenue model, the marketspace it operates in, who its main competitors are, any comparative advantages you believe the company possesses, and what its market strategy appears to be. Also try to locate information about the company's management team and organizational structure. (Check for a page labeled "the Company," "About Us," or something similar.)

2. Examine the experience of shopping on the Web versus shopping in a traditional environment. Imagine that you have decided to purchase a digital camera (or any other item of your choosing). First, shop for the camera in a traditional manner.

Describe how you would do so (for example, how you would gather the necessary information you would need to choose a particular item, what stores you would visit, how long it would take, prices, etc.). Next, shop for the item on the Web. Compare and contrast your experiences. What were the advantages and disadvantages of each? Which did you prefer and why?

3. Visit eBay and look at the many types of auctions available. If you were considering establishing a rival specialized online auction business, what are the top three market opportunities you would pursue, based on the goods and auction community in evidence at eBay? Prepare a report or electronic slide presentation to support your analysis and approach.

4. During the early days of e-commerce, first-mover advantage was touted as one way to success. On the other hand, some suggest that being a market follower can yield rewards as well. Which approach has proven to be more successful—first mover or follower? Choose two e-commerce companies that prove your point, and prepare a brief presentation to explain your analysis and position.

5. Prepare a research report (3 to 5 pages) on the current and potential future impacts of e-commerce technology, including mobile devices, on the book publishing industry.

6. Select a B2C e-commerce retail industry segment such as pet products, online gaming, gift baskets, and analyze its value chain and industry value chain. Prepare a short presentation that identifies the major industry participants in that business and illustrates the move from raw materials to finished product.

7. The ringtone industry is a profitable segment of the music industry. Research the ringtone industry in terms of industry structure, value chains, and competitive environment. Is there room in this industry for another competitor, and if so, what kind of business model and market strategy would it folllow?

PART 2

■ **CHAPTER 3**
E-commerce Infrastructure: The Internet, Web, and Mobile Platform

■ **CHAPTER 4**
Building an E-commerce Presence: Web Sites, Mobile Sites, and Apps

■ **CHAPTER 5**
E-commerce Security and Payment Systems

Technology Infrastructure for E-commerce

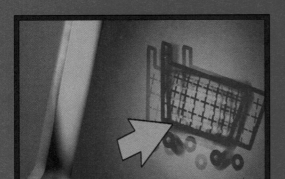

CHAPTER 3

E-commerce Infrastructure: The Internet, Web, and Mobile Platform

LEARNING OBJECTIVES

After reading this chapter, you will be able to:

- Discuss the origins of the Internet.
- Identify the key technology concepts behind the Internet.
- Describe the role of Internet protocols and utility programs.
- Discuss the impact of the mobile platform and cloud computing.
- Explain the current structure of the Internet.
- Describe the potential capabilities of the Internet of the future.
- Understand how the Web works.
- Describe how Internet and Web features and services support e-commerce.
- Understand the impact of m-commerce applications.

Google Glass:

Augment My Reality

Today, the primary means of accessing the Internet is through smartphones. Traditional desktop and laptop PCs will remain important e-commerce and Internet tools, but the action has shifted to the mobile platform. Rather than being just another channel to the Internet, mobile devices are becoming THE channel. This means the primary platform for e-commerce products and services will also change to the mobile platform. The number of mobile Internet users is expected to grow to more than 75% of all Internet users in the United States, about 200 million people, by 2016.

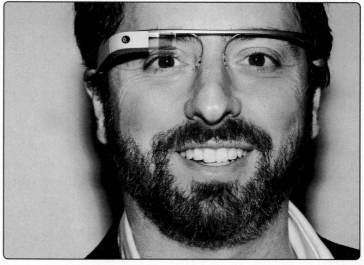

© REUTERS/Carlo Allegri

The mobile platform provides the foundation for a number of unique new services. One of the most exciting examples is augmented reality. Augmented reality refers to content (text, video, and sound) that is superimposed over live images in order to enrich the user's experience. The technology brings together location and context, helping the user understand his or her environment better. A recent study by Semico Research predicted that by the end of 2016, revenue produced by the augmented reality industry will total more than $600 billion. There is a wealth of possibilities for augmented reality, and Google is leading the way.

In 2012, Google began releasing information about its prototype augmented reality glasses, and co-founder Sergey Brin was seen wearing a trial version in public. The small, wrap-around glasses have a clear display mounted above the eye, and they stream information directly to the lenses. The wearer can use voice commands to access features of the glasses, which also have a camera that can snap pictures or record video. Most importantly, the glasses have an augmented reality display, which will allow users to overlay graphics and other images on top of their vision that adjust based on the line of sight of the wearer.

Promotional videos released by Google suggest the device will perform a wide array of functions for the user, including calling up maps, accessing reviews on the fly, displaying schedule reminders at appropriate times, and integrating fully with other Google services, like Google+. Google's involvement in augmented reality is a major step in the maturation of the technology, and Apple has filed for patents that suggest it is planning its own augmented reality foray, which may be the final push needed to put augmented reality squarely into the mainstream. Still, skeptics worry that the technology is more flash than

SOURCES: "How Augmented Reality Will Change the Way We Live," by Mez Breeze, thenextweb.com, August 25, 2012; "Augmented Reality is a New Reality for a Forward Thinking Retailer," by Allison Enright, Internetretailer.com, August 24, 2012; "Augmented Reality is Finally Getting Real," by Rachel Metz, *Technology Review*, August 2, 2012; "Is the Floor Beneath Your Feet Real?" by Bill Siwicki, Internetretailer.com, July 31, 2012; "You Will Want Google Goggles," by Farhad Manjoo, *Technology Review*, July 2012; "Google Begins Testing Its Augmented-Reality Glasses," by Nick Bilton, *New York Times*, April 4, 2012; "Apple Patent Hints at Augmented Reality Camera App," by Josh Lowensohn, News.cnet.com; August 18, 2011; "Augmented Reality Kills the QR Code Star," by Kit Eaton, Fastcompany.com, August 4, 2011; "Qualcomm's Awesome Augmented Reality SDK Now Available for iOS," Techcrunch.com, July 27, 2011; "Real Life or Just Fantasy," by Nick Clayton, *Wall Street Journal*, June 29, 2011; "Augmented Reality Comes Closer to Reality," by John Markoff, *New York Times*, April 7, 2011; "Augmented Reality's Industry Prospects May Get Very Real, Very Fast," by Danny King, Dailyfinance.com, March 11, 2011; "Even Better Than the Real Thing," by Paul Skelton, *Wall Street Journal*, February 15, 2011; "Wikitude Goes Wimbledon 2010," press release, Wikitude.com, June 20, 2010.

substance, and that it might not deliver on the optimistic earnings projections cited today. Other critics worry that the technology will be too distracting. Google engineers counter that augmented reality displays will help users to connect more seamlessly with the real world, rather than obscuring it.

It's not hard to figure out where the e-commerce might reside in these tools. How would you like your business to show up on the Google glasses of users visiting or searching for points of interest in your neighborhood? Yellow Pages is testing the use of augmented reality to overlay advertisements, paid for by businesses, to street views where its app is used. Another variation is a real estate app tested by RightMove that allows users to point their phone up and down a street and find out what is for sale or for rent, and how much it costs. It also provides contact information for each of the properties.

How much would you pay to have an online travel guide with you all the time for that next trip abroad? Yelp, TripAdvisor, and Lonely Planet are just a few of the travel companies that have introduced some aspects of augmented reality to their apps. Wikitude is an online augmented reality mobile platform that uses the same kind of wiki tools that power Wikipedia, the online encyclopedia. The application is available for the iPhone, Android, and Symbian mobile operating systems. The Wikitude browser displays information about whatever the user's phone camera is pointed at. Using the smartphone's GPS, accelerometer, and compass, the browser knows where it is located, and what direction it is pointing. The browser then accesses the Wikitude database to provide text information on the object being looked at by the user, including identifying the object or scene, history, and related points of interest.

Many companies are using augmented reality as part of their mobile applications to allow users to see how a prospective purchase would look before buying. For example, Blinds.com's Window Shopper app allows consumers to take a photo of a window in their house using their mobile phone, and then overlay different styles of blinds on the photo to see how the end result would look before they finalize their purchase. Because the top reason that people provide for not buying blinds online is not being able to see what they would look like, augmented reality is helping Blinds.com drive more online sales than ever before.

Yet another current use of augmented reality is to allow users to simulate "trying on" the product. For instance, eBay's Fashion iPhone app lets users virtually try on sunglasses using the phone's front-facing camera to take a picture of themselves and then virtually "fit" the sunglasses to their face. Watchmaker Neuvo offers a similar app that lets users virtually try on watches, while a Converse app lets you do the same with Converse shoes. Software from Zugara allows you to try on clothing from online shops.

Gaming is another area where augmented reality is expected to make a big splash. Qualcomm, a leading digital wireless telecommunication development firm, has released an augmented reality game software development kit for both Android and iOS devices. Many believe that augmented reality will ultimately become essential to consumers' mobile experiences, just as mobile devices themselves have become essential. The challenge is to get past the tendency to view augmented reality as a science fiction come to life and instead look at it as a tool that businesses and consumers can use to connect and communicate.

Τhis chapter examines the Internet, Web, and mobile platform of today and tomorrow, how it evolved, how it works, and how its present and future infrastructure enables new business opportunities.

The opening case illustrates how important it is for business people to understand how the Internet and related technologies work, and to be aware of what's new. Operating a successful e-commerce business and implementing key e-commerce business strategies such as personalization, customization, market segmentation, and price discrimination requires that business people understand Internet technology and keep track of Web and mobile platform developments.

The Internet and its underlying technology is not a static phenomenon in history, but instead continues to change over time. Computers have merged with cell phone services; broadband access in the home and broadband wireless access to the Internet via smartphones, tablet computers, and laptops is expanding rapidly; self-publishing on the Web via blogging, social networking, and podcasting now engages millions of Internet users; and software technologies such as Web services, cloud computing, and smartphone apps are revolutionizing the way businesses are using the Internet. Looking forward a few years, the business strategies of the future will require a firm understanding of these technologies to deliver products and services to consumers.

3.1 THE INTERNET: TECHNOLOGY BACKGROUND

What is the Internet? Where did it come from, and how did it support the growth of the Web? What are the Internet's most important operating principles? How much do you really need to know about the technology of the Internet?

Let's take the last question first. The answer is: it depends on your career interests. If you are on a marketing career path, or general managerial business path, then you need to know the basics about Internet technology, which you'll learn in this and the following chapter. If you are on a technical career path and hope to become a Web designer, or pursue a technical career in Web infrastructure for businesses, you'll need to start with these basics and then build from there. You'll also need to know about the business side of e-commerce, which you will learn about throughout this book.

As noted in Chapter 1, the **Internet** is an interconnected network of thousands of networks and millions of computers (sometimes called *host computers* or just *hosts*) linking businesses, educational institutions, government agencies, and individuals. The Internet provides approximately 2.3 billion people around the world (including about 239 million people in the United States) with services such as e-mail, apps, newsgroups, shopping, research, instant messaging, music, videos, and news (Internetworldstats.com, 2012). No single organization controls the Internet or how it functions, nor is it owned by anybody, yet it has provided the infrastructure for a transformation in commerce, scientific research, and culture. The word Internet is derived from the word *internetwork*, or the connecting together of two or more

Internet
an interconnected network of thousands of networks and millions of computers linking businesses, educational institutions, government agencies, and individuals

the Web

one of the Internet's most popular services, providing access to more than 100 billion Web pages

computer networks. The **Web** is one of the Internet's most popular services, providing access to billions, perhaps trillions, of Web pages, which are documents created in a programming language called HTML that can contain text, graphics, audio, video, and other objects, as well as "hyperlinks" that permit users to jump easily from one page to another. Web pages are navigated using browser software.

THE EVOLUTION OF THE INTERNET: 1961—THE PRESENT

Today's Internet has evolved over the last 60 or so years. In this sense, the Internet is not "new;" it did not happen yesterday. Although journalists talk glibly about "Internet" time—suggesting a fast-paced, nearly instant, worldwide global change mechanism—in fact, it has taken about 60 years of hard work to arrive at today's Internet.

The history of the Internet can be segmented into three phases (see **Figure 3.1**). In the first phase, the *Innovation Phase,* from 1961 to 1974, the fundamental building blocks of the Internet were conceptualized and then realized in actual hardware and software. The basic building blocks are: packet-switching hardware, a communications protocol called TCP/IP, and client/server computing (all described more fully later in this section). The original purpose of the Internet, when it was conceived in the 1960s, was to link large mainframe computers on different college campuses. This kind of one-to-one communication between campuses was previously only possible through the telephone system or private networks owned by the large computer manufacturers.

In the second phase, the *Institutionalization Phase*, from 1975 to 1995, large institutions such as the Department of Defense (DoD) and the National Science Foundation (NSF) provided funding and legitimization for the fledging invention called the Internet. Once the concepts behind the Internet had been proven in several

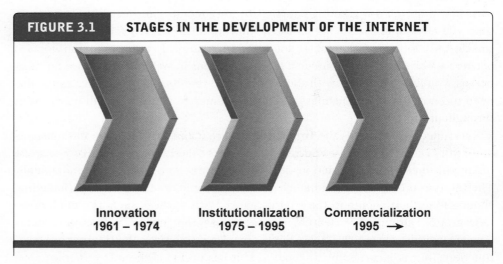

| FIGURE 3.1 | STAGES IN THE DEVELOPMENT OF THE INTERNET |

Innovation
1961 – 1974

Institutionalization
1975 – 1995

Commercialization
1995 →

The Internet has developed in three stages over a 50-year period from 1961 to the present. In the Innovation stage, basic ideas and technologies were developed; in the Institutionalization stage, these ideas were brought to life; in the Commercialization stage, once the ideas and technologies had been proven, private companies brought the Internet to millions of people worldwide.

government-supported demonstration projects, the DoD contributed $1 million to further develop them into a robust military communications system that could withstand nuclear war. This effort created what was then called ARPANET (Advanced Research Projects Agency Network). In 1986, the NSF assumed responsibility for the development of a civilian Internet (then called NSFNET) and began a 10-year-long $200 million expansion program.

In the third phase, the *Commercialization Phase*, from 1995 to the present, government agencies encouraged private corporations to take over and expand both the Internet backbone and local service to ordinary citizens—families and individuals across America and the world who were not students on campuses. By 2000, the Internet's use had expanded well beyond military installations and research universities.

THE INTERNET: KEY TECHNOLOGY CONCEPTS

In 1995, the Federal Networking Council (FNC) passed a resolution formally defining the term *Internet* as a network that uses the IP addressing scheme, supports the Transmission Control Protocol (TCP), and makes services available to users much like a telephone system makes voice and data services available to the public.

Behind this formal definition are three extremely important concepts that are the basis for understanding the Internet: packet switching, the TCP/IP communications protocol, and client/server computing. Although the Internet has evolved and changed dramatically in the last 30 years, these three concepts are at the core of the way the Internet functions today and are the foundation for Internet II.

Packet Switching

Packet switching is a method of slicing digital messages into discrete units called **packets**, sending the packets along different communication paths as they become available, and then reassembling the packets once they arrive at their destination (see **Figure 3.2**). Prior to the development of packet switching, early computer networks used leased, dedicated telephone circuits to communicate with terminals and other computers. In circuit-switched networks such as the telephone system, a complete point-to-point circuit is put together, and then communication can proceed. However, these "dedicated" circuit-switching techniques were expensive and wasted available communications capacity—the circuit would be maintained regardless of whether any data was being sent. For nearly 70% of the time, a dedicated voice circuit is not being fully used because of pauses between words and delays in assembling the circuit segments, both of which increase the length of time required to find and connect circuits. A better technology was needed.

The first book on packet switching was written by Leonard Kleinrock in 1964 (Kleinrock, 1964), and the technique was further developed by others in the defense research labs of both the United States and England. With packet switching, the communications capacity of a network can be increased by a factor of 100 or more. (The communications capacity of a digital network is measured in terms of bits per

packet switching
a method of slicing digital messages into packets, sending the packets along different communication paths as they become available, and then reassembling the packets once they arrive at their destination

packet
the discrete units into which digital messages are sliced for transmission over the Internet

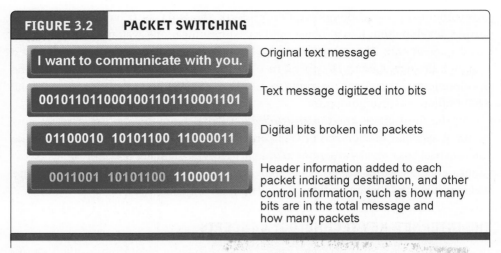

FIGURE 3.2	PACKET SWITCHING

I want to communicate with you. — Original text message

0010110110001001101110001101 — Text message digitized into bits

01100010 10101100 11000011 — Digital bits broken into packets

0011001 10101100 11000011 — Header information added to each packet indicating destination, and other control information, such as how many bits are in the total message and how many packets

In packet switching, digital messages are divided into fixed-length packets of bits (generally about 1,500 bytes). Header information indicates both the origin and the ultimate destination address of the packet, the size of the message, and the number of packets the receiving node should expect. Because the receipt of each packet is acknowledged by the receiving computer, for a considerable amount of time, the network is not passing information, only acknowledgments, producing a delay called latency.

second.[1]) Imagine if the gas mileage of your car went from 15 miles per gallon to 1,500 miles per gallon—all without changing too much of the car!

In packet-switched networks, messages are first broken down into packets. Appended to each packet are digital codes that indicate a source address (the origination point) and a destination address, as well as sequencing information and error-control information for the packet. Rather than being sent directly to the destination address, in a packet network, the packets travel from computer to computer until they reach their destination. These computers are called routers. A **router** is a special-purpose computer that interconnects the different computer networks that make up the Internet and routes packets along to their ultimate destination as they travel. To ensure that packets take the best available path toward their destination, routers use a computer program called a **routing algorithm**.

Packet switching does not require a dedicated circuit, but can make use of any spare capacity that is available on any of several hundred circuits. Packet switching makes nearly full use of almost all available communication lines and capacity. Moreover, if some lines are disabled or too busy, the packets can be sent on any available line that eventually leads to the destination point.

Transmission Control Protocol/Internet Protocol (TCP/IP)

While packet switching was an enormous advance in communications capacity, there was no universally agreed-upon method for breaking up digital messages into packets,

router

special-purpose computer that interconnects the computer networks that make up the Internet and routes packets to their ultimate destination as they travel the Internet

routing algorithm

computer program that ensures that packets take the best available path toward their destination

---

[1] A bit is a binary digit, 0 or 1. A string of eight bits constitutes a byte. A home telephone dial-up modem connects to the Internet usually at 56 Kbps (56,000 bits per second). Mbps refers to millions of bits per second, whereas Gbps refers to billions of bits per second.

routing them to the proper address, and then reassembling them into a coherent message. This was like having a system for producing stamps but no postal system (a series of post offices and a set of addresses). The answer was to develop a **protocol** (a set of rules and standards for data transfer) to govern the formatting, ordering, compressing, and error-checking of messages, as well as specify the speed of transmission and means by which devices on the network will indicate they have stopped sending and/or receiving messages.

Transmission Control Protocol/Internet Protocol (TCP/IP), which has become the core communications protocol for the Internet (Cerf and Kahn, 1974). **TCP** establishes the connections among sending and receiving Web computers, and makes sure that packets sent by one computer are received in the same sequence by the other, without any packets missing. **IP** provides the Internet's addressing scheme and is responsible for the actual delivery of the packets.

TCP/IP is divided into four separate layers, with each layer handling a different aspect of the communication problem (see **Figure 3.3**).

protocol
a set of rules and standards for data transfer

Transmission Control Protocol/Internet Protocol (TCP/IP)
the core communications protocol for the Internet

TCP
protocol that establishes the connections among sending and receiving Web computers and handles the assembly of packets at the point of transmission, and their reassembly at the receiving end

IP
protocol that provides the Internet's addressing scheme and is responsible for the actual delivery of the packets

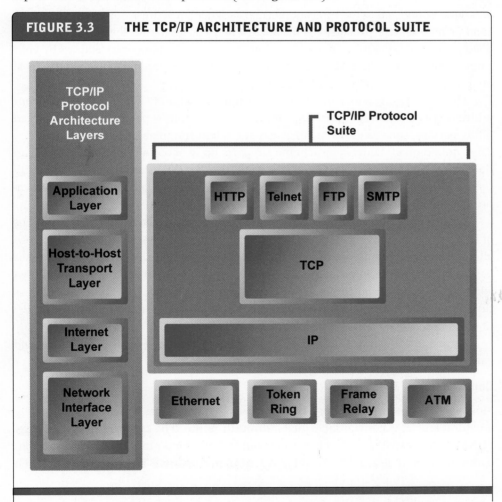

FIGURE 3.3   **THE TCP/IP ARCHITECTURE AND PROTOCOL SUITE**

TCP/IP is an industry-standard suite of protocols for large internetworks. The purpose of TCP/IP is to provide high-speed communication network links.

Network Interface Layer
responsible for placing packets on and receiving them from the network medium

Internet Layer
responsible for addressing, packaging, and routing messages on the Internet

Transport Layer
responsible for providing communication with the application by acknowledging and sequencing the packets to and from the application

Application Layer
provides a wide variety of applications with the ability to access the services of the lower layers

IPv4 Internet address
Internet address expressed as a 32-bit number that appears as a series of four separate numbers marked off by periods, such as 64.49.254.91

IPv6 Internet address
Internet address expressed as an 128-bit number

domain name
IP address expressed in natural language

Domain Name System (DNS)
system for expressing numeric IP addresses in natural language

Uniform Resource Locator (URL)
the address used by a Web browser to identify the location of content on the Web

The **Network Interface Layer** is responsible for placing packets on and receiving them from the network medium, which could be a LAN (Ethernet) or Token Ring network, or other network technology. TCP/IP is independent from any local network technology and can adapt to changes at the local level. The **Internet Layer** is responsible for addressing, packaging, and routing messages on the Internet. The **Transport Layer** is responsible for providing communication with the application by acknowledging and sequencing the packets to and from the application. The **Application Layer** provides a wide variety of applications with the ability to access the services of the lower layers. Some of the best-known applications are HyperText Transfer Protocol (HTTP), File Transfer Protocol (FTP), and Simple Mail Transfer Protocol (SMTP), all of which we will discuss later in this chapter.

IP Addresses

The IP addressing scheme answers the question "How can billions of computers attached to the Internet communicate with one another?" The answer is that every computer connected to the Internet must be assigned an address—otherwise it cannot send or receive TCP packets. For instance, when you sign onto the Internet using a dial-up, DSL, or cable modem, your computer is assigned a temporary address by your Internet Service Provider. Most corporate and university computers attached to a local area network have a permanent IP address.

There are two versions of IP currently in use: IPv4 and IPv6. An **IPv4 Internet address** is a 32-bit number that appears as a series of four separate numbers marked off by periods, such as 64.49.254.91. Each of the four numbers can range from 0–255. This "dotted quad" addressing scheme supports up to about 4 billion addresses (2 to the 32nd power). In a typical Class C network, the first three sets of numbers identify the network (in the preceding example, 64.49.254 is the local area network identification) and the last number (91) identifies a specific computer.

Because many large corporate and government domains have been given millions of IP addresses each (to accommodate their current and future work forces), and with all the new networks and new Internet-enabled devices requiring unique IP addresses being attached to the Internet, by 2011, there were only an estimated 76 million IPv4 addresses left, declining at the rate of 1 million per week. IPv6 was created to address this problem. An **IPv6 Internet address** is 128 bits, so it can support up to 2^{128} (3.4×10^{38}) addresses, many more than IPv4.

Figure 3.4 illustrates how TCP/IP and packet switching work together to send data over the Internet.

Domain Names, DNS, and URLs

Most people cannot remember 32-bit numbers. An IP address can be represented by a natural language convention called a **domain name**. The **Domain Name System (DNS)** allows expressions such as Cnet.com to stand for a numeric IP address (cnet. com's numeric IP is 216.239.113.101).[2] A **Uniform Resource Locator (URL)**, which

---

[2] You can check the IP address of any domain name on the Internet. In Windows 7 or Vista, use Start/ cmd to open the DOS prompt. Type ping < Domain Name >. You will receive the IP address in return.

FIGURE 3.4	ROUTING INTERNET MESSAGES: TCP/IP AND PACKET SWITCHING

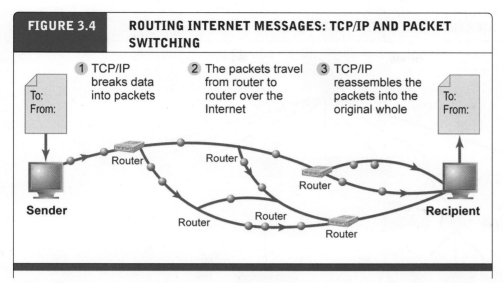

The Internet uses packet-switched networks and the TCP/IP communications protocol to send, route, and assemble messages. Messages are broken into packets, and packets from the same message can travel along different routes.

is the address used by a Web browser to identify the location of content on the Web, also uses a domain name as part of the URL. A typical URL contains the protocol to be used when accessing the address, followed by its location. For instance, the URL http://www.azimuth-interactive.com/flash_test refers to the IP address 208.148.84.1 with the domain name "azimuth-interactive.com" and the protocol being used to access the address, HTTP. A resource called "flash_test" is located on the server directory path /flash_test. A URL can have from two to four parts; for example, name1.name2.name3.org. We discuss domain names and URLs further in Section 3.4. **Figure 3.5** illustrates the Domain Name System and **Table 3.1** summarizes the important components of the Internet addressing scheme.

Client/Server Computing

While packet switching exploded the available communications capacity and TCP/IP provided the communications rules and regulations, it took a revolution in computing to bring about today's Internet and the Web. That revolution is called client/server computing and without it, the Web—in all its richness—would not exist. **Client/server computing** is a model of computing in which powerful personal computers and other Internet devices called **clients** are connected in a network to one or more server computers. These clients are sufficiently powerful to accomplish complex tasks such as displaying rich graphics, storing large files, and processing graphics and sound files, all on a local desktop or handheld device. **Servers** are networked computers dedicated to common functions that the client computers on the network need, such as file storage, software applications, utility programs that provide Web connections, and printers (see **Figure 3.6** on page 79). The Internet is a giant example of client/server computing in which millions of Web servers located around the world can be easily accessed by millions of client computers, also located throughout the world.

client/server computing
a model of computing in which powerful personal computers are connected in a network together with one or more servers

client
a powerful personal computer that is part of a network

server
networked computer dedicated to common functions that the client computers on the network need

FIGURE 3.5	THE HIERARCHICAL DOMAIN NAME SYSTEM

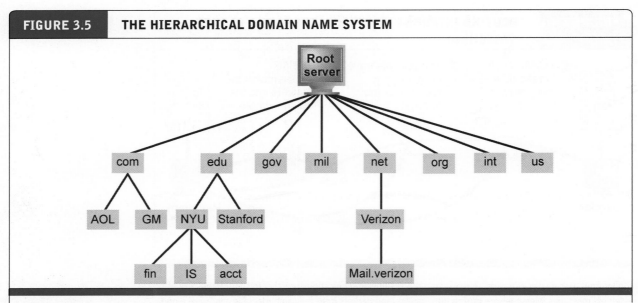

The Domain Name System is a hierarchical namespace with a root server at the top. Top-level domains appear next and identify the organization type (such as .com, .gov, .org, etc.) or geographic location (such as .uk [Great Britain] or .ca [Canada]). Second-level servers for each top-level domain assign and register second-level domain names for organizations and individuals such as IBM.com, Microsoft.com, and Stanford.edu. Finally, third-level domains identify a particular computer or group of computers within an organization, e.g., www.finance.nyu.edu.

To appreciate what client/server computing makes possible, you must understand what preceded it. In the mainframe computing environment of the 1960s and 1970s, computing power was very expensive and limited. For instance, the largest commercial mainframes of the late 1960s had 128k of RAM and 10-megabyte disk drives, and occupied hundreds of square feet. There was insufficient computing capacity to support graphics or color in text documents, let alone sound files, video, or hyperlinked documents.

With the development of personal computers and local area networks during the late 1970s and early 1980s, client/server computing became possible. Client/

TABLE 3.1	PIECES OF THE INTERNET PUZZLE: NAMES AND ADDRESSES
IP addresses	Every device connected to the Internet must have a unique address number called an Internet Protocol (IP) address.
Domain names	The Domain Name System allows expressions such as Pearsoned.com (Pearson Education's Web site) to stand for numeric IP locations.
DNS servers	DNS servers are databases that keep track of IP addresses and domain names on the Internet.
Root servers	Root servers are central directories that list all domain names currently in use for specific domains; for example, the .com root server. DNS servers consult root servers to look up unfamiliar domain names when routing traffic.

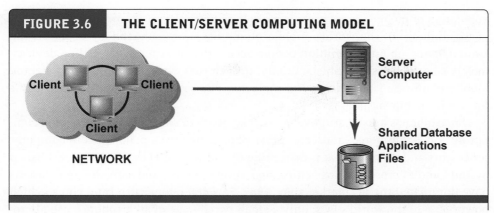

FIGURE 3.6 **THE CLIENT/SERVER COMPUTING MODEL**

In the client/server model of computing, client computers are connected in a network together with one or more servers.

server computing has many advantages over centralized mainframe computing. For instance, it is easy to expand capacity by adding servers and clients. Also, client/server networks are less vulnerable than centralized computing architectures. If one server goes down, backup or mirror servers can pick up the slack; if a client computer is inoperable, the rest of the network continues operating. Moreover, processing load is balanced over many powerful smaller computers rather than being concentrated in a single huge computer that performs processing for everyone. Both software and hardware in client/server environments can be built more simply and economically.

Today there are more than 1.6 billion personal computers in existence worldwide. Personal computing capabilities have also moved to smartphones and laptop computers (all much "thinner clients" with a bit less computing horsepower, and limited memory, but which rely on Internet servers to accomplish their tasks). In the process, more computer processing will be performed by central servers.

THE NEW CLIENT: THE MOBILE PLATFORM

There's a new client in town. In a few years, the primary means of accessing the Internet both in the United States and worldwide will be through highly portable smartphones and tablet computers, and not traditional desktop or laptop PCs. This means that the primary platform for e-commerce products and services will also change to a mobile platform.

The change in hardware has reached a tipping point. The form factor of PCs has changed from desktops to laptops and tablet computers such as the iPad (and more than 100 other competitors). Tablets are lighter, do not require a complex operating system, and rely on the Internet cloud to provide processing and storage. And, while there are an estimated 1.6 billion PCs in the world, the number of cell phones long ago exceeded the population of PCs. In 2011, there were an estimated 4 billion worldwide mobile phone users, with 243 million in the United States, around 880 million in China, and 470 million in India (eMarketer, Inc., 2012a). The population of mobile phone users is more than twice that of PC owners. About 25%, or 950 million, of the world's mobile phone users are smartphone users. In the United States, about 122 million people access the Internet using mobile devices, mostly smartphones and tablets. Briefly, the Internet world is turning into a lighter, mobile platform. The tablet is not replacing PCs so much as supplementing PCs for use in mobile situations.

Smartphones are a disruptive technology that radically alters the personal computing and e-commerce landscape. Smartphones involve a major shift in computer processors and software that is disrupting the 40-year dual monopolies established by Intel and Microsoft, whose chips, operating systems, and software applications have dominated the PC market since 1982. Few cell phones use Intel chips, which power 90% of the world's PCs; only a small percentage of smartphones use Microsoft's operating system (Windows Mobile). Instead, smartphone manufacturers either purchase operating systems such as Symbian, the world leader, or build their own, such as Apple's iPhone iOS and BlackBerry's OS, typically based on Linux and Java platforms. Smartphones do not need fans. Cell phones do not use power-hungry hard drives but instead use flash memory chips with storage up to 32 megabytes that also require much less power.

The mobile platform has profound implications for e-commerce because it influences how, where, and when consumers shop and buy.

THE INTERNET "CLOUD COMPUTING" MODEL: SOFTWARE AND HARDWARE AS A SERVICE

The growing bandwidth power of the Internet has pushed the client/server model one step further towards what is called the "cloud computing model" (**Figure 3.7**).

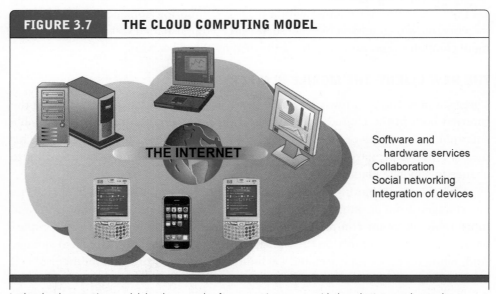

FIGURE 3.7   **THE CLOUD COMPUTING MODEL**

THE INTERNET

Software and
   hardware services
Collaboration
Social networking
Integration of devices

In the cloud computing model, hardware and software services are provided on the Internet by vendors operating very large server farms and data centers.

Cloud computing refers to a model of computing in which firms and individuals obtain computing power and software applications over the Internet, rather than purchasing the hardware and software and installing it on their own computers. Currently, cloud computing is the fastest growing form of computing, with an estimated market size in 2012 of $100 billion.

Hardware firms such as IBM, HP, and Dell have built very large, scalable cloud computing centers that provide computing power, data storage, and high-speed Internet connections to firms that rely on the Internet for business software applications. Amazon, the Internet's largest retailer, is also one of the largest providers of cloud infrastructure and software services.

Software firms such as Google, Microsoft, SAP, Oracle, and Salesforce.com sell software applications that are Internet-based. Instead of software as a product, in the cloud computing model, software is a service provided over the Internet (referred to as SaaS—software as a service). For instance, Google claims there are around 40 million active users and 4 million businesses that use Google Apps, its suite of office software applications such as word processing, spreadsheets, and calendars, that users access over the Internet. More than 100,000 firms and organizations use Salesforce.com's customer relationship management software.

Microsoft, which in the past has depended on selling boxed software to firms and individuals, is adapting to this new marketplace with its own "software plus service" (buy the boxed version and get "free" online services), Windows Live, and Online Technology initiatives.

Cloud computing has many significant implications for e-commerce. For e-commerce firms, cloud computing radically reduces the cost of building and operating Web sites because the necessary hardware infrastructure and software can be licensed as a service from Internet providers at a fraction of the cost of purchasing these services as products. This means firms can adopt "pay-as-you-go" and "pay-as-you-grow" strategies when building out their Web sites. For instance, according to Amazon, hundreds of thousands of customers use Amazon's Web Services arm, which provides storage services, computing services, database services, messaging services, and payment services. For individuals, cloud computing means you no longer need a powerful laptop or desktop computer to engage in e-commerce or other activities. Instead, you can use much less-expensive tablets or smartphones that cost a few hundred dollars. For corporations, cloud computing means that a significant part of hardware and software costs (infrastructure costs) can be reduced because firms can obtain these services online for a fraction of the cost of owning, and they do not have to hire an IT staff to support the infrastructure. These benefits come with some risks: firms become totally dependent on their cloud service providers.

OTHER INTERNET PROTOCOLS AND UTILITY PROGRAMS

There are many other Internet protocols and utility programs that provide services to users in the form of Internet applications that run on Internet clients and servers. These Internet services are based on universally accepted protocols—or standards—that are available to everyone who uses the Internet. They are not owned by any

cloud computing
model of computing in which firms and individuals obtain computing power and software over the Internet

organization, but they are services that have been developed over many years and made available to all Internet users.

Internet Protocols: HTTP, E-mail Protocols, FTP, Telnet, and SSL/TLS

HyperText Transfer Protocol (HTTP)
the Internet protocol used for transferring Web pages

Simple Mail Transfer Protocol (SMTP)
the Internet protocol used to send mail to a server

Post Office Protocol 3 (POP3)
a protocol used by the client to retrieve mail from an Internet server

Internet Message Access Protocol (IMAP)
a more current e-mail protocol that allows users to search, organize, and filter their mail prior to downloading it from the server

File Transfer Protocol (FTP)
one of the original Internet services. Part of the TCP/IP protocol that permits users to transfer files from the server to their client computer, and vice versa

Telnet
a terminal emulation program that runs in TCP/IP

Secure Sockets Layer (SSL) /Transport Layer Security (TLS)
protocols that secure communications between the client and the server

HyperText Transfer Protocol (HTTP) is the Internet protocol used to transfer Web pages (described in the following section). HTTP was developed by the World Wide Web Consortium (W3C) and the Internet Engineering Task Force (IETF). HTTP runs in the Application Layer of the TCP/IP model shown in Figure 3.3 on page 75. An HTTP session begins when a client's browser requests a resource, such as a Web page, from a remote Internet server. When the server responds by sending the page requested, the HTTP session for that object ends. Because Web pages may have many objects on them—graphics, sound or video files, frames, and so forth—each object must be requested by a separate HTTP message. For more information about HTTP, you can consult RFC 2616, which details the standards for HTTP/1.1, the version of HTTP most commonly used today (Internet Society, 1999). (An RFC is a document published by the Internet Society [ISOC] or one of the other organizations involved in Internet governance that sets forth the standards for various Internet-related technologies. You will learn more about the organizations involved in setting standards for the Internet later in the chapter.)

E-mail is one of the oldest, most important, and frequently used Internet services. Like HTTP, the various Internet protocols used to handle e-mail all run in the Application Layer of TCP/IP. **Simple Mail Transfer Protocol (SMTP)** is the Internet protocol used to send e-mail to a server. SMTP is a relatively simple, text-based protocol that was developed in the early 1980s. SMTP handles only the sending of e-mail. To retrieve e-mail from a server, the client computer uses either **Post Office Protocol 3 (POP3)** or **Internet Message Access Protocol (IMAP)**. You can set POP3 to retrieve e-mail messages from the server and then delete the messages on the server, or retain them on the server. IMAP is a more current e-mail protocol supported by all browsers and most servers and ISPs. IMAP allows users to search, organize, and filter their mail prior to downloading it from the server.

File Transfer Protocol (FTP) is one of the original Internet services. FTP runs in TCP/IP's Application Layer and permits users to transfer files from a server to their client computer, and vice versa. The files can be documents, programs, or large database files. FTP is the fastest and most convenient way to transfer files larger than 1 megabyte, which some e-mail servers will not accept. More information about FTP is available in RFC 959 (Internet Society, 1985).

Telnet is a network protocol that also runs in TCP/IP's Application Layer and is used to allow remote login on another computer. The term Telnet also refers to the Telnet program, which provides the client part of the protocol and enables the client to emulate a mainframe computer terminal. (The industry-standard terminals defined in the days of mainframe computing are VT-52, VT-100, and IBM 3250.) You can then attach yourself to a computer on the Internet that supports Telnet and run programs or download files from that computer. Telnet was the first "remote work" program that permitted users to work on a computer from a remote location.

Secure Sockets Layer (SSL)/Transport Layer Security (TLS) are protocols that operate between the Transport and Application Layers of TCP/IP and secure communications between the client and the server. SSL/TLS helps secure e-commerce communications and payments through a variety of techniques, such as message encryption and digital signatures, that we will discuss further in Chapter 5.

Utility Programs: Ping and Tracert

Packet InterNet Groper (Ping) allows you to check the connection between a client computer and a TCP/IP network (see **Figure 3.8**). Ping will also tell you the time it takes for the server to respond, giving you some idea about the speed of the server and the Internet at that moment. We will discuss Ping further in Chapter 5, because one way to slow down or even crash a domain server is to send it millions of ping requests.

Tracert is one of several route-tracing utilities that allow you to follow the path of a message you send from your client to a remote computer on the Internet. **Figure 3.9** shows the result of a message sent to a remote host using a visual route-tracing program called VisualRoute (available from Visualware).

Ping
a program that allows you to check the connection between your client and the server

Tracert
one of several route-tracing utilities that allow you to follow the path of a message you send from your client to a remote computer on the Internet

3.2	**THE INTERNET TODAY**

In 2012, there were an estimated 2.3 billion Internet users worldwide, up from 100 million users at year-end 1997. While this is a huge number, it represents only about 30% of the world's population (Internetworldstats.com, 2012). Although Internet user growth has slowed in the United States to about 1% annually, in Asia, Internet growth is about 10% annually, and by 2015, it is expected that there will be about 2.9 billion Internet users worldwide. One would think the Internet would be overloaded with such incredible growth; however, this has not been true for several reasons. First, client/server computing is highly extensible. By simply adding servers and clients, the population of Internet users can grow indefinitely. Second, the Internet architecture is built in layers so that each layer can change without disturbing developments in

FIGURE 3.8	**THE RESULT OF A PING**

```
Command Prompt                                    _ □ ×

C:\>
C:\>
C:\>ping www.yahoo.com

Pinging www.yahoo.com [204.71.200.72] with 32 bytes of data:

Reply from 204.71.200.72: bytes=32 time=100ms TTL=240
Reply from 204.71.200.72: bytes=32 time=100ms TTL=240
Reply from 204.71.200.72: bytes=32 time=130ms TTL=240
Reply from 204.71.200.72: bytes=32 time=100ms TTL=240

C:\>
```

A ping is used to verify an address and test the speed of the round trip from a client computer to a host and back.

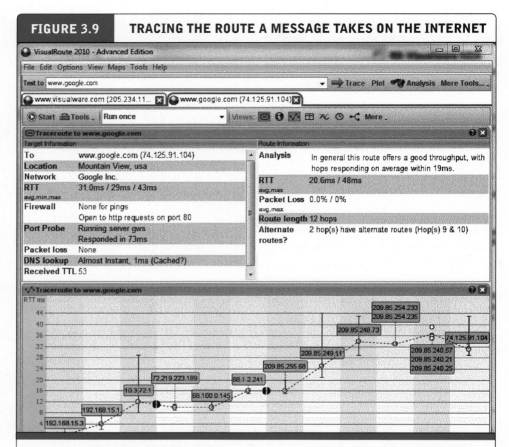

FIGURE 3.9   **TRACING THE ROUTE A MESSAGE TAKES ON THE INTERNET**

VisualRoute and other tracing programs provide some insight into how the Internet uses packet switching. This particular message traveled from a computer in Ashburn, Virginia, to San Antonio, Texas.

SOURCE: Visualware, Inc., 2011.

Network Technology Substrate layer

layer of Internet technology that is composed of telecommunications networks and protocols

Transport Services and Representation Standards layer

layer of Internet architecture that houses the TCP/IP protocol

Applications layer

layer of Internet architecture that contains client applications

Middleware Services layer

the "glue" that ties the applications to the communications networks and includes such services as security, authentication, addresses, and storage repositories

other layers. For instance, the technology used to move messages through the Internet can go through radical changes to make service faster without being disruptive to your desktop applications running on the Internet.

Figure 3.10 illustrates the "hourglass" and layered architecture of the Internet. The Internet can be viewed conceptually as having four layers: Network Technology Substrates, Transport Services and Representation Standards, Middleware Services, and Applications.[3] The **Network Technology Substrate layer** is composed of telecommunications networks and protocols. The **Transport Services and Representation Standards layer** houses the TCP/IP protocol. The **Applications layer** contains client applications such as the World Wide Web, e-mail, and audio or video playback. The **Middleware Services layer** is the glue that ties the applications to the communications networks and includes such services as security, authentication, addresses, and storage repositories. Users work with applications (such as e-mail) and rarely become

---

[3] Recall that the TCP/IP communications protocol also has layers, not to be confused with the Internet architecture layers.

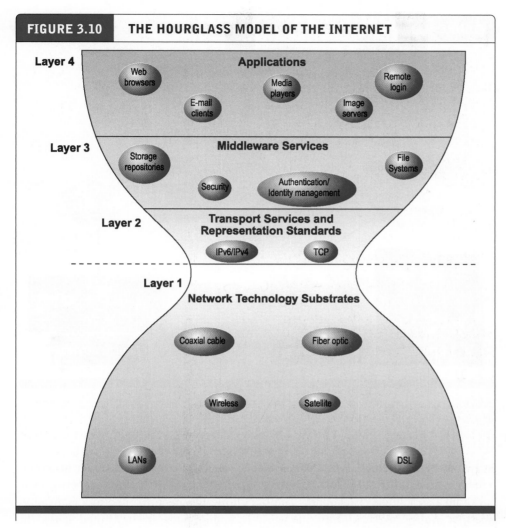

FIGURE 3.10   **THE HOURGLASS MODEL OF THE INTERNET**

Layer 4 — Applications (Web browsers, E-mail clients, Media players, Image servers, Remote login)

Layer 3 — Middleware Services (Storage repositories, Security, Authentication/Identity management, File Systems)

Layer 2 — Transport Services and Representation Standards (IPv6/IPv4, TCP)

Layer 1 — Network Technology Substrates (Coaxial cable, Fiber optic, Wireless, Satellite, LANs, DSL)

The Internet can be characterized as an hourglass modular structure with a lower layer containing the bit-carrying infrastructure (including cables and switches) and an upper layer containing user applications such as e-mail and the Web. In the narrow waist are transportation protocols such as TCP/IP.

aware of middleware that operates in the background. Because all layers use TCP/IP and other common standards linking all four layers, it is possible for there to be significant changes in the Network layer without forcing changes in the Applications Layer.

THE INTERNET BACKBONE

Figure 3.11 illustrates some of the main physical elements of today's Internet. Originally, the Internet had a single backbone, but today's Internet has several backbones that are physically connected with each other and that transfer information from one private network to another. These private networks are referred to as

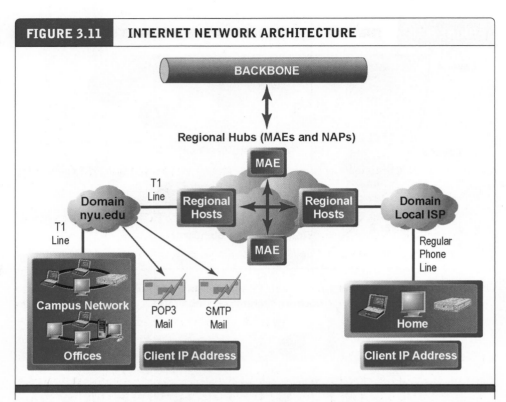

| FIGURE 3.11 | INTERNET NETWORK ARCHITECTURE |

Today's Internet has a multi-tiered open network architecture featuring multiple national backbones, regional hubs, campus area networks, and local client computers.

Network Service Provider (NSP)
owns and controls one of the major networks comprising the Internet's backbone

backbone
high-bandwidth fiber-optic cable that transports data across the Internet

bandwidth
measures how much data can be transferred over a communications medium within a fixed period of time; is usually expressed in bits per second (bps), kilobits per second (Kbps), megabits per second (Mbps), or gigabits per second (Gbps)

redundancy
Refers to multiple duplicate devices and paths in a network

Network Service Providers (NSPs), which own and control the major backbone networks (see **Table 3.2**). For the sake of clarity we will refer to these networks of backbones as a single "backbone." The **backbone** has been likened to a giant pipeline that transports data around the world in milliseconds. In the United States, the backbone is composed entirely of fiber-optic cable with bandwidths ranging from 155 Mbps to 2.5 Gbps. **Bandwidth** measures how much data can be transferred over a communications medium within a fixed period of time and is usually expressed in bits per second (bps), kilobits (thousands of bits) per second (Kbps), megabits (millions of bits) per second (Mbps), or gigabits (billions of bits) per second (Gbps).

Connections to other continents are made via a combination of undersea fiber-optic cable and satellite links. The backbones in foreign countries typically are operated by a mixture of private and public owners. The backbone has built-in redundancy so that if one part breaks down, data can be rerouted to another part of the backbone. **Redundancy** refers to multiple duplicate devices and paths in a network.

INTERNET EXCHANGE POINTS

In the United States, there are a number of hubs where the backbone intersects with regional and local networks, and where the backbone owners connect with one another (see **Figure 3.12**). These hubs were originally called Network Access Points

TABLE 3.2	MAJOR U.S. INTERNET BACKBONE OWNERS	
AT&T		Verio
AOL Transit Data Network (ATDN)		CenturyLink
Cable & Wireless		Sprint
Level 3 Communications		Verizon

(NAPs) or Metropolitan Area Exchanges (MAEs), but now are more commonly referred to as **Internet Exchange Points (IXPs)**. IXPs use high-speed switching computers to connect the backbone to regional and local networks, and exchange messages with one another. The regional and local networks are owned by local Bell operating companies (RBOCs—pronounced "ree-bocks") and private telecommunications firms; they generally are fiber-optic networks operating at more than 100 Mbps. The regional networks lease access to ISPs, private companies, and government institutions.

Internet Exchange Point (IXP)

hub where the backbone intersects with local and regional networks and where backbone owners connect with one another

CAMPUS AREA NETWORKS

Campus area networks (CANs) are generally local area networks operating within a single organization—such as New York University or Microsoft Corporation. In fact, most large organizations have hundreds of such local area networks. These organizations are sufficiently large that they lease access to the Web directly from regional and national carriers. These local area networks generally are running Ethernet (a

campus area network (CAN)

generally, a local area network operating within a single organization that leases access to the Web directly from regional and national carriers

FIGURE 3.12	SOME MAJOR U.S. INTERNET EXCHANGE POINTS (IXPs)

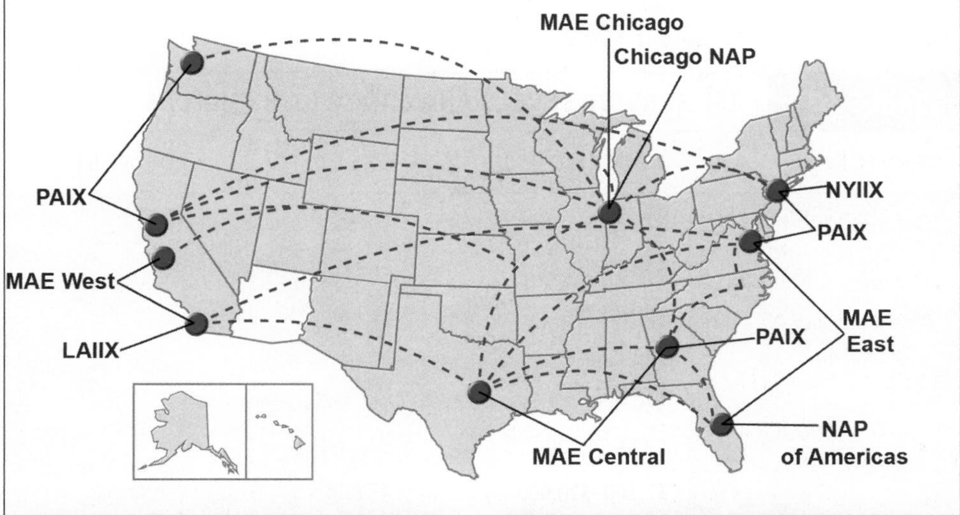

local area network protocol) and have network operating systems such as Windows Server or Linux that permit desktop clients to connect to the Internet through a local Internet server attached to their campus networks. Connection speeds in campus area networks are in the range of 10–100 Mbps to the desktop.

INTERNET SERVICE PROVIDERS

The firms that provide the lowest level of service in the multi-tiered Internet architecture by leasing Internet access to home owners, small businesses, and some large institutions are called **Internet Service Providers (ISPs)**. ISPs are retail providers. They deal with "the last mile of service" to the curb—homes and business offices. ISPs typically connect to IXPs with high-speed telephone or cable lines (45 Mbps and higher).

There are a number of major ISPs, such as AT&T, Comcast (Optimum Online), Cablevision, Cox, Time Warner Cable, Verizon, Sprint, and CenturyLink (formerly Qwest), as well as thousands of local ISPs in the United States, ranging from local telephone companies offering dial-up and DSL telephone access to cable companies offering cable modem service, to small "mom-and-pop" Internet shops that service a small town, city, or even county with mostly dial-up phone access. If you have home or small business Internet access, an ISP likely provides the service to you. Satellite firms also offer Internet access, especially in remote areas where broadband service is not available.

Table 3.3 summarizes the variety of services, speeds, and costs of ISP Internet connections. There are two types of ISP service: narrowband and broadband. **Narrowband** service is the traditional telephone modem connection now operating at 56.6 Kbps (although the actual throughput hovers around 30 Kbps due to line noise that causes extensive resending of packets). This used to be the most common form of connection worldwide but is quickly being replaced by broadband connections in the United States, Europe, and Asia. Broadband service is based on DSL, cable modem, telephone (T1 and T3 lines), and satellite technologies. **Broadband**, in the context of Internet service, refers to any communication technology that permits clients to play

Internet Service Provider (ISP)
firm that provides the lowest level of service in the multi-tiered Internet architecture by leasing Internet access to home owners, small businesses, and some large institutions

narrowband
the traditional telephone modem connection, now operating at 56.6 Kbps

broadband
refers to any communication technology that permits clients to play streaming audio and video files at acceptable speeds—generally anything above 100 Kbps

TABLE 3.3	ISP SERVICE LEVELS AND BANDWIDTH CHOICES	
SERVICE	COST/MONTH	SPEED TO DESKTOP (KBPS)
Telephone modem	$10–$25	30–56 Kbps
DSL	$15–$50	768 Kbps–7 Mbps
FiOS	$90–$130	15 Mbps–50 Mbps
Cable modem	$20–$50	1 Mbps–20 Mbps
Satellite	$20–$50	768 Kbps–5 Mbps
T1	$300–$1,200	1.54 Mbps
T3	$2,500–$10,000	45 Mbps

streaming audio and video files at acceptable speeds—generally anything above 100 Kbps. In the United States, broadband users surpassed dial-up users in 2004, and in 2012, there were an estimated 82 million broadband households (about 70% of all households) (eMarketer, Inc., 2012b).

The actual throughput of data will depend on a variety of factors including noise in the line and the number of subscribers requesting service. Service-level speeds quoted are typically only for downloads of Internet content; upload speeds tend to be much slower. T1 lines are publicly regulated utility lines that offer a guaranteed level of service, but the actual throughput of the other forms of Internet service is not guaranteed.

Digital Subscriber Line (DSL) service is a telephone technology that provides high-speed access to the Internet through ordinary telephone lines found in a home or business. Service levels range from about 768 Kbps up to 7 Mbps. DSL service requires that customers live within two miles (about 4,000 meters) of a neighborhood telephone switching center.

Cable modem refers to a cable television technology that piggybacks digital access to the Internet using the same analog or digital video cable providing television signals to a home. Cable Internet is a major broadband alternative to DSL service, generally providing faster speeds and a "triple play" subscription: telephone, television, and Internet for a single monthly payment. Cable modem services range from 1 Mbps up to 15 Mbps. Comcast, Time Warner Road Runner, Cox and Cablevision are the largest cable Internet providers.

T1 and T3 are international telephone standards for digital communication. **T1** lines offer guaranteed delivery at 1.54 Mbps, while **T3** lines offer delivery at a whopping 45 Mbps. These are leased, dedicated, guaranteed lines suitable for corporations, government agencies, and businesses such as ISPs requiring high-speed guaranteed service levels.

Satellite companies provide high-speed broadband Internet access, primarily to homes and offices located in rural areas where DSL or cable access is not available. Access speeds and monthly costs are comparable to DSL and cable, but typically require a higher initial payment for installation of a small (18-inch) satellite dish. Satellite providers typically have policies that limit the total megabytes of data that a single account can download within a set period, usually 24 hours. The major satellite providers are HughesNet, WildBlue, and StarBand.

Nearly all large business firms and government agencies have broadband connections to the Internet. Demand for broadband service has grown so rapidly because it greatly speeds up the process of downloading Web pages and increasingly, large video and audio files located on Web pages (see **Table 3.4**). As the quality of Internet service offerings expands to include Hollywood movies, music, games, and other rich media-streaming content, the demand for broadband access will continue to swell. In order to compete with cable companies, telephone companies provide an advanced form of DSL called FiOS (fiber-optic service) that provides up to 50 Mbps speeds for households, which is much faster than cable systems.

Digital Subscriber Line (DSL)
delivers high-speed access through ordinary telephone lines found in homes or businesses

cable modem
piggybacks digital access to the Internet on top of the analog video cable providing television signals to a home

T1
an international telephone standard for digital communication that offers guaranteed delivery at 1.54 Mbps

T3
an international telephone standard for digital communication that offers guaranteed delivery at 45 Mbps

TABLE 3.4	TIME TO DOWNLOAD A 10-MEGABYTE FILE BY TYPE OF INTERNET SERVICE
TYPE OF INTERNET SERVICE	**TIME TO DOWNLOAD**
NARROWBAND SERVICES	
Telephone modem	25 minutes
BROADBAND SERVICES	
DSL @ 1 Mbps	1.33 minutes
Cable modem @ 10 Mbps	8 seconds
T1	52 seconds
T3	2 seconds

INTRANETS AND EXTRANETS

The very same Internet technologies that make it possible to operate a worldwide public network can also be used by private and government organizations as internal networks. An **intranet** is a TCP/IP network located within a single organization for purposes of communications and information processing. Internet technologies are generally far less expensive than proprietary networks, and there is a global source of new applications that can run on intranets. In fact, all the applications available on the public Internet can be used in private intranets. The largest provider of local area network software is Microsoft, followed by open source Linux, both of which use TCP/IP networking protocols.

intranet
a TCP/IP network located within a single organization for purposes of communications and information processing

WHO GOVERNS THE INTERNET?

Aficionados and journalists often claim that the Internet is governed by no one, and indeed cannot be governed, and that it is inherently above and beyond the law. What these people forget is that the Internet runs over private and public telecommunications facilities that are themselves governed by laws, and subject to the same pressures as all telecommunications carriers. In fact, the Internet is tied into a complex web of governing bodies, national governments, and international professional societies. There is no one single governing organization that controls activity on the Internet. Instead, there are several organizations that influence the system and monitor its operations. Among the governing bodies of the Internet are:

- The *Internet Architecture Board (IAB)*, which helps define the overall structure of the Internet.
- The *Internet Corporation for Assigned Names and Numbers (ICANN)*, which assigns IP addresses and manages the top-level Domain Name System. ICANN was created in 1998 by the U.S. Department of Commerce.

- The *Internet Engineering Steering Group (IESG)*, which oversees the setting of standards with respect to the Internet.
- The *Internet Engineering Task Force (IETF)*, a private-sector group that forecasts the next step in the growth of the Internet, keeping watch over its evolution and operation.
- The *Internet Society (ISOC)*, which is a consortium of corporations, government agencies, and nonprofit organizations that monitors Internet policies and practices.
- The *World Wide Web Consortium (W3C)*, a largely academic group that sets HTML and other programming standards for the Web.
- The *International Telecommunication Union (ITU)*, which helps set technical standards.

While none of these organizations has actual control over the Internet and how it functions, they can and do influence government agencies, major network owners, ISPs, corporations, and software developers with the goal of keeping the Internet operating as efficiently as possible. ICANN comes closest to being a manager of the Internet and reflects the powerful role that the U.S. Department of Commerce has played historically in Internet governance.

In addition to these professional bodies, the Internet must also conform to the laws of the sovereign nation-states in which it operates, as well as the technical infrastructures that exist within each nation-state. Although in the early years of the Internet there was very little legislative or executive interference, this situation is changing as the Internet plays a growing role in the distribution of information and knowledge, including content that some find objectionable.

3.3 THE FUTURE INTERNET INFRASTRUCTURE

The Internet is changing as new technologies appear and new applications are developed. The next era of the Internet is being built today by private corporations, universities, and government agencies. To appreciate the potential benefits of the Internet of the future, you must first understand the limitations of the Internet's current infrastructure.

LIMITATIONS OF THE CURRENT INTERNET

Much of the Internet's current infrastructure is several decades old (equivalent to a century in Internet time). It suffers from a number of limitations, including limitations on bandwidth, making it slow to deliver video and data; inability to guarantee high levels of service, and instead relies on "best effort" quality of service; limitations in network architecture that create bottlenecks in content delivery; and reliance on wired cable physical network technology.

Now imagine an Internet at least 1,000 times as powerful as today's Internet, one that is not subjected to the limitations of bandwidth, protocols, architecture, physical connections, and language detailed previously. Welcome to the world of the future Internet, and the next generation of e-commerce services and products!

THE INTERNET2® PROJECT

Internet2® is an advanced networking consortium of more than 350 member institutions including universities, corporations, government research agencies, and not-for-profit networking organizations, all working in partnership to facilitate the development, deployment, and use of revolutionary Internet technologies. The broader Internet2 community includes more than 66,000 institutions across the United States and international networking partners in more than 50 countries. Internet2's work is a continuation of the kind of cooperation among government, private, and educational organizations that created the original Internet.

The advanced networks created and in use by Internet2 members provide an environment in which new technologies can be tested and enhanced. For instance, Internet2 provides a next-generation, nationwide 100 gigabit-per-second network that not only makes available a reliable production services platform for current high-performance needs but also creates a powerful experimental platform for the development of new network capabilities. The fourth generation of this network, built through a federal stimulus grant from the National Telecommunications and Information Administration's Broadband Technology Opportunities Program, began to be deployed in 2011 (see **Figure 3.13**). The hybrid optical and packet network provides 8.8 terabits

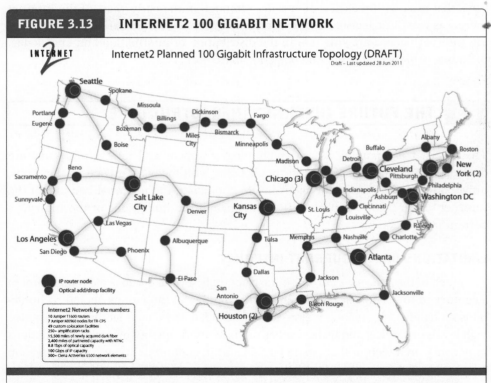

FIGURE 3.13	INTERNET2 100 GIGABIT NETWORK

Internet2 is in the process of deploying a 100 gigabit-per-second network. The network represents the first national implementation of 100 gigabit Ethernet capabilities across the entire network.

SOURCE: Internet2.edu, 2011.

of capacity with the ability to seamlessly scale as requirements grow, includes over 15,000 miles of owned fiber optic cable, and will reach into underserved areas of the country, supporting connectivity for approximately 200,000 U.S. community anchor institutions (schools, local libraries, and museums), and enabling them to provide citizens across the country with telemedicine, distance learning, and other advanced applications not possible with consumer-grade Internet services. The infrastructure will support a wide range of IP and optical services already available today and also stimulate a new generation of innovative services. The goal is to create an intelligent global ecosystem that will enable researchers, scientists, and others to "turn on" high-capacity network connections whenever and wherever they are needed.

THE FIRST MILE AND THE LAST MILE

The Internet2 project is just the tip of the iceberg when it comes to future enhancements to the Internet. The most significant private and government programs lie in in two areas: fiber-optic trunk line bandwidth and wireless Internet services. Fiber optics is concerned with the first mile or backbone Internet services that carry bulk traffic long distances. Wireless Internet is concerned with the last mile—from the larger Internet to the user's smartphone, tablet computer, or laptop.

Fiber Optics and the Bandwidth Explosion in the First Mile

Fiber-optic cable consists of up to hundreds of strands of glass that use light to transmit data. It often replaces existing coaxial and twisted pair cabling because it can transmit much more data at faster speeds, with less interference and better data security. Fiber-optic cable is also thinner and lighter, taking up less space during installation. The hope is to use fiber optics to expand network bandwidth capacity in order to prepare for the expected increases in Web traffic once Internet II services are widely adopted.

Telecommunication firms made substantial investments in fiber optic cross-country and regional cable systems in the last decade. This installed base of fiber optic cable represents a vast digital highway that is currently being exploited by YouTube (Google), Facebook, and other high-bandwidth applications. Telecommunications companies are recapitalizing and building new business models based on market prices for digital traffic. The net result is that society ultimately benefited from extraordinarily low-cost, long-haul, very high-bandwidth communication facilities that are already paid for.

Demand for fiber-optic cable has begun to strengthen as consumers demand integrated telephone, broadband access, and video from a single source. In 2011, around 19 million miles of optical fiber were installed in the United States, the most since 2000. In 2004, Verizon began building its FiOS fiber-optic Internet service, network infrastructure, and since then, it has spent $23 billion expanding the service. In 2012, there were about 5 million Verizon FiOS broadband customers. FiOS provides download speeds of up to 50 Mbps and upload speeds of up to 10 Mbps.

fiber-optic cable
consists of up to hundreds of strands of glass or plastic that use light to transmit data

The Last Mile: Mobile Internet Access

Fiber-optic networks carry the long-haul bulk traffic of the Internet—and in the future will play an important role in bringing BigBand to the household and small business. The goal of the Internet2 and similar projects is to bring gigabit and ultimately terabit bandwidth to the household over the next 20 years. But along with fiber optics, arguably the most significant development for the Internet and Web in the last five years has been the emergence of mobile Internet access.

Wireless Internet is concerned with the last mile of Internet access to the user's home, office, car, smartphone, or tablet computer, anywhere they are located. Up until 2000, the last-mile access to the Internet—with the exception of a small satellite Internet connect population—was bound up in land lines of some sort: copper coaxial TV cables or telephone lines or, in some cases, fiber-optic lines to the office. Today, in comparison, high-speed cell phone networks and Wi-Fi network hotspots provide a major alternative.

In 2012, more tablet and laptop computers with wireless networking functionality built in were sold in the United States than desktop computers. And more smartphones will be sold than PCs of any kind in 2012. Smartphones are the fastest growing mobile devices with respect to Internet access. Clearly, a large part of the future Internet will be mobile, access-anywhere broadband service for the delivery of video, music, and Web search.

Telephone-based versus Computer Network-based Wireless Internet Access There are two different basic types of wireless Internet connectivity: telephone-based and computer network-based systems.

Telephone-based wireless Internet access connects the user to a global telephone system (land, satellite, and microwave) that has a long history of dealing with thousands of users simultaneously and already has in place a large-scale transaction billing system and related infrastructure. Cellular telephones and the telephone industry are currently the largest providers of wireless access to the Internet today. **Table 3.5** summarizes the various telephone technologies used for wireless Internet access.

Smartphones, such as an iPhone, Android, or BlackBerry, combine the functionality of a cell phone with that of a laptop computer with Wi-Fi capability. This makes it possible to combine in one device music, video, Web access, and telephone service.

Wireless local area network (WLAN)-based Internet access derives from a completely different background from telephone-based wireless Internet access. Popularly known as **Wi-Fi**, WLANs are based on computer local area networks where the task is to connect client computers (generally stationary) to server computers within local areas of, say, a few hundred meters. WLANs function by sending radio signals that are broadcast over the airwaves using certain radio frequency ranges (2.4 GHz to 5.875 GHz, depending on the type of standard involved). The major technologies here are the various versions of the Wi-Fi standard and Bluetooth. Other WLAN technologies include WiMax, Ultra-Wideband (UWB), and ZigBee (see **Table 3.6**).

In a Wi-Fi network, a *wireless access point* (also known as a "hot spot") connects to the Internet directly via a broadband connection (cable, DSL telephone, or T1 line) and then transmits a radio signal to a transmitter/receiver installed in a laptop computer or

Wi-Fi
Wireless standard for Ethernet networks with greater speed and range than Bluetooth

TABLE 3.5	WIRELESS INTERNET ACCESS TELEPHONE TECHNOLOGIES		
TECHNOLOGY	SPEED	DESCRIPTION	PLAYERS
3G (THIRD GENERATION)			
CDMA2000 EV-DO HSPA (W-CDMA)	144 Kbps–2 Mbps	High-speed, mobile, always on for e-mail, browsing, instant messaging. Implementing technologies include versions of CDMA2000 EV-DO (used by CDMA providers) and HSPDA (used by GSM providers). Nearly as fast as Wi-Fi.	Verizon, Sprint, AT&T, T-Mobile, Vodafone
3.5G (3G+)			
CDMA2000 EV-DO, Rev.B	Up to 14.4 Mbps	Enhanced version of CDMA 2000 EV-DO.	Verizon, Sprint
HSPA+	Up to 11 Mbps	Enhanced version of HSPA.	AT&T, T-Mobile
4G (FOURTH GENERATION)			
Long-Term Evolution (LTE)	Up to 100 Mbps	True broadband on cell phone.	AT&T, Verizon, Sprint, T-Mobile (in 2013)

PDA, either as a PC card or built-in at manufacture (such as Intel's Centrino processor, which provides built-in support for Wi-Fi in portable devices). **Figure 3.15** illustrates how a Wi-Fi network works.

A second WLAN technology for connecting to the Internet, and for connecting Internet devices to one another, is called Bluetooth. **Bluetooth** is a personal connectivity technology that enables links between mobile computers, mobile phones, PDAs, and connectivity to the Internet (Bluetooth.com, 2012). Bluetooth is the

Bluetooth

technology standard for short-range wireless communication under 30 feet

TABLE 3.6	WIRELESS INTERNET ACCESS NETWORK TECHNOLOGIES		
TECHNOLOGY	RANGE/ SPEED	DESCRIPTION	PLAYERS
Wi-Fi (IEEE 802.11 a/b/g/n)	300 feet/ 11–70 Mbps	Evolving high-speed, fixed broadband wireless local area network for commercial and residential use	Linksys, Cisco, and other Wi-Fi router manufacturers; entrepreneurial network developers
WiMax (IEEE 802.16)	30 miles/ 50–70 Mbps	High-speed, medium-range, broadband wireless metropolitan area network	Clearwire, Sprint, Fujitsu, Intel, Alcatel, Proxim
Bluetooth (wireless personal area network)	1–30 meters/ 1–3 Mbps	Modest-speed, low-power, short-range connection of digital devices	Sony Ericsson, Nokia, Apple, HP, and other device makers

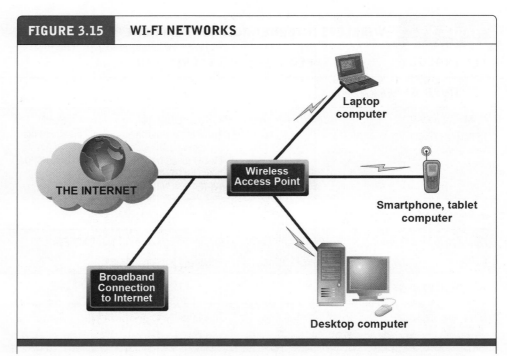

FIGURE 3.15 | **WI-FI NETWORKS**

In a Wi-Fi network, wireless access points connect to the Internet using a land-based broadband connection. Clients, which could be laptops, desktops, or tablet computers, connect to the access point using radio signals.

universal cable cutter, promising to get rid of the tangled mess of wires, cradles, and special attachments that plague the current world of personal computing.

THE FUTURE INTERNET

The increased bandwidth and expanded wireless network connectivity of the Internet of the future will result in benefits beyond faster access and richer communications. First-mile enhancements created by fiber-optic networks will enhance reliability and quality of Internet transmissions and create new business models and opportunities. Some of the major benefits of these technological advancements include latency solutions, guaranteed service levels, lower error rates, and declining costs. Widespread wireless access to the Internet will also essentially double or even triple the size of the online shopping marketspace because consumers will be able to shop and make purchases just about anywhere. This is equivalent to doubling the physical floor space of all shopping malls in America. We describe some of these benefits in more detail in the following sections.

The Internet of Things

No discussion of the future Internet would be complete without mentioning the **Internet of Things (IoT)**, also sometimes referred to as the Industrial Internet. Internet technology is spreading beyond the desktop, laptop, and tablet computer, and beyond the smartphone, to consumer electronics, electrical appliances, cars, medical devices, utility systems, machines of all types, even clothing—just about anything that can be equipped with sensors that collect data and connect to the Internet, enabling the data to be analyzed with data analytics software. The Internet of Things builds on

Internet of Things (IoT)

Use of the Internet to connect a wide variety of devices, machines, and sensors a foundation of existing technologies, such as RFID, and is being enabled by the availability of low-cost sensors, the drop in price of data storage, the development of "Big Data" analytics software that can work with trillions of pieces of data, as well implementation of IPV6, which will allow Internet addresses to be assigned to all of these new devices. Funding and research for the Internet of Things is being spearheaded by the European Union and China (where it is known as the Sensing Planet), and in the United States by companies such as IBM's Smarter Planet initiative. Although challenges remain before the Internet of Things is fully realized, it is coming closer to fruition.

3.4 THE WEB

Without the Web, there would be no e-commerce. The invention of the Web brought an extraordinary expansion of digital services to millions of amateur computer users, including color text and pages, formatted text, pictures, animations, video, and sound. In short, the Web makes nearly all the rich elements of human expression needed to establish a commercial marketplace available to nontechnical computer users worldwide.

While the Internet was born in the 1960s, the Web was not invented until 1989–1991 by Dr. Tim Berners-Lee of the European Particle Physics Laboratory, better known as CERN (Berners-Lee et al., 1994). Several earlier authors—such as Vannevar Bush (in 1945) and Ted Nelson (in the 1960s)—had suggested the possibility of organizing knowledge as a set of interconnected pages that users could freely browse (Bush, 1945; Ziff Davis Publishing, 1998). Berners-Lee and his associates at CERN built on these ideas and developed the initial versions of HTML, HTTP, a Web server, and a browser, the four essential components of the Web.

First, Berners-Lee wrote a computer program that allowed formatted pages within his own computer to be linked using keywords (hyperlinks). The pages were formatted usinng a markup language which he called HyperText Markup Language, or HTML. Click on a highlighted word, and you would be taken to other formatted pages stored on his computer. He then came up with the idea of storing his HTML pages on the Internet. Remote client computers could access these pages by using HTTP (introduced earlier in Section 3.1 and described more fully in the next section). But these early Web pages still appeared as black and white text pages with hyperlinks expressed inside brackets. The early Web was based on text only; the original Web browser only provided a line interface.

Information being shared on the Web remained text-based until 1993, when Marc Andreessen and others at the National Center for Supercomputing Applications (NCSA) at the University of Illinois created a Web browser with a graphical user interface (GUI) called Mosaic that made it possible to view documents on the Web graphically—using colored backgrounds, images, and even primitive animations.

Aside from making the content of Web pages colorful and available to the world's population, the graphical Web browser created the possibility of **universal computing**, the sharing of files, information, graphics, sound, video, and other objects across all computer platforms in the world, regardless of operating system.

universal computing
the sharing of files, information, graphics, sound, video, and other objects across all computer platforms in the world, regardless of operating system

Netscape Navigator
the first commercial Web browser

Internet Explorer
Microsoft's Web browser

hypertext
a way of formatting pages with embedded links that connect documents to one another, and that also link pages to other objects such as sound, video, or animation files

In 1994, Andreessen and Jim Clark founded Netscape, which created the first commercial browser, **Netscape Navigator**. Although Mosaic had been distributed free of charge, Netscape initially charged for its software. In August 1995, Microsoft Corporation released its own free version of a browser, called **Internet Explorer**. In the ensuing years, Netscape fell from a 100% market share to less than .5% in 2009, and many other browsers have emerged.

HYPERTEXT

Web pages can be accessed through the Internet because the Web browser software on your PC can request Web pages stored on an Internet host server using the HTTP protocol. **Hypertext** is a way of formatting pages with embedded links that connect documents to one another and that also link pages to other objects such as sound, video, or animation files. When you click on a graphic and a video clip plays, you have clicked on a hyperlink. For example, when you type a Web address in your browser such as http://www.sec.gov, your browser sends an HTTP request to the sec.gov server requesting the home page of sec.gov.

HTTP is the first set of letters at the start of every Web address, followed by the domain name. The domain name specifies the organization's server computer that is housing the document. Most companies have a domain name that is the same as or closely related to their official corporate name. The directory path and document name are two more pieces of information within the Web address that help the browser track down the requested page. Together, the address is called a Uniform Resource Locator, or URL. When typed into a browser, a URL tells it exactly where to look for the information. For example, in the following URL:

http://www.megacorp.com/content/features/082602.html

http = the protocol used to display Web pages

www.megacorp.com = domain name

content/features = the directory path that identifies where on the domain Web server the page is stored

082602.html = the document name and its format (an HTML page)

The most common domain extensions (known as general top-level domains, or gTLDs) currently available and officially sanctioned by ICANN are shown in **Table 3.7**. Countries also have domain names, such as .uk, .au, and .fr (United Kingdom, Australia, and France, respectively). These are sometimes referred to as country-code top-level domains, or ccTLDs. In 2011, ICANN removed nearly all restrictions on domain names, thereby greatly expanding the number of different domain names available. As of September 2012, more than 2000 applications for new gTLDs had been filed and ICANN announced that it would begin evaluating them as a batch beginning in December 2012, in a process that might take up to a year to complete.

TABLE 3.7	COMMON TOP-LEVEL DOMAINS		
GENERAL TOP-LEVEL DOMAIN (GTLD)	YEAR(S) INTRODUCED	PURPOSE	SPONSOR/ OPERATOR
.com	1980s	Unrestricted (but intended for commercial registrants)	VeriSign
.edu	1980s	U.S. educational institutions	Educause
.gov	1980s	U.S. government	U.S. General Services Administration
.mil	1980s	U.S. military	U.S. Department of Defense Network Information Center
.net	1980s	Unrestricted (but originally intended for network providers, etc.)	VeriSign
.org	1980s	Unrestricted (but intended for organizations that do not fit elsewhere)	Public Interest Registry (was operated by VeriSign until December 31, 2002)

SOURCE: Based on data from ICANN, 2011b.

MARKUP LANGUAGES

Although the most common Web page formatting language is HTML, the concept behind document formatting actually had its roots in the 1960s with the development of Generalized Markup Language (GML).

HyperText Markup Language (HTML)

HyperText Markup Language (HTML) is a GML that is relatively easy to use. HTML provides Web page designers with a fixed set of markup "tags" that are used to format a Web page (see **Figure 3.16**). When these tags are inserted into a Web page, they are read by the browser and interpreted into a page display. You can see the source HTML code for any Web page by simply clicking on the "Page Source" command found in all browsers. In Figure 3.16, the HTML code in the first screen produces the display in the second screen.

HTML defines the structure and style of a document, including the headings, graphic positioning, tables, and text formatting. Since its introduction, the major browsers have continuously added features to HTML to enable programmers to further refine their page layouts.

The most recent version of HTML is HTML5. HTML5 introduces features like video playback and drag-and-drop that in the past were provided by plug-ins like Adobe Flash. HTML5 applications have many of the rich interactive features found in smartphone apps. The *Insight on Technology* case, *Is HTML5 Ready for Prime Time?* examines some of the issues associated with use of HTML5.

HyperText Markup Language (HTML)
GML that is relatively easy to use in Web page design. HTML provides Web page designers with a fixed set of markup "tags" that are used to format a Web page

INSIGHT ON TECHNOLOGY

IS HTML5 READY FOR PRIME TIME?

HTML5 has been welcomed by developers far in advance of its scheduled 2014 ratification by the World Wide Web Consortium (W3C). Advocated by Apple founder Steve Jobs as the preferred method for displaying video on the Web, HTML5's video element replaces plug-ins such as Flash, QuickTime, and RealPlayer, a dramatic breakthrough in Web page design. Adobe has abandoned development of mobile Flash and agreed to use HTML5 to develop future tools.

HTML5 has become a catch-all term that encompasses not only the video element but also the use of the newest versions of Cascading Style Sheets (CSS3) and JavaScript, and another new tool, HTML5 Canvas. Multi-platform Web developers began using HTML5 because these new elements provided device independence, but soon discovered that they could do even more. The built-in functionality of mobile devices, including GPS and swiping, can be accessed, enabling m-commerce sites to build Web-based mobile apps that can replicate the native app experience.

Web-based mobile apps (HTML5 apps) work just like Web pages. When a user navigates to the page containing the mobile app, the page content, including graphics, images, and video, are loaded into the browser from the Web server, rather than residing in the mobile device hardware like a native app.

For businesses, the cost savings of HTML5 are obvious. A single HTML5 app requires far less effort to build than multiple native apps for the iOS, Android, Windows Phone, and other platforms. Embedded video and HTML5 apps can more easily be linked to and shared on social networks, encouraging viral distribution.

Some HTML5 apps can even be designed so that they can be run on mobile devices when they are offline. Differences in how apps run across different platforms and workarounds are eliminated.

The biggest challenge of HTML5 apps is to meet and then attempt to surpass the user experience and performance level of native apps. Although HTML5 sites load faster than first-generation mobile commerce sites, native apps generally still trump HTML5 apps on speed because a great deal of the interface already resides on the mobile device.

According to Tim Berners-Lee, founder and chief of the W3C, HTML5 security and access control issues are currently being addressed. For instance, HTML5 does not support digital rights management (DRM). In the past, media companies developed their own copy protection standards based on geographical region and/or whether payment had been proffered. These were enforced through their own media players. Since HTML5 does not require plug-ins to play video (or audio), and further, since HTML5 is an official W3C standard charged with remaining vendor neutral, this presents a challenge to the HTML5 working group.

Although HTML5 is being widely adopted on e-commerce and m-commerce sites, native apps aren't going anywhere. Instead, developers are incorporating HTML5 code into native apps, creating a kind of hybrid or mixed mode app. While the lure of reaching all platforms with a single product is potent, if developers cannot produce a product that equals the performance of native apps, they will stick with the side their bread is buttered on and continue to develop native apps for the top sellers.

SOURCES: "Why HTML5 Is in Trouble on the Mobile Front," by David Meyer, ZDNet, September 5, 2012; "HTML5: Don't Believe the Hype Cycle," by Dan Rowinski, ReadWriteWeb.com, August 21st, 2012; "Is HTML5 the End of Native Mobile Apps?," by Hernán Gonzalez, ClickZ.com, August 17, 2012; "What Do You Get by Adding HTML5 to Your Mobile Site?," by Bill Siwicki, Internet Retailer, April 12, 2012; "HTML5 Mobile Sites Give Apps a Run for their Money," by Bill Siwicki, Internet Retailer, February 3, 2012; "HTML5 Is Popular, Still Unfinished," by Don Clark, Wall Street Journal, November 11, 2011; "Adobe's Flash Surrender Proves Steve Jobs And Apple Were Right All Along With HTML5," by Nigam Arora, Forbes, November, 9, 2011.

FIGURE 3.16 **EXAMPLE HTML CODE (A) AND WEB PAGE (B)**

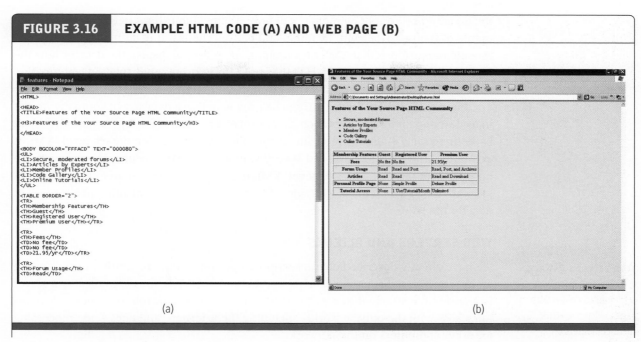

(a)   (b)

HTML is a text markup language used to create Web pages. It has a fixed set of "tags" that are used to tell the browser software how to present the content on screen. The HTML shown in Figure 3.17 (a) creates the Web page seen in Figure 3.17 (b).

eXtensible Markup Language (XML)

eXtensible Markup Language (XML) takes Web document formatting a giant leap forward. XML is a markup language specification developed by the W3C that is similar to HTML, but has a very different purpose. Whereas the purpose of HTML is to control the "look and feel" and display of data on the Web page, XML is designed to describe data and information. For example, consider the sample XML document in **Figure 3.17**. The first line in the sample document is the XML declaration, which is always included; it defines the XML version of the document. In this case, the document conforms to the 1.0 specification of XML. The next line defines the first element of

eXtensible Markup Language (XML)
a markup language specification developed by the World Wide Web Consortium (W3C) that is designed to describe data and information

---

FIGURE 3.17 **A SIMPLE XML DOCUMENT**

```
<?xml version="1.0"?>
<note>
<to>George</to>
<from>Carol</from>
<heading>Just a Reminder</heading>
<body>Don't forget to order the groceries from FreshDirect!</body>
</note>
```

The tags in this simple XML document, such as <note>, <to>, and <from> are used to describe data and information, rather than the look and feel of the document.

the document (the root element): < note >. The next four lines define four child elements of the root (to, from, heading, and body). The last line defines the end of the root element. Notice that XML says nothing about how to display the data, or how the text should look on the screen. HTML is used for information display in combination with XML, which is used for data description.

Figure 3.18 shows how XML can be used to define a database of company names in a company directory. Tags such as < Company >, < Name >, and < Specialty > can be defined for a single firm, or an entire industry. On an elementary level, XML is extraordinarily easy to learn and is very similar to HTML except that you can make up your own tags. At a deeper level, XML has a rich syntax and an enormous set of software tools, which make XML ideal for storing and communicating many types of data on the Web.

WEB SERVERS AND CLIENTS

Web server software
software that enables a computer to deliver Web pages written in HTML to client computers on a network that request this service by sending an HTTP request

We have already described client/server computing and the revolution in computing architecture brought about by client/server computing. You already know that a server is a computer attached to a network that stores files, controls peripheral devices, interfaces with the outside world—including the Internet—and does some processing for other computers on the network.

But what is a Web server? **Web server software** refers to the software that enables a computer to deliver Web pages written in HTML to client computers on a network

FIGURE 3.18 SAMPLE XML CODE FOR A COMPANY DIRECTORY

```
<?xml version="1.0"?>
<Companies>
    <Company>
         <Name>Azimuth Interactive Inc.</Name>
       <Specialties>
               <Specialty>HTML development</Specialty>
                 <Specialty>technical documentation</Specialty>
             <Specialty>ROBO Help</Specialty>
               <Country>United States</Country>
       </Specialties>
       <Location>
               <Country>United States</Country>
            <State />
             <City>Chicago</City>
       </Location>
            <Telephone>301-555-1212</Telephone>
    </Company>
    <Company>
      ...
    </Company>
   ...
</Companies>
```

This XML document uses tags to define a database of company names.

that request this service by sending an HTTP request. The two leading brands of Web server software are Apache, which is free Web server shareware that accounts for about 64% of the market, and Microsoft's Internet Information Services (IIS), which accounts for about 14% of the market.

Aside from responding to requests for Web pages, all Web servers provide some additional basic capabilities such as the following:

- *Security services*—These consist mainly of authentication services that verify that the person trying to access the site is authorized to do so.
- *FTP*—This protocol allows users to transfer files to and from the server.
- *Search engine*—Just as search engine sites enable users to search the entire Web for particular documents, search engine modules within the basic Web server software package enable indexing of the site's Web pages and content and permit easy keyword searching of the site's content.
- *Data capture*—Web servers are also helpful at monitoring site traffic, capturing information on who has visited a site, how long the user stayed there, the date and time of each visit, and which specific pages on the server were accessed. This information is compiled and saved in a log file, which can then be analyzed. By analyzing a log file, a site manager can find out the total number of visitors, average length of each visit, browser used, operating system, and the most popular destinations, or Web pages.

The term *Web server* is also used to refer to the physical computer that runs Web server software. Leading manufacturers of Web server computers include IBM, Dell, and Hewlett-Packard. Although any personal computer can run Web server software, it is best to use a computer that has been optimized for this purpose. To be a Web server, a computer must have the Web server software installed and be connected to the Internet. Every public Web server computer has an IP address. For example, if you type http://www.pearsonhighered.com/laudon in your browser, the browser software sends a request for HTTP service to the Web server whose domain name is pearsonhighered.com. The server then locates the page named "laudon" on its hard drive, sends the page back to your browser, and displays it on your screen. Of course, firms also can use Web servers for strictly internal local area networking in intranets.

Aside from the generic Web server software packages, there are actually many types of specialized servers on the Web, from **database servers** that access specific information within a database, to **ad servers** that deliver targeted banner ads, to **mail servers** that provide e-mail messages, and **video servers** that provide video clips.

A **Web client**, on the other hand, is any computing device attached to the Internet that is capable of making HTTP requests and displaying HTML pages. The most common client is a Windows or Macintosh computer, with various flavors of Unix/Linux computers a distant third. However, the fastest growing category of Web clients are mobile computers like smartphones, tablets, and netbooks outfitted with wireless Web access software. In general, Web clients can be any device—including a printer, refrigerator, stove, home lighting system, or automobile instrument panel—capable of sending and receiving information from Web servers.

database server
server designed to access specific information within a database

ad server
server designed to deliver targeted banner ads

mail server
server that provides e-mail messages

video server
server that serves video clips

Web client
any computing device attached to the Internet that is capable of making HTTP requests and displaying HTML pages, most commonly a Windows PC or Macintosh

WEB BROWSERS

A Web browser is a software program whose primary purpose is to display Web pages. Browsers also have added features, such as e-mail and newsgroups (an online discussion group or forum). The leading Web browser is Microsoft Internet Explorer, with about 49% of the market as of August 2012. Mozilla Firefox is currently the second most popular Web browser, with about 18% of the U.S. Web browser market (Marketshare.hitslink.com, 2012). The third most popular browser, with about a 17% market share, is Google's Chrome, a small, yet technologically advanced open source browser. Apple's Safari browser is fourth, with about 11% of the market.

3.5	THE INTERNET AND THE WEB: FEATURES AND SERVICES

The Internet and the Web have spawned a number of powerful software applications upon which the foundations of e-commerce are built. You can think of these all as Web services, and it is interesting as you read along to compare these services to other traditional media such as television or print media. If you do, you will quickly realize the richness of the Internet environment.

electronic mail (e-mail)

the most-used application of the Internet. Uses a series of protocols to enable messages containing text, images, sound, and video clips to be transferred from one Internet user to another

E-MAIL

Since its earliest days, **electronic mail**, or **e-mail**, has been the most-used application of the Internet. E-mail uses a series of protocols to enable messages containing text, images, sound, and video clips to be transferred from one Internet user to another. Because of its flexibility and speed, it is now the most popular form of business communication—more popular than the phone, fax, or snail mail (the U.S. Postal Service), with an estimated 145 billion e-mails sent each day (Radicati Group, 2012).

instant messaging (IM)

displays words typed on a computer almost instantaneously. Recipients can then respond immediately to the sender the same way, making the communication more like a live conversation than is possible through e-mail

INSTANT MESSAGING

Instant messaging (IM) allows you to send messages in real time, one line at a time, unlike e-mail. E-mail messages have a time lag of several seconds to minutes between when messages are sent and received. IM displays lines of text entered on a computer almost instantaneously. Recipients can then respond immediately to the sender the same way, making the communication more like a live conversation than is possible through e-mail. And although text remains the primary communication mechanism in IM, users can insert audio clips or photos into their instant messages, and even participate in video conferencing. Instant messaging over the Internet competes with wireless phone Short Message Service (SMS) texting, which is far more expensive than IM.

The major IM systems are Microsoft's Windows Live Messenger, Skype, Yahoo Messenger, Google Talk, and AIM (AOL Instant Messenger). Facebook also offers instant messaging services via Facebook Chat.

SEARCH ENGINES

Search engines identify Web pages that appear to match keywords, also called queries, typed by a user and then provide a list of the best matches (search results). Almost 60% of all adult American Internet users use a search engine on any given day, generating about 17 billion queries a month (Pew Internet & American Life Project, 2012; comScore, 2012a). There are hundreds of different search engines, but the vast majority of the search results are supplied by the top five providers (see **Figure 3.19**).

The Google search engine is continuously crawling the Web, indexing the content of each page, calculating its popularity, and caching the pages so that it can respond quickly to your request to see a page. The entire process of scanning a page takes about one-half of a second. **Figure 3.20** illustrates how Google works. Initially, few understood how to make money from search engines. That changed in 2000 when Goto.com (later Overture) allowed advertisers to bid for placement on their search engine results, and Google followed suit in 2003 with its AdWords program, which allowed advertisers to bid for placement of short text ads on Google search results. The spectacular increase in Internet advertising revenues (which have been growing at around 20%–25% annually over the last few years), has helped search engines transform themselves into major shopping tools and created an entire new industry called "search engine marketing."

ONLINE FORUMS AND CHAT

An **online forum** (also referred to as a message board, bulletin board, discussion board, discussion group, or simply a board or forum) is a Web application that

search engine
identifies Web pages that appear to match keywords, also called queries, typed by the user and then provides a list of the best matches

online forum
a Web application that allows Internet users to communicate with each other, although not in real time

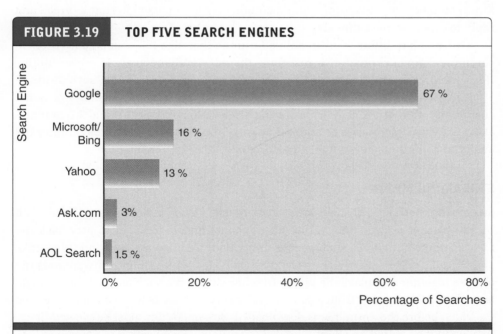

| FIGURE 3.19 | TOP FIVE SEARCH ENGINES |

Google is, by far, the leading search engine based on its percentage share of the number of searches.
SOURCE: Based on data from comScore, 2012a.

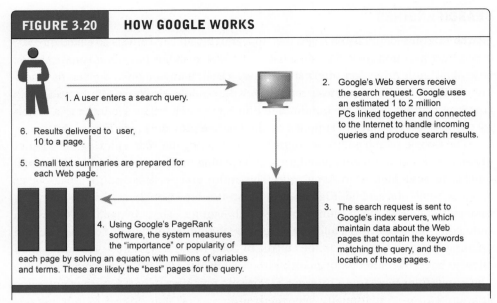

FIGURE 3.20 HOW GOOGLE WORKS

1. A user enters a search query.

2. Google's Web servers receive the search request. Google uses an estimated 1 to 2 million PCs linked together and connected to the Internet to handle incoming queries and produce search results.

6. Results delivered to user, 10 to a page.

5. Small text summaries are prepared for each Web page.

4. Using Google's PageRank software, the system measures the "importance" or popularity of each page by solving an equation with millions of variables and terms. These are likely the "best" pages for the query.

3. The search request is sent to Google's index servers, which maintain data about the Web pages that contain the keywords matching the query, and the location of those pages.

The Google search engine is continuously crawling the Web, indexing the content of each page, calculating its popularity, and caching the pages so that it can respond quickly to your request to see a page. The entire process takes about one-half of a second.

enables Internet users to communicate with each other, although not in real time. A forum provides a container for various discussions (or "threads") started (or "posted") by members of the forum, and depending on the permissions granted to forum members by the forum's administrator, enables a person to start a thread and reply to other people's threads.

online chat
enables users to communicate via computer in real time, that is, simultaneously. Unlike IM, chat can occur among several users

Online chat differs from an online forum in that, like IM, chat enables users to communicate via computer in real time, that is, simultaneously. However, unlike IM, which works only between two people, chat can occur among several users. Typically, users log in to a "chat room" where they can text message others. Some chat rooms offer virtual chat, which enable users to incorporate 2-D and 3-D graphics along with avatars (an icon or representation of the user) into their chat, or offer the ability to communicate via audio and/or video.

STREAMING MEDIA

streaming media
enables music, video, and other large files to be sent to users in chunks so that when received and played, the file comes through uninterrupted

Streaming media enables live Web video, music, video, and other large-bandwidth files to be sent to users in a variety of ways that enable the user to play back the files. In some situations, such as live Web video, the files are broken into chunks and served by specialized video servers to users in chunks. Client software puts the chunks together and plays the video. In other situations, such as YouTube, a single large file is downloaded from a standard Web server to users who can begin playing the video before the entire file is downloaded. Streamed files must be viewed "live"; they cannot be stored on client hard drives without special software. Streamed files are "played" by a software program such as Windows Media Player, Apple Quick-Time, Flash, and RealMedia Player.

COOKIES

A **cookie** is a tool used by a Web site to store information about a user. When a visitor enters a Web site, the site sends a small text file (the cookie) to the user's computer so that information from the site can be loaded more quickly on future visits. The cookie can contain any information desired by the Web site designers, including customer number, pages visited, products examined, and other detailed information about the behavior of the consumer at the site. Cookies are useful to consumers because the Web site will recognize returning patrons and not ask them to register again. Cookies are also used by advertisers to ensure visitors do not receive the same advertisements repeatedly. Cookies can also help personalize a Web site by allowing the site to recognize returning customers and make special offers to them based on their past behavior at the site. Cookies allow Web marketers to customize products and segment markets—the ability to change the product or the price based on prior consumer information (described more fully in later chapters). As we will discuss throughout the book, cookies also can pose a threat to consumer privacy, and at times they are bothersome. Many people clear their cookies at the end of every day. Some disable them entirely using tools built into most browsers.

cookie
a tool used by Web sites to store information about a user. When a visitor enters a Web site, the site sends a small text file (the cookie) to the user's computer so that information from the site can be loaded more quickly on future visits. The cookie can contain any information desired by the site designers

WEB 2.0 FEATURES AND SERVICES

Today's broadband Internet infrastructure has greatly expanded the services available to users. These new capabilities have formed the basis for new business models. Digital content and digital communications are the two areas where innovation is most rapid. Web 2.0 applications and services are "social" in nature because they support communication among individuals within groups or social networks.

Online Social Networks

If there is a "killer app" on the Internet in 2012 and going forward, it is social networks. Online social networks are described throughout this book in many chapters because they have developed very large worldwide audiences and form the basis for new advertising platforms and for social e-commerce (see chapters 6 and 10). Online social networks are services that support communication within networks of friends, colleagues, and entire professions. The largest social networks are Facebook, LinkedIn, Twitter, and Pinterest. These networks rely on user-generated content (messages, photos, and videos) and emphasize sharing of content. All of these features require significant broadband Internet connectivity and equally large cloud computing facilities to store content.

Blogs

A **blog** (originally called a **weblog**) is a personal Web page that typically contains a series of chronological entries (newest to oldest) by its author, and links to related Web pages. The blog may include a blogroll (a collection of links to other blogs) and trackbacks (a list of entries in other blogs that refer to a post on the first blog). Most blogs allow readers to post comments on the blog entries as well. The act of creating a blog is often referred to as "blogging." Blogs are either hosted by a third-party site such as

blog
personal Web page that is created by an individual or corporation to communicate with readers

Blogger.com (owned by Google), LiveJournal, TypePad, Xanga, WordPress, and Tumblr, or prospective bloggers can download software such as Movable Type to create a blog that is hosted by the user's ISP. Blog pages are usually variations on templates provided by the blogging service or software and hence require no knowledge of HTML. Therefore, millions of people without HTML skills of any kind can post their own Web pages, and share content with friends and relatives. The totality of blog-related Web sites is often referred to as the "blogosphere."

Really Simple Syndication (RSS)

The rise of blogs is correlated with a distribution mechanism for news and information from Web sites that regularly update their content. **Really Simple Syndication (RSS)** is an XML format that allows users to have digital content, including text, articles, blogs, and podcast audio files, automatically sent to their computers over the Internet. An RSS aggregator software application that you install on your computer gathers material from the Web sites and blogs that you tell it to scan and brings new information from those sites to you.

Podcasting

A **podcast** is an audio presentation—such as a radio show, audio from a movie, or simply a personal audio presentation—stored as an audio file and posted to the Web. Listeners download the files from the Web and play them on their players or computers. While commonly associated with Apple's iPod portable music player, you can listen to MP3 podcast files with any MP3 player.

Wikis

A **wiki** is a Web application that allows a user to easily add and edit content on a Web page. (The term wiki derives from the "wiki wiki" (quick or fast) shuttle buses at Honolulu Airport.) Wiki software enables documents to be written collectively and collaboratively. Most wiki systems are open source, server-side systems that store content in a relational database. The software typically provides a template that defines layout and elements common to all pages, displays user-editable source code (usually plain text), and then renders the content into an HTML-based page for display in a Web browser.

The most well-known wiki is Wikipedia, an online encyclopedia that contains more than 4 million English-language articles on a variety of topics, appears in 285 languages, and has 365 million readers worldwide. It is more popular than iTunes.

Music and Video Services

With the low-bandwidth connections of the early Internet, audio and video files were difficult to download and share, but with the huge growth in broadband connections, these files are not only commonplace but today constitute the majority of Web traffic. Spurred on by the worldwide sales of more than 410 million iOS devices (iPhones, iPads, and iPod Touches) through June 30, 2012, as well as millions of other smartphones and MP3 players, the Internet has become a virtual digital river

Really Simple Syndication (RSS)
program that allows users to have digital content, including text, articles, blogs, and podcast audio files, automatically sent to their computers over the Internet

podcast
an audio presentation—such as a radio show, audio from a movie, or simply a personal audio presentation—stored as an audio file and posted to the Web

wiki
Web application that allows a user to easily add and edit content on a Web page

of music files. Today, the iTunes Store has a catalog with more than 28 million tracks, 85,000 television episodes, and 45,000 movies, including more than 3,000 in high definition (Arar, 2012).

Online video viewing has also exploded in popularity. In July 2012, around 184 million Americans watched 37 billion videos for an average of 22.5 hours per viewer (comScore, 2012b). By far, the most common type of Internet video is provided by YouTube, with more than 4 billion videos streamed and viewed each a day (120 billion a month), most of them short clips taken from television shows, or user-generated content.

Internet Telephony

If the telephone system were to be built from scratch today, it would be an Internet-based, packet-switched network using TCP/IP because it would be less expensive and more efficient than the alternative existing system, which involves a mix of circuit-switched legs with a digital backbone. Likewise, if cable television systems were built from scratch today, they most likely would use Internet technologies for the same reasons.

Already, nearly all pre-paid phone cards use the Internet for the long distance portion of calls. About 30% of the international calls from or to the United States use the Internet. Internet telephony is not entirely new. **IP telephony** is a general term for the technologies that use **Voice over Internet Protocol (VoIP)** and the Internet's packet-switched network to transmit voice, fax, and other forms of audio communication over the Internet. VoIP avoids the long distance charges imposed by traditional phone companies.

IP telephony
a general term for the technologies that use VoIP and the Internet's packet-switched network to transmit voice and other forms of audio communication over the Internet

Voice over Internet Protocol (VoIP)
protocol that allows for transmission of voice and other forms of audio communication over the Internet

Intelligent Personal Assistants

Apple's Siri, billed as an intelligent personal assistant and knowledge navigator and released in October 2011 for the iPhone 4S, has many of the capabilities of the computer assistants found in fiction. Siri has a natural language, conversational interface, situational awareness, and is capable of carrying out many tasks based on verbal commands by delegating requests to a variety of different Web services. Siri is currently available on the iPhone 4S, the iPhone 5, the third generation iPad, and the fifth generation iPod Touch. In July 2012, Google released its version of an intelligent assistant for Android-based smartphones, which it calls Google Now. Google Now is part of the Google Search application. While Google Now has many of the capabilities of Apple's Siri, it attempts to go further by predicting what users may need based on situational awareness, including physical location, time of day, previous location history, calendar, and expressed interests based on previous activity.

3.6   MOBILE APPS: THE NEXT BIG THING IS HERE

The use of mobile Internet access devices such as smartphones, iPads and other tablet computers, and laptops in e-commerce has truly exploded in 2012. From nearly zero mobile commerce prior to 2007, today, mobile commerce revenue in the United States from mobile retail purchases ($11.3 billion), mobile advertising ($2.6 billion), location-based services ($1 billion), games ($1 billion), e-book sales ($2.1 billion), and app sales ($6.7 billion) is approaching $25 billion. Worldwide, mobile payment transactions will reach an estimated $250 billion in 2012 (Juniper Research, 2012). More than 70% of U.S. mobile phone owners are expected to use their mobile devices to research and browse products and services in 2012, and the percentage is steadily increasing. More than 35% are expected to make at least one purchase via mobile phone in 2012, more than double the number in 2010 (eMarketer, Inc., 2012c). While mobile commerce is more widespread among younger consumers, there is evidence that even those over 55 are beginning to use this channel more frequently.

Tablets are being added into the mix. More than 50% of tablet owners have reported using their tablets at least once a week to shop, particularly on nights and weekends, and often from the comfort of couch or bed. More than 40% have made a purchase using their tablet (eMarketer, 2012d). As a result, companies are rapidly increasing their investment in mobile commerce technologies. As with many other aspects of e-commerce, Amazon is a leader, with more than $2 billion in mobile sales worldwide in 2011. More than $4 billion in mobile sales worldwide were transacted using eBay (Internet Retailer, 2012).

Mobile capabilities include making sure Web sites are compatible with mobile browsers, are optimized for use on various devices (discussed further in Chapter 4), and provide downloadable mobile apps. *Insight on Technology: Apps For Everything: The App Ecosystem* gives you some further background on mobile apps.

PLATFORMS FOR MOBILE APPLICATION DEVELOPMENT

Unlike mobile Web sites, which can be accessed by any Web-enabled mobile device, apps are platform-specific. Applications for the iPhone, iPad, and other iOS devices are written in the Objective-C programming language using the iOS SDK (software developer kit). Applications for Android operating system–based phones are typically written using Java, although portions of the code may be in the C or C++ programming language. BlackBerry apps are also written in Java. Applications for Windows mobile devices are written in C or C++.

APP MARKETPLACES

Once written, applications are distributed through various marketplaces. Android apps for Android-based phones are distributed through Google Play, which is controlled by Google. iPhone applications are distributed through Apple's App Store. BlackBerry applications can be found in RIM's App World, while Microsoft operates the Windows Phone Marketplace for Windows mobile devices. Apps can also be purchased from third-party vendors such as Amazon's Appstore. It is important to distinguish "native" mobile apps, which run directly on a mobile device and rely on the device's internal operating system, from Web apps, which install into your browser, although these can operate in a mobile environment as well.

INSIGHT ON BUSINESS

APPS FOR EVERYTHING: THE APP ECOSYSTEM

When Steve Jobs introduced the iPhone in January 2007, no one—including himself—envisioned that the device would become a major e-commerce platform. The iPhone's original primary functions, beyond being a cell phone, were to be a camera, text messaging device, and Web browser. What Apple initially lacked for the iPhone were software applications that would take full advantage of its computing capabilities. The solution was software developed by outside developers who were attracted to the mission by potential profits and fame from the sale or free distribution of their software applications on a platform approved by the leading innovator in handheld computing and cellular devices.

In July 2008, Apple introduced the App Store, which provides a platform for the distribution and sale of apps by Apple as well as by independent developers. Apple hoped that the software apps—most free—would drive sales of the iPhone device. It was not expecting the App Store itself to become a major source of revenue. By 2012, however, there were an estimated 725,000 approved apps available for download from the App Store. Other smartphone developers also followed suit: there are also thousands of apps available for Android phones, Black-Berrys, and Windows phones. Analysts believe apps generated more than $2 billion for Apple in 2012.

The app phenomenon, equally virulent on Android and BlackBerry operating system platforms, has spawned a new digital ecosystem: tens of thousands of developers, a wildly popular hardware platform, and millions of consumers looking for a computer in their pocket. The range of applications among the 725,000 or so apps on the Apple platform is staggering and defies brief description. There

are so many apps that searching for a particular app can be a problem unless you know the name of the app or the developer. Google is probably the best search engine for apps. The most popular app categories are games, education, entertainment, books, and lifestyle.

The implications of the app ecosystem for e-commerce are significant. The smartphone in your pocket not only becomes a general-purpose computer, but also an always present shopping tool for consumers, as well as an entirely new marketing and advertising platform for vendors. You can shop anywhere, shop everywhere, and shop all the time, in between talking, texting, watching video, and listening to music. Almost all of the top 100 brands have a presence in at least one of the major app stores, and more than 85% have an app in the Apple App Store.

There are, of course, dangers in any ecosystem dominated by a single company. The Apple iOS platform is closed and proprietary. Apple can act as a censor of content, such as when it banished hundreds of apps with adult content. Clearly Apple is concerned the App Store might become an adult digital theme park that would turn off parents and families who are the target audience for iPhone and iPad sales.

Apps don't come with any warranty. In 2012, for the first time, Apple was forced to remove malware from its App Store. A Russian app entitled "Find and Call" purported to simplify users' contacts lists, but instead stole those contacts and uploaded the address book to a remote server, spamming those addresses. Clearly, the app ecosystem is not immune to many of the same issues that apply to the Internet and e-commerce at large.

SOURCES: "App Store Metrics," 148Apps.biz, accessed September 10, 2012; "First Instance of iOS App Store Malware Detected, Removed," by Christina Bonnington, Wired.com, July 5, 2012; "iOS Devs Earned $2.5B from Apps Year over Year," by Jolie O'Dell, VentureBeat.com, June 11, 2012; "iSuppli: Apple's App Store Will Dominate the Market Through 2014," by Leslie Horn, PCMag.com, May 4, 2011; "Apple More Than Doubles 2010 Apps Revenue, but Its Market Share Slips," by Danny King, Dailyfinance.com, February 15, 2011; "Mobile Apps and Consumer Product Brands," by Tobi Elkin, eMarketer, March 2010; "Apple Bans Some Apps for Sex-Tinged Content," by Jenna Wortham, *New York Times*, February 22, 2010.

3.7 CASE STUDY

Akamai Technologies:
Attempting to Keep Supply Ahead of Demand

In 2012, the amount of Internet traffic generated by YouTube alone was greater than the amount of traffic on the entire Internet in 2000. In the last year, Netflix's subscriber base jumped by 16 million to more than 27 million subscribers, most of whom are now streaming movies over the Internet and, in June 2012, those subscribers logged approximately one billion hours of content-viewing. Because of video streaming and the explosion in mobile devices demanding high-bandwidth applications, Internet traffic has increased 800% since 2007 and is predicted to triple by the end of 2016, primarily because of video streaming and the explosion in mobile devices demanding high-bandwidth applications. Experts call services like YouTube, Netflix, and high definition streaming video "net bombs" because they threaten the effective operation of the Internet. Large telecommunication companies argue that demand will overwhelm capacity by 2015, while other experts argue that Internet bandwidth can double every year for a very long time and easily keep up with demand.

In today's broadband environment, anyone seeking to use the Web for delivery of high-quality multimedia content such as CD-quality music and high definition video will definitely need some help. Akamai is one of the Web's major helpers. Thousands of companies, including about a third of Fortune 500 companies, use Akamai's services to speed the delivery of content. Akamai serves more than 3,000 hours of content every minute.

Slow-loading Web pages and Web content—from music to video—sometimes result from poor design, but more often than not, the problem stems from the underlying infrastructure of the Internet. The Internet was originally developed to carry text-based e-mail messages among a relatively small group of researchers, not bandwidth-hogging graphics, sound, and video files to tens of millions of people all at once. The Internet is a collection of networks that has to pass information from one network to another. Sometimes the handoff is not smooth. Every 1,500-byte packet of information sent over the Internet must be verified by the receiving server and an acknowledgment sent to the sender. This slows down not only the distribution of content such as music, but also slows down interactive requests, such as purchases, that require the client computer to interact with an online shopping cart. Moreover, each packet may go through many different servers on its way to its final destination, multiplying by several orders of magnitude the number of acknowledgments required to move a packet from New York to San Francisco. The Internet today spends much of its time and capacity verifying packets, contributing to a problem called "latency" or delay. For this reason, a single e-mail with a 1-megabyte attached PDF file can create more than 50 megabytes of Internet traffic and data storage on servers, client hard drives, and network back up drives.

Akamai was founded with the idea of expediting Internet traffic to overcome these limitations. Akamai's current products are based on the Akamai Intelligent Platform, a cloud platform made up of over 105,000 servers within over 1,000 networks in 78 countries around the world, and all within a single network hop of 90% of all Internet users. Akamai software on these servers allows the platform to identify and block security threats and provide comprehensive knowledge of network conditions. Akamai's site performance products allow customers to move their Web content closer to end users so a user in New York City, for instance, will be served pages from the New York Metro area Akamai servers. Akamai has a wide range of large corporate and government clients: 1 out of every 3 global Fortune 500 companies, the top 30 media and entertainment companies, 92 of the top 100 online U.S. retailers, all branches of the U.S. military, all the top Internet portals, all the major U.S. sports leagues, and so on. In 2012, Akamai delivered between 15% and 30% of all Web traffic, and over 2 trillion daily Internet interactions. Other competitors in the content delivery network (CDN) industry include Blue Coat, Limelight, Savvis, and Mirror Image Internet

Accomplishing this task requires that Akamai monitor the entire Internet, locating potential sluggish areas and devising faster routes for information to travel. Frequently used portions of a client's Web site, or large video or audio files that would be difficult to send to users quickly, are stored on Akamai's servers. When a user requests a song or a video file, his or her request is redirected to an Akamai server nearby and the content served from this local server. Akamai's servers are placed in Tier 1 backbone

SOURCES: "Facts & Figures," Akamai.com, accessed September 10, 2012; "The State of the Internet, 1st Quarter 2012 Report," by Akamai Technologies, Inc., August 9, 2012; "Akamai Shares Jump on Cloud-Computing Profit Boost," by Sarah Frier, Bloomberg.com, July 26, 2012; "You Think the Internet is Big Now? Akamai Needs to Grow 100-Fold," by Mathew Ingram, GigaOM.com, June 20, 2012; "Akamai Eyes Acceleration Boost for Mobile Content," by Stephen Lawson, *Computerworld*, March 20, 2012; "Akamai Now Running 105,000 Servers," by Rich Miller, datacenter-knowledge.com, March 8, 2012; "To Cash In on Wave of Web Attacks, Akamai Launches Standalone Security Business," by Andy Greenberg, Forbes.com, February 21, 2012; "Google TV, Apple TV, and Roku's Biggest Enemy: A Lack of Internet Bandwidth," by Steven Vaughan-Nichols, zdnet.com, October 8, 2010.

supplier networks, large ISPs, universities, and other networks. Akamai's software determines which server is optimum for the user and then transmits the "Akamaized" content locally. Web sites that are "Akamaized" can be delivered anywhere from 4 to 10 times as fast as non-Akamaized content.

Akamai has developed a number of other business services based on its Internet savvy, including targeted advertising based on user location and zip code, content security, business intelligence, disaster recovery, on-demand bandwidth and computing capacity during spikes in Internet traffic, storage, global traffic management, and streaming services.

Akamai also offers a product called Advertising Decision Solutions, which provides companies with intelligence generated by the Internet's most accurate and comprehensive knowledge base of Internet network activity. Akamai's massive server deployment and relationships with networks throughout the world enable optimal collection of geography and bandwidth-sensing information. As a result, Akamai provides a highly accurate knowledge base with worldwide coverage. Customers integrate a simple program into their Web server or application server. This program communicates with the Akamai database to retrieve the very latest information. The Akamai network of servers is constantly mapping the Internet, and at the same time, each company's software is in continual communication with the Akamai network. The result: data is always current. Advertisers can deliver ads based on country, region, city, market area, area code, county, zip code, connection type, and speed. You can see several interesting visualizations of the Internet that log basic real-time Web activity by visiting the Akamai Web site.

The shift towards cloud computing and the mobile platform as well as the growing popularity of streaming video have provided Akamai with new growth opportunities. As more businesses and business models are moving to the Web, Akamai has seen its client base continue to grow beyond the most powerful Internet retailers and online content providers. In 2012, Akamai launched its Aqua Mobile Accelerator service, which automatically senses the quality of a wireless Internet connection and optimizes it continuously. It also detects the type of device submitting a request for data, whether a PC-based browser, smartphone, or tablet, and optimizes content delivery for that platform.

Akamai is also acutely aware of the increase in cybercrime as more traffic migrates to the Internet. Growth in Internet traffic is good news for Akamai, but the company must also now deal with politically motivated cyberattacks, organized crime online, and state-sponsored cyberwarfare. In 2012, Akamai unveiled its Kona Site Defender tool, which offers a variety of security measures for Akamai clients. The tool protects against Distributed Denial of Service (DDoS) attacks and includes a firewall for Web applications. With so many businesses now dependent on the uninterrupted flow of content over the Internet, Akamai is in a very strong position to sell security services to its customers. However, as impressive as Akamai's operation has become, it may not be nearly enough to cope with the next 5 to 10 years of Internet growth.

Case Study Questions

1. Why does Akamai need to geographically disperse its servers to deliver its customers' Web content?

2. If you wanted to deliver software content over the Internet, would you sign up for Akamai's service? What alternatives exist?

3. What advantages does an advertiser derive from using Akamai's service? What kinds of products might benefit from this kind of service?

3.8   REVIEW

KEY CONCEPTS

- Discuss the origins of the Internet.

The history of the Internet can be divided into three phases:

- During the *Innovation Phase* (1961–1974), the Internet's purpose was to link researchers nationwide via computer.
- During the *Institutionalization Phase* (1975–1995), the Department of Defense and National Science Foundation provided funding to expand the fundamental building blocks of the Internet into a complex military communications system and then into a civilian system.
- During the *Commercialization Phase* (1995 to the present), government agencies encouraged corporations to assume responsibility for further expansion of the network, and private business began to exploit the Internet for commercial purposes.

- Identify the key technology concepts behind the Internet.

The Internet's three key technology components are:

- *Packet switching*, which slices digital messages into packets, routes the packets along different communication paths as they become available, and then reassembles the packets once they arrive at their destination.
- *TCP/IP*, which establishes the connections among sending and receiving Web computers and makes sure that packets sent by one computer are received in the sequence by the other, without any packets missing.
- *Client/server technology*, which makes it possible for large amounts of information to be stored on Web servers and shared with individual users on their client computers (which may be desktop PCs, laptops, netbooks, tablets, or smartphones).

- Discuss the impact of the mobile platform and cloud computing

- The mobile platform is becoming the primary means for accessing the Internet.
- The number of cellphone subscribers worldwide far exceeds the number of PC owners.

- The form factor of PCs has changed from desktops to laptops and tablet computers such as the iPad.
- Smartphones are a disruptive technology that radically alters the personal computing and e-commerce landscape.
- Cloud computing refers to a model of computing in which firms and individuals obtain computing power and software applications over the Internet.

■   Describe the role of Internet protocols and utility programs.

Internet protocols and utility programs make the following Internet services possible:

- *HTTP* delivers requested Web pages, allowing users to view them.
- *SMTP* and *POP* enable e-mail to be routed to a mail server and then picked up by the recipient's server, while *IMAP* enables e-mail to be sorted before being downloaded by the recipient.
- *SSL* and *TLS* ensure that information transmissions are encrypted.
- *FTP* is used to transfer files from servers to clients and vice versa.
- *Telnet* is a utility program that enables work to be done remotely.
- *Ping* is a utility program that allows users to verify a connection between client and server.
- *Tracert* lets you track the route a message takes from a client to a remote computer.

■   Explain the structure of the Internet today.

The main structural elements of the Internet are:

- The *backbone*, which is composed primarily of high-bandwidth fiber-optic cable operated by a variety of providers.
- *IXPs*, which are hubs that use high-speed switching computers to connect the backbone with regional and local networks.
- *CANs*, which are local area networks operating within a single organization that connect directly to regional networks.
- *ISPs*, which deal with the "last mile" of service to homes and offices. ISPs offer a variety of types of service, ranging from dial-up service to broadband DSL, cable modem, T1 and T3 lines, and satellite link service.
- *Governing bodies*, such as IAB, ICANN, IESG, IETF, ISOC, W3C, and ITU. Although they do not control the Internet, they have influence over it and monitor its operations.

■   Describe the potential capabilities of the Internet of the future.

Internet2 is a consortium working together to develop and test new technologies for potential use on the Internet. In addition to the Internet2 project, other groups are working to expand Internet bandwidth via improvements to fiber optics. Wireless LAN and 4G technologies are providing users of smartphones and tablet computers with increased access to the Internet and its various services. The increased bandwidth and expanded connections will result in a number of benefits, including latency solutions; guaranteed service levels; lower error rates; and declining costs.

The Internet of Things will be a big part of the Internet of the future, with more and more sensor-equipped machines and devices connected to the Internet.

■ **Understand how the Web works.**

The key concepts you need to be familiar with in order to understand how the Web works are the following:

- *Hypertext*, which is a way of formatting pages with embedded links that connect documents to one another and that also link pages to other objects.
- *HTTP*, which is the protocol used to transmit Web pages over the Internet.
- *URLs*, which are the addresses at which Web pages can be found.
- *HTML*, which is the programming language used to create most Web pages and which provides designers with a fixed set of tags that are used to format a Web page.
- *XML*, which is a newer markup language that allows designers to describe data and information.
- *Web server software*, which is software that enables a computer to deliver Web pages written in HTML to client computers that request this service by sending an HTTP request. Web server software also provides security services, FTP, search engine, and data capture services. The term Web server also is used to refer to the physical computer that runs the Web server software.
- *Web clients*, which are computing devices attached to the Internet that are capable of making HTTP requests and displaying HTML pages.
- *Web browsers*, which display Web pages and also have added features such as e-mail and newsgroups.

■ **Describe how Internet and Web features and services support e-commerce.**

Together, the Internet and the Web make e-commerce possible by allowing computer users to access product and service information and to complete purchases online. Some of the specific features that support e-commerce include:

- *E-mail*, which uses a series of protocols to enable messages containing text, images, sound, and video clips to be transferred from one Internet user to another. E-mail is used in e-commerce as a marketing and customer support tool.
- *Instant messaging*, which allows messages to be sent between two users almost instantly, allowing parties to engage in a two-way conversation. In e-commerce, companies are using instant messaging as a customer support tool.
- *Search engines*, which identify Web pages that match a query submitted by a user. Search engines assist users in locating Web pages related to items they may want to buy.
- *Online forums* (message boards), which enable users to communicate with each other, although not in real time, and *online chat*, which allows users to communicate in real time (simultaneously), are being used in e-commerce as community-building tools.
- *Streaming media*, which enables music, video, and other large files to be sent to users in chunks so that when received and played, the file comes through uninterrupted. Like standard digital files, streaming media may be sold as digital content and used as a marketing tool.

- *Cookies*, which are small text files that allow a Web site to store information about a user, are used by e-commerce as a marketing tool. Cookies allow Web sites to personalize the site to the user and also permit customization and market segmentation.

Web 2.0 features and services include:

- *Social networks*, which are online services that support communication within networks of friends, colleagues, and even entire professions.
- *Blogs*, which are personal Web pages that typically contain a series of chronological entries (newest to oldest) by the author and links to related Web pages.
- *RSS*, which is an XML format that allows users to have digital content, including text, articles, blogs, and podcast audio files, automatically sent to their computers over the Internet.
- *Podcasts*, which are audio presentations—such as a radio show, audio from a movie, or simply personal audio presentations—stored as audio files and posted to the Web.
- *Wikis*, which are Web applications that allow a user to easily add and edit content on a Web page.
- *Music and video services*, such as iTunes and digital video on demand.
- *Internet telephony*, which uses VoIP to transmit audio communication over the Internet.

■ **Understand the impact of m-commerce applications.**

- M-commerce applications are part of the larger $25 billion m-commerce market. They facilitate many aspects of this larger market, and sales of mobile apps currently account for about $6.7 billion in annual revenue.
- There are a variety of different platforms for mobile application development including Objective-C (for iOS devices), Java (BlackBerrys and Android smartphones), and C and C++ (Windows mobile devices and some BlackBerry coding).
- Mobile apps for the iPhone are distributed through Apple's App Store, for BlackBerrys through RIM's App World, for Android devices through Google Play, and for Windows mobile devices through Microsoft's Windows Phone Marketplace. There are also third-party vendors such as Amazon's Appstore.

QUESTIONS

1. What are the three basic building blocks of the Internet?
2. What is latency, and how does it interfere with Internet functioning?
3. Explain how packet switching works.
4. How is the TCP/IP protocol related to information transfer on the Internet?
5. What technological innovation made client/server computing possible?
6. What is cloud computing, and how has it impacted the Internet?
7. Why are smartphones a disruptive technology?
8. What types of companies form the Internet backbone today?
9. What function do the IXPs serve?
10. What is the goal of the Internet2 project?
11. What are some of the major limitations of today's Internet?
12. What are some of the challenges of policing the Internet? Who has the final say when it comes to content?

13. Compare and contrast the capabilities of Wi-Fi and 3G/4G wireless networks.
14. What are the basic capabilities of a Web server?
15. What are the major technological advancements that are anticipated to accompany the Internet of the future? Discuss the importance of each.
16. Why was the development of the browser so significant for the growth of the Web?
17. What advances and features does HTML5 offer?
18. Name and describe five services currently available through the Web.
19. Why are mobile apps the next big thing?

PROJECTS

1. Review the opening case on augmented reality. What developments have occurred since the date this case was written in September 2012?

2. Locate where cookies are stored on your computer. (They are probably in a folder entitled "Cookies" within your browser program.) List the top 10 cookies you find and write a brief report describing the kinds of sites that placed the cookies. What purpose do you think the cookies serve? Also, what do you believe are the major advantages and disadvantages of cookies? In your opinion, do the advantages outweigh the disadvantages, or vice versa?

3. Call or visit the Web sites of a cable provider, DSL provider, and satellite provider to obtain information on their Internet services. Prepare a brief report summarizing the features, benefits, and costs of each. Which is the fastest? What, if any, are the downsides of selecting any of the three for Internet service (such as additional equipment purchases)?

4. Select two countries (excluding the United States) and prepare a short report describing their basic Internet infrastructure. Are they public or commercial? How and where do they connect to backbones within the United States?

5. Investigate the Internet of Things. Select one example and describe what it is and how it works.

CHAPTER 4

Building an E-commerce Presence: Web Sites, Mobile Sites, and Apps

Tommy Hilfiger

Replatforms

Tommy Hilfiger is one of the world's best known premium life-style brands in the United States for the 18–35 age demographic. Founded in 1985 by Tommy Hilfiger, a young designer in New York City, the brand expanded its line of casual clothing for men, women, and children through specialty retailers, department stores, and more than 1,000 apparel stores and outlets throughout the world. In 2010, the company was purchased by Phillips-Van Heusen, owner of the Calvin Klein brand, for $3 billion. The resulting company is the world's largest clothing

© incamerastock / Alamy

company, with $5.9 billion in revenues in 2011, with Tommy Hilfiger generating $3.1 billion of those revenues.

A significant part of the company's growth since 2007 has occurred through its online stores. The company had developed a Web store in 2000 as a simple catalog of products available at retailers and then expanded into online sales by 2004. By 2006, it was clear that effective online retailing required more than just a storefront with a catalog, and more than a database responding to customer requests for products. The existing Web site did not fit the contemporary needs and expectations of customers or company merchandisers.

Hilfiger did not want to hire an entire new IT staff to rebuild its Web site, and it did not want to make the investment in hardware and telecommunications that would be required for a new Web site. Instead it turned to Art Technology Group (ATG), a firm specializing in e-commerce software and hardware solutions. The ATG e-commerce plat-form software provided Hilfiger managers with a state-of-the-art e-commerce platform with automated recommendations that can deliver a personalized experience to each customer, and easy marketing and promotional campaign support to Hilfiger managers through a cutting-edge Business Control Center. Best of all, the ATG platform solution was an on-demand, online software platform. Hilfiger did not have to buy any hardware or software infrastructure, or hire IT staff, to build the new Web site. One way to

SOURCES: "How Do You Know When It's Time to Replatform," by Jared Blank, slide presentation, June 14, 2012; PVH Corporation, "SEC Form 10-K for the Fiscal Year 2011," Securities and Exchange Commission, filed on March 28, 2012; "Tommy Hilfiger Bolsters in-store Summer Traffic via iPad App," by Rimma Kats, Mobilemarketer.com, June 30, 2011; "Virtual Fitting Room...In Reality," by Justin Disandro, Socialtechpop.com, May 5, 2011; "Interview: Jared Blank, VP E-commerce for Tommy Hilfiger," Patperdue.com, March 23, 2011; "ShopTommy.com Dresses For Online Success—On Demand," Case Study, ATG.com, June 2010; "Finding the Right Fit for Multi-Channel Commerce: American Eagle Outfitters," Case Study, ATG.com, June 2010; "Technology for the Solo Entrepreneur," by William Bulkeley, *Wall Street Journal*, May 17, 2010; "Calvin Klein Owner Buys Tommy Hilfiger," BBCnews.co.uk, March 15, 2010.

"right-size" a Web site's infrastructure is to shift the risks and costs of infrastructure to external, specialized firms that can operate the infrastructure for you. From a "look and feel" standpoint, the Web site distinctly captured the Tommy Hilfiger "vibe," also an important consideration. Advancing the brand experience through the Web site was a major driver in its redesign. The result was a smashing success: online sales for Hilfiger increased 30% in the first year of operation.

But success comes with costs: in 2011, Tommy Hilfiger decided to replatform its global IT infrastructure because of the growth in its complex business, and because of the demands of customers using its Web sites and partner sites like eBay who needed far more support as sales expanded. Hilfiger had swiftly transformed from a bricks-and-mortar retailer into a more complex retail operation with substantial online sales, and now had to deal with online service issues, returns, payments, shipping, and customer support issues on a global basis. The company turned to SAP to create a new global enterprise infrastructure and help build out its mobile Web applications not only for retail customers but also for its global suppliers and retailers.

In 2012, Hilfiger continued to build on its e-commerce success. Its Facebook page has more than 4.4 million Likes, and almost 70,000 people talking about the company's clothing on Facebook. Hilfiger has also broadened its social visual site presence through an extensive photo blog on Tumblr and a smaller presence on Pinterest. It has a Twitter feed, and an iPhone app that allows customers to try on digital versions of select pieces in virtual fitting rooms. For the iPad, Hilfiger has created the iPad Fit Guide, which uses video imaging to capture a 360-degree view of the clothing. Customers can compare the fit of different products, view alternative styling suggestions, and read about the specifics of the cut and rise of each pant.

For start-ups and small businesses, there are of course many less-costly alternatives to using a sophisticated tool like ATG's or SAP's sophisticated e-commerce platforms. For instance, one solution is to build a Web site using pre-built templates offered by Yahoo! Merchant Solutions, Amazon, eBay, Network Solutions, or hundreds of other online sites. Fees range from a few hundred dollars to several thousand. These firms host your Web site and they worry about capacity and scale issues as your firm grows. For instance, Yahoo Merchant Solutions offers three different packages: Starter, Standard, and Professional. As the business grows, you can move up to a more comprehensive package.

The cost of building Web sites has fallen drastically, not just because of the fall in hardware costs, but also because the cost of software needed to build and operate Web sites has fallen, sometimes to zero. There are thousands of open source software tools available to develop Web sites and associated databases that will cost you nothing. Some are as simple to use as blog software tools, while others require a technical background and training. Analysts believe that a Web site costing more than $1 million in 2000 could be built for less than $50,000 in 2012. However, building a Web presence yourself will cost you dearly in time, and could delay your entrance to the market. How much is your time worth? Remember, the "e" in e-commerce does not stand for easy.

In Chapter 3, you learned about e-commerce's technological foundation: the Internet, Web, and the mobile platform. In this chapter, you will examine the important factors that a manager needs to consider when building an e-commerce presence. The focus will be on the managerial and business decisions you must make before you begin, and that you will continually need to make. Although building a sophisticated e-commerce presence isn't easy, today's tools are much less expensive and far more powerful than they were during the early days of e-commerce. You do not have to be Amazon or eBay to create a successful Web e-commerce presence. In this chapter, we focus on both small and medium-sized businesses as well as much larger corporate entities that serve thousands of customers a day, or even an hour. As you will see, although the scale may be very different, the principles and considerations are basically the same.

4.1 IMAGINE YOUR E-COMMERCE PRESENCE

Before you begin to build a Web site or app of your own, there are some important questions you will need to think about and answer. The answers to these questions will drive the development and implementation of your online presence.

WHAT'S THE IDEA? (THE VISIONING PROCESS)

Before you can plan and actually build a Web presence, you need to have a vision of what you hope to accomplish and how you hope to accomplish it. The vision includes not just a statement of mission, but also identification of the target audience, characterization of the market space, a strategic analysis, an Internet marketing matrix, and a development timeline. It starts with a dream of what's possible, and concludes with a timeline and preliminary budget for development of the Web presence.

If you examine any successful Web site, you can usually tell from the home page what the vision that inspires the site is. If the company is a public company, you can often find a succinct statement of its vision or mission in the reports it files with the Securities and Exchange Commission. For Amazon, it's to become the largest marketplace on earth. For Facebook, it's to make the world more open and connected. For Google, it's to organize the world's information and make it universally accessible and useful. The Web presence you want to build may not have such all encompassing ambitions, but a succinct statement of mission, purpose, and direction is the key factor in driving the development of your project. For instance, the Tommy.com Web site reflects the brand image of Tommy Hilfiger Inc., whose primary mission is (as noted in its annual report) to combine fresh American style with unique details to give time-honored classics an updated look for customers who desire high quality, designer apparel at competitive prices under a number of different labels.

WHERE'S THE MONEY: BUSINESS AND REVENUE MODEL

Once you have defined a mission statement, a vision, you need to start thinking about where the money will be coming from. You will need to develop a preliminary idea of your business and revenue models. You don't need detailed revenue and cost projections at this point. Instead, you need a general idea of how your business will generate revenues. The basic choices have been described in Chapter 2. Basic business models are portal, e-tailer, content provider, transaction broker, market creator, service provider, and community provider (social network).

The basic revenue model alternatives are advertising, subscriptions, transaction fees, sales, and affiliate revenue. There's no reason to adopt a single business or revenue model, and in fact, many firms have multiple models. For instance, at Theknot.com, a vertical portal for the wedding industry, you will find ads, affiliate relationships, and sponsorships from major creators of wedding products and services, including a directory to local wedding planners, all of which produce revenue for Theknot.com.

WHO AND WHERE IS THE TARGET AUDIENCE

Without a clear understanding of your target audience, you will not have a successful Web presence. There are two questions here: who is your target audience and where are they on the Web? Your target audience can be described in a number of ways: demographics, behavior patterns (lifestyle), current consumption patterns (online vs. offline purchasing), digital usage patterns, content creation preferences (blogs, social networks, sites like Pinterest), and buyer personas (profiles of your typical customer). Understanding the demographics of your target audience is usually the first step. Demographic information includes age, income, gender, and location. In some cases, this may be obvious and in others, much less so. For instance, Harley-Davidson sells motorcycles to a very broad demographic range of varying ages, incomes, and locations, from 34-year-olds to 65-year-olds. Although most of the purchasers are middle-aged men, with middle incomes, many of the men ride with women, and the Harley-Davidson Web site has a collection of women's clothing and several Web pages devoted to women riders. While the majority of men who purchase Harley-Davidsons have modest incomes, a significant group of purchasers are professionals with above-average incomes. Hence, the age and income demographic target is quite broad. What ties Harley-Davidson riders together is not their shared demographics, but their love of the motorcycles and the brand, and the lifestyle associated with touring the highways of America on a powerful motorcycle that sounds like a potato popper. In contrast, a site like Theknot.com is aimed at women in the 18–34-year-old range who are in varying stages of getting married, with lifestyles that include shopping online, using smartphones and tablets, downloading apps, and using Facebook. This audience is technologically hip. These women read and contribute to blogs, comment on forums, and use Pinterest to find ideas for fashion. A "typical" visitor to Theknot.com would be a 28-year-old woman who has an engagement ring, is just starting the wedding planning process, has an income of $45,000, lives in the Northeast, and is interested in a beach wedding. There are, of course, other "typical" profiles. For each profile for your Web site you will need to develop a detailed description.

WHAT IS THE BALLPARK? CHARACTERIZE THE MARKETPLACE

The chances of your success will depend greatly on the characteristics of the market you are about to enter, and not just on your entrepreneurial brilliance. Enter into a declining market filled with strong competitors, and you will multiply your chances of failure. Enter into a market that is emerging, growing and has few competitors, and you stand a better chance. Enter a market where there are no players, and you will either be rewarded handsomely with a profitable monopoly on a successful product no one else thought of or you will be quickly forgotten because there isn't a market for your product at this point in time.

Features of the marketplace to focus on include the demographics of the market and how a Web presence fits into the market. In addition, you will want to know about the structure of the market: competitors and substitute products.

What are the features of the marketplace you are about to enter? Is the market growing, or receding in size? If it's growing, among which age and income groups? Is the marketplace shifting from offline to online delivery? If so, is the market moving towards traditional Web sites, mobile, and/or tablets? Is there a special role for a mobile presence in this market? What percentage of your target audience uses a Web site, smartphone, or tablet? What about social networks? What's the buzz on products like yours? Are your potential customers talking about the products and services you want to offer on Facebook, Twitter, or blogs? How many blogs focus on products like yours? How many Twitter posts mention similar offerings? How many Facebook Likes (signs of customer engagement) are attached to products you want to offer?

The structure of the market is described in terms of your direct competitors, suppliers, and substitute products. You will want to make a list of the top five or ten competitors and try to describe their market share, and distinguishing characteristics. Some of your competitors may offer traditional versions of your products, while others will offer new renditions or versions of products that have new features. You need to find out everything you can about your competitors. What's the market buzz on your competitors? How many unique monthly visitors (UMVs) do they have? How many Facebook Likes, Twitter followers, and/or Pinterest followers? How are your competitors using social sites and mobile devices as a part of their online presence. Is there something special you could do with social networks that your competitors do not? Do a search on customer reviews of their products. You can find online services (some of them free) that will measure the number of online conversations about your competitors, and the total share of Internet voice each of your competitors receives. Do your competitors have a special relationship with their suppliers that you may not have access to? Exclusive marketing arrangements would be one example of a special supplier relationship. Finally, are there substitutes for your products and services? For instance, your site may offer advice to the community of pet owners, but local pet stores or local groups may be a more trusted source of advice on pets.

WHERE'S THE CONTENT COMING FROM?

Web sites are like books: they're composed of a lot of pages that have content ranging from text, to graphics, photos, and videos. This content is what search engines catalog as they crawl through all the new and changed Web pages on the Internet. The content is why your customers visit your site and either purchase things or look at ads that generate revenue for you. Therefore, the content is the single most important foundation for your revenue and ultimate success.

There are generally two kinds of content: static and dynamic. Static content is text and images that do not frequently change, such as product descriptions, photos, or text that you create to share with your visitors. Dynamic content is content that changes regularly, say, daily or hourly. Dynamic content can be created by you, or increasingly, by bloggers and fans of your Web site and products. User-generated content has a number of advantages: it's free, it engages your customer fan base, and search engines are more likely to catalog your site if the content is changing. Other sources of content, especially photos, are external Web sites that aggregate content such as Pinterest, discussed in the opening case in Chapter 1.

KNOW YOURSELF: CONDUCT A SWOT ANALYSIS

SWOT analysis

describes a firm's strengths, weaknesses, opportunities, and threats

A **SWOT analysis** is a simple but powerful method for strategizing about your business and understanding where you should focus your efforts. In a SWOT analysis you describe your strengths, weaknesses, threats, and opportunities. In the example SWOT analysis in **Figure 4.1**, you will see a profile of a typical start-up venture that includes a unique approach to an existing market, a promise of addressing unmet needs in this market, and the use of newer technologies (social and mobile platforms) that older competitors may have overlooked. There are many opportunities to address a large market with unmet needs, as well as the potential to use the initial Web site as a home base and spin-off related or nearby sites, leveraging the investment in design and technology. But there are also weaknesses and threats. Lack of financial and human resources are typically the biggest weakness of start-up sites. Threats include competitors that could develop the same capabilities as you, and low market entry costs, which might encourage many more start-ups to enter the marketplace.

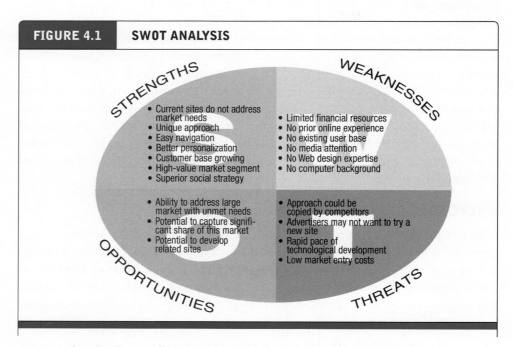

FIGURE 4.1	SWOT ANALYSIS

STRENGTHS
- Current sites do not address market needs
- Unique approach
- Easy navigation
- Better personalization
- Customer base growing
- High-value market segment
- Superior social strategy

WEAKNESSES
- Limited financial resources
- No prior online experience
- No existing user base
- No media attention
- No Web design expertise
- No computer background

OPPORTUNITIES
- Ability to address large market with unmet needs
- Potential to capture significant share of this market
- Potential to develop related sites

THREATS
- Approach could be copied by competitors
- Advertisers may not want to try a new site
- Rapid pace of technological development
- Low market entry costs

A SWOT analysis describes your firm's strengths, weaknesses, opportunities, and threats.

Once you have conducted a SWOT analysis, you can consider ways to overcome your weaknesses and build on your strengths. For instance, you could consider hiring or partnering to obtain technical and managerial expertise, and looking for financing opportunities (including friends and relatives).

DEVELOP AN E-COMMERCE PRESENCE MAP

E-commerce has moved from being a PC-centric activity on the Web to a mobile and tablet-based activity as well. While 80% or more of e-commerce today is conducted using PCs, increasingly smartphones and tablets will be used for purchasing. Currently, smartphones and tablets are used by a majority of Internet users in the United States to shop for goods and services, explore purchase options, look up prices, and access social sites. Your potential customers use these various devices at different times during the day, and involve themselves in different conversations depending on what they are doing—touching base with friends, tweeting, or reading a blog. Each of these are "touch points" where you can meet the customer, and you have to think about how you develop a presence in these different virtual places. **Figure 4.2** provides a roadmap to the platforms and related activities you will need to think about when developing your e-commerce presence.

Figure 4.2 illustrates four different kinds of an e-commerce presence: Web sites, e-mail, social media, and offline media. For each of these types there are different platforms that you will need to address. For instance, in the case of Web site presence, there are three different platforms: traditional desktop, tablets, and smartphones, each with different capabilities. And for each type of e-commerce presence there are related activities you will need to consider. For instance, in the case of Web sites, you will want to engage in search engine marketing, display ads, affiliate programs, and

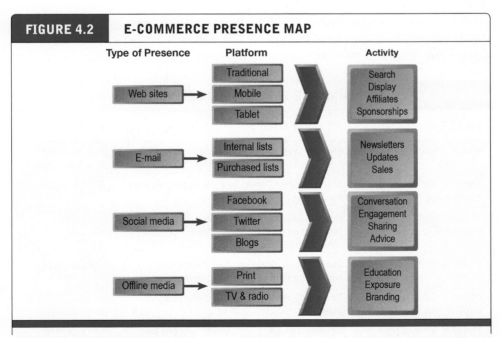

| FIGURE 4.2 | E-COMMERCE PRESENCE MAP |

An e-commerce Web presence requires firms to consider the four different kinds of Web presence, and the platforms and activities associated with each type of presence.

sponsorships. Offline media, the fourth type of e-commerce presence, is included here because many firms use multiplatform or integrated marketing where print ads refer customers to Web sites. The marketing activities in Figure 4.2 are described in much greater detail in Chapters 6 and 7.

DEVELOP A TIMELINE: MILESTONES

Where would you like to be a year from now? It's a good idea for you to have a rough idea of the time frame for developing your e-commerce presence when you begin. You should break your project down into a small number of phases that could be completed within a specified time. Six phases are usually enough detail at this point. **Table 4.1** illustrates a one-year timeline for the development of a start-up Web site devoted to teenage fashions.

HOW MUCH WILL THIS COST?

It's too early in the process to develop a detailed budget for your e-commerce presence, but it is a good time to develop a preliminary idea of the costs involved. How much you spend on a Web site depends on what you want it to do. Simple Web sites can be built and hosted with a first-year cost of $5,000 or less if all the work is done in-house by yourself and others are willing to work without pay. A more reasonable budget for a small Web start-up would be $25,000 to $50,000. Here the firm owner would develop all the content at no cost, and a Web designer and programmer would be hired to implement the initial Web site. As discussed later, the Web site would be hosted on a cloud-based server. The Web sites of large firms that offer high levels of interactivity and linkage to corporate systems can cost several hundred thousand to millions of dollars a year to create and operate.

While how much you spend to build a Web site depends on how much you can afford, and, of course, the size of the opportunity, **Figure 4.3** provides some idea of the relative size of various Web site costs. In general, the cost of hardware, software, and

TABLE 4.1	E-COMMERCE PRESENCE TIMELINE	
PHASE	ACTIVITY	MILESTONE
Phase 1: Planning	Envision Web presence; determine personnel	Web mission statement
Phase 2: Web site development	Acquire content; develop a site design; arrange for hosting the site	Web site plan
Phase 3: Web Implementation	Develop keywords and metatags; focus on search engine optimization; identify potential sponsors	A functional Web site
Phase 4: Social media plan	Identify appropriate social platforms and content for your products and services	A social media plan
Phase 5: Social media implementation	Develop Facebook, Twitter, and Pinterest presence	Functioning social media presence
Phase 6: Mobile plan	Develop a mobile plan; consider options for porting your Web site to smartphones	A mobile media plan

FIGURE 4.3	COMPONENTS OF A WEB PRESENCE BUDGET

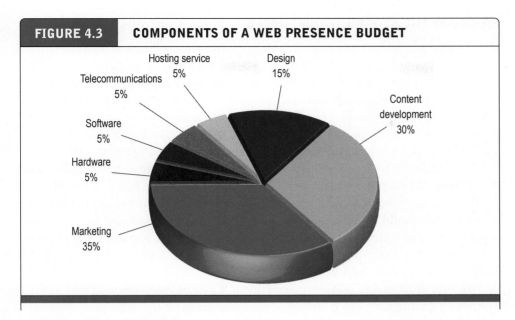

While hardware and software costs have fallen dramatically, Web sites face significant design, content development, and marketing costs.

telecommunications for building and operating a Web site has fallen dramatically (by over 50%) in the last decade, making it possible for very small entrepreneurs to build fairly sophisticated sites. At the same time, while technology has lowered the costs of system development, the costs of marketing, content development, and design have risen to make up more than half of typical Web site budgets. The longer-term costs would also have to include site and system maintenance, which are not included here.

4.2 BUILDING AN E-COMMERCE PRESENCE: A SYSTEMATIC APPROACH

Once you have developed a vision of the Web presence you want to build, it's time to start thinking about how to build and implement the Web presence. Building a successful e-commerce presence requires a keen understanding of business, technology, and social issues, as well as a systematic approach. E-commerce is just too important to be left totally to technologists and programmers.

The two most important management challenges are (1) developing a clear understanding of your business objectives and (2) knowing how to choose the right technology to achieve those objectives. The first challenge requires you to build a plan for developing your firm's presence. The second challenge requires you to understand some of the basic elements of e-commerce infrastructure. Let the business drive the technology.

Even if you decide to outsource the development effort and operation to a service provider, you will still need to have a development plan and some understanding of the basic e-commerce infrastructure issues such as cost, capability, and constraints. Without a plan and a knowledge base, you will not be able to make sound management decisions about e-commerce within your firm.

PIECES OF THE SITE-BUILDING PUZZLE

Let's assume you are a manager for a medium-sized industrial parts firm in the United States. You have been given a budget of $100,000 to develop an e-commerce presence for the firm. The purpose will be to sell and service the firm's customers, who are mostly small machine and metal fabricating shops, and to engage your customers through a blog and user forum. Where do you start? In the following sections, we will examine developing an e-commerce Web site, and then, at the end of the chapter, discuss some of the considerations involved in developing a mobile site and building mobile applications.

First, you must be aware of the main areas where you will need to make decisions (see **Figure 4.4**). On the organizational and human resources fronts, you will have to bring together a team of individuals who possess the skill sets needed to build and manage a successful e-commerce Web site. This team will make the key decisions about business objectives and strategy, technology, site design, and social and information policies. The entire development effort must be closely managed if you hope to avoid the disasters that have occurred at some firms.

You will also need to make decisions about hardware, software, and telecommunications infrastructure. The demands of your customers should drive your choices of technology. Your customers will want technology that enables them to find what they want easily, view the product, purchase the product, and then receive the product from your warehouses quickly. You will also have to carefully consider design. Once you have identified the key decision areas, you will need to think about a plan for the project.

PLANNING: THE SYSTEMS DEVELOPMENT LIFE CYCLE

systems development life cycle (SDLC)

a methodology for understanding the business objectives of any system and designing an appropriate solution

Your second step in building an e-commerce Web site will be creating a plan document. In order to tackle a complex problem such as building an e-commerce site, you will have to proceed systematically through a series of steps. One methodology is the systems development life cycle. The **systems development life cycle (SDLC)** is a methodology for understanding the business objectives of any system and designing an appropriate solution. Adopting a life cycle methodology does not guarantee success,

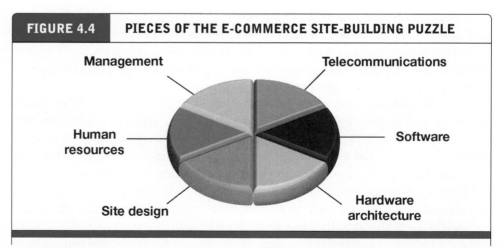

| FIGURE 4.4 | PIECES OF THE E-COMMERCE SITE-BUILDING PUZZLE |

Building an e-commerce Web site requires that you systematically consider the many factors that go into the process.

but it is far better than having no plan at all. The SDLC method also helps in creating documents that communicate objectives, important milestones, and the uses of resources to management. **Figure 4.5** illustrates the five major steps involved in the systems development life cycle for an e-commerce site:

- Systems analysis/planning
- Systems design
- Building the system
- Testing
- Implementation

SYSTEMS ANALYSIS/PLANNING: IDENTIFY BUSINESS OBJECTIVES, SYSTEM FUNCTIONALITY, AND INFORMATION REQUIREMENTS

In the systems analysis/planning step of the SDLC, you try to answer the question, "What do we want this e-commerce site to do for our business?" The key point is to let the business decisions drive the technology, not the reverse. This will ensure that your technology platform is aligned with your business. We will assume here that you have identified a business strategy and chosen a business model to achieve your strategic objectives (see Chapter 2). But how do you translate your strategies, business models, and ideas into a working e-commerce Web site?

One way to start is to identify the specific business objectives for your site, and then develop a list of system functionalities and information requirements. **Business objectives** are simply capabilities you want your site to have.

System functionalities are types of information systems capabilities you will need to achieve your business objectives. The **information requirements** for a system are the information elements that the system must produce in order to achieve

business objectives
capabilities you want your site to have

system functionalities
types of information systems capabilities you will need to achieve your business objectives

information requirements
the information elements that the system must produce in order to achieve the business objectives

FIGURE 4.5	WEB SITE SYSTEMS DEVELOPMENT LIFE CYCLE

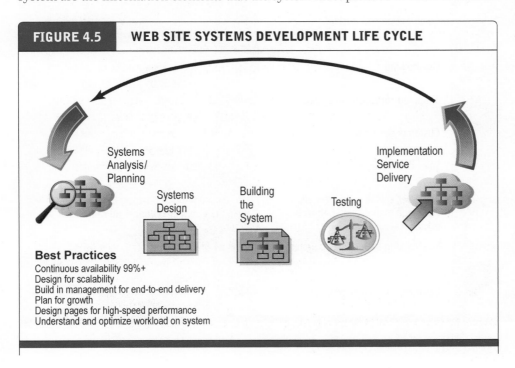

Systems Analysis/ Planning

Systems Design

Building the System

Testing

Implementation Service Delivery

Best Practices
Continuous availability 99%+
Design for scalability
Build in management for end-to-end delivery
Plan for growth
Design pages for high-speed performance
Understand and optimize workload on system

the business objectives. You will need to provide these lists to system developers and programmers so they know what you as the manager expect them to do.

Table 4.2 describes some basic business objectives, system functionalities, and information requirements for a typical e-commerce site. As shown in the table, there are nine basic business objectives that an e-commerce site must deliver. These objectives must be translated into a description of system functionalities and ultimately into a set of precise information requirements. The specific information requirements for a system typically are defined in much greater detail than Table 4.2 indicates. To a large extent, the business objectives of an e-commerce site are not that different from those of an ordinary retail store. The real difference lies in the system functionalities and information requirements. In an e-commerce site, the business objectives must be provided entirely in digital form without buildings or salespeople, 24 hours a day, 7 days a week.

SYSTEM DESIGN: HARDWARE AND SOFTWARE PLATFORMS

Once you have identified the business objectives and system functionalities, and have developed a list of precise information requirements, you can begin to consider just

TABLE 4.2	SYSTEM ANALYSIS: BUSINESS OBJECTIVES, SYSTEM FUNCTIONALITY, AND INFORMATION REQUIREMENTS FOR A TYPICAL E-COMMERCE SITE	
BUSINESS OBJECTIVE	**SYSTEM FUNCTIONALITY**	**INFORMATION REQUIREMENTS**
Display goods	Digital catalog	Dynamic text and graphics catalog
Provide product information (content)	Product database	Product description, stocking numbers, inventory levels
Personalize/customize product	Customer on-site tracking	Site log for every customer visit; data mining capability to identify common customer paths and appropriate responses
Engage customers in conversations	On-site blog	Software with blogging and community response functionality
Execute a transaction	Shopping cart/payment system	Secure credit card clearing; multiple payment options
Accumulate customer information	Customer database	Name, address, phone, and e-mail for all customers; online customer registration
Provide after-sale customer support	Sales database	Customer ID, product, date, payment, shipment date
Coordinate marketing/advertising	Ad server, e-mail server, e-mail, campaign manager, ad banner manager	Site behavior log of prospects and customers linked to e-mail and banner ad campaigns
Understand marketing effectiveness	Site tracking and reporting system	Number of unique visitors, pages visited, products purchased, identified by marketing campaign
Provide production and supplier links	Inventory management system	Product and inventory levels, supplier ID and contact, order quantity data by product

how all this functionality will be delivered. You must come up with a **system design specification**—a description of the main components in the system and their relationship to one another. The system design itself can be broken down into two components: a logical design and a physical design. A **logical design** includes a data flow diagram that describes the flow of information at your e-commerce site, the processing functions that must be performed, and the databases that will be used. The logical design also includes a description of the security and emergency backup procedures that will be instituted, and the controls that will be used in the system.

A **physical design** translates the logical design into physical components. For instance, the physical design details the specific model of server to be purchased, the software to be used, the size of the telecommunications link that will be required, the way the system will be backed up and protected from outsiders, and so on.

Figure 4.6(a) presents a data flow diagram for a simple high-level logical design for a very basic Web site that delivers catalog pages in HTML in response to HTTP requests from the client's browser, while **Figure 4.6(b)** shows the corresponding physical design. Each of the main processes can be broken down into lower-level designs that are much more precise in identifying exactly how the information flows and what equipment is involved.

BUILDING THE SYSTEM: IN-HOUSE VERSUS OUTSOURCING

Now that you have a clear idea of both the logical and physical design for your site, you can begin considering how to actually build the site. You have many choices and much depends on the amount of money you are willing to spend. Choices range from outsourcing everything (including the actual systems analysis and design) to building everything yourself (in-house). **Outsourcing** means that you will hire an outside vendor to provide the services involved in building the site rather than using in-house personnel. You also have a second decision to make: will you host (operate) the site on your firm's own servers or will you outsource the hosting to a Web host provider? These decisions are independent of each other, but they are usually considered at the same time. There are some vendors who will design, build, and host your site, while others will either build or host (but not both).

Build Your Own versus Outsourcing

Let's take the building decision first. If you elect to build your own site, there are a range of options. Unless you are fairly skilled, you should use a pre-built template to create the Web site. For example, Yahoo Merchant Solutions, Amazon Stores, and eBay all provide templates that merely require you to input text, graphics, and other data, as well as the infrastructure to run the Web site once it has been created.

If your Web site is not a sales-oriented site requiring a shopping cart, one of the least expensive and most widely used site building tools is WordPress. **WordPress** is a blogging tool with a sophisticated content management system. A **content management system (CMS)** is a database software program specifically designed to manage structured and unstructured data and objects in a Web site environment. A CMS provides Web managers and designers with a centralized control structure to manage Web site content. WordPress also has thousands of user-built plug-ins and widgets that you

system design specification
description of the main components in a system and their relationship to one another

logical design
describes the flow of information at your e-commerce site, the processing functions that must be performed, the databases that will be used, the security and emergency backup procedures that will be instituted, and the controls that will be used in the system

physical design
translates the logical design into physical components

outsourcing
hiring an outside vendor to provide the services you cannot perform with in-house personnel

WordPress
open source content management and blog Web site design tool

content management system (CMS)
organizes, stores, and processes Web site content

FIGURE 4.6	A LOGICAL AND PHYSICAL DESIGN FOR A SIMPLE WEB SITE

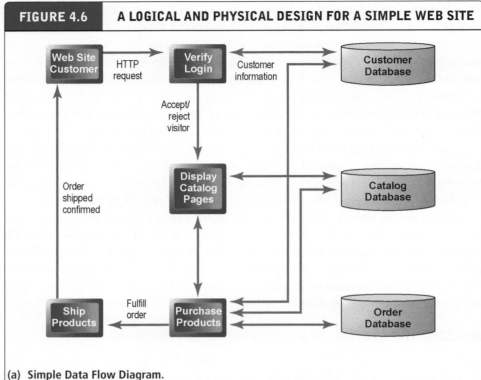

(a) Simple Data Flow Diagram.
This data flow diagram describes the flow of information requests and responses for a simple Web site.

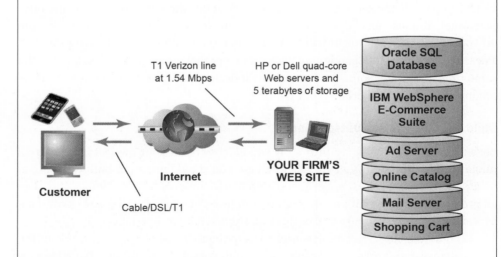

(b) Simple Physical Design.
A physical design describes the hardware and software needed to realize the logical design.

can use to extend the functionality of a Web site. Web sites built in WordPress are treated by search engines like any other Web site: their content is indexed and made available to the entire Web community. Revenue-generating ads, affiliates, and sponsors are the main sources of revenue for WordPress sites. While these are the least costly sources of a Web presence, you will be limited to the "look and feel" and functionality provided by the template and infrastructure supplied by these vendors.

If you have some experience with computers, you might decide to build the site yourself "from scratch." There are a broad variety of tools, ranging from those that help you build everything truly "from scratch," such as Adobe Dreamweaver and Microsoft Expression, to top-of-the-line prepackaged site-building tools that can create sophisticated sites customized to your needs. **Figure 4.7** illustrates the spectrum of tools available. We will look more closely at the variety of e-commerce software available in Section 4.3.

The decision to build a Web site on your own has a number of risks. Given the complexity of features such as shopping carts, credit card authentication and processing, inventory management, and order processing, the costs involved are high, as are the risks of doing a poor job. You will be reinventing what other specialized firms have already built, and your staff may face a long, difficult learning curve, delaying your entry to market. Your efforts could fail. On the positive side, you may be better able to build a site that does exactly what you want, and, more importantly, develop the in-house knowledge to allow you to change the site rapidly if necessary due to a changing business environment.

If you choose more expensive site-building packages, you will be purchasing state-of-the art software that is well tested. You could get to market sooner. However, to make a sound decision, you will have to evaluate many different packages, and this can take a long time.

In the past, bricks-and-mortar retailers in need of an e-commerce site typically designed the site themselves (because they already had the skilled staff in place and had extensive investments in information technology capital such as databases and telecommunications). However, as Web applications have become more sophisticated, larger retailers today rely heavily on vendors to provide sophisticated Web

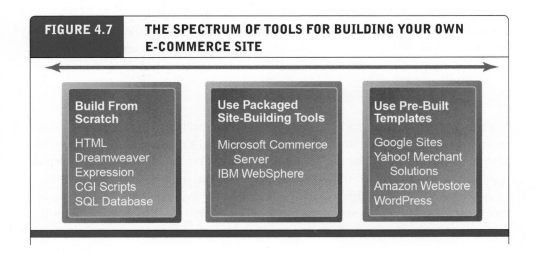

FIGURE 4.7   **THE SPECTRUM OF TOOLS FOR BUILDING YOUR OWN E-COMMERCE SITE**

Build From Scratch

HTML
Dreamweaver
Expression
CGI Scripts
SQL Database

Use Packaged Site-Building Tools

Microsoft Commerce Server
IBM WebSphere

Use Pre-Built Templates

Google Sites
Yahoo! Merchant Solutions
Amazon Webstore
WordPress

site capabilities, while also maintaining a substantial internal staff. Small start-ups may build their own sites from scratch using in-house technical personnel in an effort to keep costs low. Medium-size start-ups will often purchase a Web site design and programming expertise from vendors. Very small mom-and-pop firms seeking simple storefronts will use templates or blogging tools like WordPress. For e-commerce sites, the cost of building has dropped dramatically in the last five years, resulting in lower capital requirements for all players (see *Insight on Business: Curly Hair and Appillionaires*.)

Host Your Own versus Outsourcing

Now let's look at the hosting decision. Most businesses choose to outsource hosting and pay a company to host their Web site, which means that the hosting company is responsible for ensuring the site is "live," or accessible, 24 hours a day. By agreeing to a monthly fee, the business need not concern itself with many of the technical aspects of setting up a Web server and maintaining it, telecommunications links, nor with staffing needs.

co-location

when a firm purchases or leases a Web server (and has total control over its operation) but locates the server in a vendor's physical facility. The vendor maintains the facility, communications lines, and the machinery

You can also choose to *co-locate*. With a **co-location** agreement, your firm purchases or leases a Web server (and has total control over its operation) but locates the server in a vendor's physical facility. The vendor maintains the facility, communications lines, and the machinery.

While co-location involves renting physical space for your hardware, you can think of using a cloud service provider as renting virtual space in your provider's infrastructure. Cloud services are rapidly replacing co-location because they are less expensive, and arguably more reliable. Unlike with co-location, your firm does not own the hardware. Cloud service providers offer a standardized infrastructure, virtualization technology, and usually employ a pay-as-you-go billing system.

There are several disadvantages to outsourcing hosting. If you choose a vendor, make sure the vendor has the capability to grow with you. You need to know what kinds of security provisions are in place for backup copies of your site, internal monitoring of activity, and security track record. Is there a public record of a security breach at the vendor? Most Fortune 500 firms have their own private cloud data centers so they can control the Web environment. On the other hand, there are risks to hosting your own site if you are a small business. Your costs will be higher than if you had used a large outsourcing firm because you don't have the market power to obtain low-cost hardware and telecommunications. You will have to purchase hardware and software, have a physical facility, lease communications lines, hire a staff, and build security and backup capabilities yourself.

TESTING THE SYSTEM

unit testing

involves testing the site's program modules one at a time

system testing

involves testing the site as a whole, in a way the typical user will use the site

Once the system has been built and programmed, you will have to engage in a testing process. Depending on the size of the system, this could be fairly difficult and lengthy. Testing is required whether the system is outsourced or built in-house. A complex e-commerce site can have thousands of pathways through the site, each of which must be documented and then tested. **Unit testing** involves testing the site's program modules one at a time. **System testing** involves testing the site as a whole, in the same way a typical user would when using the site. Because there is no truly "typical"

INSIGHT ON BUSINESS

CURLY HAIR AND APPILLIONAIRES

Although big companies with national brand names dominate the e-commerce scene, there are still billions left in potential online retail sales, with additional money to be made from advertising revenues. Today's start-ups have much leaner development models made possible in part by much cheaper technology and social network sites. If you can create or identify a community of people with shared interests and issues, you'll have a built-in audience.

NaturallyCurly.com is a good example of a low-entry-cost, niche-oriented site that actually created an online community where none existed before. Two reporters with curly hair, Gretchen Heber and Michelle Breyer, started the site with $500 in 1998. They spent $200 on the domain name, and bought some curly hair products to review on the site. Their first site was built with a simple Web server and the help of a 14-year-old Web page designer.

Even without advertising on Google, they started showing up in Google searches for "curly hair" near or at the top of the search results list. In 2000, after a year of operation, they got an e-mail from Procter & Gamble asking if they would accept advertising for $2,000 a month for two years. From there, the site grew by adding additional advertising from leading hair care products companies and now generates revenue in excess of $1 million from advertising and sales of products on its online boutique for curly hair products.

The firm has moved aggressively into social marketing by establishing a Facebook page and a Twitter account. In 2011, the firm launched Curls on-the-Go, a free app that personalizes advice to its users based on their hair characteristics and preferred styles. The app is designed to sell products, provide reviews from visitors to its Web sites, and to help users find local salons. Naturallycurly.com and its affiliate sites now generate more than 2 million unique visitors a month, and the firm is profitable.

The app economy has also changed the economics of software production and e-commerce and has led to a small group of Appillionaires—a very small group of apps creators who make it big. One of the best known appillionaires is Chris Stevens, author of the Alice for the iPad app, an interactive rendering of Lewis Carroll's *Alice in Wonderland*. Within a few months of its release, Alice for the iPad was reviewed on Oprah Winfrey's television show and rose to the top ranks of apps in the iTunes store. To make the app, Stevens used just an iMac and an iPhone, along with three months of 15-hour days.

It isn't just hardware and software that are becoming less expensive, but other services as well that are vital for the success of small start-ups. Market intelligence, public relations, and even design services can be found online for a fraction of the cost of traditional service firms. It's never been cheaper to start an e-commerce company. In fact, the recession of the past few years may have been an entrepreneur's best friend. In a poor economy, failures are not so noticeable, which creates a better environment for risk-taking and innovation.

■ **SOURCES:** "Behind the Curls: TextureMedia Becomes a Big Hairy Deal," by Sandra Zaragoza, *Austin Business Journal*, August 12, 2012; "Community and the Value of a Kinky Idea," by Laura Lorber, Entrepreneur.com, August 2012; "Chris Stevens on Alice for the iPad, Book Apps, and Toronto," *Toronto Review*, January 9, 2012; "Striking It Rich In The App Store: For Developers, It's More Casino Than Gold Mine," by Chris Stevens, *FastCompany*, November 2, 2011; *Appillionaires: Secrets from Developers Who Struck It Rich on the App Store*, by Chris Stevens, Wiley, September 2011; "The NaturallyCurly Network Launches Curls on the Go," Naturallycurly.com, July 7, 2011; "Web Start Up Frenzy 2.0," by Sharon Machlis, Computerworld.com, April 29, 2010; "Launching an E-commerce Site With Social Networking," Marketingsherpa.com, March 3, 2010; "Software and Technology Services NaturallyCurly.com, Inc.," Business-Week.com, July 28, 2009; "The New Internet Startup Boom: Get Rich Slow," by Josh Quittner, Time.com, April 9, 2009.

acceptance testing
verifies that the business objectives of the system as originally conceived are in fact working

user, system testing requires that every conceivable path be tested. Final **acceptance testing** requires that the firm's key personnel and managers in marketing, production, sales, and general management actually use the system as installed on a test Internet or intranet server. This acceptance test verifies that the business objectives of the system as originally conceived are in fact working. It is important to note that testing is generally under-budgeted. As much as 50% of the software effort can be consumed by testing and rebuilding (usually depending on the quality of the initial design).

IMPLEMENTATION AND MAINTENANCE

Most people unfamiliar with systems erroneously think that once an information system is installed, the process is over. In fact, while the beginning of the process is over, the operational life of a system is just beginning. Systems break down for a variety of reasons—most of them unpredictable. Therefore, they need continual checking, testing, and repair. Systems maintenance is vital, but sometimes not budgeted for. In general, the annual system maintenance cost will roughly parallel the development cost. A $40,000 e-commerce site will likely require a $40,000 annual expenditure to maintain. Very large e-commerce sites experience some economies of scale, so that, for example, a $1 million site will likely require a maintenance budget of $500,000 to $700,000.

Why does it cost so much to maintain an e-commerce site? Unlike payroll systems, for example, e-commerce sites are always in a process of change, improvement, and correction. E-commerce sites are never finished: they are always in the process of being built and rebuilt. They are dynamic—much more so than payroll systems.

4.3   CHOOSING SOFTWARE AND HARDWARE

Much of what you are able to do at an e-commerce site is a function of the software and hardware. Along with telecommunications, hardware and software constitute the infrastructure of a Web presence. As a business manager in charge of building the site, you will need to know some basic information about both.

SIMPLE VERSUS MULTI-TIERED WEB SITE ARCHITECTURE

Prior to the development of e-commerce, Web sites simply delivered Web pages to users who were making requests through their browsers for HTML pages with content of various sorts. Web site software was appropriately quite simple—it consisted of a server computer running basic Web server software. We might call this arrangement a single-tier system architecture. **System architecture** refers to the arrangement of software, machinery, and tasks in an information system needed to achieve a specific functionality (much like a home's architecture refers to the arrangement of building materials to achieve a particular functionality). Tens of thousands of dot-com sites still perform this way. Orders can always be called in by telephone and not taken online.

However, the development of e-commerce required a great deal more interactive functionality, such as the ability to respond to user input (name and address forms), take customer orders for goods and services, clear credit card transactions on the fly,

system architecture
the arrangement of software, machinery, and tasks in an information system needed to achieve a specific functionality

consult price and product databases, and even adjust advertising on the screen based on user characteristics. This kind of extended functionality required the development of Web application servers and a multi-tiered system architecture to handle the processing loads. *Web application servers* are specialized software programs that perform a wide variety of transaction processing required by e-commerce.

In addition to having specialized application servers, e-commerce sites must be able to pull information from and add information to pre-existing corporate databases. These older databases that predate the e-commerce era are called *backend* or *legacy* databases. Corporations have made massive investments in these systems to store their information on customers, products, employees, and vendors. These backend systems constitute an additional layer in a multi-tiered site.

Figure 4.8 illustrates a simple two-tier and more complex multi-tier e-commerce system architecture. In **two-tier architecture**, a Web server responds to requests for Web pages and a database server provides backend data storage. In a **multi-tier architecture**, in contrast, the Web server is linked to a middle-tier layer that typically includes a series of application servers that perform specific tasks, as well as to a backend layer of existing corporate systems containing product, customer, and pricing information.

WEB SERVER SOFTWARE

All e-commerce sites require basic Web server software to answer requests from customers for HTML and XML pages. The leading Web server software is Apache, which works with Linux and Unix operating systems. Apache is free and can be downloaded from many sites on the Web; it also comes installed on most IBM Web servers.

Microsoft Internet Information Services (IIS) is the second major Web server software available. IIS is based on the Windows operating system and is compatible with a wide selection of Microsoft utility and support programs.

There are also at least 100 other smaller providers of Web server software, most of them based on the Unix or Sun Solaris operating systems. Note that the choice of Web server has little effect on users of your system. The pages they see will look the same regardless of the development environment. There are many advantages to the Microsoft suite of development tools—they are integrated, powerful, and easy to use. The Unix operating system, on the other hand, is exceptionally reliable and stable, and there is a worldwide open software community that develops and tests Unix-based Web server software.

Site Management Tools

Another functionality of Web server software is site management tools. **Site management tools** are essential if you want to keep your site working, and if you want to understand how well it is working. Site management tools verify that links on pages are still valid and also identify orphan files, or files on the site that are not linked to any pages. By surveying the links on a Web site, a site management tool can quickly report on potential problems and errors that users may encounter. Your customers will not be impressed if they encounter a "404 Error: Page Does Not Exist" message on your Web site. Links to URLs that have moved or been deleted are called dead links; these

two-tier architecture
e-commerce system architecture in which a Web server responds to requests for Web pages and a database server provides backend data storage

multi-tier architecture
e-commerce system architecture in which the Web server is linked to a middle-tier layer that typically includes a series of application servers that perform specific tasks as well as to a backend layer of existing corporate systems

site management tools
verify that links on pages are still valid and also identify orphan files

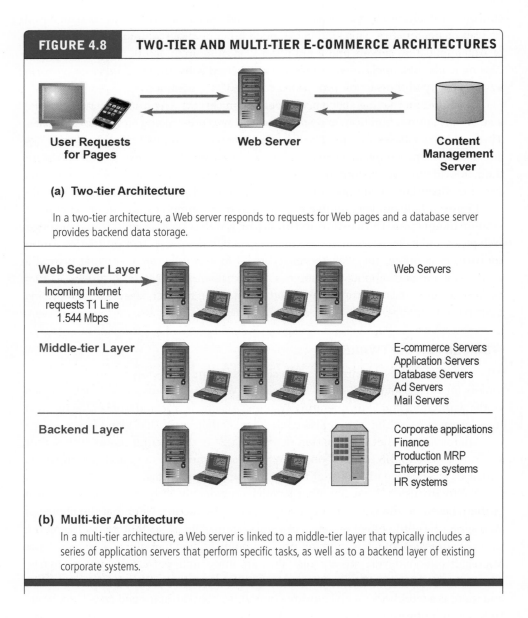

FIGURE 4.8 | **TWO-TIER AND MULTI-TIER E-COMMERCE ARCHITECTURES**

(a) Two-tier Architecture

In a two-tier architecture, a Web server responds to requests for Web pages and a database server provides backend data storage.

(b) Multi-tier Architecture

In a multi-tier architecture, a Web server is linked to a middle-tier layer that typically includes a series of application servers that perform specific tasks, as well as to a backend layer of existing corporate systems.

can cause error messages for users trying to access that link. Regularly checking that all links on a site are operational helps prevent irritation and frustration in users who may decide to take their business elsewhere to a better functioning site.

Dynamic Page Generation Tools

One of the most important innovations in Web site operation has been the development of dynamic page generation tools. The content of successful e-commerce sites is always changing, often day by day. There are new products and promotions, changing prices, news events, and stories of successful users. E-commerce sites must intensively interact with users who not only request pages but also request product, price, availability, and inventory information.

With **dynamic page generation**, the contents of a Web page are stored as objects in a database, rather than being hard-coded in HTML. When the user requests a Web page, the contents for that page are then fetched from the database. The objects are retrieved from the database using Common Gateway Interface (CGI), Active Server Pages (ASP), Java Server Pages (JSP), or other server-side programs. CGI, ASP, and JSP are described in the last section of this chapter. This technique is much more efficient than working directly in HTML code. It is much easier to change the contents of a database than it is to change the coding of an HTML page.

Dynamic page generation also enables the use of a content management system (CMS). A CMS is used to create and manage Web content. A CMS separates the design and presentation of content (such as HTML documents, images, video, audio) from the content creation process. The content is maintained in a database and dynamically linked to the Web site. A CMS usually includes templates that can be automatically applied to new and existing content, WYSIWYG editing tools that make it easy to edit and describe (tag) content, and collaboration, workflow, and document management tools. Typically, an experienced programmer is needed to install the system, but thereafter, content can be created and managed by non-technical staff. There are a wide range of commercial CMSs available, from top-end enterprise systems offered by Autonomy, EMC/Documentum, OpenText, IBM, and Oracle, to mid-market systems by Ixiasoft, PaperThin, and Ektron, as well as hosted software as a service (SaaS) versions by Clickability, CrownPeak Technology, and OmniUpdate. There are also several open source content management systems available, such as WordPress, Joomla, Drupal, OpenCms, and others.

dynamic page generation
the contents of a Web page are stored as objects in a database, rather than being hard-coded in HTML. When the user requests a Web page, the contents for that page are then fetched from the database

APPLICATION SERVERS

Web application servers are software programs that provide the specific business functionality required of a Web site. The basic idea of application servers is to isolate the business applications from the details of displaying Web pages to users on the front end and the details of connecting to databases on the back end. Application servers are a kind of middleware software that provides the glue connecting traditional corporate systems to the customer as well as all the functionality needed to conduct e-commerce. In the early years, a number of software firms developed specific separate programs for each function, but increasingly, these specific programs are being replaced by integrated software tools that combine all the needed functionality for an e-commerce site into a single development environment, a packaged software approach.

Table 4.3 illustrates the wide variety of application servers available in the marketplace. The table focuses on "sell-side" servers that are designed to enable selling products on the Web. So-called "buy-side" and "link" servers focus on the needs of businesses to connect with partners in their supply chains or find suppliers for specific parts and assemblies. These buy-side and link servers are described more fully in Chapter 12. There are several thousand software vendors that provide application server software. For Linux and Unix environments, many of these capabilities are available

Web application server
software programs that provide specific business functionality required of a Web site

TABLE 4.3	APPLICATION SERVERS AND THEIR FUNCTION
APPLICATION SERVER	FUNCTIONALITY
Catalog display	Provides a database for product descriptions and prices
Transaction processing (shopping cart)	Accepts orders and clears payments
List server	Creates and serves mailing lists and manages e-mail marketing campaigns
Proxy server	Monitors and controls access to main Web server; implements firewall protection
Mail server	Manages Internet e-mail
Audio/video server	Stores and delivers streaming media content
Chat server	Creates an environment for online real-time text and audio interactions with customers
News server	Provides connectivity and displays Internet news feeds
Fax server	Provides fax reception and sending using a Web server
Groupware server	Creates workgroup environments for online collaboration
Database server	Stores customer, product, and price information
Ad server	Maintains Web-enabled database of advertising banners that permits customized and personalized display of advertisements based on consumer behavior and characteristics
Auction server	Provides a transaction environment for conducting online auctions
B2B server	Implements buy, sell, and link marketplaces for commercial transactions

e-commerce merchant server software

software that provides the basic functionality needed for online sales, including an online catalog, order taking via an online shopping cart, and online credit card processing

free on the Internet from various sites. Most businesses—faced with this bewildering array of choices—choose to use integrated software tools called merchant server software.

E-COMMERCE MERCHANT SERVER SOFTWARE FUNCTIONALITY

E-commerce merchant server software provides the basic functionality needed for online sales, including an online catalog, order taking via an online shopping cart, and online credit card processing.

Online Catalog

A company that wants to sell products on the Web must have a list, or **online catalog**, of its products, available on its Web site. Merchant server software typically includes a database capability that will allow for construction of a customized online catalog. The complexity and sophistication of the catalog will vary depending on the size of the company and its product lines.

online catalog
list of products available on a Web site

Shopping Cart

Online **shopping carts** are much like their real-world equivalent; both allow shoppers to set aside desired purchases in preparation for checkout. The difference is that the online variety is part of a merchant server software program residing on the Web server, and allows consumers to select merchandise, review what they have selected, edit their selections as necessary, and then actually make the purchase by clicking a button. The merchant server software automatically stores shopping cart data.

shopping cart
allows shoppers to set aside desired purchases in preparation for checkout, review what they have selected, edit their selections as necessary, and then actually make the purchase by clicking a button

Credit Card Processing

A site's shopping cart typically works in conjunction with credit card processing software, which verifies the shopper's credit card and then puts through the debit to the card and the credit to the company's account at checkout. Integrated e-commerce software suites typically supply the software for this function. Otherwise, you will have to make arrangements with a variety of credit card processing banks and intermediaries.

MERCHANT SERVER SOFTWARE PACKAGES (E-COMMERCE SUITES)

Rather than build your site from a collection of disparate software applications, it is easier, faster, and generally more cost-effective to purchase a **merchant server software package** (also called an **e-commerce server suite**). Merchant server software/e-commerce suites offer an integrated environment that promises to provide most or all of the functionality and capabilities you will need to develop a sophisticated, customer-centric site. An important element of merchant sofware packages is a built-in shopping cart that can display merchandise, manage orders, and clear credit card transactions. E-commerce suites come in three general ranges of price and functionality.

merchant server software package (e-commerce server suite)
offers an integrated environment that provides most or all of the functionality and capabilities needed to develop a sophisticated, customer-centric site

Basic packages for elementary e-commerce business applications are provided by Bizland, HyperMart, and Yahoo Merchant Solutions. Webs.com also offers free Web building tools and hosting services. OSCommerce is a free, open source e-commerce suite used by many small start-up sites. PayPal can be used as a payment system on simple Web sites, and widgets can add interesting capabilities.

Midrange suites include IBM WebSphere Commerce Express Edition and Ascentium Commerce Server (formerly Microsoft Commerce Server). High-end enterprise solutions for large global firms are provided by IBM WebSphere's Commerce Professional and Enterprise Editions, ATG, GSI Commerce, Demandware, Magento, and others. There are several hundred software firms that provide e-commerce suites, which raises the costs of making sensible decisions on this matter. Many firms simply choose vendors with the best overall reputation. Quite often this turns out to be an expensive but ultimately workable solution.

WEB SERVICES AND OPEN SOURCE OPTIONS

While existing firms often have the financial capital to invest in commercial merchant server software suites, many small firms and start-up firms do not. They have to build their own Web sites, at least initially. There are really two options here, the key factor being how much programming experience and time you have. One option is to utilize the e-commerce merchant services provided by hosting sites such as Yahoo Merchant Solutions. For a $50 setup fee, and a starter plan of $39.95, the service will walk you through setting up your Web site and provide Web hosting, a shopping cart, technical help by phone, and payment processing. An e-commerce template is a pre-designed Web site that allows users to customize the look and feel of the site to fit their business needs and provides a standard set of functionality. Most templates today contain ready-to-go site designs with built-in e-commerce suite functionality like shopping carts, payment clearance, and site management tools.

open source software
software that is developed by a community of programmers and designers, and is free to use and modify

If you have considerable, or at least some, programming background, you can consider open source merchant server software. **Open source software** is software developed by a community of programmers and designers, and is free to use and modify. **Table 4.4** provides a description of some open source options.

TABLE 4.4	OPEN SOURCE SOFTWARE OPTIONS
MERCHANT SERVER FUNCTIONALITY	**OPEN SOURCE SOFTWARE**
Web server	Apache (the leading Web server for small and medium businesses)
Shopping cart, online catalog	Many providers: Zen-Cart.com, AgoraCart.com, X-Cart.com, osCommerce.com
Credit card processing	Many providers: Echo Internet Gateway; ASPDotNetStorefront. Credit card acceptance is typically provided in shopping cart software but you may need a merchant account from a bank as well.
Database	MySQL (the leading open source SQL database for businesses)
Programming/scripting language	PHP (a scripting language embedded in HTML documents but executed by the server providing server-side execution with the simplicity of HTML editing). Perl is an alternative language. JavaScript programs are client-side programs that provide user interface components. Ruby on Rails (RoR, Rails) is another popular open source Web application framework.
Analytics	Analytics keep track of your site's customer activities and the success of your Web advertising campaign. You can also use Google Analytics if you advertise on Google, which provides good tracking tools; most hosting services will provide these services as well. Other open source analytic tools include Piwik, CrawlTrack, and Open Web Analytics.

The advantage of using open source Web building tools is that you get exactly what you want, a truly customized unique Web site. The disadvantage is that it will take several months for a single programmer to develop the site and get all the tools to work together seamlessly. How many months do you want to wait before you get to market with your ideas?

One alternative to building a Web site first is to create a blog first, and develop your business ideas and a following of potential customers on your blog. Once you have tested your ideas with a blog, and attract a Web audience, you can then move on to developing a simple Web site.

THE HARDWARE PLATFORM

Whether you host your own site or outsource the hosting and operation of your site, you will need to understand certain aspects of the computing hardware platform. The **hardware platform** refers to all the underlying computing equipment that the system uses to achieve its e-commerce functionality.

hardware platform
refers to all the underlying computing equipment that the system uses to achieve its e-commerce functionality

RIGHT-SIZING YOUR HARDWARE PLATFORM: THE DEMAND SIDE

Demand on a Web site is fairly complex and depends primarily on the type of site you are operating. The number of simultaneous users in peak periods, the nature of customer requests, the type of content, the required security, the number of items in inventory, the number of page requests, and the speed of legacy applications that may be needed to supply data to the Web pages are all important factors in overall demand on a Web site system.

Certainly, one important factor to consider is the number of simultaneous users who will likely visit your site. In general, the load created by an individual customer on a server is typically quite limited and short-lived. Other factors to consider when estimating the demand on a Web site are the user profile and the nature of the content. If users request searches, registration forms, and order taking via shopping carts, then demands on processors will increase markedly.

RIGHT-SIZING YOUR HARDWARE PLATFORM: THE SUPPLY SIDE

Once you estimate the likely demand on your site, you will need to consider how to scale up your site to meet demand. We have already discussed one solution that requires very little thought: outsource the hosting of your Web site to a cloud-based service. See Chapter 3 for a discussion of cloud-based computing services. However, if you decide to host your own Web site, scalability is an important consideration. **Scalability** refers to the ability of a site to increase in size as demand warrants (see **Table 4.5**). **Vertical scaling** refers to increasing the processing power of individual components. **Horizontal scaling** refers to employing multiple computers to share the workload and increase the "footprint" of the installation.

A third alternative—improving the processing architecture—is a combination of vertical and horizontal scaling, combined with artful design decisions. **Table 4.6** lists some of the more common steps you can take to greatly improve performance of your site.

scalability
the ability of a site to increase in size as demand warrants

vertical scaling
increasing the processing power of individual components

horizontal scaling
employing multiple computers to share the workload

TABLE 4.5	VERTICAL AND HORIZONTAL SCALING TECHNIQUES
TECHNIQUE	APPLICATION
Use a faster computer	Deploy edge servers, presentation servers, data servers, etc.
Create a cluster of computers	Use computers in parallel to balance loads.
Use appliance servers	Use special-purpose computers optimized for their task.
Segment workload	Segment incoming work to specialized computers.
Batch requests	Combine related requests for data into groups, process as group.
Manage connections	Reduce connections between processes and computers to a minimum.
Aggregate user data	Aggregate user data from legacy applications in single data pools.
Cache	Store frequently used data in cache rather than on the disk.

4.4 OTHER E-COMMERCE SITE TOOLS

Now that you understand the key factors affecting the speed, capacity, and scalability of your Web site, we can consider some other important requirements.

WEB SITE DESIGN: BASIC BUSINESS CONSIDERATIONS

This is not a text about how to design Web sites. (In Chapter 6, we discuss Web site design issues from a marketing perspective.) Nevertheless, from a business manager's perspective, there are certain design objectives you must communicate to your Web site designers to let them know how you will evaluate their work. At a minimum, your customers will need to find what they need at your site, make a purchase, and leave. A Web site that annoys customers runs the risk of losing the customer forever. See **Table 4.7** for a list of the most common consumer complaints about Web sites. **Table 4.8** restates these negative experiences as positive goals for Web site design.

TABLE 4.6	IMPROVING THE PROCESSING ARCHITECTURE OF YOUR SITE
ARCHITECTURE IMPROVEMENT	DESCRIPTION
Separate static content from dynamic content	Use specialized servers for each type of workload.
Cache static content	Increase RAM to the gigabyte range and store static content in RAM.
Cache database lookup tables	Use cache tables used to look up database records.
Consolidate business logic on dedicated servers	Put shopping cart, credit card processing, and other CPU-intensive activity on dedicated servers.
Optimize ASP code	Examine your code to ensure it is operating efficiently.
Optimize the database schema	Examine your database search times and take steps to reduce access times.

TABLE 4.7	**E-COMMERCE WEB SITE FEATURES THAT ANNOY CUSTOMERS**

- Requiring user to view ad or Flash introduction before going to Web site content
- Pop-up and pop-under ads and windows
- Too many clicks to get to the content
- Links that don't work
- Confusing navigation; no search function
- Requirement to register and log in before viewing content or ordering
- Slow loading pages
- Content that is out of date
- Inability to use browser's Back button
- No contact information available (Web form only)
- Unnecessary splash/flash screens, animation, etc.
- Music or other audio that plays automatically
- Unprofessional design elements
- Text not easily legible due to size, color, format
- Typographical errors
- No or unclear returns policy

TOOLS FOR WEB SITE OPTIMIZATION

A Web site is only as valuable from a business perspective as the number of people who visit. Web site optimization (as we use it here) means how to attract lots of people to your site. The first stop for most customers looking for a product or service is to start with a search engine, and follow the listings on the page, usually starting with the top three to five listings, then glancing to the sponsored ads to the right. The higher you are on the search engine pages, the more traffic you will receive. Page 1 is much better than Page 2. So how do you get to Page 1 in the natural (unpaid) search listings? While every search engine is different, and none of them publish their algorithms for ranking pages, there are some basic ideas that work well:

TABLE 4.8	**THE EIGHT MOST IMPORTANT FACTORS IN SUCCESSFUL E-COMMERCE SITE DESIGN**
FACTOR	DESCRIPTION
Functionality	Pages that work, load quickly, and point the customer toward your product offerings
Informational	Links that customers can easily find to discover more about you and your products
Ease of use	Simple fool-proof navigation
Redundant navigation	Alternative navigation to the same content
Ease of purchase	One or two clicks to purchase
Multi-browser functionality	Site works with the most popular browsers
Simple graphics	Avoids distracting, obnoxious graphics and sounds that the user cannot control
Legible text	Avoids backgrounds that distort text or make it illegible

- **Metatags, titles, page contents:** Search engines "crawl" your site and identify keywords as well as title pages and then index them for use in search arguments. Pepper your pages with keywords that accurately describe what you say you do in your metatag site "description" and "keywords" sections of your source code. Experiment: use different keywords to see which work.

- **Identify market niches:** Instead of marketing "jewelry," be more specific, such as "Victorian jewelry," or "1950s jewelry" to attract small, specific groups who are intensely interested in period jewelry and closer to purchasing.

- **Offer expertise:** White papers, industry analyses, FAQ pages, guides, and histories are excellent ways to build confidence on the part of users and to encourage them to see your Web site as the place to go for help and guidance.

- **Get linked up:** Encourage other sites to link to your site; build a blog that attracts people and who will share your URL with others and post links in the process. List your site with Yahoo Directory. Build a Facebook page for your company, and think about using Twitter to develop a following or fan base for your products.

- **Buy ads:** Complement your natural search optimization efforts with paid search engine keywords and ads. Choose your keywords and purchase direct exposure on Web pages. You can set your budget and put a ceiling on it to prevent large losses. See what works, and observe the number of visits to your site produced by each keyword string.

- **Local e-commerce:** Developing a national market can take a long time. If your Web site is particularly attractive to local people, or involves products sold locally, use keywords that connote your location so people can find you nearby. Town, city, and region names in your keywords can be helpful, such as "Vermont cheese" or "San Francisco blues music."

TOOLS FOR INTERACTIVITY AND ACTIVE CONTENT

The more interactive a Web site is, the more effective it will be in generating sales and encouraging return visitors. Although functionality and ease of use are the supreme objectives in site design, you will also want to interact with users and present them with a lively, "active" experience. You will want to personalize the experience for customers by addressing their individual needs, and customize the content of your offerings based on their behavior or expressed desires. Simple interactions such as a customer submitting a name, along with more complex interactions involving credit cards, user preferences, and user responses to prompts, all require special programs. The following sections provide a brief description of some commonly used software tools for achieving high levels of site interactivity.

Common Gateway Interface (CGI)

Common Gateway Interface (CGI) is a set of standards for communication between a browser and a program running on a server that allows for interaction between the user and the server. CGI permits an executable program to access all the information within incoming requests from clients. The program can then generate all the output required to make up the return page (the HTML, script code, text, etc.), and send it

Common Gateway Interface (CGI)
a set of standards for communication between a browser and a program running on a server that allows for interaction between the user and the server

back to the client via the Web server. For instance, if a user clicks the My Shopping Cart button, the server receives this request and executes a CGI program. The CGI program retrieves the contents of the shopping cart from the database and returns it to the server. The server sends an HTML page that displays the contents of the shopping cart on the user's screen. Notice that all the computing takes place on the server side (this is why CGI programs and others like it are referred to as "server-side" programs).

CGI programs can be written in nearly any programming language as long as they conform to CGI standards. Currently, Perl is the most popular language for CGI scripting. Generally, CGI programs are used with Unix servers. CGI's primary disadvantage is that it is not highly scalable because a new process must be created for each request, thereby limiting the number of concurrent requests that can be handled. CGI scripts are best used for small to medium-sized applications that do not involve a high volume of user traffic.

Active Server Pages (ASP)

Active Server Pages (ASP) is Microsoft's version of server-side programming for Windows. Invented by Microsoft in late 1996, ASP has grown rapidly to become the major technique for server-side Web programming in the Windows environment. ASP enables developers to easily create and open records from a database and execute programs within an HTML page, as well as handle all the various forms of interactivity found on e-commerce sites. Like CGI, ASP permits an interaction to take place between the browser and the server. ASP uses the same standards as CGI for communication with the browser. ASP programs are restricted to use on Windows 2003/2000/NT Web servers running Microsoft's IIS Web server software.

Java, Java Server Pages (JSP), and JavaScript

Java is a programming language that allows programmers to create interactivity and active content on the client computer, thereby saving considerable load on the server. Java was invented by Sun Microsystems in 1990 as a platform-independent programming language for consumer electronics. The idea was to create a language whose programs (so-called Write Once Run Anywhere [WORA] programs) could operate on any computer regardless of operating system. This would be possible if every operating system at the time (Macintosh, Windows, Unix, DOS, and mainframe MVS systems) had a Java Virtual Machine (VM) installed that would interpret the Java programs for that environment.

By 1995, it had become clear, however, that Java was more applicable to the Web than to consumer electronics. Java programs (known as Java applets) could be downloaded to the client over the Web and executed entirely on the client's computer. Applet tags could be included in an HTML page. To enable this, each browser would have to include a Java VM. Today, the leading browsers do include a VM to run Java programs. When the browser accesses a page with an applet, a request is sent to the server to download and execute the program and allocate page space to display the results of the program. Java can be used to display interesting graphics, create interactive environments (such as a mortgage calculator), and directly access the Web server.

Active Server Pages (ASP)
a proprietary software development tool that enables programmers using Microsoft's IIS package to build dynamic pages

Java
a programming language that allows programmers to create interactivity and active content on the client computer, thereby saving considerable load on the server

Java Server Pages (JSP)

like CGI and ASP, a Web page coding standard that allows developers to dynamically generate Web pages in response to user requests

Java Server Pages (JSP), like CGI and ASP, is a Web page coding standard that allows developers to use a combination of HTML, JSP scripts, and Java to dynamically generate Web pages in response to user requests. JSP uses Java "servlets," small Java programs that are specified in the Web page and run on the Web server to modify the Web page before it is sent to the user who requested it. JSP is supported by most of the popular application servers on the market today.

JavaScript

a programming language invented by Netscape that is used to control the objects on an HTML page and handle interactions with the browser

JavaScript is a programming language invented by Netscape that is used to control the objects on an HTML page and handle interactions with the browser. It is most commonly used to handle verification and validation of user input, as well as to implement business logic. For instance, JavaScript can be used on customer registration forms to confirm that a valid phone number, zip code, or even e-mail address has been given. Before a user finishes completing a form, the e-mail address given can be tested for validity. JavaScript appears to be much more acceptable to corporations and other environments in large part because it is more stable and also it is restricted to the operation of requested HTML pages.

Web 2.0 Design Elements

widget

a small, pre-built chunk of code that executes automatically in your HTML Web page; capable of performing a wide variety of tasks

One easy way to pump up the energy on your Web site is to include some appropriate widgets (sometimes called gadgets, plug-ins, or snippets). **Widgets** are small chunks of code that execute automatically in your HTML Web page. They are pre-built and many are free. Social networks and blogs use widgets to present users with content drawn from around the Web (news headlines from specific news sources, announcements, press releases, and other routine content), calendars, clocks, weather, live TV, games, and other functionality. You can copy the code to an HTML Web page.

Mashups are a little more complicated and involve pulling functionality and data from one program and including it in another. The most common mashup involves using Google Maps data and software and combining it with other data. For instance, if you have a local real estate Web site, you can download Google Maps and satellite image applications to your site so visitors can get a sense of the neighborhood. There are thousands of Google Map mashups.

The point of these Web 2.0 applications is to enhance user interest and engagement with your Web site and brand.

4.5 DEVELOPING A MOBILE WEB SITE AND BUILDING MOBILE APPLICATIONS

Today, building a Web site is just one part of developing an e-commerce presence. Given that 122 million U.S. Internet users (about 50% of all Internet users) access the Web at least part of the time from mobile devices, firms today need to develop mobile Web sites, mobile Web apps, as well as native apps, in order to interact with customers, suppliers, and employees. Deciding which of these extended Web presence tools to use is a first step.

mobile Web site

version of a regular desktop Web site that is scaled down in content and navigation

There are three kinds of mobile e-commerce software offerings to consider, each with unique advantages and costs. A **mobile Web site** is a version of a regular Web site that is scaled down in content and navigation so that users can find what they want and move quickly to a decision or purchase. You can see the difference between a regular Web site and a mobile site by visiting the Amazon Web site from your desktop computer and then a smartphone or tablet computer. Amazon's mobile site is a cleaner, more interactive site suitable for finger navigation, and efficient consumer decision making. Like traditional Web sites, mobile Web sites run on a firm's servers, and are built using standard Web tools such as server side HTML, Linux, PHP, and SQL. Like all Web sites, the user must be connected to the Web and performance will depend on bandwidth. Generally, mobile Web sites operate more slowly than traditional Web sites viewed on a desktop computer connected to a broadband office network. Most large firms today have mobile Web sites.

A new trend in the development of mobile Web sites is the use of **responsive Web design** tools and design techniques, which make it possible to design a Web site that automatically adjusts its layout and display according to the user's screen resolution, whether a desktop, tablet, or smartphone. Responsive design tools include HTML5 and CSS3 and its three key design principles involve using flexible grid-based layouts, flexible images and media, and media queries.

A **mobile Web app** is an application built to run on the mobile Web browser built into a smartphone or tablet computer. In the case of Apple, the native browser is Safari. Generally they are built to mimic the qualities of native apps using HTML5 and Java. Mobile Web apps are specifically designed for the mobile platform in terms of screen size, finger navigation, and graphical simplicity. Mobile Web apps can support complex interactions used in games and rich media, perform real-time, on-the-fly calculations, and can be geo-sensitive using the smartphone's built-in global positioning system (GPS) function. Mobile Web apps typically operate faster than mobile Web sites but not as fast as native apps.

A **native app** is an application designed specifically to operate using the mobile device's hardware and operating system. These stand-alone programs can connect to the Internet to download and upload data, and can operate on this data even when not connected to the Internet. Download a book to an app reader, disconnect from the Internet, and read your book. Because the various types of smartphones have different hardware and operating systems, apps are not "one size fits all" and therefore need to be developed for different mobile platforms. An Apple app that runs on an iPhone cannot operate on Android phones. As you learned in Chapter 3, native apps are built using different programming languages depending on the device for which they are intended, which is then compiled into binary code, and which executes extremely fast on mobile devices, much faster than HTML or Java-based mobile Web apps. For this reason, native apps are ideal for games, complex interactions, on-the-fly calculations, graphic manipulations, and rich media advertising.

PLANNING AND BUILDING A MOBILE WEB PRESENCE

What is the "right" mobile Web presence for your firm? The answer depends on identifying the business objectives, and from these, deriving the information requirements of your mobile presence. The same kind of systems analysis and design (SAD) reasoning

responsive Web design
Tools and design principles that automatically adjust the layout of a Web site depending on user screen resolution

mobile Web app
application built to run on the mobile Web browser built into a smartphone or tablet computer

native app
application designed specifically to operate using the mobile device's hardware and operating system

described earlier in the chapter is needed for planning and building a mobile presence, although there are important differences.

The first step is to identify the business objectives you are trying to achieve. **Table 4.9** illustrates the thought process for the analysis stage of building a mobile presence. Once you have a clear sense of business objectives, you will be able to describe the kind of system functionality that is needed and specify the information requirements for your mobile presence.

After you have identified the business objectives, system functionality, and information requirements, you can think about how to design and build the system. Now is the time to consider which to develop: a mobile Web site, a mobile Web app, or a native app. From our previous discussion, if your objective is branding or building community, then a native app is recommended because you can display rich interactive media and highly interactive, efficient games. If your objective is to drive sales, advertise, or gather feedback on specific products, all of which require an online database of products, then a mobile Web site or mobile Web app is recommended because high-speed interactions are not needed, and these objectives are really just an extension of your main desktop Web site.

MOBILE WEB PRESENCE: DESIGN CONSIDERATIONS

Designing a mobile presence is somewhat different from traditional desktop Web site design because of different hardware, software, and consumer expectations. **Table 4.10** describes some of the major differences.

Designers need to take mobile platform constraints into account when designing for the mobile platform. File sizes should be kept smaller and the number of files sent to the user reduced. Focus on a few, powerful graphics, and minimize the number of images sent to the user. Simplify choice boxes and lists so the user can easily scroll and touch-select the options.

TABLE 4.9	SYSTEMS ANALYSIS FOR BUILDING A MOBILE PRESENCE	
BUSINESS OBJECTIVE	**SYSTEM FUNCTIONALITY**	**INFORMATION REQUIREMENTS**
Drive sales	Digital catalog; product database	Product descriptions, photos, SKUs, inventory
Branding	Showing how customers use your products	Videos and rich media; product and customer demonstrations
Building customer community	Interactive experiences, games with multiple players	Games, contests, forums, social sign-up to Facebook
Advertising and promotion	Coupons and flash sales for slow-selling items	Product descriptions, coupon management, and inventory management
Gathering customer feedback	Ability to retrieve and store user inputs including text, photos, and video	Customer sign-in and identification; customer database

TABLE 4.10	UNIQUE FEATURES THAT MUST BE TAKEN INTO ACCOUNT WHEN DESIGNING A MOBILE WEB PRESENCE
FEATURE	IMPLICATIONS FOR MOBILE PLATFORM
Hardware	Mobile hardware is smaller, and there are more resource constraints in data storage and processing power.
Connectivity	The mobile platform is constrained by slower connection speeds than desktop Web sites.
Displays	Mobile displays are much smaller and require simplification. Some screens are not good in sunlight.
Interface	Touch-screen technology introduces new interaction routines different from the traditional mouse and keyboard. The mobile platform is not a good data entry tool but can be a good navigational tool.

MOBILE WEB PRESENCE: PERFORMANCE AND COST CONSIDERATIONS

If you don't have an existing Web site, the most efficient process is to build a site in the first instance using responsive Web design, as previously described. If you already have a Web site that you don't want to totally redevelop, the least expensive path is to resize it to create a smartphone-friendly mobile site. Doing so typically will not require a complete redesign effort. You will need to reduce the graphics and text, simplify the navigation, and focus on improving the customer experience so you do not confuse people. Because your customers might still use a relatively slow 3G cell connection, you will need to lighten up the amount of data you send. Also, given the difficulty of customer data entry on a mobile device, you cannot expect customers to happily enter long strings of numbers or text characters. For marketing clarity, make sure the brand images used on the mobile Web site match those on the traditional Web site. Small companies can develop a mobile Web site for under $10,000 using the same consultants and servers as their existing Web site.

Building a mobile Web app that uses the mobile device's browser requires more effort and cost than developing a mobile Web site, suffers from the same limitations as any browser-based application, but does offer some advantages such as better graphics, more interactivity, and faster local calculations as, for instance, in mobile geo-location applications like Foursquare that require local calculations of position and then communication with the site's Web server.

The most expensive path to a mobile presence is to build a native app. Native apps can require more extensive programming expertise. In addition, virtually none of the elements used in your existing Web site can be reused, and you will need to redesign the entire logic of the interface and carefully think out the customer experience. For instance, there is a fairly stable HTML traditional Web site interface with buttons, graphics, videos, and ads that has developed over the last decade. This is not true for apps. There is no set of standards or expectations even on the part of users—every app looks different from every other app. This means the user confronts large variations in app design, so your interface must be quite simple and obvious. Many of the bells and whistles found on the large desktop Web site screen cannot be used in mobile apps. You'll need even greater simplification and focus. These weaknesses are also native apps' greatest strength: you have the opportunity to create a really stunning, unique customer experience where users can interact with your brand. If you want an intense branding experience with your customers, where interaction between your brand and customers is effortless and efficient, then native apps are the best choice.

The *Insight on Technology* case, *Building a Mobile Presence,* takes a further look at some of the considerations involved for three very different companies--Decker Outdoors Corporation, USAA, and Ryland Homes.

INSIGHT ON TECHNOLOGY

BUILDING A MOBILE PRESENCE

By 2013, more people will use their mobile phones than PCs to go online, and there will be one mobile device for every person on earth by 2015. The number of Web searches performed on mobile devices has more than quadrupled since 2010. Customers expect, and even demand, to be able to use a mobile device of their choice to obtain information or perform a transaction anywhere and at any time via apps or mobile sites.

Developing mobile apps or a mobile Web site has some special challenges. The user experience on a mobile device is fundamentally different from that on a PC. There are special features on mobile devices such as location-based services that give firms the potential to interact with customers in meaningful new ways. Firms need to be able to take advantage of those features while delivering an experience that is appropriate to a small screen. There are multiple mobile platforms to work with, each requiring its own version of an app. They also need to understand how and why their customers use mobile devices.

Deckers Outdoor Corporation, the parent company of brands such as UGG Australia, spent considerable time studying its customers' mobile behavior. Decker's analysis showed that when consumers use mobile devices inside a Deckers store, what is most important is a seamless interaction. Customers want to be able to look at a product on their phones and see the same information inside the store, plus some additional information, such as consumer reviews.

USAA, the giant financial services company serving members of the U.S. military and their families, is using mobile technology to refine its business processes and provide simpler and more powerful ways for customers to interact with the company. USAA launched its Web site in 2000 and went mobile 10 years later, with about 90% of its interactions with customers taking place on these two self-service channels. In 2011, USAA handled 183 million customer contacts through the mobile channel alone, and expects the mobile channel will be its primary point of contact with customers in the next two years. USAA has 100 dedicated mobile developers writing apps for devices using the iPhone, iPad, and Android operating systems, along with apps for the Black-Berry and Windows Phone. USAA developed a smartphone accident report and claims app that enables customers to snap a photo and submit a claim directly from the site of an accident using their phones. The mobile app also displays loan and credit card balances, shopping services, homeowners and auto insurance policy information, Home Circle and Auto Circle buying services, retirement products and information, ATM and taxi locators, and a community feature that lets users see what others are posting about USAA on Twitter, Facebook, and YouTube.

Ryland Homes revamped its mobile Web site in March 2011 to increase sales leads by helping potential customers with mobile phones find its locations, look at its products, register with the company, and call directly. Ryland's development team made the site easier to read and capable of fitting on a smartphone or tablet screen without requiring users to pinch and zoom. Ryland focused on features such as location-based driving directions to nearby communities, clickable phone numbers, and brief online registrations to increase the chances of making a sale. The site shows nearby communities in order of distance, based on the location of the mobile device.

SOURCES: "Mobility Transforms the Customer Relationship," by Samuel Greengard, *Baseline*, February 2012; "How Deckers Used a Mobile Application to Build Customer Traffic," by William Atkinson, *CIO Insight*, November 9, 2011; "Going Mobile: A Portable Approach to Process Improvement," Business Agility Insights, June 2012, and Google Inc., Ryland Homes Opens Doors to Local Sales with Mobile Site for Home-Buyers, 2011.

CASE STUDY

Orbitz Charts
Its Mobile Trajectory

When it comes to mobile apps and gauging their impact on consumers and business, there's no better industry to look at than the online travel industry and its airline and hotel reservation systems. And there's no better company in this industry in developing mobile apps than Orbitz Worldwide Inc., the leading online travel site. Orbitz connects consumers to plane tickets from 400 airlines, hotel rooms from 80,000 hotels worldwide, as well as rental cars, cruises, and vacation packages. On a busy day, consumers will make an estimated 2 million searches for airline reservations and more than 1 million hotel reservations. In June 2012, Orbitz released its latest Apple iOS app, which has its desktop reservation system. The new app allows users to arrange for flight, lodging, and car rental reservations in a continuous stream with minimal data entry from the user. Orbitz claims it is the fastest mobile travel app in the industry. For travelers on the go, the new app provides nearly real-time travel planning anywhere and anytime—no desktop needed.

Orbitz was the first Internet travel company to offer a WML-only (Wireless Markup Language) mobile Web site, way back in 2006. Users could check flight statuses for 27 airlines, some of which did not yet have a mobile site, and search for hotels in the largest destination markets in the United States. They also had access to a personal page dedicated to itineraries for Orbitz-booked trips and links to autodial Orbitz customer service. Additional services added in 2007 included enabling mobile users to view average wait times to get through security and available Wi-Fi services for a particular airport. A data feedback system was instituted to compute check-in delays and taxi line wait-times based on customer-inputted experiences. In 2008, Orbitz added an iPhone/iPod–specific app with the same capabilities for itinerary, flight status, WiFi availability, and wait-time checking as well as the ability to view weather and traffic conditions, reports from other travelers, and information about where to park and ground transportation.

In 2010, Orbitz launched a redesigned mobile Web site, and a unveiled a smartphone app for Google Inc.'s Android operating system along with an updated iPhone app. Users of any Web-enabled device could now access a tool set comparable to the standard e-commerce site to purchase flights, book car rentals, and secure hotel accommodations, including same-day reservations. The native apps and redesigned mobile site, developed in-house with input from an unnamed outside vendor, also offered the standard e-commerce site service called Price Assurance, which guarantees consumers an automatic refund if another Orbitz customer books the same service for less.

In Spring 2011, Orbitz was first-to-market with an m-commerce site specifically for business users. Orbitz decided that the optimal solution was to construct a mobile Web site that could be accessed from any Web-enabled device rather than build native apps

SOURCES: "Orbitz, Inc. History," FundingUniverse.com, accessed September 2, 2012; "How to Embark upon an M-commerce Redesign," by Kevin Woodward, *Internet Retailer*, August 10, 2012; "Top 10 Mobile Commerce Apps of Q2," by Rimma Kats, *Mobile Commerce Daily*, July 6, 2012; "Orbitz Revamps iPhone App with Focus on Streamlined Booking, Deals," by Lauren Johnson, *Mobile Commerce Daily*, June 22, 2012; "Orbitz Rolls Out Major Update to App for iPhone and iPod Touch," Orbitz, June 21, 2012; "Orbitz Releases New Travel App," by Emily Brennan, *New York Times*, June 21, 2012; "Orbitz Launches New iPhone App, Bets on Mobile Growth," by Erica Ogg, Gigaom.com, June 21, 2012; "Orbitz: Mobile Searches May Yield Better Hotel Deals," by Barbara De Lollis, *USA Today*, May, 10, 2012; Orbitz Worldwide Inc., Form 10-K for the fiscal year ended December 31, 2011, Securities and Exchange Commission, filed March 31, 2012; "Orbitz Launches Revamped Mobile Site, Daily Deals to Capitalize on Last-Minute Travel," by Lauren Johnson, *Mobile Commerce Daily*, December 13, 2011; "Orbitz Travels the M-commerce Site Redesign Route," by Bill Siwicki, *Internet Retailer*, December 13, 2011; "Orbitz Unveils Powerful New Mobile Website and Introduces New 'Mobile Steals' Program Offering Discounted Mobile-only Rates on Hotels," Orbitz, December 12, 2011; "Orbitz Creates Intuitive Search-and-Book Experience via iPad App," by Rimma Kats, *Mobile Commerce Daily*, July 7, 2011; "Get a Room," by Kevin Woodward, *Internet Retailer*, July 7, 2011; "Orbitz Launches New 'Orbitz Hotels' App for iPad®," Orbitz, July 6, 2011; "Orbitz for Business Debuts Mobile Booking Site Targeting Corporate Travelers," by Dan Butcher, *Mobile Commerce Daily*, April 15, 2011; "Two Travel Providers Make Mobile moves," by Katie Deatsch, *Internet Retailer*, November 16, 2010; "Orbitz Launches Native iPhone® and Android™ Applications That Allow Consumers to Shop and Book Flight, Hotel and Car Rental Options," Orbitz, Nov 15, 2010; "Orbitz for iPhone Review," by Joe Seifi, AppSafari.com, November 13th, 2008; "Orbitz Mobile," by Dennis Bournique, WAPReview.com, August 15, 2006.

for multiple different devices. The goals were to exclude no one, provide a uniform and yet native app-like experience for each type of device, and deliver full travel policy compliance for business clients. The Orbitz for Business mobile Web site delivers the same set of tools enjoyed by the consumer market, applies saved policy controls to new reservations, and delivers both global and company-specific messages on both the home page and in search results to assist business travelers in adhering to company guidelines.

In July 2011, Orbitz added a hotel-booking app for iPad users, "Hotels by Orbitz." When launched, the GPS-enabled app displays a map of the user's current location. Pins dot the map to indicate hotel locations, which can be touched to display the establishment name, address, phone number, and cost, providing instant price comparison. Hotels can also be selected from a scrolling list to the left of the map. The app provides the ability to book a hotel room in just three taps.

In 2012, Orbitz rolled out second-generation versions of its mobile site and apps, designed to meet evolving consumer expectations. Three main improvements were made to the m-commerce site. First, it was optimized to accommodate the small screen size of any Web-enabled mobile device. Second, it was updated to accommodate swiping gestures, and third, it was revamped to expedite touch screen transactions. Swiping, once the exclusive province of apps, can now be accomplished using the newest version of Hypertext Markup Language, HTML5. What's more, HTML5 enables m-commerce sites to incorporate capabilities identical to mobile apps simply by tapping into the built-in functionality of mobile devices, including GPS. Orbitz employed HTML5 to enable customers to swipe through pictures of hotels. Mobile transaction speed was given a boost through the implementation of a new proprietary global online travel agency platform. The platform speeds up page loading by essentially creating mobile Web pages on the fly from the standard e-commerce Web page and eliminating redirects. The standard Web page is passed through a page-rendering framework tool that instantly produces an HTML5 version that can exploit inherent smartphone capabilities.

Looking to capitalize on the market research findings that highlighted the burgeoning role of Web-enabled mobile devices in securing same-day accommodations, Orbitz also instituted mobile-exclusive same-day deals. These specials, called Mobile Steals, are available both on the m-commerce site and through the Hotels by Orbitz app, which was also released for the Android and iPhone. Last-minute perishable goods are available in more than 50 markets worldwide, benefitting both lodging proprietors and consumers. Proprietors are able to fill rooms that might otherwise remain vacant, and consumers enjoy savings of up to 50% off the standard rate.

In June 2012, Orbitz released a redesigned Apple iOS app. The new app allows users to arrange for flight, lodging, and car rental reservations in a continuous stream with minimal data entry from the user. Orbitz claims it is the fastest mobile travel app in the industry. For travelers on the go, the new app provides nearly real-time travel planning anywhere and anytime—no desktop needed.

In order to verify that its goals for the app had been achieved, Orbitz commissioned a speed comparison study. The travel apps, m-commerce sites, and e-commerce sites of its major competitors, including Kayak, Expedia, Priceline, and Travelocity, were pitted against the Orbitz iPhone app. The study found that Orbitz iPhone app users were able to book a typical flight, hotel reservation, and car rental twice as fast as people using its iPhone app competitors. The Orbitz iPhone app transaction speed also surpassed comparable iPad and Android apps as well as desktop e-commerce site experiences.

Orbitz's future plans include optimizing consumers' ability to fulfill future travel needs by incorporating a synchronization mechanism between their mobile devices and their desktops. Plans are also already underway to update the iPad app so that it is a full-service rather than just a hotel-booking tool.

Case Study Questions

1. When compared to traditional desktop customers, why are mobile phone users much more likely to book a room or airline reservation for the same day?

2. Why did Orbitz management decide to construct a mobile web site for corporate users rather than a native app?

3. Why did Orbitz build native apps for each mobile platform (iOS and Android) instead of a single mobile Web site?

4.7 REVIEW

KEY CONCEPTS

■ Understand the questions you must ask and answer, and the steps you should take, in developing an e-commerce presence.

Questions you must ask and answer when developing an e-commerce presence include:
- What is your vision and how do you hope to accomplish it?
- What is your business and revenue model?
- Who and where is the target audience?
- What are the characteristics of the marketplace?
- Where is the content coming from?
- Conduct a SWOT analysis
- Develop an e-commerce presence map
- Develop a timeline
- Develop a detailed budget

■ Explain the process that should be followed in building an e-commerce presence.

Factors you must consider when building an e-commerce site include:
- Hardware architecture
- Software
- Telecommunications capacity

- Site design
- Human resources
- Organizational capabilities

The systems development life cycle (a methodology for understanding the business objectives of a system and designing an appropriate solution) for building an e-commerce Web site involves five major steps:

- Identify the specific business objectives for the site, and then develop a list of system functionalities and information requirements.
- Develop a system design specification (both logical design and physical design).
- Build the site, either by in-house personnel or by outsourcing all or part of the responsibility to outside contractors.
- Test the system (unit testing, system testing, and acceptance testing).
- Implement and maintain the site.

■ **Describe the major issues surrounding the decision to outsource site development and/or hosting.**

Advantages of building a site in-house include:
- The ability to change and adapt the site quickly as the market demands
- The ability to build a site that does exactly what the company needs

Disadvantages of building a site in-house include:
- The costs may be higher.
- The risks of failure may be greater, given the complexity of issues such as security, privacy, and inventory management.
- The process may be more time-consuming than if you had hired an outside specialist firm to manage the effort.
- Staff may experience a longer learning curve that delays your entry into the market.

■ **Identify and understand the major considerations in choosing software and hardware for an e-commerce site.**

All e-commerce sites require basic Web server software to answer requests from customers for HTML and XML pages. When choosing Web server software, companies are also choosing what operating system the site will run on. Apache, which runs on the Unix system, is the market leader.

Web servers provide a host of services, including:
- Processing user requests
- Security services
- File transfer
- Search engine
- Data capture
- E-mail
- Site management tools

Dynamic server software allows sites to deliver dynamic content. Web application server programs enable a wide range of e-commerce functionality, including creating a customer database, creating an e-mail promotional program, and accepting and processing orders, as well as many other services.

E-commerce merchant server software is another important software package that provides catalog displays, information storage and customer tracking, order taking (shopping cart), and credit card purchase processing.

Speed, capacity, and scalability are three of the most important considerations when selecting an operating system, and therefore the hardware that it runs on.

■ **Identify additional tools that can improve Web site performance.**

In addition to providing a speedy Web site, companies must also strive to have a well-designed site that encourages visitors to buy. Commonly used software tools include:

- *Common Gateway Interface (CGI) scripts*—a set of standards for communication between a browser and a program on a server that allows for interaction between the user and the server
- *Active Server Pages (ASP)*—a Microsoft tool that also permits interaction between the browser and the server
- *Java applets*—programs written in the Java programming language that also provide interactivity
- *JavaScript*—used to validate user input, such as an e-mail address

■ **Understand the important considerations involved in building a mobile Web site and developing mobile applications.**

- When developing a mobile presence, it is important to understand the difference between a mobile Web site, mobile Web apps, and native apps.
- The first step is to identify business objectives, since they help determine which type of mobile presence is best.
- Design should take into account mobile platform constraints.
- Developing a mobile Web site is likely to be the least expensive option; mobile Web apps require more effort and cost; native apps are likely to be the most expensive to develop.

QUESTIONS

1. Name the main pieces of the e-commerce site-building puzzle.
2. Define the systems development life cycle and discuss the various steps involved in creating an e-commerce site.
3. Discuss the differences between a simple logical and simple physical Web site design.
4. Why is system testing important? Name the three types of testing and their relation to each other.
5. Why is a Web site so costly to maintain? Discuss the main factors that impact cost.
6. What are the main differences between single-tier and multi-tier site architecture?
7. Name the basic functionalities a Web server should provide.
8. What are the three main factors to consider when choosing the best hardware platform for your Web site?
9. Compare and contrast the various scaling methods. Explain why scalability is a key business issue for Web sites.

10. What are the most important factors impacting Web site design, and how do they affect a site's operation?

11. What are Java and JavaScript? What role do they play in Web site design?

PROJECTS

1. Go to Webs.com or NetworkSolutions.com. Both sites allow you to create a simple e-tailer Web site for a free trial period. Create a Web site. The site should feature at least four pages, including a home page, product page, shopping cart, and contact page. Extra credit will be given for additional complexity and creativity. Come to class prepared to present your e-tailer concept and Web site.

2. Visit several e-commerce sites, not including those mentioned in this chapter, and evaluate the effectiveness of the sites according to the eight basic criteria/ functionalities listed in Table 4.8. Choose one site you feel does an excellent job on all the aspects of an effective site and create an electronic presentation, including screen shots, to support your choice.

3. Imagine that you are the head of information technology for a fast-growth e-commerce start-up. You are in charge of development of the company's Web site. Consider your options for building the site in-house with existing staff, or outsourcing the entire operation. Decide which strategy you believe is in your company's best interest and create a brief presentation outlining your position. Why choose that approach? And what are the estimated associated costs, compared with the alternative? (You'll need to make some educated guesses here—don't worry about being exact.)

4. Choose one of the open source Web content management systems such as WordPress, Joomla, or Drupal or another of your own choosing and prepare an evaluation chart. Which system would you choose and why?

CHAPTER 5

E-commerce Security and Payment Systems

After reading this chapter, you will be able to:

- Understand the scope of e-commerce crime and security problems.
- Describe the key dimensions of e-commerce security.
- Identify the key security threats in the e-commerce environment.
- Describe how technology helps protect the security of messages sent over the Internet.
- Identify the tools used to establish secure Internet communications channels and protect networks, servers, and clients.
- Identify the major e-commerce payment systems in use today.

Cyberwar:

MAD 2.0

Over the past several years, Google and China have been fighting an undeclared war. In January 2010, Google was victim of a simple phishing attack that resulted in China stealing some of its proprietary source code. In March 2011, Google blamed the Chinese government for manipulating and disrupting Gmail and Google Talk. In June 2012, Google detected a possible "state-sponsored" cyberattack against their users' Gmail accounts.

At least 17 cyberespionage rings based in China have been identified. Their modus operandi is to insert spyware through phishing e-mails. Evidence suggests that this is a well-financed, centralized effort. The seven economic objectives in China's 12th Five-Year Plan (2011–2015) parallel the corporate and research targets, including biotech and technology manufacturing.

© Rafal Olechowski / Fotolia

According to 2012 congressional testimony, over the past 12 years, China has penetrated the networks of at least 760 ISPs, corporations, research universities, and government agencies, garnering an estimated $500 billion in U.S. corporate assets. Cyberespionage is a far quicker and cheaper path to economic dominance than independent research and development. The magnitude of this wealth transfer is difficult to quantify because there are so many unknown variables. How quickly can source code, blueprints, chemical formulas, and other data be translated into products that can outcompete?

In response to these revelations, the Obama administration publicly called out the Chinese government, which has staunchly denied all allegations, naming it the top cyberthreat to U.S. firms. The House of Representatives passed the Cyber Intelligence Sharing and Protection Act (CISPA) in April 2012. CISPA would allow ISPs and other Internet companies to collect, analyze, and share with the National Security Agency (NSA) and other agencies activities perceived as possible threats. Likewise, it establishes conditions and procedures through which agencies would be permitted to share evidence, including classified information, with companies. Respected digital rights advocacy groups such as the Electronic Frontier Foundation oppose CISPA because the language is so ambiguous as to not rule out ISPs, e-mail providers, and other Internet companies collecting virtu-

SOURCES: "Malware Aimed at Iran Hit Five Sites, Report Says," by John Markoff, *New York Times,* February 11, 2011; "Israeli Test on Worm Called Crucial in Iran Nuclear Delay," by William Broad, *New York Times,* January 15, 2011; "Stuxnet Malware is 'Weapon' Out to Destroy...Iran's Bushehr Nuclear Plant?", by Mark Clayton, *Christian Science Monitor,* September 21, 2010; "Steps Taken to End Impasse Over Cybersecurity Talks," by John Markoff, *New York Times,* July 16, 2010; "Obama and Cyber Defense," by L. Gordon Crovitz, *Wall Street Journal,* June 29, 2009; Cyberattack on Google Said to Hit Password System," by John Markoff, *New York Times,* April 10, 2010; *Cyber War: The Next Threat to National Security and What to Do About It,* by Richard A. Clarke and Robert K. Knake, Ecco/ HarperCollins Publishers, March 2010; "Mutually Assured Destruc- tion 2.0," *New York Times,* January 26, 2010; "Cyberwar: In Digital Combat, U.S. Finds No Easy Deterrent," by John Markoff, David Sanger, and Thom Shanker, *New York Times,* January 26, 2010; "Google, Citing Attack, Threatens to Exit China," by Andrew Jacobs, *New York Times,* January 12, 2010.

ally unlimited dossiers on their users. The corresponding Senate bill, the Cybersecurity Act of 2012, has not passed.

With CISPA stalled in Congress, and deeming it ineffectual in any event, Richard Clarke, former special adviser on cybersecurity to U.S. President George W. Bush, penned an April 2012 New York Times editorial calling on President Obama to pass an executive order. Without authorization, no government agency can step in to stop corporate attacks. Internal documents indicate that the administration is crafting an order to establish a Department of Homeland Security program, leaving current privacy protections intact. Privacy advocates favor this route because there would be no cybersecurity exception granting immunity to corporations.

While China has been busy employing cyberespionage to climb its way to the unrivaled apex of the economic heap, other nations are engaged in a different form of cyberwarfare. U.S. cyberspies concentrate on national security. Foreign governments, military, and terrorist groups are targeted for defense purposes. The Stuxnet worm is a high-visibility example of this. First discovered in June 2010, Stuxnet was designed to disable the com- puters that control the centrifuges in Iran's uranium enrichment process. A secret joint United States-Israel operation code-named Olympic Games is believed to have created Stuxnet. In another strike against Iran in April 2012, malware wiped computers in the Iranian Oil Ministry and the National Iranian Oil Company clean. Initial reports identi- fied the malware as a Trojan dubbed Flame. Flame was suspected of pursuing multiple Iranian objectives including key oil export hubs. Iran's National Computer Emergency Response Team released a tool to detect and destroy Flame in early May.

Although cyberattacks are reported as discrete incidents, they are in fact ongoing activities punctuated by major events. In the United States, the public Web, air-traffic control systems, healthcare, and telecommunications services have all been attacked. Both China and Russia have been caught trying to infiltrate the U.S. electric-power grid, leaving behind software code to be used to disrupt the system. In July 2010, after 10 years of debate, 15 nations including the United States and Russia agreed on a set of recommendations that it was hoped would lead to an international treaty banning com- puter warfare. It never materialized.

Because cyberweapons are both cheap and potent, more than 100 nations have cy- berwarfare capabilities and programs. Digital security companies can only discover a fraction of the existing malware. And because telecommunication security necessarily requires inspecting content, democratic nations' attempts to pass cybersecurity legislation will meet opposition from privacy groups. An international treaty seems our best hope of avoiding a protracted cyberwar between the world's superpowers.

With the United States refocusing its military attention on China as a dual cyber- weapon/conventional military threat, any attempt to reduce the distrust and ignorance that fuel arms races is welcome. Even if a complete ban on cyberweapons is unrealistic, measures such as prohibiting infrastructure and financial system attacks might be achiev- able. Better yet, persuading nations to agree that they will not perpetrate a first strike would go a long way in preventing cyberwarfare.

A s *Cyberwar: MAD 2.0* illustrates, the Internet and Web are increasingly vulnerable to large-scale attacks and potentially large-scale failure. Increasingly, these attacks are led by organized gangs of criminals operating globally—an unintended consequence of globalization. Even more worrisome is the growing number of large-scale attacks that are funded, organized, and led by various nations against the Internet resources of other nations. Currently there are few if any steps that individuals or businesses can take to prevent these kinds of attacks. However, there are several steps you can take to protect your business Web sites and your personal information from routine security attacks. Reading this chapter, you should start thinking about how your business could survive in the event of a large-scale "outage" of the Internet.

In this chapter, we will examine e-commerce security and payment issues. First, we will identify the major security risks and their costs, and describe the variety of solutions currently available. Then, we will look at the major payment methods and consider how to achieve a secure payment environment.

5.1   THE E-COMMERCE SECURITY ENVIRONMENT

For most law-abiding citizens, the Internet holds the promise of a huge and convenient global marketplace, providing access to people, goods, services, and businesses worldwide, all at a bargain price. For criminals, the Internet has created entirely new—and lucrative—ways to steal from the more than 1 billion Internet consumers worldwide. From products and services to cash to information, it's all there for the taking on the Internet.

It's also less risky to steal online. Rather than steal a CD at a local record store, you can download the same music for free and almost without risk from the Internet. The potential for anonymity on the Internet cloaks many criminals in legitimate-looking identities, allowing them to place fraudulent orders with online merchants, steal information by intercepting e-mail, or simply shut down e-commerce sites by using software viruses and swarm attacks. The Internet was never designed to be a global marketplace with a billion users, and lacks many basic security features found in older networks such as the telephone system or broadcast television networks.

THE SCOPE OF THE PROBLEM

Cybercrime is becoming a more significant problem for both organizations and consumers. Bot networks, DDoS attacks, Trojans, phishing, data theft, identity theft, credit card fraud, and spyware are just some of the threats that are making daily headlines. Social networks such as Facebook, Twitter, and LinkedIn have also had security breaches. But despite the increasing attention being paid to cybercrime, it is difficult to accurately estimate the actual amount of such crime, in part because many companies are hesitant to report it due to the fear of losing the trust of their customers, and because even if crime is reported, it may be difficult to quantify the actual dollar amount of the loss.

One source of information is the Internet Crime Complaint Center ("IC3"), a partnership between the National White Collar Crime Center and the Federal Bureau of Investigation. The IC3 data is useful for gauging the types of e-commerce crimes most likely to be reported by consumers. In 2011, the IC3 processed almost 315,000 Internet crime complaints, the second-highest number in its 11-year history. Over half the complainants reported a financial loss, with the total reported amount almost $500 million. The average amount of loss for those who reported a financial loss was more than $4,100. The most common complaints were for scams involving the FBI, identity theft, and advance fee fraud.

The Computer Security Institute's annual *Computer Crime and Security Survey* is another source of information. In 2011, the survey was based on the responses of 351 security practitioners in U.S. corporations, government agencies, financial institutions, medical institutions, and universities. The survey reported that 46% of responding organizations experienced a computer security incident within the past year. The most common type of attack experienced was a malware infection (67%), followed by phishing fraud (39%), laptop and mobile hardware theft (34%), attacks by botnets (29%), and insider abuse (25%). Not all of these necessarily involve e-commerce, although many do. Few companies were willing to share their estimated security loss numbers. But in the previous year's survey, of those that did report, the total loss reported was $41.5 million, with an average annual loss of $288,000. The most expensive security incidents were financial fraud, which averaged $500,000, followed by dealing with bot computers within the organization's network ($345,000) (Computer Security Institute, 2012). These figures represent only direct losses and not the costs of the security systems or personnel. Security experts believe underreporting of losses is growing in the last few years because of public attention.

Reports issued by security product providers, such as Symantec, are another source of data. Symantec issues a semi-annual *Internet Security Threat Report*, based on 64.6 million sensors monitoring Internet activity in more than 200 countries. In 2011, Symantec identified more than 405 million variants of malware versus 286 million in 2010. The sheer volume of Web-based attacks was up by more than 80% in 2011. Advances in technology have greatly reduced the entry costs and skills required to enter the cybercrime business. According to Symantec, low-cost and readily available Web attack kits, which enable hackers to create malware without having to write software from scratch, are responsible for more than 60% of all malicious activity (Symantec, 2012a).

Online credit card fraud and phishing attacks are perhaps the most high-profile form of e-commerce crimes. Although the average amount of credit card fraud loss experienced by any one individual is typically relatively small, the overall amount is substantial. The research firm CyberSource estimates online credit card fraud in the United States amounted to about $3.4 billion in 2011 (CyberSource, 2012).

Not every cybercriminal is necessarily after money. In some cases, such criminals aim to just deface, vandalize, and/or disrupt a Web site, rather than actually steal goods or services. The cost of such an attack includes not only the time and effort to make repairs to the site but also damage done to the site's reputation and image, as well as revenues lost as a result of the attack. Ponemon Institute estimates that the average loss to corporations for a breach of data security in 2011 was $5.5 million (Ponemon Institute, 2012).

So, what can we can conclude about the overall size of cybercrime? Cybercrime against e-commerce sites is dynamic and changing all the time, with new risks appearing often. The amount of losses to businesses appears to be significant but stable, and may represent a declining percentage of overall sales because firms have invested in security measures to protect against the simplest crimes. Individuals face new risks of fraud, many of which (unlike credit cards where federal law limits the loss to $50 for individuals) involve substantial uninsured losses involving debit cards and bank accounts. The managers of e-commerce sites must prepare for an ever-changing variety of criminal assaults, and keep current in the latest security techniques.

WHAT IS GOOD E-COMMERCE SECURITY?

Anytime you go into a marketplace you take risks, including the loss of privacy (information about what you purchased). Your prime risk as a consumer is that you do not get what you paid for. As a merchant in the market, your risk is that you don't get paid for what you sell. Thieves take merchandise and then either walk off without paying anything, or pay you with a fraudulent instrument, stolen credit card, or forged currency.

E-commerce merchants and consumers face many of the same risks as participants in traditional commerce, albeit in a new digital environment. Theft is theft, regardless of whether it is digital theft or traditional theft. Burglary, breaking and entering, embezzlement, trespass, malicious destruction, vandalism—all crimes in a traditional commercial environment—are also present in e-commerce. However, reducing risks in e-commerce is a complex process that involves new technologies, organizational policies and procedures, and new laws and industry standards that empower law enforcement officials to investigate and prosecute offenders. **Figure 5.1** illustrates the multi-layered nature of e-commerce security.

Good e-commerce security requires a set of laws, procedures, policies, and technologies that, to the extent feasible, protect individuals and organizations from unexpected behavior in the e-commerce marketplace.

DIMENSIONS OF E-COMMERCE SECURITY

There are six key dimensions to e-commerce security: integrity, nonrepudiation, authenticity, confidentiality, privacy, and availability.

Integrity refers to the ability to ensure that information being displayed on a Web site, or transmitted or received over the Internet, has not been altered in any way by an unauthorized party. For example, if an unauthorized person intercepts and changes the contents of an online communication, such as by redirecting a bank wire transfer into a different account, the integrity of the message has been compromised because the communication no longer represents what the original sender intended.

integrity
the ability to ensure that information being displayed on a Web site or transmitted or received over the Internet has not been altered in any way by an unauthorized party

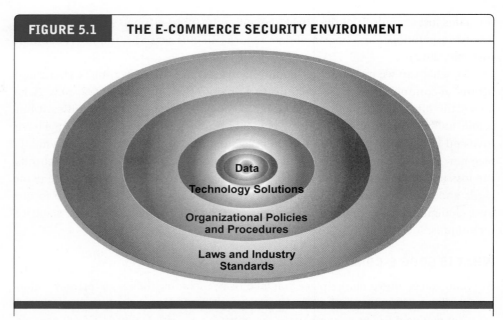

| FIGURE 5.1 | THE E-COMMERCE SECURITY ENVIRONMENT |

E-commerce security is multi-layered, and must take into account new technology, policies and procedures, and laws and industry standards.

nonrepudiation
the ability to ensure that e-commerce participants do not deny (i.e., repudiate) their online actions

Nonrepudiation refers to the ability to ensure that e-commerce participants do not deny (i.e., repudiate) their online actions. For instance, the availability of free e-mail accounts with alias names makes it easy for a person to post comments or send a message and perhaps later deny doing so. Even when a customer uses a real name and e-mail address, it is easy for that customer to order merchandise online and then later deny doing so. In most cases, because merchants typically do not obtain a physical copy of a signature, the credit card issuer will side with the customer because the merchant has no legally valid proof that the customer ordered the merchandise.

authenticity
the ability to identify the identity of a person or entity with whom you are dealing on the Internet

Authenticity refers to the ability to identify the identity of a person or entity with whom you are dealing on the Internet. How does the customer know that the Web site operator is who it claims to be? How can the merchant be assured that the customer is really who she says she is? Someone who claims to be someone he is not is "spoofing" or misrepresenting himself.

confidentiality
the ability to ensure that messages and data are available only to those who are authorized to view them

Confidentiality refers to the ability to ensure that messages and data are available only to those who are authorized to view them. Confidentiality is sometimes confused with **privacy**, which refers to the ability to control the use of information a customer provides about himself or herself to an e-commerce merchant.

privacy
the ability to control the use of information about oneself

E-commerce merchants have two concerns related to privacy. They must establish internal policies that govern their own use of customer information, and they must protect that information from illegitimate or unauthorized use. For example, if hackers break into an e-commerce site and gain access to credit card or other information, this violates not only the confidentiality of the data, but also the privacy of the individuals who supplied the information.

Availability refers to the ability to ensure that an e-commerce site continues to function as intended.

Table 5.1 summarizes these dimensions from both the merchants' and customers' perspectives. E-commerce security is designed to protect these six dimensions. When any one of them is compromised, it is a security issue. Can there be too much security? The answer is yes. Contrary to what some may believe, security is not an unmitigated good. Computer security adds overhead and expense to business operations, and also gives criminals new opportunities to hide their intentions and their crimes.

availability
the ability to ensure that an e-commerce site continues to function as intended

5.2 SECURITY THREATS IN THE E-COMMERCE ENVIRONMENT

From a technology perspective, there are three key points of vulnerability when dealing with e-commerce: the client, the server, and the communications pipeline. **Figure 5.2** illustrates what can go wrong in a typical e-commerce transaction with a consumer using a credit card to purchase a product.

In this section, we describe a number of the most common and most damaging forms of security threats to e-commerce consumers and site operators: malicious code,

TABLE 5.1	CUSTOMER AND MERCHANT PERSPECTIVES ON THE DIFFERENT DIMENSIONS OF E-COMMERCE SECURITY	
DIMENSION	CUSTOMER'S PERSPECTIVE	MERCHANT'S PERSPECTIVE
Integrity	Has information I transmitted or received been altered?	Has data on the site been altered without authorization? Is data being received from customers valid?
Nonrepudiation	Can a party to an action with me later deny taking the action?	Can a customer deny ordering products?
Authenticity	Who am I dealing with? How can I be assured that the person or entity is who they claim to be?	What is the real identity of the customer?
Confidentiality	Can someone other than the intended recipient read my messages?	Are messages or confidential data accessible to anyone other than those authorized to view them?
Privacy	Can I control the use of information about myself transmitted to an e-commerce merchant?	What use, if any, can be made of personal data collected as part of an e-commerce transaction? Is the personal information of customers being used in an unauthorized manner?
Availability	Can I get access to the site?	Is the site operational?

| FIGURE 5.2 | VULNERABLE POINTS IN AN E-COMMERCE TRANSACTION |

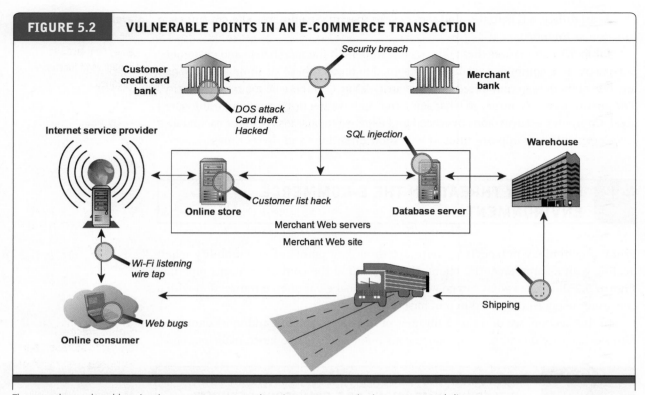

There are three vulnerable points in e-commerce transactions: Internet communications, servers, and clients.

potentially unwanted programs, phishing and identity theft, hacking and cybervandalism, credit card fraud/theft, spoofing (pharming) and spam (junk) Web sites, Denial of Service (DoS) and DDoS attacks, sniffing, insider attacks, poorly designed server and client software, social network security issues, mobile platform security issues, and finally, cloud security issues.

MALICIOUS CODE

malicious code (malware)

includes a variety of threats such as viruses, worms, Trojan horses, and bots

Malicious code (sometimes referred to as "malware") includes a variety of threats such as viruses, worms, Trojan horses, and bots. Some malicious code, sometimes referred to as an *exploit,* is designed to take advantage of software vulnerabilities in a computer's operating system, Web browser, applications, or other software components. Security firm GData reported that there were more than 2.5 million malware programs on the Internet in 2011, an increase of almost 25% from the previous year (GData Security Labs, 2011). In the past, malicious code was often intended to simply impair computers, and was often authored by a lone hacker, but increasingly the intent is to steal e-mail addresses, logon credentials, personal data, and financial information. Malicious code is also used to develop integrated malware networks that organize the theft of information and money.

One of the latest innovations in malicious code distribution is to embed it in the online advertising chain, including in Google and other ad networks. More than 1.5

million malicious ads are served every day, including "drive-by downloads" and fake anti-virus campaigns. A **drive-by download** is malware that comes with a down-loaded file that a user requests. Drive-by is now one of the most common methods of infecting computers.

A **virus** is a computer program that has the ability to replicate or make copies of itself, and spread to other files. In addition to the ability to replicate, most computer viruses deliver a "payload." The payload may be relatively benign, such as the display of a message or image, or it may be highly destructive—destroying files, reformatting the computer's hard drive, or causing programs to run improperly.

Viruses are often combined with a worm. Instead of just spreading from file to file, a **worm** is designed to spread from computer to computer. A worm does not necessarily need to be activated by a user or program in order for it to replicate itself. For example, the Slammer worm, which targeted a known vulnerability in Microsoft's SQL Server database software, infected more than 90% of vulnerable computers worldwide within 10 minutes of its release on the Internet; crashed Bank of America cash machines, especially in the southwestern part of the United States; and affected cash registers at supermarkets such as the Publix chain in Atlanta, where staff could not dispense cash to frustrated buyers.

A **Trojan horse** appears to be benign, but then does something other than expected. The Trojan horse is not itself a virus because it does not replicate, but is often a way for viruses or other malicious code such as bots or *rootkits* (a program whose aim is to subvert control of the computer's operating system) to be introduced into a computer system. A Trojan horse may masquerade as a game, but actually hide a program to steal your passwords and e-mail them to another person. Miscellaneous Trojans and Trojan downloaders and droppers (Trojans that install malicious files to a computer they have infected by either downloading them from a remote computer or from a copy contained in their own code) were found on more than 40% of computers around the world reporting malware threats to Microsoft in the fourth quarter of 2011. In May 2011, Sony experienced the largest data breach in history when a Trojan horse took over the administrative computers of Sony's PlayStation game center and downloaded personal and credit card information involving 77 million registered users.

A **backdoor** is a feature of viruses, worms, and Trojans that allows an attacker to remotely access a compromised computer. Downadup, the fourth most prevalent malicious code family in 2011, is an example of a worm with a backdoor, while Virut, a virus that infects various file types that was the fifth most common malicious code family in 2011, also includes a backdoor that can be used to download and install additional threats.

Bots (short for robots) are a type of malicious code that can be covertly installed on your computer when attached to the Internet. Around 90% of the world's spam, and 80% of the world's malware, is delivered by botnets. Once installed, the bot responds to external commands sent by the attacker; your computer becomes a "zombie" and is able to be controlled by an external third party (the "bot-herder"). **Botnets** are collections of captured computers used for malicious activities such as sending spam, participating in a DDoS attack, stealing information from computers, and storing network traffic for later analysis. The number of botnets operating world-

drive-by download
malware that comes with a downloaded file that a user requests

virus
a computer program that has the ability to replicate or make copies of itself, and spread to other files

worm
malware that is designed to spread from computer to computer

Trojan horse
appears to be benign, but then does something other than expected. Often a way for viruses or other malicious code to be introduced into a computer system

backdoor
feature of viruses, worms and Trojans that allows an attacker to remotely access a compromised computer.

bot
type of malicious code that can be covertly installed on a computer when attached to the Internet. Once installed, the bot responds to external commands sent by the attacker

botnet
collection of captured bot computers

wide is not known but is estimated to be in the thousands. Bots and bot networks are an important threat to the Internet and e-commerce because they can be used to launch very large-scale attacks using many different techniques. In March 2011, federal marshals accompanied members of Microsoft's digital crimes unit in raids designed to disable the Rustock botnet, the leading source of spam in the world with nearly 500,000 slave PCs under the control of its command and control servers located at six Internet hosting services in the United States. Officials confiscated the Rustock control servers at the hosting sites, which claimed they had no idea what the Rustock servers were doing. The actual spam e-mails were sent by the slave PCs under the command of the Rustock servers. The control servers were owned by people giving their address as Azerbaijan (Wingfield, 2011). As a result, the amount of spam sent in 2011 declined significantly compared to the previous year.

POTENTIALLY UNWANTED PROGRAMS (PUPS)

In addition to malicious code, the e-commerce security environment is further challenged by **potentially unwanted programs (PUPs)** such as adware, browser parasites, spyware, and other applications that install themselves on a computer, such as rogue security software, typically without the user's informed consent. Such programs are increasingly found on social network and user-generated content sites where users are fooled into downloading them. Once installed, these applications are usually exceedingly difficult to remove from the computer.

Adware is typically used to call for pop-up ads to display when the user visits certain sites. While annoying, adware is not typically used for criminal activities. ZangoSearch and PurityScan are examples of adware programs that open a partner site's Web pages or display the partner's pop-up ads when certain keywords are used in Internet searches. A **browser parasite** is a program that can monitor and change the settings of a user's browser, for instance, changing the browser's home page, or sending information about the sites visited to a remote computer. Browser parasites are often a component of adware. For example, Websearch is an adware component that modifies Internet Explorer's default home page and search settings.

Spyware, on the other hand, can be used to obtain information such as a user's keystrokes, copies of e-mail and instant messages, and even take screenshots (and thereby capture passwords or other confidential data). One example of spyware is Vista Antispyware 2012, which infects PCs running the Vista operating system. Vista Antispyware poses as a legitimate anti-spyware program when in fact it is malware that, when installed, disables the user's security software, alters the user's Web browser, and diverts users to scam Web sites where more malware is downloaded.

PHISHING AND IDENTITY THEFT

Social engineering relies on human curiosity, greed, and gullibility in order to trick people into taking an action that will result in the downloading of malware.

Phishing is any deceptive, online attempt by a third party to obtain confidential information for financial gain. Phishing attacks do not involve malicious code but

potentially unwanted program (PUP)
program that installs itself on a computer, typically without the user's informed consent

adware
a PUP that serves pop-up ads to your computer

browser parasite
a program that can monitor and change the settings of a user's browser

spyware
a program used to obtain information such as a user's keystrokes, e-mail, instant messages, and so on

Social engineering
exploitation of human fallibility and gullibility to distribute malware

phishing
any deceptive, online attempt by a third party to obtain confidential information for financial gain

instead rely on straightforward misrepresentation and fraud, so-called "social engineering" techniques. The most popular phishing attack is the e-mail scam letter. The scam begins with an e-mail: a rich former oil minister of Nigeria is seeking a bank account to stash millions of dollars for a short period of time, and requests your bank account number where the money can be deposited. In return, you will receive a million dollars. This type of e-mail scam is popularly known as a "Nigerian letter" scam (see **Figure 5.3**).

Thousands of other phishing attacks use other scams, some pretending to be eBay, PayPal, or Citibank writing to you for "account verification" (known as "spear phishing", or targeting a known customer of a specific bank or other type of business). Click on a link in the e-mail and you will be taken to a Web site controlled by the scammer, and prompted to enter confidential information about your accounts, such as your account number and PIN codes. On any given day, millions of these phishing attack e-mails are sent, and, unfortunately, some people are fooled and disclose their personal account information.

Phishers rely on traditional "con man" tactics, but use e-mail to trick recipients into voluntarily giving up financial access codes, bank account numbers, credit card numbers, and other personal information. Often, phishers create (or "spoof") a Web site that purports to be a legitimate financial institution and con users into entering financial information, or the site downloads malware such as a keylogger to the victim's computer. Phishers use the information they gather to commit fraudulent acts such as charging items to your credit cards or withdrawing funds from your bank

| FIGURE 5.3 | AN EXAMPLE OF A NIGERIAN LETTER E-MAIL SCAM |

This is an example of a typical Nigerian letter e-mail scam.

account, or in other ways "steal your identity" (identity theft). Phishing attacks are one of the fastest growing forms of e-commerce crime.

HACKING, CYBERVANDALISM, HACKTIVISM, AND DATA BREACHES

hacker

an individual who intends to gain unauthorized access to a computer system

cracker

within the hacking community, a term typically used to denote a hacker with criminal intent

cybervandalism

intentionally disrupting, defacing, or even destroying a site

hacktivism

cybervandalism and data theft for political purposes

data breach

occurs when an organization loses control over its information to outsiders

A **hacker** is an individual who intends to gain unauthorized access to a computer system. Within the hacking community, the term **cracker** is typically used to denote a hacker with criminal intent, although in the public press, the terms hacker and cracker tend to be used interchangeably. Hackers and crackers gain unauthorized access by finding weaknesses in the security procedures of Web sites and computer systems, often taking advantage of various features of the Internet that make it an open system that is easy to use. In the past, hackers and crackers typically were computer aficionados excited by the challenge of breaking into corporate and government Web sites. Sometimes they were satisfied merely by breaking into the files of an e-commerce site. Today, hackers have malicious intentions to disrupt, deface, or destroy sites (**cybervandalism**) or to steal personal or corporate information they can use for financial gain (data breach).

Hacktivism adds a political twist. Hacktivists typically attack governments, organizations, and even individuals for political purposes, employing the tactics of cybervandalism, denial of service attacks, data thefts, and more. LulzSec and Anonymous are two prominent hacktivist groups.

A **data breach** occurs whenever organizations lose control over corporate information to outsiders. According to Symantec, data about more than 230 million people were exposed in 2011 as a result of data breaches. Many of the data breaches resulted from a hacking campaign called Operation AntiSec run by the hacker collectives Anonymous and LulzSec, which began in the spring of 2011, and which continued into 2012, despite some arrests (Symantec, 2012a; 2012b).

CREDIT CARD FRAUD/THEFT

Theft of credit card data is one of the most feared occurrences on the Internet. Fear that credit card information will be stolen prevents users from making online purchases in many cases. Interestingly, this fear appears to be largely unfounded. Incidences of stolen credit card information are much lower than users think, around .6% of all online card transactions.

There is substantial credit card fraud in traditional commerce, but the consumer is largely insured against losses by federal law. In the past, the most common cause of credit card fraud was a lost or stolen card that was used by someone else, followed by employee theft of customer numbers and stolen identities (criminals applying for credit cards using false identities). Federal law limits the liability of individuals to $50 for a stolen credit card. For amounts more than $50, the credit card company generally pays the amount, although in some cases, the merchant may be held liable if it failed to verify the account or consult published lists of invalid cards. Banks recoup the cost of credit card fraud by charging higher interest rates on unpaid balances, and by merchants who raise prices to cover the losses.

But today, the most frequent cause of stolen cards and card information is the systematic hacking and looting of a corporate server where the information on millions of credit card purchases is stored. For instance, in March 2010, Albert Gonzalez was sentenced to 20 years in prison for organizing the largest theft of credit card numbers in American history. Along with two Russian co-conspirators, Gonzalez broke into the central computer systems of TJX, BJs, Barnes & Noble, and other companies, stealing over 160 million card numbers and costing these firms over $200 million in losses.

A central security issue of e-commerce is the difficulty of establishing the customer's identity. Currently there is no technology that can identify a person with certainty. Until a customer's identity can be guaranteed, online companies are at a much higher risk of loss than traditional offline companies.

SPOOFING (PHARMING) AND SPAM (JUNK) WEB SITES

Hackers attempting to hide their true identity often use **spoofing** tactics, misrepresenting themselves by using fake e-mail addresses or masquerading as someone else. Spoofing a Web site is also called "pharming," which involves redirecting a Web link to an address different from the intended one, with the site masquerading as the intended destination. Links that are designed to lead to one site can be reset to send users to a totally unrelated site—one that benefits the hacker.

spoofing
misrepresenting oneself by using fake e-mail addresses or masquerading as someone else

Although spoofing does not directly damage files or network servers, it threatens the integrity of a site. For example, if hackers redirect customers to a fake Web site that looks almost exactly like the true site, they can then collect and process orders, effectively stealing business from the true site. Or, if the intent is to disrupt rather than steal, hackers can alter orders—inflating them or changing products ordered—and then send them on to the true site for processing and delivery. Customers become dissatisfied with the improper order shipment, and the company may have huge inventory fluctuations that impact its operations.

DENIAL OF SERVICE (DOS) AND DISTRIBUTED DENIAL OF SERVICE (DDOS) ATTACKS

In a **Denial of Service (DoS)** attack, hackers flood a Web site with useless pings or page requests that inundate and overwhelm the site's Web servers. Increasingly, DoS attacks involve the use of bot networks and so-called "distributed attacks" built from thousands of compromised client computers. DoS attacks typically cause a Web site to shut down, making it impossible for users to access the site. For busy e-commerce sites, these attacks are costly; while the site is shut down, customers cannot make purchases. And the longer a site is shut down, the more damage is done to a site's reputation. Although such attacks do not destroy information or access restricted areas of the server, they can destroy a firm's online business. Often, DoS attacks are accom-

Denial of Service (DoS) attack
flooding a Web site with useless traffic to inundate and overwhelm the network

panied by attempts at blackmailing site owners to pay tens or hundreds of thousands of dollars to the hackers in return for stopping the DoS attack.

A **Distributed Denial of Service (DDoS)** attack uses hundreds or even thousands of computers to attack the target network from numerous launch points. DoS and DDoS attacks are threats to a system's operation because they can shut it down indefinitely. Major Web sites such as Yahoo and Microsoft have experienced such attacks, making the companies aware of their vulnerability and the need to continually introduce new measures to prevent future attacks. In August 2012, WikiLeaks, a site dedicated to the release of classified information, was hit by a massive DDoS attack that left its Web site effectively inoperable.

Distributed Denial of Service (DDoS) attack

using numerous computers to attack the target network from numerous launch points

SNIFFING

A **sniffer** is a type of eavesdropping program that monitors information traveling over a network. When used legitimately, sniffers can help identify potential network trouble-spots, but when used for criminal purposes, they can be damaging and very difficult to detect. Sniffers enable hackers to steal proprietary information from anywhere on a network, including passwords, e-mail messages, company files, and confidential reports.

sniffer

a type of eavesdropping program that monitors information traveling over a network

E-mail wiretaps are a variation on the sniffing threat. An e-mail wiretap is a method for recording or journaling e-mail traffic generally at the mail server level from any individual. E-mail wiretaps are used by employers to track employee messages, and by government agencies to surveil individuals or groups. E-mail wiretaps can be installed on servers and client computers. The USA PATRIOT Act permits the FBI to compel ISPs to install a black box on their mail servers that can impound the e-mail of a single person or group of persons for later analysis. In the case of American citizens communicating with other citizens, an FBI agent or government lawyer need only certify to a judge on the secret 11-member U.S. Foreign Intelligence Surveillance Court (FISC) that the information sought is "relevant to an ongoing criminal investigation" to get permission to install the program. Judges have no discretion. They must approve wiretaps based on government agents' unsubstantiated assertions. In the case of suspected terrorist activity, law enforcement does not have to inform a court prior to installing a wire or e-mail tap.

INSIDER ATTACKS

We tend to think of security threats to a business as originating outside the organization. In fact, the largest financial threats to business institutions come not from robberies but from embezzlement by insiders. Bank employees steal far more money than bank robbers. The same is true for e-commerce sites. Some of the largest disruptions to service, destruction to sites, and diversion of customer credit data and personal information have come from insiders—once trusted employees. Employees have access to privileged information, and, in the presence of sloppy internal security procedures, they are often able to roam throughout an organization's systems without leaving a trace. The 2010/2011 Computer Security Institute survey reports that insider abuse of systems was the fourth most frequent type of attack during the preceding 12 months, and that around 25% of survey respondents believed that insiders contributed to some portion of the firm's financial losses during the previous year.

POORLY DESIGNED SERVER AND CLIENT SOFTWARE

Many security threats prey on poorly designed server and client software, sometimes in the operating system and sometimes in the application software, including browsers. The increase in complexity and size of software programs, coupled with demands for timely delivery to markets, has contributed to an increase in software flaws or vulnerabilities that hackers can exploit. Each year, security firms identify thousands of software vulnerabilities in Internet and PC software. For instance, in its most recent semi-annual *Internet Security Threat Report,* Symantec identified almost 5,000 different software vulnerabilities. Browser vulnerabilities in particular are a popular target, as well as browser plug-ins such as for Adobe Reader. A **zero-day vulnerability** is one that has been previously unreported and for which no patch yet exists. For example, in December 2011, Adobe was hit with a zero-day vulnerability attack against its Reader and Acrobat products that persisted for over two weeks until it was able to release a patch (Symantec, 2012a). The very design of the personal computer includes many open communication ports that can be used, and indeed are designed to be used, by external computers to send and receive messages. However, given their complexity and design objectives, all operating systems and application software, including Linux and Macintosh, have vulnerabilities.

zero-day vulnerability
software vulnerability that has been previously unreported and for which no patch yet exists

SOCIAL NETWORK SECURITY ISSUES

Social networks like Facebook, Twitter, and LinkedIn provide a rich and rewarding environment for hackers. Viruses, site takeovers, identity theft, malware-loaded apps, click hijacking, phishing, and spam are all found on social networks (US-CERT, 2011). For instance, in 2011, hackers defaced Pfizer's Facebook page, took over the Twitter accounts of both USA Today and NBC News, and stole millions of LinkedIn passwords (Sophos, 2012). The Ramnit worm stole account information from more than 45,000 Facebook users. By sneaking in among our friends, hackers can masquerade as friends and dupe users into scams. Social network firms have thus far been relatively poor policemen because they have failed to aggressively weed out accounts that send visitors to malware sites (unlike Google, which maintains a list of known malware sites and patrols its search results looking for links to malware sites). Social networks are open: anyone can set up a personal page, even criminals. Most attacks are social engineering attacks that tempt visitors to click on links that sound reasonable. Social apps downloaded from either the social network or a foreign site are not certified by the social network to be clean of malware. It's "clicker beware."

MOBILE PLATFORM SECURITY ISSUES

The explosion in mobile devices has broadened opportunities for hackers. Mobile users are filling their devices with personal and financial information, making them excellent targets for hackers. In general, mobile devices face all the same risks as any Internet device as well as some new risks associated with wireless network security. While most PC users are aware their computers and Web sites may be hacked and contain malware, most cell phone users believe their cell phone is as secure as a traditional landline phone. As with social network members, mobile users are prone to think they are in a shared, trustworthy environment.

Mobile cell phone malware was developed as early as 2004 with Cabir, a Bluetooth worm affecting Symbian operating systems (Nokia phones). More recently, Ike4e.B appeared on jailbroken iPhones, turning the phones into botnet-controlled devices. Many—if not most—apps written for Android phones have poor protection for user information, and Google removed more than 100 malicious apps from the Android Market in 2011. The first malicious iPhone app was also discovered and removed from the iTunes Store. And it is not just rogue applications that are dangerous, but also popular legitimate applications that simply have little protection from hackers. ViaForensics, a mobile security firm in Chicago, found in a study of 50 popular iPhone apps that only three had adequate protection for usernames, passwords, and other sensitive data. Servers of mobile service providers like AT&T and Verizon are also vulnerable. In 2011, two computer hackers were arrested for allegedly breaking into AT&T's servers to gather e-mail addresses and other personal information of about 120,000 users of Apple's iPad, including corporate chiefs, U.S. government officials, and Hollywood moguls. The hackers did not use the information.

Vishing attacks target gullible cell phone users with verbal messages to call a certain number and, for example, donate money to starving children in Haiti. Smishing attacks exploit SMS messages. Compromised text messages can contain e-mail and Web site addresses that can lead the innocent user to a malware site. A small number of downloaded apps from app stores have also contained malware. Madware—innocent-looking apps that contain adware that launches pop-up ads and text messages on your mobile device—is also becoming an increasing problem.

Read the *Insight on Technology* case, *Think Your Smartphone Is Secure?* for a further discussion of some of the issues surrounding smartphone security.

CLOUD SECURITY ISSUES

The move of so many Internet services into the cloud also raises security risks. From an infrastructure standpoint, DDoS attacks threaten the availability of cloud services on which more and more companies are relying. Safeguarding data being maintained in a cloud environment is also a major concern. For example, researchers identified several ways data could be accessed without authorization on Dropbox, which offers

INSIGHT ON TECHNOLOGY

THINK YOUR SMARTPHONE IS SECURE?

In 2012, the biggest security danger facing smartphone users is that they will lose their phone. In reality, all of the personal and corporate data stored on the device, as well as access to corporate data on remote servers, are at risk. Smartphones are poised to become a major avenue of malware.

Many users believe their iPhones and Androids are unlikely to be hacked because Apple and Google are protecting them from malware apps, and that the carriers like Verizon and AT&T can keep the cell phone network clean from malware just as they do the land-line phone system. Telephone systems are "closed" and therefore not subject to the kinds of attacks that occur on the open Internet.

To date, there has not been a major smartphone hack, but just because it has not happened yet doesn't mean that it won't. With 116 million smartphone users in the United States, 122 million people accessing the Internet from mobile devices, business firms increasingly switching their employees to the mobile platform, and consumers using their phones for financial transactions and even paying bills, the size and richness of the smartphone target for hackers is growing.

Hackers can do to a smartphone just about anything they can do to any Internet device: request malicious files without user intervention, delete files, transmit files, install programs running in the background that can monitor user actions, and potentially convert the smartphone into a robot that can be used in a botnet to send e-mail and text messages to anyone.

Apps are one avenue for potential security breaches. Apple, Google, and RIM (BlackBerry) now offer over 1.25 million apps collectively. Apple claims that it examines each and every app to ensure that it plays by Apple's iTunes rules, but risks remain. Security company Kaspersky expects the iPhone to face an onslaught of malware within the next year. Apple iTunes app rules make some user information available to all apps by default, including the user's GPS position and name.

Security on the Android platform is much less under the control of Google because it has an open app model. As a result, the Android has been the primary smartphone target, and instances of malware on the Android platform have reportedly increased by 400%. Google does not review any of the apps for the Android platform but instead relies on technical hurdles to limit the impact of malicious code, as well as user and security expert feedback.

Beyond the threat of rogue apps, smartphones of all stripes are susceptible to browser-based malware that takes advantage of vulnerabilities in all browsers. In addition, most smartphones, including the iPhone, permit the manufacturers to remotely download configuration files to update operating systems and security protections. Unfortunately, flaws in the public key encryption procedures that permit remote server access to iPhones have been discovered, raising further questions about the security of such operations.

Some commentators dismiss these concerns as more hype than reality. But reality may be catching up with the hype.

SOURCES: "iPhone Malware: Spam App 'Find and Call' Invades App Store," by Zach Epstein, BGR.com, July 5, 2012; "iPhone Malware: Kaspersky Expects Apple's iOS to be Under Attack by Next Year," by Sara Gates, Huffington Post, May 15, 2012; "Android, Apple Face Growing Cyberattacks," by Byron Acohido, *USA Today*, June 3, 2011; "Security to Ward Off Crime on Phones," by Riva Richmond, *New York Times*, February 23, 2011; "AT&T Plans Smartphone Security Service for 2012," John Stankey, AT&T Enterprise CTO, interview May 16, 2012; "Smartphone Security Follies: A Brief History," by Brad Reed, *Network World*, April 18, 2011; "Experts: Android, iPhone Security Different But Matched," by Elinor Mills, CNET News, July 1, 2010; "Apple Security Breach Gives Complete Access to Your iPhone," by Jesus Diaz, Gizmodo.com, August 3, 2010; "iPhone Certificate Flaws, iPhone PKI Kandling flaws," by Cryptopath.com, January 2010.

a popular cloud file-sharing service. Dropbox has also experienced several security snafus, including leaving all of its users' files publicly accessible for four hours in June 2011 due to a software bug, the discovery of a security hole in its iOS app that allowed anyone with physical access to the phone to copy login credentials, and the theft of usernames and passwords in August 2012. To combat some of these issues, Dropbox has implemented a number of measures, including two-factor authentication, which relies on two separate elements—something you know, such as a password, coupled with a separately generated code. These incidents highlight the risks involved as devices, identities, and data become more and more interconnected in the cloud.

5.3 TECHNOLOGY SOLUTIONS

At first glance, it might seem like there is not much that can be done about the onslaught of security breaches on the Internet. Reviewing the security threats in the previous section, it is clear that the threats to e-commerce are very real, potentially devastating for individuals, businesses, and entire nations, and likely to be increasing in intensity along with the growth in e-commerce. But in fact a great deal of progress has been made by private security firms, corporate and home users, network administrators, technology firms, and government agencies. There are two lines of defense: technology solutions and policy solutions. In this section, we consider some technology solutions, and in the following section, we look at some policy solutions that work.

The first line of defense against the wide variety of security threats to an e-commerce site is a set of tools that can make it difficult for outsiders to invade or destroy a site. **Figure 5.4** illustrates the major tools available to achieve site security.

PROTECTING INTERNET COMMUNICATIONS

encryption

the process of transforming plain text or data into cipher text that cannot be read by anyone other than the sender and the receiver. The purpose of encryption is (a) to secure stored information and (b) to secure information transmission

Because e-commerce transactions must flow over the public Internet, and therefore involve thousands of routers and servers through which the transaction packets flow, security experts believe the greatest security threats occur at the level of Internet communications. This is very different from a private network where a dedicated communication line is established between two parties. A number of tools are available to protect the security of Internet communications, the most basic of which is message encryption.

ENCRYPTION

cipher text

text that has been encrypted and thus cannot be read by anyone other than the sender and the receiver

Encryption is the process of transforming plain text or data into **cipher text** that cannot be read by anyone other than the sender and the receiver. The purpose of encryption is (a) to secure stored information and (b) to secure information transmission. Encryption can provide four of the six key dimensions of e-commerce security referred to in Table 5.1:

• *Message integrity*—provides assurance that the message has not been altered.

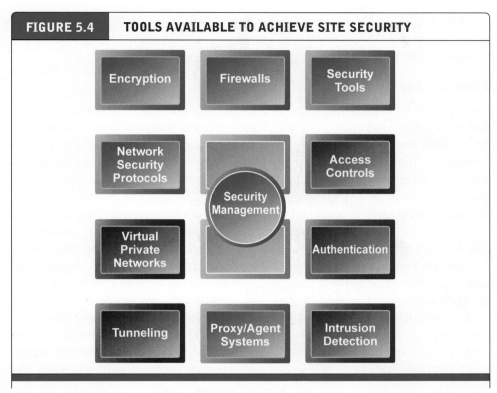

FIGURE 5.4   TOOLS AVAILABLE TO ACHIEVE SITE SECURITY

There are a number of tools available to achieve site security.

- *Nonrepudiation*—prevents the user from denying he or she sent the message.
- *Authentication*—provides verification of the identity of the person (or computer) sending the message.
- *Confidentiality*—gives assurance that the message was not read by others.

This transformation of plain text to cipher text is accomplished by using a key or cipher. A **key** (or **cipher**) is any method for transforming plain text to cipher text.

Encryption has been practiced since the earliest forms of writing and commercial transactions. Ancient Egyptian and Phoenician commercial records were encrypted using substitution and transposition ciphers. In a **substitution cipher**, every occurrence of a given letter is replaced systematically by another letter. For instance, if we used the cipher "letter plus two"—meaning replace every letter in a word with a new letter two places forward—then the word "Hello" in plain text would be transformed into the following cipher text: "JGNNQ." In a **transposition cipher**, the ordering of the letters in each word is changed in some systematic way. Leonardo Da Vinci recorded his shop notes in reverse order, making them readable only with a mirror. The word "Hello" can be written backwards as "OLLEH." A more complicated cipher would (a) break all words into two words and (b) spell the first word with every other

key (cipher)
any method for transforming plain text to cipher text

substitution cipher
every occurrence of a given letter is replaced systematically by another letter

transposition cipher
the ordering of the letters in each word is changed in some systematic way

letter beginning with the first letter, and then spell the second word with all the remaining letters. In this cipher, "HELLO" would be written as "HLO EL."

Symmetric Key Encryption

symmetric key encryption (secret key encryption)
both the sender and the receiver use the same key to encrypt and decrypt the message

In order to decipher these messages, the receiver would have to know the secret cipher that was used to encrypt the plain text. This is called **symmetric key encryption** or **secret key encryption**. In symmetric key encryption, both the sender and the receiver use the same key to encrypt and decrypt the message. How do the sender and the receiver have the same key? They have to send it over some communication media or exchange the key in person. Symmetric key encryption was used extensively throughout World War II and is still a part of Internet encryption.

The possibilities for simple substitution and transposition ciphers are endless, but they all suffer from common flaws. First, in the digital age, computers are so powerful and fast that these ancient means of encryption can be broken quickly. Second, symmetric key encryption requires that both parties share the same key. In order to share the same key, they must send the key over a presumably *insecure* medium where it could be stolen and used to decipher messages. If the secret key is lost or stolen, the entire encryption system fails. Third, in commercial use, where we are not all part of the same team, you would need a secret key for each of the parties with whom you transacted, that is, one key for the bank, another for the department store, and another for the government.

Modern encryption systems are digital. The ciphers or keys used to transform plain text into cipher text are digital strings. Computers store text or other data as binary strings composed of 0s and 1s. For instance, the binary representation of the capital letter "A" in ASCII computer code is accomplished with eight binary digits (bits): 01000001. One way in which digital strings can be transformed into cipher text is by multiplying each letter by another binary number, say, an eight-bit key number 0101 0101. If we multiplied every digital character in our text messages by this eight-bit key and sent the encrypted message to a friend along with the secret eight-bit key, the friend could decode the message easily.

public key cryptography
two mathematically related digital keys are used: a public key and a private key. The private key is kept secret by the owner, and the public key is widely disseminated. Both keys can be used to encrypt and decrypt a message. However, once the keys are used to encrypt a message, that same key cannot be used to unencrypt the message

The strength of modern security protection is measured in terms of the length of the binary key used to encrypt the data. In the preceding example, the eight-bit key is easily deciphered because there are only 2^8 or 256 possibilities. If the intruder knows you are using an eight-bit key, then he or she could decode the message in a few seconds using a modern desktop PC just by using the brute force method of checking each of the 256 possible keys. For this reason, modern digital encryption systems use keys with 56, 128, 256, or 512 binary digits. With encryption keys of 512 digits, there are 2^{512} possibilities to check out. It is estimated that all the computers in the world would need to work for 10 years before stumbling upon the answer.

Public Key Encryption

In 1976, a new way of encrypting messages called **public key cryptography** was invented by Whitfield Diffie and Martin Hellman. Public key cryptography solves the problem of exchanging keys. In this method, two mathematically related digital keys are used: a public key and a private key. The private key is kept secret by the owner, and the public key is widely disseminated. Both keys can be used to encrypt and decrypt a message. However, once the keys are used to encrypt a message, the same key cannot be used to unencrypt the message. The mathematical algorithms used to produce the keys are one-way functions. A *one-way irreversible mathematical function* is one in which, once the algorithm is applied, the input cannot be subsequently derived from the output. Most food recipes are like this. For instance, it is easy to make scrambled eggs, but impossible to retrieve whole eggs from the scrambled eggs. Public key cryptography is based on the idea of irreversible mathematical functions. The keys are sufficiently long (128, 256, and 512 bits) that it would take enormous computing power to derive one key from the other using the largest and fastest computers available. **Figure 5.5** illustrates a simple use of public key cryptography and takes you through the important steps in using public and private keys.

Public Key Encryption Using Digital Signatures and Hash Digests

In public key encryption, some elements of security are missing. Although we can be quite sure the message was not understood or read by a third party (message confidentiality), there is no guarantee the sender really is the sender; that is, there is no authentication of the sender. This means the sender could deny ever sending the message (repudiation). And there is no assurance the message was not altered somehow in transit. For example, the message "Buy Cisco @ $16" could have been accidentally or intentionally altered to read "Sell Cisco @ $16." This suggests a potential lack of integrity in the system.

A more sophisticated use of public key cryptography can achieve authentication, nonrepudiation, and integrity. **Figure 5.6** illustrates this more powerful approach.

To check the integrity of a message and ensure it has not been altered in transit, a hash function is used first to create a digest of the message. A **hash function** is an algorithm that produces a fixed-length number called a *hash* or *message digest*. A hash function can be simple, and count the number of digital 1s in a message, or it can be more complex, and produce a 128-bit number that reflects the number of 0s and 1s, the number of 00s, 11s, and so on. Standard hash functions are available (MD4 and MD5 produce 128- and 160-bit hashes) (Stein, 1998). These more complex hash functions produce hashes or hash results that are unique to every message. The results of applying the hash function are sent by the sender to the recipient. Upon receipt, the recipient applies the hash function to the received message and checks to verify the same result is produced. If so, the message has not been altered. The sender then encrypts both the hash result and the original message using the recipient's public key (as in Figure 5.5 on page 187), producing a single block of cipher text.

One more step is required. To ensure the authenticity of the message and to ensure nonrepudiation, the sender encrypts the entire block of cipher text one more time using the sender's private key. This produces a **digital signature** (also called an *e-signature*) or "signed" cipher text that can be sent over the Internet.

hash function
an algorithm that produces a fixed-length number called a hash or message digest

digital signature (e-signature)
"signed" cipher text that can be sent over the Internet

FIGURE 5.5	PUBLIC KEY CRYPTOGRAPHY—A SIMPLE CASE

STEP	DESCRIPTION
1. The sender creates a digital message.	The message could be a document, spreadsheet, or any digital object.
2. The sender obtains the recipient's public key from a public directory and applies it to the message.	Public keys are distributed widely and can be obtained from recipients directly.
3. Application of the recipient's key produces an encrypted cipher text message.	Once encrypted using the public key, the message cannot be reverse-engineered or unencrypted using the same public key. The process is irreversible.
4. The encrypted message is sent over the Internet.	The encrypted message is broken into packets and sent through several different pathways, making interception of the entire message difficult (but not impossible).
5. The recipient uses his/her private key to decrypt the message.	The only person who can decrypt the message is the person who has possession of the recipient's private key. Hopefully, this is the legitimate recipient.

In the simplest use of public key cryptography, the sender encrypts a message using the recipient's public key, and then sends it over the Internet. The only person who can decrypt this message is the recipient, using his or her private key. However, this simple case does not ensure integrity or an authentic message.

FIGURE 5.6	PUBLIC KEY CRYPTOGRAPHY WITH DIGITAL SIGNATURES

STEP	DESCRIPTION
1. The sender creates an original message.	The message can be any digital file.
2. The sender applies a hash function, producing a 128-bit hash result.	Hash functions create a unique digest of the message based on the message contents.
3. The sender encrypts the message and hash result using recipient's public key.	This irreversible process creates a cipher text that can be read only by the recipient using his or her private key.
4. The sender encrypts the result, again using his or her private key.	The sender's private key is a digital signature. There is only one person who can create this digital mark.
5. The result of this double encryption is sent over the Internet.	The message traverses the Internet as a series of independent packets.
6. The receiver uses the sender's public key to authenticate the message.	Only one person can send this message, namely, the sender.
7. The receiver uses his or her private key to decrypt the hash function and the original message. The receiver checks to ensure the original message and the hash function results conform to one another.	The hash function is used here to check the original message. This ensures the message was not changed in transit.

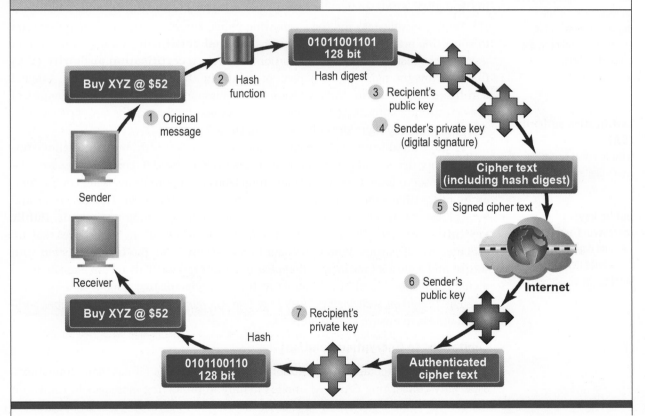

A more realistic use of public key cryptography uses hash functions and digital signatures to both ensure the confidentiality of the message and authenticate the sender. The only person who could have sent the above message is the owner or the sender using his/her private key. This authenticates the message. The hash function ensures the message was not altered in transit. As before, the only person who can decipher the message is the recipient, using his/her private key.

A digital signature is a close parallel to a handwritten signature. Like a handwritten signature, a digital signature is unique—only one person presumably possesses the private key. When used with a hash function, the digital signature is even more unique than a handwritten signature. In addition to being exclusive to a particular individual, when used to sign a hashed document, the digital signature is also unique to the document, and changes for every document.

Digital Certificates and Public Key Infrastructure (PKI)

There are still some deficiencies in the message security regime described previously. How do we know that people and institutions are who they claim to be? Anyone can make up a private and public key combination and claim to be someone they are not. Before you place an order with an online merchant such as Amazon, you want to be sure it really is Amazon.com you have on the screen and not a spoofer masquerading as Amazon. In the physical world, if someone asks who you are and you show a social security number, they may well ask to see a picture ID or a second form of certifiable or acceptable identification. If they really doubt who you are, they may ask for references to other authorities and actually interview these other authorities. Similarly, in the digital world, we need a way to know who people and institutions really are.

Digital certificates, and the supporting public key infrastructure, are an attempt to solve this problem of digital identity. A **digital certificate** is a digital document issued by a trusted third-party institution known as a **certification authority (CA)** that contains the name of the subject or company, the subject's public key, a digital certificate serial number, an expiration date, an issuance date, the digital signature of the certification authority (the name of the CA encrypted using the CA's private key), and other identifying information (see **Figure 5.7**).

In the United States, private corporations such as VeriSign, browser manufacturers, security firms, and government agencies such as the U.S. Postal Service and the Federal Reserve issue CAs. Worldwide, thousands of organizations issue CAs. A hierarchy of CAs has emerged with less-well-known CAs being certified by larger and better-known CAs, creating a community of mutually verifying institutions. **Public key infrastructure (PKI)** refers to the CAs and digital certificate procedures that are accepted by all parties. When you sign into a "secure" site, the URL will begin with "https" and a closed lock icon will appear on your browser. This means the site has a digital certificate issued by a trusted CA. It is not, presumably, a spoof site.

The *Insight on Society* story, *Web Dogs and Anonymity: Identity 2.0*, describes additional efforts to ensure online identity.

Limitations to Encryption Solutions

PKI is a powerful technological solution to security issues, but it has many limitations, especially concerning CAs. PKI applies mainly to protecting messages in transit on the Internet and is not effective against insiders—employees—who have legitimate access to corporate systems including customer information. Most e-commerce sites do not store customer information in encrypted form. Other limitations are apparent. For one, how is your private key to be protected? Most private keys will be stored on insecure desktop or laptop computers.

---

digital certificate
a digital document issued by a certification authority that contains the name of the subject or company, the subject's public key, a digital certificate serial number, an expiration date, an issuance date, the digital signature of the certification authority, and other identifying information

certification authority (CA)
a trusted third party that issues digital certificates

public key infrastructure (PKI)
CAs and digital certificate procedures that are accepted by all parties

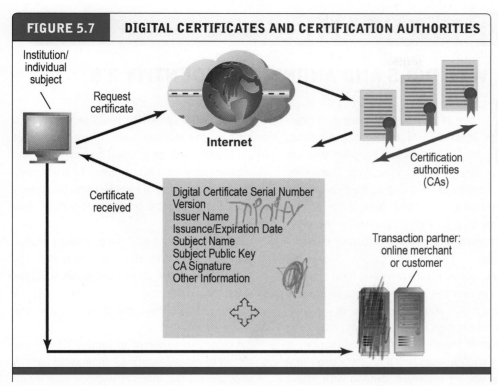

FIGURE 5.7 **DIGITAL CERTIFICATES AND CERTIFICATION AUTHORITIES**

The PKI includes certification authorities that issue, verify, and guarantee digital certificates that are used in e-commerce to assure the identity of transaction partners.

There is no guarantee the person using your computer—and your private key—is really you. For instance, you may lose your laptop or smartphone, and therefore lose the private key. Likewise, there is no assurance that someone else in the world cannot use your personal ID papers, such as a social security card, to obtain a PKI authenticated online ID in your name. If there's no real world identification system, there can be no Internet identification system. Under many digital signature laws, you are responsible for whatever your private key does even if you were not the person using the key.

SECURING CHANNELS OF COMMUNICATION

The concepts of public key encryption are used routinely for securing channels of communication.

Secure Sockets Layer (SSL) and Transport Layer Security (TLS)

The most common form of securing channels is through the *Secure Sockets Layer (SSL)* and *Transport Layer Security (TLS)* protocols. When you receive a message from a server on the Web with which you will be communicating through a secure channel, this means you will be using SSL/TLS to establish a secure negotiated session. (Notice that the URL changes from HTTP to HTTPS.) A **secure negotiated session** is a client-

secure negotiated session

a client-server session in which the URL of the requested document, along with the contents, contents of forms, and the cookies exchanged, are encrypted

INSIGHT ON SOCIETY

WEB DOGS AND ANONYMITY: IDENTITY 2.0

One of the many problems with Internet security is people sometimes don't really know just who they are dealing with on the Web. It could be anyone, even a dog, as humorously suggested by the iconic *New Yorker* magazine cartoon by Peter Steiner. On the Web, you don't know who to trust with your personal information.

It gets worse. Most Web users have multiple identities across the Web, and most Web users don't have a clue about who has what information about them, how it is used, or who has access to it. When it comes to identity, the Internet is an information asylum based on the fiction that we know who we are really dealing with in our transactions.

There are several groups trying to establish secure identity on the Internet. An international group led by large business firms and 85 governments has started a global system of authentication in an effort to reduce spam, scams, and hacking. Dubbed "Secure DNS," the system is designed to replace the existing DNS authority structure operated by private industry with a new international system operated by a consortium of countries.

The federal government, along with private industry, is also trying to fix parts of the identity problem in the United States with a program called "Identity 2.0." In April 2011, the White House unveiled a prototype identity system. The system would rely on a strong credential that would work like a combination of a digital key, a fingerprint, and perhaps a digitized photo.

The identity credential could be stored on a smart card the user carries in his or her pocket like a credit card, or it could be stored on the user's computer, or a smartphone. Internet users would not be required to have a strong credential, but they could not get access to most popular Web sites without it.

With this strong credential you would be able to sign in to any Web site requesting your ID, either by swiping the smart card or waving your smartphone, or sending a digital ID file. It's a single sign-on: you have one password and one login across all sites.

A commanding computer controlling a botnet would not be able to launch a million spam e-mails at once across the Internet without identifying itself (IP address), sending its own authentication, and using digital keys to activate all its slave computers. You would not be allowed to post to a blog or Web site without first authenticating who you are. In this plan, anonymity is not possible.

Who would control this identity system? NSTIC calls for a federation of private and public online identity systems. Banks, federal agencies, Google, the U.S. Postal Service, VeriSign, and other trusted institutions would provide the electronic smart ID cards, or digital files, once they have identified who you are. The other alternative for organizing strong identity regimes is a single federal agency. Most privacy advocates and private firms want a mix of public and private entities to control the identity ecosystem.

SOURCES: "Recommendations for Establishing an Identity Ecosystem Governance Structure," Department of Commerce, National Institute of Standards and Technology, February 2012; "A Stronger Net Security System is Deployed," John Markoff, *New York Times,* June 24, 2011; "Wave of the Future: Trusted Identities in Cyberspace," by Dan Rowinski, *New York Times,* April 20, 2011; "Enhancing Online Choice, Efficiency, Security, and Privacy," The White House, April 2011; "White House's Trusted Identities Strategy Doesn't Inspire Trust," by Matthew Harwood, Securitymanagement.com, July 27, 2010; "A Major Milestone for Internet Security," by Andrew McLaughlin, Office of Science and Technology Policy, Whitehouse.gov, July 22, 2010; "Real ID Online? New Federal Online Identity Plan Raises Privacy and Free Speech Concerns," by Lee Tien and Seth Schoen, Electronic Frontier Foundation, July 20, 2010; "Taking the Mystery Out of Web Anonymity," John Markoff, *New York Times,* July 2, 2010; "White House Strategy For Secure Cyberspace Based on Identity-theft-flawed Meatspace," by Joe Campana, Examiner.com, June 29, 2010.

server session in which the URL of the requested document, along with the contents, contents of forms, and the cookies exchanged, are encrypted (see **Figure 5.8**). For instance, your credit card number that you entered into a form would be encrypted. Through a series of handshakes and communications, the browser and the server establish one another's identity by exchanging digital certificates, decide on the strongest shared form of encryption, and then proceed to communicate using an agreed-upon session key. A **session key** is a unique symmetric encryption key chosen just for this single secure session. Once used, it is gone forever. Figure 5.10 shows how this works.

In practice, most private individuals do not have a digital certificate. In this case, the merchant server will not request a certificate, but the client browser will request the merchant certificate once a secure session is called for by the server.

SSL/TLS provides data encryption, server authentication, optional client authentication, and message integrity for TCP/IP connections. SSL/TLS addresses the issue of authenticity by allowing users to verify another user's identity or the identity of a server. It also protects the integrity of the messages exchanged. However, once the merchant receives the encrypted credit and order information, that information is typi-

session key

a unique symmetric encryption key chosen for a single secure session

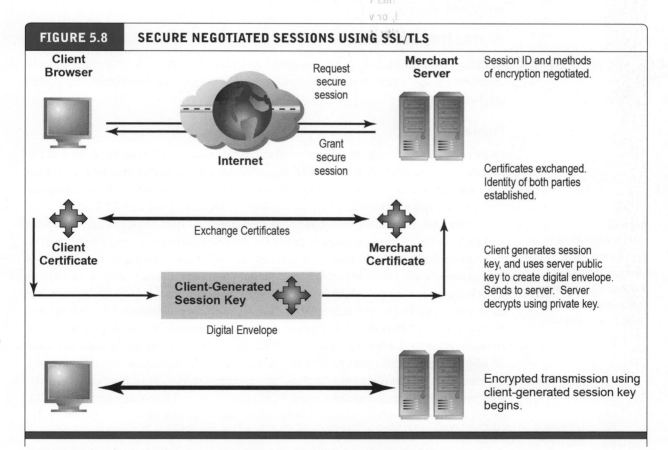

FIGURE 5.8 | SECURE NEGOTIATED SESSIONS USING SSL/TLS

Client Browser

Request secure session

Grant secure session

Internet

Merchant Server

Session ID and methods of encryption negotiated.

Exchange Certificates

Client Certificate

Merchant Certificate

Certificates exchanged. Identity of both parties established.

Client-Generated Session Key

Digital Envelope

Client generates session key, and uses server public key to create digital envelope. Sends to server. Server decrypts using private key.

Encrypted transmission using client-generated session key begins.

Certificates play a key role in using SSL/TLS to establish a secure communications channel.

cally stored in unencrypted format on the merchant's servers. While SSL/TLS provides secure transactions between merchant and consumer, it only guarantees server-side authentication. Client authentication is optional.

Virtual Private Networks (VPNs)

virtual private network (VPN)

allows remote users to securely access internal networks via the Internet, using the Point-to-Point Tunneling Protocol (PPTP)

A **virtual private network (VPN)** allows remote users to securely access a corporation's local area network via the Internet, using a variety of VPN protocols. VPNs use both authentication and encryption to secure information from unauthorized persons. VPNs are able to block message intercepts and packet sniffing (providing confidentiality and integrity). Authentication prevents spoofing and misrepresentation of identities. A remote user can connect to a remote private local network using a local ISP. The VPN protocols will establish the link from the client to the corporate network as if the user had dialed into the corporate network directly. The process of connecting one protocol through another (IP) is called *tunneling*, because the VPN creates a private connection by adding an invisible wrapper around a message to hide its content. As the message travels through the Internet between the ISP and the corporate network, it is shielded from prying eyes by an encrypted wrapper.

PROTECTING NETWORKS

Once you have protected communications as well as possible, the next set of tools to consider are those that can protect your networks, as well as the servers and clients on those networks.

Firewalls

Firewalls and proxy servers are intended to build a wall around your network and the attached servers and clients, just like physical-world firewalls protect you from fires for a limited period of time. Firewalls and proxy servers share some similar functions, but they are quite different.

firewall

refers to either hardware or software that filters communication packets and prevents some packets from entering the network based on a security policy

A **firewall** refers to either hardware or software that filters communication packets and prevents some packets from entering the network based on a security policy. The firewall controls traffic to and from servers and clients, forbidding communications from untrustworthy sources, and allowing other communications from trusted sources to proceed. Every message that is to be sent or received from the network is processed by the firewall, which determines if the message meets security guidelines established by the business. If it does, it is permitted to be distributed, and if it doesn't, the message is blocked. Firewalls can filter traffic based on packet attributes such as source IP address, destination port or IP address, type of service (such as WWW or HTTP), the domain name of the source, and many other dimensions. Most hardware firewalls that protect local area networks connected to the Internet have default settings that require little if any administrator intervention and employ simple but effective rules that deny incoming packets from a connection that does not originate from an internal request—the firewall only allows connections from servers that you requested service from.

Proxy servers (proxies) are software servers (often a dedicated computer) that handle all communications originating from or being sent to the Internet by local clients, acting as a spokesperson or bodyguard for the organization. Proxies act primarily to limit access of internal clients to external Internet servers, although some proxy servers act as firewalls as well. Proxy servers are sometimes called *dual-home systems* because they have two network interfaces. To internal computers, a proxy server is known as the *gateway*, while to external computers it is known as a *mail server* or *numeric address*.

proxy server (proxy)
software server that handles all communications originating from or being sent to the Internet, acting as a spokesperson or bodyguard for the organization

PROTECTING SERVERS AND CLIENTS

Operating system features and anti-virus software can help further protect servers and clients from certain types of attacks.

Operating System Security Enhancements

The most obvious way to protect servers and clients is to take advantage of Microsoft's and Apple's automatic computer security upgrades. Microsoft and Apple continuously update their operating systems to patch vulnerabilities discovered by hackers. These patches are autonomic; that is, when using these operating systems on the Internet, you are prompted and informed that operating system enhancements are available. Users can easily download these security patches for free.

Anti-Virus Software

The easiest and least-expensive way to prevent threats to system integrity is to install anti-virus software. Programs by McAfee, Symantec (Norton AntiVirus), and many others provide inexpensive tools to identify and eradicate the most common types of malicious code as they enter a computer, as well as destroy those already lurking on a hard drive. Anti-virus programs can be set up so that e-mail attachments are inspected prior to you clicking on them, and the attachments are eliminated if they contain a known virus or worm. It is not enough, however, to simply install the software once. Since new viruses are developed and released every day, daily routine updates are needed in order to prevent new threats from being loaded. Some premium-level anti-virus software is updated hourly.

5.4 E-COMMERCE PAYMENT SYSTEMS

For the most part, existing payment mechanisms have been able to be adapted to the online environment, albeit with some significant limitations that have led to efforts to develop alternatives. In addition, new types of purchasing relationships, such as between individuals online, and new technologies, such as the development of the mobile platform, have also created both a need and an opportunity for the development of new payment systems. In this section, we provide an overview of the major e-commerce payment systems in use today.

Online payment represented a market of more than $360 billion in 2012. Institutions and business firms that can handle this volume of transactions (mostly the large banking and credit firms) generally extract 2%–3% of the transactions in the form of fees, or about $7 to $10 billion a year in revenue. Given the size of the market, competition for online payments is spirited.

In the United States, the primary form of online payment is still the existing credit card system. Although credit card usage slipped somewhat during the recession, the total payments volume for online use of credit cards by U.S. consumers is expected to climb by over 50% in the five-year period from 2011 to 2016, compared to just a 2% increase for debit card usage during the same period. Alternative payments, although currently representing less than 20% of e-commerce transactions, are also expected to continue to make inroads into traditional payment methods (Javelin Strategy & Research, 2011). **Figure 5.9** illustrates the approximate usage of various payment types. PayPal is the most popular alternative to usage of credit and debit cards online.

In other parts of the world, e-commerce payments can be very different depending on traditions and infrastructure. Credit cards are not nearly as dominant a form of online payment as they are in the United States. If you plan on operating a Web site in Europe, Asia, or Latin America, you will need to develop different payment systems for each region.

ONLINE CREDIT CARD TRANSACTIONS

Because credit and debit cards are the dominant form of online payment, it is important to understand how they work and to recognize the strengths and weaknesses of this payment system. Online credit card transactions are processed in much the same way that in-store purchases are, with the major differences being that online merchants never see the actual card being used, no card impression is taken, and no signature is available. Online credit card transactions most closely resemble

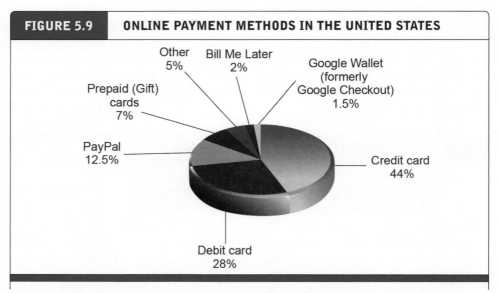

| FIGURE 5.9 | ONLINE PAYMENT METHODS IN THE UNITED STATES |

Other 5%
Bill Me Later 2%
Google Wallet (formerly Google Checkout) 1.5%
Prepaid (Gift) cards 7%
PayPal 12.5%
Credit card 44%
Debit card 28%

Traditional credit cards are still the dominant method of payment for online purchases, although alternative methods such as PayPal and mobile payments are faster growing.

SOURCES: Based on data from Internet Retailer, 2012; Javelin Strategy & Research, 2011; industry sources.

Mail Order-Telephone Order (MOTO) transactions. These types of purchases are also called Cardholder Not Present (CNP) transactions and are the major reason that charges can be disputed later by consumers. Since the merchant never sees the credit card, nor receives a hand-signed agreement to pay from the customer, when disputes arise, the merchant faces the risk that the transaction may be disallowed and reversed, even though he has already shipped the goods or the user has downloaded a digital product.

Figure 5.10 illustrates the online credit card purchasing cycle. There are five parties involved in an online credit card purchase: consumer, merchant, clearinghouse, merchant bank (sometimes called the "acquiring bank"), and the consumer's card-issuing bank. In order to accept payments by credit card, online merchants must have a merchant account established with a bank or financial institution. A **merchant account** is simply a bank account that allows companies to process credit card payments and receive funds from those transactions.

As shown in Figure 5.10, an online credit card transaction begins with a purchase (1). When a consumer wants to make a purchase, he or she adds the item to the merchant's shopping cart. When the consumer wants to pay for the items in the shopping cart, a secure tunnel through the Internet is created using SSL. Using encryption, SSL secures the session during which credit card information will be sent to the merchant and protects the information from interlopers on the Internet (2). SSL does not

merchant account
a bank account that allows companies to process credit card payments and receive funds from those transactions

FIGURE 5.10 HOW AN ONLINE CREDIT CARD TRANSACTION WORKS

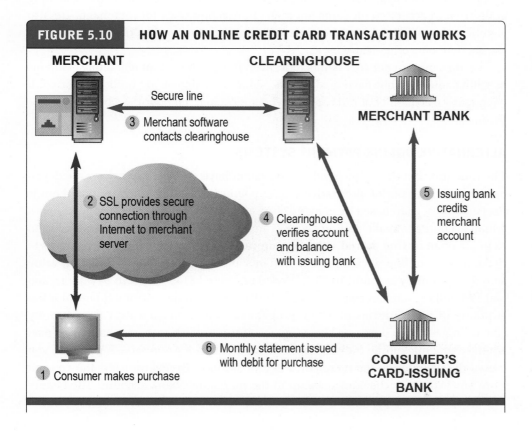

authenticate either the merchant or the consumer. The transacting parties have to trust one another.

Once the consumer credit card information is received by the merchant, the merchant software contacts a clearinghouse (3). As previously noted, a clearinghouse is a financial intermediary that authenticates credit cards and verifies account balances. The clearinghouse contacts the issuing bank to verify the account information (4). Once verified, the issuing bank credits the account of the merchant at the merchant's bank (usually this occurs at night in a batch process) (5). The debit to the consumer account is transmitted to the consumer in a monthly statement (6).

Limitations of Online Credit Card Payment Systems

There are a number of limitations to the existing credit card payment system. The most important limitations involve security, merchant risk, administrative and transaction costs, and social equity.

The existing system offers poor security. Neither the merchant nor the consumer can be fully authenticated. The merchant could be a criminal organization designed to collect credit card numbers, and the consumer could be a thief using stolen or fraudulent cards. The risk facing merchants is high: consumers can repudiate charges even though the goods have been shipped or the product downloaded. The banking industry attempted to develop a secure electronic transaction (SET) protocol, but this effort failed because it was too complex for consumers and merchants alike.

The administrative costs of setting up an online credit card system and becoming authorized to accept credit cards are high. Transaction costs for merchants are also significant—roughly 3.5% of the purchase plus a transaction fee of 20–30 cents per transaction, plus other setup fees.

Credit cards are not very democratic, even though they seem ubiquitous. Millions of young adults do not have credit cards, along with almost 100 million other adult Americans who cannot afford cards or who are considered poor risks because of low incomes.

ALTERNATIVE ONLINE PAYMENT SYSTEMS

online stored value payment system

permits consumers to make instant, online payments to merchants and other individuals based on value stored in an online account

The limitations of the online credit card system have opened the way for the development of a number of alternative online payment systems. Chief among them is PayPal. PayPal (purchased by eBay in 2002) enables individuals and businesses with e-mail accounts to make and receive payments up to a specified limit. Paypal is an example of an **online stored value payment system**, which permits consumers to make instant, online payments to merchants and other individuals based on value stored in an online account. In 2012, PayPal processed $145 billion in payments, and had 123 million active registered users. PayPal builds on the existing financial infrastructure of the countries in which it operates. You establish a PayPal account by specifying a credit, debit, or checking account you wish to have charged or paid when conducting online transactions. When you make a payment using PayPal, you e-mail the payment to the merchant's PayPal account. PayPal transfers the amount from your credit or checking account to the merchant's bank account. The beauty of PayPal is that no personal credit information has to be shared among the users, and the service can be used by individuals to pay one another even in small amounts. Issues with PayPal include its high cost (in addition to paying the credit card fee of 3.5%, PayPal tacks on a variable fee of from 1.5%–3% depending on the size of the transaction) and its lack of consumer protections when a fraud occurs or a charge is repudiated. PayPal is discussed in further depth in the case study at the end of the chapter.

Although PayPal is by far the most well-known and commonly used online credit/debit card alternative, there are a number of other alternatives as well. Amazon Payments is aimed at consumers who have concerns about entrusting their credit card information to unfamiliar online retailers. Consumers can purchase goods and services at non-Amazon Web sites using the payment methods stored in their Amazon accounts, without having to reenter their payment information at the merchant's site. Amazon provides the payment processing. Google Checkout (now merged into Google Wallet, described further in the following section on Mobile Payments) offers similar functionality, enabling consumers to sign in once and then shop online at thousands of different stores without having to reenter account information.

MOBILE PAYMENT SYSTEMS: YOUR SMARTPHONE WALLET

The use of mobile devices as payment mechanisms is already well established in Europe, Japan, and South Korea and is expanding rapidly in the United States, where the infrastructure to support mobile payment is finally being put in place, especially with the advent of smartphones equipped with near field communication chips. **Near field communication (NFC)** is a set of short-range wireless technologies used to share information among devices within about 2 inches of each other (50 mm). NFC devices are either powered or passive. A connection requires one powered unit (the initiator), and one target unpowered unit that can respond to requests from the powered unit. NFC targets can be very simple forms such as tags, stickers, key fobs, or readers. NFC peer-to-peer communication is possible where both devices are powered. An NFC-equipped smartphone, for instance, can be swiped by a merchant's reader to record a payment wirelessly and without contact. In September 2011, Google introduced Google Wallet, a mobile app designed to work with NFC chips. Google Wallet currently works with the MasterCard PayPass contactless payment card system. It is also designed to work with Android smartphones that are equipped with NFC chips, although, as of September 2012, there were few such smartphones on the market in the United States. PayPal and start-up Square are attacking the mobile payment market from a different direction, with apps and credit card readers that attach to smartphones.

In 2012, mobile retail purchases totaled around $11.6 billion.

DIGITAL CASH AND VIRTUAL CURRENCIES

Although the terms digital cash and virtual currencies are often used synonymously, they actually refer to two separate types of alternative payment systems. **Digital cash** is typically based on an algorithm that generates unique authenticated tokens representing cash value that can be used "in the real world." Examples of digital cash include Bitcoin and Ukash. Bitcoins are encrypted numbers (sometimes referred to as crypto-

near field communication (NFC)
a set of short-range wireless technologies used to share information among devices

digital cash
an alternative payment system in which unique, authenticated tokens represent cash value

currency) that are generated by a complex algorithm using a peer-to-peer network in a process referred to as "mining," that requires extensive computing power. Like real currency, Bitcoins have a fluctuating value tied to open-market trading. Like cash, Bitcoins are anonymous—they are exchanged via a 34-character alphanumeric address that the user has, and do not require any other identifying information.

virtual currency
typically circulates within an internal virtual world community or is issued by a specific corporate entity, and used to purchase virtual goods

Virtual currencies, on the other hand, typically circulate primarily within an internal virtual world community, such as Linden Dollars, created by Linden Lab for use in its virtual world, Second Life, or are associated with a specific corporation, such as Facebook Credits. Both types are typically used for purchasing virtual goods.

5.5   ELECTRONIC BILLING PRESENTMENT AND PAYMENT

In 2007, for the first time, the number of bill payments made online exceeded the number of physical checks written (Fiserv, 2007). In the $15.6 trillion U.S. economy of 2012 with an $11.1 trillion consumer sector for goods and services, there are a lot of bills to pay. No one knows for sure, but some experts believe the life-cycle cost of a paper bill for a business, from point of issuance to point of payment, ranges from $3 to $7. This calculation does not include the value of time to consumers, who must open bills, read them, write checks, address envelopes, stamp, and then mail remittances. The billing market represents an extraordinary opportunity for using the Internet as an electronic billing and payment system that potentially could greatly reduce both the cost of paying bills and the time consumers spend paying them. Estimates vary, but online payments are believed to cost between only 20 to 30 cents to process.

electronic billing presentment and payment (EBPP) system
form of online payment systems for monthly bills

Electronic billing presentment and payment (EBPP) systems are systems that enable the online delivery and payment of monthly bills. EBPP services allow consumers to view bills electronically and pay them through electronic funds transfers from bank or credit card accounts. More and more companies are choosing to issue statements and bills electronically, rather than mailing out paper versions. But even those businesses that do mail paper bills are increasingly offering online bill payment as an option to customers, allowing them to immediately transfer funds from a bank or credit card account to pay a bill somewhere else.

MARKET SIZE AND GROWTH

There were just 12 million U.S households (11% of all households) using online bill payment in 2001. In 2011, according to the financial technology firm Fiserv, an estimated 40 million U.S. households used online bill payment at a financial institution, while 53 million used biller-direct bill payment, in each case an 11% increase over 2010. Online bill payments now account for half of all bill payments, while paper checks now account for less than 25% (Fiserv, 2012).

One major reason for the surge in EBPP usage is that companies are starting to realize how much money they can save through online billing. Not only is there the savings in postage and processing, but payments can be received more quickly (3 to 12 days faster, compared to paper bills sent via regular mail), thereby improving cash flow. In order to realize these savings, many companies are becoming more aggressive in encouraging their customers to move to EBPP by instituting a charge for the privilege of continuing to receive a paper bill. Consumers are also becoming more receptive to online bill payment as they become more familiar with it.

EBPP BUSINESS MODELS

There are two main competing business models in the EBPP marketspace: biller-direct and consolidator. The biller-direct system was originally created by utility companies that send millions of bills each month. Their purpose is to make it easier for their customers to pay their utility bills routinely online. Today, telephone and credit card companies also frequently offer this service, as well as a number of individual stores. Companies implementing a biller-direct system can either develop their own system in-house (usually only an option for the very largest companies), install a system acquired from a third-party EBPP software vendor, use a third-party EBPP service bureau (the service bureau hosts a biller-branded Web site that enables consumers to view and pay bills and handles all customer enrollment, bill presentment, and payment processing), or use an application service provider (similar to a service bureau, but runs on the biller's Web site rather than being hosted on the service provider's Web site).

In the consolidator model, a third party, such as a financial institution or portal (either a general portal such as Yahoo! Bill Pay, or a focused portal such Intuit's Paytrust.com), aggregates all bills for consumers and ideally permits one-stop bill payment (pay anyone). Currently, financial institutions have been more successful than portals in attracting online bill payers. The consolidator model faces several challenges. For billers, using the consolidator model means an increased time lag between billing and payment, and also inserts an intermediary between the company and its customer. For consumers, security continues to be a major issue. Most consumers are unwilling to pay any kind of fee to pay bills online, and many are concerned about sharing personal financial information with non-financial institutions.

Supporting these two primary business models are infrastructure providers such as Fiserv, Yodlee, FIS, Online Resources, MasterCard RPPS (Remote Payment and Presentment Service), and others that provide the software to create the EBPP system or handle billing and payment collection for the biller.

5.6	CASE STUDY

Online Payment Marketplace:
Goat Rodeo

The online payment marketplace is experiencing an explosion of innovative ideas, plans, and announcements and a battle between the titans of online payment and retailing. PayPal, credit card companies, telecommunications carriers like Verizon, AT&T, and T-Mobile, mobile hardware and software companies like Apple and Google, and even large retailers like Walmart and Target are all working to develop their very own online and mobile payment systems.

Each of these titans has its own version of a future payment system that challenges the other players. They all want to help us spend money and increase the convenience of shopping. They all want to not only gather the fees that such systems can produce, but also use it to gather oceans of personal consumer information and display ads throughout the payment transaction process, along with coupons, daily deals, and flash sales based on their knowledge of the consumer. The emergence of the mobile platform of smartphones and tablets has opened the door for new firms to enter the online payment marketplace.

The overall online payment market in the United States was estimated to be worth about $362 billion in 2012 and is growing at more than 15% a year. While small compared to the total e-commerce picture, mobile commerce, driven by smartphones, tablets, and cellular networks, is growing at more than 20% a year, and a recent study by Juniper Research estimates that in 2015, mobile payment volume worldwide will reach $670 billion. And according to the Federal Reserve, U.S. consumers spent an estimated $3.3 trillion on 60 billion credit and debit card transactions in 2010. Even if a small percentage of these transactions move from plastic to mobile payments, the potential revenue is very large.

While credit and debit cards remain the dominant method of online payment, PayPal is currently the most successful alternative. PayPal allows account holders to both receive and make payments without revealing their credit card numbers, and without having to establish a credit card processing account with the credit card companies or merchant banks, offering security and convenience for both consumers and merchants. eBay purchased PayPal in 2002, and PayPal has since expanded from its eBay foundation to the larger world of online payments at e-commerce sites.

PayPal is currently the largest alternative online payment service and accounts for about 78% of the alternative payment market. In 2011, PayPal cleared about $118 billion in payments worldwide. In the mobile payment marketplace, PayPal cleared about $4 billion in payments, about 30% of the overall mobile payment market. In mobile payments, PayPal is a much smaller player than in the larger alternative payment market. This situation gives competitors an opening to challenge PayPal.

In March 2012, PayPal introduced PayPal Here, a card reader that plugs into a cell phone and can accept credit card payments, as well as check payments by taking a photo of the check. The card reader device and local accounting for payments is powered by a free smartphone app. PayPal charges 2.7% of each mobile transaction.

PayPal was late to the smartphone mobile payment market, beaten to the punch by a start-up firm called Square. Square started in 2009 with a smartphone app, credit card reader, and credit card processing service that allows anyone—businesses and individuals—to accept credit card payments. Today more than 2 million Square users are swiping away. The technology is quite simple: a square-shaped credit card reader plugs into—smartphones and tablet computers loaded with a Square app that processes the credit card information. Users can sign up online by registering a credit card with Square. Square charges merchants 2.75% of each transaction for the service, and there are no additional fees, minimums, or financial statements to file. In contrast, credit card fees for merchants typically range from 3% to 5%. Analysts believe that Square loses money on transactions less than $10, given that it must pay credit companies over 2% for their payment clearance. The future of Square will depend on the revenues it can derive from selling consumer information and placing ads on its payment system.

Square's initial credit card reader product was aimed at a market that was poorly served by credit card companies: small businesses like coffee shops, news stands, small retailers, and farmers' market merchants, as well as piano teachers, baby sitters, and taxi drivers. A poll by the National Retail Federation in 2012 found that 50% of businesses planned to use a mobile device as a cash register in the next 18 months. How many "small businesses" are there? There are 7.6 million businesses in the United States, and 6.5 million have fewer than 20 employees. These small firms employ about 30 million people and generate about $1 trillion in revenues. Mobile payment systems are aimed directly at this large, underserved marketplace.

In March 2011, Square introduced its second product: Square Register, an app for the iPad that turns the iPad into a cash register. In July 2012, Square released a new app called Pay With Square, which makes contact-less payments possible by simply entering the premises of a business, and using a photo as a personal ID in combination with a Square Register. In this system, there's no need to swipe a credit card. Using the phone's GPS, the app identifies merchants nearby that use Pay With Square. On entering the shop, you press an icon and the app sends your payment information and photo to the Square Register. After ordering your sandwich, you pay by saying your name to the merchant who checks your photo on the Square Register to ensure it's really you.

The key for all these payment systems is scale: getting enough consumers and merchants to adopt the Square dongle and purchase the iPads needed for the Square Register. Square received a tremendous boost in achieving scale in August 2012 when Starbucks agreed to use Square for all its credit card transactions in the United States. Starbucks has plenty of scale: 17,000 stores worldwide and 13,000 in the United States. Analysts believe that with Starbucks as a partner, Square will come to dominate the card swiping marketplace, and potentially play a large role in other contact-less payment schemes.

SOURCES: "Square Closes Financing Round," by Evelyn M. Rusli, *New York Times*, September 17, 2012; "Can Square Remain Hip?" by Petere Eavis, *New York Times,* August 31, 2012; "Big Retailers Team Up On Mobile Payments Plan," Reuters, August 15, 2012; "Payments Network Takes on Google," by Robin Sidel, *Wall Street Journal*, August 15, 2012; "Square Gets a Jolt From Starbucks," by Rolfe Winkler and Andrew R. Johnson, *Wall Street Journal*, August 8, 2012; "Starbucks and Square to Team Up" by Claire Cain Miller, *New York Times,* August 8, 2012; "Pay By Voice? So Long Wallet," by David Pogue, *New York Times*, July 18, 2012; "Many Competing Paths on the Road to the Phone Wallet," by Joshua Brustein, *New York Times*, May 6, 2012; "PayPal Takes on Start-Up," by Stu Woo, *Wall Street Journal*, March 16, 2012; "Retailers Join Payment Chase," by Robin Sidel, *Wall Street Journal*, March 2, 2012; "Mobile Payments: Moving Closer to a World without Wallets," by eMarketer, Inc., September 2011; "Look at All Those Zeros: Square Raises $100 Million at $1 Billion Valuation," by Tricia Duryee, Allthingsd.com, June 28, 2011; "Verizon to Add Payment Option," by Roger Cheng, *Wall Street Journal,* June 10, 2011; "Google Unveils Smartphone Pay Service, PayPal Sues," by Peter Svenson and Michael Liedtke, *Wall Street Journal*, May 27, 2011; "Payment Method Bypasses the Wallet," by Claire Cain Miller, *New York Times*, May 23, 2011; "Visa Advances Toward a Digital Wallet," by Jenna Wortham, *New York Times*, May 11, 2011; "Bill Paying Made Easier, But For a Fee," by Ann Cairns, *New York Times*, May 10, 2011; "Isis Says Carrier-backed Mobile Payments 'Accelerated,' Not 'Dialing Back,'" Matt Hamblen, *Computerworld*, May 4, 2011; "Google Sets Role in Mobile Payment," by Amir Efrati and Robin Sidel, *Wall Street Journal*, March 28, 2011; "Swiping Is the Easy Part," by Tara Bernard and Claire Miller, *New York Times*, March 21, 2011; "The Technology Behind Mobile Payments," by Nick Bilton, *New York Times*, March 21, 2011; "Your Mobile Phone is Becoming Your Wallet," by Laurie Segall, CNN Money, January 19, 2011.

While PayPal and Square duke it out in the card swiping payment market for small merchants, other payment schemes and plans that take advantage of the full capabilities of mobile devices are being announced monthly, if not daily. The greatest potential in the next five years for mobile payment systems are systems based on NFC. So-called "swipe and pay" systems, NFC enables a direct secure communication link between the consumer's smartphone and the merchant's cash register. All that's needed is to bring the smartphone in close proximity (six inches) to the cash register. The two biggest players in the NFC payment market are the telecommunication carriers' Isis system and Google's Google Wallet. A third stealth player is Merchant Customer Exchange (MCX), which is being created by some of the largest retailers in the United States.

Isis is a mobile swipe and pay venture backed by Verizon, AT&T, and T-Mobile, originally announced in 2010. To date, Isis has lined up Chase, Visa, MasterCard, Capital One, and American Express to process credit card transactions.

Google Wallet is an online payment system originally designed for desktop PCs, but Google has now extended it to include a mobile component in partnership with Sprint, Citibank, and MasterCard. Google Wallet is the only NFC system that is operational, and Google claims that it is available at 150,000 merchants. In Google's system, customers tap the merchant's NFC terminal at checkout. Called Tap & Go, Google offers its payment system with no charge to credit card companies and will not take a slice of transactions like Isis, and other mobile payment systems. Instead, Google will retain the right to display ads, coupons, loyalty programs, and daily deals by local merchants nearby on the user's mobile screen.

Merchant Customer Exchange (MCX) is an NFC payment system being developed by Walmart, Target, Sears, 7-Eleven Inc., Sunoco, and 10 other national pharmacies, supermarkets, and restaurant chains. Customers will be able to download an app to their smartphone and make purchases by tapping the phone against an NFC reader by the cash register. These nationwide merchants do not want valuable marketing assets of personal information to flow to financial service firms or Google.

The future for smartphone mobile payments is assured given the size of the players involved, the potential rewards for successful players, and the demands of consumers for a payment system that does not involve swiping plastic cards and dealing with slips of paper. But it is unlikely that all the payment systems described above will survive, and also quite likely that consumers will remain confused by all their payment options for some time yet to come.

Case Study Questions

1. What is the value proposition that Square offers consumers? How about merchants? What are some of the weaknesses of Square's system?

2. What advantages does PayPal have in the mobile payment market? What are its weaknesses?

3. What strategies would you recommend that PayPal pursue in order to translate its dominance in alternative online payments into a strong position in the emerging mobile payment market, especially in on-premise payments?

5.7 REVIEW

KEY CONCEPTS

■ **Understand the scope of e-commerce crime and security problems.**

While the overall size of cybercrime is unclear at this time, cybercrime against e-commerce sites is growing rapidly, the amount of losses is growing, and the management of e-commerce sites must prepare for a variety of criminal assaults.

■ **Describe the key dimensions of e-commerce security.**

There are six key dimensions to e-commerce security:
* *Integrity*—ensures that information displayed on a Web site or sent or received via the Internet has not been altered in any way by an unauthorized party.
* *Nonrepudiation*—ensures that e-commerce participants do not deny (repudiate) their online actions.
* *Authenticity*—verifies an individual's or business's identity.
* *Confidentiality*—determines whether information shared online, such as through e-mail communication or an order process, can be viewed by anyone other than the intended recipient.
* *Privacy*—deals with the use of information shared during an online transaction. Consumers want to limit the extent to which their personal information can be divulged to other organizations, while merchants want to protect such information from falling into the wrong hands.
* *Availability*—determines whether a Web site is accessible and operational at any given moment.

■ **Identify the key security threats in the e-commerce environment.**

The most common and most damaging forms of security threats to e-commerce sites include:
* *Malicious code*—viruses, worms, Trojan horses, and bot networks.
* *Potentially unwanted programs (adware, spyware, etc.)*—a kind of security threat that arises when programs are surreptitiously installed on your computer or computer network without your consent.
* *Phishing*—any deceptive, online attempt by a third party to obtain confidential information for financial gain.
* *Hacking and cybervandalism*—intentionally disrupting, defacing, or even destroying a site.
* *Credit card fraud/theft*—one of the most-feared occurrences and one of the main reasons more consumers do not participate in e-commerce.
* *Spoofing*—occurs when hackers attempt to hide their true identities or misrepresent themselves by using fake e-mail addresses or masquerading as someone else.
* *Denial of Service (DoS) and Distributed Denial of Service (DDoS) attacks*—hackers flood a Web site with useless traffic to inundate and overwhelm the network.
* *Sniffing*—a type of eavesdropping program that monitors information traveling over a network.

- *Insider jobs*—although the bulk of Internet security efforts are focused on keeping outsiders out, the biggest threat is from employees who have access to sensitive information and procedures.
- *Poorly designed server and client software*—the increase in complexity and size of software programs has contributed to an increase in software flaws or vulnerabilities that hackers can exploit.
- *Social network security issues*—malicious code, PUPs, phishing, data breaches, identity theft and other e-commerce security threats have all infiltrated social networks.
- *Mobile platform security issues*—the mobile platform presents an alluring target for hackers and cybercriminals, and faces all the same risks as other Internet devices, as well as new risks associated with wireless network security.
- *Cloud security issues*—as devices, identities, and data become more and more intertwined in the cloud, safeguarding data in the cloud becomes a major concern.

■ **Describe how technology helps protect the security of messages sent over the Internet.**

Encryption is the process of transforming plain text or data into cipher text that cannot be read by anyone other than the sender and the receiver. Encryption can provide four of the six key dimensions of e-commerce security:
- *Message integrity*—provides assurance that the sent message has not been altered.
- *Nonrepudiation*—prevents the user from denying that he or she sent a message.
- *Authentication*—provides verification of the identity of the person (or computer) sending the message.
- *Confidentiality*—gives assurance that the message was not read by others.

There are a variety of different forms of encryption technology currently in use. They include:
- *Symmetric key encryption*—Both the sender and the receiver use the same key to encrypt and decrypt a message.
- *Public key cryptography*—Two mathematically related digital keys are used: a public key and a private key.
- *Public key encryption using digital signatures and hash digests*—This method uses a mathematical algorithm called a hash function to produce a fixed-length number called a hash digest.
- *Digital certificates and public key infrastructure*—This method relies on certification authorities who issue, verify, and guarantee digital certificates (a digital document that contains the name of the subject or company, the subject's public key, a digital certificate serial number, an expiration date, an issuance date, the digital signature of the certification authority, and other identifying information).

■ **Identify the tools used to establish secure Internet communications channels and protect networks, servers, and clients.**

In addition to encryption, there are several other tools that are used to secure Internet channels of communication, including:
- *Secure Sockets Layer (SSL)/Transport Layer Security (TLSD)*—This is the most common form of securing channels. The SSL/TLS protocols provide data encryption, server authentication, client authentication, and message integrity for TCP/IP connections.

- *Virtual private networks (VPNs)*—These allow remote users to securely access internal networks via the Internet, using PPTP, an encoding mechanism that allows one local network to connect to another using the Internet as the conduit.

After communications channels are secured, tools to protect networks, the servers, and clients should be implemented. These include:

- *Firewalls*—software applications that act as filters between a company's private network and the Internet itself, preventing unauthorized remote client computers from attaching to your internal network.
- *Proxies*—software servers that act primarily to limit access of internal clients to external Internet servers and are frequently referred to as the gateway.
- *Operating system controls*—built-in username and password requirements that provide a level of authentication.
- *Anti-virus software*—a cheap and easy way to identify and eradicate the most common types of viruses as they enter a computer, as well as to destroy those already lurking on a hard drive.

■ Identify the major e-commerce payment systems in use today.

The major types of e-commerce payment systems in use today include:

- *Online credit card transactions,* which are the primary form of online payment system.
- *PayPal*, which is an example of an online stored value payment system that permits consumers to make instant, online payments to merchants and other individuals based on value stored in an online account.
- *Alternative payment services* such as Amazon Payments, Google Checkout/ Google Wallet, and Bill Me Later, which enable consumers to shop online at a wide variety of merchants without having to provide credit card information each time they make a purchase.
- *Mobile payment systems*, using either credit card readers attached to a smartphone (Square, PayPal Here) or near field communication (NFC) chips, which enable contactless payment.
- *Digital cash* such as Bitcoin, which is based on an algorithm that generates unique authenticated tokens representing cash value, and virtual currencies, that typically circulate within an internal virtual world or are issued by a corporation, and usually used for the purchase of virtual goods.

■ Describe the features and functionality of electronic billing presentment and payment systems.

Electronic billing presentment and payment (EBPP) systems are a form of online payment systems for monthly bills. EBPP services allow consumers to view bills electronically and pay them through electronic funds transfers from bank or credit card accounts.

QUESTIONS

1. Why is it less risky to steal online? Explain some of the ways criminals deceive consumers and merchants.
2. Explain why an e-commerce site might not want to report being the target of cybercriminals.

3. Give an example of security breaches as they relate to each of the six dimensions of e-commerce security. For instance, what would be a privacy incident?
4. How would you protect your firm against a Denial of Service attack?
5. Name the major points of vulnerability in a typical online transaction.
6. How does spoofing threaten a Web site's operations?
7. Why is adware or spyware considered to be a security threat?
8. Explain some of the modern-day flaws associated with encryption. Why is encryption not as secure today as it was earlier in the century?
9. Briefly explain how public key cryptography works.
10. Compare and contrast firewalls and proxy servers and their security functions.
11. Is a computer with anti-virus software protected from viruses? Why or why not?
12. Briefly discuss the disadvantages of credit cards as the standard for online payments. How does requiring a credit card for payment discriminate against some consumers?
13. Describe the major steps involved in an online credit card transaction.
14. How is money transferred in transactions using wireless devices?
15. Discuss why EBPP systems are becoming increasingly popular.

PROJECTS

1. Imagine you are the owner of an e-commerce Web site. What are some of the signs that your site has been hacked? Discuss the major types of attacks you could expect to experience and the resulting damage to your site. Prepare a brief summary presentation.

2. Given the shift toward mobile commerce, do a search on "mobile commerce crime." Identify and discuss the new security threats this type of technology creates. Prepare a presentation outlining your vision of the new opportunities for cybercrime.

3. Find three certification authorities and compare the features of each company's digital certificates. Provide a brief description of each company as well, including number of clients. Prepare a brief presentation of your findings.

4. Research the challenges associated with payments across international borders and prepare a brief presentation of your findings. Do most e-commerce companies conduct business internationally? How do they protect themselves from repudiation? How do exchange rates impact online purchases? What about shipping charges? Summarize by describing the differences between a U.S. customer and an international customer who each make a purchase from a U.S. e-commerce merchant.

PART **3**

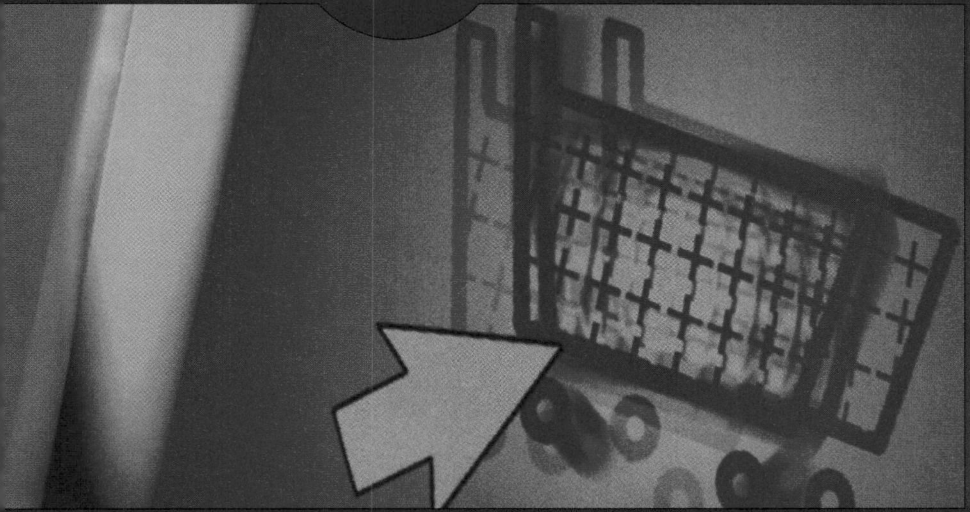

CHAPTER 6
E-commerce Marketing and
Advertising Concepts

CHAPTER 7
Ethical, Social, and Political
Issues in E-commerce

Business Concepts
and Social Issues

E-commerce Marketing and Advertising Concepts

After reading this chapter, you will be able to:

- Identify the key features of the Internet audience.
- Discuss the basic concepts of consumer behavior and purchasing decisions.
- Understand how consumers behave online.
- Identify and describe basic digital commerce marketing and advertising strategies and tools.
- Understand the costs and benefits of online marketing communications.

Facebook:

Does Social Marketing Work?

In 2012, Facebook launched its initial public offering and is now a publicly traded company. The question both investors and marketers face is straightforward: does Facebook's social marketing and advertising platform work? The answer to this question will determine Facebook's future.

Early market research has raised questions about the effectiveness of social networks as marketing platforms. Research by Goldman Sachs found that social network sites are not very effective at driving purchases. Less than 5% of online purchasers in the study ranked social network sites as the most important factor in purchasing. The most influential

© digitallife / Alamy

factors in purchasing are the retailers' Web site, search engines, display ads, and e-mails. To counter this research, Facebook commissioned a study by comScore to demonstrate the value of marketing on Facebook. Among the findings was the claim that being a fan of a brand on Facebook leads to more frequent purchases of the brand. A Facebook executive claimed that it's a myth that Facebook advertising does not work.

There are many marketing success stories, from both large Fortune 500 firms and small start-ups, that lend credibility to Facebook's claim that its social network marketing platform does, in fact, work. Currently, 88% of U.S. companies use Facebook for marketing purposes. One of the best known social media marketing campaigns is Ford Motor Company's Doug campaign, designed to attract a younger audience to its 2012 Ford Focus economy car. Ford needed a way to rebuild the brand's image, discover and engage with younger drivers, and create a market buzz that would drive people to showrooms.

Though Ford's Doug campaign was a creative use of several social media channels and a marketing success story, it was not a financial success for Facebook. Once Doug went viral there was no need to keep paying Facebook for its ads. Other large Fortune 500 advertisers report similar experiences with Facebook marketing. Only a tiny percentage of their online marketing budget goes to Facebook. While U.S. consumers spend 15% of their time online at Facebook, Facebook captures only 6.4% of total online ad spending, generating about $2 billion in U.S. ad revenues in 2012. Google remains the Internet marketing and ad giant with 2011 revenues of $38 billion. Still, there are hopeful signs that Facebook's larger advertiser base will expand. In 2012, Sony is moving 30% of its online advertising to social sites, and Diageo (maker of Smirnoff and Guinness) plans to spend $10 million on Facebook ads in 2012.

SOURCES: "Summer 2012 Online Shopper," Compete Inc., August 2012; "Facebook Marketing: Reaching Consumers in a Changing Environment," eMarketer Inc., August 2012; "Likeonomics: The Unexpected Truth Behind Earning Trust, Influencing Behavior, and Inspiring Action," by Rohit Bhargava, Wiley, 2012; "Facebook's Growth Slows," by Shayndi Raice, *Wall Street Journal*, July 27, 2012; "Facebook Combats Criticism Over Ads," by Shayndi Raice, *Wall Street Journal*, June 12, 2012; "Facebook IPO Sputters," by Shayndi Raice, *New York Times*, May 18, 2012; "Big Brands Like Facebook, But They Don't Like to Pay," by Emily Steel and Geoffrey Fowler, *Wall Street Journal*, November 2, 2012; "RIP, Doug: Ford Sends Focus Spokespuppet Packing," by Dale Buss, Brand-channel.com, September 28, 2011.

While large firms have not committed wholeheartedly to Facebook's marketing platform and are still experimenting, Facebook's real strength has been with smaller firms. One such firm is Pacific Rim, a winery in Portland, Oregon, that produces affordable Riesling wines.

Shawn Bavaresco founded Pacific Rim in 2006 with two other partners. Riesling is not a big seller like other white wines such as sauvignon blanc or pinot grigio. But the founders decided to focus on a single niche wine ignored by many retailers and wine drinkers rather than compete with wineries producing more popular varietals. And they decided to focus their marketing on millennials, people between the ages of 26 and 34, because they consume a large amount of wine and are willing to experiment with new wines. What they lacked was a committed online community of wine drinkers that shared their passion and was engaged with the brand and the wine.

In 2010, they launched a Facebook page, Pacific Rim Riesling Rules, aimed at building an online community of riesling lovers as well as creating retail point of sale. The page used contests to drive Likes, videos to engage users, animations to illustrate the wine production process, and the ability to purchase the wine directly from Pacific Rim. Pacific Rum used contests and giveaways to promote its page, generating 15,000 Likes.

Currently, the winery has 25,000 fans talking about its wines and sells 200,000 cases of wine a year. The Facebook fan base increased brand awareness among retailers, according to Bavaresco, making it much easier to convince wine retailers to sell Pacific Rim wine. Today, Pacific Rim's Facebook page has more than 29,000 Likes. You can find Pacific Rim wines at all major retailers throughout the United States. Pacific Rim was able to establish a direct connection with its customers, which is unusual in the wine industry. And most importantly, it experienced a 15% increase in revenue and 73% increase in transactions since the Facebook page launch.

The Ford and Pacific Rim examples illustrate successful uses of the Facebook platform. But in both cases, Facebook itself made little revenue. There are several Fortune 500 firms that have withdrawn from using Facebook as an advertising platform while still using Facebook's free marketing platform (Facebook pages are free). General Motors, for instance, which spends $40 million a year with Facebook, withdrew $10 million in 2012 devoted to Facebook ads because it found no relationship between its Facebook ads and purchases by consumers.

The biggest challenge facing Facebook is proving that ads on its platform lead to increases in sales, somewhere, somehow, down the line. One key issue is discovering what a Like means. Do a million Likes lead to increases in sales, and if so, by how much? What does it mean when 40% of people discussing your brand mention your Facebook campaign? No one knows at this point if Sponsored Stories work or if the new Reach Generator service will add up to new sales.

Despite having the largest online social audience in the world, it remains unclear if Facebook can monetize its user base and continue growing revenues at double-digit rates as it has done in the past. It will require several years of experimentation by marketers and Facebook to discover if social marketing on Facebook really works.

Facebook provides an example of how new Internet technologies and practices can disrupt and challenge existing industries. Perhaps no area of business has been more affected than marketing and marketing communications. As a communications tool, the Internet affords marketers new ways of contacting millions of potential customers at costs far lower than traditional media. The Internet also provides new ways—often instantaneous and spontaneous—to gather information from customers, adjust product offerings, and increase customer value. In the case of Facebook, and in the other cases in this and the following chapter, the Internet has spawned entirely new ways to identify and communicate with customers, including search engine marketing, social network marketing, behavioral targeting, recommender systems, and targeted e-mail.

The Internet was just the first transformation. Today, the mobile platform based on smartphones and tablet computers is transforming online marketing and communications yet again. The key changes in 2012 involved social networks, mobile marketing, and location-based services, including local marketing. In the next few years, the social, mobile, and local trends will accelerate as the technology improves and the always-on, social culture intensifies.

In this new environment in 2012–2013, advertisers are following huge shifts in audience away from traditional media and towards social networks, user-generated content, and online content destinations offering videos, music, and games. In this chapter, we begin by examining consumer behavior on the Web, the major types of online marketing and branding, and the technologies that support advances in online marketing. We then focus on online marketing communications, including a look at various online advertising methods and strategies.

6.1 CONSUMERS ONLINE: THE INTERNET AUDIENCE AND CONSUMER BEHAVIOR

Before firms can begin to sell their products online, they must first understand what kinds of people they will find online and how those people behave in the online marketplace. In this section, we focus primarily on individual consumers in the business-to-consumer (B2C) arena. However, many of the factors discussed apply to the B2B arena as well, insofar as purchasing decisions by firms are made by individuals.

INTERNET TRAFFIC PATTERNS: THE ONLINE CONSUMER PROFILE

We will start with an analysis of some basic background demographics of Web consumers in the United States. The first principle of marketing and sales is "know thy customer." Who uses the Web, who shops on the Web and why, and what do they buy? In 2012, around 239 million people of all ages and more than 89 million U.S. households (about 75% of all U.S. households) had access to the Internet (eMarketer, Inc., 2012a). By comparison, 98% of all U.S. households currently have televisions and 94% have telephones. Worldwide, around 2.26 billion people are online.

Although the number of new online users increased at a rate of 30% a year or higher in the early 2000s, over the last several years, this growth rate has slowed to about 2%–3% a year. E-commerce businesses can no longer count on a double-digit growth rate in the online population to fuel their revenues. The days of extremely rapid growth in the U.S. Internet population are over.

Intensity and Scope of Usage

The slowing rate of growth in the U.S. Internet population is compensated for, in part, by an increasing intensity and scope of use. Several studies show that a greater amount of time is being spent online by Internet users. Overall, users are going online more frequently, with 82% of adult users in the United States (158 million people) logging on in a typical day (Pew Internet & American Life Project, 2012a). In 2012, mobile smartphones and tablets are major new access points to the Internet and online commerce. About 122 million people, about half of all U.S. Internet users, access the Internet using a mobile device. In 2012, 102 million mobile users played games, 61 million viewed videos, 77 million visited a social site, and millions of others listened to music, shopped, and texted. (eMarketer, Inc., 2012b, 2012c). The more time users spend online, becoming more comfortable and familiar with Internet features and services, the more services they are likely to explore, according to the Pew Internet & American Life Project.

People who go online are engaging in a wider range of activities than in the past. While e-mail and using search engines remain the most-used Internet services, other popular activities include visiting social network sites like Facebook, researching products and services, catching up on news, gathering hobby-related information, watching video on a video-sharing site such as YouTube, and banking online.

Demographics and Access

The demographic profile of the Internet—and e-commerce—has changed greatly since 1995. Up until 2000, single, white, young, college-educated males with high incomes dominated the Internet. This inequality in access and usage led to concerns about a possible "digital divide." However, in recent years, there has been a marked increase in Internet usage by females, minorities, seniors, and families with modest incomes, resulting in a notable decrease—but not elimination—in the earlier inequality of access and usage. The following discussion is based on data collected in surveys conducted by the Pew Internet & American Life Project. The people least likely to go online are senior citizens, adults with less than a high school education, and those living in households earning less than $30,000 a year (Pew Internet & American Life Project, 2012b).

Gender An equal percentage (85%) of both men and women use the Internet today, in contrast to 10 years ago, when the percentage of women online compared to men was slightly higher.

Age Young adults (18–29) form the age group with the highest percentage of Internet use, at 96%. Adults in the 30–49 group (93%) are also strongly represented. Another fast-growing group online is the 65 and over segment, 58% of whom now use the Internet, more than triple the level of 2002. Although not included in the Pew Internet & American report survey, teens (12–17) actually have the highest percentage of their age group online (97%). The percentage of very young children (1–11 years) online has also spurted, to 43% of that age group (eMarketer, Inc., 2012a).

Ethnicity Variation across ethnic groups is not as wide as across age groups. In 2002, there were significant differences among ethnic groups, but this has receded. In 2012, user participation by whites is 86%, African Americans, 86%, and Hispanics, 80%. The growth rates for both Hispanics and African Americans over the period from 2002 to 2010 is higher than for whites, which has helped close the gap.

Income Level About 99% of households with income levels above $75,000 have Internet access, compared to only 75% of households earning less than $30,000. However, those households with lower earnings are gaining Internet access at faster rates than households with incomes of $75,000 and above. Over time, income differences have declined but they remain significant. Income is not significantly related to exposure or hours using the Internet.

Education Amount of education also makes a significant difference when it comes to online access. Of those individuals with less than a high school education, 61% were online in 2012, compared to 97% of individuals with a college degree or more. Even a high school education boosted Internet usage, with that segment reaching 80%. In general, educational disparities far exceed other disparities in Internet access and usage.

Overall, there remains a strong relationship between age, income, ethnicity, and education on one hand and Internet usage on the other. The so-called "digital divide" has indeed moderated, but it still persists along the income, education, age, and ethnic dimensions. Gender, income, education, age, and ethnicity also impact online behavior. According to the Pew Internet & American Life Project, adults over the age of 65, those who have not completed high school, those who make less than $30,000 a year, and Hispanics are all less likely to purchase products online. Women are slightly more likely to purchase online than men, but not significantly so. With respect to online banking, the demographics are similar—those 65 and older are less likely than any age group to bank online, while those with at least some college are more likely than those with a high school diploma or less. Online banking is also more popular with men than women. No significant differences were found in terms of ethnicity (Pew Internet & American Life Project, 2012c). Other commentators have observed that children of poorer and less educated families are spending considerably more time using their access devices for entertainment (movies, games, Facebook, and texting) than children from wealthier households. For all children and teenagers, the majority of time spent on the Internet has been labeled "wasted time" because the majority of online use is for entertainment, and not education or learning (Richtel, 2012).

Type of Internet Connection: Broadband and Mobile Impacts

While a great deal of progress has been made in reducing glaring gaps in access to the Internet, there are significant inequalities in access to broadband service. In 2012, around 83 million households had broadband service in their homes—69% of all households and 96% of Internet households (eMarketer, Inc., 2012d). Research suggests the broadband audience is different from the dial-up audience: the broadband audience is more educated and affluent. The Federal Communications Commission reports that only 50% of Hispanic and African American homes have broadband, and only 40% of those homes with less than $20,000 in annual income (Federal Communications Commission, 2012). The broadband audience is much more intensely involved with the Internet and much more capable of using the Internet. For marketers, this audience offers unique opportunities for the use of multimedia marketing campaigns, and for the positioning of products especially suited for this audience. On the other hand, the dial-up households still buy products online, visit news sites, and use social network sites—just not as frequently or intensely as broadband households. The explosive growth of smartphones and tablet computers connected to broadband cellular and Wi-Fi networks is the foundation for a truly mobile e-commerce and marketing platform, which did not exist a few years ago. more than 122 million Americans access the Internet from mobile devices, and there are more than 300 million cell phone subscriptions. More than 115 million use smartphones, and 70 million use iPad tablet computers (eMarketer, Inc., 2012e). Marketers are just beginning to use this new platform for brand development.

Media Choices and Multitasking: The Internet versus Other Media Channels

What may be of even more interest to marketers, however, is that the more time individuals spend using the Internet, the more they turn their back on traditional media. For every additional hour users spend online, they reduce their corresponding time spent with traditional media, such as television, newspapers, and radio. Traditional media are competing with the Internet for consumer attention, and so far, the Internet appears to be gaining on print media (newspapers and magazines) but not television. Television viewing has increased as the Internet has grown in popularity. About 60% of TV viewers use the Internet simultaneously (mostly chatting, searching, e-mailing, and using Facebook or Twitter). Media multitasking is rising: over 100 million U.S. adult Internet users watch television while going online. Others listen to the radio, read magazines, or newspapers. A USC study found that more than 80% of Internet users multitasked at least some of the time they spent online (USC Annenberg School, 2011). Multitasking makes measurement of media exposure difficult because people can "expand" their media time by using multiple media at once. We discuss media consumption in greater depth in Chapter 10.

PROFILES OF ONLINE CONSUMERS

Online consumer behavior parallels that of offline consumer behavior with some obvious differences. It is important to first understand why people choose the Internet channel to conduct transactions. **Table 6.1** lists the main reasons consumers choose the online channel.

TABLE 6.1	WHY CONSUMERS CHOOSE THE ONLINE CHANNEL	
REASON	PERCENTAGE OF RESPONDENTS	
24-hour shopping convenience	35.1%	
Easier to compare prices	33.1%	
Free shipping offers	31.5%	
No crowds like in mall/traditional stores	30.8%	
More convenient to shop online	29.2%	
Easier to find items online than in stores	17.5%	
Better variety online	17.4%	
No sales tax	14.9%	
Direct shipping to gift recipients	13.8%	
Easier to compare products	11.4%	

SOURCE: Based on data from eMarketer, Inc., 2011a.

While price appears on this list, overwhelmingly, consumers shop on the Web because of convenience, which in turn is produced largely by saving them time. Overall transaction cost reduction appears to be the major motivator for choosing the online channel, followed by other cost reductions in the product or service.

THE ONLINE PURCHASING DECISION

Once online, why do consumers actually purchase a product or service at a specific site? **Table 6.2** lists some of the most important factors that influence consumers' decisions to purchase online. Among the most important are price and the availability of free shipping. That the seller is someone whom the purchaser trusts is also a very important factor. The ability to make a purchase without paying tax and the availability of an online coupon are also significant factors.

But aside from individual characteristics, you also need to consider the process that buyers follow when making a purchase decision, and how the Internet environment affects consumers' decisions. There are five stages in the consumer decision process: awareness of need, search for more information, evaluation of alternatives, the actual purchase decision, and post-purchase contact with the firm. **Figure 6.1** shows the consumer decision process and the types of offline and online marketing communications that support this process and seek to influence the consumer before, during, and after the purchase decision.

As shown in Figure 6.1, traditional mass media, along with catalogs and direct mail campaigns, are used to drive potential buyers to Web sites. What's new about online purchasing is the new media marketing communications capabilities afforded by the Web: search engines, social media such as blogs, social networks and social shopping sites, online product reviews, video ads, targeted banner ads and permission e-mail, bulletin boards, chat rooms, and the like. Simply put, the Web offers marketers an

TABLE 6.2	FACTORS THAT INFLUENCE ONLINE PURCHASE DECISIONS
FACTOR	PERCENTAGE OF RESPONDENTS
Price	95%
Free shipping	90%
Trusted seller status	75%
No tax	60%
Online coupon availability	58%
Return policy	55%
Customer loyalty/rewards program	35%

SOURCE: Based on data from Channel Advisor, 2010.

extraordinary increase in marketing communications tools and power, and the ability to envelop the consumer in a very rich information and purchasing environment. Both offline and online communications tools can be used to support the online consumer decision process at each of the five stages of the process.

The stages of the consumer decision process are basically the same whether the consumer is offline or online. On the other hand, the general model of consumer behavior requires modification to take into account new factors and the unique features of the Internet that allow new opportunities to interact with the customer online also need to be accounted for. In **Figure 6.2**, we have modified the general model of consumer behavior to focus on user characteristics, product characteristics, and Web site features, along with traditional factors such as brand strength and specific market

| FIGURE 6.1 | THE CONSUMER DECISION PROCESS AND SUPPORTING COMMUNICATIONS |

MARKET COMMUNICATIONS	Awareness—Need Recognition	Search	Evaluation of Alternatives	Purchase	Post-purchase Behavior—Loyalty
Offline Communications	Mass media TV Radio Print media Social networks	Catalogs Print ads Mass media Sales people Product raters Store visits Social networks	Reference groups Opinion leaders Mass media Product raters Store visits Social networks	Promotions Direct mail Mass media Print media	Warranties Service calls Parts and repair Consumer groups Social networks
Online Communications	Targeted banner ads Interstitials Targeted event promotions Social networks	Search engines Online catalogs Site visits Targeted e-mail Social networks	Search engines Online catalogs Site visits Product reviews User evaluations Social networks	Online promotions Lotteries Discounts Targeted e-mail Flash sales	Communities of consumption Newsletters Customer e-mail Online updates Social networks

communications (advertising) and the influence of both online and offline social networks.

In the online model, Web site features, along with consumer skills, product characteristics, attitudes towards online purchasing, and perceptions about control over the Web environment come to the fore. Web site features include latency (delay in downloads), navigability, and confidence in a Web site's security. There are parallels in the analog world. For instance, it is well known that consumer behavior can be influenced by store design, and that understanding the precise movements of consumers through a physical store can enhance sales if goods and promotions are arranged along the most likely consumer tracks. Consumer skills refers to the knowledge that consumers have about how to conduct online transactions (which increases with experience). Product characteristics refers to the fact that some products can be easily described, packaged, and shipped over the Internet, whereas others cannot. Combined with traditional factors, such as brand, advertising, and firm capabilities, these factors lead to specific attitudes about purchasing at a Web site (trust in the Web site and favorable customer experience) and a sense that the consumer can control his or her environment on the Web site.

FIGURE 6.2   A MODEL OF ONLINE CONSUMER BEHAVIOR

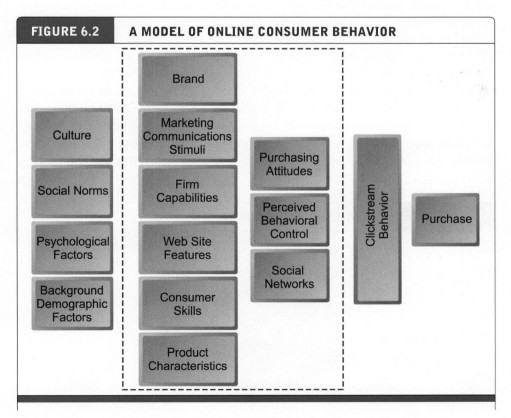

In this general model of online consumer behavior, the decision to purchase is shaped by background demographic factors, several intervening factors, and, finally, influenced greatly by clickstream behavior very near to the precise moment of purchase.

clickstream behavior

the transaction log that consumers establish as they move about the Web

Clickstream behavior refers to the transaction log that consumers establish as they move about the Web, from search engine to a variety of sites, then to a single site, then to a single page, and then, finally, to a decision to purchase. These precious moments are similar to "point-of-purchase" moments in traditional retail. A study of over 10,000 visits to an online wine store found that detailed and general clickstream behavior were as important as customer demographics and prior purchase behavior in predicting a current purchase (Van den Poel and Buckinx, 2005).

SHOPPERS: BROWSERS AND BUYERS

The picture of Internet use sketched in the previous section emphasizes the complexity of behavior online. Although the Internet audience still tends to be concentrated among the well educated, affluent, and youthful, the audience is increasingly becoming more diverse. Clickstream analysis shows us that people go online for many different reasons. Online shopping is similarly complex. Beneath the surface of the $362 billion B2C e-commerce market in 2012 are substantial differences in how users shop online.

For instance, as shown in **Figure 6.3**, about 72% of U.S. Internet users, age 14 and older, are "buyers" who actually purchase something entirely online. Another 16.5% research products on the Web ("browsers"), but purchase them offline. With the teen and adult U.S. Internet audience (14 years or older) estimated at about 209 million in 2012, online shoppers (the combination of buyers and browsers, totalling 88%) add up to a market size of around 184 million consumers. Most marketers find this number exciting.

The significance of online browsing for offline purchasing should not be underestimated. Although it is difficult to precisely measure the amount of offline sales that occur because of online product research, several different studies have found that about one-third of all offline retail purchasing is influenced by online product research, blogs, banner ads, and other Internet exposure. The offline influence varies

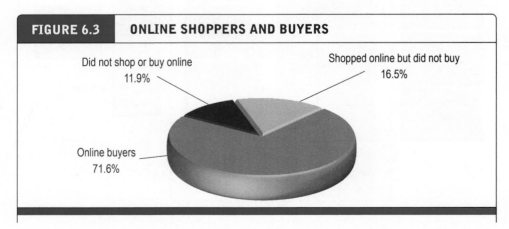

| FIGURE 6.3 | ONLINE SHOPPERS AND BUYERS |

Did not shop or buy online 11.9%

Shopped online but did not buy 16.5%

Online buyers 71.6%

About 88% of U.S Internet users, age 14 and older, shop online, either by researching products or by purchasing products online. The percentage of those actually purchasing has increased to about 72%. Only about 12% do not buy or shop online.

SOURCE: Based on data from eMarketer, Inc., 2012f.

by product. This amounts to about $1.2 trillion in annual retail sales, a truly extraordinary number (Forrester Research, 2011b).

E-commerce is a major conduit and generator of offline commerce. The reverse is also true: online traffic is driven by offline brands and shopping. While online research influences offline purchases, it is also the case that offline marketing media heavily influence online behavior including sales. Traditional print media (magazines and newspapers) and television are by far the most powerful media for reaching and engaging consumers with information about new products and directing them to the Web. Online communities and blogging are also very influential but not yet as powerful as traditional media. This may be surprising to many given the attention to social networks as marketing vehicles, but it reflects the diversity of influences on consumer behavior and the real-world marketing budgets of firms that are still heavily dominated by traditional media. Even more surprising in the era of Facebook, face-to-face interactions are a more powerful influence than participation in online social communities.

WHAT CONSUMERS SHOP FOR AND BUY ONLINE

You can look at online sales as divided roughly into two groups: small-ticket and big-ticket items. Big-ticket items include computer equipment and consumer electronics, where orders can easily be more than $1,000. Small-ticket items include apparel, books, health and beauty supplies, office supplies, music, software, videos, and toys, where the average purchase is typically less than $100. But the recent growth of big-ticket items such as computer hardware, consumer electronics, furniture, and jewelry has changed the overall sales mix. Consumers are now much more confident spending online for big-ticket items. Although furniture and large appliances were initially perceived as too bulky to sell online, these categories have rapidly expanded in the last few years. Free shipping offered by Amazon and other large retailers has also contributed to consumers buying many more expensive and large items online such as air conditioners.

INTENTIONAL ACTS: HOW SHOPPERS FIND VENDORS ONLINE

Given the prevalence of "click here" banner ads, one might think customers are "driven" to online vendors by spur-of-the-moment decisions. In fact, only a tiny percentage of shoppers click on banners to find vendors. Once they are online, 59% of consumers use a search engine as their preferred method of research for purchasing a product, 28% go to marketplaces such as Amazon or eBay, 10% go direct to retail Web sites, and 3% use other methods (Channel Advisor, 2010). E-commerce shoppers are highly intentional. Typically, they are focused browsers looking for specific products, companies, and services. Merchants can convert these "goal-oriented," intentional shoppers into buyers if the merchants can target their communications to the shoppers and design their sites in such a way as to provide easy-to-access and useful product information, full selection, and customer service, and do this at the very moment the customer is searching for the product. This is no small task.

WHY MORE PEOPLE DON'T SHOP ONLINE

A final consumer behavior question to address is: Why don't more online Web users shop online? About 28% of Internet users do not buy online. Why not? **Table 6.3** lists the major online buying concerns among Internet users in the United States.

Arguably, the largest factor preventing more people from shopping online is the "trust factor," the fear that online merchants will cheat you, lose your credit card information, or use personal information you give them to invade your personal privacy, bombarding you with unwanted e-mail and pop-up ads. Secondary factors can be summarized as "hassle factors," like shipping costs, returns, and inability to touch and feel the product.

6.2 DIGITAL COMMERCE MARKETING AND ADVERTISING STRATEGIES AND TOOLS

Internet marketing has many similarities to, and differences from, ordinary marketing. (For more information on basic marketing concepts, see Learning Track 6.1). The objective of Internet marketing—as in all marketing—is to build customer relationships so that the firm can achieve above-average returns (both by offering superior products or services and by communicating the brand's features to the consumer). These relationships are a foundation for the firm's brand. But Internet marketing, including all forms of digital marketing, is also very different from ordinary marketing because the nature of the medium and its capabilities are so different from anything that has come before.

There are four features of Internet marketing that distinguish it from traditional marketing channels. Compared to traditional print and television marketing, Internet marketing can be more personalized, participatory, peer-to-peer, and communal. Not all types of Internet marketing have these four features. For instance, there's not much difference between a marketing video splashed on your computer screen without your

TABLE 6.3	WHY INTERNET USERS DO NOT BUY ONLINE
Want to see and touch before buying	34%
Concerns about personal financial information	31%
Delivery costs are too high	30%
Concerns that returns will be a hassle	26%
Prefer to research online, then buy in a store	24%
No need to buy products online	23%
Can't speak to a sales assistant in person	14%

SOURCE: Based on data from eMarketer, Inc., 2011a.

consent and watching a television commercial. However the same marketing video can be targeted to your personal interests, community memberships, and allow you to share it with others using a Like or + tag. Marketers are learning that the most effective Internet marketing has all four of these features.

THE WEB SITE AS A MARKETING PLATFORM: ESTABLISHING THE CUSTOMER RELATIONSHIP

A firm's Web site is a major tool for establishing the initial relationship with the customer. The Web site performs four important functions: establishing the brand identity and consumer expectations, informing and educating the consumer, shaping the customer experience, and anchoring the brand in an ocean of marketing messages coming from different sources. The Web site is the one place the consumer can turn to find the complete story. This is not true of apps, e-mails, or search engine ads.

The first function of a Web site is to establish the brand's identity and to act as an anchor for the firm's other Web marketing activities, thereby driving sales revenue. This involves identifying for the consumer the differentiating features of the product or service in terms of quality, price, product support, and reliability. Identifying the differentiating features of the product on the Web site's home page is intended to create expectations in the user of what it will be like to consume the product. For instance, Coke's Web site creates the expectation that the consumer will experience happiness by opening a Coke. Ford's Web site focuses on automobile technology and high miles per gallon. The expectation created by Ford's Web site is that if you buy a Ford, you'll be experiencing the latest automotive technology and the highest mileage. At the location-based social network Web site for Foursquare, the focus is on meeting friends, discovering local places, and saving money with coupons and rewards.

Web sites also function to anchor the brand online, acting as a central point where all the branding messages that emanate from the firm's multiple digital presences, such as Facebook, Twitter, mobile apps, or e-mail, come together at a single online location. Aside from branding, Web sites also perform the typical functions of any commercial establishment by informing customers of the company's products and services. Web sites, with their online catalogs and associated shopping carts, are important elements of the online customer experience. **Customer experience** refers to the totality of experiences that a customer has with a firm, including the search, informing, purchase, consumption, and after-sales support for the product. The concept "customer experience" is broader than the traditional concept of "customer satisfaction" in that a much broader range of impacts is considered, including the customer's cognitive, affective, emotional, social, and physical relationship to the firm and its products. The totality of customer experiences will generally involve multiple retail channels. This means that, in the customer's mind, the Web site, Facebook page, Twitter feed, physical store, and television advertisements are all connected as part of his or her experience with the company.

customer experience
the totality of experiences that a customer has with a firm, including the search, informing, purchase, consumption, and after-sales support for its products, services, and various retail channels

ONLINE MARKETING AND ADVERTISING TOOLS

Below we describe the basic marketing and advertising tools for attracting consumers to a Web site: search engine marketing, display ad marketing, e-mail and permission marketing, affiliate marketing, lead generation marketing, and sponsorship marketing.

online advertising
a paid message on a Web site, online service, or other interactive medium

Companies will spend an estimated $166 billion on advertising in 2012, and an estimated $37.3 billion of that amount on **online advertising**, which includes display (banners, video, and rich media), search, mobile messaging, sponsorships, classifieds, lead generation, and e-mail, on desktop, laptop, and tablet computers, as well as mobile phones (see **Figure 6.4**) (eMarketer, Inc., 2012f).

In the last five years, advertisers have aggressively increased online spending and cut outlays on traditional channels such as newspapers and magazines (both down over 30% in the last few years) while outdoor, television, and radio advertising have shown modest growth. Over the next five years, online advertising is expected to continue to be the fastest growing form of advertising, and by 2016, it is expected to be the second largest ad channel with a 29% share.

Table 6.4 provides some comparative data on the amount of spending for certain advertising formats. The online advertising format that currently produces the highest

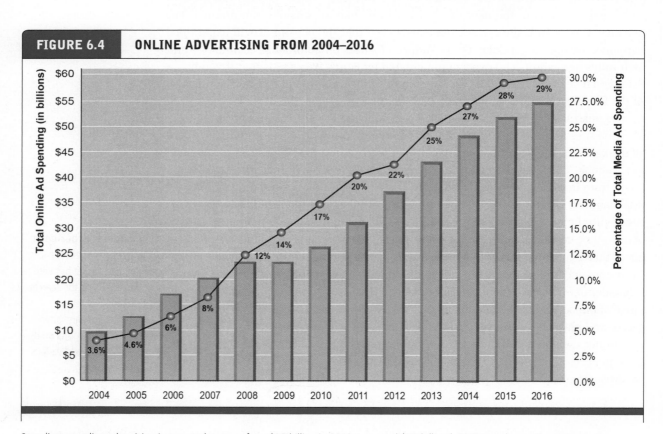

| FIGURE 6.4 | ONLINE ADVERTISING FROM 2004–2016 |

Spending on online advertising is expected to grow from $37 billion in 2012 to around $55 billion by 2016, and comprise an increasing percentage of total media ad spending.

SOURCES: Based on data from eMarketer, Inc., 2012a, 2012b.

TABLE 6.4	ONLINE ADVERTISING SPENDING FOR SELECTED FORMATS (IN BILLIONS)		
FORMAT	2012	2016	AVERAGE GROWTH RATE
Search	$17.6	$24.4	10%
Banner ads	$8.7	$11.3	8.4%
Video	$2.9	$8.0	32.6%
Classifieds	$2.6	$2.9	2.7%
Rich media	$1.8	$3.0	12.9%
Lead generation	$1.7	$2.2	7.8%
Sponsorships	$1.6	$2.9	21%
E-mail	$0.22	$0.24	2.7%
Total	$37.3	$55.3	11.6%

SOURCES: Based on data from eMarketer, Inc., 2012a.

revenue is paid search, followed by display ads, but the fastest growing online ad format is video ads.

Search Engine Marketing and Advertising

Search engines are the largest marketing and advertising platform on the Internet, and until recently, the fastest growing (see **Figure 6.5**). In 2012, companies spent an estimated $17.6 billion on search engine marketing, almost half of all spending for digital marketing. On an average day in the United States, around 114 million American adults (around 59% of the adult online population) will use a search engine (Pew Internet & American Life Project, 2012). Briefly, this is where the eyeballs are (at least for a few moments) and this is where advertising can be very effective by responding with ads that match the interests and intentions of the user. The click-through rate for search engine advertising is generally 1%–5% and has been fairly steady over the years. The top three search engine providers (Google, Microsoft/Bing, and Yahoo) supply more than 95% of all online searches.

Search engine marketing (SEM) refers to the use of search engines to build and sustain brands. **Search engine advertising** refers to the use of search engines to support direct sales to online consumers.

Search engines are often thought of as mostly direct sales channels focused on making sales in response to advertisements. While this is a major use of search engines, they are also used more subtly to strengthen brand awareness, drive traffic to other Web sites or blogs to support customer engagement, gain deeper insight into customers' perceptions of the brand, support other related advertising (for instance,

search engine marketing (SEM)
involves the use of search engines to build and sustain brands

search engine advertising
involves the use of search engines to support direct sales to online

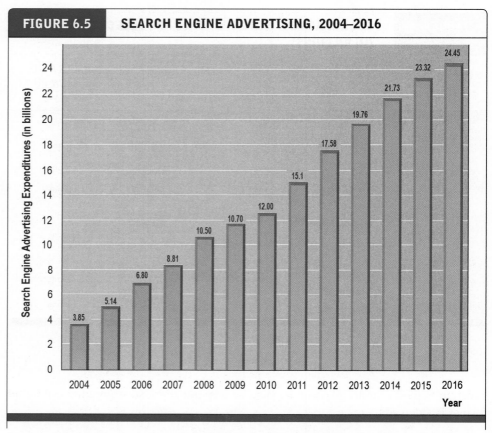

| FIGURE 6.5 | SEARCH ENGINE ADVERTISING, 2004–2016 |

Search engine advertising has grown to about 50% of all online advertising. However, its growth rate has slowed somewhat.

SOURCES: Based on data from eMarketer, Inc., 2012a.

sending consumers to local dealer sites), and to support the brand indirectly. Search engines can also provide marketers insight into customer search patterns, opinions customers hold about their products, top trending search keywords, and what their competitors are using as keywords and the customer response. For example, Pepsico, home of mega brands like Pepsi and Doritos, makes no sales on the Web, but has several branding Web sites aimed at consumers, investors, and shareholders. The focus is on building, sustaining, and updating the Pepsi collection of branded consumer goods. A search on Pepsi will generate numerous search results that link to Pepsi marketing materials.

Types of Search Engine Advertising There are at least three different types of search engine advertising: keyword paid inclusion (so-called "sponsored links"), advertising keywords (such as Google's AdWords), and search engine context ads (such as Google's AdSense). Search engine sites originally performed unbiased searches of the Web's huge collection of Web pages and derived most of their revenue from banner advertisements. This form of search engine results is often called **organic search** because the inclusion and ranking of Web sites depends on a more or less "unbiased" application of

organic search
inclusion and ranking of sites depends on a more or less unbiased application of a set of rules imposed by the search engine

a set of rules (an algorithm) imposed by the search engine. Since 1998, search engine sites slowly transformed themselves into digital yellow pages, where firms pay for inclusion in the search engine index, pay for keywords to show up in search results, or pay for keywords to show up in other vendors' ads.

Most search engines offer **paid inclusion** (also called sponsored link) programs which, for a fee, guarantee a Web site's inclusion in its list of search results, more frequent visits by its Web crawler, and suggestions for improving the results of organic searching. Search engines claim that these payments—costing some merchants hundreds of thousands a year—do not influence the organic ranking of a Web site in search results, just inclusion in the results. However, it is the case that page inclusion ads get more hits, and the rank of the page appreciates, causing the organic search algorithm to rank it higher in the organic results.

Google claims it does not permit firms to pay for their rank in the organic results, although it does allocate two to three sponsored links at the very top of their pages, albeit labeling them as "Sponsored Links." Merchants who refuse to pay for inclusion or for keywords typically fall far down on the list of results, and off the first page of results, which is akin to commercial death.

The two other types of search engine advertising rely on selling keywords in online auctions.

In **keyword advertising**, merchants purchase keywords through a bidding process at search sites, and whenever a consumer searches for that word, their advertisement shows up somewhere on the page, usually as a small text-based advertisement on the right, but also as a listing on the very top of the page. The more merchants pay, the higher the rank and greater the visibility of their ads on the page. Generally, the search engines do not exercise editorial judgment about quality or content of the ads although they do monitor the use of language. In addition, some search engines rank the ads in terms of their popularity rather than merely the money paid by the advertiser so that the rank of the ad depends on both the amount paid and the number of clicks per unit time. Google's keyword advertising program is called AdWords, Yahoo's is called Sponsored Search, and Microsoft's is called adCenter.

Network keyword advertising (**context advertising**), introduced by Google as its AdSense product in 2002, differs from ordinary keyword advertising described previously. Publishers (Web sites that want to show ads) join these networks and allow the search engine to place "relevant" ads on their sites. The ads are paid for by advertisers who want their messages to appear across the Web. Google-like text messages are the most common. The revenue from the resulting clicks is split between the search engine and the site publisher, although the publisher gets much more than half in some cases. About half of Google's revenue comes from AdWords and the rest comes from AdSense.

Search engine advertising is nearly an ideal targeted marketing technique: at precisely the moment that a consumer is looking for a product, an advertisement for that product is presented.

Consumers benefit from search engine advertising because ads for merchants appear only when consumers are looking for a specific product. There are no pop-ups, Flash animations, videos, interstitials, e-mails, or other irrelevant communications

paid inclusion
for a fee, guarantees a Web site's inclusion in its list of sites, more frequent visits by its Web crawler, and suggestions for improving the results of organic searching

keyword advertising
merchants purchase keywords through a bidding process at search sites, and whenever a consumer searches for that word, their advertisement shows up somewhere on the page

network keyword advertising (context advertising)
publishers accept ads placed by Google on their Web sites, and receive a fee for any click-throughs from those ads

to deal with. Thus, search engine advertising saves consumers cognitive energy and reduces search costs (including the cost of cars or trains needed to do physical searches for products). In a recent study, the global value of search to both merchants and consumers was estimated to be more than $800 billion, with about 65% of the benefit going to consumers in the form of lower search costs and lower prices (McKinsey, 2011).

Because search engine marketing is so effective (it has the highest click-through-rate and the highest return on ad investment), companies optimize their Web sites for search engine recognition. The better optimized the page is, the higher a ranking it will achieve in search engine result listings, and the more likely it will appear on the top of the page in search engine results. **Search engine optimization** is the process of improving the ranking of Web pages with search engines by altering the content and design of the Web pages and site. By carefully selecting key words used on the Web pages, updating content frequently, and designing the site so it can be easily read by search engine programs, marketers can improve the impact and return on investment in their Web marketing programs.

search engine optimization

techniques to improve the ranking of Web pages generated by search engine algorithms

social search

effort to provide fewer, more relevant, and trustworthy results based on the social graph

Social Search **Social search** is an attempt to use your social contacts (and your entire social graph) to provide search results. In contrast to the top search engines that use a mathematical algorithm to find pages that satisfy your query, a social search Web site reviews your friends' recommendations (and their friends), past Web visits, and use of Like buttons. One problem with Google and mechanical search engines is that they are so thorough: enter a search for "smartphone" and in .28 seconds you will receive 504 million results, some of them providing helpful information and others that are suspect. Social search is an effort to provide fewer, more relevant, and trustworthy results based on the social graph. For instance, Google has developed Google +1 as a social layer on top of its existing search engine. Users can place a +1 next to Web sites they found helpful, and their friends will be automatically notified. Subsequent searches by their friends would list the +1 sites recommended by friends higher up on the page. Facebook's Like button is a similar social search tool. So far, neither Facebook nor Google has fully implemented a social search engine. One problem with social search is that your close friends may not be interested in or have knowledge of topics that you want to explore.

Search Engine Issues While search engines have provided significant benefits to merchants and customers, they also present risks and costs. For instance, search engines have the power to crush a small business by placing its ads on the back pages of search results. Merchants are at the mercy of search engines for access to the online marketplace, and this access is dominated by a single firm, Google. How Google decides to rank one company over another in search results is not known. No one really knows how to improve in its rankings (although there are hundreds of firms who claim otherwise). Google editors intervene in unknown ways to punish certain Web sites and reward others. Using paid sponsored listings, as opposed to relying on organic search results, eliminates some of this uncertainty but not all.

Other practices that degrade the results and usefulness of search engines include:

- **Link farms** are groups of Web sites that link to one another, thereby boosting their ranking in search engines that use a PageRank algorithm to judge the "usefulness" of a site. For instance, in the 2010 holiday season, JCPenney was found to be the highest ranked merchant for a large number of clothing products. On examination, it was discovered that this resulted from Penney's hiring a search engine optimization company to create thousands of Web sites that linked to JCPenney's Web site. As a result, JCPenney's Web site became the most popular (most linked-to) Web site for products like dresses, shirts, and pants. No matter what popular clothing item people searched for, JCPenney came out on top. Experts believe this was the largest search engine fraud in history.

- **Content farms** are companies that generate large volumes of textual content for multiple Web sites designed to attract viewers and search engines. Content farms profit by attracting large numbers of readers to their sites and exposing them to ads. The content typically is not original but is artfully copied or summarized from legitimate content sites.

- **Click fraud** occurs when a competitor clicks on search engine results and ads, forcing the advertiser to pay for the click even though the click is not legitimate. Competitors can hire offshore firms to perform fraudulent clicks or hire botnets to automate the process. Click fraud can quickly run up a large bill for merchants, and not result in any growth in sales.

link farms
groups of Web sites that link to one another, thereby boosting their ranking in search engines

content farms
companies that generate large volumes of textual content for multiple Web sites designed to attract viewers and search engines

click fraud
occurs when a competitor clicks on search engine results and ads, forcing the advertiser to pay for the click even though the click is not legitimate

Display Ad Marketing

Display ads are the second largest form of online marketing and advertising. In 2012, companies spent around $13.4 billion on display ad marketing of all types, about 36% of all spending for digital marketing (eMarketer, Inc., 2012f). The display ad market is highly concentrated. The top five display ad companies are Google, Yahoo, Microsoft, Facebook, and AOL, and they account for almost 50% of U.S. display ad revenue. Display ads consist of four different kinds of ads: banner ads, rich media ads (animated ads), sponsorships, and video ads.

Banner ads are the oldest and most familiar form of display marketing. They are also the least effective and the lowest cost form of online marketing. A **banner ad** displays a promotional message in a rectangular box at the top or bottom of a computer screen. A banner ad is similar to a traditional ad in a printed publication but has some added advantages. When clicked, it brings potential customers directly to the advertiser's Web site, and the site where the ad appears can observe the user's behavior on the site. The ability to identify and track the user is a key feature of online advertising. Banner ads feature Flash video and other animations.

banner ad
displays a promotional message in a rectangular box at the top or bottom of a computer screen

Rich media ads are ads that employ animation, sound, and interactivity, using Flash, HTML5, Java, and JavaScript. Rich media ads are expected to account for about $1.8 billion in online advertising expenditures (about 5% of total online advertising) in 2012. They are far more effective than simple banner ads. For instance, one research report that analyzed 24,000 different rich media ads with more than 12 billion impressions served in North America between July and December 2011 found that exposure to rich media ads boosted advertiser site visits by nearly 300% compared to standard banner ads. Viewers of rich media ads that included video were six times more likely

rich media ad
ad employing animation, sound, and interactivity, using Flash, HTML5 Java, and JavaScript

to visit the advertiser's Web site, either by directly clicking on the ad, typing the advertiser's URL, or by searching (MediaMind, 2012a).

video ads
TV-like advertisement that appears as an in-page video commercial or before, during, or after content

Video ads are TV-like advertisements that appear as in-page video commercials or before, during, or after a variety of content. Although from a total spending standpoint, online video ads are still very small when compared to the amount spent on search engine advertising, video ads are one of the fastest growing forms of online advertisement, accounting for about $2.9 billion in online advertising spending, which is expected to almost triple to $8.0 billion by 2016. The rapid growth in video ads is due to the fact that video ads are far more effective than other display ad formats, with click-rates 12 times that of rich media and 27 times that of banner ads (MediaMind, 2012b).

The strong growth in display marketing is coming from two sources: the rapid growth of mobile devices, especially tablets, and the growing use and power of video ads and rich media ads on all platforms, from desktop PCs to tablets. Video ads are among the most powerful ads on the Internet in terms of user response and clicks.

Advertising Networks In the early years of e-commerce, firms placed ads on the few popular Web sites in existence, but by early 2000, there were hundreds of thousands of sites where ads could be displayed, and it became very inefficient for a single firm to purchase ads on each individual Web site. Most firms, even very large firms, did not have the capability by themselves to place banner ads and marketing messages on thousands of Web sites and monitor the results. Specialized marketing firms called advertising networks appeared to help firms take advantage of the powerful marketing potential of the Internet, and to make the entire process of buying and selling online ads more efficient and transparent. These ad networks have proliferated and have greatly increased the scale and liquidity of online marketing.

advertising networks
connect online marketers with publishers by displaying ads to consumers based on detailed customer information

Advertising networks represent the most sophisticated application of Internet database capabilities to date, and illustrate just how different Internet marketing is from traditional marketing. **Advertising networks** sell advertising and marketing opportunities (slots) to companies who wish to buy exposure to an online audience (advertisers). Advertising networks obtain their inventory of ad opportunities from a network of participating sites that want to display ads on their sites in return for receiving a payment from advertisers everytime a visitor clicks on an ad. These sites are usually referred to as Web publishers. Marketers buy audiences and publishers sell audiences by attracting an audience and capturing audience information. Ad networks are the intermediaries who make this market work efficiently.

Figure 6.6 illustrates how these systems work. Advertising networks begin with a consumer requesting a page from a member of the advertising network (1). A connection is established with the third-party ad server (2). The ad server identifies the user by reading the cookie file on the user's hard drive and checks its user profile database for the user's profile (3). The ad server selects an appropriate banner ad based on the user's previous purchases, interests, demographics, or other data in the profile (4). Whenever the user later goes online and visits any of the network member sites, the ad server recognizes the user and serves up the same or different ads regardless of the site content. The advertising network follows users from site to site through the use of Web tracking files (5).

FIGURE 6.6	HOW AN ADVERTISING NETWORK SUCH AS DOUBLECLICK WORKS

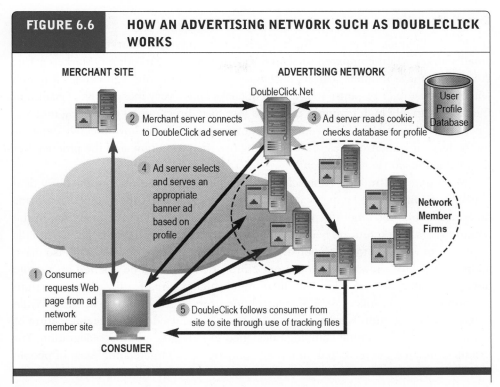

Millions of publishers have audiences to sell, and pages to fill with ads. Thousands of advertisers are looking for audiences. Ad networks are intermediaries that connect publishers with marketers.

Advertising Exchanges and Real-Time Bidding. **Ad exchanges** take the online advertising market a step further by aggregating the supply side of advertising slots available at publishers across several ad networks, and establishing a **real-time bidding process (RTB)** where marketers can bid for slots based on their marketing criteria. Want to contact males age 18 to 34, recent visitors to a car site, unmarried, high risk-taking profile, located in New York or California, urban home, and financial service industry employment? An ad exchange will allow you to bid in real time on this audience against other advertisers, and then manage the placement of ads, accounting, and measurement for your firm. Ad exchanges offer tremendous global scale and efficiency. About 60% of display ads are now placed through ad exchanges. One of the best known is Google's DoubleClick Ad Exchange, which is based on more than 100 ad networks (the supply side), and provides a computer-based market for buyers to purchase audiences (the demand side). This exchange sells audiences sliced into 1,000 interest categories. It displays more than 3 billion ads a day across 2 million Web sites worldwide, and maintains or distributes more than 100 million user profiles of Internet users (Google, 2011). These profiles are based on Web tracking files, offline purchase information, and social network data. Marketing firms, the buyers from publishers of Web sites, can target their audience and control the frequency and timing of ads during the day.

ad exchanges
create a market where many ad networks sell ad space to marketers

real-time bidding process (RTB)
online auctions where advertisers bid for audience slots

E-mail Marketing

In 2012, companies spent an estimated $220 million on e-mail marketing, a relatively small market when compared to search and display ad marketing (eMarketer, Inc. 2012f). But these numbers can be deceiving. E-mail marketing still carries a punch with solid customer response in the form of clicks and is very inexpensive. Because of the comparatively high response rates and low cost, direct e-mail marketing remains a common form of online marketing communications. Exactly how effective depends on the targeting and freshness of the mailing list, the promotion, and the product, but the average response rate is about 6%.

More than 183 million Americans use e-mail at least once a month. Daily deal firms like Groupon and LivingSocial, and flash marketers like Gilt, all built their firms on e-mail. While the amount spent on e-mail campaigns will be relatively flat in the coming years, marketers are becoming increasingly sophisticated in targeting e-mails to people most likely to be responsive. The growth of mobile devices will also drive additional e-mail campaigns. About one-third of e-mails will be opened on mobile devices in 2012, and mobile users have much higher e-mail utilization rates than desktop users. Upwards of 88% of smartphone users check their e-mail daily. While e-mail marketing often is sales oriented, it can also be used as an integral feature of a multi-channel marketing campaign designed to strengthen brand recognition. For instance, in 2012, Jeep created an e-mail campaign to a targeted audience of people who had searched on SUVs, and visited Chrysler and Jeep Facebook pages. The e-mail campaign announced a contest based on a game users could play online that involved tracking an arctic beast with a Jeep. Recipients could sign up on Facebook, Twitter, or the Jeep blog.

Today, however, e-mail no longer commands quite as much respect as it once did because of three factors: spam, software tools used to control spam that eliminate much e-mail from user inboxes, and poorly targeted purchased e-mail lists. **Spam** is "junk e-mail," and *spammers* are people who send unsolicited e-mail to a mass audience that has not expressed any interest in the product. Spammers tend to market pornography, fraudulent deals and services, scams, and other products not widely approved in most civilized societies. Legitimate direct opt-in e-mail marketing is not growing as fast as behaviorally targeted banners, pop-ups, and search engine advertising because of the explosion in spam. Consumer response to even legitimate e-mail campaigns has become more sophisticated. In general, e-mail works well for maintaining customer relationships but poorly for acquiring new customers.

While click fraud may be the Achilles' heel of search engine advertising, spam is the nemesis of effective e-mail marketing and advertising. The percentage of all e-mail that is spam is estimated at around 72% in 2012 (Symantec, 2012). Most spam originates from bot networks, which consist of thousands of captured PCs that can initiate and relay spam messages (see Chapter 5). Spam volume has declined somewhat since authorities took down the Rustock botnet in 2011. Spam is seasonally cyclical, and varies monthly due to the impact of new technologies (both supportive and discouraging of spammers), new prosecutions, and seasonal demand for products and services.

Legislative attempts to control spam have been mostly unsuccessful. Thirty-seven states in the United States have laws regulating or prohibiting spam (National

spam
unsolicited commercial e-mail

Conference of State Legislatures, 2010). State legislation typically requires that unsolicited mail (spam) contain a label in the subject line ("ADV") indicating the message is an advertisement, require a clear opt-out choice for consumers, and prohibit e-mail that contains false routing and domain name information (nearly all spammers hide their own domain, ISP, and IP address).

Congress passed the first national anti-spam law ("Controlling the Assault of Non-Solicited Pornography and Marketing" or CAN-SPAM Act) in 2003, and it went into effect in January 2004. The act does not prohibit unsolicited e-mail (spam) but instead requires unsolicited commercial e-mail messages to be labeled (though not by a standard method) and to include opt-out instructions and the sender's physical address. It prohibits the use of deceptive subject lines and false headers in such messages. The FTC is authorized (but not required) to establish a "Do Not E-mail" registry. State laws that require labels on unsolicited commercial e-mail or prohibit such messages entirely are pre-empted, although provisions merely addressing falsity and deception may remain in place. The act imposes fines of $10 for each unsolicited pornographic e-mail and authorizes state attorneys general to bring lawsuits against spammers. The act obviously makes lawful legitimate bulk mailing of unsolicited e-mail messages (what most people call spam), yet seeks to prohibit certain deceptive practices and provide a small measure of consumer control by requiring opt-out notices. In this sense, critics point out, CAN-SPAM ironically legalizes spam as long as spammers follow the rules. For this reason, large spammers have been among the bill's biggest supporters, and consumer groups have been the act's most vociferous critics.

Affiliate Marketing

Affiliate marketing is a form of marketing where a firm pays a commission to other Web sites (including blogs) for sending customers to their Web site. Affiliate marketing generally involves pay-for-performance: the affiliate or affiliate network gets paid only if users click on a link or purchase a product. In 2012, companies will spend about $2.5 billion on affiliate marketing (Forrester, 2012). Industry experts estimate that around 10% of all retail online sales are generated through affiliate programs (as compared to search engine ads, which account for more than 30% of online sales).

affiliate marketing
commissions paid by advertisers to affiliate Web sites for referring potential customers to their Web site

Visitors to an affiliate Web site typically click on ads and are taken to the advertiser's Web site. In return, the advertiser pays the affiliate a fee, either on a per-click basis or as a percentage of whatever the customer spends on the advertiser's site. Paying commissions for referrals or recommendations long pre-dated the Web.

For instance, Amazon has a strong affiliate program consisting of more than 1 million participant sites, called Associates, which receive up to 15% on sales their referrals generate. Affiliates attract people to their blogs or Web sites where they can click on ads for products at Amazon. Amazon pays affiliates a percentage on the sales generated within 24 hours of a visitor's click. Members of eBay's Affiliates Program can earn between $20 and $35 for each active registered user sent to eBay. Amazon, eBay, and other large e-commerce companies with affiliate programs typically administer such programs themselves. Smaller e-commerce firms who wish to use affiliate marketing often decide to join an affiliate network (sometimes called an affiliate broker), which acts as an intermediary. Bloggers often sign up for Google's AdSense program to attract advertisers to their sites. They are paid for each click on an ad and sometimes for subsequent purchases made by visitors.

Lead Generation Marketing

lead generation marketing
uses multiple e-commerce presences to generate leads for businesses who later can be contacted and converted into customers

Lead generation marketing uses multiple e-commerce presences to generate leads for businesses who later can be contacted and converted into customers through sales calls, e-mails, or other means. In one sense, all Internet marketing campaigns attempt to develop leads. But lead generation marketing is a specialized subset of the Internet marketing industry that provides consulting services and software tools to collect and manage leads for firms, and to convert these leads to customers. Companies spent an estimated $1.7 billion on lead generation marketing in 2012. Sometimes called "inbound marketing," lead generation marketing firms help other firms build Web sites, launch e-mail campaigns, use social network sites and blogs to optimize the generation of leads, and then manage those leads by initiating further contacts, tracking interactions, and interfacing with customer relationship management systems to keep track of customer-firm interactions. One of the foremost lead generation marketing firms is Hubspot.com, which has developed a software suite for generating and managing leads.

Sponsorship Marketing

sponsorship
a paid effort to tie an advertiser's name to information, an event, or a venue in a way that reinforces its brand in a positive yet not overtly commercial manner

A **sponsorship** is a paid effort to tie an advertiser's name to particular information, an event, or a venue in a way that reinforces its brand in a positive yet not overtly commercial manner. In 2012, companies spent about $1.6 billion for sponsorship marketing (eMarketer, Inc., 2012f). Sponsorships typically are more about branding than immediate sales. A common form of sponsorship is targeted content (or advertorials), in which editorial content is combined with an ad message to make the message more valuable and attractive to its intended audience. For instance, WebMD.com, the leading medical information Web site in the United States, offers "sponsorship sites" on the WebMD Web site to companies such as Phillips to describe its home defibrillators, and Lilly to describe its pharmaceutical solutions for attention deficit disorders among children. Social media sponsorships, in which marketers pay for mentions in social media, such as blogs, tweets, or in online video, have also become a popular tactic.

SOCIAL MARKETING AND ADVERTISING: SHARING AND ENGAGING

social marketing/ advertising
the use of online social networks and communities to build brands and drive sales

Social marketing/advertising involves the use of online social networks and communities to build brands and drive sales revenues. There are several kinds of social networks, from Facebook and Twitter, to social apps, social games, blogs, and forums (Web sites that attract people who share a community of interests or skills). In 2012, companies spent about $3.1 billion on social marketing and advertising, and this is expected to grow to about $5 billion by 2014. Next to mobile marketing, it is the fastest growing type of online marketing. Nevertheless, in 2012, it represented only 8% of all online marketing and is still dwarfed by the amount spent on search engine advertising and display advertising (eMarketer, Inc., 2012g).

Marketers cannot ignore the huge audiences that social networks such as Facebook, Twitter, and LinkedIn are gathering, which rival television and radio in size. In 2012, there were an estimated 1 billion Facebook members, 140 million active Twitter users, and more than 175 million who have joined LinkedIn worldwide. In the United States, in August 2012, Facebook had around 152 million unique visitors. Around two-thirds of the U.S. Internet population visits social sites. It's little wonder that marketers and advertisers are joyous at the prospect of connecting with this large audience. Over 80% of U.S. businesses now have Facebook pages and a presence on many other social network sites, and research has found that social network users are more likely to talk about and recommend a company or product they follow on Facebook or Twitter (eMarketer, Inc., 2012h).

There are four features of social marketing and advertising that are driving its growth:

- *Social sign-on:* Signing in to various Web sites through social network pages like Facebook. This allows Web sites to receive valuable social profile information from Facebook and use it in their own marketing efforts.

- *Collaborative shopping:* Creating an environment where consumers can share their shopping experiences with one another by viewing products, chatting, or texting. Instead of talking about the weather, friends can chat online about brands, products, and services.

- *Network notification:* Creating an environment where consumers can share their approval (or disapproval) of products, services, or content, or share their geolocation, perhaps a restaurant or club, with friends. Facebook's ubiquitous "Like" button is an example. Twitter tweets and followers are another example.

- *Social search (recommendation):* Enabling an environment where consumers can ask their friends for advice on purchases of products, services, and content. While Google can help you find things, social search can help you evaluate the quality of things by listening to the evaluations of your friends or their friends. For instance, Amazon's social recommender system can use your Facebook social profile to recommend products.

Social networks offer advertisers all the formats found on portal and search sites including banner ads (the most common), short pre-roll and post-roll ads associated with videos, and sponsorship of content. Having a corporate Facebook page is in itself an advertising portal for brands just like a Web page. Many firms, such as Coca-Cola, have shut down product-specific Web pages and instead use Facebook pages.

A typical social network advertising campaign for Facebook will include the following elements:

- Establish a Facebook page.
- Use comment and feedback tools to develop fan comments.
- Develop a community of users.
- Encourage brand involvement through videos and rich media showing product in use by real customers.
- Use contests and competitions to deepen fan involvement intensity.
- Develop display ads for use on other Facebook pages.
- Develop display ads for use in response to social search queries.

- Liberally display the Like button so fans share the experience with their friends.
- Enable e-commerce by using Facebook Connect (social sign on) to direct fans to product sale Web sites.

For more information on social marketing using Facebook, see Learning Track 6.2.

Twitter is a microblogging social networking site that allows users to send and receive 140-character messages. Twitter has an estimated 30 million users in the United States (about 12% of Internet users) (eMarketer, Inc., 2012g). Twitter claims over 140 million users worldwide. Twitter offers advertisers and marketers a chance to interact and engage with their customers in real time and in a fairly intimate, one-on-one manner. Advertisers can buy ads that look like organic tweets (the kind you receive from friends), and these ads can tie into and enhance marketing events like new product announcements or pricing changes.

There are three kinds of Twitter marketing products:

- *Promoted Tweets:* Advertisers pay to have their tweets appear in users' search results. The tweets appear as "promoted" in the search results, and the pricing is based on an auction run on the Twitter ad platform.
- *Promoted Trends:* Advertisers pay to move their hashtags (# symbol used to mark keywords in a tweet) to the top of Twitter's Trends List. Otherwise, hashtags are found by the Twitter search engine, and only those that are organically popular make it to the Trends List. Promoted Trends cost about $120,000 a day in 2012.
- *Promoted Accounts:* Advertisers pay to have their branded account moved to the top of their Who to Follow list on the Twitter home page.

While marketers are just learning how to use Twitter, researchers find that about 21% of Twitter users follow at least one brand. Millions of users flood the Twitter Web site to follow fast developing stories, celebrities, and trending topics. It is clear that Twitter's marketing platform will expand with its user base. For more information on social marketing using Twitter, see Learning Track 6.3.

There are several issues to be aware of when using social marketing and advertising. User comments can sometimes be negative and brand destruction can result. Corporate users carefully watch submissions to their social network sites. Social networks can be influential, but not under all circumstances. For instance, research has shown that social network influence may extend to closest friends but not to distant friends (influence is inversely related to size of the friendship group). The 100th most distant friend of yours couldn't care less about what you buy or think. Measuring the results of social advertising is in its infancy and not well understood. It is possible that some of your "friends" would react negatively to whatever you purchased, while others would not care or are not interested. If Facebook Likes do not turn into sales, then you will have to re-evaluate your objectives on social sites.

Blog Marketing and Advertising

Blogs have been around for a decade and are a part of the mainstream online culture (see Chapter 3 for a description of blogs). Around 23 million people write blogs, including thousands of high-ranking corporate officials, politicians, journalists, academics, and government officials, and around 72 million read blogs. Blogs play a vital role in online marketing. Around 43% of all U.S. companies used blogs for marketing in 2012. Although more firms use Twitter and Facebook, these sites have not replaced blogs, and in fact often point to blogs for long-form content. Because blog readers and creators tend to be more educated, have higher incomes, and be opinion leaders, blogs are ideal platforms for ads for many products and services that cater to this kind of an audience. Because blogs are based on the personal opinions of the writers, they are also an ideal platform to start a viral marketing campaign. Advertising networks that specialize in blogs provide some efficiency in placing ads, as do blog networks, which are collections of a small number of popular blogs, coordinated by a central management team, and which can deliver a larger audience to advertisers. For more information on social marketing using blogs, see Learning Track 6.4.

Game Advertising

The online gaming marketplace continues to expand rapidly as users are able to play games on smartphones and tablets, as well as PCs and consoles. The story of game advertising in 2012 is social, local, and mobile: social games are ascendant, mobile devices are the high-growth platform, and location-based local advertising is starting to show real traction. The objective of game advertising is both branding and driving customers to purchase moments at restaurants and retail stores.

In 2012, 102 million people played games on their mobile devices, another 40 million on consoles, and another 94 million played online games with a PC. Of the online gamers, about 76 million played social games, such as Zynga's FarmVille, CityVille, and Words With Friends. Gaming is growing at nearly 50%, driven largely by mobile app games and social site games.

Viral Marketing

Just as affiliate marketing involves using a trusted Web site to encourage users to visit other sites, **viral marketing** is a form of social marketing that involves getting customers to pass along a company's marketing message to friends, family, and colleagues. It's the online version of word-of-mouth advertising, which spreads even faster and further than in the real world. In the offline world, next to television, word of mouth is the second most important means by which consumers find out about new products. And the most important factor in the decision to purchase is the face-to-face recommendations of parents, friends, and colleagues. Millions of online adults in the United States are "influencers" who share their opinions about products in a variety of online settings. In addition to increasing the size of a company's customer base, customer referrals also have other advantages: they are less expensive to acquire since existing customers do all the acquisition work, and they tend to use online support services less, preferring to turn back to the person who referred them for advice. Also, because they cost so little to acquire and keep, referred customers begin to generate profits for a company much earlier than customers acquired through other marketing methods. There are a number of online venues where viral marketing appears. E-mail used to be the primary online venue for viral marketing ("please forward this e-mail to your

viral marketing
the process of getting customers to pass along a company's marketing message to friends, family, and colleagues

friends"), but venues such as Facebook, Google +, YouTube, blogs, and social game sites now play a major role. For example, as of August 2012, Blendtec's "Will It Blend" and Evian's "Live Young" videos headed up the top 10 viral video advertisements of all time, both with more than 100 million views on YouTube. Volkswagen's "The Force" video advertisement was in fourth place, with more than 58 million views.

MOBILE AND LOCAL MARKETING AND ADVERTISING

Mobile marketing reaches consumers via their mobile devices such as smartphones and tablet computers. Local marketing typically employs mobile devices as well, but also uses the traditional desktop platform.

Mobile Marketing and Advertising

Marketing on the mobile platform is growing rapidly although it remains a small part (7%) of the overall $37.3 billion online marketing spending. In 2012, spending on all forms of mobile marketing amounted to $2.6 billion, and it is growing at over 80% a year (eMarketer, Inc., 2012i). A number of factors are driving advertisers to the mobile platform of smartphones and tablets, including much more powerful devices, faster networks, wireless local networks, rich media and video ads, and growing demand for local advertising by small business and consumers. Most important, mobile is where the eyeballs are now and increasingly will be in the future: 122 million people access the Internet at least some of the time from mobile devices.

Although still in its infancy, mobile marketing includes the use of display banner ads, rich media, video, games, e-mail, text messaging, in-store messaging, Quick Response (QR) codes, and couponing. Over 90% of retail marketing professionals had plans for mobile marketing campaigns in 2012, and mobile is now a required part of the standard marketing budget. **Table 6.5** shows the major formats and growth rates. In 2012, search engine advertising was the most popular mobile advertising format, accounting for almost 50% of all mobile ad spending, and not surprising given that search is the second most common smartphone application (after voice and text communication). Search engine ads can be further optimized for the mobile platform by showing ads based on the physical location of the user. Display ads are also a popular format, accounting for about 36% of mobile ad spending. Display ads can be served as a part of a mobile Web site or inside apps and games. Mobile messaging generally involves SMS text messaging to consumers offering coupons or flash marketing messages. Messaging is especially effective for local advertising because consumers can be sent messages and coupons as they pass by or visit locations. Video advertising currently accounts for the smallest percentage of mobile ad spending, but it is the fastest growing format. Ad networks such as Google's AdMob, Apple's iAd, and Millennial Media are the largest providers of mobile advertising.

Mobile marketing is uniquely suited for branding purposes, raising awareness through the use of video and rich interactive media such as games. Read the *Insight on Business* case, *Mobile Marketing: Land Rover Seeks Engagement on the Small Screen*, for a further look.

TABLE 6.5	U.S. MOBILE AD SPENDING BY FORMAT AND GROWTH (2012)	
FORMAT	SPENDING (MILLIONS)	GROWTH RATE
Messaging (SMS)	$227	−9.5%
Display	$953	99%
Search	$1,280	96%
Video	$152	122%
Total	$2,612	80%

SOURCE: Based on data from eMarketer, Inc., 2012i, 2012j.

Table 6.6 provides examples of how several firms are using mobile marketing to promote their brands.

App Marketing

Apps on mobile devices constitute a new marketing platform that did not exist a few years ago. Apps are a non-browser pathway for users to experience the Web and perform a number of tasks from reading the newspaper to shopping, searching, and buying. Apps provide users much faster access to content than multi-purpose browsers. Apps are also starting to influence the design and function of traditional Web sites as consumers are attracted to the look and feel of apps, and their speed of operation. There are about a million apps on Apple iTunes and Google Apps Marketplace and another million apps provided by Internet carriers and third-party storefronts like

TABLE 6.6	MOBILE MARKETING CAMPAIGNS OF SELECTED FIRMS 2012
Kraft Foods	Created a mobile campaign to promote the launch of its new instant coffee products, Jacobs 3in1 and Jacobs 2in1..
Gatorade G Series Campaign	Uses Pandora's ad platform to place banner ads leading users to an optimized mobile Web site promoting new drink products.
Chevrolet	Chevrolet ran a mobile video advertising campaign to support the Volt, Chevrolet's hybrid car.
Ikea	Uses the Apple iAd platform to display banner ads promoting the Ikea catalog.
OfficeMax	Uses iPhone and Android platforms for loyalty marketing. OfficeMax uses SMS texting to deliver offers and daily deals.
BMW	BMW is promoting its new 3 Series and its DESIR3 campaign with short video clips in between commercial breaks while consumers are watching television shows and movies on their mobile devices.
Ford Motor Company	Uses the Mobile Posse platform for an awareness and consideration campaign for the new Ford Taurus.

INSIGHT ON BUSINESS

MOBILE MARKETING: LAND ROVER SEEKS ENGAGEMENT ON THE SMALL SCREEN

Mobile devices are used by consumers throughout the purchase cycle: over 50% of smartphone users research products before entering a store, and 36% use their phones in retail stores. The use of mobile devices to actually purchase products online (as opposed to just shopping and browsing online) is also growing commensurately. U.S. mobile commerce grew by more than 90% in 2011, and is expected to grow by 48% in 2012 to $11.6 billion. By 2015, mobile commerce is expected to nearly triple to $31 billion.

Only about half of smartphone online shoppers actually buy something using their phones, compared to more than 80% of desktop PC shoppers who actually purchase online. Many consumers feel the small screens on smartphones prevent them from examining retail products closely, and using a credit card with a smartphone is difficult. Yet nearly half of smartphone customers have purchased digital goods like books and movies, and more than a third have purchased clothing, tickets, and deals offered by firms like Gilt and Living-Social. Restaurants, museums, and entertainment venues are ideal candidates to use mobile marketing aimed at local consumers.

A good example of the use of smartphones for marketing is Land Rover's use of Apple's iAd platform to introduce the Range Rover Evoque to a new audience in 2012. The Range Rover Evoque (pronounced e-voke) is a compact SUV aimed at young urban buyers. The Evoque is a smaller, more fuel-efficient, less-polluting SUV than its much larger luxury SUV models. Land Rover wanted to introduce the car to an entirely new demographic: young affluents. The problem was how to introduce this new concept for Land Rover to an audience that most likely never intended to buy a Land Rover.

Land Rover worked with marketers to build an immersive and engaging interactive app that would allow consumers to explore and configure the interior and exterior of the car using the finger gestures of the iPhone. iAd used iTunes-based targeting to pinpoint the right audience based on the kinds of music they liked to listen to. The ad was most effective when consumers were using their favorite apps.

Using Land Rover's configuration app, customers can change the Evoque's body style, color, and wheels. They can take a photo of their car and send it to others by e-mail or SMS. There's an immersive 360-degree view of the interior that puts viewers inside the car. Using the iPhone's built-in gyroscope and accelerometer, viewers can tilt and turn the device to see a 360-degree view of the interior.

According to Land Rover, the iAd mobile marketing effort has been a success. As one Land Rover marketer noted, there's a difference between looking at a 30-second TV commercial, and someone using their iPhone to explore a new product. With the mobile ad, people are more engaged, in control, and attentive to the message. On average, people spent nearly 80 seconds whenever they engaged with the ad.

Mobile marketing is still in its infancy, and most firms are having trouble monetizing their huge and growing mobile audiences through marketing campaigns. As more and more people rely on their smartphones for shopping and purchasing, marketers cannot afford to ignore the unique capabilities of smartphones for engaging consumers.

SOURCES: "Twitter's Mobile Ads Begin to Click," by Shira Ovide, *Wall Street Journal*, June 28, 2012; "Land Rover Reaches New Audience with iAd for Brands," Apple Inc., 2012; "Land Rover iAd Campaign Delivers Highest Engagement Levels," by Chantal Tode, Mobile Marketer, August 8, 2012; "Majority of US Smartphone Owners Use Devices to Aid Shopping," eMarketer, Inc., April 12, 2012; "US Mobile Commerce Forecast," by eMarketer, Inc., [Jeffrey Grau], January 2012; "Mobile Channel Strategy," by Carrie Johnson, Forrester Research, June 2, 2011; "The Effect of Mobile On the Path to Purchase," by eMarketer, Inc., February 29, 2012.

GetJar and PocketGear, app portals like dev.appia.com, and the Amazon Appstore. An estimated one billion people used apps in 2012 worldwide, with about 200 million in the United States (eMarketer, Inc., 2012j). By 2012, more than 32 billion apps had been downloaded (Strategy Analytics, 2012).

Apps provide four potential sources of revenue for their creators and marketers: pay-per-app download of the app itself, in-app purchases, subscriptions, and advertising. According to the research firm ABI, apps produced about $9 billion in revenue in 2012, and this is expected to grow to $46 billion by 2016. The largest revenue component is in-app purchases. The most essential apps for American users are social network and community, banking, specific information (street addresses, phone numbers), search sites, and general news and information (newspapers, magazines, and news channels).

Local Marketing: The Social-Mobile-Local Nexus

Along with social marketing and mobile marketing, local marketing is the third major trend in e-commerce marketing in 2012–2013. The local search market is growing impressively (around 7% annually), and the growth of mobile devices has accelerated the growth of local search and purchasing since 2007. According to Google, local searches represented 20% of all searches, and 40% of all mobile searches in 2012. New marketing tools like local advertisements on social networks and daily deal sites are also contributing to local marketing growth.

Spending on online local ads in the United States totaled around $24 billion in 2012 and is expected to grow to more than $38 billion by 2016 (BIA/Kelsey, 2012). In contrast, spending on traditional local advertising is expected to be flat during the same time period. The most common local marketing tools are geotargeting using Google Maps (local stores appearing on a Google map), display ads in hyperlocal publications like those created by Patch Properties, aimed at narrowly defined communities, daily deals, and coupons.

The most commonly used venues include Facebook, Google, Amazon Local, Groupon, LivingSocial, LinkedIn, Yahoo, Bing, and Twitter, as well as more specific location-based offerings such as Google Places, Yahoo Local, Citysearch, YellowBook, SuperPages, and Yelp. The "daily deal" coupon sites, Groupon and LivingSocial, and location-based mobile firms such as Foursquare are also a significant part of this trend. Industry analysts believe about 92 million adult U.S. Internet users in 2012 used online coupons, and research indicates that retail stores and those in the hospitality and entertainment industries have much to gain from adding online coupons to their local search listings. Findings from comScore indicate that around 40% of U.S. Internet users search for local businesses at least once a week (comScore, 2012), so it's no surprise that search engine advertising is the most popular mobile advertising format.

MULTI-CHANNEL MARKETING: INTEGRATING ONLINE AND OFFLINE MARKETING

Without an audience, marketing is not possible. With the rapid growth of the Internet, media consumption patterns have changed greatly as consumers are more and more likely to engage with online media, from videos and news sites, to blogs, Twitter feeds,

Facebook friends, and Pinterest posts. Increasingly, marketers are using multiple online channels to "touch" customers, from e-mail to Facebook, search ads, display ads on mobile devices, and affiliate programs. Forrester Research reports, for instance, that most customers purchased online following some Web marketing influence, and nearly half of online purchases followed multiple exposures to Web marketing efforts (Forrester Research, 2011b).

Yet the average American spends only about 24% of his or her time with the Internet, and a whopping 75% with other media (**Figure 6.7**). While television accounts for a large percentage of time spent with media, setting that aside, radio, newspapers, magazines, and "other" account for an additional 36% of time spent with media, larger than the Internet per se. An increasing percentage of American media consumers multitask by using several media at once in order to increase the total media exposure. In this environment, marketers increasingly are developing multi-channel marketing programs that can take advantage of the strengths of various media, and reinforce branding messages across media. Online marketing is not the only way, or by itself the best way, to engage consumers. Internet campaigns can be significantly strengthened by also using e-mail, TV, print, and radio. The marketing communications campaigns most successful at driving traffic to a Web site have incorporated both online and offline tactics, rather than relying solely on one or the other. Several research studies have shown that the most effective online advertisements are those that use consistent imagery with campaigns running in other media at the same time.

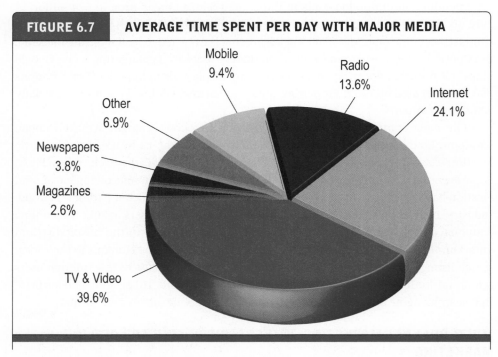

| FIGURE 6.7 | AVERAGE TIME SPENT PER DAY WITH MAJOR MEDIA |

Mobile 9.4%
Radio 13.6%
Internet 24.1%
Other 6.9%
Newspapers 3.8%
Magazines 2.6%
TV & Video 39.6%

The Internet represents only 24% of consumer exposure to media, suggesting that online marketing needs to be coupled with offline marketing to achieve optimal effectiveness.

SOURCE: Based on data from eMarketer, Inc., 2012l.

For instance, Applebee's (a national family dining chain) introduced a new menu in 2011 designed to get noon-time customers in and out of the restaurants in fourteen minutes. The marketing campaign used a multi-channel approach involving traditional TV and radio, in addition to digital media like Facebook, YouTube, and Twitter.

In 2012, the Indiana Office of Tourism Development worked with the *Indianapolis Monthly* magazine to encourage visitors to the Super Bowl in Indianapolis to try local foods and locally owned restaurants. Using Web sites, blogs, e-mail, and print media, the campaign significantly increased the sales of local restaurants.

Research by iProspect found that search queries were prompted by the following traditional media outlets: television (44%), word of mouth (41%), magazines and newspapers (35%), radio (23%), and billboards (13%) (iProspect, 2011). Offline mass media such as television and radio have nearly a 100% market penetration into the 119 million households in the United States. U.S. daily newspapers have a total circulation of around 46 million. It would be foolish for pure online companies not to use these popular media to drive traffic to the online world of commerce. In the early days of e-commerce, the Internet audience was quite different from the general population, and perhaps was best reached by using online marketing alone. This is no longer true as the Internet population becomes much more like the general population.

Insight on Business: Are the Very Rich Different from You and Me? examines how luxury goods providers use online marketing in conjunction with their offline marketing efforts.

Personalization, One-to-One Marketing, and Interest-based Advertising (Behavioral Targeting)   No Internet-based marketing technique has received more popular and academic comment than "one-to-one" or "personalized marketing." **One-to-one marketing (personalization)** segments the market on the basis of individuals (not groups), based on a precise and timely understanding of their needs, targeting specific marketing messages to these individuals, and then positioning the product vis-à-vis competitors to be truly unique. One-to-one marketing is the ultimate form of market segmentation, targeting, and positioning—where the segments are individuals.

Personalized one-to-one marketing is suitable for products (1) that can be produced in very complex forms, depending on individual tastes, (2) whose price can be adjusted to the level of personalization, and (3) where the individual's tastes and preferences can be effectively gauged.

A good example of personalization at work is Amazon or Barnesandnoble.com. Both sites greet registered visitors (based on cookie files), recommend recent books based on user preferences (stored in a user profile in their database) as well as what other consumers purchased, and expedite checkout procedures based on prior purchases.

Behavioral targeting of ads involves using the online and offline behavior of consumers to adjust the advertising message delivered online, often in real time (milliseconds from the consumer's first URL entry). The intent is to increase the efficiency of marketing and advertising, and to increase the revenue streams of firms who are in a position to behaviorally target visitors. Because "behavioral targeting" as a label has somewhat unfavorable connotations, the online advertising industry, led

one-to-one marketing (personalization)
segmenting the market based on a precise and timely understanding of an individual's needs, targeting specific marketing messages to these individuals, and then positioning the product vis-à-vis competitors to be truly unique

interest-based advertising (behavioral targeting)

using search queries and clicks on results to behaviorally target consumers

by Google, has introduced a new name for behavioral targeting. They call it **interest-based advertising**.

One of the original promises of the Web has been that it can deliver a marketing message tailored to each consumer based on this data, and then measure the results in terms of click-throughs and purchases. What's new about today's behavioral targeting is the breadth of data collected: your e-mail content, social network page content, friends, purchases online, books read or purchased, newspaper sites visited, and many other behaviors. And finally, ad exchanges take the marketing of all this information one step further. Most popular Web sites have more than 100 tracking programs on their home pages that are owned by third-party data collector firms who then sell this information in real time to the highest bidding advertiser in real-time online auctions. Ad exchanges make it possible for advertisers to retarget ads at individuals as they roam across the Internet. **Retargeting ads** involves showing the same or similar ads to individuals across multiple Web sites. Retargeted ads are nearly as effective as the original ad (eMarketer, 2011a).

retargeting ads

showing the same ad to individuals across multiple Web sites

There are four methods that online advertisers use to behaviorally target ads: search engine queries, the collection of data on individual browsing history online (monitoring the clickstream), the collection of data from social network sites, and increasingly, the integration of this online data with offline data like income, education, address, purchase patterns, credit records, driving records, and hundreds of other personal descriptors tied to specific, identifiable persons. This level of integration of both "anonymous" as well as identifiable information is routinely engaged in by Google, Microsoft, Yahoo, Facebook, and legions of small and medium-sized marketing firms that use their data, or collect data from thousands of Web sites using Web beacons and cookies. (See Chapter 6 for a more detailed discussion.) On average, online information bureaus maintain 2,000 data elements on each adult person in their database. The currency and accuracy of this data is never examined, and the retention periods are not known. Currently, there are no federal laws or regulations governing this data

customization

changing the product, not just the marketing message, according to user preferences

customer co-production

in the Web environment, takes customization one step further by allowing the customer to interactively create the product

Customization and Customer Co-Production Customization is an extension of personalization. **Customization** means changing the product—not just the marketing message—according to user preferences. **Customer co-production** means the users actually think up the innovation and help create the new product.

Many leading companies now offer "build-to-order" customized products on the Internet on a large scale, creating product differentiation and, hopefully, customer loyalty. Customers appear to be willing to pay a little more for a unique product. The key to making the process affordable is to build a standardized architecture that lets consumers combine a variety of options. For example, Nike offers customized sneakers through its Nike iD program on its Web site. Consumers can choose the type of shoe, colors, material, and even a logo of up to eight characters. Nike transmits the orders via computers to specially equipped plants in China and Korea. The sneakers cost only $10 extra and take about three weeks to reach the customer. At the Shop M&M's Web site, customers can get their own message printed on custom-made M&Ms; Timberland. com also offers online customization of its boots.

Information goods—goods whose value is based on information content—are also ideal for this level of differentiation. For instance, the New York Times—and many other content distributors—allows customers to select the news they want to see on a daily basis. Many Web sites, particularly portal sites such as Yahoo, MSN, and AOL, allow customers to create their own customized version of the Web site. Such pages frequently require security measures such as usernames and passwords to ensure privacy and confidentiality.

Dynamic Pricing and Flash Marketing The Web offers merchants the ability to dynamically change prices on the fly depending on supply and demand. One example of this phenomenon is flash marketing.

Flash marketing has proved extraordinarily effective for travel services, luxury clothing goods, and other goods. Using e-mail or dedicated Web site features to notify loyal customers (repeat purchasers), merchants offer goods and services for a limited time (usually hours) at very low prices. JetBlue has offered $14 flights between New York and Los Angeles. Deluxe hotel rooms are flash marketed at $1 a night. Companies like Rue La La, HauteLook, and Gilt Groupe are based on flash marketing techniques. Blink and you can easily miss these great prices. Gilt.com purchases overstocked items from major fashion brands and then offers them to their subscribers at discounted prices via daily e-mail and SMS flash messages. Typically, the sale of an item lasts for two hours or until the inventory is depleted. On many occasions, Gilt.com rises to the top of most frequently visited Web sites when it conducts a sale. In another example of mass retail dynamic pricing, in May 2011, Amazon used its new cloud music service to offer a flash one-day sale of Lady Gaga's latest album for 99 cents. Response was so great that Amazon's cloud servers could not meet the demand, and the offer has not been repeated.

Long Tail Marketing

Consider that Amazon sells a larger number of obscure books than it does of "hit" books (defined as the top 20% of books sold). Nevertheless, the hit books generate 80% of Amazon's revenues. Consumers distribute themselves in many markets according to a power curve where 80% of the demand is for the hit products, and demand for non-hits quickly recedes to a small number of units sold. In a traditional market, niche products are so obscure no one ever hears about them. One impact of the Internet and e-commerce on sales of obscure products with little demand is that obscure products become more visible to consumers through search engines, recommendation engines, and social networks. Hence, online retailers can earn substantial revenue selling products for which demand and price is low. In fact, with near zero inventory costs, and a good search engine, the sales of obscure products can become a much larger percentage of total revenue. Amazon, for instance, has millions of book titles for sale at $2.99 or less, many written by obscure authors. Because of its search and recommendation engines, Amazon is able to generate profits from the sale of this large number of obscure titles. This is called the "**long tail**" effect. See *Insight on Technology: The Long Tail: Big Hits and Big Misses.*

long tail
a colloquial name given to various statistical distributions characterized by a small number of events of high amplitude and a very large number of events with low amplitude

INSIGHT ON TECHNOLOGY

THE LONG TAIL: BIG HITS AND BIG MISSES

The "Long Tail" is a colloquial name given to various statistical distributions characterized by a small group of events of high amplitude and a very large group of events with low amplitude. Think Hollywood movies: there are big hits that really hit big, and thousands of films that no one ever hears about. That means 20% of the movies produce 80% of the revenue. The other 80% of the movies make up the Long Tail.

On the Internet, where search costs are tiny, and storage and distribution costs are near zero, retailers can offer millions of products for sale, many more than physical outlets. Most shoppers have a taste for both popular as well as niche products. The strength of "infinite inventory" online retailers like Amazon is that they can satisfy the broadest range of individual tastes.

There are several implications of the Long Tail phenomenon for Web marketing. Content providers focus less on the blockbusters that bust the budget, and place more emphasis on the steady base. Social networks also make the Long Tail phenomenon even stronger. One online person discovers an unheard-of niche product and shares his or her feelings with others. If a lot of people say they like an obscure product, it means more to consumers than if the same popularity attaches to a mainstream product.

But recent research casts some doubt on the revenue potential in the Long Tail. The number of DVD titles online that never get played is increasing rapidly, while the big blockbuster "winner-take-all" titles are increasing. Solid best sellers have expanded and produce the vast part of online media revenues. Over time, the number of titles in the Long Tail has exploded, and the no-play rate has expanded at music sites from 2% to 12%. The Long Tail is a very lonely, quiet place. In reality, there seems to be more selling of less (the hits) than less selling of more (the misses). A U.S. study similarly found that 10% of the music titles at Rhapsody, a music site, produced 78% of the revenues.

eBay is a company with a huge Long Tail problem that it is trying to convert into a lucrative virtue. eBay's 97 million users have stuffed its pages with over 200 million product listings, a great many of which are truly at the end of the Long Tail, desired by just a few people in the world, or worse, not even thought about by more than a few. eBay is working on a solution called Discover, which scours the listings to identify how intensely people interact with the listing, the history of the seller offering unusual items, and the emotional intensity of the product's description.

Both the Long Tail and the winner-take-all approaches have implications for marketers and product designers. In the Long Tail approach, online merchants, especially those selling digital goods such as content, should build up huge libraries of content because they can make significant revenues from niche products that have small audiences. In the winner-take-all approach, the niche products produce little revenue, and firms should concentrate on hugely popular titles and services. Surprisingly, the evidence for online digital content increasingly supports a winner-take-all perspective.

SOURCES: "Article Marketing Tips: Using Long-Tail Keywords," by Steve Shaw, Internet Business, ezinearticles.com, August 26, 2012; "Goodbye Pareto Principle, Hello Long Tail: The Effect of Search Costs on the Concentration of Product Sales," by Eric Brynjolfsson, et al., *Management Science*, July 2012; "Recommendation Networks and the Long Tail of Electronic Commerce," by Gail Oestreicher-Singer, New York University, 2012; "Long Tail Pricing in Business-to-Business Markets," by Just Schurman, Boston Consulting Group, bcgperspectives.com, July 3, 2012; "Research Commentary - Long Tails vs. Superstars: The Effect of Information Technology on Product Variety and Sales Concentration Patterns" by Erik Brynjolfsson, Yu (Jeffrey) Hu, and Michael D. Smith, Information Systerms Research, December 2010; "Anatomy of the Long Tail: Ordinary People With Extraordinary Tastes," by Sharad Goel, et al., Proceedings of the Third ACM Conference on Web Search and Data Mining, 2010; "EBay Tests Serendipitous Shopping," by Elizabeth Woyke, *Forbes*, August 22, 2011; "The Long Tail of E-commerce," by Jack Jia, *E-commerce Times*, August 18, 2011; "How Does Popularity Affect Choices? A Field Experiment," by Catherine Tucker and Juanjuan Zhang, *Management Science*, May 2011; "Keyword Strategies—The Long Tail," by Matt Daily, Searchengineguide.com, July 2010.

6.3 UNDERSTANDING THE COSTS AND BENEFITS OF ONLINE MARKETING COMMUNICATIONS

As we noted earlier, online marketing communications still comprise only a very small part of the total marketing communications universe. While there are several reasons why this is the case, two of the main ones are concerns about how well online advertising really works and about how to adequately measure the costs and benefits of online advertising. We will address both of these topics in this section. But first, we will define some important terms used when examining the effectiveness of online marketing.

ONLINE MARKETING METRICS: LEXICON

In order to understand the process of attracting prospects to your firm's Web site or Facebook page via marketing communications and converting them into customers, you will need to be familiar with Web marketing terminology. **Table 6.7** lists some terms commonly used to describe the impacts and results of online marketing for display ads, social network ads, and e-mail campaigns.

The first nine metrics focus primarily on the success of a Web site in achieving audience or market share by "driving" shoppers to the site. These measures often substitute for solid information on sales revenue as e-commerce entrepreneurs seek to have investors and the public focus on the success of the Web site in "attracting eyeballs" (viewers).

Impressions are the number of times an ad is served. **Click-through rate (CTR)** measures the percentage of people exposed to an online advertisement who actually click on the advertisement. Because not all ads lead to an immediate click, the industry has invented a new term for a long-term hit called **view-through rate (VTR)**, which measures the 30-day response rate to an ad. **Hits** are the number of HTTP requests received by a firm's server. Hits can be misleading as a measure of Web site activity because a "hit" does not equal a page. A single page may account for several hits if the page contains multiple images or graphics. A single Web site visitor can generate hundreds of hits. For this reason, hits are not an accurate representation of Web traffic or visits, even though they are generally easy to measure; the sheer volume of hits can be huge—and sound impressive—but not be a true measure of activity. **Page views** are the number of pages requested by visitors. However, with increased usage of Web frames that divide pages into separate sections, a single page that has three frames will generate three page views. Hence, page views per se are also not a very useful metric.

Stickiness (sometimes called *duration*) is the average length of time visitors remain at a Web site. Stickiness is important to marketers because the longer the amount of time a visitor spends at a Web site, the greater the probability of a purchase. In December 2011, for instance, Google's 173 million unique visitors stayed on-site an average of one and a half hours during a month's time; Yahoo's 144 million visitors stayed an average of 2 hours and 17 minutes; Facebook's 153 million visitors stayed on-site an average of almost 7 hours! While Facebook generates a great deal of stickiness, it's not the case that this translates directly into more advertisements, more sales,

impressions
number of times an ad is served

click-through rate (CTR)
the percentage of people exposed to an online advertisement who actually click on the banner

view-through rate (VTR)
measures the 30-day response rate to an ad

hits
number of http requests received by a firm's server

page views
number of pages requested by visitors

stickiness (duration)
average length of time visitors remain at a site

TABLE 6.7	MARKETING METRICS LEXICON
COMMON MARKETING DISPLAY AD METRICS	**DESCRIPTION**
Impressions	Number of times an ad is served
Click-through rate (CTR)	Percentage of times an ad is clicked
View-through rate (VTR)	Percentage of times an ad is not clicked immediately but the Web site is visited within 30 days
Hits	Number of HTTP requests
Page views	Number of pages viewed
Stickiness (duration)	Average length of stay at a Web site
Unique visitors	Number of unique visitors in a period
Loyalty	Measured variously as the number of page views, frequency of single-user visits to the Web site, or percentage of customers who return to the site in a year to make additional purchases
Reach	Percentage of Web site visitors who are potential buyers; or the percentage of total market buyers who buy at a site
Recency	Time elapsed since the last action taken by a buyer, such as a Web site visit or purchase
Acquisition rate	Percentage of visitors who indicate an interest in the Web site's products by registering or visiting product pages
Conversion rate	Percentage of visitors who become customers
Browse-to-buy ratio	Ratio of items purchased to product views
View-to-cart ratio	Ratio of "Add to cart" clicks to product views
Cart conversion rate	Ratio of actual orders to "Add to cart" clicks
Checkout conversion rate	Ratio of actual orders to checkouts started
Abandonment rate	Percentage of shoppers who begin a shopping cart purchase but then leave the Web site without completing a purchase (similar to above)
Retention rate	Percentage of existing customers who continue to buy on a regular basis (similar to loyalty)
Attrition rate	Percentage of customers who do not return during the next year after an initial purchase
SOCIAL MARKETING METRICS	
Gross rating points	Audience size times frequency of views (audience reach)
Applause ratio	Number of Likes per post
Conversation ratio	Ratio of number of comments per post
Amplification	Number of shares (or re-tweets) per post
Sentiment ratio	Ratio of positive comments to total comments
Duration of engagement	Average time on site
E-MAIL METRICS	
Open rate	Percentage of e-mail recipients who open the e-mail and are exposed to the message
Delivery rate	Percentage of e-mail recipients who received the e-mail
Click-through rate (e-mail)	Percentage of recipients who clicked through to offers
Bounce-back rate	Percentage of e-mails that could not be delivered
Unsubscribe rate	Percentage of recipients who click unsubscribe
Conversion rate (e-mail)	Percentage of recipients who actually buy

and more revenue. Equally important is what people do when they visit a Web site and not just how much time they spend there. People don't go to Facebook to buy or research goods, whereas Google visitors are more likely to visit because they are searching for something to buy (Nielsen, 2012).

The number of unique visitors is perhaps the most widely used measure of a Web site's popularity. The measurement of **unique visitors** counts the number of distinct, unique visitors to a Web site, regardless of how many pages they view. **Loyalty** measures the percentage of visitors who return in a year. This can be a good indicator of a site's Web following, and perhaps the trust shoppers place in a site. **Reach** is typically a percentage of the total number of consumers in a market who visit a Web site; for example, 10% of all book purchasers in a year will visit Amazon at least once to shop for a book. This provides an idea of the power of a Web site to attract market share. **Recency**—like loyalty—measures the power of a Web site to produce repeat visits and is generally measured as the average number of days elapsed between shopper or customer visits. For example, a recency value of 25 days means the average customer will return once every 25 days.

The metrics described so far do not say much about commercial activity nor help you understand the conversion from visitor to customer. Several other measures are more helpful in this regard. **Acquisition rate** measures the percentage of visitors who register or visit product pages (indicating interest in the product). **Conversion rate** measures the percentage of visitors who actually purchase something. Conversion rates can vary widely, depending on the success of the site. Fireclick, a provider of Web analytics software, publishes conversion rate statistics, and cites a global conversion rate of around 2%–3% (Fireclick, 2012). The **browse-to-buy ratio** measures the ratio of items purchased to product views. The **view-to-cart ratio** calculates the ratio of "Add to cart" clicks to product views. **Cart conversion rate** measures the ratio of actual orders to "Add to cart" clicks. **Checkout conversion rate** calculates the ratio of actual orders to checkouts started. **Abandonment rate** measures the percentage of shoppers who begin a shopping cart form but then fail to complete the form and leave the Web site. Abandonment rates can signal a number of potential problems—poor form design, lack of consumer trust, or consumer purchase uncertainty caused by other factors. A recent study on shopping cart abandonment found that, on average, 65% of carts were abandoned in 2012 (Baymard, 2012). Among the reasons for abandonment were security concerns, customer just checking prices, couldn't find customer support, couldn't find preferred payment option, and the item being unavailable at checkout. Given that more than 80% of online shoppers generally have a purchase in mind when they visit a Web site, a high abandonment rate signals many lost sales. **Retention rate** indicates the percentage of existing customers who continue to buy on a regular basis. **Attrition rate** measures the percentage of customers who purchase once but never return within a year (the opposite of loyalty and retention rates).

Social network marketing differs from display ad marketing because the objective is to create word-of-mouth impact and alter the interaction among your visitors, and between your visitors and your brand. While unique visitors is important, it's even more important what they do when they arrive on-site. **Conversation ratio**

unique visitors
the number of distinct, unique visitors to a site

loyalty
percentage of purchasers who return in a year

reach
percentage of the total number of consumers in a market who will visit a site

recency
average number of days elapsed between visits

acquisition rate
percentage of visitors who register or visit product pages

conversion rate
percentage of visitors who purchase something

browse-to-buy ratio
ratio of items purchased to product views

view-to-cart ratio
ratio of "Add to cart" clicks to product views

cart conversion rate
ratio of actual orders to "Add to cart" clicks

checkout conversion ratio
ratio of actual orders to checkouts started

abandonment rate
% of shoppers who begin a shopping cart, but then fail to complete it

retention rate
% of existing customers who continue to buy

attrition rate
% of customers who purchase once, but do not return within a year

conversation ratio
number of comments produced per post

applause ratio
number of Likes or Shares per post

amplification
number of re-tweets or re-shares per post

sentiment ratio
ratio of positive comments to total comments

measures the number of comments produced per post to your site. **Applause ratio** measures the number of Likes or Shares per post. **Amplification** measures the number of re-tweets or re-shares per post. All three of these measures are different dimensions of "word of mouth" advertising on social network sites. **Sentiment ratio** is the ratio of positive comments to total comments.

Facebook, Nielsen, and comScore are also measuring Facebook exposure using gross rating points, a traditional ad metric that multiplies the reach, or size, of an audience by the frequency with which that audience sees a brand. By using this metric, marketers can discuss online advertising in the same terms that they already use for TV, print, or outdoor ads (Raice, 2011; Nielsen, 2011). Facebook's application software development package provides extensive measures of user interactions and demographics. On the other hand, this metric does not measure dimensions of consumer engagement, which is the main strength of social network advertising.

E-mail campaigns have their own set of metrics. **Open rate** measures the percentage of customers who open the e-mail and are exposed to the message. Generally, open rates are quite high, in the area of 50% or greater. However, some browsers open mail as soon as the mouse cursor moves over the subject line, and therefore this measure can be difficult to interpret. **Delivery rate** measures the percentage of e-mail recipients who received the e-mail. **Click-through rate (e-mail)** measures the percentage of e-mail recipients who clicked through to the offer. Finally, **bounce-back rate** measures the percentage of e-mails that could not be delivered.

open rate
% of customers who open e-mail

delivery rate
% of e-mail recipients who received e-mail

click-through rate (e-mail)
% of e-mail recipients who clicked through to the offer

bounce-back rate
percentage of e-mails that could not be delivered

There is a lengthy path from simple online ad impressions, Web site visits, and page views to the purchase of a product and the company making a profit (see **Figure 6.8**). You first need to make customers aware of their needs for your product and somehow drive them to your Web site. Once there, you need to convince them you have the best value—quality and price—when compared to alternative providers. You then must persuade them to trust your firm to handle the transaction (by providing a secure environment and fast fulfillment). Based on your success, a percentage of customers will remain loyal and purchase again or recommend your Web site to others.

HOW WELL DOES ONLINE ADVERTISING WORK?

What is the most effective kind of online advertising? How does online advertising compare to offline advertising? The answers depend on the goals of the campaign, the nature of the product, and the quality of the Web site you direct customers toward. The answers also depend on what you measure. Click-through rates are interesting, but ultimately it's the return on the investment in the ad campaign that counts. A broader understanding of the matter requires that you consider the cost of purchasing the promotional materials and mailing lists, and the studio production costs for radio and TV ads. Also, each media has a different revenue-per-contact potential because the products advertised differ. For instance, online purchases tend to be for smaller items when compared to newspaper, magazine, and television ads (although this too seems to be changing).

Table 6.8 lists the click-through rates for various types of online marketing communications tools. There is a great deal of variability within any of these types, so the

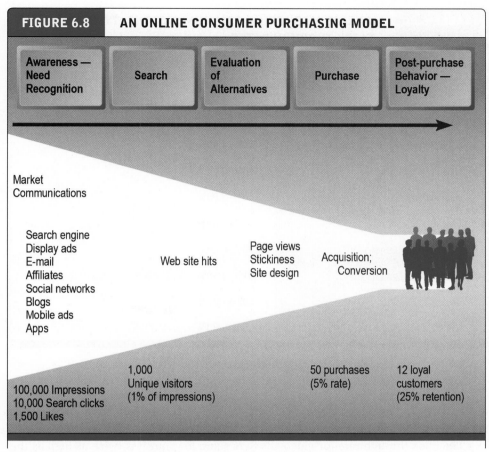

FIGURE 6.8 | AN ONLINE CONSUMER PURCHASING MODEL

| Awareness — Need Recognition | Search | Evaluation of Alternatives | Purchase | Post-purchase Behavior — Loyalty |

Market Communications

Search engine
Display ads
E-mail
Affiliates
Social networks
Blogs
Mobile ads
Apps

Web site hits

Page views
Stickiness
Site design

Acquisition; Conversion

100,000 Impressions
10,000 Search clicks
1,500 Likes

1,000
Unique visitors
(1% of impressions)

50 purchases
(5% rate)

12 loyal
customers
(25% retention)

The conversion of visitors into customers, and then loyal customers, is a complex and long-term process that may take several months.

figures in Table 7.5 should be viewed as general estimates. Click-through rates on all these formats are a function of personalization and other targeting techniques. For instance, several studies have found that e-mail response rates can be increased 20% or more by adding social sharing links. And while the average Google click-through rate is .5%, some merchants can hit 10% or more by making their ads more specific and attracting only the most interested people. Permission e-mail click-through rates have been fairly consistent over the last five years, in the 5%–6% range. Putting the recipient's name in the subject line can double the click-through rate. (For unsolicited e-mail and outright spam, response rates are much lower, even though about 20% of U.S. e-mail users report clicking occasionally on an unsolicited e-mail.)

In general, Facebook ads have a far lower click-through rate, in part because Facebook users do not go to their pages to purchase goods or experience ads of any kind. While Facebook now accounts for about one-quarter of all display advertising (1 trillion display ads a year), its share of display ad revenue is far lower because the click-through on its site is so weak. Mobile ads outperform standard banner ads by up

TABLE 6.8	ONLINE MARKETING COMMUNICATIONS: TYPICAL CLICK-THROUGH RATES
MARKETING METHODS	TYPICAL CLICK-THROUGH RATES
Display ads	.03%–.30%
Interstitials	.02%–.16%
Search engine keyword purchase	.50%–4.00%
Video and rich media	.50%–2.65%
Sponsorships	1.50%–3.00%
Affiliate relationships	.20%–.40%
E-mail marketing in-house list	5.00%–6.00%
E-mail marketing purchased list	.01%–1.50%
Social site display ads	.02%–.25%
Mobile display ads	.50%–.80%

SOURCES: Based on data from eMarketer, Inc., 2011b; 2011c; industry sources; authors' estimates.

to six times, and rich media and video ads are much more effective than banner ads (eMarketer, 2011b).

The click-through rate for video ads may seem low, but it is twice as high as the rate for display ads. The "interaction rate" (sometimes referred to as "dwell rate") with rich media ads and video ads is about 7%–8%. "Interaction" means the user clicks on the video, plays it, stops it, or takes some other action (possibly skips the ad altogether) (eMarketer, 2009; Eyeblaster, 2009). Although click-through rate is an important metric for video ads, advertising agencies also focus on other metrics to assess the success of an online video campaign, such as number of unique viewers, target impressions, brand lift, sales impact, and conversions (Brightroll, 2012).

How effective is online advertising compared to offline advertising? **Figure 6.9** provides some insight into this question. In general, the online channels (e-mail, search engine, banner ads, and video) compare very favorably with traditional channels. This explains in large part why online advertising has grown so rapidly in the last five years. Search engine advertising over the last five years has grown to be one of the most cost-effective forms of marketing communications and accounts for, in large part, the growth of Google, as well as other search engines. Surprisingly, direct opt-in e-mail is nearly twice as cost-effective as search engine advertising. This is, in part, because e-mail lists are so inexpensive compared to keywords, and because opt-in e-mail is a form of targeting people who are already interested in receiving more information.

| FIGURE 6.9 | COMPARATIVE RETURNS ON INVESTMENT |

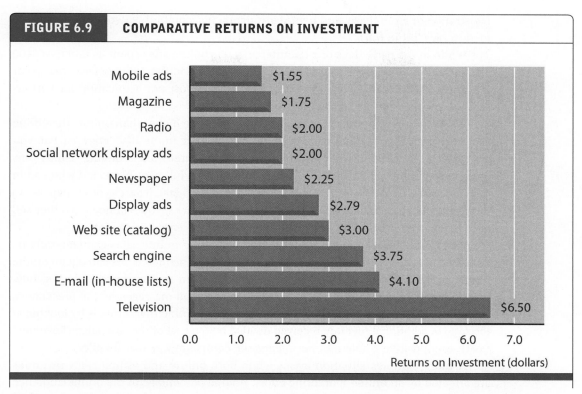

This figure shows the estimated average return on investment in dollars for every dollar spent using different types of advertising techniques. These amounts are estimates and will vary by product, effectiveness, page placement, and degree of targeting.
SOURCES: Industry sources; authors' estimates.

A study of the comparative impacts of offline and online marketing concluded that the most powerful marketing campaigns used multiple forms of marketing, including online, catalog, television, radio, newspapers, and retail store. Traditional media like television and print media remain the primary means for consumers to find out about new products even though advertisers have reduced their budgets for print media ads. The consensus conclusion is that consumers who shop multiple channels are spending more than consumers who shop only with a single channel, in part because they have more discretionary income but also because of the combined number of "touchpoints" that marketers are making with the consumers. The fastest growing channel in consumer marketing is the multi-channel shopper.

THE COSTS OF ONLINE ADVERTISING

Effectiveness cannot be considered without an analysis of costs. Initially, most online ads were sold on a barter or **cost per thousand (CPM) impressions** basis, with advertisers purchasing impressions in 1,000-unit lots. Today, other pricing models have developed, including **cost per click (CPC)**, where the advertiser pays a prenegotiated fee for each click an ad receives, **cost per action (CPA)**, where the advertiser pays a prenegotiated amount only when a user performs a specific action, such as a

cost per thousand (CPM)
advertiser pays for impressions in 1,000 unit lots

cost per click (CPC)
advertiser pays prenegotiated fee for each click an ad receives

cost per action (CPA)
advertiser pays only for those users who perform a specific action

registration or a purchase, and hybrid arrangements, combining two or more of these models (see **Table 6.9**).

While in the early days of e-commerce, a few online sites spent as much as $400 on marketing and advertising to acquire one customer, the average cost was never that high. **Table 6.10** shows the estimated average cost per acquisition for various types of media.

While the costs for offline customer acquisition are higher than online, the offline items are typically far more expensive. If you advertise in the *Wall Street Journal,* you are tapping into a wealthy demographic that may be interested in buying islands, jets, other corporations, and expensive homes in France. A full-page black and white ad in the *Wall Street Journal* National Edition costs about $350,000, whereas other papers are in the $10,000 to $100,000 range. For these kinds of prices, you will need to either sell quite a few apples or a small number of corporate jet lease agreements.

One of the advantages of online marketing is that online sales can generally be directly correlated with online marketing efforts. If online merchants can obtain offline purchase data from a data broker, the merchants can measure precisely just how much revenue is generated by specific banners or e-mail messages sent to prospective customers. One way to measure the effectiveness of online marketing is by looking at the ratio of additional revenue received divided by the cost of the campaign (Revenue/Cost). Any positive whole number means the campaign was worthwhile.

A more complex situation arises when both online and offline sales revenues are affected by an online marketing effort. A large percentage of the online audience uses the Web to "shop" but not buy. These shoppers buy at physical stores. Merchants such as Sears and Walmart use e-mail to inform their registered customers of special offers available for purchase either online or at stores. Unfortunately, purchases at physical stores cannot be tied precisely with the online e-mail campaign. In these cases, merchants have to rely on less precise measures such as customer surveys at store locations to determine the effectiveness of online campaigns.

TABLE 6.9	DIFFERENT PRICING MODELS FOR ONLINE ADVERTISEMENTS
PRICING MODEL	DESCRIPTION
Barter	Exchange of ad space for something of equal value
Cost per thousand (CPM)	Advertiser pays for impressions in 1,000-unit lots
Cost per click (CPC)	Advertiser pays prenegotiated fee for each click ad received
Cost per action (CPA)	Advertiser pays only for those users who perform a specific action, such as registering, purchasing, etc.
Hybrid	Two or more of the above models used together
Sponsorship	Term-based; advertiser pays fixed fee for a slot on a Web site

TABLE 6.10	AVERAGE COST PER CUSTOMER ACQUISITION FOR SELECT MEDIA IN THE UNITED STATES, 2012
Internet search engine	$8.50
E-mail (opt-in)	$10.00
Television	$11.00
Magazine	$19.00
Yellow pages	$20.00
Newspaper	$25.00
Online display ads	$50.00
Direct mail	$50.00

SOURCES: Industry sources; authors' estimates.

In either case, measuring the effectiveness of online marketing communications—and specifying precisely the objective (branding versus sales)—is critical to profitability. To measure marketing effectiveness, you need to understand the costs of various marketing media and the process of converting online prospects into online customers.

Instant Ads:
Real-Time Marketing on Exchanges

The holy grail of advertising and marketing is to deliver the right message to the right person at the right time. But most of the display ads shown to site visitors are marvelously irrelevant to visitors' interests, both short term and long term. For this reason, the click-through rate for banner advertising is a stunningly low 0.03%, and the price of display ads has fallen to a few cents because of their poor performance.

A part of the problem is that online display ad publishers did not know very much about you (until recently), and what they did know was quite general: gender, zip code, age, and perhaps some prior purchases. Even if they knew everything about you, the advertising networks did not have the mechanism to sell that information instantly to a potential advertiser. For this reason, banner ads displayed on the Web sites you visited in the past rarely had anything to do with your interests at the time.

Behavioral targeting and tracking of online behavior have begun to improve the situation for display advertisers by expanding the scope, breadth, and depth of personal information, making it possible for advertisers to fine-tune their display ads and to develop a much finer-grained, digital image of individual customers—real people, not just profiles. Using beacons, Web bugs, cookies, and Flash cookies, almost all the top Web sites now install tracking software onto visitor computers. A *Wall Street Journal* study of the 50 top Web sites in the United States, accounting for 40% of U.S. page views, found these sites installed 3,180 tracking files on a test computer that visited each site. Only one top-50 site installed no tracking files: Wikipedia. Over two-thirds of the tracking files were installed by 131 companies. The biggest trackers are Google, Microsoft, and Yahoo.

Today, when a user visits a site, a tracking number or cookie is assigned to the user. Often a "beacon" or Web bug is installed, which captures what people are typing on a Web site. The file keeps growing the more the user visits Web sites. So what happens to all this information about you and others? The cookie and beacon owners collect all this information and sell it to advertisers. The information and the profile are sold to advertisers usually for 10 cents a piece. Once individuals fitting a particular profile type appear at a Web site, the advertiser pays to have a pre-fabricated ad displayed to that person. The result is a more efficient market communications process, happier Internet users who see what they are interested in looking at, and users who click more often.

One thing is missing from this heady mix of behavioral tracking and targeting: immediacy. When you click on a search engine result, it's because you are interested in that product or service right now, this moment, this instant. Google, which is currently used by 75% of global Internet users, or approximately 1.5 billion people, is

SOURCES: "Ad Tech Company eXelate Raises $12M," by Ted O'Hear, Techcrunch.com, September 24, 2012; "Facebook Efforts on Advertising Face a Day of Judgment," by Somini Sengupta, *New York Times,* July 22, 2012; "Facebook Exchange and the Rise of Real-Time Ad Bidding," by Michael Baker, *Forbes,* June 14, 2012; "Facebook to Debut Ad Exchange in Bid to Boost Revenues" by Robert Hof, *Forbes,* June 13, 2012; "What's a Facebook Ad Exchange?" by Peter Kafka, *All Things Digital,* June 13, 2012; "ComScore, eXelate Cleaning Up 'Garbage In, Garbage Out,'" by Erin Griffith, *Ad Week,* August 16, 2011; "Tracking the Trackers: Early Results," by Jonathan Mayer, Stanford Center for Internet and Society, July 12, 2011; "Real-Time Bidding Becomes a $832 Million Market in 2011," by Michael Barrett, AdAgeDigital, February 8, 2011; "Google Agonizes on Privacy as Ad World Vaults Ahead," by Jessica Vascellaro, *Wall Street Journal,* August 10, 2010; "Sites Feed Personal Details to New Tracking Industry," by Julia Angwin and Tom McGinty, *Wall Street Journal,* July 30, 2010; "Yahoo Finally Allows Real-Time Bidding on Network and Exchange," Kate Kaye, ClickZ.com, March 15, 2010; "Instant Ads Set the Pace on the Web," by Stephanie Clifford, *New York Times;* March 10, 2010; "Online Ad Auctions," by Hal Varian, Draft, University of California and Google, February 16, 2009.

believed to be the largest and best repository of immediate user interests. For display ads, even targeted ones, this has not been possible, but in 2012, this situation is changing, and for the first time display advertisers, portals, and ad networks they own are building the capability to display banner ads that are based on the granular behavior of individuals just prior to displaying the ad.

The really large Web advertisers like Google, Microsoft, Facebook, and Yahoo have each developed real-time ad exchanges that permit advertisers to bid for ad spaces in the few milliseconds between a user entering a Web address (or clicking on a search query) and the page appearing, based on the data purchased from data exchanges. Ad exchanges are middlemen who stand between Web site publishers who have ad space to sell and advertisers who want to display ads to highly targeted audiences. Ad exchanges use real-time bidding (RTB) to allocate publisher ad spaces to advertisers.

Ad exchanges allow advertisers to purchase inventory in an eBay-like auction environment. Advertisers can enter the kind of ad they want from display, pre-roll to a video, or other rich media ad, enter the desired demographics and audience characteristics, and the price range, and then click a button. When users enter a Web site, they are screened in a few milliseconds to see if they fit the profile, and if so, they are shown the ad.

According to Forrester, advertisers spent $353 million in the United States on RTB advertising in 2010, and this more than doubled in 2011 to $823 million—roughly 8% of total display spending. These ad exchanges have moved closer to the ideal Web advertising environment by allowing advertisers to decide where to place their ads on the fly, based on fairly solid data on the people most likely to see the ad. This is far different from the traditional ad placement process, which placed ads weeks and months in advance of the ad being displayed.

Case Study Questions

1. Pay a visit to your favorite portal and count the total ads on the opening page. Count how many of these ads are (a) immediately of interest and relevant to you, (b) sort of interesting or relevant but not now, and (c) not interesting or relevant. Do this 10 times and calculate the percentage of the three kinds of situations. Describe what you find and explain the results using this case.

2. Advertisers use different kinds of "profiles" in the decision to display ads to customers. Identify the different kinds of profiles described in this case, and explain why they are relevant to online display advertising.

3. How can display ads achieve search-engine–like results?

4. Do you think instant display ads based on your immediately prior clickstream will be as effective as search engine marketing techniques? Why or why not?

6.5	REVIEW

KEY CONCEPTS

■ **Identify the key features of the Internet audience.**

Key features of the Internet audience include:
- *The number of users online in the United States.* In 2012, the total was around 239 million.
- *Intensity and scope of use.* Both are increasing, with around 82% of adult users in the United States logging on in a typical day and engaging in a wider set of activities.
- *Demographics and access.* Although the Internet population is growing increasingly diverse, some demographic groups have much higher percentages of online usage.
- *Media choices.* The more time individuals spend using the Internet, the less time they spend using traditional media.

■ **Discuss the basic concepts of consumer behavior and purchasing decisions.**

There are five stages in the consumer decision process:
- Awareness of need
- Search for more information
- Evaluation of alternatives
- The actual purchase decision
- Post-purchase contact with the firm

The online consumer decision process is basically the same, with the addition of two new factors:
- *Web site capabilities*—the content, design, and functionality of a site.
- *Consumer clickstream behavior*—the transaction log that consumers establish as they move about the Web and through specific sites.

■ **Understand how consumers behave online.**

Clickstream analysis shows us that people go online for many different reasons, at different times, and for numerous purposes.
- About 72% of online users are "buyers" who actually purchase something entirely online. Another 16.5% of online users research products on the Web, but purchase them offline. This combined group, referred to as "shoppers," constitutes approximately 88% of the online Internet audience.
- Online sales are divided roughly into two groups: small-ticket and big-ticket items. In the early days of e-commerce, sales of small-ticket items vastly outnumbered those of large-ticket items. However, the recent growth of big-ticket items such as computer hardware and consumer electronics has changed the overall sales mix.
- There are a number of actions that e-commerce vendors could take to increase the likelihood that shoppers and non-shoppers would purchase online more frequently. These include better security of credit card information and privacy of personal information, lower shipping costs, and easier returns.

■ Identify and describe the basic digital commerce marketing and advertising strategies and tools.

The major digital commerce marketing and advertising strategies and tools include:

- A *Web site* is the major tool for establishing the initial relationship with the customer.
- *Search engine marketing and advertising* allows firms to pay search engines for inclusion in the search engine index (formerly free and based on "objective" criteria), receiving a guarantee that their firm will appear in the results of relevant searches.
- *Display ads* are promotional messages that users can respond to by clicking on the banner and following the link to a product description or offering.
- *E-mail marketing* sends e-mail directly to interested users, and has proven to be one of the most effective forms of marketing communications.
- *Lead generation marketing* uses multiple e-commerce presences to generate leads for businesses who later can be contacted and converted into customers.
- *Affiliate marketing* involves a firm putting its logo or banner ad on another firm's Web site from which users of that site can click through to the affiliate's site.
- *Sponsorships* are paid efforts to tie an advertiser's name to particular information, an event, or a venue in a way that reinforces its brand in a positive yet not overtly commercial manner.
- *Social marketing and advertising*, on social networks, blogs, and in games, involves using the social graph to communicate brand images and directly promote sales of products and services.
- *Mobile and local marketing and advertising* involves using display ads, search engine advertising, video ads, and mobile messaging on mobile devices such as smartphones and tablet computers, often using the geographic location of the user.
- *Multi-channel marketing* (combining offline and online marketing efforts) is typically the most effective. Although many e-commerce ventures want to rely heavily on online communications, marketing communications campaigns most successful at driving traffic have incorporated both online and offline tactics.

■ Understand the costs and benefits of online marketing communications.

Key terms that one must know in order to understand evaluations of online marketing communications' effectiveness and its costs and benefits include:

- *Impressions*—the number of times an ad is served.
- *Click-through rate*—the number of times an ad is clicked.
- *View-through rate*—the 30-day response rate to an ad.
- *Hits*—the number of http requests received by a firm's server.
- *Page views*—the number of pages viewed by visitors.
- *Stickiness (duration)*—the average length of time visitors remain at a site.
- *Unique visitors*—the number of distinct, unique visitors to a site.
- *Loyalty*—the percentage of purchasers who return in a year.
- *Reach*—the percentage of total consumers in a market who will visit a site.
- *Recency*—the average number of days elapsed between visits.
- *Acquisition rate*—the percentage of visitors who indicate an interest in the site's product by registering or visiting product pages.
- *Conversion rate*—the percentage of visitors who purchase something.

- *Browse-to-buy ratio*—the ratio of items purchased to product views.
- *View-to-cart ratio*—the ratio of "Add to cart" clicks to product views.
- *Cart conversion rate*—the ratio of actual orders to "Add to cart" clicks.
- *Checkout conversion rate*—the ratio of actual orders to checkouts started.
- *Abandonment rate*—the percentage of shoppers who begin a shopping cart form, but then fail to complete the form.
- *Retention rate*—the percentage of existing customers who continue to buy on a regular basis.
- *Attrition rate*—the percentage of customers who purchase once, but do not return within a year.
- *Conversation ratio*—the number of comments produced per post to a site.
- *Applause ratio*—the number of Likes or Shares per post.
- *Amplification*—the number of re-tweets or re-shares per post.
- *Sentiment ratio*—the ratio of positive comments to total comments.
- *Open rate*—the percentage of customers who open the mail and are exposed to the message.
- *Delivery rate*—the percentage of e-mail recipients who received the e-mail.
- *Click-through rate (e-mail)*—the percentage of e-mail recipients who clicked through to the offer.
- *Bounce-back rate*—the percentage of e-mails that could not be delivered.

Studies have shown that low click-through rates are not indicative of a lack of commercial impact of online advertising, and that advertising communication does occur even when users do not directly respond by clicking. Online advertising in its various forms has been shown to boost brand awareness and brand recall, create positive brand perceptions, and increase intent to purchase.

QUESTIONS

1. Is growth of the Internet, in terms of users, expected to continue indefinitely? What, if anything, will cause it to slow?
2. Other than search engines, what are some of the most popular uses of the Internet?
3. Would you say that the Internet fosters or impedes social activity? Explain your position.
4. Research has shown that many consumers use the Internet to investigate purchases before actually buying, which is often done in a physical storefront. What implication does this have for online merchants? What can they do to entice more online buying, rather than pure research?
5. Describe a perfect market from the supplier's and customer's perspectives.
6. Explain why an imperfect market is more advantageous for businesses.
7. List some of the major advantages of having a strong brand. How does a strong brand positively influence consumer purchasing?
8. How are product positioning and branding related? How are they different?
9. Why have advertising networks become controversial? What, if anything, can be done to overcome any resistance to this technique?
10. Which of the four market entry strategies is most lucrative?
11. Compare and contrast four marketing strategies used in mass marketing, direct marketing, micromarketing, and one-to-one marketing.

12. What are some of the reasons for the decline in click-through rates on banner ads today? How can banner ads be made more effective?

13. What are some of the advantages of direct e-mail marketing?

14. Why is offline advertising still important?

PROJECTS

1. Go to www.strategicbusinessinsights.com/vals/presurvey.shtml. Take the survey to determine which lifestyle category you fit into. Then write a two-page paper describing how your lifestyle and values impact your use of the Web for e-commerce. How is your online consumer behavior affected by your lifestyle?

2. Visit Net-a-porter.com and create an Internet marketing plan for it that includes each of the following:
   - One-to-one marketing
   - Affiliate marketing
   - Viral marketing
   - Blog marketing
   - Social network marketing

   Describe how each plays a role in growing the business, and create a slide presentation of your marketing plan.

Ethical, Social, and Political Issues in E-commerce

After reading this chapter, you will be able to:

- Understand why e-commerce raises ethical, social, and political issues.
- Recognize the main ethical, social, and political issues raised by e-commerce.
- Understand basic concepts related to privacy.
- Identify the practices of e-commerce companies that threaten privacy.
- Describe the different methods used to protect online privacy.
- Understand the various forms of intellectual property and the challenges involved in protecting it.
- Understand how governance of the Internet has evolved over time.
- Explain why taxation of e-commerce raises governance and jurisdiction issues.
- Identify major public safety and welfare issues raised by e-commerce.

Internet Free Speech:
Who Decides?

Now that nearly all of our public and private life has moved online, who determines whether what we choose to say can be disseminated to the rest of the world via the Internet? Should private companies like Google, Facebook, and Twitter be able to control what is distributed? Or should this be the role of government? There now also seems to be a third possibility: any group that is powerful enough to threaten the social order appears to be able to influence what is disseminated on the Internet.

As a case in point, in July 2012, a 14-minute movie trailer from a reputed feature-length film called *The Innocence of Muslims* was released on the Internet. The amateurish trailer was a scathing,

satirical attack that ridiculed the prophet Muhammad. In September, the video suddenly went viral throughout the Arab world, via Google and other search engines in response to user queries, and on Google's YouTube. An international firestorm ensued. Islamic groups, first in the Middle East and then throughout the world, protested the video, and in some cases, riots ensued.

In response to growing unrest in the Islamic world, the Obama administration requested that Google remove links to the video on the Google search engine (refusing to answer search queries on the topic and removing references to any and all URLs where the video might be viewed), as well as remove the video from YouTube. The government argued that the video constituted "hate speech," which Google prohibits under its Terms of Service. Google disagreed, saying the video did not clearly violate its Terms of Service. However, a day after refusing to remove the video from YouTube, Google did block access to it in Egypt and Libya because, it said, the situation in those countries was exceptional and the ban was temporary. It did continue to allow the video to circulate in the rest of the world.

Nearly all developed countries, and many developing countries, have laws that prohibit "hate speech." Hate speech is defined in most of these laws (as it is in Google's Terms of Service) as speech that may promote or incite hate or violence against a group or individual. These laws often identify protected groups by disability, ethnicity, religion, gender identity, nationality, race, or other characteristic. Hate speech is prohibited in many European countries. Europe has prohibited Neo-Nazi speech and banned materials that are offensive to various religious and ethnic groups, long before the Internet existed. Generally, Google, Facebook, and Yahoo follow the requirements of local laws.

SOURCES: "Held Dear in the U.S., Free Speech Perplexing Abroad," National Public Radio, September 19, 2012; "State of the Web: Online Speech Is Only as Free as Google Wants It to Be," by Andrew Couts, Digitaltrends.com, September 18, 2012; "On the Web, a Fine Line on Free Speech Across the Globe," by Somini Sengupta, *New York Times*, September 16, 2012; "As Violence Spreads in the Arab World, Google Blocks Access to Inflammatory Video," Claire Cain Miller, *Wall Street Journal*, September 13, 2012; "Google Groups Content Policy," Google Inc., http://support.google.com/groups, September 2012; "Free Speech and the Internet," *New York Times*, July 3, 2011; "Supreme Court Plays Hooky, Leaves Student Online Free Speech Rights Murky," by David Kravets, *Wired*, November 1, 2011; "The Role of Telecommunications in Hate Crimes," National Telecommunication and Information Administration, U.S. Department of Commerce, December 1993.

For instance, Google has removed videos that ridiculed Pakistani officials and blocked access to videos that exposed private information about Turkish officials, in both instances because the content violated local laws.

In contrast, hate speech is not prohibited in the United States. The United States has a more absolutist view of the right to freedom of speech because of the First Amendment. However, as with all rights, there are limitations in the United States with respect to the right to free speech. For instance, speech can be prohibited if there is an imminent and immediate likelihood that there will be violence in close proximity to the speech in time and space. Strong advocates of free speech criticized Google for bowing to the demands of protestors in Egypt and Libya. Will freedom of speech on the Internet be determined by mobs in the street? Civil libertarians warned that to allow Google, a private corporation, to determine what is or is not published on the Web is a worrisome development. Freedom of speech is guaranteed in the Constitution, and they question whether or not Google has the right to regulate a "public speech platform." For instance, the *New York Times* has editorialized that nobody should be banned from the Internet because it is a fundamental tool for enabling free speech. Yet few of these critics would deny the editorial right of the *New York Times,* or any other newspaper, to refuse to publish any material, for whatever reason. Indeed, this happens all the time. On the other hand, Google does not believe it is a publisher that potentially can be held liable for failing to monitor content. Google believes it is a utility carrier, like a telephone company, and that therefore it cannot be held liable for content, or conspiracies, that users distribute and create on its various services.

Others question Google's administration of its own content policies: surely Google managers knew, or should have known, that distributing *The Innocence of Muslims* on YouTube would be a violation of local laws in some countries, and that they should have, and could have, anticipated the public unrest that ensued. In this view, the right to freedom of speech has limits, and one of them is imminent danger to violence. However, in this case, there was a long gap between distribution of the video and the resulting violence. Violence was not imminent, immediate, or proximate in physical space. If there are to be limits to freedom of speech on the Internet because of the potential for violence, then new criteria may be needed to replace imminence, immediacy, and proximity because these conditions are rarely met on the Internet.

Today, what speech should be protected on the Internet, and who should protect it, is suddenly not clear at all. Ironically, the very technology that was supposed to bring people together into one big global community, can have just the opposite impact, dividing nations, religions, and peoples. The Internet can become a platform for wicked individuals to sow violence with their user-generated content. Like bringing the extended family together for holidays, bringing the world's diverse populations together on YouTube can have unexpected, and even dangerous, consequences.

D etermining how or whether to regulate behavior on the Internet is just one of many ethical, social, and political issues raised by the rapid evolution of the Internet and e-commerce. For instance, as described in the opening case, whether U.S. principles of free speech should govern on the Internet, or the principles of other nations, has not been determined. These questions are not just ethical questions that we as individuals have to answer; they also involve social institutions such as family, schools, business firms, and in some cases, entire nation-states. And these questions have obvious political dimensions because they involve collective choices about how we should live and what laws we would like to live under.

In this chapter, we discuss the ethical, social, and political issues raised in e-commerce, provide a framework for organizing the issues, and make recommendations for managers who are given the responsibility of operating e-commerce companies within commonly accepted standards of appropriateness.

7.1 UNDERSTANDING ETHICAL, SOCIAL, AND POLITICAL ISSUES IN E-COMMERCE

The Internet and its use in e-commerce have raised pervasive ethical, social, and political issues on a scale unprecedented for computer technology. Entire sections of daily newspapers and weekly magazines are devoted to the social impact of the Internet. But why is this so? Why is the Internet at the root of so many contemporary controversies? Part of the answer lies in the underlying features of Internet technology itself, and the ways in which it has been exploited by business firms. Internet technology and its use in e-commerce disrupt existing social and business relationships and understandings.

Consider for instance Table 1.2 (in Chapter 1), which lists the unique features of Internet technology. Instead of considering the business consequences of each unique feature, **Table 7.1** examines the actual or potential ethical, social, and/or political consequences of the technology.

We live in an "information society," where power and wealth increasingly depend on information and knowledge as central assets. Controversies over information are often disagreements over power, wealth, influence, and other things thought to be valuable. Like other technologies, such as steam, electricity, telephones, and television, the Internet and e-commerce can be used to achieve social progress, and for the most part, this has occurred. However, the same technologies can be used to commit crimes, despoil the environment, and threaten cherished social values. Before automobiles, there was very little interstate crime and very little federal jurisdiction over crime. Likewise with the Internet: before the Internet, there was no "cybercrime."

A MODEL FOR ORGANIZING THE ISSUES

E-commerce—and the Internet—have raised so many ethical, social, and political issues that it is difficult to classify them all, and hence, complicated to see their relationship to one another. Clearly, ethical, social, and political issues are interrelated. One way to organize the ethical, social, and political dimensions surrounding

TABLE 7.1	UNIQUE FEATURES OF E-COMMERCE TECHNOLOGY AND THEIR POTENTIAL ETHICAL, SOCIAL, AND/OR POLITICAL IMPLICATIONS
E-COMMERCE TECHNOLOGY DIMENSION	**POTENTIAL ETHICAL, SOCIAL, AND POLITICAL SIGNIFICANCE**
Ubiquity—Internet/Web technology is available everywhere: at work, at home, and elsewhere via mobile devices, anytime.	Work and shopping can invade family life; shopping can distract workers at work, lowering productivity; use of mobile devices can lead to automobile and industrial accidents. Presents confusing issues of "nexus" to taxation authorities.
Global reach—The technology reaches across national boundaries, around the Earth.	Reduces cultural diversity in products; weakens local small firms while strengthening large global firms; moves manufacturing production to low-wage areas of the world; weakens the ability of all nations—large and small—to control their information destiny.
Universal standards—There is one set of technology standards, namely Internet standards.	Increases vulnerability to viruses and hacking attacks worldwide, affecting millions of people at once. Increases the likelihood of "information" crime, crimes against systems, and deception.
Richness—Video, audio, and text messages are possible.	A "screen technology" that reduces use of text and potentially the ability to read by focusing instead on video and audio messages. Potentially very persuasive messages that may reduce reliance on multiple independent sources of information.
Interactivity—The technology works through interaction with the user.	The nature of interactivity at commercial sites can be shallow and meaningless. Customer e-mails are frequently not read by human beings. Customers do not really "co-produce" the product as much as they "co-produce" the sale. The amount of "customization" of products that occurs is minimal, occurring within predefined platforms and plug-in options.
Information density—The technology reduces information costs, and raises quality.	While the total amount of information available to all parties increases, so does the possibility of false and misleading information, unwanted information, and invasion of solitude. Trust, authenticity, accuracy, completeness, and other quality features of information can be degraded. The ability of individuals and organizations to make sense out of this plethora of information is limited.
Personalization/Customization—The technology allows personalized messages to be delivered to individuals as well as groups.	Opens up the possibility of intensive invasion of privacy for commercial and governmental purposes that is unprecedented.
Social technology—The technology enables user content generation and social networking.	Creates opportunities for cyberbullying, abusive language, and predation; challenges concepts of privacy, fair use, and consent to use posted information; creates new opportunities for surveillance by authorities and corporations into private lives.

e-commerce is shown in **Figure 7.1**. At the individual level, what appears as an ethical issue—"What should I do?"—is reflected at the social and political levels—"What should we as a society and government do?" The ethical dilemmas you face as a manager of a business using the Web reverberate and are reflected in social and political debates. The major ethical, social, and political issues that have developed around e-commerce over the past 10 years can be loosely categorized into four major dimensions: information rights, property rights, governance, and public safety and welfare.

FIGURE 7.1	THE MORAL DIMENSIONS OF AN INTERNET SOCIETY

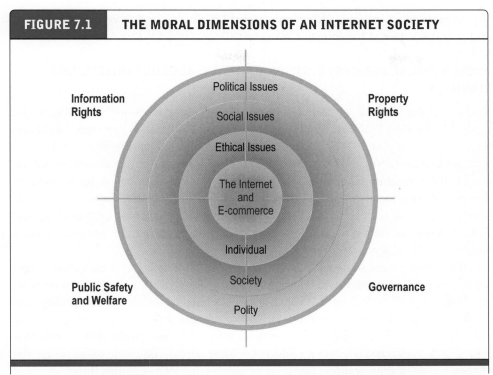

The introduction of the Internet and e-commerce impacts individuals, societies, and political institutions. These impacts can be classified into four moral dimensions: property rights, information rights, governance, and public safety and welfare.

Some of the ethical, social, and political issues raised in each of these areas include the following:

- **Information rights:** What rights to their own personal information do individuals have in a public marketplace, or in their private homes, when Internet technologies make information collection so pervasive and efficient? What rights do individuals have to access information about business firms and other organizations?

- **Property rights:** How can traditional intellectual property rights be enforced in an Internet world where perfect copies of protected works can be made and easily distributed worldwide in seconds?

- **Governance:** Should the Internet and e-commerce be subject to public laws? And if so, what law-making bodies have jurisdiction—state, federal, and/or international?

- **Public safety and welfare:** What efforts should be undertaken to ensure equitable access to the Internet and e-commerce channels? Should governments be responsible for ensuring that schools and colleges have access to the Internet? Are certain online content and activities—such as pornography and gambling—a threat to public safety and welfare? Should mobile commerce be allowed from moving vehicles?

Before examining the four moral dimensions of e-commerce in greater depth, we will briefly review some basic concepts of ethical reasoning that you can use as a guide to ethical decision making, and provide general reasoning principles about the social and political issues of the Internet that you will face in the future.

BASIC ETHICAL CONCEPTS: RESPONSIBILITY, ACCOUNTABILITY, AND LIABILITY

ethics

the study of principles that individuals and organizations can use to determine right and wrong courses of action

Ethics is at the heart of social and political debates about the Internet. **Ethics** is the study of principles that individuals and organizations can use to determine right and wrong courses of action. It is assumed in ethics that individuals are free moral agents who are in a position to make choices. When faced with alternative courses of action, what is the correct moral choice? Extending ethics from individuals to business firms and even entire societies can be difficult, but it is not impossible. As long as there is a decision-making body or individual (such as a board of directors or CEO in a business firm, or a governmental body in a society), their decisions can be judged against a variety of ethical principles.

If you understand some basic ethical principles, your ability to reason about larger social and political debates will be improved. In western culture, there are three basic principles that all ethical schools of thought share: responsibility, accountability, and liability. **Responsibility** means that as free moral agents, individuals, organizations, and societies are responsible for the actions they take. **Accountability** means that individuals, organizations, and societies should be held accountable to others for the consequences of their actions. The third principle—liability—extends the concepts of responsibility and accountability to the area of law. **Liability** is a feature of political systems in which a body of law is in place that permits individuals to recover the damages done to them by other actors, systems, or organizations. **Due process** is a feature of law-governed societies and refers to a process in which laws are known and understood, and there is an ability to appeal to higher authorities to ensure that the laws have been correctly applied.

responsibility

as free moral agents, individuals, organizations, and societies are responsible for the actions they take

accountability

individuals, organizations, and societies should be held accountable to others for the consequences of their actions

liability

a feature of political systems in which a body of law is in place that permits individuals to recover the damages done to them by other actors, systems, or organizations

due process

a process in which laws are known and understood and there is an ability to appeal to higher authorities to ensure that the laws have been correctly applied

ETHICAL PRINCIPLES

Although you are the only one who can decide which ethical principles you will follow and how you will prioritize them, it is helpful to consider some ethical principles with deep roots in many cultures that have survived throughout recorded history:

- **The Golden Rule:** Do unto others as you would have them do unto you. Putting yourself into the place of others and thinking of yourself as the object of the decision can help you think about fairness in decision making.

- **Universalism:** If an action is not right for all situations, then it is not right for any specific situation (Immanuel Kant's categorical imperative). Ask yourself, "If we adopted this rule in every case, could the organization, or society, survive?"

- **Slippery Slope:** If an action cannot be taken repeatedly, then it is not right to take at all. An action may appear to work in one instance to solve a problem, but if repeated, would result in a negative outcome. In plain English, this rule might be stated as "once started down a slippery path, you may not be able to stop."

- **Collective Utilitarian Principle:** Take the action that achieves the greater value for all of society. This rule assumes you can prioritize values in a rank order and understand the consequences of various courses of action.

- **Risk Aversion:** Take the action that produces the least harm, or the least potential cost. Some actions have extremely high failure costs of very low probability (e.g., building a nuclear generating facility in an urban area) or extremely high failure costs of moderate probability (speeding and automobile accidents). Avoid the high-failure cost actions and choose those actions whose consequences would not be catastrophic, even if there were a failure.

- **No Free Lunch:** Assume that virtually all tangible and intangible objects are owned by someone else unless there is a specific declaration otherwise. (This is the ethical "no free lunch" rule.) If something someone else has created is useful to you, it has value and you should assume the creator wants compensation for this work.

- **The New York Times Test (Perfect Information Rule):** Assume that the results of your decision on a matter will be the subject of the lead article in the *New York Times* the next day. Will the reaction of readers be positive or negative? Would your parents, friends, and children be proud of your decision? Most criminals and unethical actors assume imperfect information, and therefore they assume their decisions and actions will never be revealed. When making decisions involving ethical dilemmas, it is wise to assume perfect information markets.

- **The Social Contract Rule:** Would you like to live in a society where the principle you are supporting would become an organizing principle of the entire society? For instance, you might think it is wonderful to download illegal copies of music tracks, but you might not want to live in a society that does not respect property rights, such as your property rights to the car in your driveway, or your rights to a term paper or original art.

None of these rules is an absolute guide, and there are exceptions and logical difficulties with all of them. Nevertheless, actions that do not easily pass these guidelines deserve some very close attention and a great deal of caution because the appearance of unethical behavior may do as much harm to you and your company as the actual behavior.

Now that you have an understanding of some basic ethical reasoning concepts, let's take a closer look at each of the major types of ethical, social, and political debates that have arisen in e-commerce.

7.2 PRIVACY AND INFORMATION RIGHTS

Privacy is the moral right of individuals to be left alone, free from surveillance or interference from other individuals or organizations, including the state. Privacy is a girder supporting freedom: Without the privacy required to think, write, plan, and associate independently and without fear, social and political freedom is weakened, and perhaps destroyed. **Information privacy** is a subset of privacy. The right to

privacy
the moral right of individuals to be left alone, free from surveillance or interference from other individuals or organizations, including the state

information privacy
includes both the claim that certain information should not be collected at all by governments or business firms, and the claim of individuals to control the use of whatever information that is collected about them

information privacy includes both the claim that certain information should not be collected at all by governments or business firms, and the claim of individuals to control the use of whatever information that is collected about them. Individual control over personal information is at the core of the privacy concept.

Due process also plays an important role in defining privacy. The best statement of due process in record keeping is given by the Fair Information Practices doctrine developed in the early 1970s and extended to the online privacy debate in the late 1990s (described later in this section).

There are two kinds of threats to individual privacy posed by the Internet. One threat originates in the private sector and concerns how much personal information is collected by commercial Web sites and how it will be used. A second threat originates in the public sector and concerns how much personal information federal, state, and local government authorities collect, and how they use it. While these threats are conceptually distinct, in practice they are related as the federal government increasingly relies on Internet companies to provide intelligence on specific individuals and groups, and as Internet records held by search engine companies and others (like Amazon) are sought by legal authorities and attornies.

Today, the public discussion of privacy has broadened from a concern about tracking the behavior of individuals while they use the Internet, especially on social networks, to include the impact of mobile devices for tracking the location of people via their smartphones, and collecting information on their personal behavior including the locations they have visited. Smartphone apps that tap user information have also received critical attention. The falling costs of personal tracking technology like mobile cameras, the ubiquitous use of always-on smartphones fitted out with GPS, and the growth of powerful storage and analytic capabilities, has resulted in a torrent of data, referred to as "Big Data," pouring into marketing and law enforcement databases. Private and government investigations have found both Apple and Google are collecting personal location and behavior data, and potentially sharing this information with marketers and government agencies. The cell phone carriers receive more than a million requests each year from law enforcement agencies for call data.

In general, the Internet and the Web provide an ideal environment for both business and government to invade the personal privacy of millions of users on a scale unprecedented in history. The major ethical issues related to e-commerce and privacy include the following: Under what conditions should we collect information about others? What legitimates intruding into others' lives through unobtrusive surveillance, online tracking programs, market research, or other means? Do people have a right to be informed when Web sites are collecting data about them? The major social issues related to e-commerce and privacy concern the development of "expectations of privacy" or privacy norms, as well as public attitudes. In what areas of life should we as a society encourage people to think they are in "private territory" as opposed to public view? The major political issues related to e-commerce and privacy concern the development of statutes that govern the relations between record keepers and individuals. How should both public and private organizations—which may be reluctant to remit the advantages that come from the unfettered flow of information on individuals—be restrained, if at all? In the following section, we look first at the various practices of e-commerce companies that pose a threat to privacy.

INFORMATION COLLECTED AT E-COMMERCE SITES

As you have learned in previous chapters, e-commerce sites routinely collect a variety of information from or about consumers who visit their site and/or make purchases. Some of this data constitutes **personally identifiable information (PII)**, which is defined as any data that can be used to identify, locate, or contact an individual. Other data is **anonymous information**, composed of demographic and behavioral information, such as age, occupation, income, zip code, ethnicity, and other data that characterizes your life such as Web browsing behavior without identifying who you are. **Table 7.2** lists some of the personal identifiers routinely collected by online e-commerce sites including mobile sites and apps. This is not an exhaustive list, and in fact many Web sites collect hundreds of different data points on visitors.

Advertising networks and search engines also track the behavior of consumers across thousands of popular sites, not just at one site, via cookies, Web beacons, tracking software, spyware, and other techniques

Table 7.3 illustrates some of the major ways online firms gather information about consumers.

SOCIAL NETWORKS AND PRIVACY

Social networks pose a unique challenge for the maintenance of personal privacy because they encourage people to reveal details about their personal lives and to share them with their friends. While Google's search engine is a massive database of personal intentions, Facebook has created a massive database of friends, preferences, Likes, posts, and activities. An Austrian researcher was able to obtain his Facebook file (possible under European laws) and received a 1,222 page document of messages, photos, posts, and friends (Sengupta, 2012a). Some social networkers share these personal details with everyone on the social network. On the face of it, this would seem to indicate that people who participate in social networks voluntarily give up their rights to personal privacy. How could they claim an expectation of privacy? When everything is shared, what's private?

personally identifiable information (PII)
any data that can be used to identify, locate, or contact an individual

anonymous information
demographic and behavioral information that does not include any personal identifiers

TABLE 7.2	PERSONAL INFORMATION COLLECTED BY E-COMMERCE SITES	
Name	Gender	Education
Address	Age	Preference data
Phone number	Occupation	Transaction data
E-mail address	Location	Clickstream data
Social security number	Location history	Device used for access
Bank accounts	Likes	Browser type
Credit card accounts	Photograph	

TABLE 7.3	THE INTERNET'S MAJOR INFORMATION-GATHERING TOOLS AND THEIR IMPACT ON PRIVACY
INTERNET CAPABILITY	IMPACT ON PRIVACY
Smartphones and apps	Track location and share photos, addresses, phone numbers, search, and other behavior to marketers.
Advertising networks	Track individuals as they move among thousands of Web sites.
Social networks	Used to gather information on user-provided content such as books, music, friends, and other interests, and lifestyles.
Cookies and Super Cookies	Used to track individuals at a single site.
Third-party cookies	Cookies placed by third-party advertising networks. Used to monitor and track online behavior, searches, and sites visited.
Spyware	Records all the keyboard activity of a user.
Search engine behavioral targeting (Google and other search engines)	Uses prior search history, demographics, expressed interests, geographic, or other user-entered data to target advertising.
Shopping carts	Collect detailed payment and purchase information.
Forms	Create personal profiles.
Site transaction logs	Collect and analyze detailed information on page content viewed by users.
Search engines	Identify user social and political views and activities.
Digital wallets (single sign-on services)	Client-side wallets and software that reveal personal information to Web sites verifying the identity of the consumer.
Digital Rights Management (DRM)	Software (Windows Media Player) that requires users of online media to identify themselves before viewing copyrighted content.

But the reality is that many adult (18 or over) participants in social networks have a very keen sense of their personal privacy. Every time a leading social network has sought to use the personal information provided by participants as a method of monetizing social networks by displaying ads and targeting individuals, it has been vociferously rejected by members of the networks. Facebook is a prime example of senior management pushing the envelope of privacy, and experiencing a number of public relations reversals and growing government concern. In its most recent gaffe, Facebook had deployed facial recognition technology without any previous notice, which compromised its users' privacy by allowing them to be tagged in photos without their consent. Researchers at Carnegie Mellon found that it is possible to identify people, even their social security numbers, based on a single Facebook photograph and using facial recognition programs (Angwin, 2011; Acquisti, et al., 2011). After consumer uproar and challenges from various state attorneys general, Facebook reversed course and made it easier for users to opt out of the technology.

The result of these conflicts suggests that social network participants do indeed have a strong expectation of privacy in the sense that they want to control how "their" information is used. People who contribute user-generated content have a strong sense of ownership over that content that is not diminished by posting the information on a social network for one's friends. What's involved are some basic tenets of privacy thinking: personal control over the uses of personal information, choice, informed consent, participation in formulation of information policies, and due process. Some of these ideas are foreign to managers and owners seeking to monetize huge social network audiences. As for members who post information to everyone, not just friends, these should be seen as "public performances" where the contributors voluntarily publish their performances, just as writers or other artists do. This does not mean they want the entirety of their personal lives thrown open to every Web tracking automaton on the Internet.

MOBILE AND LOCATION-BASED PRIVACY ISSUES

As the mobile platform becomes more and more important, issues about mobile and location-based privacy are also becoming a major concern. In April 2011, a furor erupted over news that Apple iPhones and iPads and Google Android smartphones were able to track and store user location information. In 2012, investigators discovered that iOS and Android apps were funneling location information to mobile advertisers, along with users' address books and photos. In April 2012, Congress opened an investigation into the privacy policies of smartphone manufacturers, along with Facebook, Pinterest, Yahoo, Google and 30 others in the app marketplace. Twitter announced that anyone using its "Find Friends" feature on smartphones was also sending every phone number and e-mail address in their address books to the company. In July 2012, Facebook launched a new mobile advertising service that tracks what apps people use on their smartphones, and what they do while using the apps. The tracking starts when users sign on to Facebook Connect with their smartphones. Apple and Google track users' apps also. Apple disclosed that it can target ads based on the apps that a person has downloaded, while Google does not currently do this. Google and Apple do not track what users do on apps, while the Facebook program goes this additional step. Apps on both Android and Apple smartphones share user information with advertisers seeking to target their ads by location, time of day, and personal data shared with the app.

PROFILING AND BEHAVIORAL TARGETING

On an average day, around 158 million adult Americans go online (Pew Internet & American Life Project, 2012). Marketers would like to know who these people are, what they are interested in, and what they buy. The more precise the information, the more complete the information, and the more valuable it is as a predictive and marketing tool. Armed with this information, marketers can make their ad campaigns more efficient by targeting specific ads at specific groups or individuals, and they can even adjust the ads for specific groups.

Many Web sites allow third parties—including online advertising networks such as Microsoft Advertising, DoubleClick, and others—to place "third-party" cookies and

profiling
the creation of digital images that characterize online individual and group behavior

anonymous profiles
identify people as belonging to highly specific and targeted groups

personal profiles
add a personal e-mail address, postal address, and/or phone number to behavioral data

Web tracking software on a visitor's computer in order to engage in profiling the user's behavior across thousands of Web sites. A third-party cookie is used to track users across hundreds or thousands of other Web sites who are members of the advertising network. **Profiling** is the creation of digital images that characterize online individual and group behavior. **Anonymous profiles** identify people as belonging to highly specific and targeted groups, for example, 20- to 30-year-old males, with college degrees and incomes greater than $30,000 a year, and interested in high-fashion clothing (based on recent search engine use). **Personal profiles** add a personal e-mail address, postal address, and/or phone number to behavioral data. Increasingly, online firms are linking their online profiles to personal offline consumer data collected by database firms tracking credit card purchases, as well as established retail and catalog firms.

The online advertising networks such as DoubleClick and 24/7 Real Media have added several new dimensions to established offline marketing techniques. First, they have the ability to precisely track not just consumer purchases, but all browsing behavior on the Web at thousands of the most popular member sites, including browsing book lists, filling out preference forms, and viewing content pages. Second, they can dynamically adjust what the shopper sees on screen—including prices. Third, they can build and continually refresh high-resolution data images or behavioral profiles of consumers. Other advertising firms have created spyware software that, when placed on a consumer's computer, can report back to the advertiser's server on all consumer Internet use, and is also used to display advertising on the consumer's computer.

Network advertising firms argue that Web profiling benefits both consumers and businesses. Profiling permits targeting of ads, ensuring that consumers see advertisements mostly for products and services in which they are actually interested. Businesses benefit by not paying for wasted advertising sent to consumers who have no interest in their product or service. The industry argues that by increasing the effectiveness of advertising, more advertising revenues go to the Internet, which in turn subsidizes free content on the Internet. Last, product designers and entrepreneurs benefit by sensing demand for new products and services by examining user searches and profiles.

Critics argue that profiling undermines the expectation of anonymity and privacy that most people have when using the Internet, and changes what should be a private experience into one where an individual's every move is recorded. As people become aware that their every move is being watched, they will be far less likely to explore sensitive topics, browse pages, or read about controversial issues. In most cases, the profiling is invisible to users, and even hidden. Consumers are not notified that profiling is occurring.

The pervasive and largely unregulated collection of personal information online has raised significant fears and opposition among consumers. Contrary to what the online advertising industry has often said, namely, that the public really does not care about its online privacy, there is a long history of opinion polls that document the public's fear of losing control over their personal information when visiting e-commerce sites. A 2012 survey by TRUSTe and Harris Interactive found that 94% of online consumers think privacy is an important issue, with 55% saying online privacy is really important to them. Targeted advertising makes 40% of those surveyed uncomfortable. More than 75% do not allow companies to share their personal information with a third party. More than two-thirds say they have stopped doing business with an online company because of privacy concerns (TRUSTe, 2012).

THE INTERNET AND GOVERNMENT INVASIONS OF PRIVACY: E-COMMERCE SURVEILLANCE

Today, the online and mobile behavior, profiles, and transactions of consumers are routinely available to a wide range of government agencies and law enforcement authorities, contributing to rising fears among online consumers, and in many cases, their withdrawal from the online marketplace. In 2012, there was a surge in the use of cell phone tracking and surveillance of citizen movements by law enforcement authorities. While the Internet used to be thought of as impossible for governments to control or monitor, nothing could be actually further from the truth. Law enforcement authorities have long claimed the right under numerous statutes to monitor any form of electronic communication pursuant to a court order and judicial review and based on the reasonable belief that a crime is being committed. This includes the surveillance of consumers engaged in e-commerce. In the case of the Internet, this is accomplished by placing sniffer software and servers at the ISP being used by the target suspect, in a manner similar to pen registers and trap-and-trace devices used for telephone surveillance. The Communications Assistance for Law Enforcement Act (CALEA), the USA PATRIOT Act, the Cyber Security Enhancement Act, and the Homeland Security Act all strengthen the ability of law enforcement agencies to monitor Internet users without their knowledge and, under certain circumstances when life is purportedly at stake, without judicial oversight. The Patriot Act designed to combat terrorism inside the borders of the United States permits nearly unlimited government surveillance without court oversight, according to several senators.

Government agencies are among the largest users of private sector commercial data brokers, such as ChoicePoint, Acxiom, Experian, and TransUnion Corporation, that collect a vast amount of information about consumers from various offline and online public sources, such as public records and the telephone directory, and nonpublic sources, such as "credit header" information from credit bureaus (which typically contains name, aliases, birth date, social security number, current and prior addresses, and phone numbers). Acxiom is the largest private personal database in the world with records on more than 500,000 people and about 1,500 data points per person.

Retention of search engine query data is also an issue. Although the amount of time such data is retained is not governed by U.S. law, the European Union has indicated that it should not be retained for more than six months. The three major search engines (Google, Bing, and Yahoo) have varying policies. In January 2010, Microsoft agreed to reduce the amount of time that it retains certain data, such as IP addresses, to six months to comply with the E.U. standard, although it retains other data, such as cookie IDs and cross-session IDs for 18 months. Google has refused, however, and retains search records for 18 months, claiming that this amount of time is necessary for it to improve services and prevent fraud. In April 2011, Yahoo, which had previously prided itself for retaining search records for only three months, announced that it too would extend that time to 18 months, for competitive reasons.

LEGAL PROTECTIONS

In the United States, Canada, and Germany, rights to privacy are explicitly granted in, or can be derived from, founding documents such as constitutions, as well as in specific statutes. In England and the United States, there is also protection of privacy in the common law, a body of court decisions involving torts or personal injuries. For instance, in the United States, four privacy-related torts have been defined in court decisions involving claims of injury to individuals caused by other private parties: intrusion on solitude, public disclosure of private facts, publicity placing a person in a false light, and appropriation of a person's name or likeness (mostly concerning celebrities) for a commercial purpose (Laudon, 1996). In the United States, the claim to privacy against government intrusion is protected primarily by the First Amendment guarantees of freedom of speech and association, the Fourth Amendment protections against unreasonable search and seizure of one's personal documents or home, and the Fourteenth Amendment's guarantee of due process.

In addition to common law and the Constitution, there are both federal laws and state laws that protect individuals against government intrusion and in some cases define privacy rights vis-à-vis private organizations such as financial, educational, and media institutions (cable television and video rentals) (see **Table 7.4**).

Informed Consent

informed consent
consent given with knowledge of all material facts needed to make a rational decision

The concept of **informed consent** (defined as consent given with knowledge of all material facts needed to make a rational decision) also plays an important role in protecting privacy. In the United States, business firms (and government agencies) can gather transaction information generated in the marketplace and then use that information for other marketing purposes, without obtaining the informed consent of the individual. For instance, in the United States, if a Web shopper purchases books about baseball at a site that belongs to an advertising network such as DoubleClick, a cookie can be placed on the consumer's hard drive and used by other member sites to sell the shopper sports clothing without the explicit permission or even knowledge of the user. This online preference information may also be linked with personally identifying information. In Europe, this would be illegal. A business in Europe cannot use marketplace transaction information for any purpose other than supporting the current transaction, unless of course it obtains the individual's consent in writing or by filling out an on-screen form.

opt-in
requires an affirmative action by the consumer to allow collection and use of consumer information

opt-out
the default is to collect information unless the consumer takes an affirmative action to prevent the collection of data

There are traditionally two models for informed consent: opt-in and opt-out. The **opt-in** model requires an affirmative action by the consumer to allow collection and use of information. For instance, using opt-in, consumers would first be asked if they approved of the collection and use of information, and then directed to check a selection box if they agreed. Otherwise, the default is not to approve the collection of data. In the **opt-out** model, the default is to collect information unless the consumer takes an affirmative action to prevent the collection of data by checking a box or by filling out a form.

TABLE 7.4	FEDERAL PRIVACY LAWS
NAME	DESCRIPTION
GENERAL FEDERAL PRIVACY LAWS	
Freedom of Information Act of 1966	Gives people the right to inspect information about themselves held in government.
Privacy Act of 1974, as amended	Regulates the federal government's collection, use, and disclosure of data collected by federal agencies. Gives individuals a right to inspect and correct records.
Electronic Communications Privacy Act of 1986	Makes conduct that would infringe on the security of electronic communications illegal.
Computer Security Act of 1987	Makes conduct that would infringe on the security of computer-based files illegal.
Computer Matching and Privacy Protection Act of 1988	Regulates computerized matching of files held by different government agencies.
Driver's Privacy Protection Act of 1994	Limits access to personal information maintained by state motor vehicle departments to those with legitimate business purposes..
E-Government Act of 2002	Regulates the collection and use of personal information by federal agencies.
FEDERAL PRIVACY LAWS AFFECTING PRIVATE INSTITUTIONS	
Fair Credit Reporting Act of 1970	Regulates the credit investigating and reporting industry. Gives people the right to inspect credit records if they have been denied credit and provides procedures for correcting information.
Family Educational Rights and Privacy Act of 1974	Requires schools and colleges to give students and their parents access to student records and to allow them to challenge and correct information; limits disclosure of such records to third parties.
Right to Financial Privacy Act of 1978	Regulates the financial industry's use of personal financial records; establishes procedures that federal agencies must follow to gain access to such records.
Privacy Protection Act of 1980	Prohibits government agents from conducting unannounced searches of press offices and files if no one in the office is suspected of committing a crime.
Cable Communications Policy Act of 1984	Regulates the cable industry's collection and disclosure of information concerning subscribers.
Video Privacy Protection Act of 1988	Prevents disclosure of a person's video rental records without court order or consent.
Children's Online Privacy Protection Act (1998)	Prohibits deceptive practices in connection with the collection, use, and/or disclosure of personal information from and about children on the Internet.
Health Insurance Portability and Accountability Act of 1996 (HIPAA)	Requires healthcare providers and insurers and other third parties to promulgate privacy policies to consumers and establishes due process procedures.
Financial Modernization Act (Gramm-Leach-Bliley Act) (1999)	Requires financial institutions to inform consumers of their privacy policies and permits consumers some control over their records.

The Federal Trade Commission's Fair Information Practices Principles

In the United States, the Federal Trade Commission (FTC) has taken the lead in conducting research on online privacy and recommending legislation to Congress. The FTC is a cabinet-level agency charged with promoting the efficient functioning of the marketplace by protecting consumers from unfair or deceptive practices and increasing consumer choice by promoting competition. In addition to reports and recommendations, the FTC enforces existing legislation by suing corporations it believes are in violation of federal fair trade laws.

In 1998, the FTC issued its Fair Information Practice (FIP) principles, on which it has based its assessments and recommendations for online privacy. **Table 7.5** describes these principles. Two of the five are designated as basic, "core" principles that must be present to protect privacy, whereas the other practices are less central.

The FTC's FIP principles set the ground rules for what constitutes due process privacy protection procedures at e-commerce and all other Web sites—including government and nonprofit Web sites—in the United States.

In 2000, the FTC recommended legislation to Congress to protect online consumer privacy from the threat posed by advertising networks. The FTC profiling recommendations significantly strengthened the FIP principles of notification and choice, while

TABLE 7.5	FEDERAL TRADE COMMISSION'S FAIR INFORMATION PRACTICE PRINCIPLES
Notice/Awareness (core principle)	Sites must disclose their information practices before collecting data. Includes identification of collector, uses of data, other recipients of data, nature of collection (active/inactive), voluntary or required, consequences of refusal, and steps taken to protect confidentiality, integrity, and quality of the data.
Choice/Consent (core principle)	There must be a choice regime in place allowing consumers to choose how their information will be used for secondary purposes other than supporting the transaction, including internal use and transfer to third parties. Opt-in/opt-out must be available.
Access/Participation	Consumers should be able to review and contest the accuracy and completeness of data collected about them in a timely, inexpensive process.
Security	Data collectors must take reasonable steps to assure that consumer information is accurate and secure from unauthorized use.
Enforcement	There must be a mechanism to enforce FIP principles in place. This can involve self-regulation, legislation giving consumers legal remedies for violations, or federal statutes and regulation.

SOURCE: Based on data from Federal Trade Commission, 1998, 2000a.

also including restrictions on information that may be collected. Although the FTC supported industry efforts at self-regulation, it nevertheless recommended regulation to ensure that all Web sites using network advertising and all network advertisers complied.

In the last decade, the FTC's privacy approach has shifted somewhat, away from notice and choice requirements and into a harm-based approach targeting practices that are likely to cause harm or unwarranted intrusion in consumers' daily lives. However, in recent years, the FTC has recognized the limitations of both the notice-and-choice and harm-based models. In 2009, the FTC held a series of three public roundtables to explore the effectiveness of these approaches in light of rapidly evolving technology and the market for consumer data. The major concepts that emerged from these roundtables were:

- The increasing collection and use of consumer data
- Consumers' lack of understanding about the collection and use of their personal data, and the resulting inability to make informed choices
- Consumers' interest in and concern about their privacy
- Benefits of data collection and use to both businesses and consumers
- Decreasing relevance of the distinction between PII and non-PII.

As a result of the roundtables, the FTC has developed a new framework to address consumer privacy. **Table 7.6** summarizes the important aspects of this framework.

TABLE 7.6	THE FTC'S NEW PRIVACY FRAMEWORK
PRINCIPLE	**APPLICATION**
Scope	Applies to all commercial entities that collect or use consumer data; not limited to those that just collect PII.
Privacy by Design	Companies should promote consumer privacy throughout the organization and at every stage of development of products and services.
Simplified Choice	Companies should simplify consumer choice. Need not provide choice before collecting and using data for commonly accepted practices. For all other commercial data collection and use, choice is required, and should be clearly and conspicuously offered at a time and in context in which consumer is providing data.
	Some types of information or practices (children, financial, and medical information, deep packet inspection) may require additional protection through enhanced consent.
	Special choice mechanism for online behavioral advertising: "Do Not Track."
Greater Transparency	Increase transparency of data practices by making privacy notices clearer, shorter, and more standardized to enable better comprehension and comparison. Also, provide consumers with reasonable access to data about themselves, provide prominent disclosure, and obtain express affirmative consent before using consumer data in a materially different manner than claimed when data was collected.

SOURCE: Based on data from Federal Trade Commission, 2010.

Among the most noteworthy is the call for a "Do Not Track" mechanism for online behavioral advertising. The mechanism would involve placing a persistent cookie on a consumer's browser and conveying its setting to sites that the browser visits to signal whether or not the consumer wants to be tracked or receive targeted advertisements. A number of bills have been introduced in Congress to implement Do Not Track, but as yet none have been passed.

In response to growing public and congressional concern with online and mobile privacy violations, in 2011 and 2012, the FTC began taking a much more aggressive stance based on these new privacy policies. In March 2011, the FTC reached an agreement with Google concerning charges it used deceptive tactics and violated its own privacy policies when it launched its Google Buzz social network, forcing people to join the network even if they selected not to join. Under the settlement, Google agreed to start a privacy program, permit independent privacy audits for 20 years, and face $16,000 fines for every future privacy misrepresentation. This was the first time the FTC had charged a company with such violations and ordered it to start a privacy program (Federal Trade Commission, 2011). In August 2012, the FTC fined Google $22.5 million to settle charges that it had bypassed privacy settings in Apple's Safari browser to be able to track users of the browser and show them advertisements, and violated the earlier privacy settlement with the agency. This fine is the largest civil penalty levied by the FTC to date, which has been cracking down on tech companies for privacy violations and is also investigating Google for antitrust violations (Federal Trade Commission, 2012a). In August 2012, the FTC also reached a settlement with Facebook resolving charges that Facebook deceived its users by telling them they could keep their information on Facebook private, but then repeatedly allowing it to be shared and made public. The settlement requires Facebook to live up to its promises by giving consumers clear and prominent notice and obtaining their express consent before sharing their information beyond the user's privacy settings. It also requires Facebook to develop a comprehensive privacy program, and obtain independent biennial privacy audits for a period of 20 years (Federal Trade Commission, 2012b).

In March 2012, the FTC released a final report based on its work in the previous two years. The report describes industry best practices for protecting the privacy of Americans and focuses on five areas: Do Not Track, mobile privacy, data brokers, large platform providers (advertising networks, operating systems, browsers, and social media companies), and the development of self-regulatory codes. The report called for implementation of an easy to use, persistent, and effective Do Not Track system; improved disclosures for use of mobile data; making it easier for people to see the files about themselves compiled by data brokers; development of a central Web site where data brokers identify themselves; development of a privacy policy by large platform providers to regulate comprehensive tracking across the Internet; and enforcement of self-regulatory rules to ensure firms adhere to industry codes of conduct.

The European Data Protection Directive

In Europe, privacy protection is much stronger than it is in the United States. In the United States, private organizations and businesses are permitted to use PII gathered in commercial transactions for other business purposes without the prior consent of the consumer (so-called secondary uses of PII). In the United States, there is no federal agency charged with enforcing privacy laws. Instead, privacy laws are enforced largely through self-regulation by businesses, and by individuals who must sue agencies or companies in court to recover damages. This is expensive and rarely done. The European approach to privacy protection is more comprehensive and regulatory in nature. European countries do not allow business firms to use PII without the prior consent of consumers. They enforce their privacy laws by creating data protection agencies to pursue complaints brought by citizens and actively enforce privacy laws.

On October 25, 1998, the European Commission's Data Protection Directive went into effect, standardizing and broadening privacy protection in the E.U. nations. The Directive is based on the Fair Information Practices doctrine but extends the control individuals can exercise over their personal information. The Directive requires companies to inform people when they collect information about them and to disclose how it will be stored and used. Customers must provide their informed consent before any company can legally use data about them, and they have the right to access that information, correct it, and request that no further data be collected. Further, the Directive prohibits the transfer of PII to organizations or countries that do not have similarly strong privacy protection policies. This means that data collected in Europe by American business firms cannot be transferred or processed in the United States (which has weaker privacy protection laws). This would potentially interfere with a $3.5 trillion annual trade flow in goods, services, and investment between the United States and Europe.

The U.S. Department of Commerce, working with the European Commission, developed a safe harbor framework for U.S. firms. A **safe harbor** is a private self-regulating policy and enforcement mechanism that meets the objectives of government regulators and legislation, but does not involve government regulation or enforcement.

In January 2012, the E.U. issued significant proposed changes to its data protection rules, the first overhaul since 1995 (European Commission, 2012). The new rules would apply to all companies providing services in Europe, and require Internet companies like Amazon, Facebook, Apple, Google, and others to obtain explicit consent from consumers about the use of their personal data, delete information at the user's request (based on the "right to be forgotten"), and retain information only as long as absolutely necessary.

safe harbor
a private self-regulating policy and enforcement mechanism that meets the objectives of government regulators and legislation but does not involve government regulation or enforcement

PRIVATE INDUSTRY SELF-REGULATION

The online industry in the United States has historically opposed online privacy legislation, arguing that industry can do a better job of protecting privacy than government. However, individual firms such as Facebook, Apple, Yahoo, and Google have adopted policies on their own in an effort to address the concerns of the public about personal privacy on the Internet. The online industry formed the Online Privacy Alliance (OPA) in 1998 to encourage self-regulation in part as a reaction to growing public concerns and the threat of legislation being proposed by FTC and privacy advocacy groups.

The FTC and private industry in the United States has created the idea of safe harbors from government regulation. For instance, COPPA includes a provision enabling industry groups or others to submit for the FTC's approval self-regulatory guidelines that implement the protections of the FIP principles and FTC rules. In May 2001, the FTC approved the TRUSTe Internet privacy protection program under the terms of COPPA as a safe harbor.

In general, industry efforts at self-regulation in online privacy have not succeeded in reducing American fears of privacy invasion during online transactions, or in reducing the level of privacy invasion. At best, self-regulation has offered consumers notice about whether a privacy policy exists, but usually says little about the actual use of the information, does not offer consumers a chance to see and correct the information or control its use in any significant way, offers no promises for the security of that information, and offers no enforcement mechanism.

TECHNOLOGICAL SOLUTIONS

A number of privacy-enhancing technologies have been developed for protecting user privacy during interactions with Web sites such as spyware blockers, pop-up blockers, cookie managers, and secure e-mail. However, the most powerful tools for protecting privacy need to be built into browsers. Responding to pressure from privacy advocates in 2012, browsers have a number of tools that can help users protect their privacy, such as eliminating third-party cookies. One of the most powerful browser-based protections is a built-in Do Not Track capability. Microsoft, Mozilla, Google, and Apple have all committed to introducing a default Do Not Track capability by 2013. Most of these tools emphasize security—the ability of individuals to protect their communications and files from illegitimate snoopers.

7.3 INTELLECTUAL PROPERTY RIGHTS

Next to privacy, the most controversial ethical, social, and political issue related to e-commerce is the fate of intellectual property rights. Intellectual property encompasses all the tangible and intangible products of the human mind. As a general rule, in the United States, the creator of intellectual property owns it. For instance, if you personally create an e-commerce site, it belongs entirely to you, and you have exclusive rights to use this "property" in any lawful way you see fit. But the Internet potentially changes things. Once intellectual works become digital, it becomes difficult to control access, use, distribution, and copying. These are precisely the areas that intellectual property seeks to control.

Digital media differ from books, periodicals, and other media in terms of ease of replication, transmission, and alteration; difficulty in classifying a software work as a program, book, or even music; compactness—making theft easy; and difficulty in establishing uniqueness. Before widespread use of the Internet, copies of software, books, magazine articles, or films had to be stored on physical media, such as paper, computer disks, or videotape, creating some hurdles to distribution.

The Internet technically permits millions of people to make perfect digital copies of various works—from music to plays, poems, and journal articles—and then to distribute them nearly cost-free to hundreds of millions of Web users. The proliferation of innovation has occurred so rapidly that few entrepreneurs have stopped to consider who owns the patent on a business technique or method that they are using on their site. The spirit of the Web has been so free-wheeling that many entrepreneurs ignored trademark law and registered domain names that can easily be confused with another company's registered trademarks. In short, the Internet has demonstrated the potential for destroying traditional conceptions and implementations of intellectual property law developed over the last two centuries.

The major ethical issue related to e-commerce and intellectual property concerns how we (both as individuals and as business professionals) should treat property that belongs to others. From a social point of view, the main questions are: Is there continued value in protecting intellectual property in the Internet age? In what ways is society better off, or worse off, for having the concept of property apply to intangible ideas? Should society make certain technology illegal just because it has an adverse impact on some intellectual property owners? From a political perspective, we need to ask how the Internet and e-commerce can be regulated or governed to protect the institution of intellectual property while at the same time encouraging the growth of e-commerce and the Internet.

TYPES OF INTELLECTUAL PROPERTY PROTECTION

There are three main types of intellectual property protection: copyright, patent, and trademark law. In the United States, the development of intellectual property law begins in the U.S. Constitution in 1788, which mandated Congress to devise a system of laws to promote "the progress of science and the useful arts." Congress passed the first copyright law in 1790 to protect original written works for a period of 14 years, with a 14-year renewal if the author was still alive. Since then, the idea of copyright has been extended to include music, films, translations, photographs, and most recently the designs of vessels under 200 feet. The copyright law has been amended (mostly extended) 11 times in the last 40 years.

The goal of intellectual property law is to balance two competing interests—the public and the private. The public interest is served by the creation and distribution of inventions, works of art, music, literature, and other forms of intellectual expression. The private interest is served by rewarding people for creating these works through the creation of a time-limited monopoly granting exclusive use to the creator.

In the next few sections, we discuss the significant developments in each area: copyright, patent, and trademark.

COPYRIGHT: THE PROBLEM OF PERFECT COPIES AND ENCRYPTION

In the United States, **copyright law** protects original forms of expression such as writings (books, periodicals, lecture notes), art, drawings, photographs, music, motion pictures, performances, and computer programs from being copied by others for a period of time. Up until 1998, the copyright law protected works of individuals for their lifetime plus 50 years beyond their life, and works created for hire and owned by corporations, such as Mickey Mouse of the Disney Corporation, for 75 years after

copyright law
protects original forms of expression such as writings, art, drawings, photographs, music, motion pictures, performances, and computer programs from being copied by others for a minimum of 70 years

initial creation. Copyright does not protect ideas—just their expression in a tangible medium such as paper, cassette tape, or handwritten notes.

In the mid-1960s, the Copyright Office began registering software programs, and in 1980, Congress passed the Computer Software Copyright Act, which clearly provides protection for source and object code and for copies of the original sold in commerce, and sets forth the rights of the purchaser to use the software while the creator retains legal title. For instance, the HTML code for a Web page—even though easily available to every browser—cannot be lawfully copied and used for a commercial purpose, say, to create a new Web site that looks identical.

Fair Use Doctrine

doctrine of fair use
under certain circumstances, permits use of copyrighted material without permission

Copyrights, like all rights, are not absolute. There are situations where strict copyright observance could be harmful to society, potentially inhibiting other rights such as the right to freedom of expression and thought. As a result, the doctrine of fair use has been created. The **doctrine of fair use** permits teachers and writers to use copyrighted materials without permission under certain circumstances. **Table 7.7** describes the five factors that courts consider when assessing what constitutes fair use.

The fair use doctrine draws upon the First Amendment's protection of freedom of speech (and writing). Journalists, writers, and academics must be able to refer to, and cite from, copyrighted works in order to criticize or even discuss copyrighted works. Professors are allowed to clip a contemporary article just before class, copy it, and hand it out to students as an example of a topic under discussion. However, they are not permitted to add this article to the class syllabus for the next semester without compensating the copyright holder.

What constitutes fair use has been at issue in a number of recent cases, including the Google Books Library Project described in the case study at the end of the chapter, and in several recent lawsuits. In *Kelly v. Arriba Soft* (2003) and *Perfect 10,*

TABLE 7.7	FAIR USE CONSIDERATIONS TO COPYRIGHT PROTECTIONS
FAIR USE FACTOR	**INTERPRETATION**
Character of use	Nonprofit or educational use versus for-profit use.
Nature of the work	Creative works such as plays or novels receive greater protection than factual accounts, e.g., newspaper accounts.
Amount of work used	A stanza from a poem or a single page from a book would be allowed, but not the entire poem or a book chapter.
Market effect of use	Will the use harm the marketability of the original product? Has it already harmed the product in the marketplace?
Context of use	A last-minute, unplanned use in a classroom versus a planned infringement.

Inc. v. Amazon.com, Inc. et al., (2007), the Federal Circuit Court of Appeals for the 9th Circuit held that the display of thumbnail images in response to search requests constituted fair use. A similar result was reached by the district court for the District of Nevada with respect to Google's storage and display of Web sites from cache memory, in *Field v. Google, Inc.* (2006). In all of these cases, the courts accepted the argument that caching the material and displaying it in response to a search request was not only a public benefit, but also a form of marketing of the material on behalf of its copyright owner, thereby enhancing the material's commercial value. Fair use is also at issue in the lawsuit filed by Viacom against Google and YouTube described further in the next section.

The Digital Millennium Copyright Act of 1998

The **Digital Millennium Copyright Act (DMCA)** is the first major effort to adjust the copyright laws to the Internet age. This legislation was the result of a confrontation between the major copyright holders in the United States (publishing, sheet music, record label, and commercial film industries), ISPs, and users of copyrighted materials such as libraries, universities, and consumers. **Table 7.8** summarizes the major provisions of the DMCA.

The DMCA attempts to answer two vexing questions in the Internet age. First, how can society protect copyrights online when any practical encryption scheme

Digital Millennium Copyright Act (DMCA)
the first major effort to adjust the copyright laws to the Internet age

TABLE 7.8	THE DIGITAL MILLENNIUM COPYRIGHT ACT
SECTION	IMPORTANCE
Title I, WIPO Copyright and Performances and Phonograms Treaties Implementation	Makes it illegal to circumvent technological measures to protect works for either access or copying or to circumvent any electronic rights management information.
Title II, Online Copyright Infringement Liability Limitation	Requires ISPs to "take down" sites they host if they are infringing copyrights, and requires search engines to block access to infringing sites. Limits liability of ISPs and search engines.
Title III, Computer Maintenance Competition Assurance	Permits users to make a copy of a computer program for maintenance or repair of the computer.
Title IV, Miscellaneous Provisions	Requires the Copyright Office to report to Congress on the use of copyright materials for distance education; allows libraries to make digital copies of works for internal use only; extends musical copyrights to include "webcasting."

SOURCE: Based on data from United States Copyright Office, 1998.

imaginable can be broken by hackers and the results distributed worldwide? Second, how can society control the behavior of thousands of ISPs, who often host infringing Web sites or who provide Internet service to individuals who are routine infringers? ISPs claim to be like telephone utilities—just carrying messages—and they do not want to put their users under surveillance or invade the privacy of users. The DMCA recognizes that ISPs have some control over how their customers use their facilities.

There are a number of exceptions to the strong prohibitions against defeating a copyright protection scheme outlined above. There are exceptions for libraries to examine works for adoption, for reverse engineering to achieve interoperability with other software, for encryption research, for privacy protection purposes, and for security testing. Many companies, such as YouTube and Google, have latched on to the provision of the DMCA that relates to removing infringing material upon request of the copyright owner as a "safe harbor" that precludes them from being held responsible for copyright infringement. This position is currently being tested in a $1 billion lawsuit originally brought by Viacom in 2007 against Google and YouTube for willful copyright infringement.

In the Viacom case, Viacom alleges that YouTube and Google engaged in massive copyright infringement by deliberately and knowingly building up a library of infringing works to draw traffic to the YouTube site and enhance its commercial value. In response, Google and YouTube claim that they are protected by the DMCA's safe harbor and fair use, and that it is often impossible to know whether a video is infringing or not. YouTube also does not display ads on pages where consumers can view videos unless it has an agreement with the content owner. In October 2007, Google announced a filtering system (ContentID) aimed at addressing the problem. It requires content owners to give Google a copy of their content so Google can load it into an auto-identification system. The copyright owner can specify whether it will allow others to post the material. Then after a video is uploaded to YouTube, the system attempts to match it with its database of copyrighted material and removes any unauthorized material. In April 2012, a U.S. appeals court allowed the case to move forward. The court ruled that YouTube had specific knowledge or awareness of the infringing activity, and ample ability to prevent it.

The entertainment industry continues to be aggressive in pursuing online copyright infringement. In 2011, in a suit brought by the Motion Picture Association of America, a federal judge ordered DVD-streaming service Zediva to shut down. Zediva had argued that its service was just like one person lending a physical DVD to another, but just using the Web to accomplish the task. The court did not agree and said that the service threatened the growing Internet-based video-on-demand market.

File-sharing continues to be an ongoing copyright issue as well. File sharing sites keep popping up and are just as quickly being sued. Grooveshark, a U.S. digital music service that lets subscribers stream several million songs for free, is being sued by the four major music firms for copyright infringement. Grooveshark obtains its music in part by encouraging users to upload their music to Grooveshark servers in order to share with others. Grooveshark claims that under DMCA's Safe Harbor provisions, it can store music tracks as long as it agrees to take them down when asked by copyright holders (Sisario, 2012). Grooveshark argues that its users have a right to share their own music with whomever they want. In 2012, both Google and Apple have removed Grooveshark apps from their stores.

Refer back to the case study at the end of Chapter 1, *The Pirate Bay: The World's Most Resilient Copyright Infringer?* for further discussion of copyright issues in e-commerce.

PATENTS: BUSINESS METHODS AND PROCESSES

A **patent** grants the owner a 20-year exclusive monopoly on the ideas behind an invention. The congressional intent behind patent law was to ensure that inventors of new machines, devices, or industrial methods would receive the full financial and other rewards of their labor and still make widespread use of the invention possible by providing detailed diagrams for those wishing to use the idea under license from the patent's owner. Patents are obtained from the United States Patent and Trademark Office (USPTO), which was created in 1812. Obtaining a patent is much more difficult and time-consuming than obtaining copyright protection (which is automatic with the creation of the work). Patents must be formally applied for, and the granting of a patent is determined by Patent Office examiners who follow a set of rigorous rules. Ultimately, federal courts decide when patents are valid and when infringement occurs.

Patents are very different from copyrights because patents protect the ideas themselves and not merely the expression of ideas. There are four types of inventions for which patents are granted under patent law: machines, man-made products, compositions of matter, and processing methods. The Supreme Court has determined that patents extend to "anything under the sun that is made by man" (*Diamond v. Chakrabarty*, 1980) as long as the other requirements of the Patent Act are met. There are three things that cannot be patented: laws of nature, natural phenomena, and abstract ideas. For instance, a mathematical algorithm cannot be patented unless it is realized in a tangible machine or process that has a "useful" result (the mathematical algorithm exception).

In order to be granted a patent, the applicant must show that the invention is new, original, novel, nonobvious, and not evident in prior arts and practice. As with copyrights, the granting of patents has moved far beyond the original intent of Congress's first patent statute, which sought to protect industrial designs and machines. Patent protection has been extended to articles of manufacture (1842), plants (1930), surgical and medical procedures (1950), and software (1981). The Patent Office did not accept applications for software patents until a 1981 Supreme Court decision that held that computer programs could be a part of a patentable process. Since that time, thousands of software patents have been granted. Virtually any software program can be patented as long as it is novel and not obvious.

The danger of patents is that they stifle competition by raising barriers to entry into an industry. Patents force new entrants to pay licensing fees to incumbents, and thus slow down the development of technical applications of new ideas by creating lengthy licensing applications and delays.

E-commerce Patents

In 1998, a landmark legal decision, *State Street Bank & Trust v. Signature Financial Group, Inc.*, paved the way for business firms to begin applying for "business methods"

patent
grants the owner an exclusive monopoly on the ideas behind an invention for 20 years

patents. In this case, a Federal Circuit Court of Appeals upheld the claims of Signature Financial to a valid patent for a business method that allows managers to monitor and record financial information flows generated by a partner fund. Previously, it was thought business methods could not be patented. However, the court ruled there was no reason to disallow business methods from patent protection, or any "step by step process, be it electronic or chemical or mechanical, [that] involves an algorithm in the broad sense of the term" (*State Street Bank & Trust Co. v. Signature Financial Group*, 1998). The State Street decision led to an explosion in applications for e-commerce "business methods" patents.

Table 7.9 lists some of the better-known, controversial e-commerce patents. Reviewing these, you can understand the concerns of commentators and corporations. Some of the patent claims are very broad (for example, "name your price" sales methods), have historical precedents in the pre-Internet era (shopping carts), and seem "obvious" (one-click purchasing). Critics of online business methods patents argue that the Patent Office has been too lenient in granting such patents, and that in most instances, the supposed inventions merely copy pre-Internet business methods and thus do not constitute "inventions" (Harmon, 2003; Thurm, 2000; Chiappetta, 2001).

TRADEMARKS: ONLINE INFRINGEMENT AND DILUTION

trademark
a mark used to identify and distinguish goods and indicate their source

Trademark law is a form of intellectual property protection for **trademarks**—a mark used to identify and distinguish goods and indicate their source. Trademark protections exist at both the federal and state levels in the United States. The purpose of trademark law is twofold. First, trademark law protects the public in the marketplace by ensuring that it gets what it pays for and wants to receive. Second, trademark law protects the owner—who has spent time, money, and energy bringing the product to the marketplace—against piracy and misappropriation. Trademarks have been extended from single words to pictures, shapes, packaging, and colors. Some things may not be trademarked such as common words that are merely descriptive ("clock"). Federal trademarks are obtained, first, by use in interstate commerce, and second, by registration with the U.S. Patent and Trademark Office (USPTO). Federal trademarks are granted for a period of 10 years and can be renewed indefinitely.

Disputes over federal trademarks involve establishing infringement. The test for infringement is twofold: market confusion and bad faith. Use of a trademark that creates confusion with existing trademarks, causes consumers to make market mistakes, or misrepresents the origins of goods is an infringement. In addition, the intentional misuse of words and symbols in the marketplace to extort revenue from legitimate trademark owners ("bad faith") is proscribed.

dilution
any behavior that would weaken the connection between the trademark and the product

In 1995, Congress passed the Federal Trademark Dilution Act (FTDA), which created a federal cause of action for dilution of famous marks. This legislation dispenses with the test of market confusion (although that is still required to claim infringement), and extends protection to owners of famous trademarks against **dilution**, which is defined as any behavior that would weaken the connection between the trademark and the product.

TABLE 7.9	SELECTED E-COMMERCE PATENTS	
COMPANY	SUBJECT	UPDATE
Amazon	One-click purchasing	Amazon attempted to use patent originally granted to it in 1999 to force changes to Barnes & Noble's Web site, but a federal court overturned a previously issued injunction. Eventually settled out of court. In September 2007, a USPTO panel rejected some of the patent because of evidence another patent predated it, sending it back to the patent examiner for reconsideration. Amazon amended the patent, and the revised version was confirmed in March 2010.
Eolas Technologies	Embedding interactive content in a Web site	Eolas Technologies, a spin-off of the University of California, obtained patent in 1998. Eolas filed suit against Microsoft in 1999 for infringing the patent in Internet Explorer and was awarded a $520 million judgment in 2003.
Priceline	Buyer-driven "name your price" sales	Originally invented by Walker Digital, an intellectual property laboratory, and then assigned to Priceline. Granted by the USPTO in 1999. Shortly thereafter, Priceline sued Microsoft and Expedia for copying its patented business method.
Sightsound	Music downloads	Sightsound won a settlement in 2004 against Bertelsmann subsidiaries CDNow and N2K music sites for infringing its patent.
Akamai	Internet content delivery global hosting system	A broad patent granted in 2000 covering techniques for expediting the flow of information over the Internet. Akamai sued Digital Island (subsequently acquired by Cable & Wireless) for violating the patent and, in 2001, a jury found in its favor.
DoubleClick	Dynamic delivery of online advertising	The patent underlying DoubleClick's business of online banner ad delivery, originally granted in 2000. DoubleClick sued competitors 24/7 Real Media and L90 for violating the patent and ultimately reached a settlement with them.
Overture	Pay for performance search	System and method for influencing position on search result list generated by computer search engine, granted in 2001. Competitor FindWhat.com sued Overture, charging that patent was obtained illegally; Overture countered by suing both FindWhat and Google for violating patent. Google agreed to pay a license fee to Overture in 2004 to settle.
Acacia Technologies	Streaming video media transmission	Patents for the receipt and transmission of streaming digital audio and or video content originally granted to founders of Greenwich Information Technologies in 1990s. Patents were purchased by Acacia, a firm founded solely to enforce the patents, in 2001.
Soverain Software	Purchase technology	The so-called "shopping cart" patent for network-based systems, which involves any transaction over a network involving a seller, buyer, and payment system. In other words, e-commerce! Originally owned by Open Markets, then Divine Inc., and now Soverain. Soverain filed suit against Amazon for patent infringement, which Amazon paid $40 million to settle.
MercExchange (Thomas Woolston)	Auction technology	Patents on person-to-person auctions and database search, originally granted in 1995. eBay ordered to pay $25 million in 2003 for infringing on patent. In July 2007, the U.S. district court denied a motion for permanent patent injunction against eBay using the "Buy It Now" feature. MercExchange and eBay settled the dispute in 2008 on confidential terms.
Google	Search technology	Google PageRank patent was filed in 1998 and granted in 2001. Becomes non-exclusive in 2011 and expires in 2017.
Google	Location technology	Google issued a patent in 2010 for a method of using location information in an advertising system.
Apple	Social technology	Apple applied for a patent in 2010 that allows groups of friends attending events to stay in communication with each other and share reactions to live events as they are occurring.

Trademarks and the Internet

The rapid growth and commercialization of the Internet have provided unusual opportunities for existing firms with distinctive and famous trademarks to extend their brands to the Internet. These same developments have provided malicious individuals and firms the opportunity to squat on Internet domain names built upon famous marks, as well as attempt to confuse consumers and dilute famous or distinctive marks (including your personal name or a movie star's name). The conflict between legitimate trademark owners and malicious firms was allowed to fester and grow because Network Solutions Inc. (NSI), originally the Internet's sole agency for domain name registration for many years, had a policy of "first come, first served." This meant anyone could register any domain name that had not already been registered, regardless of the trademark status of the domain name. NSI was not authorized to decide trademark issues.

In response to a growing number of complaints from owners of famous trademarks who found their trademark names being appropriated by Web entrepreneurs, Congress passed the **Anticybersquatting Consumer Protection Act (ACPA)** in November 1999. The ACPA creates civil liabilities for anyone who attempts in bad faith to profit from an existing famous or distinctive trademark by registering an Internet domain name that is identical or confusingly similar to, or "dilutive" of, that trademark. The act does not establish criminal sanctions. The act proscribes using "bad-faith" domain names to extort money from the owners of the existing trademark **(cybersquatting)**, or using the bad-faith domain to divert Web traffic to the bad-faith domain that could harm the good will represented by the trademark, create market confusion, tarnish, or disparage the mark **(cyberpiracy)**. The act also proscribes the use of a domain name that consists of the name of a living person, or a name confusingly similar to an existing personal name, without that person's consent, if the registrant is registering the name with the intent to profit by selling the domain name to that person.

Trademark abuse can take many forms on the Web. **Table 7.10** lists the major behaviors on the Internet that have run afoul of trademark law.

Cybersquatting and Brandjacking

In one of the first cases involving the ACPA, E. & J. Gallo Winery, owner of the registered mark "Ernest and Julio Gallo" for alcoholic beverages, sued Spider Webs Ltd. for using the domain name Ernestandjuliogallo.com. Spider Webs Ltd. was a domain name speculator that owned numerous domain names consisting of famous company names. The Ernestandjuliogallo.com Web site contained information on the risks of alcohol use, anti-corporate articles about E. & J. Gallo Winery, and was poorly constructed. The court concluded that Spider Webs Ltd. was in violation of the ACPA and that its actions constituted dilution by blurring because the Ernestandjuliogallo.com domain name appeared on every page printed off the Web site accessed by that name, and that Spider Webs Ltd. was not free to use this particular mark as a domain name (*E. & J. Gallo Winery v. Spider Webs Ltd.*, 2001). In August 2009, a court upheld the largest cybersquatting judgment to date: a $33 million verdict in favor of Verizon against OnlineNIC, an Internet domain registration company that had used over 660 names that could easily be confused with legitimate Verizon domain names. Although there

Anticybersquatting Consumer Protection Act (ACPA)

creates civil liabilities for anyone who attempts in bad faith to profit from an existing famous or distinctive trademark by registering an Internet domain name that is identical or confusingly similar to, or "dilutive" of, that trademark

cybersquatting

involves the registration of an infringing domain name, or other Internet use of an existing trademark, for the purpose of extorting payments from the legitimate owners

cyberpiracy

involves the same behavior as cybersquatting, but with the intent of diverting traffic from the legitimate site to an infringing site

TABLE 7.10	INTERNET TRADEMARK LAW ISSUES
ACTIVITY	DESCRIPTION
Cybersquatting	Registering domain names similar or identical to trademarks of others to extort profits from legitimate holders
Cyberpiracy	Registering domain names similar or identical to trademarks of others to divert Web traffic to their own sites
Metatagging	Using trademarked words in a site's metatags
Keywording	Placing trademarked keywords on Web pages, either visible or invisible
Linking	Linking to content pages on other sites, bypassing the home page
Framing	Placing the content of other sites in a frame on the infringer's site

have not been many cases decided under the ACPA, that does not mean the problem has gone away. For instance, in 2011, MarkMonitor looked at incidents of brandjacking in the online sports apparel industry, and found almost 500 cybersquatting sites.

Cyberpiracy

Cyberpiracy involves the same behavior as cybersquatting, but with the intent of diverting traffic from the legitimate site to an infringing site. In *Ford Motor Co. v. Lapertosa*, Lapertosa had registered and used a Web site called Fordrecalls.com as an adult entertainment Web site. The court ruled that Fordrecalls.com was in violation of the ACPA in that it was a bad-faith attempt to divert traffic to the Lapertosa site and diluted Ford's wholesome trademark (*Ford Motor Co. v. Lapertosa*, 2001).

In the *Paine Webber Inc. v. Fortuny* case, the court enjoined Fortuny from using the domain name Wwwpainewebber.com—a site that specialized in pornographic materials—because it diluted and tarnished Paine Webber's trademark and diverted Web traffic from Paine Webber's legitimate site—Painewebber.com (*Paine Webber Inc. v. Fortuny*, 1999). In a more recent case, *Audi AG and Volkswagen of America Inc. v. Bob D'Amato*, the Federal Circuit Court of Appeals for the Sixth Circuit affirmed the district court's ruling that the defendant Bob D'Amato infringed and diluted the plaintiffs' Audi, Quattro, and Audi Four Rings logo marks, and violated the ACPA by operating the Audisport.com Web site (*Audi AG and Volkswagen of America Inc. v. Bob D'Amato*, 2006).

Typosquatting is a form of cyberpiracy in which a domain name contains a common misspelling of another site's name. Often the user ends up at a site very different from one they intended to visit. Harvard Business School professor Ben Edelman conducted a study in 2010 that found that there were at least 938,000 domains typosquatting on the top 3,264 ".com" Web sites, and that 57% of these domains included Google pay-per click ads.

Metatagging

The legal status of using famous or distinctive marks as metatags is more complex and subtle. The use of trademarks in metatags is permitted if the use does not mislead or confuse consumers. Usually this depends on the content of the site. A car dealer would be permitted to use a famous automobile trademark in its metatags if the dealer sold this brand of automobiles, but a pornography site could not use the same trademark, nor a dealer for a rival manufacturer. A Ford dealer would most likely be infringing if it used "Honda" in its metatags, but would not be infringing if it used "Ford" in its metatags. (Ford Motor Company would be unlikely to seek an injunction against one of its dealers.)

Keywording

The permissibility of using trademarks as keywords on search engines is also subtle and depends (1) on the extent to which such use is considered to be a "use in commerce" and causes "initial customer confusion" and (2) on the content of the search results.

Google has faced a number of lawsuits alleging that its advertising network illegally exploits others' trademarks. For instance, insurance company GEICO challenged Google's practice of allowing competitors' ads to appear when a searcher types "Geico" as the search query. In December 2004, a U.S. district court ruled that this practice did not violate federal trademark laws as long as the word "Geico" was not used in the ads' text (*Government Employees Insurance Company v. Google, Inc.*, 2004). Google quickly discontinued allowing the latter, and settled the case (Associated Press, 2005). In 2009, Google expanded its policy of allowing anyone to buy someone else's trademark as a keyword trigger for ads to more than 190 new countries. Google also announced that it would allow the limited use of other companies' trademarks in the text of some search ads, even if the trademark owner objected. In July 2009, Rosetta Stone, the language-learning software firm, filed a lawsuit against Google for trademark infringement, alleging its AdWords program allowed other companies to use Rosetta Stone's trademarks for online advertisements without permission. The suit was dismissed by a federal district court judge in August 2010, but was appealed by Rosetta Stone. In April 2012, the 4th Circuit Court of Appeals overturned the decision by the federal district court, finding that a trier of fact could find that Google could be held liable for trademark infringement. The court pointed to evidence that an internal Google study found that even sophisticated users were sometimes unaware that sponsored links were advertisements.

Currently Google allows anyone to buy anyone else's trademark as a keyword. In February 2011, Microsoft decided to follow this practice as well with Bing and Yahoo Search.

linking
building hypertext links from one site to another site

Linking

Linking refers to building hypertext links from one site to another site. This is obviously a major design feature and benefit of the Web. **Deep linking** involves bypassing the target site's home page and going directly to a content page. In *Ticketmaster Corp. v. Tickets.com*, Tickets.com—owned by Microsoft—competed directly against Ticketmaster in the events ticket market. When Tickets.com did not have tickets for an event, it would direct users to Ticketmaster's internal pages, bypassing the Ticketmaster home page. Even though its logo was displayed on the internal pages, Ticketmas-

deep linking
involves bypassing the target site's home page, and going directly to a content page

ter objected on the grounds that such "deep linking" violated the terms and conditions of use for its site (stated on a separate page altogether and construed by Ticketmaster as equivalent to a shrink-wrap license), and constituted false advertising, as well as the violation of copyright. The court found, however, that deep linking per se is not illegal, no violation of copyright occurred because no copies were made, the terms and conditions of use were not obvious to users, and users were not required to read the page on which the terms and conditions of use appeared in any event. The court refused to rule in favor of Ticketmaster, but left open further argument on the licensing issue. In an out-of-court settlement, Tickets.com nevertheless agreed to stop the practice of deep linking (*Ticketmaster v. Tickets.com*, 2000).

Framing

Framing involves displaying the content of another Web site inside your own Web site within a frame or window. The user never leaves the framer's site and can be exposed to advertising while the target site's advertising is distorted or eliminated. Framers may or may not acknowledge the source of the content. In *The Washington Post, et al. v. TotalNews, Inc.* case, The Washington Post Company, CNN, Reuters, and several other news organizations filed suit against TotalNews, Inc., claiming that TotalNews's use of frames on its Web site, TotalNews.com, infringed upon the respective plaintiffs' copyrights and trademarks, and diluted the content of their individual Web sites. The plaintiffs claimed additionally that TotalNews's framing practice effectively deprived the plaintiffs' Web sites of advertising revenue.

framing
involves displaying the content of another Web site inside your own Web site within a frame or window

The case was settled out of court. The news organizations allowed TotalNews to link to their Web sites, but prohibited framing and any attempt to imply affiliation with the news organizations (*The Washington Post, et al. v. TotalNews, Inc.*, 1997).

7.4   GOVERNANCE

Governance has to do with social control: Who will control the Internet? Who will control the processes of e-commerce, the content, and the activities? What elements will be controlled, and how will the controls be implemented? A natural question arises and needs to be answered: Why do we as a society need to "control" e-commerce? Because e-commerce and the Internet are so closely intertwined (though not identical), controlling e-commerce also involves regulating the Internet.

governance
has to do with social control: who will control e-commerce, what elements will be controlled, and how the controls will be implemented

WHO GOVERNS THE INTERNET AND E-COMMERCE?

Governance of both the Internet and e-commerce has gone through four stages. **Table 7.11** summarizes these stages in the evolution of e-commerce governance.

Prior to 1995, the Internet was a government program. Beginning in 1995, private corporations were given control of the technical infrastructure as well as the process of granting IP addresses and domain names. However, the NSI monopoly created in this period did not represent international users of the Internet, and was unable to cope with emerging public policy issues such as trademark and intellectual property

TABLE 7.11	THE EVOLUTION OF GOVERNANCE OF THE INTERNET
INTERNET GOVERNANCE PERIOD	DESCRIPTION
Government control, 1970–1994	DARPA and the National Science Foundation control the Internet as a fully government-funded program.
Privatization, 1995–1998	Network Solutions Inc. is given a monopoly to assign and track high-level Internet domains. Backbone is sold to private telecommunications companies. Policy issues are not decided.
Self-regulation, 1995–present	President Clinton and the U.S. Department of Commerce encourage the creation of a semiprivate body, ICANN, to deal with emerging conflicts and establish policies. ICANN currently holds a contract with the Department of Commerce to govern some aspects of the Internet.
Governmental regulation, 1998–present	Executive, legislative, and judicial bodies worldwide begin to implement direct controls over the Internet and e-commerce.

protection, fair policies for allocating domains, and growing concerns that a small group of firms were benefiting from growth in the Internet.

In 1995, the Department of Commerce encouraged the establishment of an international body, the Internet Corporation for Assigned Names and Numbers (ICANN), that hopefully could better represent a wider range of countries and a broad range of interests, and begin to address emerging public policy issues. ICANN was intended to be an Internet/e-commerce industry self-governing body, not another government agency.

The explosive growth of the Web and e-commerce created a number of issues over which ICANN had no authority. Content issues such as pornography, gambling, and offensive written expressions and graphics, along with commercial issue of intellectual property protection, ushered in the current era of growing governmental regulation of the Internet and e-commerce throughout the world. Currently, we are in a mixed-mode policy environment where self-regulation through a variety of Internet policy and technical bodies co-exists with limited government regulation.

Today, ICANN remains in charge of the domain name system that translates domain names (such as www.company.com) into IP addresses. It has subcontracted the work of maintaining the databases of the domain registries to several private corporations. The U.S. government controls the "A-root" server. However, these arrangements are increasingly challenged by other countries, including China, Russia, Saudi Arabia, and most of the European Union, all of whom want the United States to give up control over the Internet to an international body such as the International Telecommunication Union (ITU) (a U.N. agency). In 2005, an Internet Summit sponsored by the ITU agreed to leave control over the Internet domain servers with the United States and instead called for an international forum to meet in future years to discuss Internet policy issues (Miller and Rhoads, 2005). The position of the United States with respect to international governance of the Internet changed significantly after the terrorist attacks of September 11, 2001. Currently, the United States has no intention of diminishing its role in control over the global or domestic Internet.

Can the Internet Be Controlled?

Early Internet advocates argued that the Internet was different from all previous technologies. They contended that the Internet could not be controlled, given its inherent decentralized design, its ability to cross borders, and its underlying packet-switching technology that made monitoring and controlling message content impossible. Many still believe this to be true today. The slogans are "Information wants to be free," and "The Net is everywhere" (but not in any central location). The implication of these slogans is that the content and behavior of e-commerce sites—indeed Internet sites of any kind—cannot be "controlled" in the same way as traditional media such as radio and television. However, attitudes have changed as many governments and corporations extend their control over the Internet and the World Wide Web (Stone, 2010).

In fact, the Internet is technically very easily controlled, monitored, and regulated from central locations (such as network access points, as well as servers and routers throughout the network). For instance, in China, Saudi Arabia, Iran, North Korea, Thailand, Singapore, and many other countries, access to the Web is controlled from government-owned centralized routers that direct traffic across their borders and within the country (such as China's "Great Firewall of China," which permits the government to block access to certain U.S. or European Web sites), or via tightly regulated ISPs operating within the countries. In China, for instance, all ISPs need a license from the Ministry of Information Industry (MII), and are prohibited from disseminating any information that may harm the state or permit pornography, gambling, or the advocacy of cults. In addition, ISPs and search engines such as Google, Yahoo, and Bing typically self-censor their Asian content by using only government-approved news sources. China has also recently instituted new regulations that require cafes, restaurants, hotels, and bookstores to install Web monitoring software that identifies those using wireless services and monitors Web activity.

In the United States, government security agencies such as the FBI can obtain court orders to monitor ISP traffic and engage in widespread monitoring of millions of e-mail messages. Under the USA PATRIOT Act, passed after the World Trade Center attack on September 11, 2001, American intelligence authorities are permitted to tap into whatever Internet traffic they believe is relevant to the campaign against terrorism, in some circumstances without judicial review. Working with the large ISP firms such as AT&T, Verizon, and others, U.S. security agencies have access to nearly all Internet communications throughout the country. And many American corporations are developing restrictions on their employees' at-work use of the Web to prevent gambling, shopping, and other activities not related to a business purpose.

Public Government and Law

The reason we have governments is ostensibly to regulate and control activities within the borders of the nation. What happens in other nations, for the most part, we generally ignore, although clearly environmental and international trade issues require multinational cooperation. E-commerce and the Internet pose some unique problems to public government that center on the ability of the nation-state to govern activities within its borders. Nations have considerable powers to shape the Internet.

TAXATION

Few questions illustrate the complexity of governance and jurisdiction more potently than taxation of e-commerce sales. In the United States, sales taxes are collected by states and localities on final sales to consumers. In the United States, there are 50 states, 3,000 counties, and 12,000 municipalities, each with unique tax rates and policies. Cheese may be taxable in one state as a "snack food" but not taxable in another state (such as Wisconsin), where it is considered a basic food. Sales taxes are generally recognized to be regressive because they disproportionately tax poorer people, for whom consumption is a larger part of total income.

The development of "remote sales" such as mail order/telephone order (MOTO) retail in the United States in the 1970s broke the relationship between physical presence and commerce, complicating the plans of state and local tax authorities to tax all retail commerce. States sought to force MOTO retailers to collect sales taxes for them based on the address of the recipient, but Supreme Court decisions in 1967 and 1992 established that states had no authority to force MOTO retailers to collect state taxes unless the businesses had a "nexus" of operations (physical presence) in the state. Congress could, however, create legislation giving states this authority. But every congressional effort to tax catalog merchants has been beaten back by a torrent of opposition from catalog merchants and consumers, leaving intact an effective tax subsidy for MOTO merchants.

The explosive growth of e-commerce has once again raised the issue of how— and if—to tax remote sales. Since its inception, e-commerce has benefited from a tax subsidy of up to 13% for goods shipped to high sales-tax areas. Local retail merchants have complained bitterly about the e-commerce tax subsidy. E-commerce merchants have argued that this form of commerce needs to be nurtured and encouraged, and that in any event, the crazy quilt of sales and use tax regimes would be difficult to administer for Internet merchants. Online giants like Amazon claim they should not have to pay taxes in states where they have no operations because they do not benefit from local schools, police, fire, and other governmental services. State and local governments meanwhile see billions of tax dollars slipping from their reach. In 2012, thousands of online retailers, including Amazon, Blue Nile, eBay, and Overstock, pay no taxes in states where they do not have a presence.

In 1998, Congress passed the Internet Tax Freedom Act, which placed a moratorium on "multiple or discriminatory taxes on electronic commerce," as well as on taxes on Internet access, for three years until October 2001. Since that time, the moratorium has been extended several times, most currently until 2014.

The merger of online e-commerce with offline commerce further complicates the taxation question. Currently, almost all of the top 100 online retailers collect taxes when orders ship to states where these firms have a physical presence. But others, like eBay, still refuse to collect and pay local taxes, arguing that the so-called tax simplification project ended up with taxes for each of 49,000 zip codes, hardly a simplification. The taxation situation is also very complex in services. For instance, none of the major online travel sites collect the full amount of state and local hotel occupancy taxes, or state and local airline taxes. Instead of remitting sales tax on the full amount of the consumer's purchase, these sites instead collect taxes on the basis of the wholesale price they pay for the hotel rooms or tickets. The states have not given up on collecting hundreds of millions of dollars from Internet merchants. The *Insight on Business* case, *Internet Sales Tax Battle*, provides further information on the fight over e-commerce sales taxes.

NET NEUTRALITY

"Net neutrality" is more a political slogan than a concept. It means different things to different people. Currently, all Internet traffic is treated equally (or "neutrally") by Internet backbone owners in the sense that all activities—word processing, e-mailing, video downloading, music and video files, etc.—are charged the same flat rate regardless of how much bandwidth is used. However, the telephone and cable companies that provide the Internet backbone (Internet Service Providers or ISPs) would like to be able to charge differentiated prices based on the amount of bandwidth consumed by content being delivered over the Internet, much like a utility company charges according to how much electricity consumers use. The carriers claim they need to introduce differential pricing in order to properly manage and finance their networks.

There are three basic ways to achieve a rationing of bandwidth using the pricing mechanism: cap plans (also known as "tiered plans"), usage metering, and "highway" or "toll" pricing. Each of these plans have historical precedents in highway, electrical, and telephone pricing. **Cap pricing** plans place a cap on usage, say 300 gigabytes a month in a basic plan, with more bandwidth available in 50-gigabyte chunks for, say, an additional $50 a month. The additional increments can also be formalized as tiers where users agree to purchase, say, 400 gigabytes each month as a Tier II plan. Additional tiers could be offered.

A variation on tier pricing is to offer **speed tiers**. Comcast offers its Xfinity Platinum Internet plan with download speeds of 300 megabits per second for $300, and Verizon offers its FiOS high-speed tier for $204 a month. An alternative to cap plans is metered or **usage-based billing**. Time Warner is testing usage plans that start at five gigabytes a month (the equivalent of two high definition movie downloads) and charge $1 for every additional gigabyte (much like an electric usage meter in a home). One variation on metering is **congestion pricing**, where, as with electric "demand pricing," the price of bandwidth goes up at peak times, say, Saturday and Sunday evening from 6:00 P.M. to 12 midnight—just when everyone wants to watch a movie! Still a third pricing model is **highway (toll) pricing** where the firms that use high levels of bandwidth for their business pay a toll based on their usage of the Internet. Highway pricing is a common way for governments to charge trucking companies

cap pricing
Putting caps on bandwidth usage, charging more for additional usage in tiers of prices

speed tiers
charging more for higher speed Internet service

usage-based billing
charging on the basis of metered units of Internet service

congestion pricing
charging more for peak hour Internet service

highway (toll) pricing
charging service providers like Netflix for their use of the Internet based on their bandwidth use

INSIGHT ON BUSINESS

INTERNET SALES TAX BATTLE

In the past, retailers without a store or other physical presence in a state could not be forced to collect state sales taxes. Suffering from persistent budget pressure, states have now sought to collect taxes on e-commerce sales. As the world's largest online retailer, Amazon is at the center of the fray.

Amazon and states have battled over taxes dating back several years, with states enacting legislation enabling them to collect taxes from Amazon, and Amazon responding by relocating its operations away from those states, including Texas, Illinois, New York, New Jersey, and California.

Facing a continuing state-by-state as well as federal assault, Amazon began to negotiate deals with states in which it planned to open distribution centers. For example, in April 2012, Amazon settled its dispute with Texas when it agreed to create 2,500 local jobs over four years' time, pay an undisclosed amount to resolve its tax bill, and begin collecting sales tax from Texas residents.

Apparently fatigued by the state-by-state offensive, Amazon has thrown its support behind the Senate's attempt to impose online retail taxation, the Main Street Fairness Act. State governments and other proponents argue that this is not a new tax, it is an already owed tax that has gone uncollected. Also supporting the bill are the major retail chains, including Walmart, Best Buy, and Sears, which have predictably been grumbling for years about the unfair advantage given to Internet-only retailers.

On the opposing side is a new coalition, WE R HERE (Web Enabled Retailers Helping Expand Retail Employment), including eBay, which was not mollified by the $500,000 small business exemption. Many of eBay's small sellers and more than 1,000 other small online retailers have joined the fray, fearful of the burden of being forced to remit sales taxes to "thousands of jurisdictions."

The real sticking point appears to be the yearly sales figure that will define a "small business." While Amazon would like to see it set as low as $150,000, NetChoice, an older lobbying group to which eBay also belongs along with Overstock.com, Facebook, Expedia, VeriSign, Yahoo, Oracle, and IAC Interactive Corp, the parent company of Shoebuy.com, would like to see this figure raised to $5 million per year in remote sales.

On balance, bill proponents have the stronger hand and are likely to prevail eventually. eBay and other online marketplaces have created unique environments in which lowered barriers to entry enable entrepreneurs to either work for themselves or start their own businesses and further, they present new opportunities to developing markets to offer their goods directly to buyers. It is these small undertakings that are still in need of protection, not, it must be noted, the large retailers that now proliferate on eBay's storefronts. A $1 million annual remote sales cap would give them a leg up, support innovation where government intervention is necessary to do so, and avoid unduly burdening small sellers whose contribution to state revenue is minor in comparison.

SOURCES: "Small E-retailers Mobilize to Lobby Against Online Sales Tax Collection," by Paul Demery, Internet Retailer, September, 14, 2012; "Coalition Launched to Oppose Internet Sales Tax Legislation," by Juliana Gruenwald, NextGov Newsletter, September 13, 2012; "Amazon, Forced to Collect a Tax, Is Adding Roots," by David Streitfeld, *New York Times*, September 11, 2012; "10 Surprising Facts About Online Sales Taxes," by Robert W. Wood, *Forbes*, September 11, 2012; "Durbin Still Hopeful for Action on Net Sales Tax Bill," by Juliana Gruenwald, " *National Journal*, June 12, 2012; "Amazon.com to Begin Collecting Sales Tax on N.J. Orders Next Year," by Matt Friedman and Jarrett Renshaw, NJ.com, May 30, 2012; "Tax Revenues Continue to Grow in Early 2012," by Lucy Dadayan, The Nelson A. Rockefeller Institute of Government State Revenue Report No. 88, August, 2012; "Durbin Gains Key Support for Revitalized Internet Sales Tax Bill," by Paul Merrion, *Crain's Chicago Business*, November 9, 2011; "Revenue Declines Less Severe, But States' Fiscal Crisis Is Far From Over," by Donald J. Boyd and Lucy Dadayan, The Nelson A. Rockefeller Institute of Government State Revenue Report No. 79, April, 2010.

based on the weight of their vehicles to compensate for the damage that heavy vehicles inflict on roadways. In the case of the Internet, YouTube, Netflix, Hulu, and other heavy bandwidth providers would pay fees to the Internet carriers based on their utilization of the networks in order to compensate the carriers for the additional capacity they are required to supply to these heavy user firms. Presumably, these fees would be passed on to customers by the industry players by charging users a distribution expense. The only way to do this fairly is to charge fees to users based on how much they download, e.g., a short YouTube video might cost 10 cents, a feature-length movie might cost $1.

Plans to ration bandwidth are controversial, and in some cases bring legal, regulatory, and political scrutiny. For instance, in September 2007, Comcast, the largest ISP in the United States, began to slow down traffic and specific Web sites using the BitTorrent protocol not because the content was pirated, but because these video users were consuming huge chunks of the Comcast network capacity during peak load times. Comcast claims its policy was a legitimate effort to manage capacity. In August 2008 the Federal Communications Commission (FCC) disagreed and ordered Comcast to stop discriminating against certain Web sites. Comcast filed suit and in April 2010, a federal appeals court ruled against the FCC and for Comcast, arguing that Comcast had the right to manage its own network, including charging some users more for bandwidth or slowing down certain traffic such as BitTorrent files (Watt, 2010).

Meanwhile, public interest groups have filed suits against the FCC for not going far enough to regulate ISPs, claiming that to allow ISPs to manage their networks will reduce innovation on the Internet. Politicians of all stripes have lined up on one side or the other. The U.S. Senate in November 2011 defeated a Republican proposal to prevent the FCC from regulating the ISPs. For instance, opponents of the legislation argued that if ISPs are allowed to manage their networks, they would impose costs on heavy bandwidth users like YouTube, Netflix, Skype, and other innovative services. New start-up companies offering high-bandwidth innovative services might not be able to get traction if they had to charge their customers for network distribution. Supporters of the FCC net neutrality regulations argue that, without net neutrality, Netflix or Hulu customers might find their cable company (which also happens to be their Internet service provider) blocking Internet access to online streaming video from Netflix in order to force customers to use the cable company's on-demand movie rental platform from which the cable company makes a much larger profit.

In the end, net neutrality is about generating revenue for content distributors and Internet service providers. Keep your eyes on the money.

7.5 PUBLIC SAFETY AND WELFARE

Governments everywhere claim to pursue public safety, health, and welfare. This effort produces laws governing everything from weights and measures to national highways, to the content of radio and television programs. Electronic media of all kinds (telegraph, telephone, radio, and television) have historically been regulated by governments seeking to develop a rational commercial telecommunications environment and to control the content of the media—which may be critical of government or offensive to powerful groups in a society. Historically, in the United States, newspapers and print media have been beyond government controls because of constitutional guarantees of freedom of speech. Electronic media such as radio and television have, on the other hand, always been subject to content regulation because they use the publicly owned frequency spectrum. Telephones have also been regulated as public utilities and "common carriers," with special social burdens to provide service and access, but with no limitations on content.

In the United States, critical issues in e-commerce center around the protection of children, strong sentiments against pornography in any public media, efforts to control gambling, and the protection of public health through restricting sales of drugs and cigarettes.

PROTECTING CHILDREN

Pornography is an immensely successful Internet business. The most recent statistics with respect to revenues generated by online pornography are now several years old and range widely. However, it is probably safe to estimate that the online pornography industry in 2012 generated more than $3 billion in revenue.

To control the Web as a distribution medium for pornography, in 1996, Congress passed the Communications Decency Act (CDA). This act made it a felony criminal offense to use any telecommunications device to transmit "any comment, request, suggestion, proposal, image, or other communications which is obscene, lewd, lascivious, filthy, or indecent" to anyone, and in particular, to persons under 18 years of age (Section 502, Communications Decency Act of 1996). In 1997, the Supreme Court struck down the CDA as an unconstitutional abridgement of freedom of speech protected by the First Amendment. While the government argued the CDA was like a zoning ordinance designed to allow "adult" Web sites for people 18 years of age or over, the Court found the CDA was a blanket proscription on content and rejected the "cyberzoning" argument as impossible to administer. In 2002, the Supreme Court struck down another law, the Child Pornography Prevention Act of 1996, which made it a crime to create, distribute, or possess "virtual" child pornography that uses computer-generated images or young adults rather than real children, as overly broad (*Ashcroft v. Free Speech Coalition*).

In 2001, Congress passed the Children's Internet Protection Act (CIPA), which requires schools and libraries in the United States to install "technology protection measures" (filtering software) in an effort to shield children from pornography. In June 2003, the Supreme Court upheld CIPA, overturning a federal district court that found the law interfered with the First Amendment guarantee of freedom of expression. The Supreme Court, in a 6–3 opinion, held that the law's limitations on access to the Internet posed no more a threat to freedom of expression than limitations on access to books that librarians choose for whatever reason not to acquire. The dissenting justices found this analogy inappropriate and instead argued the proper analogy was if librarians were to purchase encyclopedias and then rip out pages they thought were or might be offensive to patrons. All the justices agreed that existing blocking software was overly blunt, unable to distinguish child pornography from sexually explicit material (which is protected by the First Amendment), and generally unreliable (Greenhouse, 2003a). Other legislation such as the 2002 Domain Names Act seeks to prevent unscrupulous Web site operators from luring children to pornography using misleading domain names or characters known to children. The 2003 Protect Act is an omnibus bill intended to prevent child abuse that includes prohibitions against computer-generated child pornography. Part of that statute was previously held to be unconstitutional by the Eleventh Circuit Court of Appeals, but in May 2008, the Supreme Court reversed the circuit court and upheld the provision (Greenhouse, 2008).

The Children's Online Privacy Protection Act (COPPA) (1998) prohibits Web sites from collecting information on children under the age of 13. It does permit such data collection if parental consent is obtained. Because COPPA does not interfere with speech or expression, it has not been challenged in the courts. Unfortunately, it has been impossible to verify a person's age when they sign up for an account at Web sites, and in many cases, parents are helping children under 13 years of age to sign up for sites like Facebook (which has an official policy prohibiting users under age 13). Since 1998, entirely new technologies like social networks, online tracking, advertising networks, online gaming, and mobile apps have appeared that are now being used to gather data on children and which were not specifically addressed in COPPA or FTC regulations. Responding to these changes in technology and public pressure, the FTC announced a new set of rules in early September 2012. The new rules seek to prohibit online tracking of children across the Web with cookies or any other technology such as persistent identifiers; prohibit ad networks from following children across the Web and advertising to them without parental consent; make clear that mobile devices are subject to COPPA, including games and software apps; and make clear that third-party data collection firms that collect data on Web sites are responsible for any unlawful data collection. The new rules potentially will prevent Facebook from tracking the Likes of children generated when they click on the Like software plugin on other Web sites because the Like button is a tracking device that sends information back to Facebook. A *Consumer Reports* study in June 2012 discovered that Facebook has more than 5 million children registered even though its policies forbid underage members (Reuters, 2012). The new rules are opposed by the Interactive Advertising Bureau trade group, and many well-known firms who market products like breakfast cereal and fast foods to children. These firms point out that they do not knowingly collect information on children, but a study of 54 Web sites in 2011 found that sites aimed at children (Disney.com and Nick.com) use tracking technologies extensively to follow children when they are online.

CIGARETTES, GAMBLING, AND DRUGS: IS THE WEB REALLY BORDERLESS?

In the United States, both the states and the federal government have adopted legislation to control certain activities and products in order to protect public health and welfare. Cigarettes, gambling, medical drugs, and of course addictive recreational drugs, are either banned or tightly regulated by federal and state laws (see *Insight on Society: The Internet Drug Bazaar*). Yet these products and services are ideal for distri-

INSIGHT ON SOCIETY

THE INTERNET DRUG BAZAAR

Rogue drug outlets on the Internet have created an Internet drug bazaar that threatens public health and safety. According to a study done by the Treatment Research Institute at the University of Pennsylvania, addictive and potentially lethal medications are available without prescription from more than 2 million Web sites around the world, with many sites based in countries that impose little if any regulation on pharmaceuticals. According to the National Association of Boards of Pharmacy (NABP), 97% of more than 10,600 Web sites it has analyzed operate without compliance with U.S. pharmacy laws and provide an outlet for counterfeit drugs to enter the United States, fueling prescription drug use and misuse.

A U.S. study found that only two of 365 so-called Internet pharmacies it surveyed were legitimate. In many countries, the report said, trafficking in illegal prescription drugs now equals or exceeds the sale of heroin, cocaine, and amphetamines. While properly regulated Internet pharmacies offer a valuable service by increasing competition and access to treatments in underserved regions, Web pharmacies are a long way from proper regulation.

The sale of drugs without a prescription is not the only danger posed by the Internet drug bazaar. Rogue online pharmacy sites may be selling counterfeit drugs or unapproved drugs. But despite these dangers, online pharmacies remain alluring and are one of the fastest growing business models, with, oddly, senior citizens—usually some of the most law-abiding citizens—leading the charge for cheaper drugs. The main attraction of online drug sites is price. U.S. citizens can often save 50%–75% by purchasing from online pharmacies located in other countries.

Currently, a patchwork regulatory structure governs the sale of drugs online. At the federal level, the 1938 Food, Drug, and Cosmetic Act (FDCA) requires that certain drugs may only be purchased with a valid doctor's prescription and must be dispensed by a state-licensed pharmacy. To get around this requirement, some online pharmacies use questionnaires to diagnose disease and have these questionnaires reviewed by doctors who write the prescription.

The Ryan Haight Online Pharmacy Consumer Act bans the sale of prescription drugs over the Internet without a prescription issued by a medical practitioner who has examined the patient in person at least once. The Act requires online pharmacies to comply with pharmacy licensing laws in every state where they do business, and to register with the FDA before beginning to sell drugs online. This requirement is virtually unenforceable because foreign online pharmacies can easily run their Web sites from an offshore location. Still, a 2011 report found that 55%–75% of rogue pharmacies were using U.S.–based servers or domain name registrars, bringing them within the ambit of U.S. law.

In the meantime, the Food and Drug Administration recommends that consumers look for the NABP Verified Internet Pharmacy Practices Sites (VIPPS) seal, which verifies that the site is legitimate with respect to conformance with state laws, and requires a prescription for controlled drugs. So far, 32 major Internet pharmacies have signed on.

SOURCES: Legitscript.com, accessed October 4, 2012; VIPPS, National Association of Boards of Pharmacy, October 1, 2012; "The Wrong Way to Stop Fake Drugs," by Roger Bate, *New York Times*, April 22, 2012; "In Whom We Trust: The Role of Certification Agencies in Online Drug Markets," by Roger Bate et al, NBER Working Paper, March 2012; "Internet Drug Outlet Identification Program: Progress Report for State and Federal Regulators: July 2011," Nabp.net, July 11, 2011; "Drug Dealers on the Internet: Is the DEA Enforcing the Ryan Haight Act?", Legitscript.com, June 2011; "Increase in Internet Access Parallels Growth in Prescription Drug Abuse," Massgeneral.org, May 12, 2011; "Rogue Pharmacies Still a Problem For Search Engines," by Lance Whitney, CNET News, August 19, 2009; "FDA Warns Drug Firms Over Internet Ads," by Jerod Favole, *Wall Street Journal*, April 4, 2009; "Ryan Haight Online Pharmacy Consumer Protection Act," H.R. 6353, 110th Congress, 2008.

bution over the Internet through e-commerce sites. Because the sites can be located offshore, they can operate beyond the jurisdiction of state and federal prosecutors. Or so it seemed until recently. In the case of cigarettes, state and federal authorities have been quite successful in shutting down tax-free cigarette Web sites within the United States by pressuring PayPal and credit card firms to drop cigarette merchants from their systems. The major shipping companies—UPS, FedEx, and DHL—have been pressured into refusing shipment of untaxed cigarettes. Philip Morris has also agreed not to ship cigarettes to any resellers that have been found to be engaging in illegal Internet and mail order sales.

Gambling also provides an interesting example of the clash between traditional jurisdictional boundaries and claims to a borderless, uncontrollable Web. The online gambling market, based almost entirely offshore—primarily in the United Kingdom and various Caribbean Islands—grew by leaps and bounds between 2000 and 2006, generating as much as $50 billion to $60 billion a year, and with much of the action (some estimate up to 50%) coming from customers based in the United States. Although the federal government contended online gambling was illegal under U.S. federal law (the "Wire Act" of 1961 prohibits use of wire communications for sports betting), they were initially unable to stop it, with various federal courts offering mixed opinions. However, in the summer of 2006, federal officials turned up the heat and arrested two executive officers of offshore gambling operations as they passed through the United States, leading their companies to cease U.S. operations. Then in October 2006, Congress passed the Unlawful Internet Gambling Enforcement Act, which makes it a crime to use credit cards or online payment systems for Internet betting. This effectively bars online gambling companies from operating legally in the United States, and shortly thereafter a number of the leading, publicly traded companies suspended their business in the United States.

By the end of 2011, however, the Justice Department reversed its stance against Internet gambling, removing a major obstacle for states like New York and Illinois that want to legalize online gambling so they can tax the proceeds. In June 2012, the State of Delaware became the first state to legalize online gambling in all its forms. With the promise of enormous profits, Amazon, Facebook, Apple, and Zynga are rumored to be developing online betting apps. The ethical issues surrounding online gambling may have less influence on the public debate than the need for new tax revenues, and for firms, the hope for additional revenues.

The Google Books Settlement:
Is It Fair?

Google's goal is to provide access to "all the world's information," but a problem arises when what Google wants to put on its servers does not belong to them. We're all familiar with the copyrighted music and video situation, where firms often operate offshore, beyond the law (or so they think), and enable, induce, and encourage Internet users to illegally download copyrighted material without paying a dime for it, while in the meantime raking in millions of advertising dollars from companies willing to advertise on their networks.

But Google is no criminal organization. For a firm whose motto is "Don't be evil," it seems out of character for it to initiate a program of scanning millions of copyrighted books it does not own and then, without permission, providing its search engine users with access to those books without charge, while selling ad space and pocketing millions for its own account without sharing that revenue with publishers or authors. One major difference between Google and most file-sharing firms is that Google has very deep pockets filled with cash, and they are based in the United States, making it an excellent legal target.

In 2004, Google announced a program it first called Google Print and now just calls Google Books. There are two parts to the project. Under the Partner Program,

© Cyberstock / Alamy

publishers give permission to Google to scan their books, or make scans available, and then make parts of the work, or simply bibliographic information (title, author, and publisher), available on Google's search engine. No problem there: publishers and authors get a chance to find a wider market, and Google sells more ads. Publishers may even choose to sell online editions of their books on their own Web sites. And publishers were promised a hefty 70% of the display ad revenues and book sales (far better than Amazon's cut of book sales, which is about 50%).

It's the second part of the project that became controversial. Under the Library Project, Google proposed to scan millions of books in university and public libraries, allow users to search for key phrases, and then display "relevant" portions of the text ("snippets"), all without contacting the publisher or seeking permission or paying a royalty fee. Google gave the publishing industry until November 2005 to opt out by providing Google with a list of books they did not want included. In addition, Google proposed to scan millions of books for which the copyright has lapsed and make those available on its servers for free. In these early days, Google's public stance towards authors and publishers seemed to be, "Stop us if you can."

Google has the backing of a number of prestigious libraries, but not all librarians agree. Some believe this is a marvelous extension of public access to library collections, while other librarians fear it is harmful to book authors and publishers. A number of well-known libraries, such as the Smithsonian Institution and the Boston Public Library, as well as a consortium of 19 research and academic libraries in the Northeast, have refused to participate, in part because of restrictions that Google wants to place on the collection. Libraries that work with Google must agree to make the material unavailable to other commercial search services. Google claims it is performing a public service by making an index of books, and relevant portions, available to millions on the Internet, and perhaps even helping publishers sell new copies of books that currently sit on dusty library shelves. Not surprisingly, Google wants a monopoly on the books it has scanned.

In 2005, the publishing industry struck back at Google's book-scanning program and two lawsuits were filed in federal court in New York, one a class-action suit by the Authors Guild and the second by five major publishing companies (McGraw-Hill, Pearson Education, Penguin Group, Simon & Schuster, and John Wiley & Sons), claiming copyright infringement. Patricia Schroeder, president of the publishers' consortium, the American Association of Publishers (AAP), alleged that Google was claiming the right to unilaterally change copyright law and copy anything unless somebody tells them "No." Schroeder noted that Google keeps talking about how what it is doing is good for the world, but that in her view, they are just stealing people's property. Or, as one commentator put it, it's like having a thief break into your house and clean the kitchen—it's still breaking and entering.

Google, on the other hand, claimed its use was "fair" under the "fair use" doctrine that has emerged from a number of court decisions issued over the years, and which is codified in the Copyright Act in 1976. The copying and lending of books by libraries has been considered a fair use since the late 1930s under a "gentleman's agreement" between libraries and publishers, and a library exemption was codified as Section 108 of the Copyright Act of 1976. Libraries loan books to patrons for a limited period, and

SOURCES: "Google Deal Gives Publishers a Choice: Digitize or Not," by Claire Cain Miller, *New York Times*, October 4, 2012; "Suit Over Google Book Scanning Delayed on Appeal," by Chad Bray, *Wall Street Journal*, September 17, 2012; "Google Suit Gets Class-Action Status," by Jeffrey A. Trachtenberg, *Wall Street Journal,* May 31, 2012; "Authors Organizations File Fresh Lawsuit Challenging Google Library Scans and Pending 'Orphan Works' Access," by Michael Cader, PublishersLunch, September 13, 2011; "Judge Rejects Google Books Settlement," by Amir Efrati and Jeffrey A. Trachtenberg, *Wall Street Journal,* March 23, 2011; "Judge Rejects Google's Deal to Digitize Books," by Miguel Helft, *New York Times,* March 22, 2011; "What Is Google Editions?" by Peter Osnos, Theatlantic.com, July 10, 2010; "11th Hour Filings Oppose Google's Book Settlement," by Miguel Helft, *New York Times,* September 9, 2009; "Congress to Weigh Google Books Settlement," *New York Times,* September 9, 2009; "Tech Heavyweights Put Google's Books Deal in Crosshairs," by Jessica Vascellaro and Geoffrey Fowler, *Wall Street Journal,* August 21, 2009; "Probe of Google Book Deal Heats Up," by Elizabeth Williamson, J. Trachtenberg and J. Vascellaro, *Wall Street Journal,* June 10, 2009; "Justice Department Opens Antitrust Inquiry Into Google Books Deal," by Miguel Helft, *New York Times,* April 29, 2009; *The Authors Guild, Inc., Association of American Publishers, Inc., et al., v. Google Inc.,* Preliminary Settlement, Case 1:05-cv-08136-JES Document 56, Filed 10/28/2008; "Publishers Sue Google to Stop Scanning," by David A. Vise, Washington Post, October 20, 2005; *The McGraw-Hill Companies, et al., v. Google Inc.,* United States Southern District Court, Southern District of New York, October 19, 2005.

must purchase at least one copy. Many people read books borrowed from libraries and recommend them to friends, who often buy the books rather than take the time and effort to go to a library. Libraries are also considered by many in the publishing industry as helping to market a book to a larger public, and libraries are believed to be performing a public service by increasing literacy and education.

In 2008, Google agreed to a settlement of the lawsuit with the authors and publishers. In return for the nonexclusive right to sell books scanned into its database, place advertisements on those pages, display snippets, and make other commercial uses of its database of scanned books, Google agreed to pay about $125 million to the parties. All books that Google digitizes will be listed in the central registry available to the public on the Internet. In 2009, a group of companies and organizations, including Microsoft, Yahoo, and Amazon, the American Association of Publishers, members of the Author's Guild, and publishers in the European Union all filed briefs with the court disputing the settlement. The technology companies formed the Open Book Alliance to oppose the settlement. They were joined by privacy protection groups who claimed that Google would be able to track whatever e-books people accessed and read. In September 2009, representatives of those groups spoke out at a hearing sponsored by the European Commission against the proposed deal. They said it would give Google too much power, including exclusive rights to sell out-of-print works that remain under copyright, a category that includes millions of books.

The Justice Department is continuing its investigation into the antitrust implications of the settlement. Critics argue the settlement will create a de facto monopoly position for Google, make it difficult for competitors to enter the field, and give Google broad copyright immunity. The settlement provides that Google's access to publishers' books is "non-exclusive," but competitors would have to scan all the same books over again in order to establish a competitive position, something that experts believe is financially prohibitive. Google, they argue, would end up owning the digital book, which is like owning the libraries of the future. Google counters that the settlement will expand digital access to millions of books that are gathering dust on library shelves.

Currently, Google has reportedly scanned about 20 million of the estimated 130 million books in the world. About 2 million of those are in the public domain, and can be viewed for free through Google's Book Search. Google Book users can also view previews of another 2 million books that are in copyright and in print, under agreements with various publishers. The remainder of the scanned books are out of print but still in copyright. These are currently available only in short "snippet view." The settlement would have allowed users to preview longer parts of those works and potentially purchase them in their entirety, but in March 2011, Federal Judge Denny Chin rejected the settlement, throwing the project into legal limbo once again. The judge suggested that copyright owners be given the right to "opt in" to the settlement rather than "opt out" as originally proposed. An "opt in" structure had previously been rejected by Google as unworkable.

In September 2011, in a related action, the Authors Guild filed a new lawsuit related to the Library Project, suing Google, the university consortium HathiTrust, and five universities that are participating in the book-scanning project. The suit charges that the scanning of 9.5 million works in the HathiTrust repository constitutes massive copyright infringement, and also takes issue with HathiTrust's planned October 2011 launch of its Orphan Works Project, which would make available scans of books it had concluded were available after failing to locate valid copyright holders. Interestingly, as soon as the list was made public, a crowdsourcing effort quickly located some of the authors that purportedly could not be found. That suit must also wind its way through the legal process, presenting a further bar to Google's efforts to provide access to, and potentially profit from, all of the books in the world.

In 2012, the legality of the Google Books project was still up in the air. In May 2012, Judge Chin granted class-action certification to the lawsuit, allowing authors to sue Google as a group. Google had argued that copyright claims needed to be brought individually by authors, which would have made things much more difficult for them in their fight against Google. After Google appealed Judge Chin's latest decision, the case was once again delayed. In October 2012, Google and the publishers reached an out-of-court settlement (after seven years of litigation) that allows the publishers to choose whether to permit Google to scan their out-of-print books that are still under copyright. If Google scans these permitted books, then it must provide the publishers with a digital copy for their own use. The economic value of this victory for publishers is difficult to perceive. Google will be giving away the scanned books for free and receive revenue from ads displayed on some book pages. It's unlikely the publishers will be able to sell these e-books when free books will be available.

Case Study Questions

1. Who is harmed by the Library Project? Make a list of harmed groups, and for each group, try to devise a solution that would eliminate or lessen the harm.

2. Why is Google pursuing the Library Project? What is in it for Google? Make a list of benefits to Google.

3. If you were a librarian, would you support the Library Project? Why or why not?

4. Why have firms like Amazon, Yahoo, and Microsoft opposed the Library Project? Why would a firm like Sony support Google?

5. Do you think the Library Project will result in a de facto monopoly in e-books, or will there be other competitors?

7.7	**REVIEW**

KEY CONCEPTS

- **Understand why e-commerce raises ethical, social, and political issues.**

Internet technology and its use in e-commerce disrupts existing social and business relationships and understandings. Suddenly, individuals, business firms, and political institutions are confronted by new possibilities of behavior for which understandings, laws, and rules of acceptable behavior have not yet been developed. Many business firms and individuals are benefiting from the commercial development of the Internet, but this development also has costs for individuals, organizations, and societies. These costs and benefits must be carefully considered by those seeking to make ethical and socially responsible decisions in this new environment, particularly where there are as yet no clear-cut legal or cultural guidelines.

- **Recognize the main ethical, social, and political issues raised by e-commerce.**

The major issues raised by e-commerce can be loosely categorized into four major dimensions:
- *Information rights*—What rights do individuals have to control their own personal information when Internet technologies make information collection so pervasive and efficient?
- *Property rights*—How can traditional intellectual property rights be enforced when perfect copies of protected works can be made and easily distributed worldwide via the Internet?
- *Governance*—Should the Internet and e-commerce be subject to public laws? If so, what law-making bodies have jurisdiction—state, federal, and/or international?
- *Public safety and welfare*—What efforts should be undertaken to ensure equitable access to the Internet and e-commerce channels? Do certain online content and activities pose a threat to public safety and welfare?

- **Understand basic concepts related to privacy.**

To understand the issues concerning online privacy, you must first understand some basic concepts:
- *Privacy* is the moral right of individuals to be left alone, free from surveillance or interference from others.
- *Information privacy* includes both the claim that certain information should not be collected at all by governments or business firms, and the claim of individuals to control the use of information about themselves.
- *Due process* as embodied by the Fair Information Practices doctrine, informed consent, and opt-in/opt-out policies also plays an important role in privacy.

- **Identify the practices of e-commerce companies that threaten privacy.**

Almost all e-commerce companies collect some personally identifiable information in addition to anonymous information and use cookies to track clickstream behavior of visitors. Advertising networks and search engines also track the behavior of consumers across thousands of popular sites, not just at one site, via cookies, spyware, search engine behavioral targeting, and other techniques

■ **Describe the different methods used to protect online privacy.**

There are a number of different methods used to protect online privacy. They include:

- Legal protections deriving from constitutions, common law, federal law, state laws, and government regulations. In the United States, rights to online privacy may be derived from the U.S. Constitution, tort law, federal laws such as the Children's Online Privacy Protection Act (COPPA), the Federal Trade Commission's Fair Information Practice principles, and a variety of state laws. In Europe, the European Commission's Data Protection Directive has standardized and broadened privacy protection in the European Union nations.
- Industry self-regulation via industry alliances that seek to gain voluntary adherence to industry privacy guidelines and safe harbors. Some firms also hire chief privacy officers.
- Privacy-enhancing technological solutions include secure e-mail, anonymous remailers, anonymous surfing, cookie managers, disk file-erasing programs, policy generators, and privacy policy readers.

■ **Understand the various forms of intellectual property and the challenge of protecting it.**

There are three main types of intellectual property protection: copyright, patent, and trademark law.

- *Copyright law* protects original forms of expression such as writings, drawings, and computer programs from being copied by others for a minimum of 70 years. It does not protect ideas—just their expression in a tangible medium. "Look and feel" copyright infringement lawsuits are precisely about the distinction between an idea and its expression. If there is only one way to express an idea, then the expression cannot be copyrighted. Copyrights, like all rights, are not absolute. The doctrine of fair use permits certain parties under certain circumstances to use copyrighted material without permission. The Digital Millennium Copyright Act (DMCA) is the first major effort to adjust the copyright laws to the Internet age. The DMCA implements a World Intellectual Property Organization treaty, which declares it illegal to make, distribute, or use devices that circumvent technology-based protections of copyrighted materials, and attaches stiff fines and prison sentences for violations.
- *Patent law* grants the owner of a patent an exclusive monopoly to the ideas behind an invention for 20 years. Patents are very different from copyrights in that they protect the ideas themselves and not merely the expression of ideas. There are four types of inventions for which patents are granted under patent law: machines, man-made products, compositions of matter, and processing methods. In order to be granted a patent, the applicant must show that the invention is new, original, novel, nonobvious, and not evident in prior arts and practice. Most of the inventions that make the Internet and e-commerce possible were not patented by their inventors. This changed in the mid-1990s with the commercial development of the World Wide Web. Business firms began applying for "business methods" and software patents.

- *Trademark protections* exist at both the federal and state levels in the United States. The purpose of trademark law is twofold. First, trademark law protects the public in the marketplace by ensuring that it gets what it pays for and wants to receive. Second, trademark law protects the owner who has spent time, money, and energy bringing the product to market against piracy and misappropriation. Federal trademarks are obtained, first, by use in interstate commerce, and second, by registration with the U.S. Patent and Trademark Office (USPTO). Trademarks are granted for a period of 10 years and can be renewed indefinitely. Use of a trademark that creates confusion with existing trademarks, causes consumers to make market mistakes, or misrepresents the origins of goods is an infringement. In addition, the intentional misuse of words and symbols in the marketplace to extort revenue from legitimate trademark owners ("bad faith") is proscribed. The Anticybersquatting Consumer Protection Act (ACPA) creates civil liabilities for anyone who attempts in bad faith to profit from an existing famous or distinctive trademark by registering an Internet domain name that is identical or confusingly similar to, or "dilutive" of, that trademark. Trademark abuse can take many forms on the Web. The major behaviors on the Internet that have run afoul of trademark law include cybersquatting, cyberpiracy, metatagging, keywording, linking, and framing.

■ Understand how governance of the Internet has evolved over time.

Governance has to do with social control: who will control e-commerce, what elements will be controlled, and how the controls will be implemented. Governance of both the Internet and e-commerce has gone through four stages:
- *Government control (1970–1994).* During this period, DARPA and the National Science Foundation controlled the Internet as a fully government-funded program.
- *Privatization (1995–1998).* Network Solutions was given a monopoly to assign and track high-level Internet domain names. The backbone was sold to private telecommunications companies and policy issues remained undecided.
- *Self-regulation (1995–present).* President Clinton and the Department of Commerce encouraged creation of ICANN, a semi-private body, to deal with emerging conflicts and to establish policies.
- *Governmental regulation (1998–present).* Executive, legislative, and judicial bodies worldwide began to implement direct controls over the Internet and e-commerce.

We are currently in a mixed-mode policy environment where self-regulation, through a variety of Internet policy and technical bodies, co-exists with limited government regulation.

■ Explain why taxation of e-commerce raises governance and jurisdiction issues.

E-commerce raises the issue of how—and if—to tax remote sales. The national and international character of Internet sales is wreaking havoc on taxation schemes in the United States that were built in the 1930s and based on local commerce and local jurisdictions. E-commerce has benefited from a tax subsidy since its inception. E-commerce merchants have argued that this new form of commerce needs to be nurtured and encouraged, and that in any event, the crazy quilt of sales and use tax regimes would be difficult to administer for Internet merchants. In 1998, Congress passed the Internet Tax Freedom Act, which placed a moratorium on multiple or discriminatory taxes on electronic commerce, and any taxation of Internet access, and since that time has extended the moratorium three times, most recently until November 2014. In November 2002, delegates from 32 states approved model legislation designed to create a system to tax Web sales, and by 2007, 15 states had agreed to support the program. Although there appears to be acquiescence among large Internet retailers to the idea of some kind of sales tax on e-commerce sales, insistence on uniformity will delay taxation for many years, and any proposal to tax e-commerce will likely incur the wrath of U.S. e-commerce consumers.

■ **Identify major public safety and welfare issues raised by e-commerce.**

Critical public safety and welfare issues in e-commerce include:
- The protection of children and strong sentiments against pornography.
- Efforts to control gambling and restrict sales of cigarettes and drugs. In the United States, cigarettes, gambling, medical drugs, and addictive recreational drugs are either banned or tightly regulated by federal and state laws. Yet these products and services are often distributed via offshore e-commerce sites operating beyond the jurisdiction of federal and state prosecutors. At this point, it is not clear that the Web will remain borderless or that e-commerce can continue to flaunt national, state, and local laws with impunity.

QUESTIONS

1. What basic assumption does the study of ethics make about individuals?
2. What are the three basic principles of ethics? How does due process factor in?
3. Explain Google's position that YouTube does not violate the intellectual property rights of copyright owners.
4. Define universalism, slippery slope, the *New York Times* test, and the social contract rule as they apply to ethics.
5. Explain why someone with a serious medical condition might be concerned about researching his or her condition online, through medical search engines or pharmaceutical sites, for example. What is one technology that could prevent one's identity from being revealed?
6. Name some of the personal information collected by Web sites about their visitors.
7. How does information collected through online forms differ from site transaction logs? Which potentially provides a more complete consumer profile?
8. How is the opt-in model of informed consent different from opt-out? In which type of model does the consumer retain more control?
9. What are the two core principles of the FTC's Fair Information Practice principles?
10. How do safe harbors work? What is the government's role in them?
11. Name three ways online advertising networks have improved on, or added to, traditional offline marketing techniques.
12. Explain how Web profiling is supposed to benefit both consumers and businesses.

13. How could the Internet potentially change protection given to intellectual property? What capabilities make it more difficult to enforce intellectual property law?

14. What does the Digital Millennium Copyright Act (DMCA) attempt to do? Why was it enacted? What types of violations does it try to prevent?

15. Define cybersquatting. How is it different from cyberpiracy? What type of intellectual property violation does cybersquatting entail?

16. What is deep linking and why is it a trademark issue? Compare it to framing—how is it similar and different?

17. What are some of the tactics that illegal businesses, such as betting parlors and casinos, successfully use to operate outside the law on the Internet?

PROJECTS

1. Go to Google, click the Options icon in the upper-right corner of the home page, and then click on Search Settings. Examine its SafeSearch filtering options available on the Preferences page. Surf the Web in search of content that could be considered objectionable for children using each of the options. What are the pros and cons of such restrictions? Are there terms that could be considered inappropriate to the filtering software but be approved by parents? Name five questionable terms. Prepare a brief presentation to report on your experiences and to explain the positive and negative aspects of such filtering software.

2. Develop a list of privacy protection features that should be present if a Web site is serious about protecting privacy. Then, visit at least four well-known Web sites and examine their privacy policies. Write a report that rates each of the Web sites on the criteria you have developed.

3. Review the provisions of the Digital Millennium Copyright Act of 1998. Examine each of the major sections of the legislation and make a list of the protections afforded property owners and users of copyrighted materials. Do you believe this legislation balances the interests of owners and users appropriately? Do you have suggestions for strengthening "fair use" provisions in this legislation?

4. Visit at least four Web sites that take a position on e-commerce taxation, beginning with the National Conference of State Legislatures (Ncsl.org) and the National Governors Association (Nga.org). You might also include national associations of local businesses or citizen groups opposed to e-commerce taxation. Develop a reasoned argument for, or against, taxation of e-commerce.

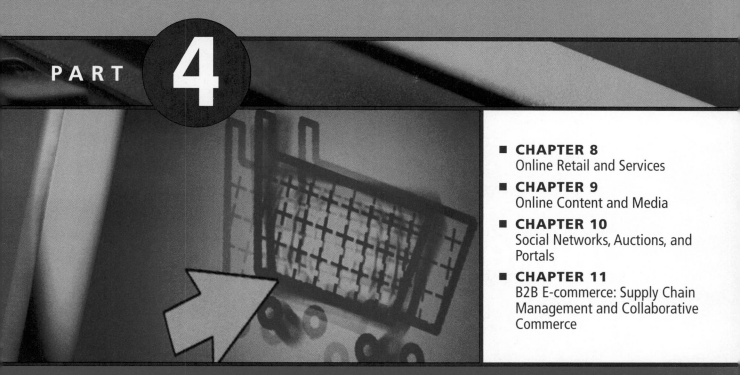

PART **4**

■ **CHAPTER 8**
Online Retail and Services

■ **CHAPTER 9**
Online Content and Media

■ **CHAPTER 10**
Social Networks, Auctions, and Portals

■ **CHAPTER 11**
B2B E-commerce: Supply Chain Management and Collaborative Commerce

E-commerce in Action

Online Retail and Services

After reading this chapter, you will be able to:

- Understand the environment in which the online retail sector operates today.
- Describe the major features of the online service sector.
- Discuss the trends taking place in the online financial services industry.
- Describe the major trends in the online travel services industry today.
- Identify current trends in the online career services industry.

Blue Nile Sparkles

for Your Cleopatra

Blue Nile, the world's leading online jewelry marketplace, offers an online selection of about 80,000 diamonds for that special someone. Back in the early days of e-commerce, no one ever thought that the Internet would be a place where fine jewelry was sold. Diamonds represent a significant cost, and there is significant uncertainty about their value and pricing. But jewelry and high-fashion retailers are leading the second act of online retailing, bursting on the scene with high-growth rates and spectacular average sales transaction levels.

© Ken Gillespie Photography / Alamy

The $65 billion traditional jewelry industry is a byzantine, fragmented collection of about 25,000 specialty jewelry stores and another 100,000-plus that sell jewelry along with other products. To supply this fragmented market, several layers of wholesalers and middlemen intervene, from rough diamond brokers to diamond cutters, diamond wholesalers, jewelry manufacturers, jewelry wholesalers, and finally, regional distributors. The fragmented supply and distribution chains add to huge markups. Currently, the typical retail store markup for diamonds is between 50% and 100%. Blue Nile's markup is only 30%.

Blue Nile's 2011 revenues were $348 million, up from $332 million in 2010, but the company experienced slower sales in the critical fourth quarter, which accounts for the lion's share of Blue Nile's revenues. International sales (in more than 40 countries worldwide) continued to be a bright spot, growing from $43.3 million in 2010 to $55.9 million in 2011. In the first half of 2012, Blue Nile's sales bounced back from the tough final quarter of 2011, increasing 13 percent over 2011 totals and landing the company at the top of lists of the strongest online retailers. International sales continued to grow as well.

Blue Nile's online competitors include Tiffany, Ice.com, Bidz, an online auction jewelry discount site, Tiffany, and even Amazon. Together, these companies are transforming the jewelry business. Blue Nile, for instance, has simplified the supply-side of diamonds by ordering and paying for a diamond, after the customer has ordered it. Blue Nile has cut out several supply-side layers of middlemen and instead deals directly with wholesale diamond owners and jewelry manufacturers.

Blue Nile minimizes its inventory costs and limits its risk of inventory markdowns. On the sell side of distribution, Blue Nile has eliminated the expensive stores, sales clerks,

SOURCES: "Blue Nile's New Direction, and What it Says about Our Industry," by Rob Bates, JCKOnline.com, September 7, 2012; "Blue Nile Carries the Week in the Internet Retailer Online Retail Index," by Thad Rueter, Internetretailer.com, August 6, 2012; "Blue Nile Announces Second Quarter 2012 Financial Results," Bluenile.com, August 2, 2012; "Blue Nile Announces Fourth Quarter and Fiscal Year 2011 Financial Results," Blue-nile.com, February 15, 2012; "Customer Says 'I Do' To a $300,000 Mobile Transaction," by Bill Siwicki, InternetRetailer.com, September 15, 2011; "Blue Nile CEO: More Shoppers Saying 'I Do,'" by Christina Berk, Cnbc.com, November 29, 2010; "Shopping on a Phone Finds Its Customer," by Geoffrey Fowler, *Wall Street Journal,* November 26, 2010; "Blue Nile Works to Build Repeat Business," Internet Retailer, September 22, 2010; "Blue Nile's App Is a Girl's Best Friend (And Maybe a Boy's Too)," by Christina Berk, Cnbc.com, September 16, 2010; "Selling Information, Not Diamonds," by Kaihan Krippendorf, Fastcompany.com, September 1, 2010; "Blue Nile Sparkles," by Kaihan Krippendorf, Fastcom-pany.com, August 30, 2010; "Digital Bling: Diamonds For Sale Online," by Wendy Kaufman, NPR.org, February 14, 2010; "Blue Nile Gets Makeover to Please Ladies," by Geoffrey Fowler, *Wall Street Journal,* September 1, 2009; "New Blue Site Hits Web," *New York Times,* September 1, 2009; "Blue Nile Aims to Sparkle With Re-designed Web Site," Internet Retailer, September 1, 2009; "Blue Nile: A Guy's Best Friend," by Jay Greene, *Business Week,* May 29, 2008.

and beautiful but expensive glass cases. Instead, Blue Nile offers a Web site at which it can aggregate the demand of thousands of unique visitors for diamonds and present them with a more attractive shopping experience than a typical retail store. The result of ratio-nalizing the supply and distribution chain is much lower markups. For example, Blue Nile will purchase a pair of oval emerald and diamond earrings from a supplier for $850 and charge the consumer $1,020. A traditional retailer would charge the consumer $1,258.

Blue Nile has improved the shopping experience primarily by creating a trust- and knowledge-based environment that reduces consumer anxiety about the value of diamonds. In essence, Blue Nile and the other online retailers give the consumer as much information as a professional gemologist would give them. The Web site contains educational guides to diamonds and diamond grading systems, and provides independent quality ratings for each diamond provided by nonprofit industry associations, such as the GIA. There's a 30-day, money-back, no-questions-asked guarantee. The company's focus is "empowering the cus-tomer with information." And empower they do. The average customer visits the Web site repeatedly over several weeks, views at least 200 pages, and typically calls Blue Nile's live customer service line at least once. Repeat business accounts for around 25% of revenue.

In 2009, Blue Nile rebuilt its Web site, strengthening its appeal to its mostly male customer base while attempting to draw more women to the site. The new site removed the left menu so common to older Web designs, enlarged the pictures, added visualiza-tion software so visitors can see the jewelry with shadows and sparkles, expanded the product detail, and improved the search engine. In 2010, it introduced a mobile Web site and iPhone/iPad app, and reported that traffic and sales from both are growing rapidly. The iPhone app provides users with a quick way to set specifications for a diamond and see the price. In 2012, 25% of Blue Nile's traffic comes to it via smartphones, and the average smartphone shopper spends more than the traditional Web shopper. The biggest smartphone sale to date: a $300,000 engagement ring!

In 2012, Blue Nile began a shift in its strategy driven by the possibility that online retailers will have to begin collecting Internet sales taxes in most jurisdictions (see the *Insight on Business* case, *Internet Sales Tax Battle,* in Chapter 7). The company is moving towards fashion jewelry and higher price points and away from simply offering the lowest prices. Blue Nile has begun offering a proprietary line of high-end jewelry, and has added a design director and a new chief merchant to retool its product offerings. Still, even with additional sales taxes, Blue Nile's Internet-based distribution methods and lack of overhead from physical stores will allow them to continue to offer competitive prices.

So far, the "Blue Nile" effect of lower margins and Internet efficiency has mainly impacted the small mom-and-pop jewelry stores. About 3,000 small retailers have disap-peared in the last few years for a variety of reasons. The big retailers, such as Tiffany, Zales, and others, sell more than Blue Nile, and continue to benefit from consumer inter-est in diamond engagement and wedding rings. Both Tiffany and Zales have active Web sites. Tiffany's site is primarily a branding site, but it has greatly improved its online graphics and online sales capabilities. The Zales site is a much more effective sales site than Tiffany's, with a marvelous build-a-ring capability, but still not quite up to the level of Blue Nile with respect to certification. Still, Blue Nile will have to keep a keen watch on its competitors, who are not far behind, to keep its edge online.

The Blue Nile case illustrates some of the advantages that a pure-play, start-up retail company has over traditional offline retailers, and some of the disadvantages. A pure-play consumer service company can radically simplify the existing industry supply chain and develop an entirely new Web-based distribution system that is far more efficient than traditional retail outlets. At the same time, an online pure-play retailer can create a better value proposition for the customer, improving customer service and satisfaction in the process. On the other hand, pure-play start-up companies often have razor-thin profit margins, lack a physical store network to bolster sales to the non-Internet audience, and are often based on unproven business assumptions that, in the long term, may not prove out. In contrast, large offline retailers such as Walmart, JCPenney, Sears, and Target have established brand names, a huge real estate investment, a loyal customer base, and extraordinarily efficient inventory control and fulfillment systems. As we shall see in this chapter, traditional offline catalog merchants are even more advantaged. We will also see that, in order to leverage their assets and core competencies, established offline retailers need to cultivate new competencies and a carefully developed business plan to succeed on the Web.

As with retail goods, the promise of pure-online service providers is that they can deliver superior-quality service and greater convenience to millions of consumers at a lower cost than established bricks-and-mortar service providers, and still make a respectable return on invested capital. The service sector is one of the most natural avenues for e-commerce because so much of the value in services is based on collecting, storing, and exchanging information—something for which the Web is ideally suited. And, in fact, online services have been extraordinarily successful in attracting banking, brokerage, travel, and job-hunting customers. The quality and amount of information online to support consumer decisions in finance, travel, and career placement is extraordinary, especially when compared to what was available to consumers before e-commerce.

The online service sector—like online retail—has shown both explosive growth and some recent impressive failures. Despite the failures, online services have established a significant beachhead and are coming to play a large role in consumer time on the Internet. In areas such as brokerage, banking, and travel, online services are an extraordinary success story, and are transforming their industries. As with the retail sector, many of the early innovators—delivery services such as Kozmo and Webvan and consulting firms such as BizConsult.com—are gone. However, some early innovators, such as E*Trade, Schwab, Expedia, and Monster, have been successful, while many established service providers, such as Citigroup, JPMorgan Chase, Wells Fargo, Bank of America, and the large airlines, have developed successful online e-commerce service delivery sites. In Sections 7.5–7.7 of this chapter, we take a close look at three of the most successful online services: financial services (including insurance and real estate), travel services, and career services.

8.1 ONLINE RETAIL

By any measure, the size of the U.S. retail market is huge. In a $15.6 trillion economy, personal consumption of retail goods and services accounts for about $11.1 trillion (about 71%) of the total gross domestic product (GDP) (Bureau of Economic Analysis, U.S. Department of Commerce, 2012). The retail industry is composed of many different types of firms (see **Figure 8.1**). Each of these segments offers opportunities for online retail, and yet in each segment, the uses of the Internet may differ. Some eating and drinking establishments use the Web to inform people of their physical locations and menus, while others offer delivery via Web orders (although this has not been a successful model). Retailers of durable goods typically use the Web as an informational tool rather than as a direct purchasing tool, although this is beginning to change as consumers have begun to purchase furniture and building supplies over the Internet. For instance, automobile manufacturers still do not directly sell cars over the Web, but they do provide information to assist customers in choosing among competing models. The MOTO sector is the most similar to the online retail sales sector. In the absence of physical stores, MOTO retailers distribute millions of physical catalogs (their largest expense) and operate large telephone call centers to accept orders. They have developed extraordinarily efficient order fulfillment centers that generally ship customer orders within 24 hours of receipt. MOTO was the fastest growing retail segment throughout the 1970s and 1980s. MOTO was the last "techno-

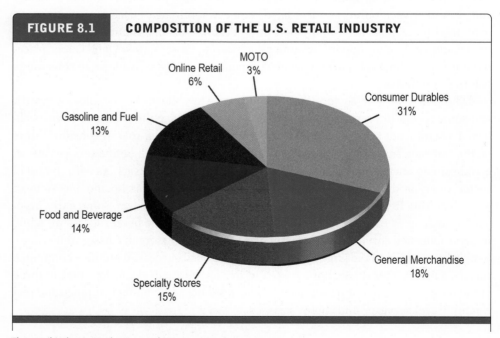

FIGURE 8.1 | **COMPOSITION OF THE U.S. RETAIL INDUSTRY**

The retail industry can be grouped into seven major segments.
SOURCE: Based on data from U.S. Census Bureau, 2012.

logical" retailing revolution that preceded e-commerce. Because of their experience in fulfilling small orders rapidly, MOTO firms are advantaged when competing in e-commerce, and the transition to e-commerce has not been difficult for these firms.

ONLINE RETAILING

Online retail is perhaps the most high-profile sector of e-commerce on the Web. Over the past decade, this sector has experienced both explosive growth and spectacular failures.

E-commerce Retail: The Vision

In the early years of e-commerce, literally thousands of entrepreneurial Web-based retailers were drawn to the marketplace for retail goods, simply because it was one of the largest market opportunities in the U.S. economy. Many entrepreneurs initially believed it was easy to enter the retail market. Early writers predicted that the retail industry would be revolutionized, literally "blown to bits"—as prophesized by two consultants in a famous Harvard Business School book (Evans and Wurster, 2000). The basis of this revolution would be fourfold. First, because the Internet greatly reduced both search costs and transaction costs, consumers would use the Web to find the lowest-cost products. Several results would follow. Consumers would increasingly drift to the Web for shopping and purchasing, and only low-cost, high-service, quality online retail merchants would survive. Economists assumed that the Web consumer was rational and cost-driven—not driven by perceived value or brand, both of which are nonrational factors.

Second, it was assumed that the entry costs to the online retail market were much less than those needed to establish physical storefronts, and that online merchants were inherently more efficient at marketing and order fulfillment than offline stores. The costs of establishing a powerful Web site were thought to be minuscule compared to the costs of warehouses, fulfillment centers, and physical stores.

Third, as prices fell, traditional offline physical store merchants would be forced out of business. New entrepreneurial companies—such as Amazon—would replace the traditional stores. It was thought that if online merchants grew very quickly, they would have first-mover advantages and lock out the older traditional firms that were too slow to enter the online market.

Fourth, in some industries—such as electronics, apparel, and digital content—the market would be disintermediated as manufacturers or their distributors entered to build a direct relationship with the consumer, destroying the retail intermediaries or middlemen. In this scenario, traditional retail channels—such as physical stores, sales clerks, and sales forces—would be replaced by a single dominant channel: the Web.

Many predicted, on the other hand, a kind of hypermediation based on the concept of a virtual firm in which online retailers would gain advantage over established offline merchants by building an online brand name that attracted millions of customers, and outsourcing the expensive warehousing and order fulfillment functions—the original concept of Amazon and Drugstore.com.

As it turned out, few of these assumptions and visions were correct, and the structure of the retail marketplace in the United States, with some notable exceptions, has not been blown to bits, disintermediated, or revolutionized in the traditional meaning of the word "revolution." With several notable exceptions, online retail has often not been successful as an independent platform on which to build a successful "pure-play" Web-only business. As it turns out, the consumer is not primarily price-driven when shopping on the Internet but instead considers brand name, trust, reliability, delivery time, convenience, ease of use, and above all "the experience," as at least as important as price.

The Online Retail Sector Today

Although online retailing is one of the smallest segments of the retail industry, constituting about 5%–6% of the total retail market today, it is growing at a faster rate than its offline counterparts, with new functionality and product lines being added every day (see **Figure 8.2**). Due to the recession, online retail revenues were basically flat from 2008 to 2009, but they since have resumed their upward trajectory. When we refer to online retail, we will not be including online services revenues such as travel, job-hunting, or the purchase of digital downloads such as software applications and music. Instead, for the purposes of this chapter, online retail refers solely to sales of physical

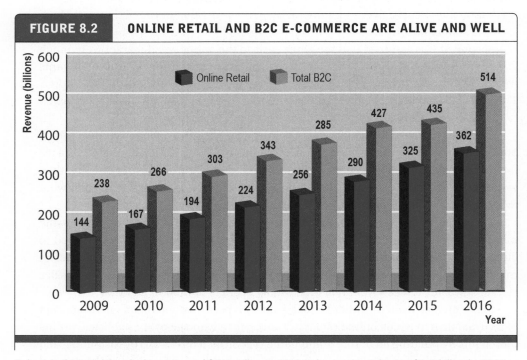

FIGURE 8.2   ONLINE RETAIL AND B2C E-COMMERCE ARE ALIVE AND WELL

Online retail revenues reached an estimated $224 million in 2012 and are estimated to top $362 billion by 2016. Total B2C e-commerce revenues (including travel, other services, and digital downloads) are projected to reach around $514 billion by 2016.

SOURCES: Based on data from eMarketer, 2012a; author estimates.

goods over the Internet. The Internet provides a number of unique advantages and challenges to online retailers. **Table 8.1** summarizes these advantages and challenges.

Despite the high failure rate of online retailers in the early years, more consumers than ever are shopping online. For most consumers, the advantages of shopping on the Web overcome the disadvantages. It is estimated that around 72% of Internet users over the age of 14 (around 150 million people) bought at an online retail store in 2012, generating about $224 billion in online retail sales. The average shopper is spending more on the Internet each year, and finding many new categories of items to buy. For instance, in 2003, the average annual amount spent online by users was $675, but by 2012, it had jumped to around $1,500 (eMarketer, Inc., 2012a, 2005).

The primary beneficiaries of this growing consumer support are not only the pure online companies, but also the established offline retailers who have the brand-name recognition, supportive infrastructure, and financial resources to enter the online marketplace successfully. The top online retail firms ranked by online sales consist of pure-play online retailers for whom the Internet is the only sales channel, such as Amazon (in first place) and Newegg (in 13th); multi-channel firms that have

TABLE 8.1	ONLINE RETAIL: ADVANTAGES AND CHALLENGES
ADVANTAGES	CHALLENGES
Lower supply chain costs by aggregating demand at a single site and increasing purchasing power	Consumer concerns about the security of transactions
Lower cost of distribution using Web sites rather than physical stores	Consumer concerns about the privacy of personal information given to Web sites
Ability to reach and serve a much larger geographically distributed group of customers	Delays in delivery of goods when compared to store shopping
Ability to react quickly to customer tastes and demand	Inconvenience associated with return of damaged or exchange goods
Ability to change prices nearly instantly	Overcoming lack of consumer trust in online brand names
Ability to rapidly change visual presentation of goods	Added expenses for online photography, video, and animated presentations
Avoidance of direct marketing costs of catalogs and physical mail	Online marketing costs for search, e-mail, and displays
Increased opportunities for personalization, customization	Added complexity to product offerings and customer service
Ability to greatly improve information and knowledge delivered to consumer	Greater customer information can translate into price competition and lower profits
Ability to lower consumers' overall market transaction costs	

established brand names and for whom e-commerce plays a relatively small role when compared to their offline physical store channels, such as Staples (2nd), Walmart (4th), Office Depot (6th), Sears (8th), Best Buy (11th), OfficeMax (12th), and Macy's (14th), and manufacturers of computer and electronic equipment, such as Apple (3rd), Dell (5th), and Sony (16th). The top 25 retailers account for over 60% of all online retail.

Multi-Channel Integration

Clearly one of the most important e-commerce retail themes of 2012–2013, and into the future, is the ability of offline traditional firms such as Walmart, Target, JCPenney, Staples, and others to continue to integrate their Web and mobile operations with their physical store operations in order to provide an "integrated shopping customer experience," and leverage the value of their physical stores. **Table 8.2** illustrates some of the various ways in which traditional retailers have integrated the Web, the mobile

TABLE 8.2	RETAIL E-COMMERCE: MULTI-CHANNEL INTEGRATION METHODS
INTEGRATION TYPE	**DESCRIPTION**
Online order, in-store pickup	Probably one of the first types of integration.
Online order, store directory, and inventory	When items are out of stock online, customer is directed to physical store.
In-store kiosk Web order, home delivery	When retail store is out of stock, customer orders in store and receives at home. Presumes customer is Web familiar.
In-store retail clerk Web order, home delivery	Similar to above, but the retail clerk searches Web inventory if local store is out of stock as a normal part of the in-store checkout process.
Web order, in-store returns, and adjustments	Defective or rejected products ordered on the Web can be returned to any store location.
Online Web catalog	Online Web catalog supplements offline physical catalog and often the online catalog has substantially more product on display.
Manufacturers use online Web site promotions to drive customers to their distributors' retail stores	Consumer product manufacturers such as Colgate-Palmolive and Procter & Gamble use their Web channels to design new products and promote existing product retail sales.
Gift card, loyalty program points can be used in any channel	Recipient of gift card, loyalty program points can use it to purchase in-store, online, or via catalog, if offered by merchant.
Mobile order, Web site and physical store sales	Apps take users directly to specially formatted Web site for ordering, or to in-store bargains.
Geo-fencing mobile notification, in-store sales	Use of smartphone geo-location technology to target ads for nearby stores and restaurants.

platform, and store operations to develop nearly seamless multi-channel shopping. This list is not exclusive, and retailers continue to develop new links between channels.

The most significant changes in retail e-commerce in 2012 were the explosive growth in social e-commerce, the growing ability of firms to market local services and products through the use of location-based marketing, and not least, the rapidly growing mobile platform composed of smartphones and tablet computers. In retail circles, tablets are being called "the ultimate shopping machine," enabling consumers to browse media-rich online catalogs just like they used to do with physical catalogs, and then buy when they feel the urge.

Social e-commerce refers to marketing and purchasing on social network sites like Facebook, Twitter, Tumblr, and others. To date, these sites have not become major locations from which consumers actually purchase products. Instead they have developed into major marketing and advertising platforms, directing consumers to external Web sites to purchase products. For instance, over 25% of the 4.8 trillion display ads shown in the United States in 2012 appeared on Facebook, more than double that of Yahoo (comScore, 2012a). It is estimated that social commerce reached $3 billion in 2012 and is expected to almost double, to $5 billion, in 2013.

Whereas in the past only large firms could afford to run marketing and ad campaigns on the Web, this changed radically with the development of local marketing firms like Groupon and LivingSocial, and tens of others, who make it possible for consumers to receive discount deals and coupons from local merchants based on their geographic location. Using billions of daily e-mails, these so-called daily deal sites have sold millions of coupons to purchase local goods and services at steep discounts. For the first time, local merchants can inexpensively use the Web to advertise their products and services. It is estimated that local commerce generated about $2.9 billion in revenues in 2012, and this is expected to grow to around $7 billion by 2015 (eMarketer, Inc, 2011a).

Social and local e-commerce are enabled by the tremendous growth in mobile Internet devices, both smartphones and tablet computers. It is estimated that mobile commerce generated over $4 billion in sales at Amazon in 2012, and around $11.6 billion overall. In 2012, about 35% of smartphone users made a purchase with their phone, and it is estimated that this percentage will grow to over 42% by 2015. More than 40% of tablet owners made a purchase using their tablet in 2012 (eMarketer, Inc., 2011b; 2012b).

8.2   ONLINE RETAIL BUSINESS MODELS

So far, we have been discussing online retail as if it were a single entity. In fact, as we briefly discussed in Chapter 2, there are four main types of online retail business models: virtual merchants, multi-channel merchandisers (sometimes referred to as bricks-and-clicks or clicks-and-bricks), catalog merchants, and manufacturer-direct firms. In addition, there are small mom-and-pop retailers that use eBay, Amazon, and Yahoo Stores sales platforms, as well as affiliate merchants whose primary revenue derives from sending traffic to their "mother" sites. Each of these different types of online retailers faces a different strategic environment, as well as different industry and firm economics.

VIRTUAL MERCHANTS

virtual merchant
single-channel Web firms that generate almost all of their revenue from online sales

Virtual merchants are single-channel Web firms that generate almost all their revenue from online sales. Virtual merchants face extraordinary strategic challenges. They must build a business and brand name from scratch, quickly, in an entirely new channel and confront many virtual merchant competitors (especially in smaller niche areas). Because these firms are totally online stores, they do not have to bear the costs associated with building and maintaining physical stores, but they face large costs in building and maintaining a Web site, building an order fulfillment infrastructure, and developing a brand name. Customer acquisition costs are high, and the learning curve is steep. Like all retail firms, their gross margins (the difference between the retail price of goods sold and the cost of goods to the retailer) are low. Therefore, virtual merchants must achieve highly efficient operations in order to preserve a profit, while building a brand name as quickly as possible in order to attract sufficient customers to cover their costs of operations. Most merchants in this category adopt low-cost and convenience strategies, coupled with extremely effective and efficient fulfillment processes to ensure customers receive what they ordered as fast as possible. In addition to Amazon, successful virtual merchants include Newegg, Netflix, Zappos (now part of Amazon), Overstock.com, Drugstore.com, Buy.com, Gilt Group, Wayfair, Rue La La, Blue Nile (profiled in the opening case), Bluefly, Hayneedle, Net-a-Porter, and Shoebuy.

MULTI-CHANNEL MERCHANTS: BRICKS-AND-CLICKS

bricks-and-clicks
companies that have a network of physical stores as their primary retail channel, but have also introduced online offerings

Also called multi-channel merchants, **bricks-and-clicks** companies have a network of physical stores as their primary retail channel, but have also introduced online offerings. These are multi-channel firms such as Walmart, Sears, JCPenney, Staples, OfficeMax, Costco, Macy's, Target, and other brand-name merchants. While bricks-and-clicks merchants face high costs of physical buildings and large sales staffs, they also have many advantages such as a brand name, a national customer base, warehouses, large scale (giving them leverage with suppliers), and a trained staff. Acquiring customers is less expensive because of their brand names, but these firms face challenges in coordinating prices across channels and handling returns of Web purchases at their retail outlets. However, these retail players are used to operating on very thin margins and have invested heavily in purchasing and inventory control systems to control costs, and in coordinating returns from multiple locations. Bricks-and-clicks companies face the challenge of leveraging their strengths and assets to the Web, building a credible Web site, hiring new skilled staff, and building rapid-response order entry and fulfillment systems. According to Internet Retailer, in 2011, the chain retailers accounted for around $65 billion (around 30%) of all online retail sales. However, there remains much room for growth (Internet Retailer, 2012).

JCPenney is a prime example of a traditional merchant based on physical stores and a catalog operation moving successfully to a multi-channel online store. In 2011, JCPenney.com ranked 20th on Internet Retailer's list of the top 500 retail Web sites ranked by annual sales. JCPenney opened its Web site for business in 1998 and placed its full catalog inventory online. At JCPenney.com, customers can buy family clothing, jewelry, shoes, accessories, and home furnishings. And whether they buy merchandise in a bricks-and-mortar store, through the catalog, or on the Internet, customers can return items either at a store or through the mail. Indeed, the current essence of multi-channel retailing is the nearly complete integration of offline and online sales and operations while presenting a single branded experience to the customer. A second feature of successful multi-channel retailing is understanding customer preferences so that each channel sells products appropriate to that channel. For instance, not only can customers pick up and return at a local store what they order from JCPenney.com, but they can also order items from the store's counters that are only available online. The in-store point-of-sale system is integrated with Penney's Web catalog, and they both share a common inventory system. Many items are too expensive to hold in physical store inventory, but they can be offered economically on the Web site. The company has also invested in state-of-the-art interactivity and imaging tools for the Web site, such as a tool that lets shoppers mix and match 142,000 combinations of window treatments, and fitting guides that enable shoppers to zoom in on products such as jeans and create more custom-fitted orders. It has also embraced social media, with a presence on Facebook, YouTube, and Twitter, and mobile commerce. Its mobile site has won praise for its performance. It has also begun to advertise using the mobile platform, running ads inside the Hulu Plus iPhone app that let users shop via JCPenney's mobile site (JCPenney, 2012; Internet Retailer, 2012).

CATALOG MERCHANTS

Catalog merchants such as Lands' End, L.L.Bean, CDW Corp., PC Connection, Cabela's, and Victoria's Secret are established companies that have a national offline catalog operation, but who have also developed online capabilities. Catalog merchants face very high costs for printing and mailing millions of catalogs each year—many of which have a half-life of 30 seconds after the customer receives them. Catalog merchants typically have developed centralized fulfillment and call centers, extraordinary service, and excellent fulfillment in partnership with package delivery firms such as FedEx and UPS. Catalog firms have suffered in recent years as catalog sales growth rates have fallen. As a result, catalog merchants have had to diversify their channels either by building stores (L.L.Bean), being bought by store-based firms (Sears purchased Lands' End), or by building a strong Web presence.

catalog merchants
established companies that have a national offline catalog operation that is their largest retail channel, but who have recently developed online capabilities

Catalog merchants face many of the same challenges as bricks-and-mortar stores—they must leverage their existing assets and competencies to a new technology environment, build a credible Web presence, and hire new staff. Catalog firms are uniquely advantaged, however, because they already possess very efficient order entry and fulfillment systems. Nevertheless, in 2011, according to Internet Retailer, catalog merchants generated combined Web sales of about $22.3 billion (Internet Retailer, 2012).

LandsEnd.com is one of the most successful online catalog merchants. Lands' End started out in 1963 in a basement of Chicago's tannery district selling sailboat equipment and clothing, handling 15 orders on a good day. Since then it expanded into a direct catalog merchant, distributing over 200 million catalogs annually and selling a much expanded line of "traditionally" styled sport clothing, soft luggage, and products for the home. Lands' End launched its Web site in 1995 with 100 products and travelogue essays. Located in Racine, Wisconsin, it has since grown into one of the Web's most successful apparel sites. Lands' End has always been on the leading edge of online retailing technologies, most of which emphasize personal marketing and customized products. Lands' End was the first e-commerce Web site to allow customers to create a 3-D model of themselves to "try on" clothing. Lands' End "Get Live Help" enables customers to chat online with customer service representatives; Lands' End Custom allows customers to create custom-crafted clothing built for their personal measurements. In 2003, Lands' End was purchased by Sears (which itself was purchased by Kmart in 2004) but retains an independent online presence and catalog operation. Sears has incorporated many of Lands' End's online techniques into its own Web site, Sears.com.

MANUFACTURER-DIRECT

manufacturer-direct
single- or multi-channel manufacturers who sell directly online to consumers without the intervention of retailers

Manufacturer-direct firms are either single- or multi-channel manufacturers that sell directly online to consumers without the intervention of retailers. Manufacturer-direct firms were predicted to play a very large role in e-commerce, but this has generally not happened. The primary exceptions are computer hardware, where firms such as Apple, Dell, Sony, and Hewlett-Packard account for over 70% of computer retail sales online, and apparel manufacturers, such as Ralph Lauren, Nike, Under Armour, Fossil, Crocs, Jones Retail, and Vera Bradley. Most consumer products manufacturers do not sell directly online, although this has started to change. For instance, in 2010, Procter & Gamble launched PGeStore.com, which carries over 50 different Procter & Gamble brands. Overall, according to Internet Retailer, consumer brand manufacturers accounted for about $20.3 billion in online retail sales in 2011 (Internet Retailer, 2012).

Manufacturer-direct firms face channel conflict challenges. Channel conflict occurs when physical retailers of products must compete on price and currency of inventory directly against the manufacturer, who does not face the cost of maintaining inventory, physical stores, or sales staffs. Firms with no prior direct marketing experience face the additional challenges of developing a fast-response online order and fulfillment system, acquiring customers, and coordinating their supply chains with market demand. Switching from a supply-push model (where products are made prior to orders received based on estimated demand and then stored in warehouses awaiting sale) to a demand-pull model (where products are not built until an order is received) has proved extremely difficult for traditional manufacturers. Yet for many products, manufacturer-direct firms have the advantage of an established national brand name, an existing large customer base, and a lower cost structure than even catalog merchants because they are the manufacturer of the goods and thus do not pay profits to anyone else. Therefore, manufacturer-direct firms should have higher margins.

One of the most frequently cited manufacturer-direct retailers is Dell Inc., the world's largest direct computer systems supplier, providing corporations, government agencies, small-to-medium businesses, and individuals with computer products and services ordered straight from the manufacturer's headquarters in Austin, Texas. Although sales representatives support corporate customers, individuals and smaller businesses buy direct from Dell by phone, fax, and via the Internet, with about $4.6 billion in sales generated online in 2011 (ranking 2nd only to Apple among consumer brand manufacturers and 5th on Internet Retailer's list of top 500 online retailers) (Internet Retailer, 2012).

To extend the benefits of its direct sales model, Dell has aggressively moved sales, service, and support online. Each month, the company typically has about 7 million unique visitors at Dell.com, where it maintains an estimated 80 country-specific Web sites. Dell's Premier service enables companies to investigate product offerings, complete order forms and purchase orders, track orders in real time, and review order histories all online. For its small business customers, it has created an online virtual account executive, as well as a spare-parts ordering system and virtual help desk with direct access to technical support data.

COMMON THEMES IN ONLINE RETAILING

We have looked at some very different companies in the preceding section, from entrepreneurial Web-only merchants to established offline giants. Online retail is the fastest growing channel in retail commerce, has the fastest growing consumer base, and has growing penetration across many categories of goods. On the other hand, profits for many start-up ventures have been difficult to achieve, and it took even Amazon eight years to show its first profit.

The reasons for the difficulties experienced by many online retailers in achieving profits are also now clear. The path to success in any form of retail involves having a central location in order to attract a larger number of shoppers, charging high enough prices to cover the costs of goods as well as marketing, and developing highly efficient inventory and fulfillment systems so that the company can offer goods at lower costs than competitors and still make a profit. Many online merchants failed to follow these fundamental ideas, and lowered prices below the total costs of goods and operations, failed to develop efficient business processes, failed to attract a large enough audience to their Web sites, and spent far too much on customer acquisition and marketing. By 2012, the lessons of the past have been learned, and far fewer online merchants are selling below cost, especially if they are start-up companies. There's also been a change in consumer culture and attitudes. Whereas in the past consumers looked to the Web for really cheap prices, in 2012, they look to online purchasing for convenience, time savings, and time shifting (buying retail goods at night from the sofa). Consumers have been willing to accept higher prices in return for the convenience of shopping online and avoiding the inconvenience of shopping at stores and malls. This allows online merchants more pricing freedom.

A second common theme in retail e-commerce is that, for the most part, disintermediation did not occur and the retail middleman did not disappear. Indeed, virtual merchants, along with powerful offline merchants who moved online, maintained their powerful grip on the retail customer, with some notable exceptions in electronics and software. Manufacturers—with the exception of electronic goods—have used the Web primarily as an informational resource, driving consumers to the traditional retail channels for transactions.

A third theme is that in order to succeed online, established merchants need to create an integrated shopping environment that combines their catalog, store, and online experiences into one. Customers want to shop wherever they want, using any device, and at any time. Established retailers have significant fulfillment, inventory management, supply chain management, and other competencies that apply directly to the online channel. To succeed online, established retailers need to extend their brands, provide incentives to consumers to use the online channel (which given the same prices for goods is more efficient to operate than a physical store), avoid channel conflict, and build advertising campaigns using online search engines such as Google, Yahoo, and Bing, and shopping comparison sites, as described further in *Insight on Technology: Using the Web to Shop 'Till You Drop.*

A fourth theme is the growth of online specialty merchants selling high-end, fashionable and luxury goods such as diamonds (Blue Nile), jewelry (Tiffany), and high fashion (Emporio Armani and Gilt.com) or selling discounted electronics (BestBuy.com), apparel (Gap.com), or office products (OfficeDepot.com). These firms are demonstrating the vitality and openness of the Internet for innovation and extending the range of products available on the Web. Many virtual merchants have developed large, online customer bases, as well as the online tools required to market to their customer base.

A final theme is the continuing extraordinary growth in social commerce, local marketing and commerce, and mobile commerce. In the space of five years since the first iPhone appeared, the mobile platform has emerged as a retail marketing and shopping tool, which will greatly expand e-commerce, potentially driving e-commerce to 20% of all commerce in the next five years. Local merchants will be a major benefactor of the growing mobile commerce platform. In an equally short time, Americans have begun to spend a quarter of their Internet time on social network sites where they share attitudes and experiences about business firms, products, and services. In a few years, social sites will turn into large purchasing venues.

8.3 ONLINE SERVICES

The service sector is typically the largest and most rapidly expanding part of the economies in advanced industrial nations such as the United States and in European and some Asian countries. In the United States, the service sector (broadly defined) employs about four out of every five workers and accounts for about 75% of all economic activity. E-commerce in the service sector offers extraordinary opportunities to deliver information, knowledge, and transaction efficiencies.

The major service industry groups are finance, insurance, real estate, travel, professional services such as legal and accounting, business services, health services, and educational services. Business services include activities such as consulting, advertis-

INSIGHT ON TECHNOLOGY

USING THE WEB TO SHOP 'TILL YOU DROP

Comparison shopping sites allow consumers to compare prices, features, and consumer reviews of products. When visitors click on a product and price they like, they are taken to the merchant's Web site where they can make the purchase. The merchant pays the Web site a fee or commission for sending the customer. The top comparison shopping sites include Nextag, PriceGrabber, Shopping.com, and Shopzilla/BizRate. According to Channel Advisor, a leading e-commerce software and services provider, comparison shopping sites drive about 15% of e-commerce, making them an important channel for retailers.

Shopping sites make money by charging participating merchants on a per-click basis regardless of whether a sale is made. A twist on shopping search engines is comparison shopping coupon systems. Sites like Wow-Coupons, CurrentCodes, FatWallet, and Bing Deals search the Web for deals and coupons.

Comparison shopping sites focused originally on tracking online prices for electronic consumer goods and computers. Consumer electronics are fairly commoditized products by a few branded manufacturers, with standard features, making it relatively easy to compare one product to another. You can refine your search as you move along the purchase process, and explore the reputations of dealers before you decide to purchase.

However, although Shopping.com tracks over 60 million products and about 2,700 different brands, very few of these items are so-called "soft goods" purchased by women, who have risen to comprise the majority of purchasing power on the Web. Women are much more likely to be looking for soft goods, such as apparel, jewelry, accessories, luggage, and gifts. In fact, these are among the fastest growing consumer product categories on the Web. For this reason, the shopping comparison sites are currently adding soft goods to their services.

But the process of comparison shopping for soft goods is not as simple as for hard goods such as digital TVs or digital cameras. In more complex product areas, such as apparel or jewelry, industry standards do not exist. One solution is to focus on the brands of soft goods and not the price: bags from Gucci, sweaters from Benetton, and mountain climbing gear from REI. Yahoo and search engines such as Bing and Google are moving closer to the brand model of comparison shopping as price becomes a less powerful factor in consumer purchases of soft goods.

As more attention focuses on comparison shopping sites, the sites themselves continue to innovate and add features, including mobile offerings, improved search time, and third-party reviews. As the number of shoppers using mobile to make purchases continues to rise rapidly, comparison shopping on mobile has grown as well.

In 2012, perhaps the biggest news in comparison shopping came from Google when it announced that its free Google Product Search service would become a paid service called Google Shopping. This was bad news to merchants who were used to receiving this service for free from Google, but Google's unbeatable amounts of eyeballs and potential traffic will likely be too much for most merchants to ignore. Search engines like Google and Bing are in direct competition with the stand-alone comparison shopping sites for business.

SOURCES: "Survey: Younger Shoppers Increasingly Using Mobiles To Buy and Compare," by Natasha Lomas, TechCrunch.com, September 28, 2012; "The 10 Best Shopping Engines," by Andrew Davis, Searchenginewatch.com, June 19, 2012; "The New Google Shopping: 15 FAQs," by Mary Weinstein, Cpcstrategy.com, June 14, 2012; "Nextag's Radar Picks Up a Smartphone App," by Kevin Woodward, *Internet Retailer*, August 24, 2011; "PriceGrabber Adds Price Alerts and Local Availability to its Mobile Apps," by Katie Deatsch, *Internet Retailer*, January 5, 2011; "Comparison Shopping Engines: Strategies for Smaller Merchants," *Practical eCommerce*, August 25, 2010; "Amazon Moves Up in a Ranking of Comparison Shopping Sites," by Don Davis, *Internet Retailer*, July 20, 2010; "Beyond Compare," by Don Davis, *Internet Retailer*, May 27, 2010; "8 Top Sites for Online Shopping Deals," by Jennifer Mulrean, moneycentral.msn.com, September 14, 2009; "Shopzilla Site Redo—You Get What You Measure," by Philip Dixon, en.oreilly.com, June 24, 2009.

transaction brokering
acting as an intermediary
to facilitate a transaction

ing and marketing, and information processing. Within these service industry groups, companies can be further categorized into those that involve **transaction brokering** (acting as an intermediary to facilitate a transaction) and those that involve providing a "hands-on" service. For instance, one type of financial service involves stockbrokers who act as the middle person in a transaction between buyers and sellers. Online mortgage companies such as LendingTree.com refer customers to mortgage companies that actually issue the mortgage. Employment agencies put a seller of labor in contact with a buyer of labor. The service involved in all these examples is brokering a transaction.

In contrast, some industries perform specific hands-on activities for consumers. In order to provide their service, these professionals need to interact directly and personally with the "client." For these service industries, the opportunities for e-commerce are somewhat different. Currently, doctors and dentists cannot treat patients over the Internet. However, the Internet can assist their services by providing consumers with information, knowledge, and communication.

With some exceptions (for example, providers of physical services, such as cleaning, gardening, and so on), perhaps the most important feature of service industries (and occupations) is that they are knowledge- and information-intense. In order to provide value, service industries process a great deal of information and employ a highly skilled, educated workforce. For instance, to provide legal services, you need lawyers with law degrees. Law firms are required to process enormous amounts of textual information. Likewise with medical services. Financial services are not so knowledge-intensive, but require much larger investments in information processing just to keep track of transactions and investments.

Services differ in the amount of personalization and customization required, although just about all services entail some personalization or customization. Some services, such as legal, medical, and accounting services, require extensive personalization—the adjustment of a service to the precise needs of a single individual or object. Others, such as financial services, benefit from customization by allowing individuals to choose from a restricted menu. The ability of Internet and e-commerce technology to personalize and customize service, or components of service, is a major factor undergirding the extremely rapid growth of e-commerce services. Future expansion of e-services will depend in part on the ability of e-commerce firms to transform their customized services—choosing from a list—into truly personalized services, such as providing unique advice and consultation based on a digital yet intimate understanding of the client (at least as intimate as professional service providers).

8.4 ONLINE FINANCIAL SERVICES

The online financial services sector is a shining example of an e-commerce success story, but one with many twists and turns. While the innovative, pure-online firms such as E*Trade have been instrumental in transforming the brokerage industry, the impacts of e-commerce on the large, powerful banking, insurance, and real estate firms have been delayed by consumer resistance and the lack of industry innovation.

For instance, online-only banks have not displaced or transformed the large national banks or even regional and local banks. But e-commerce has nevertheless transformed the banking and financial industries, as the major institutions have deployed their own online applications to service an increasingly connected online customer base. A 2011 survey by the American Bankers Association found that 62% of customers preferred online banking compared with any other method (American Bankers Association, 2012). Insurance has become more standardized and easier to purchase on the Web. Although security is still a concern, consumers are much more willing to trust online sites with their financial information than in the past. Firms such as Mint.com (now owned by Quicken), SmartyPig, and Credit Karma continue to show growth. Multi-channel, established financial services firms—the slow followers—also continue to show modest gains in online transactions of about 2%–4% annually.

ONLINE FINANCIAL CONSUMER BEHAVIOR

Surveys show that consumers are attracted to financial sites because of their desire to save time and access information rather than save money, although saving money is an important goal among the most sophisticated online financial households. According to financial services technology provider Fiserv, around 79 million households used online banking in 2011 compared to just 46.7 million in 2005. Over 53 million households paid bills directly at company Web sites, and over 40 million used online bill payment at a financial institution (Fiserv, 2012). Most online consumers use financial services sites for mundane financial management, such as checking balances of existing accounts, and paying bills, most of which were established offline. Once accustomed to performing mundane financial management activities, consumers move on to more sophisticated capabilities such as using personal financial management tools, making loan payments, and considering offers from online institutions. The number of people using mobile devices for financial service needs is also surging. According to FiServ, about 25% of online households had used a mobile banking service, primarily to check their account balance, pay bills, and transfer money (FiServ, 2012).

ONLINE BANKING AND BROKERAGE

NetBank and Wingspan Bank pioneered online banking in the United States in 1996 and 1997, respectively. Traditional banks had developed earlier versions of telephone banking but did not use online services until 1998. Although late by a year or two, the established brand-name national banks have taken a substantial lead in market share as the percentage of their customers who bank online has grown rapidly. **Table 8.3** lists the top five online banks in 2012, ranked by the percentage of all Web visits to online banks. The top banks are all large, national banks. In 2011, Capital One acquired ING Direct, leaving VirtualBank as one of the last pure online banks.

It is estimated that around 107 million U.S. consumers conducted some online banking activity in 2012, and this number is expected to grow 4%–5% a year, to around 116 million by 2014 (eMarketer, Inc., 2010; comScore, 2010a) (see **Figure 8.3**). Over 32 million in the United States access banking information from a mobile device (comScore, 2012b).

TABLE 8.3	TOP ONLINE BANKS: OCTOBER 2012
BANK (RANKED BY VISITORS)	PERCENTAGE OF TOTAL WEB BANK VISITS
Wells Fargo Online Banking	8.98%
Chase Online	7.85%
Bank of America Online Banking	2.58%
Capital One Online Banking	2.54%
PNC Online Banking	2.05%

SOURCES: Based on data from eMarketer, Inc., 2012c.

The history of online brokerage has been similar to that of online banking. Early innovators such as E*Trade have been displaced from their leadership positions in terms of numbers of online accounts by discount broker pioneer Charles Schwab and financial industry giant Fidelity (which has more mutual fund customers and more funds under management than any other U.S. firm).

According to Nielsen Net Ratings, an estimated 20 million U.S. investors traded online on 2012, a number expected to increase to approximately 29 million by 2013.

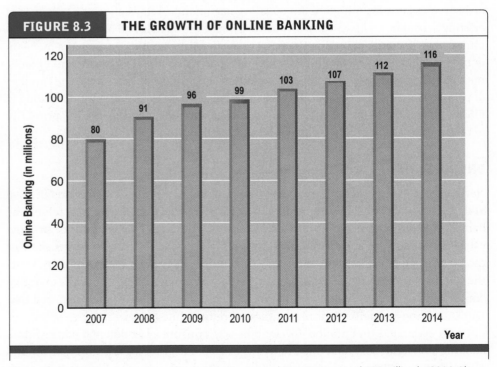

| FIGURE 8.3 | THE GROWTH OF ONLINE BANKING |

The number of Internet users using online banking is expected to grow to around 116 million by 2014. About 60% of the U.S. Internet population visits at least one of the top 20 online banks. Increases in mobile banking may impact these numbers over the next three years.

SOURCES: Based on data from comScore, 2010a; eMarketer, 2010; authors' estimates.

According to comScore, almost 10 million use a mobile device to access brokerage or stock information (comScore, 2012b).

Multi-Channel vs. Pure Online Financial Services Firms

Online consumers prefer to visit financial services sites that have physical outlets or branches. In general, multi-channel financial services firms that have both physical branches or offices and solid online offerings are growing faster than pure-online firms that have no physical presence, and they are assuming market leadership as well. Traditional banking firms have literally thousands of branches where customers can open accounts, deposit money, take out loans, find home mortgages, and rent a safety deposit box. Top online brokerage firms do not have the same physical footprint as the banks do, but each has a strong physical presence or telephone presence to strengthen its online presence. Fidelity has urban walk-in service center branches, but it relies primarily on the telephone for interacting with investors. Charles Schwab has investment centers around the country as an integral part of its online strategy. Pure-online banks and brokerages cannot provide customers with some services that still require a face-to-face interaction.

Financial Portals and Account Aggregators

Financial portals are sites that provide consumers with comparison shopping services, independent financial advice, and financial planning. Independent portals do not themselves offer financial services, but act as steering mechanisms to online providers. They generate revenue from advertising, referral fees, and subscription fees. For example, Yahoo's financial portal, Yahoo Finance, offers consumers credit card purchase tracking, market overviews, real-time stock quotes, news, financial advice, streaming video interviews with financial leaders, and Yahoo Bill Pay, an EBPP system. Other independent financial portals include Intuit's Quicken.com, MSN's MSN Money, CNNMoney, and America Online's Money & Finance channel. A host of financial portal sites have sprung up to help consumers with financial management and planning such as Mint.com (owned by Quicken), SmartPiggy, and Credit Karma.

financial portals
sites that provide consumers with comparison shopping services, independent financial advice, and financial planning

Account aggregation is the process of pulling together all of a customer's financial (and even nonfinancial) data at a single personalized Web site, including brokerage, banking, insurance, loans, frequent flyer miles, personalized news, and much more. For example, a consumer can see his or her TD Ameritrade brokerage account, Fidelity 401(k) account, Travelers Insurance annuity account, and American Airlines frequent flyer miles all displayed on a single site. The idea is to provide consumers with a holistic view of their entire portfolio of assets, no matter what financial institution actually holds those assets.

account aggregation
the process of pulling together all of a customer's financial (and even nonfinancial) data at a single personalized Web site

The leading provider of account aggregation technology is Yodlee. It uses screen-scraping and other techniques to pull information from over 12,000 different data sources.

ONLINE MORTGAGE AND LENDING SERVICES

During the early days of e-commerce, hundreds of firms launched pure-play online mortgage sites to capture the U.S. home mortgage market. Early entrants hoped to radically simplify and transform the traditional mortgage value chain process, dramatically speed up the loan closing process, and share the economies with consumers by offering lower rates.

By 2003, over half of these early-entry, pure-online firms had failed. Early pure-play online mortgage institutions had difficulties developing a brand name at an affordable price and failed to simplify the mortgage generation process. They ended up suffering from high start-up and administrative costs, high customer acquisition costs, rising interest rates, and poor execution of their strategies.

Despite this rocky start, the online mortgage market is slowly growing; it is dominated by established online banks and other online financial services firms, traditional mortgage vendors, and a few successful online mortgage firms.

More than half of all mortgage shoppers research mortgages online, but few actually apply online because of the complexity of mortgages. Most mortgages today are written by intermediary mortgage brokers, with banks still playing an important origination role but generally not servicing mortgages they originate.

ONLINE INSURANCE SERVICES

In 1995, the price of a $500,000 20-year term life policy for a healthy 40-year-old male was $995 a year. In 2012, the same policy could be had for around $400—a decline of about 60%—while other prices have risen 15% in the same period. In a study of the term life insurance business, Brown and Goolsbee discovered that Internet usage led to an 8%–15% decline in term life insurance prices industry-wide (both offline and online), and increased consumer surplus by about $115 million per year (and hence reduced industry profits by the same amount) (Brown and Goolsbee, 2000). Price dispersion for term life policies initially increased, but then fell as more and more people began using the Internet to obtain insurance quotes.

Unlike books and CDs, where online price dispersion is higher than offline, and in many cases online prices are higher than offline, term life insurance stands out as one product group supporting the conventional wisdom that the Internet will lower search costs, increase price comparison, and lower prices to consumers. Term life insurance is a commodity product, however, and in other insurance product lines, the Web offers insurance companies new opportunities for product and service differentiation and price discrimination.

Like the online mortgage industry, the online insurance industry has been very successful in attracting visitors who are looking to obtain prices and terms of insurance policies. While many national insurance underwriting companies initially did not offer competitive products directly on the Web because it might injure the business operations of their traditional local agents, the Web sites of almost all of the major firms now provide the ability to obtain an online quote. Even if consumers do not actually purchase insurance policies online, the Internet has proven to have a powerful influence on consumer insurance decisions by dramatically reducing search costs and changing the price discovery process. Some of the leading online insurance services companies are InsWeb, Insure.com, Insurance.com, QuickQuote, and NetQuote.

ONLINE REAL ESTATE SERVICES

During the early days of e-commerce, real estate seemed ripe for an Internet revolution that would rationalize this historically local, complex, and local agent-driven industry that monopolized the flow of consumer information. Potentially, the Internet and e-commerce might have disintermediated this huge marketspace, allowing buyers and sellers, and owners to transact directly, lower search costs to near zero, and dramatically reduce prices. However, this did not happen. What did happen is extremely beneficial to buyers and sellers, as well as to real estate agents. At one point, there were an estimated 100,000 real estate sites on the Internet worldwide. Many of these sites have disappeared. However, the remaining online sites have started to make headway toward transforming the industry. In addition, most local real estate brokers in the United States have their own agency Web sites to deal with clients, in addition to participating with thousands of other agencies in multiple listing services that list homes online. Some of the major online real estate sites are Realtor.com, HomeGain, RealEstate.com, ZipRealty, Move.com, Craigslist, Zillow, and Trulia.

Real estate differs from other types of online financial services because it is impossible to complete a property transaction online. Clearly, the major impact of Internet real estate sites is in influencing offline decisions. The Internet has become a compelling method for real estate professionals, homebuilders, property managers and owners, and ancillary service providers to communicate with and provide information to consumers. According to a survey conducted by the National Association of Realtors, 90% of buyers surf the Internet to search for a home. Although buyers also use other resources, most start the search process online and then contact an agent, with about 85% purchasing through an agent. Almost 40% of buyers said that they first learned of the home that they ultimately purchased via the Internet (National Association of Realtors, 2010).

The primary service offered by real estate sites is a listing of houses available. Realtor.com, the official site of the National Association of Realtors, is one of the top Web sites in terms of market share of visits. Realtor.com listed over 4 million homes, and had over 9 million unique visitors in October 2012. The offerings have become sophisticated and integrated. Listings typically feature detailed property descriptions, multiple photographs, and virtual 360-degree tours. Consumers can link to mortgage lenders, credit reporting agencies, house inspectors, and surveyors. There are also online loan calculators, appraisal reports, sales price histories by neighborhood, school district data, crime reports, and social and historical information on neighborhoods. Some online real estate brokers now charge substantially less than traditional offline brokers who typically charge 6% of the sale price.

Despite the revolution in available information, there has not been a revolution in the industry value chain. The listings available on Web sites are provided by local multiple listing services supported by local real estate agents. Sometimes, addresses of the houses are not available, and online users are directed to the local listing agent who is hired by the seller of house. Traditional hands-on real estate brokers will show the house and handle all transactions with the owner to preserve their fees, typically ranging from 5% to 6% of the transaction.

9.6 ONLINE TRAVEL SERVICES

Online travel is one of the most successful B2C e-commerce segments. The Internet is becoming the most common channel used by consumers to research travel options, seek the best possible prices, and book reservations for airline tickets, hotel rooms, rental cars, cruises, and tours. Today, more travel is booked online than offline. Online travel services revenues reached almost $120 billion in 2012, and are expected to continue growing to over $150 billion by 2016 (see **Figure 8.4**) (eMarketer, Inc., 2012d).

WHY ARE ONLINE TRAVEL SERVICES SO POPULAR?

Online travel sites offer consumers a one-stop, convenient, leisure and business travel experience where travelers can find content (descriptions of vacations and facilities),

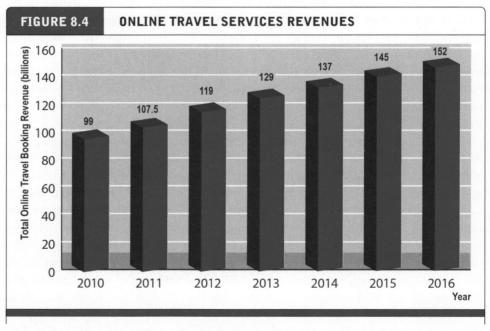

| FIGURE 8.4 | ONLINE TRAVEL SERVICES REVENUES |

U.S. online leisure/unmanaged business travel service revenues has resumed growing and is expected to reach over $150 billion by 2016.

SOURCE: Based on data from eMarketer, Inc., 2012d.

community (chat groups and bulletin boards), commerce (purchase of all travel elements), and customer service (usually through call centers). Online sites offer much more information and many more travel options than traditional travel agents. For suppliers—the owners of hotels, rental cars, and airlines—the online sites aggregate millions of consumers into singular, focused customer pools that can be efficiently reached through on-site advertising and promotions. Online sites create a much more efficient marketplace, bringing consumers and suppliers together in a low-transaction cost environment.

Travel services appear to be an ideal service for the Internet, and therefore e-commerce business models should work well for this product. Travel is an information-intensive product requiring significant consumer research. It is a digital product in the sense that travel requirements—planning, researching, comparison shopping, reserving, and payment—can be accomplished for the most part online in a digital environment. On the travel reservation side, travel does not require any "inventory": there are no physical assets. And the suppliers of the product—owners of hotels, airlines, rental cars, vacation rooms, and tour guides—are highly fragmented and often have excess capacity. Always looking for customers to fill vacant rooms and rent idle cars, suppliers will be anxious to lower prices and willing to advertise on Web sites that can attract millions of consumers. The online agencies—such as Travelocity, Expedia, and others—do not have to deploy thousands of travel agents in physical offices across the country but can instead concentrate on a single interface with a national consumer audience.

THE ONLINE TRAVEL MARKET

There are four major sectors in the travel market: airline tickets, hotel reservations, car rentals, and cruises/tours. Airline tickets are the source of the greatest amount of revenue in online travel. Airline reservations are largely a commodity. They can be easily described over the Web. According to a 2011 survey, 57% of respondents purchased airline tickets on the airline's Web site, while 22% used a travel booking Web site such as Expedia or Orbitz. Only 5% reported using a traditional travel agent (MarketTools, 2011). The same is true with car rentals; most people can reliably rent a car over the phone or the Web and expect to obtain what they ordered.

ONLINE TRAVEL INDUSTRY DYNAMICS

Because much of what travel agency sites offer is a commodity, and thus they face the same costs, competition among online providers is intense. Price competition is difficult because shoppers, as well as online site managers, can comparison shop easily. Therefore, competition among sites tends to focus on scope of offerings, ease of use, payment options, and personalization. Some well-known travel sites are listed in **Table 8.4**.

The online travel services industry has gone through a period of consolidation with stronger offline, established firms such as Sabre Holdings (which now owns Travelocity, Lastminute, and Site59, among others) purchasing weaker and relatively inexpensive online travel agencies in order to build stronger multi-channel travel sites. Orbitz and

TABLE 8.4	MAJOR ONLINE TRAVEL SITES
NAME	DESCRIPTION
LEISURE/UNMANAGED BUSINESS TRAVEL	
Expedia	Largest online travel service; leisure focus.
Travelocity	Second-largest online travel service; leisure focus. Owned by Sabre Holdings.
TripAdvisor	Travel shopping bot that searches for the lowest fares across all other sites.
Orbitz	Began as supplier-owned reservation system; now part of Orbitz Worldwide, a public company.
Priceline	Name Your Price model; leisure focus.
CheapTickets	Discount airline tickets, hotel reservations, and auto rentals. Part of Orbitz Worldwide.
Hotels.com	Largest hotel reservation network; leisure and corporate focus. Owned by Expedia.
Hotwire	Seeks out discount fares based on airline excess inventory. Owned by Expedia.
MANAGED BUSINESS TRAVEL	
GetThere.com	Corporate online booking solution (COBS). Owned by Sabre Holdings.
Travelocity Business	Full-service corporate travel agency.

Expedia have also been involved in the industry consolidation. Orbitz was initially an industry consortium, then went public, then was purchased by Cendant (along with other travel firms such as CheapTickets and Trip.com), then sold by Cendant to Blackstone Group, and finally went public again in 2007. Expedia, originally begun by Microsoft, was purchased by Barry Diller's conglomerate IAC/InterActiveCorp, but has now been spun off as an independent company once again, picking up IAC's Hotels.com, Hotwire, TripAdvisor, and TravelNow in the process.

Mobile devices and apps used for pre-trip planning, booking, check-in, and context and location-based destination information are also transforming the online travel industry (see also the case study on Orbitz's mobile strategy in Chapter 4). For instance, it is estimated that over 36 million people used a mobile device to research travel in 2012, and that number is expected to double, to over 72 million by 2016 (eMarketer, 2012e). During the past year, most of the major airlines have launched apps for a variety of mobile platforms to enable flight research, booking, and management.

Social media is also having a big impact on the online travel industry. User-generated content and online reviews are having an increasing influence on travel-buying decisions. The *Insight on Society* story, *Phony Reviews,* examines some of the issues this presents for the industry.

INSIGHT ON SOCIETY

PHONY REVIEWS

In the United Kingdom, TripAdvisor, a consumer review aggregator, is under investigation by the U.K. Advertising Standards Authority as a result of complaints of fraudulent reviews. According to online reputation management KwikChex, as many as 10 million of the most current reviews on TripAdvisor could be fake. KwikChex alleges that hotels are paying people to create false identities and post favorable reviews on their properties, and also to slam competing venues. Some establishments offer guests future discounts for "honest but positive" reviews. In 2012, TripAdvisor was told by the ASA to remove wording on its site claiming that its reviews were "trusted and honest."

For sites like Yelp, which are primarily focused on business ratings and reviews, the growth in phony reviews presents a considerable challenge. The authenticity and accuracy of reviews are critically important to Yelp's success, but garnering a high review score is equally important to the restaurants and other businesses listed on the site. If site visitors have no reason to trust Yelp's reviews, there isn't much incentive for those visitors to return in the future. With this in mind, Yelp has begun to remove suspect reviews from its site, including those from a Californian marketing and business networking group. Members of the group were giving five-star reviews to all of the other members of the group to inflate their ratings. Yelp caught on and removed those reviews

from its site. Yelp is also developing its own algorithm which are intended to detect phony reviews.

TripAdvisor also claims it uses an algorithm to help filter out false reviews, although it rejects requiring would-be reviewers to supply a reservation number in order to prove that they have actually stayed at the property that they are reviewing. According to TripAdvisor, it takes the authenticity of its reviews very seriously, and has numerous methods to ensure their legitimacy, including automated site tools and a team of review integrity experts. It also relies on the review community itself to identify suspicious content and trolls the sites where businesses advertise for fake reviewers.

There may soon be another tool in TripAdvisor's toolbox. Researchers at Cornell University have developed an algorithm that they say can identify language features specific to fake and truthful reviews. To train the algorithm, they created a database of 20 truthful and 20 fake reviews for 20 hotels, for a total of 800 reviews. According to the researchers, the algorithm accurately identified fake reviews 90% of the time based on the type of language used. The algorithm has attracted the attention of a number of companies, including TripAdvisor, Hilton, and several specialist travel sites.

Are the days of phony reviews over as a result? Probably not. So best to take what you read with a grain of salt, discarding both the overwhelmingly positive and the unrelentingly negative reviews.

SOURCES: "Yelp Reviews: Can You Trust Them? Some Firms Game the System," by Jessica Guynn and Andrea Chang, *Los Angeles Times,* July 4, 2012; "TripAdvisor Told to Stop Claiming Reviews are 'Trusted and Honest,'" *Daily Mail,* February 1, 2012; "A Lie Detector Test for Online Reviewers," by Karen Weise, *BusinessWeek,* September 29, 2011; "Cornell Researchers Work to Spot Fake Reviews," by Emma Court, *The Cornell Daily Sun,* September 23, 2011; "TripAdvisor Called into Question Over 'Fake' Reviews," by Melanie Naylor, Boston.com, September 7, 2011; "Investigation Launched into TripAdvisor Following Claims up to 10 Million Reviews are Fake," News.com.au, September 5, 2011; "TripAdvisor's Fake Reviews Sickness Goes Critical," by Phillip Butler, Argophilia.com, September 2, 2011; "TripAdvisor's Fake Battle," by Gulliver, *The Economist,* August 22, 2011; "The Yelp Wars: False Reviews, Anti-SLAPP, and Slander — What's Ethical in Online Reviewing?", by Kathleen Miles, Scpr.org, August 25, 2011; "In a Race to Out-Rave, 5-Star Web Reviews Go for $5," by David Streitfeld, *New York Times,* August 19, 2011.

8.6 ONLINE CAREER SERVICES

Next to travel services, one of the Internet's most successful online services has been job services (recruitment sites) that provide a free posting of individual resumes, plus many other related career services; for a fee, they also list job openings posted by companies. Career services sites collect revenue from other sources as well, by providing value-added services to users and collecting fees from related service providers.

The online job market is dominated by two large players: CareerBuilder (which provides job listings for AOL and MSN), with about 15 million unique monthly visitors in October 2012, and Monster, with about 18 million. (Yahoo HotJobs, which had been the third large player, was acquired by Monster for $225 million in 2010.) Other popular sites include Indeed (24 million unique visitors), SimplyHired (5.5 million), and SnagAJob (5.8 million). These top sites generate more than $1 billion annually in revenue from employers' fees and consumer fees. Rising unemployment during late 2008 to 2010 has led to an increasing number of Americans seeking jobs and career opportunities online, with career services and development Web sites among the top 10 fastest growing site categories (comScore, 2010b, 2011). The professional social network site LinkedIn is also becoming an increasingly important player in this market (see the opening case in Chapter 11). In 2011, it added a plug-in, Apply with LinkedIn, that allows job seekers to easily submit their LinkedIn profile to an employer's Web site.

Traditionally, companies have relied on five employee recruitment tools: classified and print advertising, career expos (or trade shows), on-campus recruiting, private employment agencies (now called "staffing firms"), and internal referral programs. In comparison to online recruiting, these tools have severe limitations. Print advertising usually includes a per-word charge that limits the amount of detail employers provide about a job opening, as well as a limited time period within which the job is posted. Career expos do not allow for pre-screening of attendees and are limited by the amount of time a recruiter can spend with each candidate. Staffing firms charge high fees and have a limited, usually local, selection of job hunters. On-campus recruiting also restricts the number of candidates a recruiter can speak with during a normal visit and requires that employers visit numerous campuses. And internal referral programs may encourage employees to propose unqualified candidates for openings in order to qualify for rewards or incentives offered.

Online recruiting overcomes these limitations, providing a more efficient and cost-effective means of linking employers and potential employees, while reducing the total time to hire. Online recruiting enables job hunters to more easily build, update, and distribute their resumes while gathering information about prospective employers and conducting job searches.

IT'S JUST INFORMATION: THE IDEAL WEB BUSINESS?

Online recruitment is ideally suited for the Web. The hiring process is an information-intense business process that involves discovering the skills and salary requirements of individuals and matching them with available jobs. In order to accomplish this matchup, there does not initially need to be face-to-face interaction, or a great deal of personalization. Prior to the Internet, this information sharing was accomplished

TABLE 8.5	POPULAR ONLINE RECRUITMENT SITES
RECRUITMENT SITE	BRIEF DESCRIPTION
GENERAL RECRUITMENT SITES	
CareerBuilder	Provides job search centers for more than 9,000 Web sites, and 140 newspapers; 1.6 million jobs listed.
Monster	Public company offering general job searches in 50 countries.
Yahoo HotJobs	General job searches. Purchased by Monster in 2010 for $225 million.
Indeed.com	Job site aggregator
SimplyHired	Job site aggregator
Craigslist	Popular classified listing service focused on local recruiting
NICHE JOB SITES	
SnagAJob	Part-time and hourly jobs
USAJobs	Federal government jobs
HigherEdJobs	Education industry
EngineerJobs	Engineering jobs
Dice	Information technology jobs

locally by human networks of friends, acquaintances, former employers, and relatives, in addition to employment agencies that developed paper files on job hunters. The Internet can clearly automate this flow of information, reducing search time and costs for all parties. **Table 8.5** lists some of the most popular recruitment sites.

Why are so many job hunters and employers using Internet job sites? Recruitment sites are popular largely because they save time and money for both job hunters and employers seeking recruits. For employers, the job boards expand the geographical reach of their searches, lower costs, and result in faster hiring decisions.

For job seekers, online sites are popular not only because their resumes can be made widely available to recruiters but also because of a variety of other related job-hunting services. The services delivered by online recruitment sites have greatly expanded since their emergence in 1996. Originally, online recruitment sites just provided a digital version of newspaper classified ads. Today's sites offer many other services, including skills assessment, personality assessment questionnaires, personalized account management for job hunters, organizational culture assessments, job search tools, employer blocking (prevents your employer from seeing your posting), employee blocking (prevents your employees from seeing your listings if you are their employer), and e-mail notification. Online sites also provide a number of educational services such as resume writing advice, software skills preparation, and interview tips.

OpenTable:
Your Reservation Is Waiting

OpenTable is the leading supplier of reservation, table management, and guest management software for restaurants. More than 25,000 restaurants in the United States, Canada, Mexico, the United Kingdom, Germany, and Japan use the OpenTable hardware and software system. This system automates the reservation-taking and table management process, while allowing restaurants to build diner databases for improved guest recognition and targeted e-mail marketing. The OpenTable Web site, OpenTable for Mobile Web (its mobile Web site), and OpenTable Mobile (its mobile app), provide a fast, efficient way for diners to find available tables in real time. The Web sites and app connect directly to the thousands of computerized reservation systems at OpenTable restaurants, and reservations are immediately recorded in a restaurant's electronic reservation book.

OpenTable's revenue comes from two sources. Restaurants pay a one-time fee for on-site installation and training, a monthly subscription fee of $199 for software and hardware, and a $1 transaction fee for each restaurant guest seated through online reservations. The online reservation service is free to diners. The business model encourages diners to assist in viral marketing. When an individual makes a reserva-

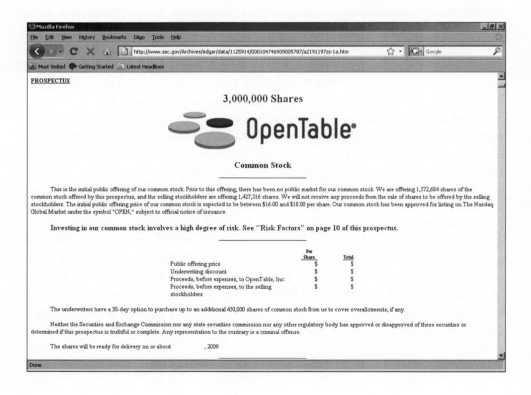

tion, the site "suggests" that they send e-vites to their dinner companions directly from OpenTable.com. The e-vites include a link back to the OpenTable site.

The founders of OpenTable knew that dealing with restaurants as a single market would be difficult. They also realized that the Internet was changing things for diners by providing them with instant access to reviews, menus, and other information about dining options. And there was no method for making reservations online—we all know reserving by phone is time-consuming, inefficient, and prone to errors. For diners to use an online reservation system, they would need real-time access to a number of local restaurants, and the ability to instantly book confirmed reservations around the clock.

OpenTable's initial strategy of paying online restaurant reviewers for links to its Web site and targeting national chains for fast expansions got the company into 50 cities, but it was spending $1 million a month and bringing in only $100,000 in revenue. The original investors still felt there was a viable business to be built, and they made a number of management changes, including installing investor and board member Thomas Layton, founder of CitySearch.com, as OpenTable's CEO. Layton cut staff, shut down marketing efforts, and got the company out of all but four cities: Chicago, New York, San Francisco, and Washington, D.C.

The company retooled its hardware and software to create the user-friendly ERB system, and deployed a door-to-door sales force to solicit subscriptions from high-end restaurants. The combination of e-commerce, user-friendly technology, and the personal touch worked. The four markets OpenTable targeted initially developed into active, local networks of restaurants and diners that continue to grow. OpenTable has implemented the same strategy across the country, and now includes approximately 25,000 OpenTable restaurant customers. In 13 years, the company has seated approximately 350 million diners, and it is currently averaging 10 million diners seated per month.

In 2009, the company chose an aggressive strategy, going ahead with an initial public offering (IPO) despite a terrible economy and worse financial markets. So far, the gamble has paid off. On its first day of trading, OpenTable's shares climbed 59%. The share price at the end of September 2012 was in the mid-$40 range, more than double the $20 IPO price. Since then, the company has continued to grow and has shown no signs of slowing down in 2012.

The company has benefited from having e-commerce revenue streams from subscription fees and per-transaction charges, instead of from advertising, and restaurant owners report that the software is easy to use. OpenTable's market is susceptible to network effects: the more people use it, the more utility the system delivers.

While OpenTable is the biggest, most successful online player in the restaurant reservations market, it does have competitors. MenuPages.com offers access to restaurant menus and reviews, but visitors to the site can't make reservations, and the site covers only eight U.S. cities. Urbanspoon.com offers a reservation service, but its technology is not compatible with OpenTable, so those reservations must be entered manually into the OpenTable system. Like OpenTable, Urbanspoon charges $1 for each diner. Looming on the horizon is Google, which purchased online restaurant

SOURCES: "OpenTable Shares Drop After Analyst Cuts Rating," Businessweek.com, September 17, 2012; "OpenTable Hits 15 million Restaurant Reviews," by Anita Li, Mashable.com, September 6, 2012; "OpenTable, Inc. Form 10-Q," filed with the SEC, August 6, 2012; "OpenTable Inc. Announces Fourth Quarter and Full Year 2011 Financial Results," Opentable.com, February 7, 2012; "Google Buys Zagat to View the OpenTable, Yelp," by Alexei Oreskovic, Reuters, September 8, 2011; OpenTable 10-Q for the quarterly period ended June 30, 2011, Sec.gov, August 4, 2011; Form 10-K for the year ended December 31, 2010, Sec.gov, March 9, 2011; "Behind Open-Table's Success," Kevin Kelleher, CNNMoney.com, September 23, 2010; "OpenTable Introduces the Next Generation of Its Electronic Reservation Book Software," RestaurantNews.com, August 17, 2010; "OpenTable: the Hottest Spot in Town," by Maha Atal, CNNMoney.con, August 14, 2009; "OpenTable Unveils Version 2.0 of its iPhone App," AppScout.com, August 14, 2009; "Gadgetell: Fight for Your Dinner: Urbanspoon vs. Open Table," NewsFactor.com, August 8, 2009; "Urbanspoon is Now Taking Online Reservations: Takes on OpenTable," by Frederic Lardinois, ReadWriteWeb.com, August 7, 2009; "Yelp vs. OpenT-able—Where Should Restaurants Spend Their Marketing Dollars," Dinner Rush Blog, reservationdc. wordpress.com, July 19, 2009; May 22, 2009; "What Media Companies Could Learn from OpenTable," The Media Wonk, May 20, 2009; Open Table S-1/A Amendment #6, filed with the Securities and Exchange Commission, May 19, 2009.

guide Zagat in September 2011, raising the specter that it might try to compete with OpenTable, although Zagat does not yet possess that functionality.

The company's international strategy is to replicate the successful U.S. model by focusing initially on building a restaurant customer base. OpenTable believes the localized versions of its software will compare favorably against competitive software offerings, enabling them to expand across a broad selection of local restaurants.

The company is well-positioned for future growth. Its size, track record of growth, and high customer satisfaction rates should continue to work in its favor.

Case Study Questions

1. Why will OpenTable competitors have a difficult time competing against Open-Table?

2. What characteristics of the restaurant market make it difficult for a reservation system to work?

3. How did OpenTable change its marketing strategy to succeed?

4. Why would restaurants find the SaaS model very attractive?

8.8   REVIEW

KEY CONCEPTS

■ **Understand the environment in which the online retail sector operates today.**

Personal consumption of retail goods and services comprise about 71% and account for about $11.1 trillion of total GDP. The retail industry can be divided into seven major firm types:
- General merchandise
- Durable goods
- Specialty stores
- Food and beverage
- Gasoline and fuel
- MOTO
- Online retail firms

Each type offers opportunities for online retail. The MOTO sector is the most similar to the online retail sales sector, and MOTO retailers are among the fastest growing online retail firms.

During the early days of e-commerce, some predicted that the retail industry would be revolutionized, based on the following beliefs:
- Greatly reduced search costs on the Internet would encourage consumers to abandon traditional marketplaces in order to find the lowest prices for goods. First movers who provided low-cost goods and high-quality service would succeed.

- Market entry costs would be much lower than those for physical storefront merchants, and online merchants would be more efficient at marketing and order fulfillment than their offline competitors because they had command of the technology (technology prices were falling sharply).
- Online companies would replace traditional stores as physical store merchants were forced out of business.
- In certain industries, the "middleman" would be eliminated (disintermediation) as manufacturers or their distributors entered the market and built a direct relationship with the consumer. This cost savings would ensure the emergence of the Web as the dominant marketing channel.
- In other industries, online retailers would gain the advantage over traditional merchants by outsourcing functions such as warehousing and order fulfillment, resulting in a kind of hypermediation, in which the online retailer gained the upper hand by eliminating inventory purchasing and storage costs.

Today, it has become clear that few of the initial assumptions about the future of online retail were correct. Also, the structure of the retail marketplace in the United States has not been revolutionized. The reality is that:

- Online consumers are not primarily cost-driven—instead, they are as brand-driven and influenced by perceived value as their offline counterparts.
- Online market entry costs were underestimated, as was the cost of acquiring new customers.
- Older traditional firms, such as the general merchandising giants and the established catalog-based retailers, are taking over as the top online retail sites.
- Disintermediation did not occur. On the contrary, online retailing has become an example of the powerful role that intermediaries play in retail trade.

■ **Identify the challenges faced by the different types of online retailers.**

There are four major types of online retail business models, and each faces its own particular challenges:

- *Virtual merchants* are single-channel Web firms that generate all of their revenues from online sales. Their challenges include building a business and a brand name quickly, many competitors in the virtual marketplace, and substantial costs to build and maintain a Web site.
- *Multi-channel merchants* (bricks-and-clicks) have a network of physical stores as their primary retail channel, but have also begun online operations. Their challenges include high cost of physical buildings, high cost of large sales staffs, and the need to coordinate prices across channels.
- *Catalog merchants* are established companies that have a national offline catalog operation as their largest retail channel, but who have recently developed online capabilities. Their challenges include high costs for printing and mailing, the need to leverage their existing assets and competencies to the new technology environment, and building a credible Web site.
- *Manufacturer-direct merchants* are either single- or multi-channel manufacturers who sell to consumers directly online without the intervention of retailers. Their challenges include channel conflict, quickly developing a rapid-response online order and fulfillment system, and switching from a supply-push to a demand-pull model.

■ **Describe the major features of the online service sector.**

The service sector is the largest and most rapidly expanding part of the economy of advanced industrial nations. The major service industry groups are financial services, insurance, real estate, business services, and health services. Within these service industry groups, companies can be further categorized into those that involve transaction brokering and those that involve providing a "hands-on" service. With some exceptions, the service sector is by and large a knowledge- and information-intense industry. For this reason, many services are uniquely suited to e-commerce and the strengths of the Internet.

The rapid expansion of e-commerce services in the areas of finance, including insurance and real estate, travel, and job placement, can be explained by the ability of these firms to:

- Collect, store, and disseminate high-value information
- Provide reliable, fast communication
- Personalize and customize service or components of service

E-commerce offers extraordinary opportunities to improve transaction efficiencies and thus productivity in a sector where productivity has so far not been markedly affected by the explosion in information technology.

■ **Discuss the trends taking place in the online financial services industry.**

The online financial services sector is a good example of an e-commerce success story, but the success is somewhat different than what had been predicted in the early days of e-commerce. Today, the multi-channel established financial firms are growing the most rapidly and have the best prospects for long-term viability. Key features of the online banking and brokerage industries include the following:

- Multi-channel firms that have both physical branches and solid online offerings have assumed market leadership over the pure-online firms that cannot provide customers with many services that still require hands-on interaction.
- Customer acquisition costs are significantly higher for Internet-only banks and brokerages that must invest heavily in marketing versus their established brand-name bricks-and-mortar competitors, which can simply convert existing branch customers to online customers at a much lower cost.
- Financial portals provide comparison shopping services and steer consumers to online providers for independent financial advice and financial planning.
- Account aggregation is another rapidly growing online financial service, which pulls together all of a customer's financial data on a single personalized Web site.
- During the early days of e-commerce, a radically altered online mortgage and lending services market was envisioned in which the mortgage value chain would be simplified and the loan closing process speeded up, with the resulting cost savings passed on to consumers. Affordably building a brand name, the resulting high customer acquisition costs, and instituting these value chain changes proved to be too difficult. Today, the established banks and lenders are reaping the benefits of a relatively small but growing market.

Key features of the online insurance industry include the following:

- Term life insurance stands out as one product group supporting the early visions of lower search costs, increased price transparency, and the resulting consumer savings. However, in other insurance product lines, the Web offers insurance companies new opportunities for product and service differentiation and price discrimination.

Key features of the online real estate services industry include the following:

- The early vision that the historically local, complex, and agent-driven real estate industry would be transformed into a disintermediated marketplace where buyers and sellers could transact directly has not been realized. What has happened has been beneficial to buyers, sellers, and real estate agents alike.
- Since it is not possible to complete a property transaction online, the major impact of the online real estate industry is in influencing offline purchases.
- The primary service is a listing of available houses, with secondary links to mortgage lenders, credit reporting agencies, neighborhood information, loan calculators, appraisal reports, sales price histories by neighborhood, school district data, and crime reports.
- The industry value chain, however, has remained unchanged. Home addresses are not available online and users are directed back to the local listing agent for further information about the house.

■ **Discuss the major trends in the online travel services industry today.**

Online travel services attract the largest single e-commerce audience and the largest slice of B2C revenues. The Internet has become the most common channel used by consumers to research travel options. It is also the most common way for people to search for the best possible prices and book reservations for airline tickets, rental cars, hotel rooms, cruises, and tours. Some of the reasons why online travel services have been so successful include the following:

- Online travel sites offer consumers a one-stop, convenient, leisure and business travel experience where travelers can find content, community, commerce, and customer service. Online sites offer more information and travel options than traditional travel agents. They also bring consumers and suppliers together in a low transaction cost environment.
- Travel is an information-intensive product as well as a digital product in the sense that travel requirements can be accomplished for the most part online. Since travel does not require any inventory, suppliers (which are highly fragmented) are always looking for customers to fill excess capacity. Also, travel services do not require an expensive multi-channel physical presence. For these reasons, travel services appear to be particularly well suited for the online marketplace.
- Corporations are increasingly outsourcing their travel offices entirely to vendors who can provide Web-based solutions, high-quality service, and lower costs.

The major trends in online travel services include the following:

- The online travel services industry is going through a period of consolidation as stronger offline, established firms purchase weaker and relatively inexpensive online travel agencies in order to build stronger multi-channel travel sites that combine physical presence, television sales outlets, and online sites.
- Mobile devices and apps and social media also are having a big impact on the online travel industry.

■   Identify current trends in the online career services industry.

Next to travel services, job-hunting services have been one of the Internet's most successful online services because they save money for both job hunters and employers.

Online recruiting can also serve to establish market prices and terms, thereby identifying both the salary levels for specific jobs and the skill sets required to achieve those salary levels. This should lead to a rationalization of wages, greater labor mobility, and higher efficiency in recruitment and operations as employers are able to more quickly fill positions.

QUESTIONS

1. Why were so many entrepreneurs drawn to start businesses in the online retail sector initially?
2. Which segment of the offline retail business is most like online retailing? Why?
3. Describe the technological retail revolution that preceded the growth of e-commerce. What were some of the innovations that made later online retailing possible?
4. Name two assumptions e-commerce analysts made early on about consumers and their buying behavior that turned out to be false.
5. Explain the distinction between disintermediation and hypermediation as it relates to online retailing.
6. Compare and contrast virtual merchants and bricks-and-clicks firms. What other type of online retailer is most like the virtual merchant?
7. What is the difference between a supply-push and a demand-pull sales model? Why do most manufacturer-direct firms have difficulty switching to one of these?
8. What is the biggest deterrent to growth of the online insurance industry nationally?
9. Define channel conflict and explain how it currently applies to the mortgage and insurance industries.
10. Name and describe the four types of services provided by financial services firms on the Web.
11. How have travel services suppliers benefited from consumer use of travel Web sites?
12. Name and describe five traditional recruitment tools companies have used to identify and attract employees. What are the disadvantages of such tools compared to online career sites?
13. In addition to matching job applicants with available positions, what larger function do online job sites fill? Explain how such sites can affect salaries and going rates.

PROJECTS

1. Find the Securities and Exchange Commission Web site at Sec.gov, and access the EDGAR archives, where you can review 10-K filings for all public companies. Search for the 10-K report for the most recent completed fiscal

year for two online retail companies of your choice (preferably ones operating in the same industry, such as Staples Inc. and Office Depot Inc.). Prepare a presentation that compares the financial stability and prospects of the two businesses, focusing specifically on the performance of their respective Internet operations.

2. Examine the financial statements for Amazon and Best Buy Co., Inc. What observations can you make about the two businesses? Which one is stronger financially and why? Which one's business model appears to be weaker and why? If you could identify two major problem areas for each, what would they be? Prepare a presentation that makes your case.

3. Conduct a thorough analysis—strategic and financial—of one of the following companies or another of your own choosing: Bluefly Inc., Drugstore.com, Inc., or 1-800-Flowers.com, Inc. Prepare a presentation that summarizes your observations about the company's Internet operations and future prospects.

4. Find an example not mentioned in the text of each of the four types of online retailing business models. Prepare a short report describing each firm and why it is an example of the particular business model.

5. Drawing on material in the chapter and your own research, prepare a short paper describing your views on the major social and legal issues facing online retailers.

6. Conduct a thorough analysis—strategic and financial—of one of the following Web sites: Progressive.com, Insure.com, or Insweb.com. Prepare a presentation that summarizes your observations about the company's operations and future prospects.

7. Choose a services industry not discussed in the chapter (such as legal services, medical services, accounting services, or another of your choosing). Prepare a 3- to 5-page report discussing recent trends affecting online provision of these services.

8. Together with a teammate, investigate the use of mobile apps in the financial services industries. Prepare a short joint presentation on your findings.

9. Find at least two examples of companies not mentioned in the text that act as transaction brokers and at least two examples of companies that provide a hands-on service. Prepare a short memo describing the services each company offers and explaining why the company should be categorized as a transaction broker or a hands-on service provider.

Online Content and Media

After reading this chapter, you will be able to:

- Identify the major trends in the consumption of media and online content, and the major revenue models for digital content delivery.
- Understand digital rights management.
- Understand the key factors affecting the online publishing industry.
- Understand the key factors affecting the online entertainment industry.

YouTube

and the Emerging Internet Broadcasting System (IBS)

Y ouTube is on its way to developing a new kind of television network, one based on the Internet. This new network will go head to head with cable and broadcast television giants competing for viewers, and of course, advertising dollars, which make it all happen. YouTube today supports 4 billion video streams a day, in some cases rivaling the audience sizes of cable and broadcast television, still the most popular source of video in the United States. The most popular television shows in 2012 (*The Big Bang Theory* and *American Idol*) routinely draw six million viewers each, and they stay for the full show. Reruns and syndication over the lifetime of the show can easily triple these numbers.

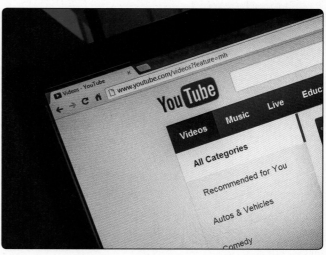

© Ingvar Björk / Alamy

Television advertising in the United States generates $70 billion in revenues, dwarfing YouTube's expected $3.2 billion in revenue in 2012. In the last few years, rivals such as Hulu, Apple, and Amazon have developed new Internet audiences for high-quality video, both from television series to movie rentals. And there's the problem: While YouTube's overall unique audience in the United States is about 146 million a month in 2012, it cannot easily be "monetized" if that audience only stays for an average of 14 minutes.

YouTube has figured out the solution to this problem: improve the quality and length of videos so visitors stay longer. There are three sources of high-quality entertainment videos in the United States: Hollywood studios, broadcast and cable television producers, and independent producers. YouTube is coming closer to being both a producer of video content and the world's largest Internet video distributor. In reality, it is becoming a third platform, right alongside cable television and broadcast television. YouTube is being joined by other Internet juggernauts Apple, Netflix, and Amazon, all of whom are reshaping the television and movie video industry. Together, these new Internet broadcasters threaten to disrupt the highly successful 50-year-old cable television industry, reshaping television and movies with their Internet Broadcasting System.

In 2011, Google initiated a number of new projects to improve the quality and advertising potential of its videos. Like its rivals who hold dominant positions in Internet distribution (Apple, Facebook, Netflix, and Microsoft), YouTube has reached out to Hollywood movie and New York television producers to offer streaming movies and television series. It has struck deals with Sony, Lionsgate, television networks, and MGM to rent full-length movies and television series. In April 2012, YouTube and MGM struck a deal to bring 600 new rental titles to YouTube. Google is late to the streaming movie

SOURCES: "Felix Baumgartner Jump: Record 8m Watch Live on YouTube," by John Plunkett, *The Guardian*, October 14, 2012; "YouTube to Double Down on Its 'Channel' Experiment," by Amir Efrati, *New York Times*, July 30, 2012; "CW Network's Rush to Web Rankles Some TV Stations," by Sam Schechner and Christopher Stewart, *Wall Street Journal*, April 19, 2012; "Youths Are Watching, but Less Often on TV," by Brian Stelter, *New York Times*, February 8, 2012; "Wall Street Journal Launches Video Channel For YouTube," *Wall Street Journal*, February 1, 2012; "New YouTube Channel is All About Games, Brands," by Tom Loftus, *Wall Street Journal*, January 30, 2012; "Hulu to Create More Original Shows," by Sam Schechner and Christopher Stewart, *Wall Street Journal*, January 17, 2012; "Food Network Executive to Run YouTube Channel," by Brian Stelter, *New York Times*, January 29, 2012; "New Rules for the Way We Watch," by David Carr, *New York Times*, December 24, 2011; "YouTube Announces Channels: Video Site Will Feel a Little More Like Cable TV," by D.M. Levine, *Adweek*, October 28, 2011; "New Layer of Content Amid Chaos on YouTube," by Ben Sisario, *New York Times*, March 12, 2011.

business, compared to Netflix, with 20,000 titles, and Amazon, with 5,000 streaming titles tied to its Prime Advantage program of free shipping. All these Web broadcasters have to share ad revenues with the copyright owners of the content, reducing profitability. One possible solution to this profit-reducing situation is for Web broadcasters to create their own content designed specifically for the Web audience of 12- to 34-year-olds who are watching less TV on traditional television sets than 34+ viewers, and instead, watching their tablets and smartphones more.

In October 2011, YouTube announced an $100 million initiative to create 100 YouTube channels. The idea is for Google to provide seed funding of up to several million dollars for independent and even well-known sources to produce video content and develop their brands online. Control over content is entirely with the producers, and Google receives all the ad revenue until the seed money is repaid, and then splits the ad revenues thereafter. About 50 channels are online in 2012, running the gamut from the IGN Entertainment game channel, MyIsh (a channel for discovering new music), celebrity channels (Madonna), a slew of sports channels (ESPN for kids), to the *Wall Street Journal*'s channel featuring *Off Duty*, a daily lifestyle show, and regular contributions from the *Journal*'s name-brand reporters. Yes, that's right: the *Wall Street Journal* newspaper is a major new online source of video, along with the *New York Times* and other papers. Foodies don't despair: Bruce Seidel, who produced shows for the Food Network, including the *Iron Chef*, is working with a YouTube media company, Electus, to produce a food channel that will drive the Internet food conversation. YouTube is providing $5 million in seed money to Electus. Electus, a production studio, is not an amateur outfit, formed by Ben Silverman, former co-chairman of NBC Entertainment, and owned by Barry Diller's IAC Inc., a firm with 30 years of television and Internet content development.

While YouTube's channels are aimed at niche audiences (just like the hundreds of cable channels), collectively they will play to an audience of 800 million people worldwide, who are viewing 4 billion hours of video each month. The YouTube content will not require a monthly subscription fee (outside of an Internet connection), and content will be paid for by advertising (as in existing television systems). Moreover, the user determines the schedule for on-demand viewing and the device on which to view the show. What's not to like?

To celebrate its early success with launching video channels, YouTube hosted 1,000 top advertisers, agencies, and content producers in May 2012 in New York in a coordinated effort called Digital Content Newfronts. YouTube joined Web broadcasters Yahoo, AOL, Microsoft, and Hulu in an effort to tap off a portion of the $70 billion TV ad budget. YouTube was pushing ad packages for up to $62 million to advertisers for multi-channel slots, with single-channel ad packages selling for $2–$4 million. By August 2012, YouTube had secured commitments for $150 million in advertising.

Across town, the traditional cable and television advertising industry was holding its annual meeting called the Upfronts, where advertisers, agencies, and TV executives haggle over the next year's advertising packages. The cable and broadcast television audience for 12–34-year-olds has begun to shrink for the first time since basic cable television began in 1976 with Ted Turner's network. The implication for the traditional television industry is that advertising dollars will slip away to the new Internet Broadcasting System.

The opening case illustrates how online content distributors like YouTube are both moving into premium content production and sales, and also becoming Internet stores for traditional television and movie content, possibly rivaling existing cable and satellite distributors. If consumers can find their favorite television shows and movies online, then why should they pay for cable or satellite TV? If consumers can watch their favorite shows on a smartphone or tablet, why should they buy a TV? As Internet users increasingly change their reading and viewing habits, spurred on by the growth of mobile media devices, they are challenging existing business models that worked for decades to support newspapers, books, magazines, television, and Hollywood movies. Clearly, the future of content—news, music, and video—is online. Today, the print industry, including newspapers, books, and magazines, is having a difficult time coping with the movement of their readership to the Web. Broadcast and cable television, along with Hollywood and the music labels, are also wrestling with outdated business models based on physical media. Established media giants are continuing to make extraordinary investments in unique online content, new technology, new digital distribution channels, and entirely new business models. Internet giants like Apple, Google, Amazon, and Facebook are competing to dominate online content distribution. In this chapter, we focus primarily on the publishing and entertainment industries as they attempt to transform their traditional media into Web-deliverable forms and experiences for consumers, while at the same time, earning profits.

9.1 ONLINE CONTENT

No other sector of the American economy has been so challenged by the Internet and the Web than the content industries. The online content industries are organized into two major categories: the print industries (newspapers, books, and magazines), and the online entertainment industries of television, feature-length movies, radio, video games, and music. Together, the online content industries generated revenues of about $15 billion in 2012 (including the online versions of print products).

As a communications medium, the Web is, by definition, a source of online content as well as a powerful new distribution platform. In this chapter, we will look closely at publishing (newspapers, books, and magazines) and entertainment (music, film, games, and television). These industries make up the largest share of the commercial content marketplace, both offline and online. In each of these industries, there are powerful offline brands, significant new pure-play online providers and distributors, consumer constraints and opportunities, a variety of legal issues, and new mobile technology platforms that offer an entirely new content distribution system in the form of smartphones and tablet computers.

CONTENT AUDIENCE AND MARKET: WHERE ARE THE EYEBALLS AND THE MONEY?

The average American adult spends around 4,200 hours each year consuming various media, twice the amount of time spent at work (2,000 hours/year) (see **Figure 9.1**). U.S. entertainment and media (E & M) revenues (both online and offline) in 2012 were estimated to be $488 billion, and they are expected to grow at a compound rate of 6% to a total of $598 billion in 2016 (U.S. Census Bureau, 2012; PWC, 2012). Sales of tablets and smartphones have created new revenue streams for entertainment and media firms as consumer behavior changes in response to the new technologies. Content is no longer tied to physical products, and can be delivered over the Internet to multiple mobile devices, reducing costs for consumers. Currently, online digital E&M revenue is 24% of total E&M revenue, or $117 billion in 2012. Analysts estimate that by 2016, digital E&M revenue will be 32% of E&M revenue or about $188 billion (PWC, 2012).

Media Utilization

The proliferation of new mobile media devices—tablets and smartphones—has led to an increase in the total amount of time spent listening to radio, watching TV and movies, and reading books, newspapers, and even magazines. An increasing percentage of this media engagement is digital, although traditional TV and radio audiences

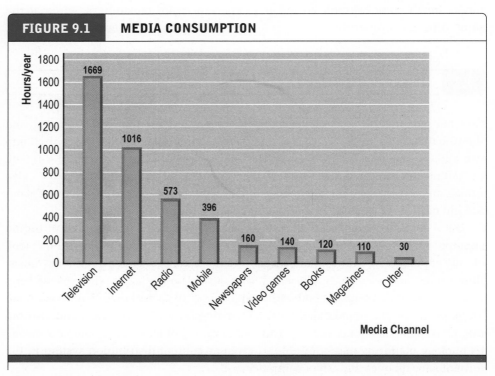

FIGURE 9.1   MEDIA CONSUMPTION

Each American spends around 4,200 hours annually, on average, consuming various media, mostly television, the Internet, radio, and mobile media, including games.

SOURCES: Based on data from eMarketer, Inc., 2012a; authors' estimates.

remain stable (Arbitron, 2012). The most popular medium is television, followed by the Internet, and then radio. Together, these three media account for more than 77% of the hours spent consuming various media. While the Internet is currently second, far behind television, Internet utilization has been growing rapidly (U.S. Census Bureau, 2012). Nielsen, a media rating service, reports that television viewing is down slightly in 2012 (.5%).

Internet and Traditional Media: Cannibalization versus Complementarity

Several studies reveal that time spent on the Internet reduces consumer time available for other media (Pew Internet & American Life Project, 2011). This is often referred to as "cannibalization" where one media form consumes another, or where one supplier's product reduces sales of another. True, there has been a massive shift of the general audience to the Web, and once there, a large percentage of time is spent on viewing content. Yet more recent data finds a more complex picture. Despite the availability of the Internet on high-resolution tablet computers, television viewing remains strong, video viewing on all devices has increased, and the reading of all kinds of books, including physical books, has increased. Total music consumption measured in hours a day listening to music has increased dramatically even as CDs decline, and movie consumption has increased dramatically even as DVD sales decline markedly. The impact of the Internet on media appears to be increasing the total demand for media, and even in some cases, stimulating demand for traditional products like books. It is also the case that content firms' physical products—printed newspapers, magazines, music CDs, and movie DVDs—are being replaced by digital versions.

Multimedia use reduces the cannibalization impact of the Internet for some visual and aural media, but obviously not for reading physical books or newspapers. And even for these print media, the Internet is simply an alternative source; Internet users are increasing the time they spend online reading newspapers, magazines, and even books. Ironically, the new mobile media platform of smartphones and tablet computers has led to an explosion in reading of both newspapers and books, but digital versions, not the printed versions. Content is not being cannabalized even though the Internet is cannibalizing physical media.

Media Revenues

An examination of media revenues reveals a somewhat different pattern when compared to media consumption (see **Figure 9.2**). Television accounts for 28% of media revenues, print media (books, newspapers, and magazines) accounts for 37%, video games 9%, Internet media (video) 7%, music media (radio and recorded music) 11%, and box office 4%. Internet media, while small now, is growing at 12% annually, far faster than traditional media revenues.

Three Revenue Models for Digital Content Delivery: Subscription, A La Carte, and Advertising-Supported (Free and Freemium)

There are three revenue models for delivering content on the Internet. The two "pay" models are subscriptions (usually all you can eat) and a la carte (pay for what you

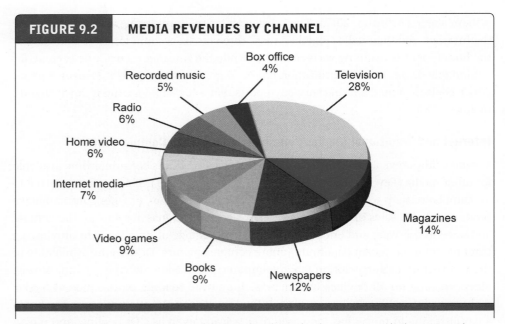

FIGURE 9.2 | **MEDIA REVENUES BY CHANNEL**

- Box office 4%
- Television 28%
- Recorded music 5%
- Radio 6%
- Home video 6%
- Internet media 7%
- Video games 9%
- Books 9%
- Newspapers 12%
- Magazines 14%

Traditional media still dominate the entertainment and media market, but Internet media (streaming videos, music, and content) is the fastest growing segment.

SOURCES: Based on data from industry sources; authors' estimates.

use). The third model uses advertising revenue to provide content for free (to users), usually with a "freemium" (higher price) option. There is also completely free, user-generated content, which we will discuss later. Contrary to early analysts' projections that "free" would drive "paid" out of business ("information wants to be free"), it turns out that both models are viable now and in the near future. Consumers increasingly choose to pay for high-quality, convenient, and unique content, and they have gladly accepted "free" advertiser-supported content when that content is deemed not worth paying for but entertaining nevertheless. There's nothing contradictory about all three models working in tandem and cooperatively: free content can drive customers to paid content, as the recorded music firms have discovered with services like Pandora.

Online Content Consumption

Now let's look at what kinds of online content Internet users purchase or view online (**Figure 9.3**). Nearly 50% of Internet users read newspapers and 43% listen to radio, the two most popular activities. Casual games (41%) and TV shows (41%) are nearly as popular, followed by movies and music downloads and streams. E-book consumption (23%) has grown at triple-digit rates since the Kindle was introduced in 2007 and the iPad in 2010. What this reveals is that Internet users retain their affinity to traditional formats—newspapers, radio, TV shows, and music tracks and albums—and bring these tastes to the Internet.

Figure 9.4 shows the estimated revenues from the online entertainment and media industries, projected to 2015. In 2012, total paid online content was estimated

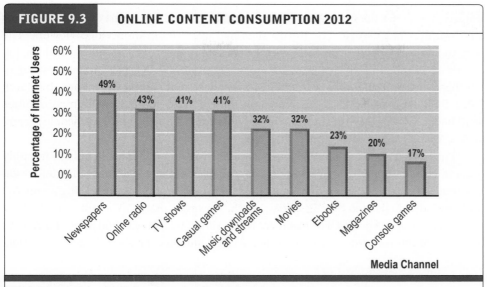

FIGURE 9.3   **ONLINE CONTENT CONSUMPTION 2012**

SOURCES: Based on data from industry sources; authors' estimates.

to be $11.2 billion, and is expected to reach $17 billion by 2015. Online video (including premium movies) and music are the largest and projected fastest growing online segments, followed by TV.

Now let's look at the fastest growing paid content area: videos (which includes movies, short videos, and TV shows). This audience is huge and growing very rapidly.

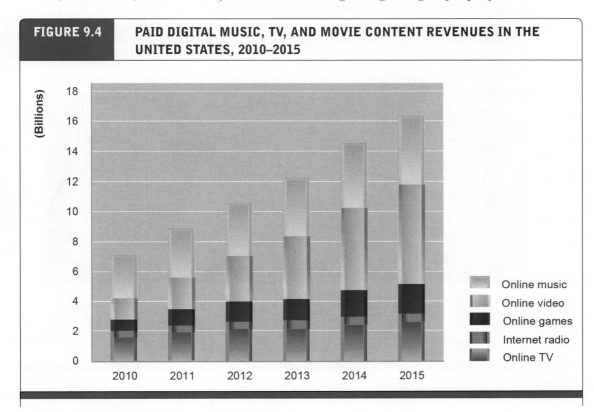

FIGURE 9.4   **PAID DIGITAL MUSIC, TV, AND MOVIE CONTENT REVENUES IN THE UNITED STATES, 2010–2015**

SOURCES: Based on data from industry sources; authors' estimates.

Figure 9.5 shows the top online video sites in March 2012 in terms of unique viewers and minutes per viewer. The top 10 sites had over 180 million video viewers. The largest site was Google (YouTube) with 157 million viewers of 17.6 million videos, followed by Yahoo, and the fast growing music video site, VEVO. The monetary value of all these videos is that they attract large audiences that can be shown ads. In March 2012, 9.5 billion video ads were shown on the Internet, about 3.9 billion ad minutes watched, reaching 52% of the Internet population (about 120 million people) (comScore, 2012).

The overall size of the online video audience (with more than 180 million monthly unique viewers in the United States) is about the same size as the traditional television audience. There are 115 million households with televisions, representing about 200 million individuals who tune in every month. However, major TV events tend to draw a much higher viewership. For instance, 111.3 million people watched Super Bowl XLVI in 2012. No Internet video has drawn such a large audience during a single time period.

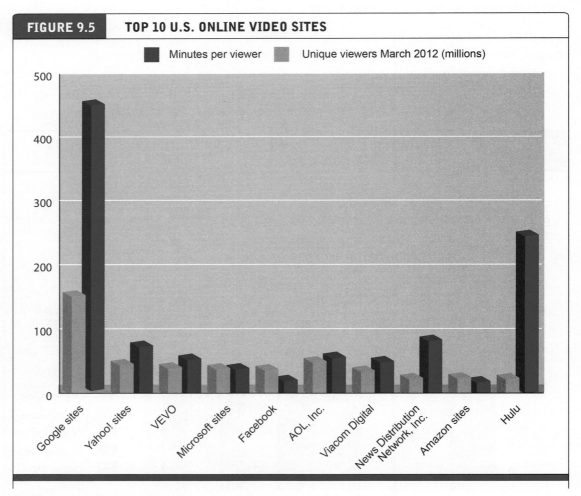

FIGURE 9.5 | **TOP 10 U.S. ONLINE VIDEO SITES**

SOURCES: Based on data from comScore, 2012

Free or Fee: Attitudes About Paying for Content and the Tolerance for Advertising

In the early years of online content, multiple surveys found that large majorities of the Internet audience expected to pay nothing for online content although equally large majorities were willing to accept advertising as a way to pay for free content. In reality, on the early Web, there wasn't much high-quality content. By 2012, attitudes towards paying for content had greatly changed. Until Internet services such as iTunes arrived, few thought the "fee" model could compete with the "free" model, and most Internet aficionados and experts concluded that information on the Internet wants to be free. Cable TV systems (networks themselves) offer a totally different history: they always charged for service and content, and cable TV experts never thought information wanted to be free. Neither did the Hollywood and New York media companies that paid for and provided the content to television and movie theaters. In 2012, millions of Internet users pay for high-quality content delivered on a convenient device such as a smartphone or tablet computer. Like cable TV, Apple iTunes charges for service and content as well. In a demonstration of just how much quality online content is worth paying for, by 2012, Apple had sold 20 billion songs, 450 million TV shows, and more than 100 million movies. Pandora, the second largest source of Internet music, and the largest streaming service, has 20 million monthly unique visitors. While an estimated 16 million Internet users in the United States still download songs from illegal P2P sites, 80 million bought music from legal sites in 2012, generating $3.6 billion in sales (eMarketer, Inc., 2012a). Most experts thought free would drive out fee models. Yet the percentage of illegal downloaders in the United States shrank from 16% to 9% of Internet users in the last two years (NPD Group, 2011). Worldwide, iTunes has more than 400 million customers with credit cards on file.

DIGITAL RIGHTS MANAGEMENT (DRM) AND WALLED GARDENS

Content producers—newspapers, book publishers, television, movie, and music producers—generate revenue and profits from their creations, and they protect these revenue streams through copyright. In the digital age, when exact copies and widescale distribution of works is possible, protecting the copyrights to content is a major challenge.

Digital rights management (DRM) refers to a combination of technical (both hardware and software) and legal means for protecting digital content from unlimited reproduction and distribution without permission. Essentially, DRM can prevent users from purchasing and making copies for widespread distribution over the Internet without compensating the content owners. Newer cloud-based digital services have made traditional DRM software less useful. Most music firms with subscription services use technologies that limit the time period that a song can be played without re-subscribing. For instance, songs downloaded from Rhapsody, the largest music subscription service, will not play after 30 days unless the user pays the monthly subscription fee. And if you don't pay, you will lose access to all your songs. Movies streamed from Netflix are technically difficult for the average user to capture and share. Likewise, music streamed from Pandora is cumbersome to record and share. These newer digital services, including both Apple and Amazon, use a kind of DRM

digital rights management (DRM)
refers to the combination of technical and legal means for protecting digital content from unlimited reproduction without permission

called "walled garden" to restrict the widespread sharing of content. E-books purchased from Amazon can only be played on Kindles or Kindle apps running on smartphones, tablets, computers, or browsers. By locking the content to a physical device, or a digital stream with no local storage, the appliance makers derive additional revenues and profits by locking customers into their service or device.

9.2   THE ONLINE PUBLISHING INDUSTRY

Nothing is quite so fundamental to a civilized society as reading text. Text is the way we record our history, current events, thoughts, and aspirations, and transmit them to all others in the civilization who can read. Even videos require scripts. Today, the publishing industry (composed of books, newspapers, magazines, and periodicals) is a $82 billion media sector based originally on print, and now moving rapidly to the Internet (U.S. Census Bureau, 2012). The Internet offers the text publishing industry an opportunity to move toward a new generation of newspapers, magazines, and books that are produced, processed, stored, distributed, and sold over the Web, available anytime, anywhere, and on any device. The same Internet offers the possibility of destroying many existing print-based businesses that may not be able to make this transition and remain profitable.

ONLINE NEWSPAPERS

Newspapers in 2012 are the most troubled segment of the publishing industry, troubles that result almost exclusively from the availability of alternatives to the printed newspaper, as well as a sluggish response by management to the opportunities on the Internet for news, if not newspapers. Also important is the failure of newspaper management to protect its valuable content from being distributed for free by headline aggregators such as Yahoo, MSN, and Google, as well as tens of millions of bloggers and tweeters. These search firms can index online newspaper content, and provide search results to users' queries (as they display ads to those same users and derive revenue). While these search firms do link to the actual newspaper articles, they have in the meantime generated revenue for themselves based on the newspaper article contents. There wouldn't be a Google or Yahoo news functionality without traditional reporters and editors who work for newspapers and create the content. As you may have noticed, a single, original, high-quality newspaper article generates hundreds if not thousands of Internet knockoff articles on blogs, news aggregation sites, and content generator sites.

Over 60% of newspapers have reduced news staff in the last three years, and 61% report shrinking the size of the newspaper. Readership has been declining for 10 years, print edition advertising is down 15% a year, subscriptions are down, and old print readers are not being replaced by young readers, who instead get their news online. To make matters worse, in the slow growth period of 2009–2012, online ads declined another 28%, and the amount spent on Internet advertising in general now equals that spent on newspaper advertising. Alternative online sources such as Yahoo, Google, and even blogs, have became major sources of news for many Americans. Much of this "news" is redistributed content generated by newspapers! Alternatives to newspaper classified ads like Craigslist have decimated newspaper classified revenues.

But there is some good news too. Online readership of newspapers is growing at more than 10% a year. New reading devices from smartphones to e-readers, iPads, and tablet PCs connected to wireless networks offer opportunities for online newspapers to be read everywhere. A new Internet culture is supportive of paying for quality content. Newspaper owners, faced with extinction, are exploring ways to protect their content, and are introducing paid "premium" news and views, a la carte purchase of articles, subscriptions to digital versions, and online apps for mobile devices.

Audience Size and Growth

According to the Newspaper Association of America, in 2012, print newspapers had around 46 million paid subscribers, down from 62 million in 1990. On an average day, 49 million people read a print newspaper and 150 million read a newspaper online. Nearly 50% of all Web users on a typical day visit an online newspaper. The online audience increases the overall footprint of the newspaper media.

There are more than 10,000 online newspapers in the world. Globally, online newspaper readership is growing at 17% a year. According to comScore, online newspapers experienced very strong growth in recent quarters. (See **Figure 9.6** for a list of the top eight.) The online newspapers attract a wealthy and consumer-intense demographic, reaching 64% of 25- to 34-year-olds and 75% of individuals in households

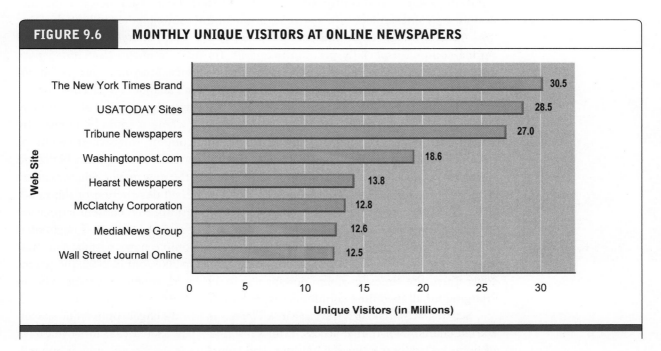

FIGURE 9.6 **MONTHLY UNIQUE VISITORS AT ONLINE NEWSPAPERS**

Online newspaper readership is expanding rapidly as more people get their news online, and as smartphone and tablet apps become more widespread.

SOURCES: Based on data from Myers, 2012.

earning more than $100,000 a year on average throughout the quarter. The online newspaper audience is also highly engaged, generating 4.1 billion page views each month, spending nearly 3.4 billion minutes browsing the sites (comScore, 2011). The average online visitor stayed on the site for 35 to 45 minutes. Online newspapers are the dominant local Web site: 62% of Internet users look for local news on a local newspaper Web site. Given this huge online newspaper audience, it is clear that the future of newspapers lies in the online mobile market even as readership and subscriptions to the traditional print newspapers continue to decline at a steady pace.

Next to social networks, newspapers produce the largest online audiences of any media, and in that sense, contrary to popular opinion, are one of the most successful forms of online content to date. The Internet provides existing branded newspapers the opportunity to extend their brands to a new online audience, and also gives entrepreneurial firms the opportunity to offer services—such as classified job listings—on the Web that were previously delivered by newspapers. Online newspapers are the top choice for local news and information for Internet users in the United States.

While newspapers have done an excellent job at increasing their Web presence and audience, few have reached break-even operations. Instead, online classified and advertising revenues have not kept pace with the fall in revenues from their traditional print editions.

Newspaper Business Models

The online newspaper industry has gone through several business models, from fee to free, and most recently, struggling to return to a fee-based metered and subscription business model. In the past, a few online newspapers such as the *New York Times*, *Wall Street Journal*, and *Financial Times* (U.K.) charged for some or all online content, especially premium content. In the case of the *New York Times*, access to the *New York Times* archives was a paid service. Most newspapers did not charge for online content, and even the *New York Times* abandoned its Times Select subscription service for archived content. The result was that content generated by newspapers became freely available across the Web, where it could be indexed by search engines that redistributed the headlines and content. Newspaper headlines became the primary content on Google News and Yahoo News. Newspapers benefited from this because a Google listing brought readers to the newspaper, where readers could be exposed to advertising. In 2012, the threatened destruction of the newspaper industry caused newspaper management to rethink free content supported by online ads placed at the newspapers' sites. The Associated Press has negotiated licensing agreements with Google, Yahoo, and other online news portals. The *Wall Street Journal* was prepared to abandon the fee model in 2008, but in 2009, the parent News Corp., the largest owner of newspapers in the world, announced plans to begin charging for all its online content across the world.

Starting in March 2011, the *New York Times*, the world's largest online newspaper, started charging for online access. Print subscribers pay $300 a year for seven days of home or business-delivered editions, and complete free access to any online editions from the Web to smartphone apps. Unlimited digital access is about $420 a year. Those who are not a print or digital subscriber are limited to 10 free articles a month, after which readers will have to become digital subscribers at $15 to $35 a month depending on the devices used to access the *Times*. In the first month of operation, the online edition had 100,000 paid subscribers, and in March 2012, the paper hit 480,000 paid subscribers. The *Times* online subscriptions produce more than $200 million in revenue, nearly 10% of its overall revenues.

Tablet computers and e-readers offer newspapers an opportunity to connect directly with their readers anytime and anywhere using digital newsstands such as Google and Apple newsstand apps, where newspapers can display their apps. NewspaperDirect is an online store that has same-day online editions of nearly 2,210 newspapers from 94 countries in 54 languages. Unlimited subscriptions are $29.00 a month, economy editions are $9.95 for 31 articles, and most individual articles cost 99 cents. See the *Insight on Society* case, *Can Apps and Video Save Newspapers?*

E-BOOKS AND ONLINE BOOK PUBLISHING

In April 2000, Stephen King, one of America's most popular writers, published a novella called *Riding the Bullet*. This novella was only available as an e-book. King was the first major fiction writer to create an e-book-only volume of a new work. King's publisher, Simon & Schuster, arranged for sales online through online retailers such as Amazon. In the first day, there were 400,000 downloads, so many that Amazon's servers crashed several times. More than 600,000 downloads occurred in the first week. While Amazon gave the book away for free in the first two weeks, when it began charging $2.50 for a 66-page novella—about the same price per page as a standard King hardcover novel—sales continued to be brisk.

Ten years later, on April 15, 2010, Amanda Hocking, an unknown and unpublished self-publisher from Austin, Minnesota, uploaded one of her vampire novels, *My Blood Approves*, to Amazon's self-publishing site, and later to Barnes & Noble e-book store. Her novels had been rejected by many of the publishing houses in New York. By March 2011, she had sold more than 1 million copies of her e-books, which generally sell for 99 cents to $2.99, and earned more than $2 million. Starting out with sales of 5 to 10 books a day, Hocking's sales have reached as many as 100,000 a day when she first publishes a novel. In the same month, she signed a traditional publishing contract worth $2 million with St. Martin's Press. In 2012, Hocking is listed as one of the Amazon 99 cent millionaires.

In the space of a decade, e-books have gone from an unusual experiment by a major author, to an everyday experience for millions of Americans, and an exciting new market for authors. Sales of e-books have exploded in a few short years, and the process of writing, selling, and distributing books has radically changed. E-books sales in 2012 were expected to be $4.2 billion dollars (see **Figure 9.7**). An entire new channel for self-published authors now exists, a channel not controlled by the major New York publishing houses and their professional editors. In essence, by passing professional editors and publishers, authors can now "crowdsource" the distribution of their books. Recognizing the booming self-publishing market, Penguin (the second largest trade book publisher in the world after Random House) purchased the self-publishing company Author Solutions in July 2012. Author Solutions has published 150,000 authors and more than 190,000 books. Other publishers have made similar

INSIGHT ON SOCIETY

CAN APPS AND VIDEO SAVE NEWSPAPERS?

The initial reaction of the newspaper industry to the Internet and Web was to build Web sites as a way to attract an Internet audience and advertisers. It didn't work. But because of the Internet, newspaper readership is actually up, not down. In 2012, more than half of newspaper readers get their news from an online edition. Online readership is growing: over 113 million people read newspapers online in 2012, nearly half of all adult users of the Internet, and readership is growing at 10% a year. The social, local, mobile platform driven by smartphones and tablet computers offers newspapers many new opportunities to attract subscribers and advertisers. There are four factors that might just keep newspapers around.

The first is the paid subscription business model. Newspapers are increasingly using a freemium business model and charging for online content. Information wants to be expensive if it's current, relevant, accurate, and timely. The *Wall Street Journal* led the way in the United States with an online premium service: $260 a year for both the print and online editions, and $207 a year for the digital edition. Today, the *Journal* has nearly 600,000 online subscribers, 80,000 of whom use tablets and smartphones.

The *New York Times* led the pay revolution for general-purpose newspapers by announcing a paid subscription freemium service in 2011. Today, the *Times* has more than 450,000 online subscribers, although the ad revenue does not match the revenues lost from declining physical paper sales. In May 2012, the *Times* reduced the number of free articles to 10 per day in an effort to encourage more paid subscriptions.

The second factor is the arrival of the mobile platform, which is proving to be a boon for online newspapers. In a survey by comScore, over 67% of online newspaper readers said they use multiple devices—PCs, tablets, and/or smartphones. Apps enable the newspapers to charge a la carte for articles, develop different versions at different price points, personalize the content, and above all, protect the content from being copied without payment. From a customer experience point of view, high-resolution tablets are uniquely suited for the large format, pictures, and videos found in today's online newspapers.

The third factor is video content. If you visit online or app-based newspapers, you'll see that online newspapers are increasingly differentiated from traditional print newspapers because of extensive use of video. Online newspapers are redesigning themselves to be more like CNN or MSNBC television shows. Ads displayed alongside videos pay over $50 per CPM (cost per thousand clicks), whereas ordinary display ads pay only $5 per CPM or less. For newspapers starved for revenue, the future is video, driven by a professional reporting and editorial staff.

The final factor is that news is predominantly local. In 2012, there are over 500 local online newspapers supported by local advertisers. While not as sophisticated in their use of video or apps, these local papers are building a strong local readership, and hopefully a successful business model.

There are many challenges ahead for the newspaper industry. Online revenues are not high enough right now to overcome the loss of ad revenues from the print editions but they are a fast growing revenue stream. These revenues soften the blow of declining print revenues, and give newspapers some breathing room to innovate and experiment. So far, the experiments online have been successful.

SOURCES: "Newspaper Websites See Increases in Unique and Average Daily Visitors in First Quarter," by Marianna Hendricks, Newspaper Association of America, April 25, 2012; "Smart Devices Attract News Readers," eMarketer, April 11, 2012; "New York Times Nears Half-million Online Subscriber Mark, Halves Free Article Allowance to Celebrate," New York Times Communications Group, March 12, 2012; "Papers Put Faith in Paywalls," by Russell Adams, *Wall Street Journal*, March 4, 2012.

FIGURE 9.7	E-BOOK SALES

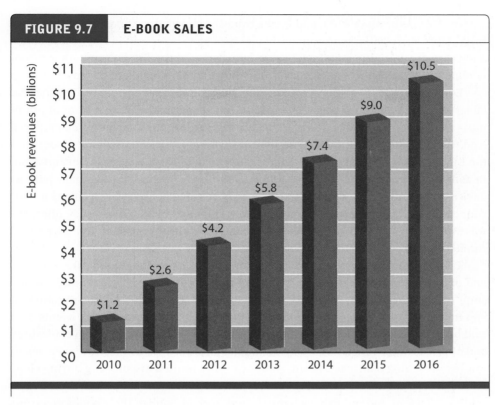

E-book sales have exploded as a result of the rival Amazon and Apple e-book platforms.
SOURCE: Based on data from eMarketer, Inc., 2012b.

purchases in the hope that successful books and authors will emerge from the burgeoning online author crowd (Bosman, 2012).

Amazon and Apple: The New Digital Media Ecosystems

Prospects for e-books picked up in 2001 with the introduction of Apple's iPod, which later became a platform for e-books (iPod Touch). In 2004, Sony introduced the first e-ink reader (Sony Librie). In 2007, the iPhone smartphone was released with a high definition color screen that could be used to read books.

The future of e-books was finally and firmly established when Amazon introduced its Kindle in 2007 to a skeptical public and critical industry observers. The early Kindle readers used electronic ink technology, providing a higher resolution than PCs and a longer battery life than portable book readers. The early Kindle had 16 megabytes of memory and could store 200 books. More important, the reader was linked to the Internet through AT&T's cell network, permitting users to access Amazon's bookstore where they could browse, search, and purchase e-books. Amazon's bookstore is the largest online bookstore on the Internet. Today the Kindle Fire is no longer simply an e-book reader, but rather a media and entertainment portable device.

In 2012, Amazon's e-book and media store contained an estimated 1 million book titles. More than 800 million Kindles of all types have been sold in the United States, and there are 46 million adults who use e-readers like the Kindle (and other e-book readers like the Barnes & Noble Nook, and tablet computers like the iPad).

E-books received another large boost in 2010 when Apple introduced its first iPad tablet computer. With its large 11.7" screen and access to the iTunes Store of online music, video, TV, and book content, the iPad was an ideal media entertainment device. And with its high-resolution screen, the iPad was an even better e-book reader than the Kindle, albeit not easily slipped into a purse. While Amazon got the jump on Apple in dedicated e-book readers, Apple's approach from the beginning was a multipurpose device that could handle movies, music, magazines, and books, as well having a Wi-Fi connection to the Internet. Apple's iBookstore at launch in 2010 had 60,000 titles, and was estimated to have about 150,000 titles in 2012 (much smaller than Amazon's store). Apple has sold about 84 million iPads since 2007.

The result of the Amazon and Apple ecosystems, combining hardware, software, and online mega stores, is an explosion in online book content, readership, authorship, marketing, and at least a partial upending of the traditional book publishing and marketing channels. In the traditional process, authors worked with agents, who sold book manuscripts to editors and publishers, who sold books through bookstores, and at prices determined largely by the publishers. Because bookstores had a vested interest in selling books at a profit, there was only limited discounting during clearance sales. In the new publishing model, authors still write books, but then bypass traditional agent and publisher channels and instead publish their books electronically on the Amazon or Apple online stores. Prices are determined by the author, usually much lower than traditional books depending on the popularity of the author, and the platform takes a percentage of the sale (usually 30%). New self-published authors typically give away their early works to develop an audience, and then, when an audience appears, charge a small amount for their books, typically 99 cents to $2.99. Marketing occurs by word of mouth on social networks, author blogs, and public readings. While a small percentage of all books are produced this way, it is a growing and popular form of publishing and striking it rich, sometimes. They're called "99 cent millionaires," and there's enough around to arouse the passions of thousands of potential writers of the great American novel, as well as lesser genres from police procedurals to paranormal romance writers.

What Are the Challenges of the Digital E-Book Platform?

Despite, or because, of the rapid growth in e-books, the book publishing industry is in stable, even robust condition. There are two major challenges facing book publishers. Responses to these challenges will shape the future existence of the book publishing industry as we know it. These two challenges are cannibalization and finding the right business model.

cannibalization

when sales of new digital products replace sales of traditional products

Cannibalization in digital markets refers to the potential for new digital products to rapidly reduce the sales of existing physical products. This can be a threat to digital content firms insofar as the prices and profits available from selling digital products are much lower than prices and profits from physical products. Sometimes the situation is complicated by large online digital distributors such as Amazon, who want to maximize their sales of physical devices by offering free or low-priced content, and have little short-term interest protecting the profits of content owners and producers. Both the music and newspaper industries have suffered cannibalization, with revenues declining by 50% or more over the last decade. The evidence from book publishing is mixed so far. Overall, book publishing revenues in 2011 were $27.2 billion, down 2.5% from 2010. As digital revenues have expanded, print book sales have gone down about $1 billion from the previous year. The overall picture that emerges is that the rapid growth of e-books and online sales has lowered sales of physical books in brick-and-mortar stores. However, much of this lost revenue is being made up by the growth in e-book sales online. Total readership has increased with the popularity of e-books and the widespread adoption of Kindles and iPads.

Finding the right business model is also a challenge. The e-book industry is composed of intermediary retailers (both brick-and-mortar stores and online merchants), traditional publishers, technology developers, device makers (e-readers), and vanity presses (self-publishing service companies). Together, these players have pursued a wide variety of business models and developed many alliances in an effort to move text onto the computer screen.

Interactive Books: Converging Technologies

The future of e-books will also depend in part on changes in the concept of a book. The modern book is not really very different from the first two-facing page, bound books that began to appear in seventeenth-century Europe. The traditional book has a very simple, non-digital operating system: text appears left to right, pages are numbered, there is a front and back cover, and text pages are bound together by stitching or glue. In educational and reference books, there is an alphabetical index in the back of the book that permits direct access to the book's content. While these traditional books will be with us for many years given their portability, ease of use, and flexibility, a parallel new world of interactive e-books is expected to emerge in the next five years. Interactive books combine audio, video, and photography with text, providing the reader with a multimedia experience thought to be more powerful than simply reading a book. In 2012, Apple released iBook Author, an app to help authors create interactive books. Hundreds of children's books are already built as interactive books. Some experts believe that traditional print books will be curiosities by 2020.

MAGAZINES REBOUND ON THE TABLET PLATFORM

Magazines in the United States reached their peak circulation in the early 1980s, with more than 40 million people reading some kind of weekly or monthly magazine. Most Americans got their national and international news from the three weekly news magazines, *Time*, *Newsweek*, and *U.S. News and World Report*. The "glossies," as general-interest magazines were known, attracted readers with superb writing, short form articles, and stunning photography brought to life by very high-resolution color printing (Vega, 2012).

Circulation fell after 2000 in part because of the Internet. At first, the Internet and the Web did not have much impact on magazine sales, in part because the PC was no match for the high-resolution, large-format pictures found in, say, *Life* or *Time*. Eventually, as screens improved, as video on the Web became common, and the economics of color publishing changed, magazine circulation began to plummet and advertisers turned their attention to the digital platform on the Web, where readers were increasingly getting their news, general-interest journalism, and photographic accounts of events.

Magazine newsstand sales dropped from 22 million units in 2001 to 11 million in 2011 (Sass, 2011). Yet special-interest, celebrity, homemaking, and automobile magazines remained stable. In the last half of 2011, sales continued a fall of nearly 10% from the previous year. Increasingly, magazine readers were turning to the Internet for celebrity gossip and news, unusual stories, pictures, and video.

Despite the shrinkage of print subscription and newsstand sales, the growth of digital magazine sales has been extraordinary. Almost one-third of the Internet population in the United States (about 74 million people) read magazines online, and digital magazine circulation has doubled in 2012 to 3.29 million copies. More than 35% of tablet computer owners read magazine content once a week (eMarketer, Inc., 2012a). Popular Web sites like Pinterest, an image-collecting site that attracts millions of women, and Facebook, Yahoo, and Twitter, are the largest drivers of traffic to digital magazines (Vega, 2012). The widespread adoption of tablet computers has helped create the "visual Internet," where glossy magazine publishers, who are inherently oriented to richly detailed color photography, can display their works and advertisements to great advantage.

With hundreds of popular online magazines to choose from, magazine aggregators like Zinio and Apple's Newsstand make it possible for customers to find their favorite magazines using a single app. A **magazine aggregator** is a Web site or app that offers users online subscriptions and sales of many digital magazines.

magazine aggregator
a Web site or app that provides subscriptions and sales of many digital magazines

9.3 THE ONLINE ENTERTAINMENT INDUSTRY

The entertainment industry is generally considered to be composed of four traditional, commercial players and one new arrival: television, radio broadcasting, Hollywood films, music, and video games (the new arrival). **Figure 9.8** illustrates the estimated relative sizes of these commercial entertainment markets as of 2012. By far, the largest entertainment producer is television (broadcast, satellite, and cable), and then motion pictures, followed by music, radio, and video games (both stand-alone and online games). While online, computer, and console games have grown to be larger than film box office revenues, total Hollywood film revenues dwarf the game industry when DVD sales and rentals, licensing, and ancillary products are added.

Along with the other content industries, the entertainment segment is undergoing a transformation brought about by the Internet. Several forces are at work. Accelerated platform development such as the iPhone/iPad video and music platform, other smartphones and tablets, the Amazon music and video platform, not to mention the Netflix streaming platform, have changed consumer preferences and increased demand for music, video, television, and game entertainment delivered over Internet

---

| **FIGURE 9.8** | **THE FIVE MAJOR PLAYERS IN THE ENTERTAINMENT INDUSTRY: 2012 ESTIMATED REVENUES** |

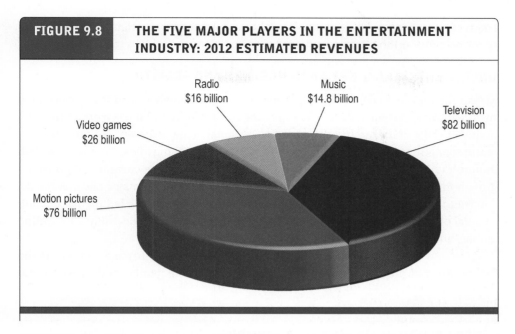

SOURCES: Based on data from industry sources; authors' estimates.

---

devices whether in subscription or a la carte pay-per-view forms. Other social network platforms are also spurring the delivery of entertainment content to desktop and laptop PCs and smartphones. Facebook is attempting to become an important entertainment distribution site. iTunes and other legitimate music subscription services like Pandora, Spotify, and Rhapsody have demonstrated a viable business model where millions of consumers are willing to pay reasonable prices for high-quality content, portability, and convenience. The growth in broadband has obviously made possible both wired and wireless delivery of all forms of entertainment over the Internet, potentially displacing cable and broadcast television networks. The development of high-quality customer experiences at online entertainment sites has in many cases eliminated the need for digital rights management restrictions. Closed platforms, like the Kindle, also work to obviate the need for DRM. Subscription services for streaming music and video are inherently copyright-protected because the content is never downloaded to a computer (similar to cable TV). All of these forces combined in 2012 to bring about a transformation in the entertainment industries.

The ideal Internet content e-commerce world would allow consumers to watch any movie, listen to any music, watch any TV show, and play any game, when they want, where they want, and using whatever Internet device is convenient. Consumers would be billed monthly for these services by a single provider of Internet service. This idealized version of a convergent media world is many years away, but clearly this is the direction of the Internet-enabled entertainment industry.

When we think of the producers of entertainment in the offline world, we tend to think about television networks such as ABC, Fox, NBC, HBO, or CBS; Hollywood film studios such as MGM, Disney, Paramount, and Twentieth Century Fox; and music labels such as Sony BMG, Atlantic Records, Columbia Records, and Warner Records.

Interestingly, none of these international brand names have a significant entertainment presence on the Internet.

ONLINE ENTERTAINMENT AUDIENCE SIZE AND GROWTH

Measuring the size and growth of the Internet content audience is far less precise than measuring a television audience. Recognizing the difficulties of measuring an Internet audience, let's first examine the use of "traditional" entertainment content, such as feature-length movies, music, online TV, online radio, and games; then we will look at non-traditional online entertainment. **Figure 9.9** shows the current and projected growth for commercial online entertainment revenues for the major players: music, Internet radio, online TV, online games, and online video. Music led the list of commercial entertainment revenues in 2012, followed by online video, online TV, online games, and Internet radio.

There will be some interesting changes by 2015. Video surpasses music as the largest form of online entertainment. Online TV, online games, and radio remain

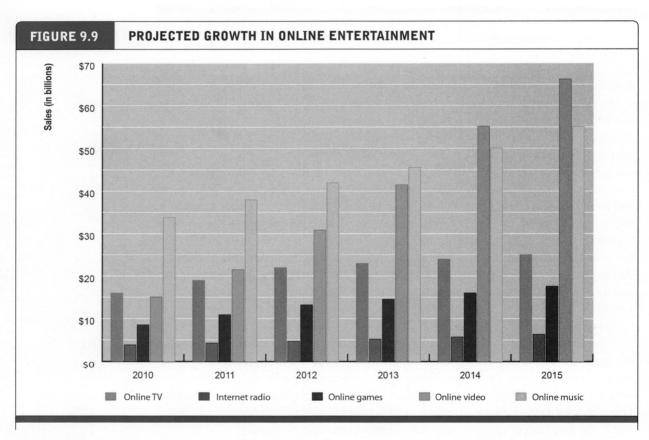

| FIGURE 9.9 | PROJECTED GROWTH IN ONLINE ENTERTAINMENT |

Among commercial forms of mass entertainment, online music downloads engaged the largest number of people and generated the largest revenues on the Web in 2012. However, online video and games will grow dramatically in the next four years, with video becoming larger than music in 2015 revenues.

SOURCES: Based on data from industry sources; authors' estimates.

relatively smaller generators of revenue, declining in significance when compared to music and video.

TELEVISION AND PREMIUM VIDEO

In 2012, about 170 million Americans watched video online, about 70% of the Internet population (Nielsen, 2012a). Increasingly, the TV household is a cross-platform phenomenon. Every week, Americans watch about 35 hours of TV on traditional TV sets, but nearly 6 hours using a computer, 2.5 hours watching time-shifted TV using a digital video recorder or cable system with cloud storage, and 7 minutes watching video on a smartphone. While teens continue to spend more time texting than ever, 70% of college students ages 18 to 30 report watching streamed television shows (eMarketer, Inc., 2011a). Netflix is the second largest distributor of premium online video with $3.2 billion in 2012 revenues (half of which come from streaming video), 24 million subscribers, and annual growth at 50%. The largest online video distributor is Apple's iTunes (which provides downloads or cloud storage but not streaming). Netflix is close to exceeding iTunes video revenues.

The television industry, the major source of premium video on the Internet, is beginning a transition to a new delivery platform, the Internet and mobile smartphones and tablet computers. This transition closely follows an earlier but related transition to digital video recorders and "time-shifting" by consumers who no longer were constrained by television executives' programming and scheduling decisions. The current transition to Internet delivery of television is not leading to a decline in traditional television viewing, which has in fact increased. The new platform is just changing how, when, and where consumers can watch TV. Cloud computing, the storage and streaming of content from large Internet datacenters rather than on individual personal devices, has created a large shift away from ownership of content, and a focus instead on access to content anywhere, anytime, from any device. Social networks have enabled a new kind of "social TV" where consumers share comments while viewing television shows. The most important activity in today's television household may not be what's on screen, but instead what's being said about what's on screen. Television rating agencies today do not have a methodology for measuring this kind of engagement.

Expansion of broadband networks, especially those serving mobile devices such as Wi-Fi and high-speed cellular networks, and the growth of cloud servers, has enabled the growth of a whole new class of television distributors. Cloud distributors, like Apple's iCloud service, allow users to purchase video and movies, store them in iCloud, and view the entertainment from any device, anywhere. Whereas the dominant way consumers obtained a TV signal in the past was from over-the-air broadcasters, cable TV, or satellite distributors, a new "over-the-top" channel has developed led by powerful technology companies such as Apple, Google, Hulu, VUDU, Netflix, and many others, all of whom offer consumers access to television shows and some full-length feature movies. **Over-the-top (OTT)** entertainment services refers to the use of the Internet to deliver online entertainment services to the home. "Over-the-top" refers to the fact that the entertainment service rides "on top" of other network services like cable TV and telephone service. It's as if we have a new Internet Broadcasting System

over-the-top (OTT)
use of the Internet to deliver entertainment services to the home on cable TV or FiOS networks

with many new players. This new network is obviously a threat to cable television and the other distributors, who, in turn, have their on-demand services for television series and movies.

The Internet and the new mobile platform have also changed the viewing experience. The best screen when commuting or traveling is the smartphone and tablet. More importantly, Internet-enabled social networks like Facebook and Twitter have made TV viewing a social experience shared among neighbors, friends, and colleagues. In the past, television was often a social event involving family and friends in the same room watching a single TV show. The social circle has expanded to include Facebook and Twitter friends in different locations, changing television from a "lean back and enjoy" experience into a "lean forward and engage" experience. Reality television shows encourage viewers to tweet while watching, and run a scrolling bar of viewer tweets. About 20% of viewers start watching a TV show after hearing about it on a social network. TV viewers are multitasking: co-viewing shows while texting, commenting, and chatting on line while the show unfolds. Around 32% of Internet users will use social media while watching TV, and this jumps to 64% for users who own smartphones and tablets (eMarketer, Inc., 2012b). Nearly 60% are watching TV show clips on social networks.

MOVIES

The Hollywood movie industry is going through a difficult transition from a reliance on DVDs, its primary revenue generator over the last decade, to a new marketplace where consumers want to watch videos on their PCs, tablet computers, and their smartphones. Americans spent more money on online videos (both streaming and purchased films) than they did on DVDs. Consumers downloaded or streamed an estimated 3.4 billion movies in 2012, versus renting or purchasing 2.4 billion DVDs (IHS iSuppli, 2012a). A little over 60 million Americans watched movies online in 2012 (see **Figure 9.10**). Consumers increasingly want access to cloud-stored movies rather than downloading entire movies to their devices. There are many parallels with the television industry: a very rapid growth in the mobile platform, expansion of cloud computing to support instant streaming of movies, and a change in consumer behavior in which movie viewing becomes both more individualized (watch whatever you want on your phone) and more social (let's text as we watch the movie). Both the television and movie industries are concentrated oligopolies with little competition. Pundits may write about the "indie" television movement, along with indie films built for the Internet, and the hundreds of millions of non-premium movies on YouTube. But these sub-premium efforts produce sub-premium revenues or no revenues at all.

While the movie box office attendance in 2011 hit a 16-year low, and DVD sales continued to drop, Hollywood is nevertheless weathering the digital onslaught far better than the music industry. Hollywood has a potent weapon in its corner: no one goes online to see zeroes and ones. Instead, they go to online entertainment sites to be happy, sad, awed, romantically stimulated, or agitated. The future of online movies is very bright: it is expected to rise continuously worldwide through 2016 (IHS, 2012b). Hollywood has few competitors. Also, movies are far larger than music tracks and much more difficult to illegally download and move around the Web without detec-

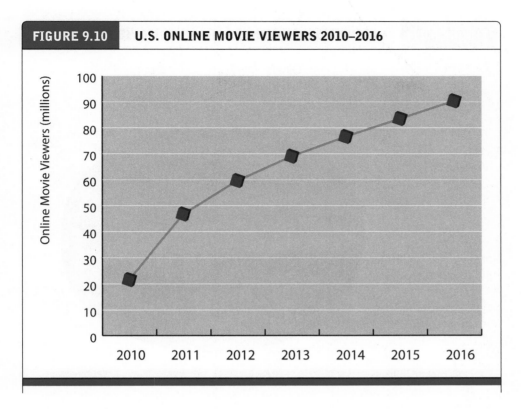

FIGURE 9.10 **U.S. ONLINE MOVIE VIEWERS 2010–2016**

SOURCE: Based on data from eMarketer, Inc., 2012d.

tion. And unlike the music labels, who allowed a single distributor (Apple iTunes) to dominate online sales, the movie producers have Apple, Google (YouTube), Amazon, Netflix, Hulu, VUDU, and others competing for distribution rights.

In 2012, for the first time, consumers viewed more and paid more for Web-based movie downloads, rentals, and streams than for DVDs or related physical products (eMarketer, Inc., 2012c). As with television, the demand for feature-length Hollywood movies appears to be expanding in part because of the growth of smartphones and tablets. In addition, the surprising resurgence of music videos, led by VEVO, is attracting millions of younger viewers on smartphones and tablets.

The size of the online movie business is difficult to ascertain because TV show rentals and premium video are often lumped together. Nevertheless, industry observers estimate the total online movie market at about $1 billion in 2012. To put this in perspective, the total annual revenues of Hollywood studios when all revenue streams are combined is about $70 billion. So at this point, the Internet and online distribution is a tiny part of the overall picture, but one that is growing very rapidly. Netflix is the largest Internet video distributor (44% of online video and movie revenues) by far, followed by Apple, and then a host of smaller services (IHS iSuppli, 2012b) (see **Figure 9.11**).

The online movie industry is a complex web of competing forces with conflicting interests. The existing Hollywood movie industry, which creates the products that produce the revenues, is threatened by the piracy of its products, loss of control

| FIGURE 9.11 | ONLINE MOVIE BUSINESS SHARE OF MOVIE REVENUES |

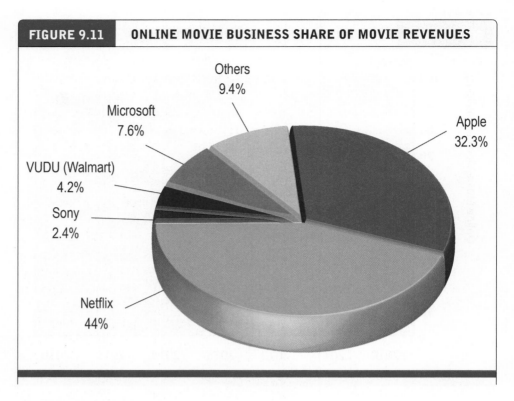

SOURCE: Based on data from IHS iSuppli, 2012.

over its traditional and very profitable distribution channels (largely movie theaters, television networks, and retailers of its DVD products), and the growth of powerful technology players such as Apple, Google, and Amazon, who own online movie stores and also sell the physical devices used to watch movies.

The movie industry estimates that it loses over $5 billion a year in pirated movies copied from DVDs, early production copies, and in-theater videoing. But video piracy appears not to be growing. A Google research paper found that searches for pirated movies peaked in 2008, and have been dropping steadily, while searches for online rentals and streaming are up (Google, 2011). Insofar as searches are an indicator of consumer interest and intent, the public interest in pirated movies is declining rapidly. A recent academic study found no evidence that U.S. box office receipts since 2003 have been negatively impacted by BitTorrent (a popular protocol for peer-to-peer sharing of copyrighted materials), and that international piracy increases when Hollywood studios delay release of films in foreign countries (Danaher and Waldfogel, 2012).

However, the estimated losses due to piracy pale in comparison to the fall in DVD sales: in 2008, DVD sales of physical units were $10 billion, and by 2012 were estimated to be less than $4 billion. The DVD format is rapidly declining just as the digital rental, digital download-and-own, streaming, and video-on-demand markets show striking growth. Netflix is estimated to have had 28.5 million customers in 2012, the majority of which stream movies and television. Digital streaming grew to $1 billion in sales in 2011 (about a 20% increase), and sales of movies through digital download services like Apple's iTunes rose 9% to $554 million (DEG, 2012). The download movie market is dominated by Apple (65%), Microsoft's Zune Video Marketplace, and Walmart's VUDU, where you can rent a movie for as little as $3.99 or purchase a digital downloaded copy for $14 to $16.

Insight on Technology: Hollywood and the Internet: Let's Cut a Deal describes how Hollywood studios and Internet distributors are cutting deals to provide more video and movie content online.

MUSIC

In 2012, the online radio audience reached over 100 million listeners in the United States, four times larger than in 2002. Online radio consists of AM/FM station streams, and Internet pure-play programming from firms like Pandora, Spotify, and Songza. The growth of online radio provides a large opportunity for music labels and artists, while at the same time threatening their very existence because online streaming digital revenues are so much smaller than the CD-driven revenues, or broadcast station ad revenues in the past.

In 2011, the top-selling CD album was Adele's *21* with more than 5.8 million units sold. It was also the top-selling digital download album, with 1.8 million units sold. Both were a record in terms of sales for any album since 2004. After 12 years of bad digital news, with some predicting the record industry would collapse and albums were dead, the music industry is staging a steady comeback from the abyss created by new technology, and, in part, its own obstinacy.

More than any of the other content industries, the recorded music industry has suffered the most from the onslaught of digital devices and Internet distribution. For most of its history, the music industry depended on a variety of physical media to distribute music--acetate records, vinyl recordings, cassette tapes, and finally CD-ROMs. At the core of its revenue was a physical product. Since the 1950s, that physical product was an album—a collection of bundled songs that sold for a much higher price than singles. The Internet changed all that when, in 2000, a music service called Napster begin distributing pirated music tracks over the Internet to consumers using their PCs as record players. Despite the collapse of Napster due to legal challenges, hundreds of other illegal sites showed up, resulting in music industry revenues falling from $14 billion in 1999 to an estimated $5.4 billion in 2012. The appearance of powerful mobile media players beginning in 2001 that could be connected to the Internet, like Apple's iPod, iPhone, and iPad, further eroded sales of CD albums. With the growth of cloud computing and cloud-based music services, by 2012, the very concept of "owning" music has begun to shift instead to "access" to music from any device, anywhere.

The music industry initially resisted the development of legal digital channels of distribution, but ultimately and reluctantly struck deals with Apple's new iTunes Store in 2003, as well as with several small subscription music services, for online distribution. Nevertheless, revenues from the sales of digital downloads of individual songs from iTunes selling for 99 cents paled in comparison to revenues produced by CD albums selling for $15. Internet downloads of individual songs, which unbundled the album, decimated revenues as users created their own collections of songs. Despite

INSIGHT ON TECHNOLOGY

HOLLYWOOD AND THE INTERNET: LET'S CUT A DEAL

In tough times, people go to the movies. Despite the continuing effects of the recession, global box office sales were up to $32 billion in 2011, a record, and 3% higher than the previous year. Internet sales, rentals, and movie subscriptions are estimated to be about $1 billion in 2012. The year also boasted the continuing success of some of the highest-grossing movies of all time. If only all movies could produce results like these, Hollywood would be golden again.

But Hollywood is facing several problems moving forward to a world where most people will be watching movies on the Internet. Although the Internet is Hollywood's fastest growing segment, it's also the least profitable. A second problem is that Hollywood does not control its own Internet distribution network, but instead is forced to rely on the likes of Netflix, Apple, Amazon, and Google.

Netflix continues to dominate online movie revenues. At one time, Apple had a 70% share of Internet movie revenue, and Hollywood studios feared Apple would be able to dominate Internet distribution and dictate prices. Now with Netflix dominating the streaming market, Hollywood fears it will be forced to sell its product for a pittance compared to DVD prices. For this reason, Hollywood has been restricting the release of movies to Netflix.

In 2012, more and more large firms, such as Google, Walmart, and Best Buy, entered the streaming market, and competed with one another for Hollywood movies, driving up prices. Amazon also struck a deal with Viacom to purchase TV episodes and movies to stock its forthcoming streaming service.

One result of all this competition for Hollywood content is rising prices paid by the distributors, and a feeling in Hollywood that they can maintain some semblance of control over their fate, unlike the music industry. In fact, the prices being paid by Netflix and others exceed those paid by cable television video-on-demand services. Netflix spent nearly $2 billion in 2012 for content to stream to its 24 million subscribers. As a result, its profits fell significantly and its share price tanked from $250 in 2011 to $60 in 2012.

The movie industry itself has launched a new movie service called UltraViolet that would possibly give new life to DVDs. Designed to cut down on piracy, and make it possible for consumers to watch their movies on multiple devices, customers will purchase DVDs in retail stores and register the DVD serial number at the same time on the UltraViolet service. Once registered, consumers can watch a digital version of their movies stored on Walmart cloud servers streamed to their smartphones, tablets, or PCs.

In the end, Hollywood and the Internet need each other, and the only question is how to find the price, define the terms of trade, and cut a deal where both parties come out winners.

SOURCES: "Netflix Passes Apple to Take Lead in Online Movie Business," by Dan Graziano, BGR.com, June 6, 2012; "Theatrical Market Statistics," Motion Picture Industry Association, March 2012; "Walmart to Give Hollywood a Hand," by Michelle Kung, Wall Street Journal, February 28, 2012; "Web Deals Cheer Hollywood, Despite Drop in Moviegoers," by Brooks Barnes, New York Times, February 24, 2012; "For Wal-Mart, a Rare Online Success," by Miguel Bustillo and Karen Talley, Wall Street Journal, August 20, 2011; "Painful Profits From Web Video," by Sam Schechner, Wall Street Journal, August 15, 2011; "YouTube Is Said to Be Near a Major Film Rental Deal," by Brooks Barnes and Claire Cain Miller, New York Times, April 26, 2011.

the growth of Amazon, Walmart, and other online retailers of CDs, consumers increasingly shifted to digital downloads and, more recently, streams.

In 2011, for the first time in history, revenue from digital downloads and streams accounted for a majority (52%) of industry revenues. While the industry makes about 32 cents from a downloaded song, it makes less than a penny (about .63 of a penny) on a streamed version of the same song. This revenue is split with the artists who receive .32 of a penny. *Rolling Stone* calculated that a very popular song selling one million streams would produce revenue of $3,166 for the artist and a similar amount for the music label.

Yet in 2012, the outlook for the music industry was cautiously optimistic. It's a different industry from what it was, no longer totally dependent on highly profitable physical products, less able to sell bundled music as albums, but with a rapidly growing demand for its high-quality, popular products from a variety of Internet distributors who are competing with one another to buy musical content. The explosive growth in smartphones and tablets has further driven demand for cloud-based streaming music access. Online music monthly listening hours in the United States have doubled from 606 million in 2009 to 1,301 million in 2011, according to AccuStream Research. **Figure 9.12** shows consumer spending on digital music (both downloads and streams), which

| FIGURE 9.12 | CONSUMER SPENDING ON DIGITAL MUSIC |

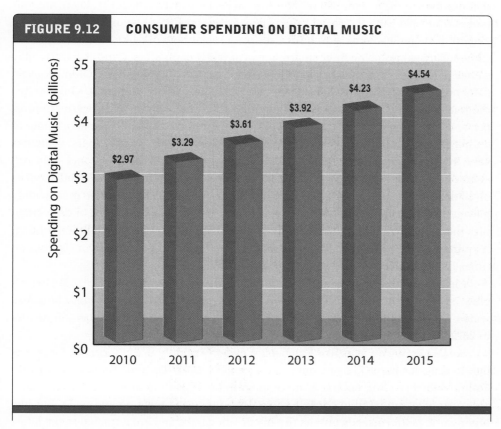

SOURCE: Based on data from eMarketer, Inc., 2012f.

is expected to reach $4.54 billion in 2015, up from $3.61 billion in 2012 (IFPI, 2012; eMarketer, Inc., 2012f).

The most popular streaming services are Amazon (Cloud Player), Apple (iTunes Match), Google (Google Play), iHeartRadio, Last.fm, MOGH, Pandora, Rdio, Slacker, and Spotify. Streaming music services are currently growing at nearly 100% annually although this is expected to slow. Next to iTunes, Pandora's is the second largest music service with over 150 million subscribers in 2012.

The streaming services use a variety of different business models: ad-supported, subscription fees, and device sales. Internet radio streaming services like Pandora and Spotify make over 85% of their revenue from advertisements, mostly to music sites where consumers can purchase CDs or downloads. In return for free but limited music, users agree to be exposed to ads. Less than 15% of revenues come from subscription fees for premium services. Amazon, Apple, and Google are not interested in music as a source of revenue, but rather in the sale of physical devices (from Kindles, to smartphones and tablets) which have much higher profit margins.

GAMES

No Internet media content form has grown as explosively as online games. Well over 100 million Internet users play some kind of game online in the United States, and that number swells to over 300 million worldwide (Wakabayachi, 2012). There are four types of Internet gamers. Casual gamers play games on a PC or laptop computer. Social gamers play games using a Web browser on a social network like Facebook. Mobile gamers play games using their smartphones or tablet computers. Console gamers play games online (or offline) using a console like Xbox, PlayStation, or Wii. Often, console gamers are connected over the Internet to enable group play. **Figure 9.13** illustrates the relative size of these four online gaming audiences and their future growth prospects. Because people play games in a variety of different venues, the total number of online gamers is on the order of 105 million, about 40% of all Internet users. Estimates vary, but industry analysts peg annual sales of console games (hardware and software) at around $17.5 billion for 2012, and sales of subscriptions, virtual goods, and services on social, mobile, and casual gaming platforms at around $8 billion. The most widely played mobile casual game is *Angry Birds*. In *Angry Birds,* players launch birds at green pigs hiding inside buildings using a sling shot to blast away the pig and the building. As mindless as this sounds, *Angry Birds* had been downloaded more than 700 million times by 2012 (Anderson, 2012).

Clearly, the fastest growing gaming venue is the mobile smartphone market, which grew 26% in 2012. The smallest audience, and slowest growing, is the console games venue. Social and casual gaming—often lumped together in a single number—grew 10% in 2012, but is expected to slow over time to about 5% in 2016.

Social gaming on sites like Facebook grew very rapidly in 2010–2012 in large part due to the success of Zynga games like *Farmville, CityVille,* and *Words With Friends.* Online social gaming enlarged the demographic of gamers to include women and older people, compared to console gamers who tend to be young and male. But like other game platforms, consumers tire of current games and are attracted to the latest market entrants. Users of various Zynga "ville" games have fallen in 2012 by up to 35%.

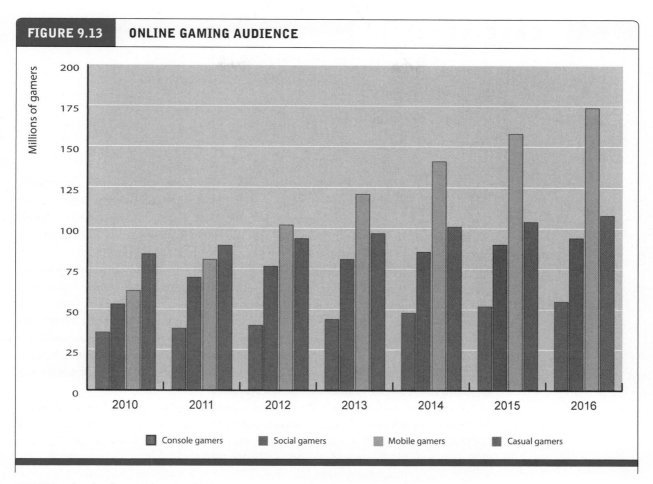

FIGURE 9.13   ONLINE GAMING AUDIENCE

SOURCE: Based on data from eMarketer, Inc., 2012g.

While casual and social gaming rapidly grows, nearly all these online and mobile games are free and users do not stay in the games very long. These two features make it difficult for gaming firms to monetize their user base by showing advertisements and charging for services. Zynga has chosen a different route to profits by relying on the sales of virtual goods to its customers with mixed results. For a discussion of Zynga's struggle to define a workable business model, see the chapter ending case, *Zynga Bets on Online Games*.

Zynga
Bets on Online Games

Until 2012, Zynga was riding high. Zynga was the leader in a movement that brought online games to the social network platform. Zynga's games on Facebook have over 182 million active users. Its most popular games include *FarmVille*, *CityVille*, *Mafia Wars*, and *Words with Friends*. In 2011, Zynga generated $1.1 billion in revenue selling virtual goods. Zynga's 2011 revenues were twice 2010 revenues, and in two previous years it grew by several hundred percent a year to become the fastest growing mobile gaming service in history. But Zynga showed a $400 million loss in 2011 and plunging stock prices amid signs that the growth of new users was slowing, veteran players were leaving, and the firm was having a hard time coming up with new enticing games. Although Zynga is expanding to other social networks such as Google +, it remains heavily dependent on Facebook, where it is one of hundreds of businesses located almost exclusively on Facebook, and where it can directly appeal to Facebook's 1 billion members worldwide.

Founded in 2007 by Mark Pincus and a group of other entrepreneurs, Zynga is the leading developer of social network games. In October 2012, its *ChefVille*, *Texas HoldEm Poker, FarmVille2,* and *Zynga Slingo* were the top four Facebook apps in terms of monthly average users, each of them with between 35 million to 39 million users. Zynga's games generate 3 terabytes of data every day. Since its inception, Zynga has made data analytics a priority for guiding the management of its games and the busi-

ness decisions of the company. Zynga is not interested in individual user information, but instead in the trends displayed in the aggregated data it collects. The company relies heavily on its data to improve user retention and to increase collaboration among its gamers. Zynga uses a reporting team and an analytics team to work with the data and create concrete recommendations for increasing sales. Zynga's analytics system is, in reality, a very sophisticated customer relationship management system. If a gold halo around a virtual angel's head causes more purchases of virtual angels, then the change is made. Zynga's audience demographics are perhaps not what you would think. Like most social games, the audience is slightly more female, older (average age is 46 years), and wealthier than console or other online gamers.

Zynga went public in December 16, 2011, after delaying earlier efforts throughout the year due to questions about its accounting. Earlier in the year, other IPOs for Groupon, LinkedIn, and Zillow had gone well, with their share prices zooming upwards on the first day of trading in true Internet-frenzy style. Not so for Zynga: its shares, which were priced at $10, giving the company a value of $20 billion, fell to $9.50 in a matter of minutes. Since then, Zynga has faced a difficult time maintaining investor confidence.

Zynga's business model is to offer free games aimed at a larger, more casual gaming audience, and to make money by selling "virtual goods" in games initially, and later by exploiting the advertising possibilities of the games. The idea of "free games" is a blow to the existing video game business that depends on selling video games. The idea of virtual goods has been around for years, most notably in Second Life and other virtual worlds, where users can buy apparel and accessories for their in-game avatars. But Zynga's attention to detail and ability to glean important information from countless terabytes of data generated by its users on a daily basis has set it apart. For example, analytics have shown that Zynga's gamers tend to buy more in-game goods when they are offered as limited edition items. Zynga sells about 38,000 virtual goods every second of operation.

Zynga also benefits from using Facebook as its game platform. When users install a Zynga application, they allow Zynga access to all of their profile information, including their names, genders, and lists of friends. Zynga then uses that information to determine what types of users are most likely to behave in certain ways. If Zynga updates its games, it sends messages to all your friends whether they play the game or not. By carefully analyzing the online behavior of its customers, Zynga hopes to determine which types of users are most likely to become "whales," or big spenders that buy hundreds of dollars of virtual goods each month and account for most of Zynga's profits.

Zynga's games also make heavy use of Facebook's social features. For example, in *CityVille*, users must find friends to fill fictional posts at their "City Hall" to successfully complete the structure. All of Zynga's games have features like this, but Facebook hasn't always fully supported all of Zynga's efforts. Facebook apps were formerly able to send messages directly to Facebook members, but Facebook disabled the feature after complaints that it was a form of spam.

After releasing exceptionally poor second quarter results in July 2012, Zynga's stock plunged 40%. Revenue growth had "slowed" down to 19% from 32% in the prior quarter. Investors had been expecting a doubling in sales for most of 2012. Selling at under $3 a share in July 2012, the company lost 70% of its IPO value in about six

SOURCES: "Facebook Apps Leaderboard," Appdata.com, accessed October 2012; "It's Too Late for Gambling to Save Zynga," by Jeff John Roberts, Gigaom.com, October 8, 2012; "Zynga to Launch Real-Money Gambling Online Games in 2013," by Dean Takahashi, Venturebeat.com, July 26, 2012; "Zynga Stock Dives on Loss," by John Letzing and Shayndi Raice, *New York Times,* July 26, 2012; "Zynga's Facebook Games Continue to Shed Players by the Millions," by Paul Tassi, *Forbes,* May 23, 2012; Zynga Inc., "Form 10K for the Fiscal Year Ending December 31, 2011," Securities and Exchange Commission, February 28, 2012; "Testing the Durability of Zynga's Virtual Business," by Rolfe Winkler, *Wall Street Journal,* September 28, 2011; "Zynga Filing Shows Slowing Growth," by Shayndi Raice and Randall Smith, *Wall Street Journal,* September 21, 2011; "Virtual Products, Real Profits," *Wall Street Journal,* September 9, 2011, Jacquelyn Gavron; "Vertica: The Analytics Behind all the Zynga Games," ReadWrite Enterprise, July 18, 2011; "Crikey! Zynga's IPO By the Numbers," by Mathew Lynley, VentureBeat, July 1, 2011; "Social Gaming," by Paul Verna, eMarketer, January 2011.

months. Factors contributing to Zynga's decline included lack of new hit games and increased churn rate. In late summer 2012, Zynga was reported to be looking at online gambling as the answer to its problems. CEO Mark Pincus announced that Zynga would launch its first online gambling poker game involving real money in the first half of 2013, most likely outside the United States, since online gambling using real money is still illegal in most states and under U.S. federal law.

No one knows the long-term prospects of Zynga, even if it succeeds in launching its new online gambling initiative. It faces significant competition from established players, such as PokerStars and other upstarts like Big Fish Casino that have already beat Zynga to the table. In addition, its primary business in virtual goods looks increasingly suspect. What has sold on Zynga in the past are fashionable virtual goods, and what comes into fashion often goes quickly out of fashion. Perhaps the biggest risk for Zynga is that it is still almost totally reliant on Facebook, to whom it pays 30% of all revenues from its games including ad revenue. It has also agreed to use Facebook Credits as the sole means of payment by its users for the next five years. (Facebook Credits is Facebook's internal virtual payment system—users buy Facebook Credits to pay vendors on Facebook. Facebook Credits are not good anywhere else on the Web.) The customer base is also very narrow, with the virtual goods revenues coming from only 5% of the users. Advertising currently produces less than 10% of Zynga's revenues. In the last year, Zynga has been working to get its games on other platforms like Google +, Yahoo, and the iPhone and iPad in order to reduce its dependence on Facebook. It has also been working to expand its international presence. However, it is not clear if Zynga is going to continue to be able to dominate the games market in the future. Instead, Zynga has many competitors with a chance to succeed.

Case Study Questions

1. Do you think Zynga would be a good advertising platform? What kinds of companies would be interested in reaching this audience, and how should the ads be presented to users?

2. How could firms use the Zynga platform to develop and sell branded virtual goods? Assume you were a manufacturer of sporting goods and wanted to use Zynga as a marketing platform. What concerns would you have about the Zynga platform? How would you use its social character to extend the reach of your campaign?

3. How would you judge the competitive situation facing Zynga?

9.5 REVIEW

KEY CONCEPTS

■ **Identify the major trends in the consumption of media and online content, and the major revenue models for digital content delivery.**

Major trends in the consumption of media and online content include the following:

• The average American adult spends around 4,200 hours per year consuming various media. The most hours are spent viewing television, followed by using the Internet and listening to the radio.

• Although several studies indicate that time spent on the Internet reduces consumer time available for other media, recent data reveals a more complex picture, as Internet users multitask and consume more media of all types than do non-Internet users.

• In terms of revenue, print media (books, newspapers, and magazines) accounts for the most revenue (37%), followed by television (28%) and radio and recorded music (11%).

• The three major revenue models for digital content delivery are the subscription, a la carte, and advertising-supported (free and freemium) models.

• Online newspapers, online radio, online TV shows, and casual games are the top four categories of online content.

• The fastest growing paid content area is videos.

■ **Understand Digital Rights Management (DRM)**

• Digital rights management (DRM) refers to the combination of technical and legal means for protecting digital content from reproduction without permission.

• Walled gardens are a kind of DRM that restrict the widespread sharing of content.

■ **Understand the key factors affecting the online publishing industry.**

Key factors affecting online newspapers include:

• *Audience size and growth.* Although the newspaper industry as a whole is the most troubled part of the publishing industry, online readership of newspapers is growing at more than 10% a year, fueled by new reading devices such as smartphones, e-readers, and tablet computers, and online newspapers produce the largest online audience of any media, next to social networks.

• *Revenue models and results.* Online newspapers predominantly rely upon an advertising model. Some also supplement revenues by using a subscription revenue model.

Key factors affecting e-books and online book publishing include:

• *Audience size and growth.* E-book sales have exploded, fueled by the Amazon Kindle, Barnes & Noble Nook, and Apple iPad. The mobile platform of smartphones and tablets has made millions of books available online at a lower price than print books. The future of the book will be digital although printed books will not disappear for many years.

- *Challenges.* The two primary challenges of the digital e-book platform are cannibalization and finding the right business model.

Key factors affecting online magazines include:

- *Online audience and growth:* Digital magazine sales have soared, with almost a third of the Internet population now reading magazines online.
- *Magazine aggregation:* Magazine aggregators (Web sites or apps) offer users online subscriptions and sales of many digital magazines.

■ **Understand the key factors affecting the online entertainment industry.**

There are five main players in the entertainment sector: television, motion pictures, music, video games, and radio broadcasting. The entertainment segment is currently undergoing great change, brought about by the Internet and the mobile platform. Consumers have begun to accept paying for content and also beginning to expect to be able to access online entertainment from any device at any time.

Key factors include the following:

- *Audience size and growth.* While music downloads are the most popular form of entertainment, the fast-paced growth of online video sees videos overtaking music in 2014–2015 as the most popular online entertainment. In addition, Internet users are defining new forms of non-traditional entertainment that do not involve the traditional media titans, such as blogs and user-generated content on social network sites.
- *The emergence of streaming services and the mobile platform.* In the movie and television industries, two major trends are the move to consumers purchasing streaming services, from Amazon, Apple, Hulu, and other channels and the continued increase in online purchases and downloads. Although physical sales of products (DVDs) are dropping significantly, more and more consumers are purchasing movies and television episodes on new mobile devices, such as smartphones and tablets. The music industry is experiencing similar trends as the movie industry: the growth of streaming services, or Internet radio, the continued expansion of online purchases, and increased downloads on mobile devices. However, the unbundling of a traditional music product, the album, into individual songs, has decimated music industry revenues. Of the four types of gamers—casual, social, mobile, and console—the greatest growth is anticipated for mobile gamers, as the mobile market is rapidly expanding along all e-commerce fronts.

QUESTIONS

1. What are the basic revenue models for online content, and what is their major challenge?
2. What effect is the growth of tablet computing having on online entertainment and content?
3. What techniques do music subscription services use to enforce DRM?
4. How has the Internet impacted the content that newspapers can offer?
5. What changes have occurred for newspapers in the classified ads department?
6. What are the key challenges facing the online newspaper industry?
7. How has the Internet changed the packaging, distribution, marketing, and sale of traditional music tracks?

8. How has streaming technology impacted the television industry?
9. Why is the growth of cloud storage services important to the growth of mobile content delivery?
10. Has the average consumer become more receptive to advertising-supported Internet content? What developments support this?
11. What factors are needed to support successfully charging the consumer for online content?
12. Why are apps helping the newspaper and magazine industries where Web sites failed?

PROJECTS

1. Go to Amazon and explore the different digital products that are available. Prepare a presentation to convey your findings to the class.

2. Examine and report on the progress made with respect to the delivery of movies on demand over the Internet.

3. Choose a magazine that is available both online and as a physical magazine. How is the online magazine similar? How is it different? Prepare a short report discussing this issue.

CHAPTER 10

Social Networks, Auctions, and Portals

After reading this chapter, you will be able to:

- Explain the difference between a traditional social network and an online social network.
- Describe the different types of social networks and online communities and their business models.
- Describe the major types of auctions, their benefits and costs, and how they operate.
- Understand when to use auctions in a business.
- Describe the major types of Internet portals.
- Understand the business models of portals.

Social Network Fever

Spreads to the Professions

When social networks first appeared a decade ago, it was widely believed the phenomenon would be limited to crazed teenagers already captive to online games and video game consoles. Most of the technorati in Silicon Valley and Wall Street felt this was a blip on the horizon, and their full attention was occupied by search engines, search engine marketing, and ad placement. But when the population of social network participants pushed past 50 million and on to 75 million, even the technical elite woke up to the fact that these huge audiences were not just a bunch of teenagers. Instead, a wide slice of American society was participating. Steve Ballmer, CEO

Courtesy of Carol Traver

of Microsoft, expressed the conviction as early as September 2007 that social networks would have some staying power, although he tempered that outlook with reservations about just how long that would be, given their youthful appeal and faddish nature. This was just before Microsoft paid $250 million for a small stake in Facebook, which valued the company at $15 billion. Trying to sound convincing, the month before his company spent $1.65 billion for YouTube, Google CEO Eric Schmidt asserted his belief that despite prevailing opinion, social networks were a bona fide business opportunity.

By October 2012, Facebook had grown to about 1 billion subscribers worldwide, challenging Google and Yahoo for face time with the Internet audience. The social network craze obviously has awakened the technology giants, but they focus mostly on the really huge audiences attracted to general social network sites such as Facebook, Twitter, and YouTube. However, in the background there is a fast-growing collection of social networks that are aimed at communities of practitioners or specific interest groups.

Take LinkedIn, for example, probably the best-known and most popular business network site. LinkedIn is an online network with more than 175 million worldwide members in over 200 countries, representing 170 different industries. Two new members join LinkedIn approximately every second. LinkedIn allows a member to create a profile, including a photo, to summarize his or her professional accomplishments. Members' networks include their connections, their connections' connections, as well as people they know, potentially linking them to thousands of others. How members use LinkedIn depends somewhat on their position. Top executives use the site mainly for industry networking and promoting their businesses. Middle managers use LinkedIn primarily to keep in touch with others and also for industry networking. Lower-level employees typically use the site for job searching and networking with co-workers. On May 18, 2011, LinkedIn went public in what was, at the time, the biggest Internet IPO since Google, raising more than $350

SOURCES: "About Us," LinkedIn.com Press Center, accessed October 10, 2012; "LinkedIn Corporation Market Cap," YCharts.com, accessed October 10, 2012; "Number of Active Users at Facebook Over the Years," Associated Press, October, 4, 2012; "Thirty-Seven Percent of Companies Use Social Networks to Research Potential Job Candidates, According to New CareerBuilder Survey," by Ryan Hunt, Career-Builder.com, April 18, 2012; "Managing Your Online Image Across Social Networks" The Reppler Effect, September 27, 2011; "LinkedIn Hits $10 Billion Market Cap; Valuation Ethereal," by Eric Savitz, *Forbes*, May 19, 2011; "How Professionals Use LinkedIn," eMarketer, August 5, 2011; "LinkedFA Offers Network for Financial Advisors," by David F. Carr, *Information Week*, June 1, 2011; "All About LinkedIn, Knowledge@Wharton, May 20, 2011; "The Social Network That Gets Down to Business," by Miguel Helft, *New York Times*, September 29, 2010; "Online Reputation in a Connected World," Cross-Tab Marketing, January 2010; "Influence Marketing With Social Networks," by Lee Oden, Toprank-blog.com, September 16, 2009; "Online Social Networks Go to Work," by Xeni Jardin, Msnbc.com, September 16, 2009.

million and giving it a company valuation of $8.9 billion. The company priced its IPO at $45 per share. As of October 2012 its stock had risen to approximately $112 per share, making its market capitalization now well over $11.65 billion.

Those with a particular interest in the stock market can choose from a crop of Web sites aimed at stock investors who want to share their ideas with other investors. These social networks are not just bulletin boards with anonymous comments, but active communities where users are identified and ranked according to the performance of their stock picks. One network is SocialPicks. SocialPicks is a community where stock investors exchange ideas and track the performance of financial bloggers. Like the larger social network sites, the financial sites allow users to connect with other investors, discuss issues focused on the stock market, and sometimes just show off investing prowess. The Motley Fool, one of the best-known online stock investment services, started its CAPS stock-rating social network in 2006 and has around 170,000 members.

You can find similar social network sites for a variety of specific professional groups such as health care (DailyStrength.org), law (LawLink), physicians (Sermo), wireless industry executives (INmobile.org), advertising professionals (AdGabber), and financial advisors (LinkedFA). These social networks encourage members to discuss the realities of their professions and practices, sharing successes and failures. There are also general business social networks designed more to develop a network for career advancement, such as Ecademy and Ryze. The rapid growth of professional social networks, linked to industry and careers, demonstrates how widespread and nearly universal the appeal of social networks is. While e-mail remains the Web's most popular activity, it is about to be eclipsed by social networks. What explains the very broad attraction to social networks? E-mail is excellent for communicating with other individuals, or even a small group. But e-mail is not very good at getting a sense of what others in the group are thinking, especially if the group numbers more than a dozen people. The strength of social networks lies in their ability to reveal group attitudes and opinions, values, and practices.

Professionals who join social networks need to be careful about the content they provide, and the distribution of this content. As business social networks have grown, and as the number of participants expands, employers are finding them a great place to discover the "inner" person who applies for a job. An April 2012 survey by CareerBuilder, the most widely used employment site in the United States, found that 37% of employers use social networks to screen job candidates and another 11% plan to begin doing so. However six months earlier, Reppler, an online identity management service, surveyed 300 hiring professionals. An astonishing 91% reported that they used social network screening, 47% of those upon receiving an application, 27% after detailed conversation with the prospective employee, and another 4% right before making an offer. Almost 70% of those using this tool reported rejecting a candidate based upon information they discovered. Provocative photos and references to drinking and drugs are the most common factors in deciding not to offer a job. For this reason, it wise to use Facebook's and other sites' maximum privacy settings, and release to the public only the most innocuous content. Likewise, be cautious of social network sites that do not provide "take down" policies, which allow users to remove embarrassing materials from their pages.

I n this chapter, we discuss social networks, auctions, and portals. One might ask, "What do social networks, auctions, and portals have in common?" They are all based on feelings of shared interest and self-identification—in short, a sense of community. Social networks and online communities explicitly attract people with shared affinities, such as ethnicity, gender, religion, and political views, or shared interests, such as hobbies, sports, and vacations. The auction site eBay started as a community of people interested in trading unwanted but functional items for which there was no ready commercial market. That community turned out to be huge—much larger than anyone expected. Portals also contain strong elements of community by providing access to community-fostering technologies such as e-mail, chat groups, bulletin boards, and discussion forums.

10.1 SOCIAL NETWORKS AND ONLINE COMMUNITIES

The Internet was designed originally as a communications medium to connect scientists in computer science departments around the continental United States. From the beginning, the Internet was intended, in part, as a community-building technology that would allow scientists to share data, knowledge, and opinions in a real-time online environment (see Chapter 3) (Hiltzik, 1999). The result of this early Internet was the first "virtual communities" (Rheingold, 1993). As the Internet grew in the late 1980s to include scientists from many disciplines and university campuses, thousands of virtual communities sprang up among small groups of scientists in many disciplines that communicated regularly using Internet e-mail, listservs, and bulletin boards. The first articles and books on the new electronic communities began appearing in the mid- to late 1980s. One of the earliest online communities, The Well, was formed in San Francisco in 1985 by a small group of people who once shared an 1,800-acre commune in Tennessee. It is now a part of Salon.com, an online community and magazine. The Well (Whole Earth 'Lectronic Link) is an online community that now has thousands of members devoted to discussion, debate, advice, and help (Hafner, 1997; Rheingold, 1998). With the development of the Web in the early 1990s, millions of people began obtaining Internet accounts and Web e-mail, and the community-building impact of the Internet strengthened. By 2012, 157 million Americans and 1.4 billion people worldwide belonged to online social networks.

Currently, social network participation is one of the most common usages of the Internet. About two-thirds of all Internet users in the United States—about 158 million Americans—use social networks on a regular basis, about 67% of all Internet users and 50% of all adults (eMarketer, 2012a). Facebook has about 1 billion active users worldwide (about 190 million in the North America) (Facebook, 2012). The Google+ social network has over 100 million worldwide users and 27 million in the United States (Gaudin, 2012).

WHAT IS AN ONLINE SOCIAL NETWORK?

social network

involves a group of people, shared social interaction, common ties among members, and people who share an area for some period of time

online social network

an area online, where people who share common ties can interact with one another

So exactly how do we define an online social network, and how is it any different from, say, an offline social network? Sociologists, who frequently criticize modern society for having destroyed traditional communities, unfortunately have not given us very good definitions of social networks and community. One study examined 94 different sociological definitions of community and found four areas of agreement. **Social networks** involve (a) a group of people, (b) shared social interaction, (c) common ties among members, and (d) people who share an area for some period of time (Hillery, 1955). This will be our working definition of a social network. Social networks do not necessarily have shared goals, purposes, or intentions. Indeed, social networks can be places where people just "hang out," share space, and communicate.

It's a short step to defining an **online social network** as an area online where people who share common ties can interact with one another. The Internet removes the geographic and time limitations of offline social networks. To be in an online network, you don't need to meet face to face, in a common room, at a common time.

THE GROWTH OF SOCIAL NETWORKS AND ONLINE COMMUNITIES

Facebook, Twitter, LinkedIn, Google+, Pinterest, and Tumblr are all examples of popular online communities. **Figure 10.1** shows the top 10 social network sites, which together account for well over 90% of the Internet's social network activity. While social networks originally attracted mostly young Internet users, social networks today are not just about teens and college students, but a much larger social phenomenon. More than 50% of Facebook's users are over 35.

While Facebook and Twitter dominate the news, a new kind of social network is appearing, and growing much faster than Facebook with respect to unique visitors and subscribers. These new sites are attracting marketers and advertisers as well. For instance, Pinterest, described in the opening case in Chapter 1, is a visually oriented site that allows users to curate their tastes and preferences, expressed in visual arts. You can think of Pinterest as a visual blog. Users post images to an online "pinboard." The images can come from any source. Users can also "re-pin" images they see on Pinterest. Pinterest's membership has skyrocketed since its launch and had more than 25 million monthly unique visitors in the United States in August 2012. Tumblr is an easy-to-use blogging site with tools for visual and text curating, sharing with others, and re-blogging contents. Tumblr started in 2007 and has 30 million users. **Table 10.1** describes some other social sites that are more focused.

The number of unique visitors is just one way to measure the influence of a site. Time on site is another important metric. The more time people spend on a site, called engagement, the more time to display ads and generate revenue. In this sense, Facebook is three times more addictive and immersive than the other top sites on the Web. In the United States, Facebook visitors spend about seven hours a month on Facebook, compared to about three hours on Yahoo, and only 1.5 hours on Google (eMarketer, Inc., 2012a).

The amount of advertising revenue generated by sites is perhaps the ultimate metric for measuring the business potential of Web sites and brands. The top four search engine companies (Google, Yahoo, Microsoft, and AOL) will generate about

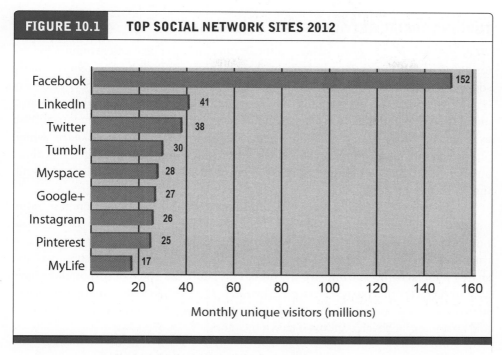

FIGURE 10.1 TOP SOCIAL NETWORK SITES 2012

SOURCES: Based on data from comScore, 2012a; Gaudin, 2012; McGee, 2012.

$17.5 billion in U.S. advertising revenue in 2012 (eMarketer, Inc., 2012b). In contrast, social network sites in the United States in 2012 generated only about $3.1 billion in advertising revenue (eMarketer, Inc., 2012c). Social network sites are the fastest growing form of Internet usage, but they are not yet as powerful as traditional search engines/portals in terms of ad dollars generated. A part of the problem is that subscribers do not go to social network sites to seek ads for relevant products, nor pay attention to the ads that are flashed before their eyes (see Chapter 6).

TABLE 10.1 OTHER FAST-GROWING SOCIAL SITES

SOCIAL NETWORK	DESCRIPTION
Path	Personal journal for sharing photos, text
Stumbleupon	A search platform for sharing interests
Flickr	The original social photo-sharing site
Instagram	Social photo-sharing site (now owned by Facebook)
Ning	Platform for creating personal social networks
Polyvore	Topic-focused social network (fashion)
deviantART	Web site focused on art, sharing of images
Vevo	Video and music sharing site

TURNING SOCIAL NETWORKS INTO BUSINESSES

While the early social networks had a difficult time raising capital and revenues, today's top social network sites are now learning how to monetize their huge audiences. Early social network sites relied on subscriptions, but today, most social networks rely on advertising or the investments of venture capitalists. Users of portals and search engines have come to accept advertising as the preferred means of supporting Web experiences rather than paying for it. One important exception is LinkedIn, which offers free memberships to individual job seekers but charges professional recruiters and business firms for premium services. **Figure 10.2** shows the amount of ad spending on social networks.

Social networks have had a profound impact on how businesses operate, communicate, and serve their customers. The most visible business firm use of social networks is as a marketing and branding tool. More than 90% of the Fortune 500 have established Facebook pages, where "fans" can follow the business and its products and share opinions with the company and other fans. More than 80% of corporations have Twitter feeds for this purpose as well (Newman, 2011). A less visible marketing use of networks is as a powerful listening tool that has strengthened the role of customers and customer feedback systems inside a business.

TYPES OF SOCIAL NETWORKS AND THEIR BUSINESS MODELS

There are many types and many ways of classifying social networks and online communities. While the most popular general social networks have adopted an advertising model, other kinds of networks have different revenue sources. Social networks have

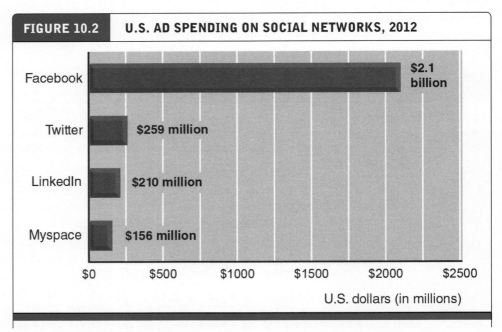

FIGURE 10.2 **U.S. AD SPENDING ON SOCIAL NETWORKS, 2012**

SOURCE: Based on data from eMarketer, 2012c.

different types of sponsors and different kinds of members. For instance, some are created by firms such as IBM for the exclusive use of their sales force or other employees (intra-firm communities or B2E [business-to-employee] communities); others are built for suppliers and resellers (inter-organizational or B2B communities); and others are built by dedicated individuals for other similar persons with shared interests (P2P [people-to-people] communities). In this chapter, we will discuss B2C communities for the most part, although we also discuss briefly P2P communities of practice.

Table 10.2 describes in greater detail the five generic types of social networks and online communities: general, practice, interest, affinity, and sponsored. Each type of community can have a commercial intent or commercial consequence. We use this schema to explore the business models of commercial communities.

SOCIAL NETWORK FEATURES AND TECHNOLOGIES

Social networks have developed software applications that allow users to engage in a number of activities. Not all sites have the same features, but there is an emerging feature set among the larger communities. Some of these software tools are built into the site, while others can be added by users to their profile pages as widgets (described in earlier chapters). **Table 10.3** describes several social network functionalities.

THE FUTURE OF SOCIAL NETWORKS

Social networking is currently one of the most popular online activities. Will it stay that way or grow even more popular? Today's social network scene is highly concentrated with the top site, Facebook, garnering about 50% of the social network audience,

TABLE 10.2	TYPES OF SOCIAL NETWORKS AND ONLINE COMMUNITIES
TYPE OF SOCIAL NETWORK / COMMUNITY	**DESCRIPTION**
General	Online social gathering place to meet and socialize with friends, share content, schedules, and interests. Examples: Facebook, Pinterest, Tumblr, and Myspace.
Practice	Social network of professionals and practitioners, creators of artifacts such as computer code or music. Examples: Just Plain Folks (musicians' community) and LinkedIn (business).
Interest	Community built around a common interest, such as games, sports, music, stock markets, politics, health, finance, foreign affairs, or lifestyle. Examples: E-democracy.org (political discussion group) and PredictWallStreet (stock market site).
Affinity	Community of members who self-identify with a demographic or geographic category, such as women, African Americans, or Arab Americans. Examples: BlackPlanet (African American community and social network site) and iVillage (focusing on women).
Sponsored	Network created by commercial, government, and nonprofit organizations for a variety of purposes. Examples: Nike, IBM, Cisco, and political candidates.

TABLE 10.3	SOCIAL NETWORK FEATURES AND TECHNOLOGIES
FEATURE	**DESCRIPTION**
Profiles	User-created Web pages that describe themselves on a variety of dimensions
Friends network	Ability to create a linked group of friends
Network discovery	Ability to find other networks and find new groups and friends
Favorites	Ability to communicate favorite sites, bookmarks, content, and destinations
Games, widgets, and apps	Apps and games on the site, such as those offered by Facebook
E-mail	Ability to send e-mail within the social network site to friends
Storage	Storage space for network members' content
Instant messaging	Immediate one-to-one contact with friends through the community facility
Message boards	Posting of messages to groups of friends and other groups' members
Online polling	Polling of member opinion
Chat	Online immediate group discussion; Internet relay chat (IRC)
Discussion groups	Discussion groups and forums organized by topic
Experts online	Certified experts in selected areas respond to queries
Membership management tools	Ability of site managers to edit content, and dialog; remove objectionable material; protect security and privacy

which has declined from a few years ago when Facebook represented over 65% of the market. Relative to other sites then, Facebook's growth has slowed, while newer social network sites have grown explosively. Moreover, the success of Facebook is likely to attract some powerful competitors with their own ideas of how to build online versions of the social graph, namely, Google, Apple, and Amazon. See the *Insight on Technology* case *Facebook Has Friends*.

Many Facebook users report "network fatigue" caused by spending too much time keeping up with their close and distant friends on many social networks. An Associated Press poll found that 80% of users said they had never been influenced by an ad on the site, and 43% said Facebook would fade away as new platforms appear (Oreskovic, 2012; Murphy, 2012). The fears that many users have about the privacy of their posts and content is also another factor in people either not joining Facebook, or pulling back from engagement.

The financial future of social networks is to become advertising and sales platforms. But social networks are not yet proven advertising platforms that drive sales. The relationship between Likes and sales is not clear yet. Response rates to display ads on Facebook are far lower than on portal sites like Yahoo, or search ads like Google. In part this reflects the sentiment of users who go onto social sites without the intention of purchasing anything.

INSIGHT ON TECHNOLOGY

FACEBOOK HAS FRIENDS

In October 2012, Facebook had an estimated 1 billion users worldwide. Facebook seems to have attained social network dominance, but its growth rate has slowed down, and minutes of engagement with the site have also begun to plateau. By September 2012, Facebook's stock price had sunk to $20 a share, down from its IPO price of $38, amid questions about the efficacy of its ad business.

Facebook faces increasing competition from other fledgling networks and services, such as Tumblr. A micro-blogging site, Tumblr is growing at more than 200% a year. It's free, with no ads, forced banner ads, or logos, but just like Facebook, at some point Tumblr will have to monetize its audience, and earn revenue with premium features.

Facebook is also facing competition from giants of the Web, like Google and Microsoft. Google launched its Google+ social network in June 2011. Google+ is based on the idea (similar to Tumblr) of sharing with multiple separate groups of friends, called "circles," who form the collection of real-world social networks that people participate in.

Other features of Google+ include group video chatting (called "Hangouts") and group mobile audio and video chatting (called "Huddles"). It is fully integrated with other Google products like Gmail, so you can drag and drop friends from your Gmail lists to request they join one of your circles. Google+ is advertising-supported, you betcha!

By the end of September 2012, Google+ had reached 27 million registered users. While Google+ is a contender for social network power, it lacks the engagement of other sites like Face-book, Tumblr, and Pinterest. For instance, the average Facebook user in the United States spends nearly seven hours a month on Facebook, whereas Google+ users spend three minutes.

Not to be outdone, Microsoft invested $250 million in Facebook in October 2007 for a 1.6% stake. This valued Facebook at $15 billion, and was a sign of Microsoft's desperation at the time. However, Facebook and Microsoft have shared only a few technologies so far. Microsoft's search engine Bing is used by Facebook users. In May 2011, Microsoft purchased Skype, the Internet-based telephone service. Facebook needs Skype because it does not have a peer-to-peer network of its own that can handle video and voice services for users.

It's unlikely that Microsoft will be satisfied with its tiny slice of Facebook. In May 2012, Microsoft launched a social network called So.cl (pronounced "social"). So.cl is designed to help students find and share interesting Web pages, combining social with Bing search. So.cl has developed partnerships with several universities, including New York University.

While Facebook is the dominant social network site now, given the strength of its competitors, it is likely there will be many powerful social networks for users to join. Journalists are already reporting a kind of "social network fatigue," where users are simply getting tired of following and updating their Facebook, Twitter, Tumblr, and LinkedIn networks. The next generation of entrepreneurs may solve this problem by creating an inter-network, an inter-operable system where users can participate in all their networks from one interface. But for now, the big players in this field are determined to build their own walls (pun intended).

■ **SOURCES:** "Apple Officials Said to Consider Stake in Twitter," by Evelyn Rusli and Nick Bilton, *New York Times*, July 27, 2012; "Microsoft Launches New Social Network to Compete With Google," by Kelly Clay, *Forbes*, May 21, 2012; "The Mounting Minuses at Google+," by Amir Efrati, *Wall Street Journal*, February 28, 2012; "Google is Now in the Top Ten Social Networking Sites," by Matt Rosoff, *Business Insider*, September 26, 2011; "Google+ Traffic Floodgates Open," Rolfe Winkler, *Wall Street Journal*, September 22, 2011; "Microsoft Social Networking Accident Makes Perfect Sense," Nick Kolakowski, *eWeek*, July 18, 2011; "Going in Google+ Circles," by Katherine Boehret, *Wall Street Journal*, July 13, 2011; "Google Makes Facebook Look Socially Awkward," Rolfe Winkler, *Wall Street Journal*, July 7, 2011; "Google Takes on Friend Sprawl," by Amir Efrati, *Wall Street Journal*, June 29, 2010; "Another Try by Google to Take On Facebook," by Claire Cain Miller, *New York Times*, June 28, 2011.

10.2 ONLINE AUCTIONS

Online auction sites are among the most popular consumer-to-consumer (C2C) e-commerce sites on the Internet, although the popularity of auctions and their growth rates have slowed in recent years due to customers' preferences for a "buy now" fixed-price model. The market leader in C2C auctions is eBay, which has 100 million active users in the United States and over 300 million items listed on any given day within 18,000 categories. In August 2012, eBay had around 75 million unique visitors, placing it 11th on the list of top 50 Web properties (comScore, 2012b). In 2011, eBay had $5.4 billion in net revenues from its Marketplaces segment, a 12% increase from 2010, and the total worth of goods sold was $68 billion (Gross Market Value) (eBay, 2012). eBay is further discussed in the case study at the end of this chapter. In the United States alone, there are several hundred auction sites, some specializing in unique collectible products such as stamps and coins, others adopting a more generalist approach in which almost any good can be found for sale. Increasingly, established portals and online retail sites—from Yahoo and MSN to JCPenney and Sam's Club—are adding auctions to their sites. Auctions constitute a significant part of B2B e-commerce, and more than a third of business procurement officers use auctions to procure goods. What explains the extraordinary popularity of auctions? Do consumers always get lower prices at auctions? Why do merchants auction their products if the prices they receive are so low?

DEFINING AND MEASURING THE GROWTH OF AUCTIONS AND DYNAMIC PRICING

auctions

markets in which prices are variable and based on the competition among participants who are buying or selling products and services

Auctions are markets in which prices are variable and based on the competition among participants who are buying or selling products and services. Auctions are one type of **dynamic pricing**, in which the price of the product varies, depending directly on the demand characteristics of the customer and the supply situation of the seller. There is a wide variety of dynamically priced markets, from simple haggling, bartering, and negotiating between one buyer and one seller, to much more sophisticated public auctions in which there may be thousands of sellers and thousands of buyers, as in a single stock market for a bundle of shares.

dynamic pricing

the price of the product varies, depending directly on the demand characteristics of the customer and the supply situation of the seller

In dynamic pricing, merchants change their prices based on both their understanding of how much value the customer attaches to the product and their own desire to make a sale. Likewise, customers change their offers to buy based on both their perceptions of the seller's desire to sell and their own need for the product. If you as a customer really want the product right now, you will be charged a higher price in a dynamic pricing regime, and you will willingly pay a higher price than if you placed less value on the product and were willing to wait several days to buy it. For instance, if you want to travel from New York to San Francisco to attend a last-minute business conference, and then return as soon as possible, you will be charged twice as much as a tourist who agrees to stay over the weekend.

fixed pricing

one national price, everywhere, for everyone

In contrast, traditional mass-market merchants generally use **fixed pricing**—one national price, everywhere, for everyone. Fixed pricing first appeared in the nineteenth century with the development of mass national markets and retail stores that could sell to a national audience. Prior to this period, all pricing was dynamic and local, with prices derived through a process of negotiation between the customer and the merchant. Computers and the development of the Internet have contributed to a return of dynamic pricing. The difference is that with the Internet, dynamic pricing can be conducted globally, continuously, and at a very low cost.

Auctions—one form of dynamic pricing mechanism—are used throughout the e-commerce landscape. The most widely known auctions are **consumer-to-consumer (C2C) auctions**, in which the auction house is simply an intermediary market maker, providing a forum where consumers—buyers and sellers—can discover prices and trade. Less well known are **business-to-consumer (B2C) auctions**, where a business owns or controls assets and uses dynamic pricing to establish the price. Established merchants on occasion use B2C auctions to sell excess goods. This form of auction or dynamic pricing will grow along with C2C auctions.

Some leading online auction sites are listed in **Table 10.4**. Auctions are not limited to goods and services. They can also be used to allocate resources, and bundles of resources, among any group of bidders. For instance, if you wanted to establish an optimal schedule for assigned tasks in an office among a group of clerical workers, an auction in which workers bid for assignments would come close to producing a nearly optimal solution in a short amount of time (Parkes and Ungar, 2000). In short, auctions—like all markets—are ways of allocating resources among independent agents (bidders).

consumer-to-consumer (C2C) auctions
auction house acts as an intermediary market maker, providing a forum where consumers can discover prices and trade

business-to-consumer (B2C) auctions
auction house sells goods it owns, or controls, using various dynamic pricing models

WHY ARE AUCTIONS SO POPULAR? BENEFITS AND COSTS OF AUCTIONS

The Internet is primarily responsible for the resurgence in auctions. Although electronic network-based auctions such as AUCNET in Japan (an electronic automobile auction for used cars) were developed in the late 1980s, these pre-Internet auctions required an expensive telecommunications network to implement. The Internet provides a global environment and very low fixed and operational costs for the aggregation of huge buyer audiences, composed of millions of consumers worldwide, who can use a universally available technology (Internet browsers) to shop for goods.

Benefits of Auctions

Aside from the sheer game-like fun of participating in auctions, consumers, merchants, and society as a whole derive a number of economic benefits from participating in Internet auctions. These benefits include:

- **Liquidity:** Sellers can find willing buyers, and buyers can find sellers.
- **Price discovery:** Buyers and sellers can quickly and efficiently develop prices for items that are difficult to assess, where the price depends on demand and supply, and where the product is rare.
- **Price transparency:** Public Internet auctions allow everyone in the world to see the asking and bidding prices for items.

- **Market efficiency:** Auctions can, and often do, lead to reduced prices, and hence reduced profits for merchants, leading to an increase in consumer welfare—one measure of market efficiency.

- **Lower transaction costs:** Online auctions can lower the cost of selling and purchasing products, benefiting both merchants and consumers. Like other Internet markets, such as retail markets, Internet auctions have very low (but not zero) transaction costs.

- **Consumer aggregation:** Sellers benefit from large auction sites' ability to aggregate a large number of consumers who are motivated to purchase something in one marketspace.

- **Network effects:** The larger an auction site becomes in terms of visitors and products for sale, the more valuable it becomes as a marketplace for everyone by providing liquidity and several other benefits listed previously, such as lower transaction costs, higher efficiency, and better price transparency.

Risks and Costs of Auctions for Consumers and Businesses

There are a number of risks and costs involved in participating in auctions. In some cases, auction markets can fail—like all markets at times. (We describe auction market failure in more detail later.) Some of the more important risks and costs to keep in mind are:

- **Delayed consumption costs:** Internet auctions can go on for days, and shipping will take additional time.

- **Monitoring costs:** Participation in auctions requires your time to monitor bidding.

- **Equipment costs:** Internet auctions require you to purchase a computer system, pay for Internet access, and learn a complex operating system.

- **Trust risks:** Online auctions are the single largest source of Internet fraud. Using auctions increases the risk of experiencing a loss.

- **Fulfillment costs:** Typically, the buyer pays fulfillment costs of packing, shipping, and insurance, whereas at a physical store these costs are included in the retail price.

Auction sites such as eBay have taken a number of steps to reduce consumer participation costs and trust risk. For instance, auction sites attempt to solve the trust problem by providing a rating system in which previous customers rate sellers based on their overall experience with the merchant. Although helpful, this solution does not always work. Auction fraud is the leading source of e-commerce complaints to federal law enforcement officials.

Market-Maker Benefits: Auctions as an E-commerce Business Model

Online auctions have been among the most successful business models in retail and B2B commerce. eBay, the Internet's most lucrative auction site, has been profitable nearly since its inception. The strategy for eBay has been to make money off every stage in the auction cycle. eBay earns revenue from auctions in several ways: transaction fees based on the amount of the sale, listing fees for display of goods, financial service fees from payment systems such as PayPal, and advertising or placement

TABLE 10.4	**LEADING ONLINE AUCTION SITES**
GENERAL	
eBay	The world market leader in auctions: 75 million visitors a month and millions of products.
uBid	Marketplace for excess inventory from pre-approved merchants.
eBid	In business since 1998. Operates in 18 countries, including U.S. Currently, the top competitor to eBay. Offers much lower fees.
Bid4Assets	Liquidation of distressed assets from government and the public sector, corporations, restructurings, and bankruptcies.
Auctions.samsclub	Sam's Club brand merchandise in a variety of categories.
SPECIALIZED	
BidZ	Live auction format for online jewelry.
Racersauction	Specialized site for automobile racing parts.
Philatelic Phantasies	Stamp site for professionals, monthly online stamp auction.
Teletrade	America's largest fully automated auction company of certified coins including ancient gold, silver, and copper coins. Also offers sports cards.
Baseball-cards.com	The Internet's first baseball card store. Offers weekly auctions of baseball, football, basketball, hockey, wire photos, and more.
Oldandsold	Online auction service specializing in quality antiques. Dealers pay a 3% commission on merchandise sold.

fees where sellers pay extra for special services such as particular display or listing services.

However, it is on the cost side that online auctions have extraordinary advantages over ordinary retail or catalog sites. Auction sites carry no inventory and do not perform any fulfillment activities—they need no warehouses, shipping, or logistical facilities. Sellers and consumers provide these services and bear these costs. In this sense, online auctions are an ideal digital business because they involve simply the transfer of information.

TYPES AND EXAMPLES OF AUCTIONS

There are four major different types of auctions:

English Auctions The **English auction** is the easiest to understand and the most common form of auction on eBay. Typically, there is a single item up for sale from a single seller. There is a time limit when the auction ends, a reserve price below which the seller will not sell (usually secret), and a minimum incremental bid set. Multiple buyers bid against one another until the auction time limit is reached. The highest

English auction
most common form of auction; the highest bidder wins

bidder wins the item (if the reserve price of the seller has been met or exceeded). English auctions are considered to be seller-biased because multiple buyers compete against one another—usually anonymously.

Traditional Dutch Auctions In the traditional Dutch auction in Aalsmeer, Holland, 5,000 flower growers—who own the auction facility—sell bundles of graded flowers to 2,000 buyers. The Dutch auction uses a clock visible to all that displays the starting price growers want for their flowers. Every few seconds, the clock ticks to a lower price. When buyers want to buy at the displayed price, they push a button to accept the lot of flowers at that price. If buyers fail to bid in a timely fashion, their competitors will win the flowers. The auction is very efficient: on average, Aalsmeer conducts 50,000 transactions daily for 20 million flowers.

Dutch Internet auction

public ascending price, multiple unit auction. Final price is lowest successful bid, which sets price for all higher bidders

Dutch Internet Auctions In **Dutch Internet auctions**, such as those on eBay, OnSale, and others, the rules and action are different from the classical Dutch auction. The Dutch Internet auction format is perfect for sellers that have many identical items to sell. Sellers start by listing a minimum price, or a starting bid for one item, and the number of items for sale. Bidders specify both a bid price and the quantity they want to buy. The uniform price reigns. Winning bidders pay the same price per item, which is the lowest successful bid.

Name Your Own Price auction

auction where users specify what they are willing to pay for goods or services

Name Your Own Price Auctions The **Name Your Own Price** auction was pioneered by Priceline, and is the second most-popular auction format on the Web. Although Priceline also acts as an intermediary, buying blocks of airline tickets and vacation packages at a discount and selling them at a reduced retail price or matching its inventory to bidders, it is best known for its Name Your Own Price auctions, where users specify what they are willing to pay for goods or services, and multiple providers bid for their business. Prices do not descend and are fixed: the initial consumer offer is a commitment to purchase at that price. In 2011, Priceline had more than $4.35 billion in revenues, and in 2012, attracted around 15 million unique visitors a month.

demand aggregators

suppliers or market makers who group unrelated buyers into a single purchase in return for offering a lower purchase price. Prices on multiple units fall as the number of buyers increases

Group Buying Auctions: Demand Aggregators A **demand aggregator** facilitates group buying of products at dynamically adjusted discount prices based on high-volume purchases. Online demand aggregation is built on two principles. First, sellers are more likely to offer discounts to buyers purchasing in volume, and, second, buyers increase their purchases as prices fall. Prices are expected to adjust dynamically to the volume of the order and the motivations of the vendors. In general, demand aggregation is suitable for MRO products (commodity-like products) that are frequently purchased by a large number of organizations in high volume.

Professional Service Auctions Perhaps one of the more interesting uses for auctions on the Web is eBay's marketplace for professional services, Elance. This auction is a sealed-bid, dynamic-priced market for freelance professional services from legal and marketing services to graphics design and programming. Firms looking for professional services post a project description and request for bid on Elance. Providers of services bid for the work. The buyer can choose from among bidders on the basis of both cost and perceived quality of the providers that can be gauged from the feedback of clients posted on the site.

WHEN TO USE AUCTIONS (AND FOR WHAT) IN BUSINESS

There are many different situations in which auctions are an appropriate channel for businesses to consider. For much of this chapter, we have looked at auctions from a consumer point of view. The objective of consumers is to receive the greatest value for the lowest cost. Now, switch your perspective to that of a business. Remember that the objective of businesses using auctions is to maximize their revenue (their share of consumer surplus) by finding the true market value of products and services, a market value that hopefully is higher in the auction channel than in fixed-price channels. **Table 10.5** provides an overview of factors to consider:

- **Type of product:** Online auctions are most commonly used for rare and unique products for which prices are difficult to discover, and there may have been no market for the goods.

- **Product life cycle:** For the most part, businesses have traditionally used auctions for goods at the end of their product life cycle and for products where auctions yield a higher price than fixed-price liquidation sales. However, products at the beginning of their life cycle are increasingly being sold at auction. Early releases of music, books, videos, games, and digital appliances can be sold to highly motivated early adopters who want to be the first in their neighborhood with new products.

- **Channel management:** Established retailers such as JCPenney and Walmart, and manufacturers in general, must be careful not to allow their auction activity to interfere with their existing profitable channels.

- **Type of auction:** Sellers obviously should choose auctions where there are many buyers and only a few, or even one, seller. English ascending-price auctions such

TABLE 10.5	FACTORS TO CONSIDER WHEN CHOOSING AUCTIONS
CONSIDERATIONS	DESCRIPTION
Type of product	Rare, unique, commodity, perishable
Stage of product life cycle	Early, mature, late
Channel-management issues	Conflict with retail distributors; differentiation
Type of auction	Seller vs. buyer bias
Initial pricing	Low vs. high
Bid increment amounts	Low vs. high
Auction length	Short vs. long
Number of items	Single vs. multiple
Price-allocation rule	Uniform vs. discriminatory
Information sharing	Closed vs. open bidding

as those at eBay are best for sellers because as the number of bidders increases, the price tends to move higher.

- **Initial pricing:** Research suggests that auction items should start out with low initial bid prices in order to encourage more bidders to bid (see "Bid increments" below). The lower the price, the larger the number of bidders will appear. The larger the number of bidders, the higher the prices move.

- **Bid increments:** It is generally safest to keep bid increments low so as to increase the number of bidders and the frequency of their bids. If bidders can be convinced that, for just a few more dollars, they can win the auction, then they will tend to make the higher bid and forget about the total amount they are bidding.

- **Auction length:** In general, the longer auctions are scheduled, the larger the number of bidders and the higher the prices can go. However, once the new bid arrival rate drops off and approaches zero, bid prices stabilize. Most eBay auctions are scheduled for seven days.

- **Number of items:** When a business has a number of items to sell, buyers usually expect a "volume discount," and this expectation can cause lower bids in return. Therefore, sellers should consider breaking up very large bundles into smaller bundles auctioned at different times.

- **Price allocation rule:** Most buyers believe it is "fair" that everyone pay the same price in a multi-unit auction, and a uniform pricing rule is recommended. eBay Dutch Internet auctions encourage this expectation. The idea that some buyers should pay more based on their differential need for the product is not widely supported.

- **Closed vs. open bidding:** Closed bidding has many advantages for the seller, and sellers should use this approach whenever possible because it permits price discrimination without offending buyers.

Auction Prices: Are They the Lowest?

It is widely assumed that auction prices are lower than prices in other fixed-price markets. Empirical evidence is mixed on this assumption. But there are many reasons why auction prices might be higher than those in fixed-price markets for items of identical quality, and why auction prices in one auction market may be higher than those in other auction markets. Consumers are not driven solely by value maximization, but instead are influenced by many situational factors, irrelevant and wrong information, and misperceptions when they make market decisions (Simonson and Tversky, 1992). Auctions are social events—shared social environments, where bidders adjust to one another (Hanson and Putler, 1996). Briefly, bidders base their bids on what others previously bid, and this can lead to an upward cascading effect (Arkes and Hutzel, 2000). In a study of hundreds of eBay auctions for Sony PlayStations, CD players, Mexican pottery, and Italian silk ties, Dholakia and Soltysinski (2001) found that bidders exhibited **herd behavior** (the tendency to bid higher for items based on the higher bids of others).

herd behavior
the tendency to bid higher for items based on the higher bids of others

WHEN AUCTION MARKETS FAIL: FRAUD AND ABUSE IN AUCTIONS

Online and offline auction markets can be prone to fraud, which produces information asymmetries between sellers and buyers and among buyers, which in turn causes auction markets to fail. Some of the possible abuses and frauds include:

- **Bid rigging**: Agreeing offline to limit bids or using shills to submit false bids that drive prices up.
- **Price matching:** Agreeing informally or formally to set floor prices on auction items below which sellers will not sell in open markets.
- **Shill feedback, defensive:** Using secondary IDs or other auction members to inflate seller ratings.
- **Shill feedback, offensive:** Using secondary IDs or other auction members to deflate ratings for another user (feedback bombs).
- **Feedback extortion:** Threatening negative feedback in return for a benefit.
- **Transaction interference:** E-mailing buyers to warn them away from a seller.
- **Bid manipulation:** Using the retraction option to make high bids, discovering the maximum bid of the current high bidder, and then retracting the bid.
- **Non-payment after winning:** Blocking legitimate buyers by bidding high, then not paying.
- **Shill bidding:** Using secondary user IDs or other auction members to artificially raise the price of an item.
- **Transaction non-performance:** Accepting payment and failing to deliver.
- **Non-selling seller:** Refusing payment or failing to deliver after a successful auction.
- **Bid siphoning:** E-mailing another seller's bidders and offering the same product for less.

According to the Internet Crime Complaint Center (IC3), Internet auto-auction fraud was one of the top 10 types of fraud reported in 2011. Victims of auto-auction fraud scams reported more than $8.2 million in losses, and an average reported loss of more than $2,000 (National White Collar Crime Center/FBI, 2012). Auction sites have sought to reduce these risks through various methods including:

- **Rating systems:** Previous customers rate sellers based on their experience with them and post them on the site for other buyers to see.
- **Watch lists:** These allow buyers to monitor specific auctions as they proceed over a number of days and only pay close attention in the last few minutes of bidding.
- **Proxy bidding:** Buyers can enter a maximum price they are willing to pay, and the auction software will automatically place incremental bids as their original bid is surpassed.

eBay and many other auction sites have investigation units that receive complaints from consumers and investigate reported abuses. Nevertheless, with millions of visitors per week and hundreds of thousands of auctions to monitor, eBay is highly dependent on the good faith of sellers and consumers to follow the rules.

10.3 E-COMMERCE PORTALS

Portals are the most frequently visited sites on the Web if only because they often are the first page to which many users point their browser on startup. The top portals such as Yahoo, MSN, and AOL have hundreds of millions of unique visitors worldwide each month. The original portals in the early days of e-commerce were search engines. Consumers would pass through search engine portals on their way to rich, detailed, in-depth content on the Web. But portals evolved into much more complex Web sites that provide news, entertainment, maps, images, social networks, in-depth information, and education on a growing variety of topics all contained at the portal site. Portals today seek to be a sticky destination site, not merely a gateway through which visitors pass. In this respect, Web portals are very much like television networks: destination sites for content supported by advertising revenues. Portals today want visitors to stay a long time—the longer the better. For the most part they succeed: portals are places where people linger for a long time.

THE GROWTH AND EVOLUTION OF PORTALS

Web portals have changed a great deal from their initial function and role. As noted above, most of today's well-known portals, such as Yahoo, MSN, and AOL, began as search engines. The initial function provided by portals was to index Web page content and make this content available to users in a convenient form. Early portals expected visitors to stay only a few minutes at the site. Today, portals provide three important services: search and navigation of the Web; e-commerce purchasing; and content.

Because the value of portals to advertisers and content owners is largely a function of the size of the audience each portal reaches, and the length of time visitors stay on site, portals compete with one another on reach and unique visitors. *Reach* is defined as the percentage of the Web audience that visits the site in a month (or some other time period), and *unique visitors* is defined as the number of uniquely identified individuals who visit in a month. Portals are inevitably subject to network effects: The value of the portal to advertisers and consumers increases geometrically as reach increases, which, in turn, attracts still more customers. These effects have resulted in the differentiation of the portal marketspace into three tiers: a few general-purpose mega portal sites that garner 60%–80% of the Web audience, second-tier general-purpose sites that hover around 20%–30% reach, and third-tier specialized vertical market portals that attract 2%–10% of the audience. The top five portals/search engines (Google, Yahoo, MSN/Bing, AOL, and Ask.com) account for more than 95% of online searches. A similar pattern of concentration is observed when considering the audience share of portals/search engines as illustrated in **Figure 10.3**. For more insight into the nature of the competition and change among the top portals, read *Insight on Business: The Transformation of AOL*.

| FIGURE 10.3 | THE TOP 5 PORTAL/SEARCH ENGINE SITES IN THE UNITED STATES |

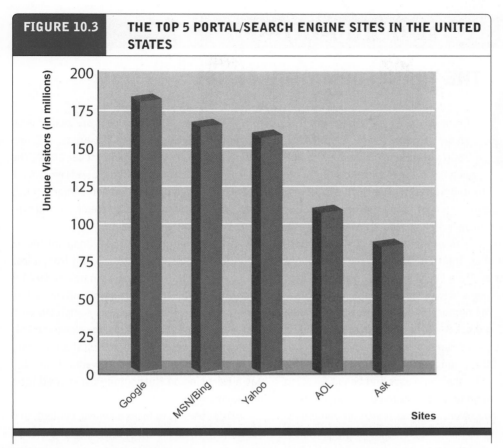

SOURCE: Based on data from comScore, 2012b.

TYPES OF PORTALS: GENERAL-PURPOSE AND VERTICAL MARKET

There are two primary types of portals: general-purpose portals and vertical market portals. **General-purpose portals** attempt to attract a very large general audience and then retain the audience on-site by providing in-depth vertical content channels, such as information on news, finance, autos, movies, and weather. General-purpose portals typically offer Web search engines, free e-mail, personal home pages, chat rooms, community-building software, and bulletin boards. Vertical content channels on general-purpose portal sites offer content such as sports scores, stock tickers, health tips, instant messaging, automobile information, and auctions.

Vertical market portals (sometimes also referred to as destination sites or vortals) attempt to attract highly focused, loyal audiences with a deep interest either in community or specialized content—from sports to the weather. In addition to their focused content, vertical market portals have recently begun adding many of the features found in general-purpose portals. For instance, in addition to being a social network, you can also think of Facebook as a portal—the home page for millions of users, and a gateway to the Internet. Facebook is an affinity group portal because it is based on friendships among people. Facebook offers e-mail, search (Bing), games, and apps. News is limited.

general-purpose portals

attempt to attract a very large general audience and then retain the audience on-site by providing in-depth vertical content

vertical market portals

attempt to attract highly focused, loyal audiences with a deep interest in either community or specialized content

INSIGHT ON BUSINESS

THE TRANSFORMATION OF AOL

From its inauspicious beginnings as an online game server for the Atari 2600 video game console to its dizzying heights as the leading ISP in the United States, to its equally staggering decline after its failed merger with Time Warner, somehow AOL has found a way to survive.

AOL rose to prominence as a subscription-based dial-up Internet provider, and was bought in 2000 by Time Warner for $165 billion. That merger is new viewed as the worst in corporate history. The number of AOL subscribers peaked in 2002 and has declined ever since as broadband Internet becomes more widespread.

In 2007, long since spun off from Time Warner, AOL changed gears and began focusing on developing and distributing premium content. To that end, AOL acquired a slew of companies to help lay the foundation, including the critical acquisition of the Huffington Post in March 2011 for $315 million. The ability to expand its video content was a major reason for the acquisition. Launched in the summer of 2012, HuffPost Live is an online cable news network with a social component. AOL also has teams of video producers in both New York and Los Angeles that are creating branded entertainment video. Only YouTube now exceeds AOL in the number of online video offerings.

Aiming to become a one-stop shop for consumers delivering the content they want when they want it, the AOL On Network debuted in April 2012. More than 420,000 videos are available on 14 channels divided into subject areas. iOS and Android apps were released in October 2012. The opposite approach from HuffPost Live is embraced. Organized, selected, programmed content, much more like traditional TV, is offered here and syndicated out to different outlets.

AOL's second quarter 2012 financial report in July 2012 registered a turnaround from a loss of $11.8 million in 2011 to earnings of $970.8 million in 2012. This was mainly attributed to a one-time patent deal that was completed with Microsoft in June. Revenue decline slowed to 2%, the smallest in seven years, and total advertising revenue was up 6%. So far, revenue from display advertising on Huffington Post showed little improvement.

AOL's strategy to focus on video, content, and display advertising is risky. One-third of the company's revenue is still derived from its dwindling dial-up subscriptions. However, in August 2012, AOL instituted a $600 million stock buyback and one-time cash dividend of $5.15 per share to recompense investors for the completed Microsoft patent deal. It also enjoyed a tripling of its stock price from the previous year, and appears well positioned to capitalize on the popularity of online video. The combination is likely to mollify investors in the short term while AOL continues to work towards consistent user growth, which the company says will signify that its turnaround is complete.

SOURCES: "AOL: You've Got Apps," *New York Business Journal*, October 4, 2012; "AOL," Wikipedia.com, accessed September 26, 2012; "AOL CEO Tim Armstrong: 'We Haven't Won Yet'," by Daniel Terdiman, News.cnet.com, September 11, 2012; "AOL's Triple-Pronged Approach to Online Video," by Troy Dreier, Streamingmedia.com, August/September 2012; "$1.1B Microsoft Patent Deal Done, AOL Buys Back $600M In Stock, Offers Dividend Of $5.15 Per Share," by Ingrid Lunden,TechCrunch.com, August 27th, 2012; "AOL Dialup Just Had Its 'Best' Quarter In A Decade, And Still Has 3 Million Subscribers," by Dan Frommer, SplatF.com, July 26, 2012; "AOL Says Patch Continues to Double Its Revenue from Last Year," by Steve Myers, Poynter.org, July 25, 2012; "AOL's Ad Revenue Up; Armstrong Bullish on Video," by Tanzina Vega, *New York Times*, July 25, 2012; "AOL Buys TechCrunch, 5Min and Thing Labs," by Jessica E. Vascellaro and Emily Steel, *New York Times*, September 29, 2010; "Eleven Years of Ambition and Failure at AOL," by Saul Hansell, *New York Times*, July 24, 2009; "Daring to Dream of a Resurgent AOL," by Saul Hansell, *New York Times*, July 23, 2009; "Before Spin-off, AOL Tries for that Start-up Feeling," *New York Times*, July 20, 2009.

General-purpose sites such as Yahoo try to be all things to all people, and attract a broad audience with both generalized navigation services and in-depth content and community efforts. For instance, Yahoo has become the Web's largest source of news: more people visit Yahoo News than any other news site including online newspapers.

As a general matter, the general-purpose portals are very well-known brands, while the vertical content and affinity group portals tend to have less well-known brands. **Figure 10.4** lists examples of general-purpose portals and the two main types of vertical market portals.

PORTAL BUSINESS MODELS

Portals receive income from a number of different sources. The revenue base of portals is changing and dynamic, with some of the largest sources of revenue declining. **Table 10.6** summarizes the major portal revenue sources.

The business strategies of both general-purpose and vertical portals have changed greatly because of the rapid growth in search engine advertising and intelligent ad placement networks such as Google's AdSense, which can place ads on thousands of Web sites based on the content of the Web site. General portal sites such as AOL and Yahoo did not have well-developed search engines, and hence have not grown as fast as Google, which has a powerful search engine. Microsoft, for instance, has invested billions of dollars in its Bing search engine to catch up with Google. On the other hand, general portals have content, which Google did not originally have, although it added to its content by purchasing YouTube and adding Google sites devoted to news,

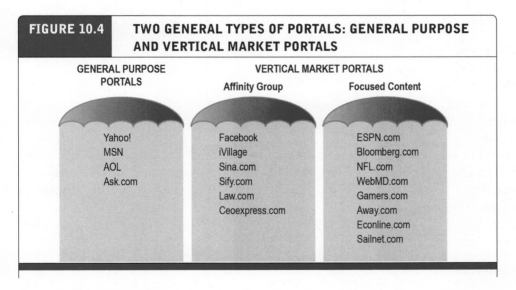

| FIGURE 10.4 | TWO GENERAL TYPES OF PORTALS: GENERAL PURPOSE AND VERTICAL MARKET PORTALS |

GENERAL PURPOSE PORTALS	VERTICAL MARKET PORTALS	
	Affinity Group	Focused Content
Yahoo!	Facebook	ESPN.com
MSN	iVillage	Bloomberg.com
AOL	Sina.com	NFL.com
Ask.com	Sify.com	WebMD.com
	Law.com	Gamers.com
	Ceoexpress.com	Away.com
		Econline.com
		Sailnet.com

There are two general types of portals: general-purpose and vertical market. Vertical market portals may be based on affinity groups or on focused content.

TABLE 10.6	TYPICAL PORTAL REVENUE SOURCES
PORTAL REVENUE SOURCE	DESCRIPTION
General advertising	Charging for impressions delivered
Tenancy deals	Fixed charge for guaranteed number of impressions, exclusive partnerships, "sole providers"
Commissions on sales	Revenue based on sales at the site by independent providers
Subscription fees	Charging for premium content
Applications and games	Games and apps are sold to users; advertising is placed within apps

financial information, images, and maps. Yahoo and MSN visitors stay on-site a long time reading news, content, and sending e-mail. Facebook users stay on-site and linger three times as long as visitors to traditional portals like Yahoo. For this reason social network sites, Facebook in particular, are direct competitors of Yahoo, Google, and the other portals. General portals are attempting to provide more premium content focused on sub-communities of their portal audience. Advertisers on portals are especially interested in focused, revenue-producing premium content available on Web portals because it attracts a more committed audience.

eBay Evolves

With the unveiling of its new, more reserved logo in September 2012, eBay announced its arrival to the mainstream. Gone are the jaunty, incongruent block letters that characterized the offbeat startup auction site founded by Pierre Omidyar in 1995. In their place, the bold primary colors intact, is a symmetrical set of block letters staidly observing the same parallel bottom line. With eBay now deriving 70% of its revenue from traditional e-commerce, and peer-to-peer auctions taking a backseat, the time had come.

The transformation began in November 2007, when former CEO Meg Whitman exited and was replaced by former Bain & Company managing director, John Donahoe. For many buyers, the novelty of online auctions had worn off, and they were returning to easier and simpler methods of buying fixed-price goods from fixed-price retailers such as Amazon, which, by comparison, had steady growth during the same time period. Search engines and comparison shopping sites were also taking away some of eBay's auction business by making items easier to find on the Web.

Donahoe's three-year revival plan moved eBay away from its origins as an online flea market, and at first it began to resemble an outlet mall where retailers sold out-of-season, overstocked, refurbished, or discontinued merchandise. From there it was

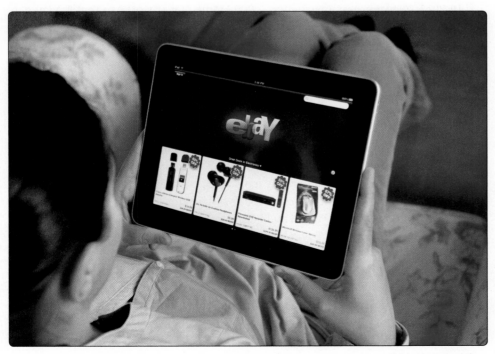

© Iain Masterton / Alamy

SOURCES: "eBay Hits 100m Mobile App Download Mark," by Dervedia Thomas, Dailydeal-media.com, September 29, 2012; "With Setify, eBay Goes Back To Its Roots And Creates The Nerdiest Pinterest Ever," by Christina Chaey, *Fast Company*, September 25, 2012; "eBay: We Need to Behave More Like a Retailer," by Sarah Shearman, Tamebay.com, September 25, 2012; "eBay Logo Gets a Refresh; The Time Felt Right After 17 Years," by Mark Tyson, Hexus.com, September 14, 2012; "eBay Bans Magic Spells and Potions," by Katy Waldman, Slate.com, August 17, 2012; "Behind eBay's Comeback," by James B. Stewart, *New York Times*, July 27, 2012; "Bill Me Later, eBay's Credit Version of PayPal, Helps Company's Profits but Exposes It to Risk," by Alistair Barr, MercuryNews.com, July 12, 2012; "PayPal Strength Helps eBay Exceed Forecasts," by Somini Sengupta, *New York Times*, April 18, 2012; "eBay Favors Big-Box Retailers in Holiday Promotions," by Ina Steiner, eCommerce-Bytes.com, December, 16, 2011; "How Jack Abraham is Reinventing eBay," by Danielle Sacks, *Fast Company*, June 22, 2011; "Connecting the Dots on eBay's Local Shopping Strategy," by Leena Rao, Techcrunch.com, May 15, 2011; "eBay CEO Sees Opportunities in Online and Offline Commerce," by Scott Morrison, *Wall Street Journal,* February 10, 2011; "eBay Says Big Growth Is Not Over," by Verne G. Kopytoff, *New York Times*, February 6, 2011; "eBay Mobile Sales Rise to $2 Billion, Reach Top End of Forecast," by Joseph Galante, Bloomberg.com, January 5, 2011.

a straightforward progression to partnering with firms such as Toys"R"Us to simply serve as another channel for current merchandise.

Small sellers were encouraged to shift away from the auction format and move toward the fixed-price sales model. The fee structure was adjusted, listing fees for fixed-price sales were lowered, improvements were made to the search engine, and rather than displaying ending auctions first, a formula was devised that took into account price and seller reputation so that highly rated merchants appeared first and received more exposure.

Unsurprisingly, the growing pains during this period included increasing complaints from sellers about excessive fees and eBay's favoritism toward big retailers. The hundreds of thousands of people who support themselves by selling on eBay and many millions more who use eBay to supplement their income often felt slighted. With its stock continuing to drop from its $58 high in 2004 to a low of just over $10 in early 2009, analysts' faith that Donahoe could turn things around had dwindled. Fearing that eBay had strayed too far from its original corporate culture and that competition from Amazon and Google Search presented serious threats, most forecasters were negative or neutral on eBay's chance of recovery. This pessimism discounted eBay's history of sensible growth marked by a number of canny purchases.

Its signature purchase is, of course, PayPal, whose payment services enable the exchange of money between individuals over the Internet. At a decade old, this acquisition was the key to eBay's endurance through the lean years and the propeller that pushed it towards the future. At times accounting for as much as 40% of eBay's revenues, it was responsible for 32% of eBay's growth from the first quarter of 2011 through the first quarter of 2012. With active registered accounts up 12% over that same time period, and half its growth accruing from abroad, PayPal was clearly an asset ripe for further development.

In 2012, a system was installed in 2,000 Home Depot stores so that PayPal card holders could either swipe their cards or use a PIN and their cell phone number to pay for purchases. Other bricks-and-mortar venues will be similarly equipped in the near future. Further expansion is a credit card processing device called PayPal Here that allows small businesses to use smartphones and tablets to accept credit cards. In direct competition with Square, eBay plans to enable consumers to "check in" so that they can be personally greeted, complete purchases without a mobile device or a credit card, and receive a text message as their receipt.

The 2008 addition of BillMeLater to the PayPal wallet, an instant credit product offered at checkout, has also proved, so far, to be farsighted. BML, which lets online customers pay several months after they have made purchases, logged 64% loan growth between 2010 and 2011, making it one of eBay's fastest growing business segments. BML can reduce funding costs for PayPal and help it to develop into a true financial product. Currently, more than 50% of PayPal purchases are funded using Visa and MasterCard credit and debit cards, which come with substantial fees. Reducing this cost would naturally increase profit margins. Now ranked the third most popular online payment service behind PayPal and Amazon's payment service, BML was used by consumers to complete 14% of purchases in 2011, a stunning jump from just 1% in 2010.

PayPal's success gave the Marketplaces segment time to rebound. And recover it did. In 2012, it delivered double-digit growth and eBay stock rose to its highest level in six years, close to $50 in September 2012. As impressive and encouraging as the Marketplaces turnaround was, it was another of eBay's astute investments that truly fueled its resurgence—mobile technology. eBay recognized the coming mobile revolution even before the first iPhone or the establishment of the App Store, according to Olivier Ropars, senior director of Mobile Commerce. This prescience resulted in two significant September 2012 milestones—the 100 millionth download of eBay mobile apps and the 100 millionth mobile listing. eBay not only has a core app, but also an eBay Motors app, an eBay Fashion app, and a RedLaser price checking app, which they expect to drive mobile sales to $10 billion by the end of 2012, nearly double 2011.

While many other acquisitions through the years have also helped to transform eBay from an online garage sale to a mainstream competitor with Amazon, its adoption of the "social, mobile, local" driving theme has been central to its survival. Positioning itself at the center of the online—offline—mobile triangle by offering a wide variety of services that enable merchants to more easily integrate their cross-channel retailing was the key to its 2012 resurgence and to its continued success.

Case Study Questions

1. Contrast eBay's original business model with its latest proposed business model.

2. What are the problems that eBay is currently facing? How is eBay trying to solve these problems?

3. Are the solutions eBay is seeking to implement good solutions? Why or why not? Are there any other solutions that eBay should consider?

4. Who are eBay's top three competitors online, and how will eBay's new strategy help it compete? Will eBay be providing a differentiated service to customers?

10.5 REVIEW

KEY CONCEPTS

■ **Explain the difference between a traditional social network and an online social network.**

Social networks involve:
- A group of people
- Shared social interaction
- Common ties among members
- A shared area for some period of time

By extension, an online social network is an area online where people who share common ties can interact with one another.

■ **Describe the different types of social networks and online communities and their business models.**

Types of social networks include:
- *General communities:* Members can interact with a general audience segmented into numerous different groups.
- *Practice networks:* Members can participate in discussion groups and get help or simply information relating to an area of shared practice.
- *Interest-based communities:* Members can participate in focused discussion groups on a shared interest.
- *Affinity communities:* Members can participate in focused discussions with others who share the same affinity or group identification, such as religion, ethnicity, gender, sexual orientation, or political beliefs.
- *Sponsored communities:* Members can participate in online communities created by government, nonprofit, or for-profit organizations for the purpose of pursuing organizational goals.

■ **Describe the major types of auctions, their benefits and costs, and how they operate.**

Auctions are markets where prices vary (dynamic pricing) depending on the competition among the participants who are buying or selling products or services. They can be classified broadly as C2C or B2C, although generally the term C2C auction refers to the venue in which the sale takes place, for example, a consumer-oriented Web site such as eBay, which also auctions items from established merchants. A B2C auction refers to an established online merchant that offers its own auctions. There are also numerous B2B online auctions for buyers of industrial parts, raw materials, commodities, and services. Within these three broad categories of auctions are several major auction types classified based upon how the bidding mechanisms work in each system:
- *English auctions:* A single item is up for sale from a single seller. Multiple buyers bid against one another within a specific time frame, with the highest bidder winning the object, as long as the high bid has exceeded the reserve bid set by the seller, below which he or she refuses to sell.
- *Traditional Dutch auctions:* Sellers with many identical items sold in lots list a starting price and time for the opening of bids. As the clock advances, the price for each lot falls until a buyer offers to buy at that price.
- *Dutch Internet auctions:* Sellers with many identical items for sale list a minimum price or starting bid, and buyers indicate both a bid price and a quantity desired. The lowest winning bid that clears the available quantity is paid by all winning bidders. Those with the highest bid are assured of receiving the quantity they desire, but only pay the amount of the lowest successful bid (uniform pricing rule).
- *Name Your Own Price or reverse auctions:* Buyers specify the price they are willing to pay for an item, and multiple sellers bid for their business. This is one example of discriminatory pricing in which winners may pay different amounts for the same product or service depending on how much they have bid.
- *Group buying or demand aggregation auctions:* In the group-buying format, the more users who sign on to buy an item, the lower the item's price falls. These are generally B2B or B2G sites where small businesses can collectively receive discount prices for items that are purchased in high volumes.

Benefits of auctions include:

- *Liquidity:* Sellers and buyers are connected in a global marketplace.
- *Price discovery:* Even difficult-to-price items can be competitively priced based on supply and demand.
- *Price transparency:* Everyone in the world can see the asking and bidding prices for items, although prices can vary from auction site to auction site.
- *Market efficiency:* Consumers are offered access to a selection of goods that would be impossible to access physically, and consumer welfare is often increased due to reduced prices.
- *Lower transaction costs:* Merchants and consumers alike are benefited by the reduced costs of selling and purchasing goods compared to the physical marketplace.
- *Consumer aggregation:* A large number of consumers who are motivated to buy are amassed in one marketplace—a great convenience to the seller.
- *Network effects:* The larger an auction site becomes in the numbers of both users and products, the greater the benefits become, and therefore the more valuable a marketplace it becomes.

Costs of auctions include:

- *Delayed consumption:* Auctions can go on for days, and the product must then be shipped to the buyer. Buyers will typically want to pay less for an item they cannot immediately obtain.
- *Monitoring costs:* Buyers must spend time monitoring the bidding.
- *Equipment costs:* Buyers must purchase, or have already purchased, computer systems and Internet service, and learned how to operate these systems.
- *Trust risks:* Consumers face an increased risk of experiencing a loss, as online auctions are the largest source of Internet fraud.
- *Fulfillment costs:* Buyers must pay for packing, shipping, and insurance, and will factor this cost into their bid price.

Auction sites have sought to reduce these risks through various methods including rating systems, watch lists, and proxy bidding.

■ Understand when to use auctions in a business.

Auctions can be an appropriate channel for businesses to sell items in a variety of situations. The factors for businesses to consider include:

- *The type of product:* Rare and unique products are well suited to the auction marketplace as are perishable items such as airline tickets, hotel rooms, car rentals, and tickets to plays, concerts, and sporting events.
- *The product life cycle:* Traditionally, auctions have been used by businesses to generate a higher profit on items at the end of their life cycle than they would receive from product liquidation sales. However, they are now more frequently being used at the beginning of a product's life cycle to generate premium prices from highly motivated early adopters.
- *Channel management:* Businesses must be careful when deciding whether to pursue an auction strategy to ensure that products at auction do not compete with products in their existing profitable channels. This is why most established

retail firms tend to use auctions for products at the end of their life cycles or to have quantity purchasing requirements.

- *The type of auction:* Businesses should choose seller-biased auctions where there are many buyers and only one or a few sellers, preferably using the English ascending price system to drive the price up as high as possible.
- *Initial pricing:* Auction items should start with a low initial bid in order to attract more bidders, because the more bidders an item has, the higher the final price will be driven.
- *Bid increments:* When increments are kept low, more bidders are attracted and the frequency of their bidding is increased. This can translate into a higher final price as bidders are prodded onward in small steps.
- *Auction length:* In general, the longer an auction runs, the more bidders will enter the auction, and the higher the final price will be. However, if an auction continues for too long, the bid prices will stabilize and the cost of posting the auction may outweigh the profit from any further price increases.
- *Number of items:* If a business has a large quantity of items to sell, it should break the lot up into smaller bundles and auction them at different times so that buyers do not expect a volume discount.
- *Price allocation rule:* Because most buyers are biased toward the uniform pricing rule, sellers should use different auction markets, or auction the same goods at different times in order to price discriminate.
- *Closed vs. open bidding:* Closed bidding should be used whenever possible because it benefits a seller by allowing price discrimination. However, open bidding can sometimes be beneficial when herd behavior kicks in, causing multiple bids on highly visited auctions, while overlooked and lightly trafficked auctions for the same or comparable items languish. This generally occurs when there are few objective measures of a product's true value in the marketplace.

■ Describe the major types of Internet portals.

Web portals are gateways to the more than 100 billion Web pages available on the Internet. Originally, their primary purpose was to help users find information on the Web, but they evolved into destination sites that provided a myriad of content from news to entertainment. Today, portals serve three main purposes: navigation of the Web, content, and commerce. Among the major portal types are:

- *Enterprise portals:* Corporations, universities, churches, and other organizations create these sites to help employees or members navigate to important content such as corporate news or organizational announcements.
- *General-purpose portals:* Examples are AOL, Yahoo, and MSN, which try to attract a very large general audience by providing many in-depth vertical content channels.
- *Vertical market portals:* Also called destination sites, they attempt to attract a highly focused, loyal audience with an intense interest in either a community they belong to or an interest they hold.
- *Affinity groups:* Statistical aggregates of people who identify themselves by their attitudes, values, beliefs, and behavior.
- *Focused content portals:* These sites contain in-depth information on a particular topic that all members are interested in.

QUESTIONS

1. What factors enable online social networks to prosper today?
2. What is an affinity community, and what is its business model?
3. List and briefly explain three of the benefits of auction markets.
4. Under what conditions does a seller bias exist in an auction market? When does a buyer bias exist?
5. What is a demand aggregator and how does it work?
6. What three characteristics define a portal site today?
7. What is a vertical market portal, and how might recent trends in consumer behavior prove advantageous to this business model?
8. What are the two main types of vertical market portals, and how are they distinguished from one another?
9. List and briefly explain the main revenue sources for the portal business model.

PROJECTS

1. Visit one for-profit-sponsored and one nonprofit-sponsored social network. Create a presentation to describe and demonstrate the offering at each site. What organizational objectives is each pursuing? How is the for-profit company using community-building technologies as a customer relations management tool?

2. Examine the use of auctions by businesses. Go to any auction site of your choosing and look for outlet auctions or auctions directly from merchants. Research at least three products for sale. What stage in the product life cycle do these products fall into? Are there quantity purchasing requirements? What was the opening bid price? What are the bid increments? What is the auction duration? Analyze why these firms have used the auction channel to sell these goods and prepare a short report on your findings.

3. Find two examples of an affinity portal and two examples of a focused-content portal. Prepare a presentation explaining why each of your examples should be categorized as an affinity portal or a focused-content portal. For each example, surf the site and describe the services each site provides. Try to determine what revenue model each of your examples is using and, if possible, how many members or registered visitors the site has attracted.

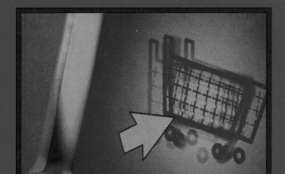

CHAPTER 11

B2B E-commerce: Supply Chain Management and Collaborative Commerce

After reading this chapter, you will be able to:

- Define B2B commerce and understand its scope and history.
- Understand the procurement process, the supply chain, and collaborative commerce.
- Identify the main types of B2B e-commerce: Net marketplaces and private industrial networks.
- Understand the four types of Net marketplaces.
- Identify the major trends in the development of Net marketplaces.
- Identify the role of private industrial networks in transforming the supply chain.
- Understand the role of private industrial networks in supporting collaborative commerce.

Volkswagen

Builds Its B2B Platform

olkswagen AG is the world's third largest car manufacturer, producing 8.3 million cars, trucks, and vans in 2011, and generating over $206 billion in revenue, up 25% from the year before. In addition to the Volkswagen brand, the Volkswagen Group also owns luxury carmakers such as Porsche, Audi, Bentley, Scania Bugatti, and Lamborghini, and family carmakers SEAT in Spain and Skoda in the Czech Republic. The company has almost 500,000 employees and operates plants in Europe, Africa, the Asian/Pacific rim, and the Americas. In the first half of 2012, Volkswagen Group continued its expansion despite a slowdown in Europe. New investments in China, India, and Mexico, along with a strong American market, pushed sales revenues up 22%, and its share of the global passenger car market to 12.4%, making Volkswagen the second largest producer in the world, behind General Motors.

© Julian Clune / Alamy

The various companies and 61 production plants in the Volkswagen Group annually purchase components, automotive parts, and indirect materials worth about 95 billion euros, or about $123 billion (which constitutes about 60% of Volkswagen's annual revenue). Obviously, the procurement process and relationships with suppliers are absolutely critical for Volkswagen's success.

Today, the Volkswagen Group manages almost all of its procurement needs via the Internet. It began building its Internet platform, VWGroupSupply.com, in 2000. The Volkswagen Group was looking for ways to create more efficient relationships with its suppliers and reduce the cost of paper-based procurement processes. However, the company did not want to automate procurement using a public independent exchange or an industry consortium because it would have had to adapt its own business processes to a common framework that could be used by many different organizations. Volkswagen hoped that by building its own B2B network, it could compete more effectively against other automakers. Volkswagen decided, for instance, not to participate in Covisint, the giant automotive industry consortium backed by major car manufacturers such as Ford, General Motors, and DaimlerChrysler, which provided procurement and other supply chain services for these companies, other automotive manufacturers, and their suppliers.

Instead, Volkswagen opted for a private platform that would allow it to integrate its suppliers more tightly with its own business processes, and where it could control more

SOURCES: "Facts and Figures," Volkswagen Group Supply, September 2012; Annual Report 2011, Volkswagen Group, March 9, 2012; "e-Procurement within the Volkswagen Group," by Alex Smith, Littleknowhow.com, September 25, 2011; "Customer Specific Quality Requirements of the Volkswagen Group," IATF Global Certification Body Conference, February 10, 2011; "Automotive B2B Developments at Odette25," GXS.com, June 22, 2010; "Best Practices: VW Revs Up its B2B Engine," by Martin Hoffman, *Optimize*, March 2004.

precisely who was invited to participate. VWGroupSupply now handles over 90% of all global purchasing for the Volkswagen Group, including all automotive and parts components. It is one of the most comprehensive e-procurement systems in the global automotive industry. Volkswagen refers to it as the Group Business Platform. From an initial seven applications in 2003, the platform now offers over 60 different online applications, such as requests for quotations (RFQs), contract negotiations, catalog purchases, purchase order management, engineering change management, vehicle program management, and payments, among others. The Volkswagen Group developed the platform using technology from a number of vendors, including Ariba, IBM, and i2 Technologies.

Suppliers of all sizes can access VWGroupSupply with standard Web browser software. The Web site is limited to suppliers who have done business with one or more companies in the Volkswagen Group and potential new suppliers who go through an authorization process. Currently, over 45,000 suppliers are registered, and there are over 206,000 users. The system maintains a common data repository with details on each supplier concerning procurement, logistics, production, quality, technical design, and finance.

VWGroupSupply's online catalog currently contains about 2.5 million items from 590 global suppliers. There are 14,200 internal users of the online catalog who have conducted over 1.5 million transactions with a value totaling 380 million euros ($447 million). The catalog uses the eCl@ss standard for classifying its contents. All suppliers who participate in the catalog ordering process classify their products using this standard.

Online negotiations involve multiple bids by suppliers for various purchasing contracts. VWGroupSupply ensures that all participants meet its technical and commercial qualifications. Before an online solicitation begins, the system informs vendors about the data and precise rules governing negotiations. About 13,000 different vendors have taken part in online negotiations. In 2011, VWGroupSupply conducted around 2,500 online contract negotiations online, with a value of 2.6 billion euros ($3.3 billion).

Shifts in market demand have a drastic impact on Volkswagen's production activities and affect the ability of suppliers to deliver. Production bottlenecks can result if suppliers are unprepared for a sudden upsurge in demand. If suppliers stock too much inventory, they may incur excess costs from running at overcapacity. VWGroupSupply has an application called electronic Capacity Management (eCAP) to alert both Volkswagen and its suppliers to changes in trends in advance. eCAP enables suppliers to track Volkswagen's continually updated production plans and materials requirements in real time online. This capability captures information about participating suppliers' planned maximum and minimum capacities. If Volkswagen production requirements go beyond these limits, the system sets off an alarm so both parties can react quickly. eCAP maintains information on over 400 suppliers and 4,000 critical parts.

The VWGroupSupply case illustrates the exciting potential for B2B e-commerce to lower production costs, increase collaboration among firms, speed up new product delivery, and ultimately revolutionize both the manufacturing process inherited from the early twentieth century and the way industrial products are designed and manufactured. VWGroupSupply is an example of just one type of B2B e-commerce, but there are many other equally promising efforts to using the Internet to change the relationships among manufacturers and their suppliers. In the fashion industry, the combination of high-speed value chains coupled with equally high-speed trendy design, not only clears shelves (and reduces the likelihood of clearance sales), but increases profits by increasing value to consumers (Cachon and Swinney, 2011).

In 2012—2013, the most important themes in B2B e-commerce involve growing industry concern with supply chain risk and volatility, along with a growing public concern with the accountability of supply chains—in particular, violations of developed-world expectations of working conditions in third-world factories that play a key role in the production of goods sold in more developed countries. What many firms have learned in the last decade is that supply chains can strengthen or weaken a company depending on a number of factors related to supply chain efficiency such as community engagement, labor relations, environmental protection, and sustainability. Thousands of smaller firms are now able to participate in B2B systems as low-cost cloud-based computing and software-as-a-service (SaaS) become widely available.

11.1 B2B E-COMMERCE AND SUPPLY CHAIN MANAGEMENT

The trade between business firms represents a huge marketplace. The total amount of B2B trade in the United States in 2012 was about $11.5 trillion, with B2B e-commerce (online B2B) contributing about $4.1 trillion of that amount (U.S. Census Bureau, 2012a; authors' estimates). By 2016, B2B e-commerce should grow to about $5.6 trillion in the United States.

The process of conducting trade among business firms is complex and requires significant human intervention, and therefore, consumes significant resources. Some firms estimate that each corporate purchase order for support products costs them, on average, at least $100 in administrative overhead. Administrative overhead includes processing paper, approving purchase decisions, spending time using the telephone and fax machines to search for products and arrange for purchases, arranging for shipping, and receiving the goods. Across the economy, this adds up to trillions of dollars annually being spent for procurement processes that could potentially be automated. If even just a portion of inter-firm trade were automated, and parts of the entire procurement process assisted by the Internet, then literally trillions of dollars might be released for more productive uses, consumer prices potentially would fall, productivity would increase, and the economic wealth of the nation would expand. This is the promise of B2B e-commerce. The challenge of B2B e-commerce is changing existing patterns and systems of procurement, and designing and implementing new Internet-based B2B solutions.

DEFINING AND MEASURING THE GROWTH OF B2B COMMERCE

total inter-firm trade
the total flow of value among firms

B2B commerce
all types of inter-firm trade

Before the Internet, business-to-business transactions were referred to simply as *trade* or the *procurement process*. The term **total inter-firm trade** refers to the total flow of value among firms. Today, we use the term **B2B commerce** to describe all types of inter-firm trade to exchange value across organizational boundaries. B2B commerce includes the following business processes insofar as they involve inter-firm trade: customer relationship management, demand management, order fulfillment, manufacturing management, procurement, product development, returns, logistics/transportation, and inventory management (Barlow, 2011). This definition of B2B commerce does not include transactions that occur within the boundaries of a single firm—for instance, the transfer of goods and value from one subsidiary to another, or the use of corporate intranets to manage the firm. We use the term **B2B e-commerce** (or **B2B digital commerce**) to describe specifically that portion of B2B commerce that is enabled by the Internet. The links that connect business firms in the production of goods and services are referred to as "the supply chain." **Supply chains** are a complex system of organizations, people, business processes, technology, and information, all of which need to work together to produce products efficiently (Global Supply Chain Forum, 2012). Today's supply chains are often global, connecting the smartphones in New York to the shipyards in Los Angeles and Quindow, and to the Foxconn factories that produce the phones. They are also local and national in scope.

B2B e-commerce (B2B digital commerce)
that portion of B2B commerce that is enabled by the Internet

supply chain
the links that connect business firms with one another to coordinate production

THE EVOLUTION OF B2B COMMERCE

B2B commerce has evolved over a 35-year period through several technology-driven stages (see **Figure 11.1**). The first step in the development of B2B commerce in the mid-1970s was **automated order entry systems** that involved the use of telephone modems to send digital orders to health care products companies such as Baxter Healthcare. This early technology was replaced by personal computers using private networks in the late 1980s, and by Internet workstations accessing electronic online catalogs in the late 1990s.

automated order entry systems
involve the use of telephone modems to send digital orders

By the late 1970s, a new form of computer-to-computer communication called **electronic data interchange (EDI)** emerged. We describe EDI in greater detail later in this chapter, but at this point, it is necessary only to know that EDI is a communications standard for sharing business documents such as invoices, purchase orders, shipping bills, product stocking numbers (SKUs), and settlement information among a small number of firms. Virtually all large firms have EDI systems, and most industry groups have industry standards for defining documents in that industry.

electronic data interchange (EDI)
a communications standard for sharing business documents and settlement information among a small number of firms

Electronic storefronts emerged in the mid-1990s along with the commercialization of the Internet. **B2B electronic storefronts** are perhaps the simplest and easiest form of B2B e-commerce to understand, because they are just online catalogs of products made available to the public marketplace by a single supplier—similar to Amazon for the B2C retail market. Owned by the suppliers, they are seller-side solutions and seller-biased because they show only the products offered by a single supplier.

B2B electronic storefronts
online catalogs of products made available to the public marketplace by a single supplier

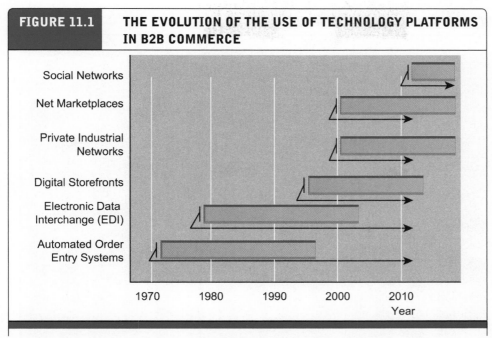

FIGURE 11.1 THE EVOLUTION OF THE USE OF TECHNOLOGY PLATFORMS IN B2B COMMERCE

B2B commerce has gone through many stages of development since the 1970s. Each stage reflects a major change in technology platforms from mainframes to private dedicated networks, and finally to the Internet. In 2012, social networks—both private and public—are being used to coordinate decision-making in B2B commerce.

Net marketplaces emerged in the late 1990s as a natural extension and scaling-up of the electronic storefronts. There are many different kinds of Net marketplaces, which we describe in detail in Section 11.2, but the essential characteristic of a Net marketplace is that they bring hundreds to thousands of suppliers—each with electronic catalogs and potentially thousands of purchasing firms—into a single Internet-based environment to conduct trade.

Private industrial networks also emerged in the late 1990s as natural extensions of EDI systems and the existing close relationships that developed between large industrial firms and their trusted suppliers. Described in more detail in Section 11.3, **private industrial networks** (sometimes also referred to as a *private trading exchange*, or *PTX*) are Internet-based communication environments that extend far beyond procurement to encompass supply chain efficiency enhancements and truly collaborative commerce. Private industrial networks permit buyer firms and their principal suppliers to share product design and development, marketing, inventory, production scheduling, and unstructured communications.

THE GROWTH OF B2B E-COMMERCE 2000–2016

During the period 2012–2016, B2B e-commerce is projected to grow from about 40% to 42% of total inter-firm trade in the United States, or from $4.1 trillion in 2012 to $5.6 trillion in 2016 (see **Figure 11.2**).

Net marketplace
brings hundreds to thousands of suppliers and buyers into a single Internet-based environment to conduct trade

private industrial networks (private trading exchange, PTX)
Internet-based communication environments that extend far beyond procurement to encompass truly collaborative commerce

| FIGURE 11.2 | GROWTH OF B2B COMMERCE 2000–2016 |

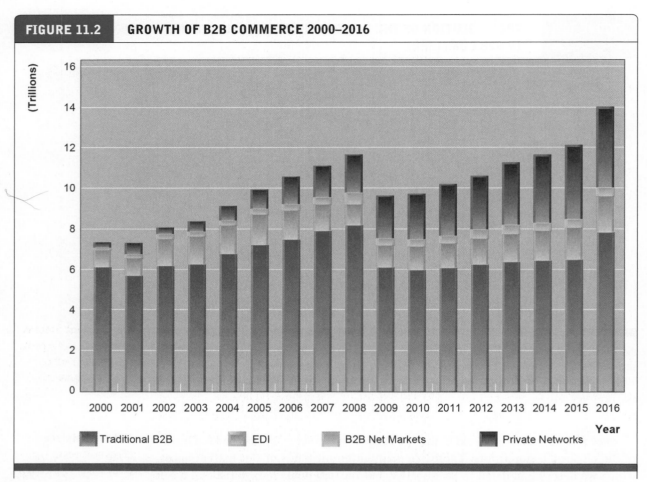

Private industrial networks are the fastest growing form of online B2B e-commerce, which includes EDI, B2B Net marketplaces, and private industrial markets.

SOURCES: Based on data from U.S. Census Bureau, 2012a; authors' estimates.

POTENTIAL BENEFITS AND CHALLENGES OF B2B E-COMMERCE

Regardless of the specific type of B2B e-commerce, as a whole, Internet-based B2B commerce promises many strategic benefits to participating firms—both buyers and sellers—and impressive gains for the economy as a whole. B2B e-commerce can:

- Lower administrative costs
- Lower search costs for buyers
- Reduce inventory costs by increasing competition among suppliers (increasing price transparency) and reducing inventory to the bare minimum
- Lower transaction costs by eliminating paperwork and automating parts of the procurement process
- Increase production flexibility by ensuring delivery of parts "just in time"
- Improve quality of products by increasing cooperation among buyers and sellers and reducing quality issues

- Decrease product cycle time by sharing designs and production schedules with suppliers
- Increase opportunities for collaborating with suppliers and distributors
- Create greater price transparency—the ability to see the actual buy and sell prices in a market
- Increase the visibility and real-time information sharing among all participants in the supply chain network.

While there are many potential benefits to B2B e-commerce supply chains, there are also considerable risks and challenges. Read *Insight on Society: Where's My iPad? Apple's Supply Chain Risks and Vulnerabilities* for a look at the impact the recent earthquake in Japan has had on global supply chains, as well as the reputational risk posed by supply chains.

THE PROCUREMENT PROCESS AND THE SUPPLY CHAIN

The subject of B2B e-commerce can be complex because there are so many ways the Internet can be used to support the exchange of goods and payments among organizations, efficient supply chains, and collaboration. At the most basic level, B2B digital e-commerce is about changing the **procurement process** (how business firms purchase goods they need to produce goods they will ultimately sell to consumers) of thousands of firms across the United States and the world.

One way to enter this area of Internet-based B2B commerce is to examine the existing procurement business process (see **Figure 11.3**). Firms purchase goods from a set of suppliers, and they in turn purchase their inputs from a set of suppliers. The supply chain includes not just the firms themselves, but also the relationships among them and the processes that connect them.

There are seven separate steps in the procurement process. The first three steps involve the decision of who to buy from and what to pay: searching for suppliers of specific products; qualifying both the seller and the products they sell; and negotiating prices, credit terms, escrow requirements, quality, and scheduling of delivery. Once a supplier is identified, purchase orders are issued, the buyer is sent an invoice, the goods are shipped, and the buyer sends a payment. Each of these steps in the procurement process is composed of many separate business processes and sub-activities. Each of these activities must be recorded in the information systems of the seller, buyer, and shipper. Often, this data entry is not automatic and involves a great deal of manual labor, telephone calls, faxes, and e-mails.

Types of Procurement

Two distinctions are important for understanding how B2B e-commerce can improve the procurement process. First, firms make purchases of two kinds of goods from suppliers: direct goods and indirect goods. **Direct goods** are goods integrally involved in the production process; for instance, when an automobile manufacturer purchases sheet steel for auto body production. **Indirect goods** are all other goods not directly involved in the production process, such as office supplies and maintenance products.

procurement process
how firms purchase goods they need to produce goods for consumers

direct goods
goods directly involved in the production process

indirect goods
all other goods not directly involved in the production process

INSIGHT ON SOCIETY

WHERE'S MY IPAD? SUPPLY CHAIN RISK AND VULNERABILITY

Technology, globalization of trade, and high levels of wage disparity between the developed and undeveloped worlds have led to a massive outsourcing of manufacturing around the world. Today, every component of every manufactured product is carefully examined by company engineers and financial managers with an eye to finding the lowest cost and highest quality manufacturer in the world. Production inevitably tends to concentrate at single firms that are given very high order volumes if they can meet the price. Large orders make lower prices easier to grant because of scale economies. But when you concentrate production globally on a few suppliers, you also concentrate risk.

Computers, cell phones, Caterpillar earth movers, Boeing airplanes, and automobiles from Toyota, Ford, GM, and Honda are just a few of the complex manufactured goods that rely on parts and subassemblies made thousands of miles away from their assembly plants. Most of these manufacturers know who their first-tier suppliers are but don't have a clue as to who supplies their suppliers, and so on down the line of the industrial spider's web that constitutes the real world of supply chains.

Take the Apple iPad. IHS iSuppli is a market research firm that tears apart consumer electronic devices to discover how they are made, who makes the components, and where they are made, in order to obtain market intelligence on producer prices and profits. In its teardown of the iPad 2, it identified at least five major components sourced from Japanese suppliers. When a catastrophic earthquake rocked Japan in 2011, several of these sub-suppliers were directly impacted. After the quake, the consumer order delivery delays reached eight weeks.

The new iPad released in March 2012 suggests that Apple has changed its supply chain sourcing in order to lessen the risk of disruption. It's unclear if using multiple suppliers all from the same region mitigates Apple's supply chain risk, or if it is an effort to extract lower prices from competing suppliers.

Supply chains can also produce reputational risks when key suppliers engage in unacceptable labor and environmental policies and practices. For instance, for much of 2012, Apple was under attack in the United States and Europe after an audit by the Fair Labor Association found that workers at several assembly plants operated by Apple contractor Foxconn were exposed to toxic chemicals and forced to work over 60 hours a week under dangerous work conditions.

Apple was not the only manufacturer that learned a lesson in supply chain risk from the Japanese earthquake: Boeing was without carbon fiber airframe assemblies made in Japan; Ford and GM closed factories for lack of Japanese transmissions; and Caterpillar reduced production at its factories worldwide as it attempted to secure alternative suppliers.

One might think that in the so-called global and Internet economy, computer-based supply chains could quickly and effortlessly adjust to find new suppliers for just about any component or industrial material in a matter of minutes. Think again. New supply chains will need to be built that optimize not just cost but also survivability in the event of common disasters. They must also take into account efforts to reform labor and environmental practices of those involved in the supply chain.

■ **SOURCES:** "Disruptions: Too Much Silence on Working Conditions," by Nick Bilton, *New York Times*, April 8, 2012; "Audit Faults Apple Supplier," by Jessica Vascellaro, *Wall Street Journal*, March 30, 2012; "Under the Hood of Apple's Tablet," by Don Clark, *Wall Street Journal*, March 16, 2012; "In China, Human Costs Are Built Into an iPad," by Charles Duhigg and David Barboza, New York Times, January 25, 2012; "Japan: The Business After Shocks," by Andrew Dowell, *Wall Street Journal*, March 25, 2011; "Some Worry the Success of Apple Is Tied to Japan," by Miguel Helft, *New York Times*, March 22, 2011; "Crisis Tests Supply Chain's Weak Links," by James Hookway and Aries Poon, *Wall Street Journal*, March 18, 2011; "Caterpillar Warns of Supply Problems From Quake," by Bob Tita, *Wall Street Journal*, March 18, 2011; "Lacking Parts, G.M. Will Close Plant," by Nick Bunkley, *New York Times*, March 17, 2011.

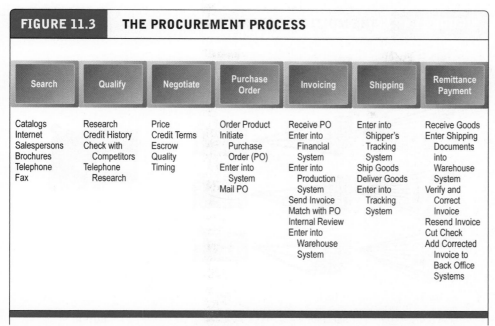

FIGURE 11.3 — **THE PROCUREMENT PROCESS**

Search	Qualify	Negotiate	Purchase Order	Invoicing	Shipping	Remittance Payment
Catalogs	Research	Price	Order Product	Receive PO	Enter into	Receive Goods
Internet	Credit History	Credit Terms	Initiate	Enter into	Shipper's	Enter Shipping
Salespersons	Check with	Escrow	Purchase	Financial	Tracking	Documents
Brochures	Competitors	Quality	Order (PO)	System	System	into
Telephone	Telephone	Timing	Enter into	Enter into	Ship Goods	Warehouse
Fax	Research		System	Production	Deliver Goods	System
			Mail PO	System	Enter into	Verify and
				Send Invoice	Tracking	Correct
				Match with PO	System	Invoice
				Internal Review		Resend Invoice
				Enter into		Cut Check
				Warehouse		Add Corrected
				System		Invoice to
						Back Office
						Systems

The procurement process is a lengthy and complicated series of steps that involves the seller, buyer, and shipping companies in a series of connected transactions.

Often these goods are called **MRO goods**—products for maintenance, repair, and operations.

Second, firms use two different methods for purchasing goods: contract purchasing and spot purchasing. **Contract purchasing** involves long-term written agreements to purchase specified products, with agreed-upon terms and quality, for an extended period of time. Generally, firms purchase direct goods using long-term contracts. **Spot purchasing** involves the purchase of goods based on immediate needs in larger marketplaces that involve many suppliers. Generally, firms use spot purchasing for indirect goods, although in some cases, firms also use spot purchasing for direct goods.

According to several estimates, about 80% of inter-firm trade involves contract purchasing of direct goods, and 20% involves spot purchasing of indirect goods (Kaplan and Sawhney, 2000). This finding is significant for understanding B2B e-commerce.

Although Figure 11.3 captures some of the complexity of the procurement process, it is important to realize that firms purchase thousands of goods from thousands of suppliers. The suppliers, in turn, must purchase their inputs from their suppliers. Large manufacturers such as Ford Motor Company have over 20,000 suppliers of parts, packaging, and technology. The number of secondary and tertiary suppliers is at least as large. Together, this extended **multi-tier supply chain** (the chain of primary, secondary, and tertiary suppliers) constitutes a crucial aspect of the industrial infrastructure of the economy. **Figure 11.4** depicts a firm's multi-tier supply chain.

The supply chain depicted in Figure 11.4 is a three-tier chain simplified for the sake of illustration. In fact, large Fortune 1000 firms have thousands of suppliers, who in turn have thousands of smaller suppliers. The complexity of the supply chain

MRO goods
products for maintenance, repair, and operations

contract purchasing
involves long-term written agreements to purchase specified products, under agreed-upon terms and quality, for an extended period of time

spot purchasing
involves the purchase of goods based on immediate needs in larger marketplaces that involve many suppliers

multi-tier supply chain
the chain of primary, secondary, and tertiary suppliers

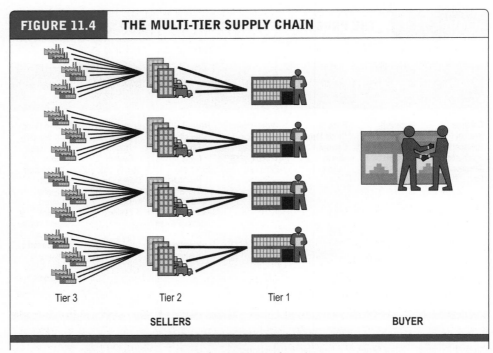

FIGURE 11.4 | **THE MULTI-TIER SUPPLY CHAIN**

Tier 3   Tier 2   Tier 1

SELLERS   BUYER

The supply chain for every firm is composed of multiple tiers of suppliers.

suggests a combinatorial explosion. Assuming a manufacturer has four primary suppliers and each one has three primary suppliers, and each of these has three primary suppliers, then the total number of suppliers in the chain (including the buying firm) rises to 53. This figure does not include the shippers, insurers, and financiers involved in the transactions.

Immediately, you can see from Figure 11.4 that the procurement process involves a very large number of suppliers, each of whom must be coordinated with the production needs of the ultimate purchaser—the buying firm. You can also understand how difficult it is to "manage" the supply chain, or obtain "visibility" into the supply chain simply because of its size and scope.

TRENDS IN SUPPLY CHAIN MANAGEMENT AND COLLABORATIVE COMMERCE

It is impossible to comprehend the actual and potential contribution of Internet-based B2B commerce, or the successes and failures of B2B e-commerce vendors and markets, without understanding ongoing efforts to improve the procurement process through a variety of supply chain management programs that long preceded the development of e-commerce.

supply chain management (SCM) refers to a wide variety of activities that firms and industries use to coordinate the key players in their procurement process. For the most part, today's procurement managers still work with telephones, e-mail, fax machines, face-to-face conversations, and instinct, relying on trusted long-term suppliers for their strategic purchases of goods directly involved in the production process.

supply chain management (SCM)
refers to a wide variety of activities that firms and industries use to coordinate the key players in their procurement process

There have been a number of major developments in supply chain management over the last two decades that set the ground rules for understanding how B2B e-commerce works (or fails to work). These developments include just-in-time and lean production, supply chain simplification, adaptive supply chains, sustainable supply chains, electronic data interchange (EDI), supply chain management systems, and collaborative commerce (Supply Chain Digest, 2012a).

Just-in-Time and Lean Production

One of the significant costs in any production process is the cost of in-process inventory: the parts and supplies needed to produce a product or service. **Just-in-time production** is a method of inventory cost management that seeks to eliminate excess inventory to a bare minimum. In just-in-time production, the parts needed for, say, an automobile, arrive at the assembly factory a few hours or even minutes before they are attached to a car. Payment for the parts does not occur until the parts are attached to a vehicle on the production line. In the past, producers used to order enough parts for a week or even a month's worth of production, creating huge, costly buffers in the production process. These buffers assured that parts would almost always be available, but at a large cost. **Lean production** is a set of production methods and tools that focuses on the elimination of waste throughout the customer value chain. It is an extension of just-in-time beyond inventory management to the full range of activities that create customer value. Originally, just-in-time and lean methods were implemented with phones, faxes, and paper documents to coordinate the flow of parts in inventory.

just-in-time production
a method of inventory cost management that seeks to eliminate excess inventory to a bare minimum.

lean production
a set of production methods and tools that focuses on the elimination of waste throughout the customer value chain

Supply Chain Simplification

Many manufacturing firms have spent the past two decades reducing the size of their supply chains and working more closely with a smaller group of "strategic" supplier firms to reduce both product costs and administrative costs, while improving quality. Following the lead of Japanese industry, for instance, the automobile industry has systematically reduced the number of its suppliers by over 50%. Instead of open bidding for orders, large manufacturers have chosen to work with strategic partner supply firms under long-term contracts that guarantee the supplier business and also establish quality, cost, and timing goals. These strategic partnership programs are essential for just-in-time production models, and often involve joint product development and design, integration of computer systems, and tight coupling of the production processes of two or more companies. **Tight coupling** is a method for ensuring that suppliers precisely deliver the ordered parts at a specific time and to a particular location, ensuring the production process is not interrupted for lack of parts.

tight coupling
a method for ensuring that suppliers precisely deliver the ordered parts, at a specific time and particular location, to ensure the production process is not interrupted for lack of parts

Supply Chain Black Swans: Adaptive Supply Chains

While firms have greatly simplified their supply chains in the last decade, they have also sought to centralize them by adopting a single, global supply chain system that integrates all the firm's vendor and logistics information into a single enterprise-wide system. Large software firms like Oracle, IBM, and SAP encourage firms to adopt a "one world, one firm, one database" enterprise-wide view of the world in order to achieve scale economies, simplicity, and to optimize global cost and value.

Beginning in earnest in 2000, managers in developed countries used these new technological capabilities to push manufacturing and production to the lowest cost labor regions of the world, specifically China and South East Asia. As it turns out, there were many risks and costs to this strategy of concentrating production in China and Asia in a world of economic, financial, political, and even geological instability. For instance, in the global financial crisis of 2007–2009, relying on suppliers in parts of Europe where currencies and interest rates fluctuated greatly exposed many firms to higher costs than anticipated. Suddenly, key suppliers could not obtain financing for their production or shipments. In March 2011, following the earthquake and tsunami in Japan, key suppliers in Japan were forced to shut down or slow production because of nuclear contamination of the entire Fukushima region where, as its turns out, major Japanese and American firms had automobile parts factories. As a result, General Motors could no longer obtain transmissions for its Volt electric car, and had to shut down a truck factory in Louisiana due to a lack of parts from Japan. Japanese and other global firms could not obtain batteries, switches, and axle assemblies. Production lead times in the automobile industry were very short, and inventories of parts were intentionally very lean, with only a few weeks supply on hand. And then, in October of 2011, torrential rains in Thailand led to flooding of many of its key industrial regions, and the wiping out of a significant share of the world's electronics components from hard disk drives to automobile sub-systems, cameras, and notebook PCs (Supply Chain Digest, 2012b; Hookway, 2012).

By 2012, the risks and costs of extended and concentrated supply chains had begun to change corporate strategies. To cope with unpredictable world events, firms are taking steps to break up single global supply chain systems into regional or product-based supply chains, with some level of centralization, but substantial autonomy for the smaller systems. Using regional supply chains, firms can decide to locate some production of parts in Latin America, rather than all their production or suppliers in a single country such as Japan. They will be able to move production around the world to temporary "safe harbors." This may result in higher short-term costs, but provide substantial, longer term risk protection in the event any single region is disrupted. Increasingly, supply chains are being built based on the assumption that global disruptions in supply are inevitable, but not predictable (Simchi-Levi, et. al., 2011;Malik, et. al., 2011). The focus in 2012 shifted to "optimal-cost," not low-cost, supply chains, and more distributed manufacturing along with more flexible supply chains that can shift reliably from high-risk to low-risk areas. Regional manufacturing means shorter supply chains that can respond rapidly to changing consumer tastes and demand levels (Cachon and Swinney, 2011).

Accountable Supply Chains: Labor Standards

Accountable supply chains are those where the labor conditions in low-wage, underdeveloped producer countries are visible and morally acceptable to ultimate consumers in more developed industrial societies. For much of the last century, American and European manufacturers with global supply chains with large offshore production facilities sought to hide the realities of their offshore factories from Western reporters and ordinary citizens. For global firms with long supply chains, "visibility" did not mean their consumers could understand how their products were made.

Beginning in 2000, and in part because of the growing power of the Internet to empower citizen reporters around the world, the realities of global supply chains have slowly become more transparent to the public. For instance, for much of the past decade, beginning in 1997, Nike, the world's largest manufacturer of sporting goods, has been under intense criticism for exploiting foreign workers, operating sweat shops, employing children, and allowing dangerous conditions in its subcontractor factories. As a result, Nike has introduced significant changes to its global supply chain.

With the emergence of truly global supply chains, and political changes at the World Trade Organization, which opened up European and American markets to Asian goods and services, many—if not most—of the electronics, toys, cosmetics, industrial supplies, footwear, apparel, and other goods consumed in the developed world are made by workers in factories in the less developed world, primarily in Asia and Latin America. Unfortunately, but quite understandably, the labor conditions in these factories in most cases do not meet the minimal labor standards of Europe or America even though these factories pay higher wages and offer better working conditions than other local jobs in the host country. In many cases, the cost for a worker of not having a job in what—to Western standards—are horrible working conditions is to sink deeper into poverty and even worse conditions. Many point out that labor conditions were brutal in the United States and Europe in the 19th and early 20th century when these countries were building industrial economies, and therefore, whatever conditions exist in offshore factories in 2012 are no worse than developed countries in their early years of rapid industrialization.

A number of groups in the last decade have contributed to efforts to make global supply chains transparent to reporters and citizens, and to develop minimal standards of accountability. Among these groups are the National Consumers League, Human Rights First, the Maquilla Solidarity Network, the Global Fairness Initiative, the Clean Clothes Campaign, the International Labor Organization (UN), and the Fair Labor Association (FLA). The FLA is a coalition of business firms with offshore production and global supply chains, universities, and private organizations. For member firms, the FLA conducts interviews with workers, makes unannounced visits to factories to track progress, and investigates complaints. They are also one of the major international labor standard-setting organizations (Fair Labor Organization, 2012).

In March 2012, the FLA released its investigation of Hon Hai Precision Industry Company (a Taiwan-based company known as Foxconn), which is the assembler of nearly all iPhones and iPads in the world. Foxconn operates what is alleged to be the largest factory in the world in Longhua, Shenzhen, where over 250,000 workers assemble electronics goods. The audit of working conditions at Foxconn was authorized by Apple, a member of the FLA, and was based on 35,000 surveys of workers at the Longhua factory. The report found over 50 legal and code violations (sometimes in violation of Chinese laws) including requiring too many hours of work a week (over 60), failing to pay workers for overtime, and hazardous conditions that injured workers (Fair Labor Association, 2012).

Sustainable Supply Chains: Lean, Mean and Green

"Sustainable business" is a call for business to take social and ecological interests, and not just corporate profits, into account in all their decision-making throughout the firm. No small request. Since the United Nations World Commission on Environment and Development (WCED) published the first comprehensive report on sustainable business in 1987, firms around the globe have struggled with these concepts and in some cases ignored or resisted them as simply a threat to sustained profitability. The commission's report (*Our Common Future*) argued for a balance of profits, social community development, and minimal impact on the world environment, including of course, the carbon footprint of business. By 2012, the consensus among major firms in Europe, Asia, and the United States has become that in the long term, and through careful planning, sustainable business is just good business because it means using the most efficient environment-regarding means of production, distribution, and logistics. These efficient methods create value for consumers, investors, and communities.

Notions of sustainable business have had a powerful impact on supply chain thinking. In part, these efforts are good risk management: all advanced countries have substantially strengthened their environmental regulations. It makes good business sense for firms to prepare methods and operations suitable to this new environment.

For instance, all the major textiles brands and retailers have announced plans for a more sustainable supply chain in textiles. One of the world's truly ancient industries, textiles supports millions of workers while consuming extraordinary resources: it takes 1,000 gallons of water to make one pound of finished cotton (your jeans, for instance). While growing cotton has its issues (fertilizer), the subsequent dying, finishing, and cleaning of cotton makes it the number one industrial polluter on Earth (cKinetics, 2010). It's not a small matter then that Walmart, Gap, Levi's, Nike, and other large players in the industry are taking steps to reduce the environmental impact of their operations by improving the efficiency of the entire supply and distribution chains.

Electronic Data Interchange (EDI)

As noted in the previous section, B2B e-commerce did not originate with the Internet, but in fact has its roots in technologies such as EDI that were first developed in the mid-1970s and 1980s. EDI is a broadly defined communications protocol for exchanging documents among computers using technical standards developed by the American National Standards Institute (ANSI X12 standards) and international bodies such as the United Nations (EDIFACT standards).

EDI was developed to reduce the cost, delays, and errors inherent in the manual exchanges of documents such as purchase orders, shipping documents, price lists, payments, and customer data. EDI differs from an unstructured message because its messages are organized with distinct fields for each of the important pieces of information in a commercial transaction such as transaction date, product purchased, amount, sender's name, address, and recipient's name.

EDI has evolved significantly since the 1980s (see **Figure 11.5**). EDI has evolved through three stages. Stage 1 attempted to automate the flow of documents. Stage 2 attempted to eliminate documents like purchase orders by sharing production schedules with their suppliers that described exactly where and when supplies would be

FIGURE 11.5	THE EVOLUTION OF EDI AS A B2B MEDIUM

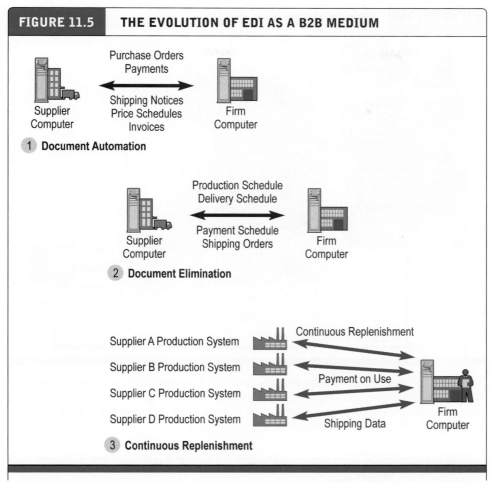

EDI has evolved from a simple point-to-point digital communications medium to a many-to-one enabling tool for continuous inventory replenishment.

needed. Stage 3 supplier firms were given access to online production schedules and it was up to them to make sure goods arrived in time to support the production schedule.

Supply Chain Management Systems: Mobile B2B in Your Palm

Supply chain simplification, lean production, focusing on strategic partners in the production process, enterprise systems, and continuous inventory replenishment, are the foundation for contemporary **supply chain management (SCM) systems**. Supply chain management systems continuously link the activities of buying, making, and moving products from suppliers to purchasing firms, as well as integrating the demand side of the business equation by including the order entry system in the process. With an SCM system and continuous replenishment, inventory is greatly reduced and production begins only when an order is received (see **Figure 11.6**). These systems enable just-in-time and lean-production methods. The growing use of smartphones has led software firms like SAP and Oracle to develop mobile apps for

supply chain management (SCM) systems
continuously link the activities of buying, making, and moving products from suppliers to purchasing firms, as well as integrating the demand side of the business equation by including the order entry system in the process

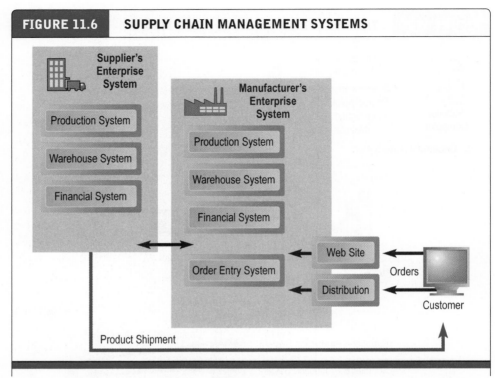

| FIGURE 11.6 | SUPPLY CHAIN MANAGEMENT SYSTEMS |

SCM systems coordinate the activities of suppliers, shippers, and order entry systems to automate order entry through production, payment, and shipping business processes. Increasingly customers, as well as employees working throughout the supply chain, are using smartphones and mobile apps to place and coordinate orders.

personal computers, smartphones, and other consumer devices to connect firms with their supply chain partners.

HP has a Web-based, order-driven supply chain management system that begins with either a customer placing an order online or the receipt of an order from a dealer. The order is forwarded from the order entry system to HP's production and delivery system. From there, the order is routed to one of several HP contractor supplier firms. One such firm is Synnex in Fremont, California. At Synnex, computers verify the order with HP and validate the ordered configuration to ensure the PC can be manufactured (e.g., will not have missing parts or fail a design specification set by HP). The order is then forwarded to a computer-based production control system that issues a bar-coded production ticket to factory assemblers. Simultaneously, a parts order is forwarded to Synnex's warehouse and inventory management system. A worker assembles the computer, and then the computer is boxed, tagged, and shipped to the customer. The delivery is monitored and tracked by HP's supply chain management system, which links directly to one of several overnight delivery systems operated by Airborne Express, Federal Express, and UPS. The elapsed time from order entry to shipping is 48 hours. With this system, Synnex and HP have eliminated the need to hold PCs in inventory, reduced cycle time from one week to 48 hours, and reduced errors. HP has extended this system to become a global B2B order tracking, reporting, and support system for large HP customers (Synnex Corporation, 2012; Hewlett-Packard, 2012). In 2010, HP began a simplification of B2B applications from over 300 applications down to 30. Many of these applications were inherited from acquired companies (Gardner, 2010).

Collaborative Commerce

Collaborative commerce is a direct extension of supply chain management systems, as well as supply chain simplification. **Collaborative commerce** is defined as the use of digital technologies to permit organizations to collaboratively design, develop, build, and manage products through their life cycles. This is a much broader mission than EDI or simply managing the flow of information among organizations. Collaborative commerce involves a definitive move from a transaction focus to a relationship focus among the supply chain participants. Rather than having an arm's-length adversarial relationship with suppliers, collaborative commerce fosters sharing of sensitive internal information with suppliers and purchasers. Managing collaborative commerce requires knowing exactly what information to share with whom. Collaborative commerce extends beyond supply chain management activities to include the collaborative development of new products and services by multiple cooperating firms.

Although collaborative commerce can involve customers as well as suppliers in the development of products, for the most part, it is concerned with the development of a rich communications environment to enable inter-firm sharing of designs, production plans, inventory levels, delivery schedules, and the development of shared products (see **Figure 11.7**).

collaborative commerce
the use of digital technologies to permit organizations to collaboratively design, develop, build, and manage products through their life cycles

FIGURE 11.7   ELEMENTS OF A COLLABORATIVE COMMERCE SYSTEM

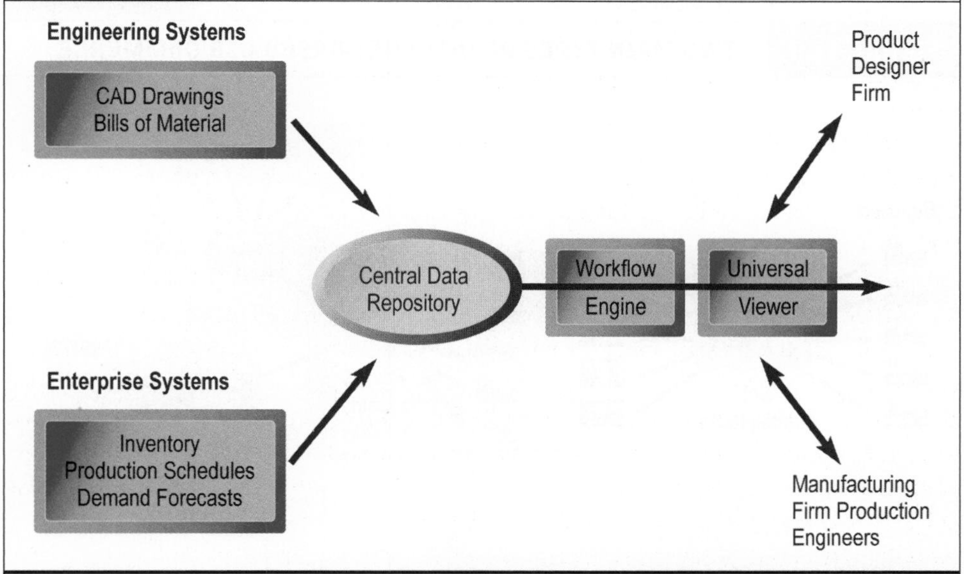

A collaborative commerce application includes a central data repository where employees at several different firms can store engineering drawings and other documents. A workflow engine determines who can see this data and what rules will apply for displaying the data on individual workstations. A viewer can be a browser operating on a workstation.

SOCIAL NETWORKS AND B2B: THE EXTENDED SOCIAL ENTERPRISE

It's a short step from collaboration with vendors, suppliers, and customers, to a more personal relationship based on conversations with participants in the supply chain using social networks—both private and public. Here, the conversations and sharing of ideas are more unstructured, situational, and personal. Procurement officers, managers of supply chains, and logistics managers are people too, and they participate in the same social network culture provided by Facebook, Twitter, Tumblr, Instagram, and a host of other public social networks as we all do. Being able to respond to fast moving developments that affect supply chains requires something more than a Web site, e-mail, or telephone calls. Social networks can provide the intimate connections among customers, suppliers, and logistics partners that are needed to keep the supply chain functioning, and to make decisions based on current conditions (Red Prairie, 2012).

Participants in the supply chain network are tapping into their tablet computers, smartphones, and social network sites for purchasing, scheduling, exception handling, and deciding with their B2B customers and suppliers. In many cases, supply chain social networks are private—owned by the largest firm in the supply chain network. In other cases, firms develop Facebook pages to organize conversations among supply chain network members.

MAIN TYPES OF INTERNET-BASED B2B COMMERCE

There are two generic types of Internet-based B2B commerce systems: Net marketplaces (which tend to be public) and private industrial networks (see **Figure 11.8**).

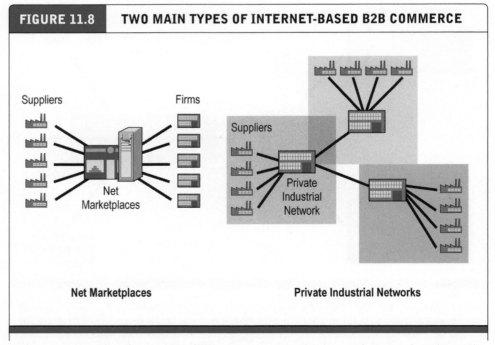

FIGURE 11.8   **TWO MAIN TYPES OF INTERNET-BASED B2B COMMERCE**

There are two main types of Internet-based B2B commerce: Net marketplaces and private industrial networks.

Within each of these general categories are many different subtypes that we discuss in the following sections (Yoo, et al., 2011).

Net marketplaces (also referred to as exchanges) bring together potentially thousands of sellers and buyers into a single digital marketplace operated over the Internet. Net marketplaces are transaction-based, support many-to-many as well as one-to-many relationships, and bear some resemblance to financial markets such as the New York Stock Exchange. There are many different types of Net marketplaces, with different pricing mechanisms, biases, and value propositions that will be explored in Section 11.2 (Kerrigan, et al., 2001). Private industrial networks bring together a small number of strategic business partner firms that collaborate to develop highly efficient supply chains and satisfy customer demand for products. Private industrial networks are relationship-based, support many-to-one or many-to-few relationships, and bear some resemblance to internal collaborative work environments. There are many different types of private industrial networks, as discussed in Section 11.3. Private industrial networks are by far the largest form of B2B e-commerce and account for over 10 times as much revenue as Net marketplaces.

11.2 NET MARKETPLACES

One of the most compelling visions of B2B e-commerce is that of an electronic marketplace on the Internet that would bring thousands of fragmented suppliers into contact with hundreds of major purchasers of industrial goods for the purpose of conducting "frictionless" commerce. The hope was that these suppliers would compete with one another on price, transactions would be automated and low cost, and as a result, the price of industrial supplies would fall. By extracting fees from buyers and sellers on each transaction, third-party intermediary market makers could earn significant revenues. These Net marketplaces could scale easily as volume increased by simply adding more computers and communications equipment.

In pursuit of this vision, well over 1,500 Net marketplaces sprang up in the early days of e-commerce. Unfortunately, many of them have since disappeared and the population is expected to stabilize at about 200. Still, many survive, and they are joined by other types of Net marketplaces—some private and some public—based on different assumptions that are quite successful.

TYPES OF NET MARKETPLACES

Although each of these distinctions helps describe the phenomenon of Net marketplaces, they do not focus on the central business functionality provided, nor are they capable by themselves of describing the variety of Net marketplaces.

In **Figure 11.9**, we present a classification of Net marketplaces that focuses on their business functionality; that is, what these Net marketplaces provide for businesses seeking solutions. We use two dimensions of Net marketplaces to create a four-cell classification table. We differentiate Net marketplaces as providing either indirect goods (goods used to support production) or direct goods (goods used in production), and we distinguish markets as providing either contractual purchasing (where

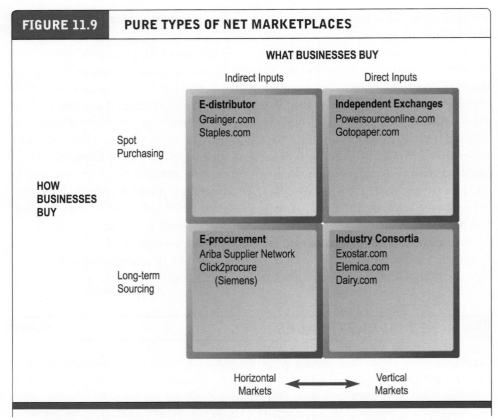

FIGURE 11.9 **PURE TYPES OF NET MARKETPLACES**

There are four main types of Net marketplaces based on the intersection of two dimensions: how businesses buy and what they buy. A third dimension—horizontal versus vertical markets—also distinguishes the different types of Net marketplaces.

purchases take place over many years according to a contract between the firm and its vendor) or spot purchasing (where purchases are episodic and anonymous—vendors and buyers do not have an ongoing relationship and may not know one another). The intersection of these dimensions produces four main types of Net marketplaces that are relatively straightforward: e-distributors, e-procurement networks, exchanges, and industry consortia. Note, however, that in the real world, some Net marketplaces can be found in multiple parts of this figure as business models change and opportunities appear and disappear. Nevertheless, the discussion of "pure types" of Net marketplaces is a useful starting point.

Each of these Net marketplaces seeks to provide value to customers in different ways. We discuss each type of Net marketplace in more detail in the following sections.

E-distributors

E-distributors are the most common and most easily understood type of Net marketplace. An **e-distributor** provides an electronic catalog that represents the products of thousands of direct manufacturers (see **Figure 11.10**). An e-distributor is the equivalent of Amazon for industry. E-distributors are independently owned intermediaries

e-distributor

provides electronic catalog that represents the products of thousands of direct manufacturers

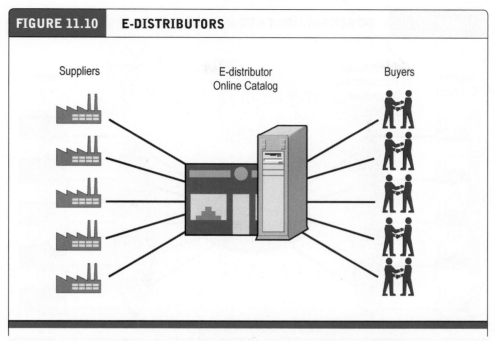

| FIGURE 11.10 | E-DISTRIBUTORS |

E-distributors are firms that bring the products of thousands of suppliers into a single online electronic catalog for sale to thousands of buyer firms. E-distributors are sometimes referred to as one-to-many markets, one seller serving many firms.

that offer industrial customers a single source from which to order indirect goods (often referred to as MRO) on a spot, as-needed basis. A significant percentage of corporate purchases cannot be satisfied under a company's existing contracts, and must be purchased on a spot basis. E-distributors make money by charging a markup on products they distribute.

The most frequently cited example of a public e-distribution market is W.W. Grainger. Grainger is involved in both long-term systematic sourcing as well as spot sourcing, but its emphasis is on spot sourcing. Grainger's business model is to become the world's leading source of MRO suppliers, and its revenue model is that of a typical retailer: it owns the products, and takes a markup on the products it sells to customers. At Grainger.com, users get an electronic online version of Grainger's famous seven-pound catalog, plus other parts not available in the catalog (adding up to around 900,000 parts), and complete electronic ordering and payment (W.W. Grainger Inc., 2012). Another example is McMaster-Carr.com, a New Jersey-based industrial parts mecca for manufacturers around the world.

E-procurement

An **e-procurement Net marketplace** is an independently owned intermediary that connects hundreds of online suppliers offering millions of maintenance and repair parts to business firms who pay fees to join the market (see **Figure 11.11**). E-procurement Net marketplaces are typically used for long-term contractual purchasing of indirect goods (MRO); they create online horizontal markets, but they

e-procurement Net marketplace

independently owned intermediary that connects hundreds of online suppliers offering millions of maintenance and repair parts to business firms who pay fees to join the market

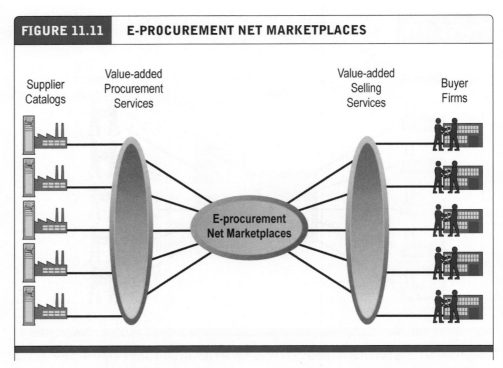

FIGURE 11.11   E-PROCUREMENT NET MARKETPLACES

E-procurement Net marketplaces aggregate hundreds of catalogs in a single marketplace and make them available to firms, often on a custom basis that reflects only the suppliers desired by the participating firms.

also provide for members' spot sourcing of MRO supplies. E-procurement companies make money by charging a percentage of each transaction, licensing consulting services and software, and assessing network use fees (Trkman and McCormack, 2010).

E-procurement companies expand on the business model of simpler e-distributors by including the online catalogs of hundreds of suppliers and offering value chain management services to both buyers and sellers. **Value chain management (VCM) services** provided by e-procurement companies include automation of a firm's entire procurement process on the buyer side and automation of the selling business processes on the seller side. For purchasers, e-procurement companies automate purchase orders, requisitions, sourcing, business rules enforcement, invoicing, and payment. For suppliers, e-procurement companies provide catalog creation and content management, order management, fulfillment, invoicing, shipment, and settlement.

Ariba stands out as one of the poster children of the B2B age, a firm born before its time. Promising to revolutionize inter-firm trade, Ariba started out in 1996 hoping to build a global business network linking buyers and sellers—sort of an eBay for business. With little revenue, the stock shot past $1,000 a share by March 2000. But sellers and buyers did not join the network in large part because they did not understand the opportunity, were too wedded to their traditional procurement processes, and did not trust outsiders to control their purchasing and vendor relationship. Today, Ariba

value chain management (VCM) services

include automation of a firm's entire procurement process on the buyer side and automation of the selling business processes on the seller side

is a leading provider of collaborative business commerce solutions (Ariba, 2012; Levy, 2010; Vance, 2010).

Exchanges

An **exchange** is an independently owned online marketplace that connects hundreds to potentially thousands of suppliers and buyers in a dynamic, real-time environment (see **Figure 11.12**). Although there are exceptions, exchanges generally create vertical markets that focus on the spot-purchasing requirements of large firms in a single industry, such as computers and telecommunications, electronics, food, and industrial equipment. Exchanges were the prototype Internet-based marketplace in the early days of e-commerce; as noted earlier, over 1,500 were created in this period, but most have failed.

Exchanges make money by charging a commission on the transaction. The pricing model can be through an online negotiation, auction, RFQ, or fixed buy-and-sell prices. The benefits offered to customers of exchanges include reduced search cost for parts and spare capacity. Other benefits include lower prices created by a global marketplace driven by competition among suppliers who would, presumably, sell goods at very low profit margins at one world-market price. The benefits offered suppliers are access to a global purchasing environment and the opportunity to unload production overruns (although at very competitive prices and low profit margins). Even though they are

exchange
independently owned online marketplace that connects hundreds to potentially thousands of suppliers and buyers in a dynamic, real-time environment

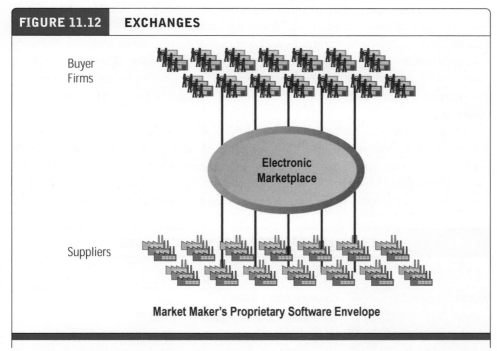

FIGURE 11.12   EXCHANGES

Buyer Firms

Electronic Marketplace

Suppliers

Market Maker's Proprietary Software Envelope

Independent exchanges bring potentially thousands of suppliers to a vertical (industry-specific) marketplace to sell their goods to potentially thousands of buyer firms. Exchanges are sometimes referred to as many-to-many markets because they have many suppliers serving many buyer firms.

private intermediaries, exchanges are public in the sense of permitting any bona fide buyer or seller to participate.

Inventory Locator Service (ILS) is an exchange that has its roots as an offline intermediary, serving as a listing service for aftermarket parts in the aerospace industry. Upon opening in 1979, ILS initially provided a telephone and fax-based directory of aftermarket parts to airplane owners and mechanics, along with government procurement professionals. As early as 1984, ILS incorporated e-mail capabilities as part of its RFQ services, and by 1998, it had begun to conduct online auctions for hard-to-find parts. In 2012, ILS maintained an Internet-accessible database of over 5 billion aerospace and marine industry parts, and has also developed an eRFQ feature that helps users streamline their sourcing processes. The network's 22,000 subscribers in 93 different countries access the site over 60,000 times a day (Inventory Locator Service, 2012). **Table 11.1** lists a few other examples of some current independent exchanges.

Industry Consortia

industry consortium
industry-owned vertical market that enables buyers to purchase direct inputs (both goods and services) from a limited set of invited participants

An **industry consortium** is an industry-owned vertical market that enables buyers to purchase direct inputs (both goods and services) from a limited set of invited participants (see **Figure 11.13**). Industry consortia emphasize long-term contractual purchasing, the development of stable relationships (as opposed to merely an anonymous transaction emphasis), and the creation of industry-wide data standards and synchronization efforts. Industry consortia are more focused on optimizing long-term supply relationships than independent exchanges, which tend to focus more on short-term transactions. The ultimate objective of industry consortia is the unification of supply chains within entire industries, across many tiers, through common data definitions, network standards, and computing platforms. In addition, industry consortia, unlike independent exchanges described previously, take their marching orders from the industry and not from venture capitalists or investment bankers. This means any profits from operating industry consortia are returned to industry business firms.

Industry consortia make money in a number of ways. Industry members usually pay for the creation of the consortia's capabilities and contribute initial operating capital. Then industry consortia charge buyer and seller firms transaction and subscription fees. Industry members—both buyers and sellers—are expected to reap benefits far greater than their contributions through the rationalization of the

TABLE 11.1	EXAMPLES OF INDEPENDENT EXCHANGES
EXCHANGE	FOCUS
PowerSource Online	Computer parts exchange
Converge	Semiconductors and computer peripherals
Smarterwork	Professional services from Web design to legal advice
Active International	Trading in underutilized manufacturing capacity
IntercontinentalExchange	International online marketplace for over 600 commodities

FIGURE 11.13   **INDUSTRY CONSORTIA**

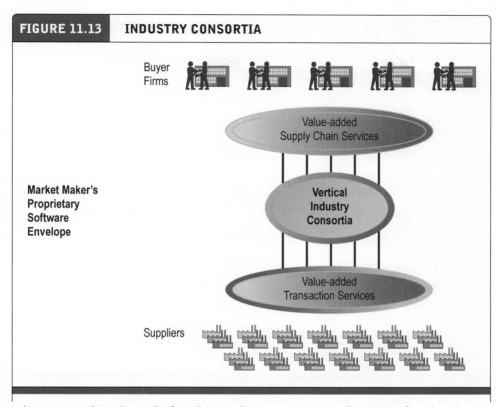

Industry consortia bring thousands of suppliers into direct contact with a smaller number of very large buyers. The market makers provide value-added software services for procurement, transaction management, shipping, and payment for both buyers and suppliers. Industry consortia are sometimes referred to as many-to-few markets, where many suppliers (albeit selected by the buyers) serve a few very large buyers, mediated by a variety of value-added services.

procurement process, competition among vendors, and closer relationships with vendors.

Exostar is one example of an industry consortium. Its founding partners include BAE Systems, Boeing, Lockheed Martin, Raytheon, and Rolls-Royce, all companies in the aerospace industry. Exostar has taken a slow but steady approach to building its technology platform. It has kept its focus on the direct procurement and supply chain needs of its largest members, and taken its time developing a portfolio of technology solutions that meet its needs. Its current products include Supply Pass, an integrated suite of tools that enables suppliers to handle buyer transactions via the Internet; SourcePass, which provides a dynamic bidding environment for buyers and sellers; and ProcurePass, which enables buyers to handle supplier transactions online, among others. As of September 2012, Exostar served a community of more than 70,000 trading partners (Exostar, 2012). **Table 11.2** lists some examples of other industry consortia.

TABLE 11.2	INDUSTRY CONSORTIA BY INDUSTRY (SEPTEMBER 2012)
INDUSTRY	NAME OF INDUSTRY CONSORTIA
Aerospace	Exostar
Automotive	SupplyOn
Chemical	Elemica
Food	Dairy.com
Hospitality	Avendra
Medical Services, Supplies	GHX (Global Healthcare Exchange)
Paper and Forest Products	PaperFiber
Shipping	OceanConnect
Textiles	The Seam (Cotton Consortium)
Transportation	Transplace

11.3   PRIVATE INDUSTRIAL NETWORKS

Private industrial networks today form the largest part of B2B e-commerce, both on and off the Internet. Industry analysts estimate that in 2012, over 50% of B2B expenditures by large firms will be for the development of private industrial networks. Private industrial networks can be considered the foundation of the "extended enterprise," allowing firms to extend their boundaries and their business processes to include supply chain and logistics partners.

WHAT ARE PRIVATE INDUSTRIAL NETWORKS?

As noted at the beginning of this chapter, private industrial networks are direct descendants of existing EDI networks, and they are closely tied to existing ERP systems used by large firms. A private industrial network (sometimes referred to as a private trading exchange, or PTX) is a Web-enabled network for the coordination of trans-organizational business processes (sometimes also called collaborative commerce). **A trans-organizational business process** requires at least two independent firms to perform (Laudon and Laudon, 2012). For the most part, these networks originate in and closely involve the manufacturing and related support industries, and therefore we refer to them as "industrial" networks, although in the future they could just as easily apply to some services. These networks can be industry-wide, but often begin and sometimes focus on the voluntary coordination of a group of supplying firms centered about a single, very large manufacturing firm. Private industrial networks can be viewed as "extended enterprises" in the

trans-organizational business process
process that requires at least two independent firms to perform

sense that they often begin as ERP systems in a single firm, and are then expanded to include (often using an extranet) the firm's major suppliers. **Figure 11.14** illustrates a private industrial network originally built by Procter & Gamble (P&G) in the United States to coordinate supply chains among its suppliers, distributors, truckers, and retailers.

In P&G's private industrial network shown in Figure 11.14, customer sales are captured at the cash register, which then initiates a flow of information back to distributors, P&G, and its suppliers. This tells P&G and its suppliers the exact level of demand for thousands of products. This information is then used to initiate production, supply, and transportation to replenish products at the distributors and retailers. This process is called an efficient customer response system (a demand-pull production model), and it relies on an equally efficient supply chain management system to coordinate the supply side. GE, Dell Computer, Cisco Systems, Microsoft, IBM, Nike, Coca-Cola, Walmart, Nokia, and Hewlett-Packard are among the firms operating successful private industrial networks.

Perhaps no single firm better illustrates the benefits of developing private industrial networks than Walmart, described in *Insight on Business: Walmart Develops a Private Industrial Network*.

PRIVATE INDUSTRIAL NETWORKS AND COLLABORATIVE COMMERCE

Private industrial networks can do much more than just serve a supply chain and efficient customer response system. They can also include other activities of a single large manufacturing firm, such as design of products and engineering diagrams, as well as marketing plans and demand forecasting. Collaboration among businesses can take many forms and involve a wide range of activities—from simple supply chain management to coordinating market feedback to designers at supply firms (see **Figure 11.15**).

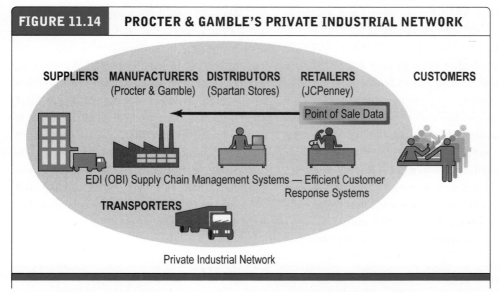

| FIGURE 11.14 | PROCTER & GAMBLE'S PRIVATE INDUSTRIAL NETWORK |

Procter & Gamble's private industrial network attempts to coordinate the trans-organizational business processes of the many firms it deals with in the consumer products industry.

INSIGHT ON BUSINESS

WALMART DEVELOPS A PRIVATE INDUSTRIAL NETWORK

Walmart is a well known for having the most efficient B2B supply chain in the world. With sales of more than $443 billion for the fiscal year ending January 31, 2012, Walmart has been able to use information technology to achieve a decisive cost advantage over competitors. But the rapid expansion in Walmart's international operations will require an even more capable private industrial network than what is now in place.

From the 1980s to the early 2000s, Walmart continually upgraded its original EDI-based network, called Retail Link. In 2002, Walmart switched to an entirely Internet-based private network. In 2007, Walmart's rapid global growth forced it to hire SAP to build a global financial management system. Walmart had finally started to outgrow its homegrown systems.

Despite the economic slowdown in 2011–2012, Walmart's sales grew. In 2011, Walmart's revenues of $443 billion were up 6.4% from 2010, and its net income was $15.77 billion, up from $15.36 billion. In the first half of 2012, sales continued to grow by over 4%. The future of Walmart's SCM lies in business analytics— working smarter—rather than simply making the movement and tracking of goods more efficient.

Like other large global firms, Walmart's global supply chain has been criticized for exploiting labor in underdeveloped countries where it buys products and in home markets where it sells them; bribing officials to look the other way; destroying environments; and wasting energy. In response to critics, Walmart has

taken a number of steps. Walmart has set a goal of reducing carbon emissions in its supply chain by 20 million metric tons by 2015, and a goal of 100% renewable energy use in the United States. Walmart has made less progress in its labor policies: In January 2012, the ABP pension fund blacklisted Walmart for failing to comply with the United Nations' Global Compact principles. The Global Compact presents a set of core values relating to human rights, labor standards, the environment, and anti-corruption efforts. In April 2012 the Department of Justice opened an investigation into widespread allegations that Walmart had bribed Mexican officials to expand its stores and supply chain in Mexico.

Walmart's success spurred its competitors in the retail industry to develop industry-wide private industrial networks such as Global NetXchange (now Agentrics) in an effort to duplicate the success of Walmart. Walmart executives have said Walmart would not join these networks, or any industry-sponsored consortium or independent exchange, because doing so would only help its competitors achieve what Walmart has already accomplished with Retail Link. To compete with the efficiencies attained by Walmart, other retailers, such as JCPenney, have implemented their own extensive private industrial networks to link suppliers to their stores' inventories directly over the Internet. Target Stores has even given over some of its inventory control and product selection to its largest apparel provider, TAL Apparel Ltd. of Hong Kong.

SOURCES: "How Walmart is Changing Supplier Sustainability-Again," by Aran Rice, Renewablechoice.com, May 30, 2012; "Wal-Mart's Dirty Partners," by Josh Eidelson, Salon.com, July 6, 2012; "The Walmart Model and the Human Cost of Our Low Priced Goods," by Juan De Lara, *The Guardian*, July 25, 2012; "Supply Chain News: Walmart, Sustainability, and Troubles in Mexico," by Dan Gilmore, *Supply Chain Digest*, April 26, 2012; "Retail Giant Optimizes Supply Chain Processes With Quintiq Software," *Supply&Demand Chain Executive*, February 15, 2012; "Walmart Adds $7 Billion Through Acquisition in 2011," by Nate Holmes, InstoreTrends.com, May 11, 2012.

| FIGURE 11.15 | PIECES OF THE COLLABORATIVE COMMERCE PUZZLE |

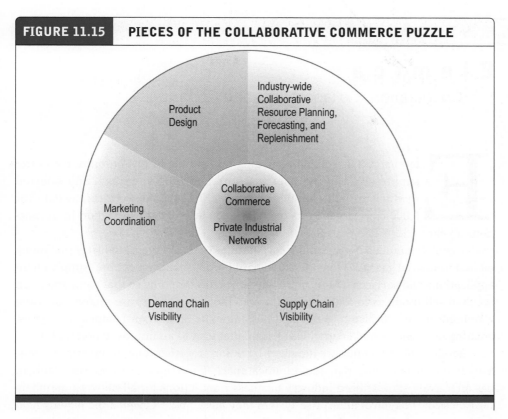

Collaborative commerce involves many cooperative activities among supply and sales firms closely interacting with a single large firm through a private industrial network.

One form of collaboration—and perhaps the most profound—is industry-wide **collaborative resource planning, forecasting, and replenishment (CPFR)**, which involves working with network members to forecast demand, develop production plans, and coordinate shipping, warehousing, and stocking activities to ensure retail and wholesale shelf space is replenished with just the right amount of goods. If this goal is achieved, hundreds of millions of dollars of excess inventory and capacity could be wrung out of an industry. This activity alone is likely to produce the largest benefits and justify the cost of developing private industrial networks.

A second area of collaboration is *demand chain visibility*. In the past, it was impossible to know where excess capacity or supplies existed in the supply and distribution chains. These excess inventories would raise costs for the entire industry and create extraordinary pressures to discount merchandise, reducing profits for everyone.

A third area of collaboration is *marketing coordination and product design*. Manufacturers that use or produce highly engineered parts use private industrial networks to coordinate both their internal design and marketing activities, as well as related activities of their supply and distribution chain partners.

collaborative resource planning, forecasting, and replenishment (CPFR)
involves working with network members to forecast demand, develop production plans, and coordinate shipping, warehousing, and stocking activities to ensure that retail and wholesale shelf space is replenished with just the right amount of goods

11.4   **CASE STUDY**

Elemica:
Cooperation, Collaboration, and Community

Elemica is a B2B industry trading hub aiming to revolutionize the entire supply chain of the chemical, tire and rubber, energy, and selected manufacturing industries worldwide. In 2012, Elemica connected over 5,000 companies to its network and clears over $100 billion in transactions a year.

Originally founded by 22 leading corporations in the chemical industry (including oil and industrial gases) to provide cloud-based order management and supply chain applications and services, Elemica provides one-stop shopping so that companies can buy and sell products to one another through their own enterprise systems or using a Web alternative. It also helps companies automate all of their business processes, creating efficiencies and economies of scale that lead to an improved bottom line.

Elemica unites community members by linking together their enterprise systems. This is the "social glue" that sets Elemica apart. The Elemica commerce platform has effectively standardized industry business transactions for all network members regardless of the type of enterprise system they have, and it's leveled the playing field for trade partners who are less technically sophisticated.

Elemica's QuickLink ERP connectivity enables companies to link their internal IT systems through a neutral platform so that information is moved into each company's database while maintaining confidentiality and security. Elemica facilitates transactions of all types, including order processing and billing and logistics management. Elemica's revenue comes from charging transaction fees on a per-transaction basis.

Elemica integrates information flow among global trading partners using a cloud-based business process network. Companies need only one connection to Elemica rather than a variable number of connections and infrastructure to all its trade partners. Once a company connects to Elemica, it can have access to thousands of other customers.

Unlike the automobile industry or the airline industry, where a few companies dominate, the $1.3 trillion chemical industry is made up of many companies of all sizes. The top 10 companies generate only 10% of the industry's annual revenue total, and the largest player, Dow Chemical, is responsible for 2%. In addition, unlike many other industries, chemical companies often buy the output from other chemical companies to use as raw materials for their products. Thus, chemical companies are often customers of one another as well as competitors.

Elemica's business model has been successful primarily because it addresses the needs of chemical, tire and rubber, energy and selected manufacturing companies of all sizes. It does this by offering multiple options for connecting to its hub system, multiple products that can be used alone or in combination, and by ensuring that only one connection integrated with a client's enterprise system is needed for all transactions.

With Elemica, companies benefit from improved operational efficiency, reduced costs due to elimination of redundant systems and excess inventory, and a much higher percentage of safe and reliable deliveries. The flexibility of Elemica's solutions and network combines simplification, standardization, and efficiency. And clients have increased their profitability and improved cash flow through faster payment.

A number of very large companies use Elemica's platform. In Europe, Shell Oil started using Elemica after recognizing that it had ongoing problems with the coordination of paperwork processing and deliveries. These delays were costing Shell money. Once Shell began using Elemica, things improved. Today, paperwork is processed 24 hours a day, and truck waiting time has been cut from an average of two hours to an average of 15 minutes.

Dow Chemical began to transition to full procurement automation with Elemica in 2007. More than 300 of their MRO suppliers are now linked to Elemica's platform. Errors are down 75%, and Dow has achieved economies of scale that have led to meaningful financial savings. Elemica helped Dow unify multiple, disparate business processes, reduced the cost of getting contracted items from suppliers, and increased efficiency in procurement, operations, IT, and accounts payable.

Air Products & Chemicals, Inc. is a global provider of gases and chemicals with 22,000 employees worldwide, and $10 billion in revenue. A major customer asked them for online ordering, but the initial method proposed would have required considerable additional work for both parties. Since both companies were connected to Elemica, there was a better option—the Elemica Supply Chain Hosted Solution.

SOURCES: "About Elemica," Elemica.com, August 31, 2012; "Elemica Introduces Transportation Management Solution," Elemica Corporation, February 16, 2012; "Elemica Wins 2011 SDCExec Green Supply Chain Award for Helping Clients Incorporate Sustainability Within Their Supply Chains," Elemica Corporation, November 29, 2011; "Elemica Procurement Case Study: Dow," Elemica Corporation, September 2010; "Elemica Order Management Case Study: BP," Elemica Corporation, September 2010; "Elemica Case Study: LanXess," Elemica Corporation, September 2010; "Elemica and Rubber-Network Merge," SDCExec.com, August 25, 2009; "Case Study: Elemica," http://www.ebusiness-watch. org/studies, August 25, 2009; "Once Elemica Tackled the Hard Part, the Rest Was Easy," SupplyChainBrain.com, August 5, 2009; "Elemica Merger with Rubber Network," Philly.com, August 3, 2009; "Elemica Automates B2B Transactions Between Trading Partners—Speeding Up Orders by 78%," Softwareag.com, January 2009; "Top Chemical Company Selects Elemica's Business Process Network to Automate Global Procurement," Redorbit.com, December 18, 2008; "Elemica: Standards and Business," by Mike McGuigan, CEO, November 6, 2007, www.pidx.org/ events/upload/Elemica. ppt; "Elemica: Simplification + Efficiency = Increased Profitability," by Fran Keeth, Elemica Business Leadership Forum, Philadelphia, Pennsylvania, wwwstatic.shell.com, September 13, 2005; "The Journey of Elemica: An e-Commerce Consortium," by Andrew Liveris, Business Group President, Performance Chemicals. Strategic Alliances Conference, www.dow. com/ebusiness/news/ecs peech. htm, April 9, 2002.

Elemica has also developed a sustainability program. Elemica says it has delivered more than 160 million messages since 2004, which equates to 1,666 cubic meters of landfill space, 18,160,002 liters of water saved in paper production, 17,434 trees, and 196,128 kilograms of CO_2 emissions. In February 2012, Elemica introduced a transportation management solution (ETM) powered by Oracle. Available as a cloud-based software-as-a-service (SaaS) on a subscription basis, ETM will enable Elemica member firms to optimize logistics and transportation business processes, resulting in supply chain savings and a reduction of carbon emissions.

Case Study Questions

1. If you were a small chemical company, what concerns would you have about joining Elemica?

2. Elemica provides a community for participants where they can transact, coordinate, and cooperate to produce products for less. Yet these firms also compete with one another when they sell chemicals to end-user firms in the automobile, airline, and manufacturing industries. How is this possible?

3. Review the concept of private industrial networks and describe how Elemica illustrates many of the features of such a network.

11.5 REVIEW

KEY CONCEPTS

■ Define B2B commerce and understand its scope and history.

Before the Internet, business-to-business transactions were referred to simply as *trade* or the *procurement process*. Today, we use the term *B2B commerce* to describe all types of computer-assisted inter-firm trade, and the term *Internet-based B2B commerce* or *B2B e-commerce* to describe specifically that portion of B2B commerce that uses the Internet to assist firms in buying and selling a variety of goods to each other.

In order to understand the history of B2B commerce, you must understand several key stages including:

- *Automated order entry systems*, developed in the 1970s, used the telephone to send digital orders to companies.
- *EDI* or *electronic data interchange*, developed in the late 1970s, is a communications standard for sharing various procurement documents including invoices, purchase orders, shipping bills, product stocking numbers (SKUs), and settlement information for an industry.
- *Electronic storefronts* emerged in the 1990s along with the commercialization of the Internet. They are online catalogs containing the products that are made available to the general public by a single vendor.

- *Net marketplaces* emerged in the late 1990s as a natural extension and scaling-up of the electronic storefront. Net marketplaces bring hundreds of suppliers, each with its own electronic catalog, together with potentially thousands of purchasing firms to form a single Internet-based marketplace.
- *Private industrial networks* also emerged in the late 1990s with the commercialization of the Internet as a natural extension of EDI systems and the existing close relationships that developed between large industrial firms and their suppliers.

■ Understand the procurement process, the supply chain, and collaborative commerce.

- The *procurement process* refers to the way business firms purchase the goods they need in order to produce the goods they will ultimately sell to consumers. Firms purchase goods from a set of suppliers who in turn purchase their inputs from a set of suppliers. These firms are linked in a series of connected transactions.
- The *supply chain* is the series of transactions that links sets of firms that do business with each other. It includes not only the firms themselves but also the relationships between them and the processes that connect them.

There are seven steps in the procurement process:
- Searching for suppliers for specific products
- Qualifying the sellers and the products they sell
- Negotiating prices, credit terms, escrow requirements, and quality requirements
- Scheduling delivery
- Issuing purchase orders
- Sending invoices
- Shipping the product

Each step is composed of separate sub-steps that must be recorded in the information systems of the buyer, seller, and shipper. There are two different types of procurements and two different methods of purchasing goods:
- *Purchases of direct goods*—goods that are directly involved in the production process.
- *Purchases of indirect goods*—goods needed to carry out the production process but that are not directly involved in creating the end product.
- *Contract purchases*—long-term agreements to buy a specified amount of a product. There are pre-specified quality requirements and pre-specified terms.
- *Spot purchases*—for acquisition of goods that meet the immediate needs of a firm. Indirect purchases are most often made on a spot-purchase basis in a large marketplace that includes many suppliers.

The term *multi-tier supply chain* is used to describe the complex series of transactions that exists between a single firm with multiple primary suppliers, the secondary suppliers who do business with those primary suppliers, and the tertiary suppliers who do business with the secondary suppliers.

Trends in supply chain management (the activities that firms and industries use to coordinate the key players in their procurement process) include:
- *Supply chain simplification,* which refers to the reduction of the size of a firm's supply chain.

- *Supply chain management systems,* which coordinate and link the activities of suppliers, shippers, and order entry systems to automate the order entry process from start to finish.
- *Collaborative commerce,* which is the use of digital technologies to permit the supplier and the purchaser to share sensitive company information in order to collaboratively design, develop, build, and manage products throughout their life cycles.

■ Identify the main types of B2B commerce: Net marketplaces and private industrial networks.

There are two generic types of B2B commerce and many different subtypes within those two main categories of Internet commerce:

- *Net marketplaces,* which are also referred to as exchanges or hubs, assemble hundreds to thousands of sellers and buyers in a single digital marketplace on the Internet. They can be owned by either the buyer or the seller, or they can operate as independent intermediaries between the buyer and seller.
- *Private industrial networks* bring together a small number of strategic business partners who collaborate with one another to develop highly efficient supply chains and to satisfy customer demand for product. They are by far the largest form of B2B commerce.

■ Understand the four types of Net marketplaces.

There are four main types of "pure" Net marketplaces:

- *E-distributors* are independently owned intermediaries that offer industrial customers a single source from which to make spot purchases of indirect or MRO goods. E-distributors operate in a horizontal market that serves many different industries with products from many different suppliers.
- *E-procurement Net marketplaces* are independently owned intermediaries connecting hundreds of online suppliers offering millions of MRO goods to business firms who pay a fee to join the market. E-procurement Net marketplaces operate in a horizontal market in which long-term contractual purchasing agreements are used to buy indirect goods.
- *Exchanges* are independently owned online marketplaces that connect hundreds to thousands of suppliers and buyers in a dynamic real-time environment. They are typically vertical markets in which spot purchases can be made for direct inputs (both goods and services). Exchanges make money by charging a commission on each transaction.
- *Industry consortia* are industry-owned vertical markets where long-term contractual purchases of direct inputs can be made from a limited set of invited participants. Consortia serve to reduce supply chain inefficiencies by unifying the supply chain for an industry through a common network and computing platform.

■ Identify the major trends in the development of Net marketplaces.

- In the early days of e-commerce, independent exchanges were the prototype Internet-based marketplace; however, most of them did not succeed, failing to attract enough players to achieve liquidity.

- Industry consortia sprang up partly in reaction to the earlier development of independently owned exchanges that were viewed by large industries as interlopers who would not directly serve their needs.
- The failure of the early exchanges is one reason Net marketplaces are changing so rapidly. Participants have come to realize that the real value of B2B e-commerce will only be realized when it succeeds in changing the entire procurement system, the supply chain, and the process of collaboration among firms.

■ **Identify the role of private industrial networks in transforming the supply chain.**

- Private industrial networks, which presently dominate B2B commerce, are Web-enabled networks for coordinating trans-organizational business processes (collaborative commerce). These networks range in scope from a single firm to an entire industry.
- Although the central purpose of private industrial networks is to provide industry-wide global solutions to achieve the highest levels of efficiency, they generally start with a single sponsoring company that "owns" the network.
- Private industrial networks are transforming the supply chain by focusing on continuous business process coordination between companies.

■ **Understand the role of private industrial networks in supporting collaborative commerce.**

Collaboration among businesses can take many forms and involve a wide range of activities. Some of the forms of collaboration used by private industrial networks include the following:

- *CPFR* or *industry-wide collaborative resource planning, forecasting, and replenishment* involves working with network members to forecast demand, develop production plans, and coordinate shipping, warehousing, and stocking activities. The goal is to ensure that retail and wholesale shelf space is precisely maintained.
- *Supply chain and distribution chain visibility* refers to the fact that, in the past, it was impossible to know where excess capacity existed in a supply or distribution chain. Eliminating excess inventories by halting the production of overstocked goods can raise the profit margins for all network members because products will no longer need to be discounted in order to move them off the shelves.
- *Marketing and product design collaboration* can be used to involve a firm's suppliers in product design and marketing activities as well as in the related activities of their supply and distribution chain partners.

QUESTIONS

1. Explain the differences among total inter-firm trade, B2B commerce, and B2B e-commerce.
2. List at least five potential benefits of B2B e-commerce.
3. Name and define the two distinct types of procurements firms make. Explain the difference between the two.
4. Name and define the two methods of purchasing goods.
5. Define the term supply chain and explain what SCM systems attempt to do. What does supply chain simplification entail?
6. How do the value chain management services provided by e-procurement companies benefit buyers? What services do they provide to suppliers?

7. What are the three dimensions that characterize an e-procurement market based on its business functionality? Name two other market characteristics of an e-procurement Net marketplace.
8. Identify and briefly explain the anti-competitive possibilities inherent in Net marketplaces.
9. List three of the objectives of a private industrial network.
10. What is the main reason why many of the independent exchanges developed in the early days of e-commerce failed?
11. Explain the difference between an industry consortium and a private industrial network.
12. What is CPFR, and what benefits could it achieve for the members of a private industrial network?

PROJECTS

1. Choose an industry and a B2B vertical market maker that interests you. Investigate the site and prepare a report that describes the size of the industry served, the type of Net marketplace provided, the benefits promised by the site for both suppliers and purchasers, and the history of the company. You might also investigate the bias (buyer versus seller), ownership (suppliers, buyers, independents), pricing mechanism(s), scope and focus, and access (public versus private) of the Net marketplace.

2. Examine the Web site of one of the e-distributors listed in Figure 11.9, and compare and contrast it to one of the Web sites listed for e-procurement Net marketplaces. If you were a business manager of a medium-sized firm, how would you decide where to purchase your indirect inputs—from an e-distributor or an e-procurement Net marketplace? Write a short report detailing your analysis.

3. Assume you are a procurement officer for an office furniture manufacturer of steel office equipment. You have a single factory located in the Midwest with 2,000 employees. You sell about 40% of your office furniture to retail-oriented catalog outlets such as Quill in response to specific customer orders, and the remainder of your output is sold to resellers under long-term contracts. You have a choice of purchasing raw steel inputs—mostly cold-rolled sheet steel—from an exchange and/or from an industry consortium. Which alternative would you choose and why? Prepare a presentation for management supporting your position.

Index

A

AAP (American Association of Publishers), 301, 302
abandonment rate, 244, 245
Acacia Technologies, 285
acceptance testing, 136, 138
account aggregators, 329
accountability, 264
accountable supply chains, 424-425
ACPA (Anticybersquatting Consumer Protection Act) (1999), 286
acquiring bank, 193
acquisition rate, 244, 245
Active International, 436
Active Server Pages. *See* ASP
Acxiom, 271
ad exchanges, 227, 253
ad servers, 103
adCenter (Microsoft), 223
AdGabber (social network), 384
AdMob (Google), 234
Adobe, 100, 177
Adobe Acrobat, 177
Adobe Dreamweaver, 135
Adobe Reader, 177
AdSense (Google), 222, 223, 230, 403
Advanced Research Projects Agency Network. *See* ARPANET
advertising
  behavioral targeting, 239, 252, 268, 269-270, 276
  interest-based advertising, 240
  newspapers, 356
  online advertising, 220
  online content and, 355
  pricing models for, 250-251
  print newspaper advertising, 356
  retargeting ads, 240
  television advertising, 347
  word-of-mouth advertising, 233, 246
  See also online marketing/advertising
advertising networks, 226, 233, 268, 269, 270
advertising revenue model, 38-39, 40
adware, 172
AdWords (Google), 105, 222, 223
affiliate marketing, 229-230
affiliate revenue model, 40
affinity group portal, 401
age, of Internet audience, 210-211
Agentrics, 440

aggregator software, 108
AgoraCart.com, 144
AIM (AOL Instant Messenger), 104
Air Products & Chemicals, Inc., 443
airline industry, 54, 156-158, 313, 333
Akamai, 112-114, 285
Akamai Aqua Mobile Accelerator service, 114
Akamai Intelligent Platform, 113
Akamai software, 113
Alice for the iPad (app), 137
Amazon
  about, 4, 15, 22, 41, 44, 45, 317
  affiliate program, 229
  business model, 43
  cloud-based music model, 47
  cloud computing, 81
  digital rights management (DRM), 355-356
  e-books, 361-362
  European data protection rules, 277
  flash marketing by, 241
  Google book-scanning lawsuit, 302
  long tail marketing, 241
  m-commerce, 110
  marketing by, 239
  mobile Web site, 151
  movie rights, 369
  music industry and, 54
  one-click purchasing, 285
  online gambling app, 299
  streaming movies, 348
  streaming music, 374
  taxation and, 294
  template for Web sites, 122
  Twitter and, 36
  value webs, 56-57
  videos, 347
  vision statement for, 123
Amazon Appstore, 237
Amazon Associates, 229
Amazon Cloud Player, 47, 374
Amazon Kindle, 361-362, 365
Amazon Local, 44
Amazon Payments, 195
Amazon Prime Advantage, 348
Amazon Web Services, 81
American Association of Publishers. *See* AAP
amplification, 244, 246
Ancestry.com, 39

Anderson, Chris, 61
Andreessen, Marc, 62, 97, 98
Android apps, 110, 111
Android phones
  location-based privacy issues, 269
  payment systems, 195
  security of, 178, 179
Angry Birds (game), 374
Anonymous (hacker collective), 174
anonymous information, 267
anonymous profiles, 270
anti-spam legislation, 229
anti-virus software, 191
Anticybersquatting Consumer Protection Act. *See* ACPA
AOL, 43, 46, 225, 329, 401, 402, 403
AOL Instant Messenger. *See* AIM
AOL Search, 105
Apache, 103, 139, 144
app marketplaces, 110
Appillionaires, 137
applause ratio, 244, 246
Apple
  about, 22, 23, 318, 322
  App Store, 63, 110, 111
  augmented reality, 69
  cloud-based music model, 47
  default Do Not Track capability, 278
  digital rights management (DRM), 355-356
  e-commerce patents, 285
  European data protection rules, 277
  iOS platform, 111
  iOS SDK, 110
  labor issues, 420
  location-based privacy issues, 269
  movies, 369, 370
  music industry and, 54
  online gambling app, 299
  privacy policy, 277
  security and, 191
  streaming music, 374
  supply chain risk, 420
  Twitter and, 36
  videos, 347
Apple iAd, 234, 236
Apple iBookstore, 362
Apple iCloud, 367
Apple iPad, 4, 109-111, 122, 178, 199, 269, 362, 371, 420, 425
Apple iPhone, 4, 80, 109, 110, 111, 178,

179, 269, 371, 425
Apple iPod, 371
Apple iPod Touch, 109
Apple iTunes, 43, 47, 179, 235, 355, 362, 365, 367, 371, 384
Apple QuickTime, 100, 106
Apple Safari, 104, 276
Apple Siri, 109
Applebees, marketing by, 239
application servers, 139, 145-146
Applications layer, 75, 76, 82, 84, 85
Apply with LinkedIn, 336
apps, 8
    defined, 7
    location-based privacy issues, 269
    as marketing platform, 235, 237
    newspapers, 360
    rogue apps, 179
    security and, 179
    See also mobile apps
Appthority, 23
Aqua Mobile Accelerator service (Akamai), 114
Ariba, 50, 434-435
ARPANET (Advanced Research Projects Agency Network), 73
Ascentium Commerce Server (software), 143
Ashcroft v. Free Speech Coalition (2002), 296
Ask.com, 43, 46, 105, 401
ASP (Active Server Pages), 141, 149
ASPDotNetStorefront, 144
AT&T, 88, 178, 179, 200
ATG (Art Technology Group), 121, 143
attrition rate, 244, 245
auctions, 392
    See also online auctions
Auctions.samsclub, 395
Audi AG and Volkswagen of America Inc. v. Bob D'Amato (2006), 287
augmented reality, 69
AuthenTec, 23
authentication, 181
authentication services, 103
authenticity, 168, 169
Author Solutions, 359
Author's Guild, Google book-scanning lawsuit, 302
auto-auction fraud scam, 399
automated order entry systems, 416
automobile industry, 54, 423, 424
Autonomy (company), 141
availability, 169
Avendra (industry consortium), 438

B

B2B commerce, 416
B2B (business-to-business) e-commerce, 415-444
    about, 15
    benefits and challenges of, 418-419
    business models, 49-51
    defined, 14, 416
    described, 416
    growth of, 416-418
    history of, 416-418
    mobile B2B SCM systems, 427-429
    net marketplaces, 417, 430, 431-438
    private industrial networks, 51, 417, 430, 431, 438-441
    procurement process, 419, 421-422
    revenue statistics, 418
    social networks and, 430
    statistics, 14
    supply chain management, 422-429
B2B electronic storefronts, 416
B2C (business-to-consumer) auctions, 383
B2C (business-to-consumer) e-commerce
    about, 15
    business models, 42-43, 45-49
    defined, 13
    statistics, 13
backbone, 85-86, 87
backdoor, 171
Ballmer, Steve, 383
bandwidth, 86, 88
Bank of America, 313, 328
banking, online, 211, 327-328
banner ads, 217, 225
Barnes & Noble, 45
Barnesandnoble.com, marketing by, 239
Baseball-cards.com, 395
Bavaresco, Shawn, 208
"beacons," 252
behavioral targeting, 239, 252, 268, 269-270, 276
Berners-Lee, Tim, 97, 100
BestBuy, 318, 324, 372
bid manipulation, at auctions, 399
bid rigging, at auctions, 399
bid siphoning, at auctions, 399
Bid4Assets (auction site), 395
Bidz (auction site), 311, 395
Big Data, 266
"Big Data" analytics software, 97
big-ticket items, 217
biller-direct system, 197
BillMeLater, 406
Bing (Microsoft), 43, 46, 106, 237, 401, 403

bit (binary digit), 74
Bit9, 23
Bitcoins, 195-196
bits per second (unit). See bps
BitTorrent, 370
Bizland (company), 143
BizRate, 325
Bizrate Insights, 3-4
BlackBerry (smartphone), 80, 110, 111
Blackstone Group, 334
Blendtec, 234
Blinds.com, 70
Bling Deals, 325
blog networks, 233
Blogger.com (Google), 108
"blogosphere," 108
blogroll, 107
blogs, 107-108, 232
Blue Coat, 113
Blue Nile, 45, 311-312, 320, 324
Bluefly, 43, 320
Bluetooth, 94, 95-96
BMW, 235
Boeing, 420
books
    revenues, 352
    See also e-books
"bot-herder," 171
bot networks, 172, 174, 228
botnets, 166, 171-172
bots, 171, 172
bounce-back rate, 244, 246
bps (bits per second), 74, 86
brand identity, 219
Breyer, Michelle, 37
bricks-and-clicks, 43, 45, 320-321
Brin, Sergey, 69
broadband technology, 88, 89, 90, 212, 367
broadcast model, 11
brokerage services, online, 328-329
browse-to-buy ratio, 244, 245
browser parasite, 172
browsers. See Web browsers
bulletin boards, 105
Bush, Vannevar, 97
business models, 35-64
    B2B e-commerce, 49-51
    B2C e-commerce, 42-43, 45-49
    defined, 37
    EBPP, 197
    elements of, 37-42
    newspapers, 358-359
    online auctions, 394-395
    online retail sector, 319-324
    portals, 403-404

social networks, 388-389
business objectives, 131
business plan, 37
business processes, 37, 58
See also business models
business strategy, 57-59
business-to-business e-commerce. *See* B2B (business-to-business) e-commerce
business-to-consumer auctions. *See* B2C auctions
business-to-consumer e-commerce. *See* B2C (business-to-consumer) e-commerce
"buy-side" servers, 141
Buy.com, 320
byte, 74

C

C and C+, 110
C2C (consumer-to-consumer) auctions, 393
C2C (consumer-to-consumer) e-commerce, 14, 15
CA. *See* certification authority
Cabela's, 321
Cabir (worm), 178
Cable Communications Policy Act of 1984, 273
cable modem, 89, 90
cable TV, 355
Cablevision, 88, 89
CALEA. *See* Communications Assistance for Law Enforcement Act
CAN-SPAM Act (Controlling the Assault of Non-Solicited Pornography and Marketing Act), 229
Canada, privacy guarantees in, 272
cannibalization, 351, 362-363
CANs (campus area networks), 87-88
cap pricing, 293
Capital One, 327, 328
car rentals, 333
Carbonite, 43, 49
Cardholder Not Present. *See* CNP transactions
Career Builder, 337
career services, 336-337
CareerBuilder (social network), 336, 384
cart conversion rate, 244, 245
Cascading Style Sheets. *See* CSS3
catalog merchants, 43, 321-322
Caterpillar, supply chain risk, 420
CBSSports.com, 43
ccTLDs (country-code top-level domains), 98
CDA (Communications Decency Act)

(1996), 296
CDW Corp., 321
cell phones. *See* mobile phones; smartphones
Cendant, 334
CenturyLink, 88
certification authority (CA), 186, 187
CGI (Common Gateway Interface), 141, 148-149
channel conflict, 322
Charles Schwab, 313, 328, 329
Chase Online, 328
chat. *See* online chat
CheapTickets, 54, 334
checkout conversion rate, 244, 245
ChefVille (game), 376
chemical industry, 54
Chestnut, Ben, 61
Chevrolet, 235
Child Pornography Prevention Act (1996), 296
children, legal protections for, 295-297
Children's Internet Protection Act. *See* CIPA
Children's Online Privacy Protection Act. *See* COPPA
Chin, Judge Denny, 302, 303
China
  cyberwarfare and, 163, 164
  Internet control in, 291
ChoicePoint, 271
Chrome (Google), 104
cigarette sales, online, 297, 299
CIPA (Children's Internet Protection Act) (2001), 296
cipher, 181
cipher text, 180
circuit-switched networks, 73
CISPA (Cyber Intelligence Sharing and Protection Act), 163
Citigroup, 313
CitySearch.com, 237, 339
CityVille (game), 233, 374, 376, 377
Clark, Jim, 98
Clarke, Richard, 164
Class C network, 76
Clean Clothes Campaign, 425
clearinghouse, for credit card transactions, 194
click fraud, 225, 228
click-through rate (CTR), 243, 244, 246-248
Clickability (company), 141
clickstream behavior, 216, 240
client/server computing, 72, 73, 77-79
client software, security, 177

clients, 77, 79, 191
cloud-based business models, 47
cloud computing
  about, 79, 114
  defined, 81
  described, 80-81
  digital services, 355
  e-commerce and, 6, 81
  entertainment industry, 367
  hosting, 136
  movies and, 368
  security, 178, 180
  software, 81
cloud music streaming, 47
Cloud Player (Amazon), 47
CMS (content management system), 133, 141
CNN.com, 43
CNNMoney, 329
CNP transactions (Cardholder Not Present), 193
co-location, 136
Coke, 219
collaborative commerce, 429, 439, 441
Collaborative resource planning, forecasting, and replenishment (CPFR), 441
collaborative shopping, 23
collective utilitarian principle, 265
Comcast, 88, 89, 295
Comcast Optimum Online, 88
Commerce Server (Ascentium), 143
commercial transactions, 7
commoditization, 58
Common Gateway Interface. *See* CGI
Communications Assistance for Law Enforcement Act (CALEA), 271
Communications Decency Act. *See* CDA
community providers, 43, 45
comparison shopping, 325
competition, 54
competitive advantage, 38, 41
competitive environment, 38, 40
complementary resources, 41
computer crime. *See* cybercrime
Computer Crime and Security Survey, 166
Computer Matching and Privacy Protection Act of 1988, 273
Computer Security Act of 1987, 273
Computer Security Institute, 166
computers. *See* PCs; tablets
comScore, marketing metrics, 246
confidentiality, 168, 169, 181
congestion pricing, 293
consent, informed consent, 272, 277
console gamers, 374, 375

consolidator model, 197
consumer behavior
  big-ticket items, 217
  browsers and buyers, 216-217
  choosing online shopping, 213
  clickstream behavior, 216, 240
  comparison shopping, 325
  intentionality, 217
  media multitasking, 212
  model of online behavior, 215
  online financial services, 327
  purchasing decision, 213-216
  research methods, 217
  small-ticket items, 217
consumer profile, online marketing, 209-212
Consumer Reports, 39
consumer-to-consumer auctions. *See* C2C auctions
consumer-to-consumer e-commerce. *See* C2C (consumer-to-consumer) e-commerce
Consumerreports.org, 40
consumers
  broadband vs. mobile access, 212
  buyers vs. browsers, 216-217
  consumer profile, 209-212
  customer experience, 219
  decision process, 213, 214
  demographics, 210-211
  See also consumer behavior
content delivery network (CDN) industry, 113
content farms, 225
content management system. *See* CMS
content providers, 43, 45-46
context advertising, 222, 223
contract purchasing, 421
Controlling the Assault of Non-Solicited Pornography and Marketing Act. *See* CAN-SPAM Act
Converge (exchange), 436
conversation ratio, 244, 245-246
Converse app, 70
conversion rate, 244, 245
cookies
  about, 107, 252, 268, 272
  defined, 107
  super cookies, 268
  third-party cookies, 268, 269-270
COPPA (Children's Online Privacy Protection Act) (1998), 273, 277-278, 297
copyright, 279-283
  defined, 279-280
  Digital Millennium Copyright Act (DMCA), 4, 281-283

fair use doctrine, 280-281
  Google Books Library Project, 280
  patent different from, 283
Copyright Act (1976), 301
copyright infringement
  case study, 28-30
  Grooveshark case, 282-283
  Pinterest, 4
  The Pirate Bay, 28-30
  Viacom case, 281, 282
copyright law, 279
cost competition, 58, 59
cost per action (CPA), 249-250
cost per click (CPC), 249
cost per thousand (CPM) impressions, 249
Costco, 320
country-code top-level domains. *See* ccTLDs
coupons, mobile marketing, 234
Cox, 88, 89
CPA. *See* cost per action
CPC. *See* cost per click
CPM. *See* cost per thousand (CPM) impressions
CPRF. *See* Collaborative resource planning, forecasting, and replenishment
crackers, 174
Craigslist, 14, 15, 331, 337
CrawlTrack (software), 144
credit card fraud/theft, 166, 174-175
credit card payment, 143, 144, 192-194, 198
Credit Karma, 327
crime. *See* cybercrime
Crocs, 322
"crowdsourcing," 359
CrownPeak Technology (company), 141
cryptocurrency, 195-196
CSS3 (Cascading Style Sheets), 100
CTR. *See* click-through rate
Curls-on-the-Go (app), 137
CurrentCodes, 325
customer co-production, 240-241
customer experience, 219
customization, 9, 11, 52, 240, 262, 326
Cyber Intelligence Sharing and Protection Act. *See* CISPA
Cyber Security Enhancement Act, 271
cybercrime, 114
  click fraud, 225, 228
  cyberpiracy, 286, 287
  cybersquatting, 286, 287
  identity theft, 174
  scope of problem, 165-167

typosquatting, 287
cyberespionage, 164
cyberpiracy, 286, 287
cybersecurity legislation, 163, 164
CyberSource, 166
cybersquatting, 286, 287
cybervandalism, 174
cyberwarfare, 163-164
cyberzoning, 296

D

daily deal sites, 319
DailyStrength.org, 384
Dairy.com (industry consortium), 438
D'Amato, Bob, 287
data breaches, 174
data brokers, 271
data capture, Web servers, 103
database servers, 103
DDoS attacks (Distributed Denial of Service attacks), 114, 171, 176, 178
dead links, 139
debit cards, 198
Deckers Outdoor Corp., 155
deep linking, 288
"deep Web," 16-17
delivery rate, 244, 246
Dell, 36, 43, 318, 322, 323
Dell.com, 323
demand aggregator, 396
demand chain visibility, 441
demand-pull model, 322
Demandware (company), 143
Denial of Service attacks. *See* DoS attacks
destination sites, 401
dev.appia.com, 237
deviantART (social site), 387
Diageo, Facebook advertising, 207
dial-up connection, 89, 212
dial-up modem, 74
Diamond v. Chakrabarty (1980), 283
Dice (Web site), 337
differentiation, 57, 58
Diffie, Whitfield, 182
digital books. *See* e-books
digital cash, 195-196
digital certificates, 186, 187
digital commerce. *See* e-commerce
digital content. *See* online content
Digital Content Newsfronts, 348
"digital divide," 211
digital marketing. *See* online marketing/advertising
digital media, intellectual property rights, 278
Digital Millennium Copyright Act. *See*

DMCA

digital rights management (DRM), 355-356
  closed platforms and, 365
  defined, 355
  HTML5 and, 100
  privacy and, 268
digital signature, 183, 185, 186
digital subscriber line. *See* DSL
digital wallets, privacy and, 268
digitally enabled transactions, 7
Diller, Barry, 348
dilution, 284
direct goods, 419
discussion boards, 105
discussion groups, 105
disintermediation, 19, 315, 323-324
display ad marketing, 225-227, 234, 235, 248, 319
Distributed Denial of Service attacks. *See* DDoS attacks
DMCA (Digital Millennium Copyright Act), 4, 281-283
DNS (Domain Name System), 76, 78
DNS servers, 78
"Do Not E-mail" registry, 229
"Do Not Track" system, 276, 278
doctrine of fair use, 280-281
DoD. *See* U.S. Department of Defense
domain extensions, 98
Domain Name System. *See* DNS
domain names
  checking IP address of, 76
  defined, 76
  described, 76, 79, 98-99
  registering, 286
  trademark law, 286-287
  typosquatting, 287
Domain Names Act (2002), 297
Donahoe, John, 405
DoS attacks (Denial of Service attacks), 175-176
dot-com crash, 18, 22
DoubleClick (Google), 227, 269-270, 272, 285
DoubleClick Ad Exchange (Google), 227
Dow Chemical, 443
Downadup (worm), 171
Dreamweaver (Adobe), 135
drive-by download, 171
Driver's Privacy Protection Act of 1994, 273
Dropbox, 178, 180
drug sales, online, 297-299
Drugstore.com, 45, 320
Drupal (CMS), 141

DSL (digital subscriber line), 89, 90
dual-home systems, 191
due process, 264
duration, 243, 244, 245
duration of engagement, 244
Dutch auctions, 396
Dutch Internet auctions, 396
dwell rate, 248
dynamic content, 125-126
dynamic page generation, 141
dynamic page generation tools, 140-141
dynamic pricing, 241, 392, 393

E

E. & J. Gallo Winery v. Spider Webs Ltd. (2001), 286
e-books, 6, 359, 361-364
e-commerce
  basic business concepts, 24, 32
  behavioral approaches to, 27
  budget for, 128-129
  business models, 35-64, 123-124
  business strategy, 57-59
  cloud computing and, 6, 81
  collaborative shopping, 23
  consolidation phase, 20, 21
  consumer profile, 209-212
  defined, 7, 8
  enablers, 51
  ethical, social, and commercial issues, 261-303
  evolution of, 17-21
  features of, 8-11
  financing of, 20
  government surveillance, 271-272
  history of, 5, 17-21
  industry structure and, 53-54
  information density, 9, 11, 52, 262
  information rights and privacy, 267
  intellectual property and, 279
  interactivity, 9, 10, 52, 148-149, 262
  Internet infrastructure and, 51
  invention phase, 18-20, 21
  major trends in, 5-6
  marketplace characterization, 124-125
  mobile app ecosystem and, 111
  online browsing with offline purchasing, 216-217
  online presence for, 123-136
  patents, 283-284, 285
  payment systems, 191-200
  portals, 43, 46, 329, 400-404
  privacy, 24, 25-26
  purchase decision making, 213-214
  re-invention phase, 18, 20-21
  revenue models, 38-39, 123-124

  richness, 9, 10, 52, 262
  security, 165-191
  social technology, 9, 11, 52, 262
  SWOT analysis, 126-127
  target audience, 124
  taxation, 5, 6, 292-293, 294
  technical approaches to, 27
  technology, 6, 23-24, 32, 52
  timeline with milestones, 128
  types, 13-15
  ubiquity, 8-9, 52, 262
  universal standards, 9, 10, 52, 262
  visioning by, 123
  See also B2B e-commerce; B2C e-commerce; C2C e-commerce; local e-commerce; m-commerce; online retail sector; online service sector; social e-commerce
e-commerce business models
  B2B e-commerce, 49-51
  B2C e-commerce, 42-43, 45-49
  defined, 37
  enablers, 51
  freemium business model, 61-62, 63, 360
  online retail sector, 319-324
  See also business models
e-commerce enablers, 51
e-commerce patents, 283-284, 285
e-commerce portals, 43, 46, 329, 400-404
e-commerce security, 167, 168
  authenticity, 168, 169
  availability, 169
  confidentiality, 168, 169
  integrity, 167, 169
  nonrepudiation, 168, 169
  privacy, 7, 24, 25-26, 168, 169
  threats to, 165-167, 169-180
  vulnerable points, 169-170
  See also security
e-commerce server suites, 143-144
e-commerce Web presence
  about, 129-130
  annoying features, 147
  application servers, 139, 145-146
  architecture, 146
  budget for, 128-129
  building the system, 133, 135-136
  components of, 130
  content for, 125-126
  credit card processing, 143
  customization, 9, 11, 52, 240, 262, 326
  design, 146-147
  development life cycle, 131
  driving search engines to site, 147-148
  dynamic page generation tools, 140-141

global reach, 9-10, 52, 262
hardware, 146-147
hosting, 136
implementation and maintenance, 138
improving, 146-147
information density, 9, 11, 52, 262
information richness, 9, 10, 52, 262
interactivity, 9, 10, 52, 148-149, 262
map for, 127-128
as marketing platform, 219
merchant server software, 142-144
metrics, 243-246
online catalog, 143
personal information collected at, 267
personalization, 9, 11, 52, 239, 262, 326
planning of, 130-131
shopping cart, 143, 244, 245, 268
site management tools, 139-140
social technology, 9, 11, 52, 262
software, 138-146
successful site design, 147
system architecture, 138-139
system design, 132-133, 134
systems analysis, 131-132
target audience, 124
testing the system, 136, 138
ubiquity, 8-9, 52, 262
universal standards, 9, 10, 52, 262
Web server software, 102-103, 139-141, 144
Web services, 144
Web site optimization, 147-148
e-distributors, 49-50, 432-433
E-Government Act of 2002, 273
e-mail
    about, 384
    defined, 104
    for marketing, 228-229, 233, 248
    marketing metrics, 244, 246, 247-248
    protocols, 82
    spam, 228
    wiretaps, 176
e-mail marketing, 228-229, 244, 246, 247-248
e-mail scam letter, 173
e-mail wiretaps, 176
e-procurement, 50
e-procurement firm, 50
e-procurement net marketplace, 433-435
e-signature, 183
e-tailers, 43, 45
E*Trade, 39, 43, 313, 326, 328
eBay
    about, 4, 15, 198, 395
    Affiliates Program, 229
    augmented reality, 70

business model, 39, 40, 43, 48
    case study, 405-407
    fraud and abuse, 399
    long tail marketing, 242
    mobile apps, 407
    taxation and, 294
    template for Web sites, 122
eBid (auction site), 395
EBPP systems. *See* electronic billing
    presentment and payment (EBPP)
    systems
Ecademy (social network), 384
eCAP. *See* electronic Capacity
    Management
Echo Internet Gateway, 144
Edelman, Ben, 287
EDI (electronic data interchange), 416,
    426-427
education, of Internet audience, 211
eHarmony, 39
Ektron (company), 141
Elance, 396
electronic billing presentment and
    payment (EBPP) systems, 196
electronic Capacity Management
    (eCAP), 414
Electronic Communications Privacy Act
    of 1986, 273
electronic data interchange. *See* EDI
Electronic Frontier Foundation, 163
electronic mail. *See* e-mail
Electus, 348
Elemica (industry consortium), 438,
    442-444
embezzlement, Internet insider attacks,
    176-177
EMC Corporation, 23
EMC/Documentum (company), 141
employee recruitment, 336
employees, Internet insider attacks by,
    176-177
Emporio Armani, 324
encryption, 180-187, 193
    defined, 180
    limitations to, 186-187
    public key cryptography, 182-185
    public key infrastructure (PKI), 186
    secret key encryption, 182
    symmetric key encryption, 182
England, privacy guarantees in, 272
English auctions, 395-396
entertainment industry, 349, 364-377
Eolas Technologies, 285
Epionions, 40
ESPN.com, 43
ethical and social issues, 261-303

basic ethical concepts, 264
ethical principles, 264-265
governance, 263, 289-292
information property rights, 24, 45-46,
    263, 278-289
of Internet society, 263-265
public safety and welfare, 263, 295-297,
    299
See also privacy
ethical principles, 264-265
ethics, 264
See also ethical and social issues
ethnicity, of Internet audience, 211
Etsy, 14, 43
Europe
    informed consent, 272, 277
    privacy legislation, 276-277
European Commission Data Protection
    Directive, 277-278
European Union
    data protection rules, 277
    query data retention period, 271
Evernote, 62, 63
Evian, viral marketing, 234
exchange of value, 7
exchanges, 50, 431, 435-436
    See also net marketplaces
Exostar, 437, 438
Expedia, 43, 54, 157, 313, 333, 334
Experian, 271
exploit, 170
Expression (Microsoft), 135
eXtensible Markup Language. *See* XML

F

Facebook
    about, 3, 4, 15, 45, 93, 104, 107, 319, 386
    ad exchanges, 253
    ad spending by, 388
    as affinity group portal, 401
    Beacon program, 25
    behavioral targeting by, 240
    business model, 43, 63
    children and tracking technology, 297
    competition of, 391
    Connect feature, 26
    as entertainment distribution site, 365
    European data protection rules, 277
    facial recognition program, 26
    facial recognition technology, 268
    FTC privacy settlement, 276
    growth of, 6, 383
    IPO, 22, 26
    "Like" button, 231, 246, 390
    local marketing, 237
    location-based privacy issues, 269

magazines and, 364
marketing metrics, 246, 247
as marketing platform, 207-208
"network fatigue," 390
online gambling app, 299
online marketing, 225, 228, 247-248
privacy and, 25-26, 268, 276
privacy policy, 277
for screening job candidates, 384
security and, 177
social marketing, 207-209, 231-232
Sponsored Stories, 25-26
stickiness, 243, 245
television viewing and, 368
use statistics, 231, 387
viral marketing, 234
vision statement for, 123
Zynga and, 376
Facebook Chat, 104
Facebook commerce. *See* social
  e-commerce
Facebook Connect, 269
Facebook Credits, 196, 378
Facebook Exchange, 26
facial recognition technology, 268
Fair Credit Reporting Act of 1970, 273
Fair Information Practices (FIP) prin-
  ciples, 266, 274-275
Fair Labor Association (FLA), 425
fair use doctrine, 280-281
  Google book-scanning program,
  300-303
Family Educational Rights and Privacy
  Act of 1974, 273
The Fancy, 4
FarmVille (game), 233, 374, 376
FarmVille2 (game), 376
FatWallet, 325
FBI, 291
FDCA (Food, Drug, and Cosmetic Act)
  (1938), 298
Federal Networking Council (FNC), 73
Federal Reserve, 186
Federal Trademark Dilution Act of 1995
  (FTDA), 284, 286
"fee" model, 355
fiber-optic cable, 93
fiber-optic networks, 94, 96
fiber optics, 93
Fidelity, 328, 329
Field v. Google, Inc. (2006), 281
file-sharing, 282
File Transfer Protocol. *See* FTP
financial fraud, 166
financial model. *See* revenue model
Financial Modernization Act (Gramm-

Leach-Bliley Act) (1999) 273
financial portals, 329
financial services, 326-332
financing, of e-commerce, 20
FiOS (fiber-optic service), 88, 89
FIP principles. *See* Fair Information
  Practices (FIP) principles
Fireclick, 245
Firefox (Mozilla), 104
firewalls, 190
firm value chain, 55-56
firm value webs, 56-57
First Amendment rights, 260, 272, 296
first-mover advantage, 41, 46
first movers, 19, 41, 46
FIS (company), 197
Fiserv (company), 197
fixed pricing, 392-393
FLA. *See* Fair Labor Association
Flame (Trojan), 164
Flash, 100, 106
flash marketing, 234, 241
flash memory, 80
Flickr (social site), 387
FNC. *See* Federal Networking Council
focus strategy, 59
Food, Drug, and Cosmetic Act. *See* FDCA
Ford Motor Co.
  cyberpiracy lawsuit by, 287
  Facebook advertising by, 207
  mobile marketing by, 235
  supply chain risk, 420
  Web site, 219
Ford Motor Co. v. Lapertosa (2001), 287
forms, privacy and, 268
forums. *See* online forums
Fossil, 322
4G (wireless Internet), 95
Foursquare, 237
Foxconn, 425
framing, 287, 289
"free" model, 355
free speech, 259-260
Freedom of Information Act of 1966, 273
freemium business model, 61-62, 63, 360
friction-free commerce, 19
FTC. *See* U.S. Federal Trade Commission
FTDA. *See* Federal Trademark Dilution
  Act of 1995
FTP (File Transfer Protocol), 76, 82, 103

G

gambling, online, 299
game advertising, 233
gaming, 374-376
  augmented reality, 70

gaming advertising, 233
  statistics, 233
Gap.com, 39, 324, 426
gateway, 191
Gatorade, 235
Gbps (unit), 86
GData Security Labs, 170
GEICO, 288
gender, of Internet audience, 210
Genealogy.com, 39
General Motors, 208, 420, 424
general-purpose portals, 400, 401, 403
general top-level domains. *See* gTLDs
geotargeting, 237
Germany, privacy guarantees in, 272
GetJar, 237
GetThere.com, 334
GHX (industry consortium), 438
Gilt Group, 228, 241, 320
Gilt.com, 324
Glam Media, 62
Glaser, Will, 60
Global Compact, 440
Global Fairness Initiative, 425
Global NetXchange, 440
global reach, 9-10, 52, 262
Gmail (Google), 48, 163
Go2Paper.com, 15
Golden Rule, 264
Gonzalez, Albert, 175
Google (company)
  about, 16, 22, 44, 46, 81, 93, 391
  augmented reality glasses, 69, 70
  book-scanning program, 300-303
  business model, 43
  cloud-based music model, 47
  cyberwarfare, 163-164
  default Do Not Track capability, 278
  e-commerce patents, 285
  European data protection rules, 277
  growth of, 383
  intelligent personal assistant, 109
  Internet free speech, 259-260
  local marketing, 237
  location-based privacy issues, 269
  online applications, 48
  online marketing, 225
  online newspapers, 356, 358
  privacy policy, 277
  restaurant software, 340
  search query data retention period, 271
  streaming movies, 347-348, 372
  streaming music, 374
  time spent on, 386
  trademark infringement cases against,
  288

Twitter and, 36
unique visitors, 401
Viacom copyright infringement case, 282
videos, 347
vision statement for, 123
YouTube acquisition, 383
Google (search engine), 105, 106
ad exchanges, 253
click-through rate, 247
search algorithms and choices, 224
social search, 224, 240
stickiness, 243
Google +, 69, 385, 387, 391
Google +1, 224
Google AdMob, 234
Google AdSense, 222, 223, 230, 403
Google AdWords, 105, 222, 223
Google Analytics, 144
Google Apps, 49, 81, 235
Google Blogger.com, 108
Google Books, 300-303
Google Books Library Project, 280, 301-303
Google Buzz, 276
Google Checkout, 192, 195
Google Chrome, 104
Google ContentID, 282
Google Docs, 48
Google DoubleClick, 227, 269-270, 272, 285
Google DoubleClick Ad Exchange, 227
Google Maps, 48, 150, 237
Google Music Beta, 47
Google News, 358
Google Now, 109
Google Offers, 44
Google Places, 237
Google Play, 47, 374
Google Print, 300
Google Product Search, 325
Google Shopping, 325
Google Talk, 104
Google Wallet, 192, 195, 200
Goto.com, 105
governance, 263, 289-292
See also legislation
Government Employees Insurance Company v. Google, Inc. (2004), 288
government surveillance, 271-272
Gpbs (unit), 74
Gramm-Leach-Bliley Act (Financial Modernization Act) (1999), 273
graphical user interface. See GUI
Grooveshark, 282-283
gross rating points, 244

group buying auctions, 396
Groupon
about, 15, 319
business model, 44
IPO, 22, 377
online marketing, 228, 237
GSI Commerce (company), 143
gTLDs (general top-level domains), 98
guest management software, 338-340
GUI (graphical user interface), 97

H
hackers, 174, 175, 178, 179
hacktivism, 174
hardware, for e-commerce Web Site, 145-147
hardware platform, 145
Harley-Davidson, 124
hash, 183
hash function, 183, 185
hate speech, 259, 260
HathiTrust, 302, 303
Hayneedle, 320
headline aggregators, 356
Health Insurance Portability and Accountability Act of 1966. See HIPAA
Heber, Gretchen, 137
Hellman, Martin, 182
herd behavior, at auctions, 398
Hewlett Packard. See HP
HigherEdJobs, 337
highway (toll) pricing, 293
HIPAA (Health Insurance Portability and Accountability Act of 1966), 273
hits, 243, 244
Hocking, Amanda, 359
Home Depot, 406
HomeGain, 331
Homeland Security Act, 271
Hon Hai Precision Industry Company, 425
horizontal marketplaces, 50
horizontal scaling, 145, 146
host computers, 71
hosting, 136
"hot spot," 94
hotel industry, 335
Hotels by Orbitz (app), 157
Hotels.com, 43, 334
Hotwire, 334
HP (Hewlett Packard), 81, 322, 428-429
HTML (HyperText Markup Language), 16, 72, 97, 99, 101
HTML5
about, 99, 100
digital rights management (DRM) and,

100
swiping, 157
HTML5 Canvas, 100
HTTP (HyperText Transfer Protocol), 76, 82, 97, 98
HTTP/1.1, 82
Hubspot.com, 230
HughesNet, 89
Hulu, 39, 295, 347, 369
Human Rights First, 425
hyperlinks, 72, 97, 139
HyperMart (company), 143
hypertext, 98
Hypertext Markup Language. See HTML
HyperText Transfer Protocol. See HTTP

I
IAB (Internet Architecture Board), 90
IAC/InterActiveCorp., 334, 348
iAd (Apple), 234, 236
IBM, 81, 97, 141, 423
IBM WebSphere Commerce Enterprise Edition, 143
IBM WebSphere Commerce Express Edition, 143
IBM WebSphere Commerce Professional Edition, 143
iBookstore, 362
IC3 (Internet Crime Complaint Center), 166, 399
ICANN (Internet Corporation for Assigned Names and Numbers), 90, 91, 98, 290
Ice.com, 311
iCloud (Apple), 47, 367
Identity 2.0, 188
identity credential, 188
identity theft, 174
IESG (Internet Engineering Steering Group), 91
IETF (Internet Engineering Task Force), 82, 91
iHeartRadio, 374
IHS iSuppli, 420
IIS. See Internet Information Services
Ike4e.B (worm), 178
Ikea, 235
ILS. See Inventory Locator Service
IM. See instant messaging
IMAP (Internet Message Access Protocol), 82
impressions, 243, 244
inbound marketing, 230
income level, of Internet audience, 211
Indeed.com, 337
indirect goods, 419

Industrial Internet, 96
industry consortia, 50-51, 436-438
industry structure, 53-54
industry value chain, 54-55
information asymmetry, 8
information content, content providers, 43, 45-46
information density, 9, 11, 52, 262
information privacy, 265-267
information requirements, 131-132
information richness, 9, 10, 52, 262
information rights, 263, 265-267
information society, 261
informed consent, 272, 277
infrastructure. See technology
ING Direct, 327
Inmobile.org, 384
insider abuse, 166
insider attacks, 176-177
Instagram (social site), 12, 22, 387
Instagram Effect, 23
instant messaging (IM), 104
insurance services, online, 330-331
Insurance.com, 331
Insure.com, 331
InsWeb, 331
integrity, 167, 169
Intel, 80
Intel Centrino Processor, 95
intellectual property, 45-46
intellectual property law
    case studies, 28
    copyright, 279-283
    copyright infringement, 4, 28-30
    patents, 279, 283-284
    trademark, 279, 284, 286-289
intellectual property rights, 24, 45-46, 278-289
intelligent personal assistants, 109
intentionality, 217
interaction rate, 248
interactive books, 363
interactivity, 9, 10, 52, 148-149, 262
IntercontinentalExchange, 436
interest-based advertising, 240
international law
    intellectual property, 29
    privacy guarantees in, 272, 277-278
    See also Europe
International Telecommunication Union. See ITU
Internet
    backbone of, 85-86, 87
    as client/server computing example, 77
    Commercialization Phase, 72, 73

consumer profile, 209-212
controllability of, 291
defined, 7, 16, 71, 73
development timeline, 72-73
drug sales online, 299
e-commerce and, 51
ethical, social, and commercial issues, 261-303
features and services, 104-109
free speech, 259-260
future of, 91-97
gambling, 299
governance, 263, 289-292
governing bodies of, 90-91
growth of, 15-16
history of, 72-73, 385
hourglass model of, 84-85
information rights and privacy, 265-267
Innovation Phase, 72
Institutionalization Phase, 72-73
intellectual property rights, 278-279
latency, 113
limitations of, 91
net neutrality, 293, 295
network architecture of, 84-85, 86
present status of, 83-91
purpose of, 114
security, 165-191
speed of, 112-114
technology concepts, 73-83
trademarks and, 286-289
traffic statistics, 112
use statistics, 83, 210
utility programs, 83
See also security; Web
Internet Architecture Board. See IAB
Internet auctions. See online auctions
Internet Broadcasting System (IBS), 347-348
Internet Corporation for Assigned Names and Numbers. See ICANN
Internet crime. See cybercrime
Internet Crime Complaint Center. See IC3
Internet drug bazaar, 298
Internet drug sales, 297-299
Internet Engineering Steering Group. See IESG
Internet Engineering Task Force. See IETF
Internet Exchange Points. See IXPs
Internet Explorer (Microsoft), 98, 104
Internet gambling, 299
Internet host, 16
Internet Information Services (IIS), 103, 139

Internet Layer, 75, 76
Internet marketing. See online marketing/advertising
Internet Message Access Protocol. See IMAP
Internet of Things (IoT), 96-97
Internet pharmacies, 298
Internet Protocol. See IP
Internet security. See security
Internet Security Threat Report (Symantec), 166, 177
Internet Service Providers. See ISPs
Internet Society. See ISOC
Internet Tax Freedom Act (1998), 292
Internet telephony, 109
Internet2®, 73, 92-93
intranets, 90
Intuit, Twitter and, 36
Intuit Paytrust.com, 197
Inventory Locator Service (ILS), 436
iOS platform (Apple), 111
iOS SDK (software developer kit), 110
IoT. See Internet of Things
IP (Internet Protocol), 75
IP addresses, 76, 78, 290
IP telephony, 109
iPad
    about, 4, 109-111, 122, 178, 199, 269, 362, 371, 420
    location-based privacy issues, 269
    mobile apps, 109-111
    mobile payment apps, 199
    Pinterest on, 4
    platform for mobile apps, 110
    security and, 178
    security chain labor issues, 425
    Siri, 109
    supply chain labor for, 425
    Tommy Hilfiger app, 122
iPhone
    about, 80, 111
    location-based privacy issues, 269
    mobile apps, 110
    music, 371
    Orbitz app, 158
    Pinterest on, 4
    security and, 178, 179
    security chain labor issues, 425
    Siri, 109
iPod, 371
iPod Touch, 109
IPOs, 22
IPv4 Internet addresses, 76
IPv6 Internet addresses, 76
Iran, cyberwarfare against, 164
Isis system, 200

ISOC (Internet Society), 82, 91
ISPs (Internet Service Providers), 88, 295
ITU (International Telecommunication Union), 91, 290-291
iTunes, 43, 47, 179, 235, 355, 362, 365, 367, 371, 374
Ixiasoft (company), 141
IXPs (Internet Exchange Points), 86-87

J

Japan earthquake, supply chain management and, 424
Java, 110, 149
Java applets, 149
Java Server Pages. *See* JSP
Java "servlets," 150
Java Virtual Machine (VM), 149
JavaScript, 100, 144, 150
JCPenney, 5, 45, 318, 320, 321
Jeep, online marketing by, 228
JetBlue, flash marketing, 241
jewelry sales, online, 311-312
job sites, 46, 48
Jobs, Steve, 100, 111
Jones Retail, 322
Joomla (CMS), 141
JPMorgan Chase, 313
JSP (Java Server Pages), 141, 150
just-in-time production, 423
Juxtapost, 4

K

Kaspersky (software), 179
Kayak, 157
Kazaa, 54
Kbps (unit), 86
Kelly v. Arriba Soft (2003), 280-281
key (encryption), 181
keyword advertising, 222, 223
keyword paid inclusion, 222, 223
keywords, 148, 222, 224, 287
Kindle, 361-362, 365
Kindle Fire, 361
King, Stephen, 359
Kleinrock, Leonard, 73
Kmart, 322
Kozmo, 313
Kraft Foods, 235
KwikChex, 335

L

labor conditions, supply chain, 425
Land Rover, 236
Lands' End, 321, 322
LandsEnd.com, 322
LANs (local area networks), 78, 87-88

Lapertosa (company), 287
laptop computers, use statistics, 94
Last.fm, 374
Lastminute, 333
latency, 113
LawLink (social network), 384
Layton, Thomas, 339
lead generation marketing, 230
lean production, 423
legislation
    copyright, 4, 279, 281-283
    cybersecurity, 164
    FTC privacy approach, 274-276, 278
    government surveillance of personal information, 271
    informed consent, 272, 277
    patents, 279, 283-284, 285
    privacy, 272-277
    protecting children, 296-297
    spamming, 228-229
    taxation of e-commerce, 292, 294
    trademark, 286-287
leverage, 41
Levi's, 426
liability, 264
LillianVernon.com, 43
Limelight (company), 113
Linden Dollars, 196
link farms, 225
"link" servers, 141
LinkedIn
    about, 22, 45, 107, 383-384
    ad spending by, 388
    business model, 43
    IPO, 376, 383-384
    local marketing, 237
    security, 177
    use statistics, 231, 387
linking, 287, 288-289
Linux, 90, 141
Lionsgate, 347
LiveJournal (software), 108
LivingSocial, 228, 237, 319
L.L. Bean, 321
LLBean.com, 39, 43, 59
local area networks. *See* LANs
local e-commerce, 15
local marketing, 237, 319, 324
localization, 44
location-based services, 155, 269
logical design, 133, 134
Lonely Planet, augmented reality, 70
long tail marketing, 241, 242
Lookout, 23
loyalty, 244, 245
LulzSec (hacker collective), 174

M

m-commerce (mobile e-commerce), 6, 15, 324
    Orbitz case study, 156-158
    revenue statistics, 110
    Web site, 150-155
    See also mobile apps
m-commerce Web presence, 150-155
    design, 152-153
    performance and cost, 153-154
    planning and building, 151-153
M&M, product customization, 240
Macy's, 318, 320
madware, 178
MAEs (Metropolitan Area Exchanges), 87
Mafia Wars (game), 376
magazine aggregator, 364
magazines, 352, 363-364
Magento (company), 143
Mail Order-Telephone Order. *See* MOTO transactions
mail servers, 103, 191
MailChimp, 61-62
Main Street Fairness Act, 294
mainframe computing, 78
malware (malicious code), 166, 170-172
    backdoor, 171
    botnets, 166, 171-172
    bots, 171, 172
    defined, 170
    drive-by downloads, 171
    mobile apps and, 111
    mobile platform and, 178
    payload, 171
    rootkits, 171
    virus, 171
management team, 38, 42
Manteresting, 4
manufacturer-direct firms, 322-323
Maquilla Solidarity Network, 425
market creators, 43, 48
market entry costs, 10
market liquidity, 50
market opportunity, 38, 40
market strategy, 38, 41-42
marketing
    behavioral targeting, 239, 252, 268, 269-270, 276
    customer co-production, 240-241
    customization, 9, 11, 52, 240, 262, 326
    differentiation of products, 58
    dynamic pricing, 241, 392, 393
    flash marketing, 241
    interest-based advertising, 240
    long tail marketing, 241, 242

one-to-one marketing, 239-240
  online marketing vs., 218-219
  personalization, 9, 11, 52, 239, 262, 326
  retargeting ads, 240
  See also online marketing/advertising
marketing coordination and product
  design, 441
marketplace, 8, 9
marketplace characterization, 124-125
marketspace, 9, 40
markup languages, 99, 101-102
mashups, 150
MasterCard PayPass, 195
MasterCard RPPS (Remote Payment and
  Presentment Service), 197
Match.com (company), 39
Mattel.com, 43
Mbps (unit), 86
MCX. *See* Merchant Customer Exchange
media
  cannibalization, 351, 362-363
  integrating online and offline market-
    ing, 238
  multitasking on various, 212
  revenues by channel, 351, 352
  time spent per day on, 238
  See also online content
MenuPages.com, 339
MercExchange, 285
merchant account, 193
Merchant Customer Exchange (MCX),
  200
merchant server software, 142-144
merchant server software package, 143
message boards, 105
message digest, 183
messaging, for mobile marketing, 234,
  235
metatags, 148, 287-288
Metropolitan Area Exchanges. *See* MAEs
MGM, 347
Microsoft, 80, 81, 90, 98
  ad exchanges, 253
  behavioral targeting by, 240
  Bing search engine, 43, 46, 106, 237,
    401, 403
  cloud computing, 81
  default Do Not Track capability, 278
  Google book-scanning lawsuit, 302
  investment in Facebook, 391
  keywords and, 288
  movies, 370
  online marketing, 225
  query data retention period, 271
  security and, 191
  social networks and, 383

Tickets.com, 288-289
  Twitter and, 36
Microsoft Active Server Pages (ASP), 141,
  149
Microsoft adCenter, 223
Microsoft Advertising, 269-270
Microsoft Bing, 43, 46, 106, 237, 401, 403
Microsoft Commerce Server, 143
Microsoft Expression, 135
Microsoft Internet Explorer, 98, 104
Microsoft Internet Information Services
  (IIS), 103, 139
Microsoft Windows Live, 81
Microsoft Windows Live Messenger, 104
Microsoft Windows Media Player, 106
Microsoft Windows Mobile, 80
Microsoft Windows Phone Marketplace,
  110
Microsoft Zune Video Marketplace, 371
Middleware Services layer, 84-85
Millenial Media, 234
"mining," 196
Mint.com, 327
Mirror Image Internet (company), 113
mixed mode apps, 100
mobile apps, 109-111
  app marketplaces, 110
  case study, 156-158
  developing, 166
  e-mail marketing, 228
  location-based privacy issues, 269
  for m-commerce, 151
  as marketing platform, 235, 237
  newspapers, 360
  platform, 110
  security and, 178, 179
  travel industry and, 334
  Web-based, 100
mobile devices, 15, 334
mobile e-commerce. *See* m-commerce
mobile Internet access, 17, 94-96
mobile marketing, 234-237
mobile payment systems, 195
mobile phones
  about, 79
  access to, 212
  location-based privacy issues, 269
  marketing/advertising on, 234-237
  payment systems, 195, 199, 200
  security of, 177, 178, 179
  travel industry and, 334
  use statistics, 79-80, 212
mobile platform
  about, 79-80, 114
  for apps, 110
  e-commerce and, 5, 6, 69

marketing/advertising on, 234-237
  online newspapers and, 360
  security, 178
Mobile Steals (app), 157
mobile Web app, 151
mobile Web presence. *See* m-commerce
  Web presence
mobile Web site, 150-155
modems, 88, 89
MOGH, 374
Monster.com, 43, 46, 313, 336, 337
moral issues. *See* ethical and social issues
mortgage services, online, 330
Mosaic (GUI), 62, 97, 98
motion pictures, 365
MOTO transactions (Mail Order-Telephone Order), 193, 292, 314-315
Move.com, 331
movies, 368-371
  DVD sales of, 368-369
  revenues, 365
  streaming, 106, 112, 370-371, 372
Mozilla, default Do Not Track capability,
  278
Mozilla Firefox, 104
Mpbs (unit), 74
MRO goods, 421
MSN, 43, 46, 356, 404
MSN Money, 329
multi-channel marketing, 237-242
multi-channel merchants, 320-321
multi-tier architecture, 139, 140
multi-tier supply chain, 421-422
multimedia, 351
multitasking, 212
music
  cloud music streaming, 47
  online, 371, 373-374
  revenues, 365
  streaming media, 47, 106, 374
music industry, 29
music services, 108-109
music subscription services, 365
My Blood Approves (Hocking), 359
MyLife, 387
MyPoints, 40
Myspace (social site), 387, 388
MySQL, 144

N
NABP (National Association of Boards of
  Pharmacy), 298
name your own price auctions, 396
NAPs (Network Access Points), 86-87
Napster, 54, 371
narrowband technology, 88, 90

National Association of Boards of
    Pharmacy. *See* NABP
National Association of Realtors, 331
National Consumers League, 425
National Science Foundation. *See* NSF
native apps, 151, 153
NaturallyCurly.com, 137
NBC News, 177
near field communication. *See* NFC
Nelson, Ted, 97
Net-a-Porter, 320
net marketplaces, 430, 431-438
    defined, 417
    described, 417
    e-distributors, 49-50, 432-433
    e-procurement net marketplace,
      433-435
    exchanges, 50, 431, 435-436
    industry consortia, 50-51, 436-438
    types, 431-432
net neutrality, 293, 295
NetBank, 327
Netflix, 44, 112, 295, 320, 355, 367, 369,
    370
NetQuote, 331
Netscape, 62, 98, 150
Netscape Navigator (browser), 8, 98
NetWitness, 23
Network Access Points. *See* NAPs
network effect, 19-20
network externalities, 10
"network fatigue," 390
Network Interface Layer, 75, 76
network keyword advertising, 223
Network Service Providers. *See* NSPs
Network Solutions Inc. (NSI), 122, 286,
    289
network technology, 76
Network Technology Substrate layer, 84,
    85
networks, security, 190-191
New Enterprise Associates, 44
New York Times, 240-241, 358-359, 360
New York Times test, 265
Newegg, 317, 320
News Corp., 358
newspapers
    advertising, 356
    as apps, 360
    business models, 358-359
    consumption statistics, 353
    online, 356-359
    revenues, 352, 353
Nextag, 325
NFC (near field communication), 195,
    200

Nielsen, marketing metrics, 246
Nigerian letter scam, 173
Nike, 240, 322, 425, 426
Ning (social site), 62, 387
"no free lunch" rule, 265
nonrepudiation, 168, 169, 181, 183
NSF (National Science Foundation), 72,
    73
NSI. *See* Network Solutions Inc.
NSPs (Network Service Providers), 86
numeric address, 191

O

OceanConnect (industry consortium),
    438
Office Depot, 318, 324
Office Max, 235, 318, 320
Oldandsold (auction site), 395
Omidyar, Pierre, 405
OmniUpdate (company), 141
one-click purchasing, 285
one-to-one marketing, 239-240
online advertising, 220
    See also online marketing/advertising
online auctions, 392-399
    B2C auctions, 383
    benefits of, 393-394
    business model, 394-395
    C2C auctions, 383
    choosing, 397
    fraud and abuse in, 399
    herd behavior, 398
    leading sites, 393, 395
    prices at, 398
    risks and cost for, 394
    types, 395-396
    when to use, 397-398
online banking, 211, 327-328
online bill payment, 196-197
online brokerage services, 328-329
online browsing, for offline purchasing,
    216-217
online career services, 336-337
online catalog, 143
online chat, 106
online communities
    history of, 385, 386
    See also social networks
online content, 349-356
    advertising and, 355
    consumption statistics, 352, 353
    content providers, 43, 45-46
    digital rights management (DRM),
      355-356
    entertainment industry, 349, 364-377
    gaming, 70, 233, 374-376

paying for content, 355
    premium content production, 347-349
    print media, 349
    publishing industry, 356-364
    revenue models for, 351-352
    revenue statistics, 352-353
    usage statistics, 350-351
online drug sales, 299
online entertainment industry, 349,
    364-377
    movies, 368-371
    over-the-top (OTT) entertainment
      services, 367
    size and growth, 366-367
    television, 367-368
online financial service sector, insurance
    services, 330-331
online financial services, 326-332
    account aggregators, 329
    banking, 211, 327-328
    brokerage, 328-329
    financial portals, 329
    mortgages, 330
online forums, 105-106
online gambling, 299
online gaming, 70, 233, 374-376
online information bureaus, 240
online insurance services, 330-331
online job market, 336
online magazines, 363-364
online marketing/advertising, 209,
    209-253, 220-227
    ad exchanges, 227
    advertising networks, 226, 233, 268,
      269, 270
    adware, 172
    affiliate marketing, 229-230
    banner ads, 217, 225
    behavioral targeting, 239, 252, 268,
      269-270, 276
    blogs, 232
    broadband vs. mobile impacts, 212
    browsers and buyers, 216-217
    click-through rate (CTR), 243, 244,
      246-248
    consumer decision-making process,
      212-214
    consumer profile, 209-212
    context ads, 222, 223
    cookies, 107, 252, 268, 269-270, 272
    costs of, 249-251
    customer co-production, 240-241
    customization, 9, 11, 52, 240, 262, 326
    display ad marketing, 225-227, 234,
      235, 248, 319
    dynamic pricing, 241, 392, 393

e-mail marketing, 228-229, 244, 246, 247-248
  establishing customer relationship, 219
  features of, 218-219
  flash marketing, 241
  game advertising, 233
  geotargeting, 237
  history of, 20-21
  inbound marketing, 230
  interest-based advertising, 240
  Internet audience for, 209-218
  keyword advertising, 223
  keywords, 222
  lead generation marketing, 230
  local marketing, 237, 319, 324
  long tail marketing, 241, 242
  metrics, 243-246
  mobile marketing/advertising, 234-237
  multi-channel marketing, 237-242
  network keyword advertising, 223
  objective of, 218
  one-to-one marketing, 239-240
  paid inclusion, 222, 223
  personalization, 9, 11, 52, 239, 262, 326
  pricing models for, 250-251
  real-time bidding (RTB), 227
  retargeting ads, 240
  rich media ads, 225-226
  search engines and, 105, 221-225, 234, 235
  social marketing, 207-209, 230-234, 388
  spending statistics for, 220-221
  sponsored links, 222, 223
  sponsorship marketing, 230
  video ads, 226
  viral marketing, 233-234
online mortgage services, 330
online music, 371, 373-374
online newspapers, 356-359
online payment systems. See payment systems
online pharmacies, 298
Online Privacy Alliance (OPA), 277
online radio, 371
online real estate services, 331-332
online recruiting, 336
Online Resources (company), 197
online retail sector, 313, 314-325
  advantages and challenges, 317
  bricks-and-clicks, 43, 45, 320-321
  business models, 319-324
  catalog merchants, 43, 321-322
  common themes, 323-324
  current status, 316-317
  manufacturer-direct firms, 322-323
  multi-channel merchants, 320-321

virtual merchants, 320
  vision of, 315-316
online service sector, 313, 324-334
  career services, 336-337
  financial services, 326-332
  real estate services, 331-332
  travel services, 332-335
online social networks, 386
  See also social networks
online stock brokers, 46, 48
online stored value payment systems, 194-195
online travel services, 332-335
OnlineNIC, 286-287
OPA. See Online Privacy Alliance
Open Book Alliance, 302
open rate, 244, 246
open source software, 144-145
Open Text (company), 141
Open Web Analytics, 144
OpenCms, 141
OpenTable (Web site), 338-340
Operation AntiSec, 174
opt-in model, 272
opt-out model, 229, 272
optimal cost supply chains, 424
optimization, 147-148
Optimum Online (Comcast), 88
Oracle, 81, 141, 423
Orbitz
  about, 54, 333-334
  business model, 43
  case study, 156-158
  mobile apps, 156-158
Orbitz for Business mobile Web site, 157
organic search, 222-223
organizational development, 38, 42
organized crime, 114
osCommerce.com, 143, 144
Our Common Future (WCED), 426
outsourcing, 133, 136
over-the-top (OTT) entertainment services, 367
Overstock.com, 320
Overture (company), 105, 285

P

Pacific Rim, 208
packet-switched networks, 74, 77, 109
packet switching, 72, 73-74, 77
packets, 73, 77
page views, 243, 244
paid inclusion, 222, 223
paid subscription model, 360
Paine Webber Inc. v. Fortuny (1999), 287
Pandora

about, 365,
  business m
Pandora Medi
Pandora One,
PaperFiber (in
PaperThin (con
Patch Propertie
patents, 279, 28
Path (social site),
PATRIOT Act. See USA PATRIOT Act
Pay with Square, 199
payload, 171
payment systems, 191-200
  credit card usage, 192-194, 198
  cryptocurrency, 195-196
  digital cash, 195-196
  electronic billing presentment and payment (EBPP) systems, 196
  merchant account, 193
  mobile payment systems, 195
  online bill payment, 196-197
  online payment statistics, 198
  online stored value payment systems, 194-195
  PayPal, 143, 192, 194, 198-199, 406
  virtual currencies, 196
PayPal, 143, 192, 194, 198-199, 406
PayPal Here, 199
Paytrust.com, 197
PC Connection, 321
PCs (personal computers), 78, 79, 155
Penguin (publisher), 359
Pepsico, 222
Perfect 10, Inc. v. Amazon.com, Inc., et al., 281
perfect information rule, 265
Perl, 144
personal information, privacy of, 266
personal profiles, 270
personalization, 9, 11, 52, 239, 262, 326
personally identifiable information (PII), 267
PGeStore.com, 322
pharming, 175
Philatelic Phantasies (auction site), 395
Phillips-Van Heusen, 121
phishing, 166, 172-173
PHP (language), 144
physical design, 133, 134
PII. See personally identifiable information
Pincus, Mark, 376, 378
ping (Packet InterNet Groper), 83
Pinterest, 3-5, 22, 43, 45, 107, 364, 386, 387
Pinterest Mobile, 4

oftware), 144

See public key infrastructure

planning, of e-commerce Web presence, 130-131

PlayStation, 374

PNC, 328

PocketGear, 237

podcast, 108

Polyvore (social site), 4, 387

Ponemon Institute, 167

POP3 (Post Office Protocol 3), 82

portal business model, 46

portals, 43, 46, 329, 400-404

"posting," 106

potentially unwanted programs. See PUPs

PowerSource Online, 436

pre-paid phone cards, 109

prescription drugs, online sale, 298

price discovery, 10

PriceGrabber, 325

Priceline, 43, 48, 157, 285, 334, 396

privacy
  about, 7, 24, 25-26, 168, 169
  "beacons," 252
  behavioral targeting, 239, 252, 268, 269-270, 276
  cookies, 107, 252, 268, 269-270, 272
  defined, 265
  "Do Not Track" mechanism, 276
  European Data Protection Directive, 277-278
  Facebook and, 25-26, 268, 276
  government surveillance, 271-272
  information privacy, 265-267
  location-based technology, 269
  mobile platform and, 269
  Online Privacy Alliance (OPA), 277
  personal information, 266
  private industry self-regulation, 277
  profiling, 269, 270
  social networks and, 267-269
  technological solutions, 278
  Web bugs, 252
  Web tracking software, 270, 297

Privacy Act of 1974, 273

privacy by design, FTC privacy framework, 275

Privacy Protection Act of 1980, 273

private industrial networks, 51, 417, 430, 431, 438-441

private trading exchanges (PTXs), 51, 417, 438

Procter & Gamble, 322, 439

procurement process, 419, 421-422
  contract purchasing, 421

defined, 419

overview of, 421

spot purchasing, 421

steps in, 419

type of, 419-420

See also supply chain

professional service auctions, 396

profiling, 269, 270

profit, 57

programming languages, 144

Promoted Accounts, 36, 232

Promoted Trends, 36, 232

Promoted Tweets, 36, 232

property rights, 263

Protect Act (2003), 297

protocols, 75, 77

proxy servers (proxies), 191

PTXs. See private trading exchanges

public key cryptography, 182-185

public key infrastructure (PKI), 186

public safety and welfare, 263, 295-297, 299
  media regulation, 295-296
  protecting children, 296-297

publishing industry, 356-364
  e-books, 6, 359, 361-364
  magazines, 352, 363-364
  online newspapers, 356-359

PUPs (potentially unwanted programs), 172

PurityScan, 172

Q

QR codes, 234

Qualcomm, 70

queries, 105

Quicken.com, 329

QuickQuote, 331

QuickTime (Apple), 100, 106

Qwest, 88

R

Racersauction, 395

radio
  online, 371-372
  revenues, 352, 365

Rails. See Ruby on Rails

Ralph Lauren, 322

Ramnit (worm), 177

RBOCs, 87

Rdio, 374

reach, 10, 244, 245, 400

real estate services, online, 331-332

real-time bidding (RTB), 227, 253

RealEstate.com, 331

Really Simple Syndication. See RSS

RealMedia Player, 106

RealPlayer, 100

Realtor.com, 331

recency, 244, 245

record industry, 29

recorded music industry
  cloud music streaming, 47
  industry structure, 53-54

redundancy, 86

REI, 45

responsibility, 264

responsive Web design, 151

restaurant reservation software, 338-340

retargeting ads, 240

retention rate, 244, 245

revenue model (financial model), 38-39
  defined, 38
  for online content, 351-352
  for portals, 404

reverse auction, 48

RFC, 82

RFID, 97

Rhapsody.com, 39, 43, 46, 47, 242, 355, 365

rich media ads, 225-226

richness, 9, 10, 52, 262

Riding the Bullet (King), 359

Right to Financial Privacy Act of 1978, 273

RightMove, augmented reality, 70

RIM App World, 110

risk aversion, 265

RocketLawyer, 43, 49

rogue apps, 179

rogue online pharmacies, 298

root servers, 78

rootkits, 171

Ropars, Olivier, 407

RoR. See Ruby on Rails

Rosetta Stone, 288

route-tracing utilities, 83, 84

routers, 74, 77

routing algorithm, 74

RSS (Really Simple Syndication), 108

RTB. See real-time bidding

Ruby on Rails (RoR, Rails), 144

Rue La La, 320

Russia, cyberwarfare and, 164

Rustock (botnet), 172, 228

Ryan Haight Online Pharmacy Consumer Act, 298

Ryland Homes, 155

Ryze (social network), 384

S

SaaS (software as a service), 141

Sabre Holdings, 333
Safari (Apple), 104, 276
safe harbors, 277, 424
Sailnet, 43
sales revenue model, 39, 40
Salesforce.com, 81
Salon.com, 385
SAP, 81, 423
satellite companies, 88, 89
Savvis (company), 113
scalability, 145
scam letter, 173
Schmidt, Eric, 383
Schroeder, Patricia, 301
Sciarra, Paul, 3
SCM. *See* supply chain management
scope strategy, 59
scripting languages, 144
SDLC. *See* systems development life
    cycle
The Seam (industry consortium), 438
search costs, 10
search engine advertising, 221
search engine marketing/advertising, 6,
    221, 223-224, 248
search engine optimization, 224
search engines, 103, 105, 148
    defined, 105
    for online marketing and advertising,
    221-225, 234, 235, 248
    organic search, 222-223
    privacy and, 268
    query data retention period, 271-272
    revenues, 386-387
    risks and problems with, 224-225
    search techniques, 222-223, 224
    social search, 224
Sears, 5, 200, 250, 318, 320, 321, 322
Sears.com, 43
second-level servers, 78
Second Life (virtual reality game), 196
secret key encryption, 182
Secure DNS, 188
secure electronic transaction protocol.
    See SET protocol
secure negotiated session, 187, 189
Secure Sockets Layer. *See* SSL
security, 23, 165-191
    anti-virus software, 191
    cloud computing and, 178, 180
    e-commerce, 165-191
    e-mail wiretaps, 176
    encryption, 180-187, 193
    exploits, 170
    firewalls, 190
    insider attacks, 176-177

    mobile apps and, 178, 179
    mobile platform and, 178
    networks and, 190-191
    proxy servers (proxies), 191
    social networks and, 177
    SSL (Secure Sockets Layer), 82-83, 187,
    189, 193-194
    suspected terrorist activity, 176
    technology solutions, 180-191
    threats to, 165-167, 169-180
    TLS (Transport Layer Security), 82-83,
    187, 189
    VPNs (virtual private networks), 190
    vulnerable points, 169-170
    zero-day vulnerability, 177
    See also cybercrime; cyberespionage;
    cybervandalism; cyberwarfare; e-com-
    merce security; security threats
security services, 103
security threats, 165-167, 169-180
    backdoor, 171
    botnets, 166, 171-172
    bots, 171, 172
    browser parasite, 172
    click fraud, 225, 228
    credit card fraud/theft, 166, 174-175
    data breaches, 174
    DDoS attacks (Distributed Denial of
    Service attacks), 114, 171, 176, 178
    DoS attacks (Denial of Service attacks),
    175-176
    drive-by download, 171
    hacking, 174, 175, 178, 179
    identity theft, 174
    madware, 178
    malicious code (malware), 111, 168,
    170-172
    Nigerian letter scam, 173
    pharming, 175
    phishing, 166, 172-173
    PUPs (potentially unwanted programs),
    172
    rootkits, 171
    smishing, 178
    sniffers, 176
    social engineering and, 172, 173, 177
    spam, 228
    spear phishing, 173
    spoofing, 173, 175
    spyware, 172
    Trojan horses, 164, 171
    viruses, 171
    vishing, 178
    worms, 171
"sell-side" servers, 141
SEM. *See* search engine marketing/

    advertising
Sensing Planet, 97
sentiment ratio, 244, 246
Sermo (social network), 384
server software, security, 177
servers, 77, 79, 191
service providers, 43, 48-49
session key, 189
SET protocol (secure electronic transac-
    tion protocol), 194
7-Eleven Inc., 200
Sharp, Evan, 3
Shell Oil, 443
shill bidding, at auctions, 399
shill feedback, at auctions, 399
Shoebuy, 320
Shop M&M, 240
Shopify, 3
shopping carts, 143, 244, 245, 268
Shopping.com, 325
Shopzilla, 325
Short Message Service texting. *See* SMS
    texting
Sightsound, 285
Silbermann, Ben, 3
Simple Mail Transfer Protocol. *See* SMTP
simplified choice, FTC privacy frame-
    work, 275
SimplyHired, 336, 337
Siri (iPhone feature), 109
site management tools, 139-140
site transaction logs, privacy and, 268
Site59, 333
Skype, 104, 295, 391
Slacker, 374
"slippery slope," 264
small-ticket items, 217
Smarter Planet Initiative (IBM), 97
Smarterwork (exchange), 436
smartphones
    about, 69, 80
    augmented reality, 70
    described, 94
    e-commerce and, 5, 127, 319
    location-based privacy issues, 269
    marketing/advertising on, 234-237
    mobile apps, 109-111
    payment systems, 195, 199, 200
    privacy, 268
    security and, 177, 178, 179
    use statistics, 80
SmartyPig, 327
smishing, 178
SMS texting, 104, 234, 235, 241
SMTP (Simple Mail Transfer Protocol),
    76, 82

SnagAJob, 336, 337
sniffing, 176, 271
social contract rule, 265
social e-commerce, 14-15, 319, 324
social engineering, 172, 173, 177
social gaming, 374-375
social marketing/advertising, 207-209,
    230-234
  blogs, 232-233
  collaborative shopping, 231
  defined, 230
  elements of, 231-232
  with Facebook, 231-232
  features driving growth, 231
  game advertising, 233
  metrics, 244, 245-246
  network notification, 231
  social search (recommendation), 231
  social sign on, 231
  with Twitter, 232
  viral marketing, 233-234
social media
  IPOs, 22
  marketing using, 207-209, 230-234
  online travel industry, 334
"social media" bubble, 22
social media sponsorships, 230
"social network fatigue," 391
social networks, 385-391
  about, 3, 6, 107
  B2B (business-to-business) e-commerce, 430
  business models, 388-389
  defined, 386
  e-commerce and, 5
  features and technologies, 389, 390
  future of, 389-390
  Groupon, 44
  history of, 386, 417
  marketing and, 207-209, 230-234
  monetizing, 388
  "network fatigue," 390
  online auctions, 392-399
  privacy and, 267-269
  revenues, 387
  for screening job candidates, 384
  security, 177
  stock market and, 384
  television viewing and, 368
  types of, 389
  use statistics, 385
social search, 224
social technology, 9, 11, 52
SocialPicks (social network), 384
software
  aggregator software, 108

Akamai software, 113
analytic tools, 144
anti-virus software, 191
ASP (Active Server Pages), 141, 149
"Big Data" analytics software, 97
  for blogging, 108
CGI programs, 141, 148-149
client software, 177
cloud computing, 81
e-commerce suites, 143-144
JavaScript, 100, 144, 150
JSP (Java Server Pages), 141, 150
mashups, 150
merchant server software, 142-144
open source software, 144-145
patents for computer programs, 283
restaurant reservation software,
338-340
route tracing programs, 83, 84
server software, 177
sniffer software, 271
"software plus service," 81
value chain management software, 50
Web server software, 102-103, 139-141,
144
  for Web site construction, 135
  widgets, 150
  wiki software, 108
  zero-day vulnerability, 177
software as a service. See SaaS
software patents, 283
Solaris OS, 139
Solera Networks, 23
Sony, 171, 318, 322, 347
SonyStyle.com, 43
Soverain Software, 285
spam, 228
spammers, 228-229
spear phishing, 173
speed tiers, 293
Spider Webs Ltd., 286
sponsored links, 222, 223
Sponsored Search (Yahoo), 223
sponsorship marketing, 230
spoofing, 173, 175
spot purchasing, 421
Spotify, 61, 365, 374
Sprint, 88
spyware, 172, 268
Square (device), 22, 195, 199, 406
Square Register, 199
SSL (Secure Sockets Layer), 82-83, 187,
  189, 193-194
"staffing firms," 336
Staples, 45, 318, 320
StarBand, 89

Starbucks, 22, 36, 199
state law, spamming, 229
state-sponsored cyberwarfare, 114
State Street Bank & Trust v. Signature
    Financial Group, Inc. (1998), 283-284
static content, 125
Steiner, Peter, 188
Stevens, Chris, 137
stickiness, 38, 243, 244, 245
stock offerings, 22
streaming media, 47, 106-107, 112,
    370-371, 372, 374
Stumbleupon (social site), 387
Stuxnet (worm), 164
StyleCaster, 4
subscription revenue model, 39, 40
substitution cipher, 181
Sun Microsystems, 149
Sun Solaris OS, 139
Sunoco, 200
super cookies, 268
SuperPages, 237
supply chain
  defined, 416
  labor standards, 424-425
  multi-tier, 421-422
supply chain management (SCM),
    422-429
  accountable supply chains, 424-425
  adaptive supply chains, 423-424
  collaborative commerce, 429, 439, 441
  defined, 422
  EDI (electronic data interchange), 416,
  426-427
  just-in-time production, 423
  lean production, 423
  sustainable supply chains, 425
  tight coupling, 423
supply chain management (SCM)
  systems, 427-429
supply chain simplification, 423
supply-push model, 322
SupplyOn (industry consortium), 438
suspected terrorist activity, 176
sustainable business, 426
sustainable supply chains, 425
"swipe and pay" systems, 200
swiping, 157
SWOT analysis, 126-127
Symantec, 166, 174, 177
Symbian, 80
symmetric key encryption, 182
Synnex, 428
system architecture, 138-139
system design specification, 133
system functionalities, 131

system testing, 136
systems development life cycle (SDLC), 130

T
T-Mobile, 200
T1 lines, 88, 89, 90
T3 lines, 88, 89, 90
table management software (restaurants), 338-340
tablets, 79
    m-commerce, 110, 127, 319
    mobile apps, 109-111
    use statistics, 80, 94
TAL Apparel Ltd., 440
Tap & Go (payment system), 200
Target, 200, 318, 320, 440
tax simplification project, 293
taxation, 5, 6, 292-293, 294
TCP (Transmission Control Protocol), 73, 75
TCP/IP (Transmission Control Protocol/Internet Protocol)
    architecture, 75-76
    defined, 75
    described, 72, 74-75, 76, 77
TD Ameritrade, 329
technology
    about, 7
    e-commerce and, 6, 23-24, 32, 52
    of the Internet, 71-83
    privacy-enhancing technologies, 278
    universal standards, 9, 10, 52, 262
telephone-based wireless Internet access, 94, 95
telephone modems, 88, 90
telephony, 109
Teletrade (auction site), 395
television
    cloud distributors, 367
    revenues, 352, 365
television advertising, 347
television viewing, 212
Telnet, 82
testing, Web sites, 136, 138
Texas HoldEm Poker (game), 376
The Pirate Bay, 28-30
Theknot.com, 124
"thinner clients," 79
third-level domains, 78
third-party cookies, 268, 269-270
3G (wireless Internet), 95
3.5G (wireless Internet), 95
Ticketmaster Corp. v. Tickets.com (2000), 289-290
Tickets.com, 288-289

tiered plans, 293
Tiffany, 311, 312, 324
tight coupling, 423
Timberland.com, product customization, 240
Time Warner, 402
Time Warner Cable, 88, 89
Time Warner Road Runner, 89
TLS (Transport Layer Security), 82-83, 187, 189
toll pricing, 293
Tommy Hilfiger Inc.
    case study, 121-122
    vision statement, 123
top-level domains, 78
total inter-firm trade, 416
TotalNews, Inc., lawsuit against, 289
touch points, 127
tracert (software), 83
tracing programs, 83, 84
trackbacks, 107
tracking, 270, 297
trademark, 279, 284, 286-289
    cyberpiracy, 286, 287
    cybersquatting, 286, 287
    defined, 284
    framing, 287, 289
    keywording, 287
    linking, 287, 288-289
    metatagging, 287-288
    typosquatting, 287
traditional Dutch auctions, 396
trans-organizational business process, 438
transaction brokers, 43, 46, 48, 326
transaction costs, 9
transaction fee revenue model, 39, 40
Transmission Control Protocol. *See* TCP
Transmission Control Protocol/Internet Protocol. *See* TCP/IP
transparency, FTC privacy framework, 275
Transplace (industry consortium), 438
Transport Layer, 75, 76, 82
Transport Layer Security. *See* TLS
Transport Services and Representation Standards layer, 84, 85
transposition cipher, 181
TransUnion Corp., 271
travel industry, 54, 156-158
travel services, online, 332-335
TravelNow, 334
Travelocity, 43, 54, 157, 333
Travelocity Business, 334
TripAdvisor, 70, 334, 335
Trip.com, 334

Trojan horse, 164, 171
Trulia, 331
trust, 218
TRUSTe protection, 278
Tumblr, 12, 108, 319, 387, 391
tunneling, 190
24/7 Real Media, 270
Twitter
    about, 3, 4, 12, 35, 45, 107, 232, 319, 386
    ad spending by, 388
    business model, 35-37, 43
    Enhanced Profile Pages, 36
    growth of, 6, 35
    local marketing, 237
    location-based privacy issues, 269
    magazines and, 364
    Promoted Accounts, 36, 232
    Promoted Trends, 36, 232
    Promoted Tweets, 36, 232
    social marketing and, 231, 232
    television viewing and, 368
    use statistics, 231, 232, 387
two-tier architecture, 139
TypePad (software), 108
typosquatting, 287

U
uBid (auction site), 395
ubiquity, 8-9, 52, 262
UGG Australia, 155
Ukash, 195
Ultra-Wideband. *See* UWB
UltraViolet (movie service), 372
U.N. Global Compact, 440
U.N. International Labor Organization, 425
U.N. World Commission on Environment and Development (WCED), 426
Under Armour, 322
Uniform Resource Locator. *See* URL
unique visitors, 244, 245, 400
unit testing, 136
United States, privacy guarantees in, 272
universal computing, 97
universal standards, 9, 10, 52, 262
universalism, 264
Unix OS, 139, 141
Unlawful Internet Gambling Enforcement Act (2006), 299
unsubscribe rate, 244
Urbanspoon.com, 339
URL (Uniform Resource Locator), 76-77, 98
U.S. Department of Commerce, 90, 91, 290
U.S. Department of Defense (DoD), 72,

73
U.S. Federal Trade Commission (FTC), 274-276, 278, 297
U.S. Foreign Intelligence Surveillance Court (FISC), 176
U.S. Patent and Trademark Office (USPTO), 283
U.S. Postal Service, 186
USA PATRIOT Act, 176, 271, 291
USA Today, 177
USAA, 155
usage-based billing, 293
USAJobs, 337
utility programs, 83
UWB (Ultra-Wideband), 94

V

value chain management (VCM) services, 434
value chain management software, 50
value chains, 54-55
value proposition, 37-38
value webs, 56-57
VCM services. *See* value chain management (VCM) services
venture capital firms, 22, 23
Vera Bradley, 322
VeriSign, 186
Verizon
   about, 88, 93, 178, 179, 200
   cybersquatting lawsuit by, 286-287
vertical market portals, 400, 401, 403
vertical marketplaces, 50
vertical scaling, 145, 146
Vevo (social site), 387
Via-Forensics, 178
Viacom copyright infringement case, 281, 282
Victoria's Secret, 321
video, streaming media, 106
video ads, 226, 248
video games, revenues, 352, 353, 365
video "net bombs," 112
Video Privacy Protection Act of 1988, 273
video servers, 103
video services, 109
video sites, 354
view-through rate (VTR), 243, 244
view-to-cart ratio, 244, 245
viral marketing, 233-234
virtual currencies, 196
virtual merchant, 43
virtual merchants, 320
virtual private networks. *See* VPNs
virtual reality, 69
VirtualBank, 327

virus (malware), 171
Virut (virus), 171
VisaNow.com, 43
vishing, 178
visioning process, 123
Vista Antispyware, 172
visual blog, 386
"visual collection" space, 4
VisualRoute (software), 83, 84
VoIP (Voice over Internet Protocol), 109
Volkswagen, 287, 413-414, 415
vortals, 43, 401
VPNs (virtual private networks), 190
VTR. *See* view-through rate
VUDU, 369, 370, 371
VWGroupSupply.com, 413

W

W3C (World Wide Web Consortium), 82, 91
Wall Street Journal, 358, 360
"walled garden," 356
Walmart
   about, 5, 45, 318, 320
   e-mail advertising by, 250
   MCX payment system, 200
   private industrial network, 440-441
   streaming movies, 372
   sustainable supply chain, 426
   VUDU, 369, 370, 371
Walmart.com, business model, 43
The Washington Post, et al. v. TotalNews, Inc. (1997), 289
Watchmaker Neuvo, 70
Wayfair, 320
WCED. *See* U.N. World Commission on Environment and Development
WE R HERE (Web Enabled Retailers Helping Expand Retail Employment), 294
Web (World Wide Web)
   as communications medium, 349
   "deep Web," 16-17
   defined, 7, 16, 72
   described, 16-17, 72
   growth of, 16-17
   history of, 97-98
   security, 165-191
   technology of, 97-99, 101-104
   See also search engines
Web 2.0, 11-12, 107-109, 150
Web 2.0 applications, 48, 49
Web application servers, 139, 141, 145-146
Web browsers, 104
Web bugs, 252

Web clients, 103
Web pages, Search engine optimization, 224
Web portals, 400-404
   See also e-commerce portals
Web searches, 155
Web server software, 102-103, 139-141, 144
Web servers, 103, 136, 144
Web services, 144
Web Services (Amazon), 81
Web site optimization, 147-148
Web sites
   active content, 148-149
   annoying features, 147
   application servers, 139, 145-146
   architecture, 146
   budget for, 128-129
   building, 133, 135-136
   content for, 125-126
   customization, 9, 11, 52, 240, 262, 326
   design, 146-147
   dynamic page generation tools, 140-141
   framing, 287, 289
   global reach, 9-10, 52, 262
   hosting, 136
   improving, 146-147
   information density, 9, 11, 52, 262
   information richness, 9, 10, 52, 262
   interactivity, 9, 10, 52, 148-149, 262
   linking, 287, 288-289
   for m-commerce, 150-155
   for marketing, 219
   merchant server software, 142-144
   metrics, 243-246
   mobile Web sites, 150-155
   optimization, 147-148
   outsourcing, 133, 136
   personalization, 9, 11, 52, 239, 262, 326
   reach, 10, 244, 245, 400
   recency, 244, 245
   shopping cart, 143, 244, 245, 268
   site management tools, 139
   social technology, 9, 11, 52, 262
   software and hardware, 138-146
   stickiness, 38, 243, 244, 245
   successful site design, 147
   system architecture, 138-139
   system design, 132-133, 134
   target audience, 124
   templates to build, 122, 144
   testing the system, 136, 138
   ubiquity, 8-9, 52, 262
   unique visitors, 244, 245, 400
   Web server software, 102-103, 139-141, 144

Web services, 144
  widgets, 150
  See also e-commerce Web presence;
    m-commerce Web presence
Web tracking software, 270, 297
Web video, 106
weblogs. *See* blogs
WebMD.com, 230
Webs.com, 143
Websearch, 172
WebSphere Commerce Enterprise
  Edition (IBM), 143
WebSphere Commerce Express Edition
  (IBM), 143
WebSphere Commerce Professional
  Edition (IBM), 143
Webvan, 313
The Well, 385
Wells Fargo, 313, 328
Westergren, Tim, 60
Whitman, Meg, 405
Wi-Fi, 94, 95, 96
widgets, 150
Wii, 374
WikiLeaks, 176
Wikipedia, about, 12, 70, 108
wikis, 108
Wikitude, 70
WildBlue, 89
WiMax, 94, 95
Windows Live (Microsoft), 81
Windows Live Messenger (Microsoft),
  104
Windows Media Player (Microsoft), 106
Windows Mobile, 80
Windows mobile devices, 110
Windows Phone Marketplace (Micro-
  soft), 110
Wingspan Bank, 327
"Wire Act" (1961), 299
wireless access point, 94-95
wireless Internet, 94, 95
Wireless Markup Language. *See*
  WML-only mobile Web site
wiretaps, 176
WLAN-based Internet access, 94, 95
  See also Wi-Fi
WML-only mobile Web site, 156
Woolston, Thomas, 285
WORA programs (Write Once Run
  Anywhere), 149
word-of-mouth advertising, 233, 246
WordPress, 108, 133, 135, 136, 141
Words With Friends (game), 233, 374,
  376
World Trade Organization, 425

World Wide Web. *See* Web
World Wide Web Consortium. *See* W3C
worms, 171
Wow-Coupons, 325
WSJ.com, 40, 43, 46
W.W. Grainger, 49, 59, 433

X
X-Cart.com, 144
Xanga (software), 108
Xbox, 374
Xboxlive.com, 39
XML (eXtensible Markup Language),
  101-102

Y
Yahoo
  about, 35, 46, 59, 106, 403
  ad exchanges, 253
  behavioral targeting by, 240
  business model, 40, 43
  Google book-scanning lawsuit, 302
  growth of, 383
  keywords and, 288
  local marketing, 237
  magazines and, 364
  newspapers, 356, 358
  online marketing, 225, 319
  privacy policy, 277
  revenue, 38-39
  search engine, 403
  search query data retention period,
    271-272
  stickiness, 243
  time spent on, 386, 404
  use statistics, 105, 401
Yahoo Bill Pay, 197, 329
Yahoo Finance, 329
Yahoo HotJobs, 336, 337
Yahoo Local, 237
Yahoo Merchant Solutions, 112, 143
Yahoo Messenger, 104
Yahoo News, 358
Yahoo Sponsored Search, 223
Yammer, 22
Yellow Pages, 70
YellowBook, 237
Yelp, 70, 237, 335
Yodlee, 197, 329
YouTube
  about, 3, 12, 93, 106, 112, 347
  acquisition by Google, 383, 403
  Internet free speech, 259-260
  movie rights, 369
  net neutrality, 295
  Viacom copyright infringement case,

282
  viral marketing, 234

Z
Zagat, 340
Zales, 312
ZangoSearch, 172
Zappos, 320
Zediva, 282
Zen-Cart.com, 144
Zenprise, 23
zero-day vulnerability, 177
Zillow, 331, 376
ZipRealty, 331
"zombie" computer, 171
Zuckerberg, Mark, 25
Zugara (Web site), 70
Zune Video Marketplace, 371
Zynga, 22, 233, 299, 374-378
Zynga Slingo (game), 376

References and Credits

References

For a full list of references cited in this book, see www.azimuthinteractive.com/essentials1e.

Credits

CHAPTER 1
p. 3, Pinterest, © Blaize Pascall/Alamy; Figure 1.3, based on data from eMarketer, Inc., © 2012, used with permission; p. 28, Pirate Bay, © Tommy (Louth)/Alamy.

CHAPTER 2
p. 35, Twitter, © Kennedy Photography/Alamy; Figure 2.1, Ancestry.com, © Ancestry.com, 2012; p. 60, Pandora.com, © NetPhotos/Alamy.

CHAPTER 3
p. 69; Sergey Brin, © REUTERS/Carlo Allegri; Figure 3.9, © Visualware, Inc., 2012. Used with permission; Figure 3.13, from Internet2.edu, © 2012; p. 112, Akamai.com © 2012 Akamai Technologies, Inc.

CHAPTER 4
p. 121, Hilfiger Denim, © incamerastock/Alamy.

CHAPTER 5
p. 163, CyberAttack, © Rafal Olechowski/Fotolia; Figure 5.3, © keith morris/Alamy.

CHAPTER 6
p. 207, Facebook © digitallife/Alamy; Figure 6.3 and 6.7, based on data from eMarketer, Inc.,© 2012, used with permission; Tables 6.1 and 6.3, based on data from eMarketer, Inc. © 2011, used with permission; Table 6.5, based on data from eMarketer, Inc. © 2012, used with permission; Figure 6.4, and Table 6.4, based on data from eMarketer, Inc., 2012, used with permission.

CHAPTER 7
p. 259, Free Speech, © kentoh/Shutterstock, p. 300, Google books, © Cyberstock/Alamy.

CHAPTER 8
p. 311, © Ken Gillespie Photography/Alamy; Figure 8.4 and Table 8.3, based on data from eMarketer, Inc., © 2012, used with permission.

CHAPTER 9
p. 347, © Ingvar Bjork/Alamy; Figures 9.7, 9.10, and 9.13, based on data from eMarketer, Inc., © 2012, used with permission; p. 376, Zynga.com, © M40S Photos/Alamy.

CHAPTER 10
p. 383, courtesy of Carol Traver; Figure 10.2, based on data from eMarketer, Inc., © 2012, used with permission; p. 405, eBay, © Iain Masterton/Alamy.

CHAPTER 11
p. 413, VW, © Julian Clune/Alamy; p. 442, Elemica, © 2013, Elemica, Inc.